# MANAGING UNCERTAINTY

**R. BRUCE MCPHERSON
ROBERT L. CROWSON**
UNIVERSITY OF ILLINOIS AT CHICAGO

**NANCY J. PITNER**
UNIVERSITY OF SOUTHERN CALIFORNIA

# MANAGING UNCERTAINTY

## ADMINISTRATIVE
## THEORY AND PRACTICE
## IN EDUCATION

**CONSULTING EDITOR: RAPHAEL O. NYSTRAND**
UNIVERSITY OF LOUISVILLE

CHARLES E. MERRILL PUBLISHING COMPANY
A BELL & HOWELL COMPANY
COLUMBUS TORONTO LONDON SYDNEY

Published by
Charles E. Merrill Publishing Co.
*A Bell & Howell Company*
Columbus, Ohio 43216

This book was set in Caledonia and Frutiger
Production Editor: Ben Shriver
Cover Designer: Cathy Watterson
Text Designer: Ben Shriver

Library of Congress Catalog Card Number: 85-72565
International Standard Book Number: 0–675–20232–9
Printed in the United States of America
1  2  3  4  5  6  7  8  9  10—89  88  87  86

*for Carolyn, Janet, and Steve*

# *F*OREWORD

This book is timely and good. Authenticity is one of its hallmarks. It is the most comprehensive linkage of theory and practice in the current literature of educational administration; moreover, it is very well done. As the authors emphasize, the arenas of theory and practice should not be unbridgeable; thus, they choose to write a volume of equal value to practitioners in the field, especially principals and superintendents, and to professors and graduate students who immerse themselves in the affairs of theory.

Why is this book so well done? The principal reason is the quality of the authors' experience and scholarship. They have addressed the task of book writing in a manner that allows for the best exhibition of the team's strengths. Each of the authors has been either an elementary or secondary teacher and/or school administrator at the building or central office level, including the superintendency. They know city, suburban, and rural school settings, and, although they now inhabit university environments, they have maintained a close contact with practitioners. Furthermore, each is well versed in the history of research in educational administration specifically, as well as in the social sciences generally. Their writing reflects, too, a more than casual acquaintance with the humanities. Often points are clarified or strengthened through reference to thinkers such as C. P. Snow or John Dewey. Poetry serves a similar purpose, as do citations to newspaper stories.

The book is so readable. Parents, school board members, and other lay persons interested in schools will find it insightful and, above all, interesting. The authors employ two writing styles deliberately. A "Studs Terkel style," as the authors describe it, is used to illustrate the perspectives of persons in the field. Those portions of the book are spritely, vital, alive with the emotions, sentiments, ideas, and insights of practitioners with years in the trenches. The other style is consistent with academic tradition, rich in documentation, thorough in coverage, but engaging for theorists and practitioners alike.

The authors have linked so well practice with theory with practice. As one who has tried to do the same thing, I admire how remarkably effective they have been in achieving that outcome. One of the principal reasons for their success in my judgment is that they were very deliberate at the start in selecting that linkage as their objective. They set out systematically to do so. Consequently the five parts structure, the sequencing of the chapters, the insertion of questions, the use of point-counterpoint, even the choice of writing styles discussed above contribute to that objective. Unique too, is the insertion of the authors as persons into the manuscript. You gain a sense of who the authors are as people, what they value, what they respect and admire from the worlds of practice and scholarship.

They have drawn heavily from both worlds for data. The practitioners' world was searched through skillful interviewing of persons chosen for their areas of work (principals and superintendents) and their ability to comment insightfully on their experience. The scholars' world was searched for ideas, concepts, frameworks, and theories that illuminate the experiences of those in the field and provide the basis for organizing content in chapter form.

For me, the interviews, as well as the case studies included in Part Five, were made incredibly interesting because of some of the persons who were selected as speakers. I knew Ike Baker, for example, throughout his twenty-year tenure as superintendent in Park Forest, Illinois. What Ike says has special meaning for me. He was an outstanding superintendent; you can rely on his judgment about so many things. Through such a connection the book becomes a book with real people and actual problems against which to juxtapose concepts and theories of your own. It is fine reading. You will like it.

Luvern L. Cunningham
Novice G. Fawcett Professor of
Educational Administration
The Ohio State University

# PREFACE

|  |  |
|---|---|
| Princess Ida: | Where is our lady surgeon? |
| Sacharissa: | Madam, here! |
| Princess Ida: | We shall require your skills to heal the wounds<br>Of those who fall. |
| Sacharissa: | (alarmed) What, heal the wounded? |
| Princess Ida: | Yes! |
| Sacharissa: | And cut off real live legs and arms? |
| Princess Ida: | Of course! |
| Sacharissa: | I wouldn't do it for a thousand pounds. |
| Princess Ida: | Why, how is this? Are you fainthearted, girl?<br>You've often cut them off in theory! |
| Sacharissa: | In theory I'll cut them off again<br>With pleasure, and as often as you like,<br>But not in practice. |

W.S. Gilbert
A. Sullivan
*Princess Ida* (Act III)
1884

With dramatic knives as sharp as those of Sacharissa the surgeon, Gilbert and Sullivan slice away at one of the favorite presumptions in the field (among others) of educational administration. It is a good deal easier, these two gentlemen argue, to do something in theory than in practice, or, put more bluntly, it is a good deal easier to *think* about something and do nothing than it is to *do* something. Many of us chuckle over this scene from *Princess Ida* because we really do tend to believe that theoreticians think and practitioners act, and only rarely will the twain step into each other's shoes. We seem comfortable with this dichotomy, from our aisle seats in the theater and from our desk chairs in school districts and college buildings.

The view of the authors of this book, however, is a different one. We side with the position that theory and practice in educational administration are virtually inseparable. It is for this reason that our book is written both for active principals and superintendents, on one hand, and university professors and their graduate students, on the other hand. Frankly, it would have been easier in many respects to write a book for one group or the other, to prepare a strategic manual for practitioners or a conventional scholarly textbook. We prefer to believe that organizational theory and the practice of educational administration are related matters of mutual concern to scholars and field administrators. People in both those roles need to be reading some of the same professional books.

The interplay between theory and practice is found throughout the book. A typical chapter begins with an excerpt describing the experience and ideas of a practicing educational administrator, followed by a practice to theory transition; then comes a substantive consideration of organizational theory (with references back to the administrator who opened the chapter); we finish with a theory to practice conclusion. Moreover, we have chosen quite deliberately to expose the reader to a wide variety of roles and locales in this corner of the profession of education—we see an inner-city elementary principal; an exurban assistant superintendent; a university chancellor; a suburban superintendent; a community college dean; a nun who is principal of a Catholic high school; a federal government official; an independent school headmaster; a state department planner. In the pages that follow the reader will encounter men and women, whites, blacks, and Hispanics, as we portray the heterogeneity that exists today in our professional group. The interviews, vignettes, and case studies that we offer bring verisimilitude to our discussion in a direct and sometimes emotional manner.

Two brief confessions seem appropriate here. Some sections of the book move away from theory into historical and philosophic perspectives. In addition, a certain tone pervades parts of the book that may appear unusual in an organizational theory textbook—particularly in the speaking voice of The Professor. These approaches have seemed natural to us as a means for constructing a book of increased depth and greater readability.

We wish to acknowledge the assistance of some people by name, as well as others who must remain anonymous. Before doing that we state our appreciation to our universities during the preparation of the manuscript—the University of Illinois at Chicago, the University of Oregon, and the University of Southern California—for providing superior environments for scholarly endeavor. Merrill editors Vicki Knight and Beverly Kolz provided the consistent balance between encouragement and questioning that we needed throughout the project. Series Editor Ray Nystrand challenged us to write a singular book, and we hope that we have been at least partially responsive to his hopes. We thank our reviewers: Samuel Moore, Michigan State University; Robert Schulz, University of Louisville; Jerry McGee, Sam Houston State University; Rodney T. Ogawa, University of Utah; Walter G. Hack, Ohio State University; and Lloyd E. McCleary, University of Utah. We particularly thank those who were most severe in their critiques of early drafts; they prompted substantial changes for the better in the book. Charles Glenn of the Bureau of Equal Educational Opportunity, Department of Education, Commonwealth of Massachusetts was generous in permitting us to use materials from a presentation he made to the Illinois State Board of Education as we developed one of our case studies. Patricia Brieschke, then a graduate student but now an administrator for the Chicago Public Schools, provided timely research, writing, and editorial assistance for chapters 3 and 6. Merry Mastny supervised her first-rate word processing section (including Debbie Allen, Lynn Casey, Sam Karnick, Mike Korenchan, Tina Ku, Monique Lambert, Kirt Menon, Schulamite Yuan) as the book entered and exited the computer. Her skill, patience, and remarkable good humor are recalled fondly. The administrators who were willing to share aspects of their lives with us and with you deserve particular commendation. Some asked that we use their names, while others preferred a pseudonym (and, in those cases, we also transplanted the speaker to a fictional locale). The choice they made was dictated, in every case, by their desire to be candid. Talking to these practitioners, developing their stories, and mutually editing the results undoubtedly provided as much fun as one can find in the writing of a long book. We trust that we have done them justice. Finally, we bow to family and friends for the kind of daily support that makes the solitude of writing possible and, for the most part, satisfying. The travail of the other parts is for us alone to remember.

The three authors are responsible for the content of this book. But many others—our teachers and mentors over the years, our professional colleagues—are responsible, too, as they have helped and influenced us. That is the way they wanted it, and even if sections of this book set their teeth on edge, that is the way they would want it now. This inescapable responsibility is one that we also accept (hopefully with the same integrity) as we are tied to a new generation of scholars and writers. It is a burden that every teacher shoulders in the spirit of Chaucer's scholarly companion, the Clerk of Oxenford, of whom it was said, "Gladly wolde he lerne and gladly teche."

# CONTENTS

# ONE

## *PRACTICE AND THEORY IN EDUCATIONAL ADMINISTRATION*

# Examining Theory and Practice: The Structure and Purpose of the Book

We believe that theory and practice in educational administration are critically interactive. They are intertwined, even symbiotic, these perspectives from the ivory tower and the trenches.

Few textbooks in educational administration have considered theory and practice in meaningful juxtaposition. Some are highly theoretical and far removed from the real problems of administrative life. Others, more frequently, are judgmentally prescriptive—offering how-to-do-it nostrums without an adequate exploration of underlying belief systems. This all-too-common separation of theory from practice is quite understandable. The technology of administration is poorly developed in both arenas; neither theory nor practice in educational administration has progressed far. Indeed, for us to attempt to treat both in one volume runs the risk of being shallow on two fronts.

Nevertheless, it is our purpose in this book to seek some balance —to provide the reader with a current review of alternative theoretical perspectives on the administration of educational organizations; to examine the improvement of practice by seeing situations through alternative theoretical lenses; and to encourage the practice of theory through seeking to understand vignettes and cases drawn from the lives of educational administrators. Generally, we refrain from offering the reader a set of answers. Certainly this is true in Part Two, the major section of the book. In Part Three we do point to some useful administrative strategies, and in Part Four we reconsider some ideas that have stood the test of time. Although in both Parts Three and Four we offer our sense of the implications of theory for practice, most often we dispense questions rather than answers. Our examination tends to be many-sided, as alternative, even competing, theories are examined.

Our book begins, as the reader will soon discover, with a mythical interviewer and a flesh and blood interviewee. As we developed the book, we talked with practicing administrators in a variety of settings—about their careers, their feelings and beliefs, their problems and solutions they have found. We believe that the examination of theory is enriched and clarified if it is set alongside the reality of the administrative job. Therefore, each of the substantive, theoretical portions of this book is introduced by an educational administrator examining, in his or her own words, some highlights from a hard-chiseled career. All of the stories are real, and many are rich and intriguing. Most of the names are fictionalized, although some respondents specifically asked that we not mask their identities. These vignettes or fragments of oral history are used, most of all, to suggest that theory and practice come together in the working lives of *people*—people trying to do the best they can amidst the ambiguity and the uncertainty of an institution that is inadequately understood.

As the reader will quickly note, the book contains two distinct writing styles. The Studs Terkel approach of our interviewer is deliberately informal and free-flowing. The intent is to provide a setting for and to convey the special world of the practitioner—a world of happenstance and variety, of puzzling complexity, of victory and defeat, of small and large concerns. The working lives of people, to be understood—even to be analyzed at all theoretically—require applying some empathy to them. One needs to attain a feeling that blood like ours flows through their veins, that their experiences *are* ours, that we can appreciate and analyze their problems on *their* terms. Thus, the style of writing in parts of this book is relaxed, even chatty, reflecting administrative lives that are informative and often compelling.

This is also a serious book on the subject of organizational theory in education. In a more formal, traditional academic style of writing, we seek to convey the growing scope of available theory, as a complement to the varied world of the practitioner. Our chapters on organizational theory in education are often long and complex. Each chapter examines multiple theoretical perspectives and offers a substantial review of the existing literature. The explanation of theory requires careful writing, and we have chosen, in much of our examination, to concentrate on breadth (an introduction to many theoretical perspectives) rather than depth (the full development of just a few theories). We hope to whet the appetite of the reader rather than to satisfy it. Our synthesis of current theory is certainly no substitute for the library, for either the graduate student or the practicing administrator who wishes to learn more.

This is a book about educational administration. For two reasons its theoretical focus is upon organizational theory. First, organizational theory has yet to receive the attention it warrants in education. Second, research on the theory of organizations generally has blossomed in recent years. Our discussion of theory focuses in Part Two of the book upon five key areas of administration. These are the production of educational outcomes; the coordination and control of educational organizations; the management of commitment; the adaptation of the organization to its environment; and the provision of managerial leadership. Why these topics? They are not comprehensive, certainly. We do not provide the almost obligatory historical review of administrative thought in education (e.g., the scientific management movement followed by the human relations approach, and so on). Neither is our choice of topics conventional. We provide a chapter on the subject of commitment in place of the usual treatment of motivation. We lead off, in our examination of organizational theory, with a chapter on outcomes, in lieu of the expected treatise on goal-setting.

Our choice of key issues for illumination in the book has been informed by two central considerations. On one hand, our practitioners' interest in the study of organizations leads us to focus upon the question of managerial control. And we prefer to present the issue of control in its more problematic form as the task of managing the *uncertainty* of education. Each of our theory chapters, and each of the topics addressed in Part Three of the book (e.g., problem finding, negotiating), has been selected with that theme in mind. The management of organizational uncertainty, as a continuing thread of practical administrative concern, is the primary organizing focus of this book.

On the other hand, our choice of key topics has been influenced by the availability of theoretical alternatives. Consider the point made by Edgar Lee Masters in one of the poetic epitaphs from his *Spoon River Anthology*:

Dippold the Optician

What do you see now?
Globes of red, yellow, purple.
Just a moment! And now?
My father and mother and sisters.
Yes! And now?
Knights at arms, beautiful women, kind faces.
Try this.
A field of grain—a city.
Very good! And now?
A young woman with angels bending over her.
A heavier lens! And now?
Many women with bright eyes and open lips.
Try this.
Just a goblet on a table.
Oh I see! Try this lens!
Just an open space—I see nothing in particular.
Well, now!
Pine trees, a lake, a summer sky.
That's better, and now?
A book.
Read a page for me.
I can't. My eyes are carried beyond the page.
Try this lens.
Depths of air.
Excellent! And now?
Light, just light, making everything below it a toy world.
Very well, we'll make the glasses accordingly.

We, too, seek to provide more than one pair of glasses. There are choices among theoretical perspectives—each with its own view of the world, each with its own shades of meaning and interpretation, each with its own implications for practice. Try

---

"Dippold the Optician" reprinted by the kind permission of Mrs. Ellen C. Masters and MacMillan Publishing Company.

this lens. Try that one. Where would this perspective lead you? Is there something to be learned by looking at the same problem in quite another way?

Each of our theoretical chapters offers alternatives—a number of sets of glasses, or lenses, for the reader to try out. The reader who is a past, present, or future administrator must eventually choose his or her own perspective. We present theoretical material in such a manner as to indicate that choices do exist, but *the obligation is upon the practitioner and not the scholar to make good sense of the particular, through a clear understanding of the general.* We take this position not to avoid responsibility, but out of respect for the unique conditions faced by working administrators. Tests of efficacy are better applied by these women and men than by us.

Our book, following a brief introductory Part One, has four additional parts. In Part Two, we present the five substantive chapters on organizational theory. Each chapter is preceded by a vignette of a practitioner—an illustrative excerpt from our interviews with administrators at work. A postscript to each chapter returns to comment on the vignette, after the examination of theory. It will become apparent to the reader, in Part Two, that this book is unconventional in one final sense. Many of the illustrations (and the practitioner interviews) reflect problems in the administration of organizations other than public elementary and secondary schools. Although we recognize differences by level and type of schooling, we nevertheless seek to enrich our discussion through the examination of educational organizations broadly conceived—including colleges and universities, and private and parochial schools.

In Parts Three, Four, and Five of the book, we focus upon practice: specifically upon the improvement of practice through theory and the working out of theory. Continuing to draw upon the lives of practicing administrators, we ask "What opportunities are there for bringing school management closer to its theoretical roots?" Part Three analyzes administrative practice in education—hoping to offer new or revitalized directions in managerial strategy (i.e., in the management of uncertainty) developing out of our increased attention to organizational principles applicable to education. Problem finding, negotiating order, and the role of the administrator as teacher comprise the topics. A concluding chapter in Part Four suggests some enduring fundamentals in the search for administrative control of uncertainty in education—fundamentals that flow (as modern as ever) out of the work of Jacob Getzels and Chester Barnard. Inevitably, the thinking administrator must be drawn to the question: "What *should* the organization be doing?" Moral responsibility in educational administration is as fundamental to practice as its theoretical foundations.

Finally, in the last section of the book, Part Five, we present eight instructional cases. Each of the cases is drawn from the actual experience of an educational administrator. Each is designed to encourage the application of theory to practice. Indeed, by book's end we will ask the reader to engage in the practice *of* theory—to continue and extend a lifelong dialogue, reflecting and searching over the complexity and confusion of the work-a-day world of the educational administrator through the deeper insights gained from examining alternative theoretical interpretations of that world.

# 2

## Examining Practice:
## The Search for Useful Theory

### THE PROFESSOR

As much as I hated flying, I was looking forward to this assignment. I really did have the qualifications, and my contact at the Association of School Administrators knew all about them when he called.

> Let's see. You were a teacher and a principal, and then a superintendent in public school systems in New Hampshire and Connecticut. About thirty years altogether. And now an associate professor of educational administration. I'll bet you enjoy being off the firing line at this point.

They always said that, but I admitted it was true. Associate professor with tenure in a small public university along the East Coast. They had needed someone with field experience to work with their master's and doctoral students. I was the token practitioner on the faculty. The doctorate from Pennsylvania State University bought a modicum of initial respect from my new colleagues, and soon they discovered that I was intrigued by theoretical issues as well. I never thought I'd be *doing* any research once the dissertation was on the shelf, but life had its twists.

What had ASA wanted from me? I had been a member for a number of years, and I had even contributed to some of their administrative training sessions, but this was different. Unexpected, intriguing—it was the way all the good consulting jobs started out. Several telephone conversations and an afternoon briefing in the ASA offices near the Mall in Washington made it reasonably clear. They were after a series of interviews of educational administrators in the Studs

Terkel style, and then a longish article, maybe a monograph, on what these men and women did, and some of their thoughts and feelings about their work and their careers. I reminded the younger man across the desk that Terkel's *Working* had failed miserably on Broadway, but he just shrugged. I tried another tack. The thrill of victory and the agony of defeat?

> **Well, maybe not quite so melodramatic, although you'll get some of that. We want a piece that will take the masks off, that will show these administrators as flesh and blood people grappling with serious problems, usually not of their own making. Men and women from different backgrounds. Different races and ethnic origins. A spread of communities. Most of the important roles. We'll give them anonymity if they want it, so they can really do some soul searching.**

I supposed that I was only going to meet winners.
   No. Not all heroes and heroines, but no villains.
Why me?

> **Well, the strong experience in the first place. You ought to be able to get these administrators comfortable enough to lay it on the line. And we've done our homework on you. The interviews you included in that article you published last year in *Educational Leadership* were interesting and well-written. You don't seem to be bogged down with as much jargon as most professors.**

He was going to add for my age, but I could see him bite his tongue. Bless you, young man. They'd identify the administrators and get their cooperation. Could I fly to Chicago to their national convention and do the interviewing there? I extracted a promise that I could use the material for a book that I was beginning to prepare with several colleagues.

> **Oh, the usual thing—organizational theory, but with a particular slant toward the practicing school administrator. Something I hope you might read and find interesting, if we can ever get it to a printer.**

We worked out some interview questions, I blocked out the time on my schedule, and here I was on a DC 10 hurtling toward O'Hare International Airport in Chicago. I was tired, but I knew I couldn't sleep. So I stared out the window and let my mind wander a bit.
   A sociologist studying educational administrators could search through library card catalogs and stacks for journals, memoirs, and autobiographies and find only frustration. No, my ilk had been almost consistently inarticulate with respect to writing about themselves and their work. I thought of a recent exception, largely because it had been so captivating and revealing. Roald Campbell—I think he's at the University of Utah now, after an illustrious career at Ohio State and Chicago—had published a memoir.[1] Detailed, personal, so candid. A chance to learn more about one of the names in the field, a truly respected and influential educational administrator. Wouldn't you love to read the book about how Benjamin Willis ran the Chicago Public Schools, or the book about Francis Keppel's efforts as United States Commissioner of Education at a time when federal involvement in American education accelerated, or the book about how Joseph

Cronin bridged the gap between the life of the professor and the role of state superintendent of education? You could learn a lot from autobiographies or even biographies of the lives of these educational administrators. I had read Studs Terkel's *Working*[2] over the Christmas holiday in preparation for this journey. I counted 133 interviews, and there were several teachers and a professor of communications, but not an educational administrator. We know more about crooks than we do about principals and superintendents—either as professionals or as human beings. I wonder why.

Is it that they do less interesting work than doctors, lawyers, ministers, businessmen, and military leaders? Well, their work may appear less glamorous to the American public, and yet many parents would *value* the work of a local school principal on behalf of their child as much or even more than routine services from these other professionals. Is it that their work is less difficult? I doubt it. Few would underestimate the rigor and pressure of the job of a large city school superintendent. Are they less interesting as people than their counterparts in other professions? Principals such as Elliott Shapiro in New York and Joseph Rosen in Chicago, or superintendents such as Mark Shedd in Philadelphia and Sidney Marland in Pittsburgh, or Adrienne Bailey at the College Board, or higher education administrators such as Clark Kerr from California and Jon Silber from Boston, or state school officers such as Dolores Colburg and Ewald Nyquist, or educational administration professors such as Mark Hanson of the University of California, Riverside, and David Clark of Indiana University—if you knew any of these front-runners, you would argue to the contrary.

Educational administrators have been around a long time, since early in the nineteenth century, but we're just beginning to recognize the need to tell our colleagues and our clients about ourselves. We've learned, often under fire, that in organizations as vulnerable to public criticism as schools and universities, the high-silhouette administrator provides a clear and convenient target. Where is the payoff in being reflective and introspective? Why develop a taste and capacity for professional writing beyond the need to whip out reports and documents and public information pieces?

Teachers have been underpaid in American society, but they've been respected, at least in the abstract. Administrators may have been overpaid at times, but generally they've not been respected. We're still searching for respect.

Well, you've a chance to change just a bit of that. I wondered if any of my prey were on this plane. Not many people of any kind aboard on Sunday afternoon. After a while, I walked up to the first row of coach seats. Administrators wouldn't be in first class on public money. I walked back down the aisle. "Pardon me, but are you going to the ASA convention by any chance?" Smiles, shrugs, disclaimers. But then a steady look that could hide a twinkle. "Yes, I am. You, too?" I sat down in the empty aisle seat and introduced myself, and he responded. I recognized the name from my list.

## IKE BAKER

*He is sixty going on forty, and he has just retired. He is living in Florida, after more than thirty years of service with the same suburban Chicago school district.*

*For twenty-two of these years he was superintendent of the community's elementary schools. The roots he established as an administrator, and for his own family, are in contrast with a childhood spent on the move—with a father in a government service position that required frequent transfers. Ike credits his parents with a liberalism and a sense of social commitment that were hallmarks of his own career. He takes pride in a professional past devoted to experimentation, innovation, and change. In recent years Ike spent a good deal of effort trying to hold together (sometimes even being forced to dismantle) that which he had worked so hard to build. Despite that, he is retiring on a relatively high note—relaxed and confident, looking forward to new interests as a retiree.*

Ike had flown from Florida to Washington to visit one of his sisters, and then he had picked this flight out of a hat.

> Look, I've got lots of family and friends to see in Chicago. I'm definitely not going to sit in the Hilton at the ASA convention for three days. How about interviewing me now? That time I'm supposed to meet you really won't be very convenient.

I took out my spiral pad, and we began.

### When did you come to Park Forest? What attracted you?

Believe it or not, I started out as a custodian. I was hired by Bob Anderson—*the* Bob Anderson. He was quite a guy. I really hadn't planned to go into education. I have an undergraduate background in biology from Roosevelt and a master's degree from Northwestern. I started working on a doctorate at Northwestern in genetics, but I had to eat, and I had run out of GI-Bill money. I'd heard about Park Forest as a community, and I inquired. Anderson grabbed me and put me into science and math teaching, and later he pushed me into administration. In the meantime I took four courses at Indiana to get certified. Anyway, when I was first hired, Anderson asked me what I wanted to do. I told him I needed work that summer, and he said there was lots of painting to be done around the new buildings. So I signed on as custodian for the summer before I began teaching. It was great. I really got to know the facilities, and a paycheck was coming in over the summer.

Bob Anderson was Park Forest's first superintendent, and he set the tone for the district. He had just finished his doctorate at Chicago. The town did quite a search, looking for a creative guy to fit the innovative ideas of the community. Anderson advocated nongraded schooling, and he was a strong administrator. He had a policy, for example, from the first, that really blew minds in this district. He said that if parents pull kids out of school for a trip, to Florida or something, we'd reassign them to a different school when they return. He was that kind of guy—an innovator, but one *very much in charge.* He was at Park Forest five years. Then he went off to Harvard, and now he's in Texas.

### Your career spanned three interesting decades in American public education—the 1950s, the 1960s, and the 1970s. What were the high and low points?

I'll admit I'm a little down psychologically right now. I came in during the building era—the postwar boom. It was really exciting those first few years. We all had boundless energy—putting up buildings, developing new ideas, creating programs in a brand new, preplanned suburban community. The town encouraged and expected creativity; it was part of the whole atmosphere. Now, especially in the last five years, the message is quite different. I came in with the feeling, like Bob Anderson, that you're here to make an impact on kids' education. In the last five years, it's boiled down to just try to hold it all together financially. The number one problem is just plain financial survival.

The universities could be much more help in this. I didn't feel as an administrator that I lacked skills in financial management, but in these troubled times you need to learn some new tricks. The banks and other private sources have helped out a lot more than the universities. The banks taught us some things you can do to refinance your debt, to get a bond issue without having to go to the people, and how to establish and then abolish a working cash fund. The universities were asleep at the switch. I used to like to jab the professors. I'd tell them that they knew theory, but they weren't helping school finance in practice. There's no one touching the real problems in school finance today. The professors are all into theory, but they don't realize that the whole ship is going down.

Another thing that I can't really say is a low point, but it sure has been a change: This is the whole relationship between a board and its superintendent. The board of education is probably *the* major responsibility of the superintendent. You've really got to see yourself as an educator of the board, one who has to bring along seven different people. The board represents the community, and it shouldn't be a rubber stamp. But things *were* different when I came in. My first board president told me, "I have a business to run, I'm busy as hell. When something comes up, call me, but we expect *you* to run the schools." The message then was *build, innovate, experiment* with new reading programs and the like. What you did when you went before the board was report to them what you've done, recount your successes, bring them up to date. The superintendent rarely had much contact with anyone but the board president. I did insist on bothering him daily. I called him every day for about a 15-minute conversation. But that was it.

Earlier the board was mainly a male-dominated, businessmen's club. Now, a later snapshot: The businessmen have opted out, and the gap has been filled by women. They're terrifically bright, active, and committed people. Most of them are younger than my own daughter. They're fully involved with the school system, and they're certainly not the kind of people you simply give an end-of-year report to. These new-style boards have had to learn a lot about public education and how to get good leadership. The Illinois Association of School Boards has helped a lot. For example, they had meetings on how to write goals, how to set objectives for the superintendent and themselves, and for the school district. It was great! It gave a board the feeling that it has some control over the process. We sat down for hours, on Saturdays, and worked it all out. It helped me work with the board; we were doing it together. We got into the quality of education in the district, not just the purchase order kinds of things. They weren't reluctant to push on some issues.

It has gone from my doing the job to a much more involved board now. It isn't any less satisfactory. I've even changed my philosophy from the notion that a board wouldn't know a good school or a good principal if they stumbled over one. Now, the board helps choose administrators. Earlier I picked them. Some were great, and some were jerks. I caught hell for the jerks, but the earlier norm was that the *superintendent* made the decisions. I'd get all the problems resolved by myself. *I* like the change, but most superintendents want to be in charge. They fail to recognize that the board represents the community and now wants more and more to be involved. You still have to keep this in balance. Some boards will take over completely. Involvement breeds a desire for more and more, so you have to be very political.

## Did the system give you room to do what you really wanted to do?

Park Forest is unique in that respect. There was no old power structure, and I guess I've been accepted as kind of one of the pioneers of the community. It really is a model community. The people here believe their own press clippings. This all makes it a unique place in which to operate. I was never under pressure from anyone in the village over who's to get hired as a teacher or a custodian, or who gets the contract to fix the school roof. In another community *every* decision to hire someone, make a purchase, or let a contract carries some political influence behind it. We've never had that here. I'm certainly not walking away from a bad community situation, even though we've had to close four schools and drop forty tenured teachers and cut programs recently. It's tough, and I'm very disappointed at the need for it, but not from a community standpoint.

## Tell me about that desegregation effort.

It was the right community with the right superintendent at the right time. It was eleven years ago. Mike Bakalis had become state superintendent in Illinois, and he really took charge in the area of desegregation. Bakalis challenged 25 districts in the state for being outside of the guidelines for racial balance. We had one school, Beacon Hill, that served a section of the next town, Chicago Heights. The area isn't in the town of Park Forest, but it is part of our school district. Anyway, Beacon Hill had been a classic case of block busting. In just 18 months it went from all-white to all-black. Thus, we had nine elementary schools in the district—eight of them white and one all black. We didn't meet Bakalis' racial enrollment guidelines.

Beacon Hill was a tough school, equal to some in the inner city. The housing was HUD 235, and falling apart. The people living there really had nothing better than a survival life style. Bakalis and his people helped us. They came out, met our board, leveled with them. They told us we could do it, or we could wait and let a judge do it and see the control of our schools taken right out of our hands. Mike gave us $100,000 just to study the issue and plan what to do for a year. And the head of Mike's Chicago office, Bob Lyons, almost lived with us for a while, helping out. Bob grew up in segregation himself, and he knew all the right things to do. He even brought out a Harvard law professor to talk to us—running down all the court cases that apply to the issue, educating us thoroughly. Of course, there was a pretty big fight in the community, and lots of people were upset. We had to change attendance boundaries and bus kids. That's always tough. But the board held fast. Later, two of our members were voted off, and desegregation opponents took their place—which surprised me because the village had never done that sort of thing before.

Desegregation was certainly a prime success of my tenure in Park Forest. Most superintendents lose their jobs in the process of desegregating. I was there for 11 more years. We've studied the effects pretty closely too. We've tracked the test scores for 11 years. There's still a gap statistically but less than ever before. Also, they're not having riots at the high school anymore. The kids now go to school together before reaching high school, and they've learned how to get along. Today, the board tends to be low key about it all, but they're solidly behind the desegregation process.

### How did you find out what you were supposed to do as a superintendent?

Well, without any real undergraduate background at all in education, I guess I wasn't badly spoiled. Later, after rising through the ranks into administration I profited from my graduate work at the University of Chicago. It came at just the right time. I wasn't hungry enough to go on to complete the doctorate, but I plugged into what they were trying to get across. People like Vern Cunningham and Alan Thomas helped me. They were great—they changed my leadership style. Hey, there *is* a way to move institutions! Maybe you *can* get a group of principals to provide some leadership! You've got to get people involved, though, and guide them with your own expectations.

I guess I also found out something about being an administrator from my parents. My mother was born in Italy, my father in Texas. My dad is a University of Chicago grad, and they met in Chicago. I was born in Chicago, and we lived there till I was five. Mother taught kindergarten in Samaritan House, a settlement house in the Little Italy area of Chicago. She took me with her each day after I was two and a half. Both my parents were social activists and liberals, and I owe them a lot. They certainly passed their frame of reference on to me.

### Is there an issue you really blew as superintendent?

Our first school closing was an absolute fiasco. In all, we've closed four schools. The last one went very well. We've learned how. With the first one, I just went to the board and said, "We should close Wildwood." "Why that one?" they asked. "Well, it's the smallest. I don't know. Why not Wildwood?" It was really bad. We didn't have any criteria. We hadn't given it any thought and went at it unprepared. Well, Wildwood is still open today, as a special education school. By the time we'd reached our fourth closing, we'd figured it out. We had meetings on the closing nearly every night—wore the opposition down. And that fourth one was the proposed closing of one of our two junior highs—which is tough for the community. Most of us as superintendents never had any classes in closing schools, but we learned fast.

### What counsel would you give to a young person just starting out today on a career as educational administrator?

I'd emphasize more academic preparation today than I had. Perhaps an MBA plus an education degree or a law degree. I guess the entrée into the superintendency today is the doctorate—but you have to be prepared uniquely today. A doctorate alone isn't enough. You have to know how to deal with lots of different situations. The whole area of the economics of public education; I feel adequate in that area, but I wish I had a much broader perspective. I've had to cut teachers and programs—it's hard to learn how to handle that. I guess another thing is that you can't be an effective superintendent without a job. And the secret to keeping one is human relations, particularly with respect to the board. You have to educate the board. School boards now want alternatives—and lots of superintendents still try to provide them with only *one*. It's hard for many older superintendents to realize that the board has the final responsibility, not the superintendent.

Another thing we've got to stop doing is always fighting as a profession. We're much too fragmented. The super school board is the state legislature. We still haven't learned that that's where the power is—and you've got to manipulate it. Instead we fight. Teachers against administrators, against board associations, against the state education department. The message we give to the legislature really hurts us. And so many administrators refuse to recognize state politics at all. I got involved in a state legislative committee a while back and found that most superintendents around the state either can't or won't talk to state legislators. It's a shame. Legislators are hungry to talk to superintendents. You can't imagine how hard it is to get most of the superintendents around the state to do such a simple thing as to send off a telegram to Springfield urging a piece of legislation forward. They just don't understand the importance. We're really naive about the whole function of influencing state government. Pressure? We don't know anything at all, really, about how to apply it.

**Have you ever reached the breaking point?**

No, never. I enjoyed every moment of it. I even enjoyed the strike. Our teachers organized about 15 years ago. I helped them. I'm pro-labor, and I was quite in sympathy with what the teachers were trying to do. I was too dumb at the time to realize that a lot of the stuff I was willing to give in on in those early contracts was going too far. Our attorney warned us on a lot of things. I listened to him sometimes, sometimes not. Overall, I was too easy, gave too much. We now have nine different kinds of leave in our contract—a teacher can get leave from us for just about anything. It has been a learning process.

*Now* it's an adversarial relationship, but it certainly wasn't 15 years ago. And, it certainly was different when they went out on strike. I actually enjoyed it—because we were so far ahead of the teachers it was unbelievable. I was all set up for the strike. We had worked with the board and prepared them—what to say, what not to say, how to handle the media. We played it cool and just didn't make any mistakes. One thing I wouldn't give in on. We recognized their right to strike—and they were out for two weeks—but we weren't about to give them a free ride. They had to take a loss of pay for their strike time. We fought over it, but eventually the teachers did agree to a loss of pay for one week. Throughout those years I was fortunate in having a chance to work with good union leaders. The working relationship between the superintendent and the leadership in the union is critical. Good leaders are needed on both sides of the table.

All in all, I can't say there was anything near a breaking point. I must say there were some distinctly better highs sometimes than at other times—and the best were certainly the early years, the honeymoon period. It was a terrific time, a fun time, with lots of challenges. I like challenges. I tend to get a bit down with routine.

**Why did you pick this particular time to retire?**

The public statement was that I'd been here long enough, and the school system needed new leadership to deal with the problems of today. Actually, it's quite simply this. I became superintendent when I was 37; we raised five children; and when I reached 50, Margaret began urging me to decide, to set a time when we would call it quits. I said we'd get out early—when I was 55. Well, I was 60 when I retired. There wasn't any direct pressure from the family to hold me to my promise, but it was there. Over time you build up enemies. Twenty years is a long time as superintendent. I probably should have gone two or three years earlier.

**What are you going to do now?**

Well, I'm not too retired. I was interested in science when I was younger—particularly meteorology. I worked in a weather bureau for a while as a kid, and I served with the Army Air Force in Europe during the war, with a fighter group, and I engaged in meteorology there. I'd have liked to continue with it after the war, but people with such training were a dime-a-dozen then. That interest has always been there, though, and in recent years I've used it in doing a lot of boating and flying. I taught meteorology to boatmen with the U.S. Power Squadron, but we sold our boat and I learned to fly, so now I'm interested in meterology from the flying end. I might also do a little flight instruction, and I'm getting involved with a unique educational institution for senior citizens near our place in Florida. Port Charlotte University. It's not a university at all, but a great place for people to come to learn just about anything someone else is able to teach.

## *FROM PRACTICE TO THEORY*

I checked in at the Michigan Avenue hotel, chucked my bags into the small room, and set my watch back an hour. Still several hours before Donald Riddle would arrive. Ike Baker had talked about the desire of people for leadership, and the fact that leaders build up enemies over the years. Those that are assertive (and Ike was in that category) do, they really do. Five to seven years was about all a superintendent could count on in one place, but Ike had tripled that. What kind of leadership *do* people want, that they won't reject out of hand? Some administrators in education discover the secret, but most don't. You either think you're the ultimate boss and act like one, or you develop the habit of sharing leadership. Finding it and nourishing it and creating a *system* of leadership. Not very complicated, but hard to get in your head and even harder to pull off. Ike had figured it out. You could tell from the way he had changed the process of school closings in his district. Anyone could pinpoint the solution, but it took a shrewd administrator to find the way to reach that solution on the job.

In truth, Americans like to set up their leaders. Select them, give them a honeymoon, and then whack away at their knees. It's not sheer meanness really, or cynicism, just a quaint way we have in this republic of keeping our leaders honest and responsive. Ike had lived through suburban growth, and then he had to suffer through the decline of the 1970s. Not easy for a builder. And hadn't we all been trained to be builders?

Ike recognized the separation that seems to occur at times between theory and practice, but as a superintendent he tried to make the connections. For him the university provided mixed blessings. Studying while he was a superintendent, he found his graduate work indispensable. But if the theory from the ivory tower couldn't help him, he merely found some from another location. "The banks and other private sources have helped out a lot more than the universities." It was as if he believed that he had to have useful theory in order to be successful in the school system and school community. In fact, once when he didn't have a solid theoretical base, when he was flying by the seat of his pants, he failed. That was when he wanted to close Wildwood. It was still open when he left Park Forest. But even there he found a way to induce theory out of difficult experience. It involved a different way of looking at the problem of decline and the processes that could lead a school district to some acceptable solutions. It was a new bag of tricks *plus* the new theory that finally managed to get some schools closed as the organization continued to shrink.

The administrator seems to be standing in the right place to make these key connections between theory and practice. He or she has to borrow some theory, or sometimes invent it, and then use it to refine or even change practice. Those Wildwood parents had a quite different conceptual framework from Ike, and they used it to shore up an effective political position. It's not just a matter of being sure what the problem really is. The administrator had to discover the right theory to illuminate that problem. Ike was a perennial student—and a perennial teacher—always looking for the broader perspective. He refused to believe that the space between theory and practice was really there. Maybe that's the best way to look at the issue after all. Like the carnival barker, "Now you see it, now you don't." With the top educational administrators, the ones who get the job done and survive quite nicely, the gap between theory and practice is temporary or nonexistent. Between the aloof scholar and the omniscient practitioner, the gap is the Grand Canyon.

It was time for a cup of coffee.

## NOTES

[1]Roald F. Campbell, *The Making of a Professor* (Salt Lake City, Utah: Publishers Press, 1981).
[2]Studs Terkel, *Working* (New York: Random House, 1972).

# 3

## Examining Theory:
## The Search for
## a Link with Practice

The theory–practice issue has been called a "durable controversy,"[1] and Whitehead observed that "there is a sense of déja-vu, a feeling of disquiet that after so many years of discussion this impasse remains unresolved. . . ."[2] What is the relationship between theory and practice? Is it more than an interaction between reflection and practice for educational administrators? More than a rationale for organizing activities in a particular way? Asking these questions will not push any researcher or practitioner to the frontier of educational thought. These questions have been raised innumerable times by philosophers over the ages. It is not particularly curious that the theory–practice relationship in educational administration has come to be characterized by an identifiable strain of controversy—a split, a gap, a dialectic—for it is a problem which can be traced directly to the age-old polarity between knowing and doing, or the tension between theoretical and practical wisdom.

Since the turn of the century the field of educational administration has been biased toward the practical. In the 1950s, interest in educational phenomena moved away from a preoccupation with practical consequences and direct experience. Optimism characterized what has been called the theory movement, when educational administration was first seen as an applied social science. Disenchantment followed when "unrealistically high expectations for quick infusions of new knowledge via theory-based research"[3] were not met. This dissatisfaction, Willower tells us, is "chronic and essentially incurable."[4] However, it may not be simply a distinction between theory and practice, but rather a distinction between kinds of theory, that lies beneath the theory–practice tension.

## Pure Theory vs. Pragmatic Theory

Clark describes a confrontation which stands as an excellent example of the pull between theory and practice. After spending many hours watching a construction project, he noted:

> Two of the construction engineers were discussing the drilling of rivet holes in a large steel beam. The older man took a piece of chalk and, after eyeing the beam, simply walked its length and made a number of marks. The younger man was obviously upset; and after a one-sided argument the older man left and went on to his next job, whereupon the younger man took out what seemed to me to be a very new slide rule and list of tables and began his calculations. After some time the young man took out *his* piece of chalk and, referring to his notes, marked the same beam with increasing consternation. His chalk marks were almost identical to those of the older engineer.[5]

It would be easy, if mistaken, to believe that only the younger engineer worked from a theoretical base. The veteran engineer who chose the right rivet holes without a slide rule or benefit of mathematical calculation also operated with a theory—an implicit or unconscious set of assumptions for procedure which he had learned by trial and error. Clark points out that people who use this kind of pragmatic theory are wrong more often than they are correct, and he calls for an end to reliance on informal theory and methods when formal theory and methods are available.

Clark reminds us that Herbert Simon made a distinction between two types of theories: *descriptive theory*, which accurately describes and predicts the behavior of people in organizations, and *prescriptive theory*, which offers the most practical solution, given the constraints of objectives, setting, tasks, people, methods, and resources. The opportunity to combine theory and practice in the future will be found in prescriptive theory, according to Clark. Yet other researchers eschew the urge to make theory prescriptive. Whitehead contends that prescriptions "are substitutes for thought" and asks "Have practitioners no intelligence of their own?"[6] They do, of course, and Clark suggests that the special knowledge of both of the engineers in our example above is valuable. Much of the theory presented in this book is descriptive rather than prescriptive. The test of theory is its ability to assist the administrator in understanding the practice of educational organizations.

Here, at the beginning of our book, we would like to characterize two interesting yet quite variant ways of viewing the relationship of theory and practice in educational administration. The first is more popular, and yet it is the second that is more appealing to us.

## Theory vs. Practice

The first position holds that theory and practice do not mesh in education generally, and in the field of educational administration in particular. The cartoon that might be sketched is one of two groups of men and women separated by a thick and high wall. On one side, theorists and researchers in long academic gowns are lounging against the wall, disdainful and disrespectful of the world of practice. On the other side of the wall, two groups of practitioners are to be found. One is angry, trying to climb the wall, shaking fists at the scholars because of the vagueness and inutility of their theories. The other group ignores the existence of the scholars and the wall altogether. It is neither a pretty nor a happy picture.

Halpin has some advice for academicians who want to help practitioners:

> The first step is for the scientist to rid himself of the prejudice that his skill in constructing theoretical models is somehow more respectable than skill in the direct observation of human events. Never let us underestimate the consummate skill needed for the direct observation of human behavior. Both skills are needed, and neither is less respectable than the other.[7]

He also speaks to the arrogance that can be found on both sides of the wall.

> If we are to freshen our observations of organizational life, we somehow must rid ourselves of clichés, slogans, and meaningless words. Ironically, the less aware a superintendent is of the emptiness of his clichés, the more vehemently does he seem to brandish them. The hypnosis by words is one source of the arrogance of the practical man who knows what he knows and is having no part of anyone else's way of knowing. But he is not alone in arrogance; for totally different reasons, the theoretically oriented scientist flees from the reality of direct intuitive and observational experience. Deprived of the knowledge such direct experience can furnish, he becomes arrogant about the theoretical models he has constructed.[8]

Like Halpin, other adherents of this stance are eager to see the wall come tumbling down.

Several recent debates in the literature of educational administration give evidence of the persistently uneasy relationship of theory and practice. Duhamel offers three plausible explanations for the incongruency: inadequate theory definition; misunderstanding among practitioners about the theory–practice relationship; and the lack of fit between current practice and traditional theory. He blames the disjointedness on the differing orientations and purposes of theorists and practitioners who rarely engage in dialogue. The practitioner focuses on specific problems, while the theorist tries to extend solutions to various situations and points in time. He warns that "theory, in and of itself, is not a panacea. It cannot now, and I doubt if it ever will, fully and accurately describe educational administration in all its variety and richness."[9]

In his response to Duhamel, Whitehead warns against making either theory or practice "the captive mistress of the other." He calls for a conceptual leap which "will allow theory and practice to be seen as equal and necessary partners in a common enterprise." He feels it imperative for the academic researcher in educational administration to "point out the failings, inconsistencies, and injustices of educational systems."[10] Practitioners should not be able to enjoy total freedom in defining and solving problems, contends Whitehead. He accuses practitioners of not being responsive to scholars, and he states that the practical, day-to-day problems which researchers and theorists address can only be solved by compromise on the part of practitioners. Further, Whitehead notes that practitioners complain that theorists do address real problems, but then they refuse to grant access to those problems, much like one who hangs up a "Do not disturb" sign on his hotel room and then objects to the manager when the room is not cleaned.

Discontent with theory in educational administration is mirrored also in the Greenfield–Griffiths debate in the 1970s, which was precipitated by Greenfield's critical address at the International Intervisitation Programme.[11] Greenfield criticized established theoretical perspectives on the basis that they encourage a dualism between people and organizations which separates the organization from the feelings, actions, beliefs, and purposes of the people who comprise the organization. Greenfield called for a phenomenological mode of research to inform theory rather than confirm it. In reaction, Griffiths reaffirmed traditional thinking about theory development, rejected phenomenology as "rudimentary" and "naive," and warned against developing phenomenological theories of administration.[12] Of course, Greenfield's "new" perspective is no longer new. The two viewpoints coexist more peacefully now, as we have become convinced of the need for a variety of research perspectives. Rigid polarization of perspectives serves no purpose. Walker, for example, has noted the need for repeated and systematic observations of organizations from as many perspectives as imagination can conjure.[13]

The state of the art of theory in education administration has changed slowly in recent years. Willower examines this evolution, providing tangible evidence of the progress of theory development.[14] Most theories, he says, are packages which are more conceptually fragmented than integrated. He cites articles by Bidwell, Griffiths, and Corwin[15] which have examined theories in relationship to educational organizations. From these comprehensive reviews he concludes that to date conceptual work in educational administration— from social system and role theory, leadership theory, and decision-making theory to bureaucratic theory and economic and political theories—is more theoretical orientation than it is theory. In other words, we have had thrusts of inquiry from which we can use some ideas, but these thrusts have only laid the groundwork for theory development in educational administration.

One of the problems Willower sees in theory development in educational administration—quite outside the problem of linking theory to practice—is usually that neither explicitly defined variables nor deductively ordered theoretical propositions have emerged. He calls for more deductive clarity so that those who are interested in these theoretical frameworks do not have to study by "excavation." He observes that "some theorists are practicing construction without blueprints."[16]

Some researchers search for the great theory of educational administration or the paradigm that will transform it as a field of study, while others are content to offer elegant fragments of theory which may help explain one small piece at a time of the practitioner's reality. Some demand a more scientifically rigorous approach to the field of educational administration (Willower sees the field maturing in this regard), while others are not certain that this direction may be most fruitful (Greenfield doubts that science can ever guide the administrator's hand). The tension persists. The debate is prolonged. What is not in dispute is the picture of the educational administrator's world that is provided by recent studies—a workplace of constant movement, activity, simultaneous events, and tremendously diverse individuals and groups of people. It is a world of pressing practical problems which need to be solved, a world in which the attempt at problem solving will be made either with or without the aid of explicit theory.

### Theory and Practice

The second, less popular but, to us, attractive position on the subject in question maintains that the problems of linking theory and practice in educational administration have been exaggerated. Practitioners constantly inform their work with theory —imported from the university as well as home-grown in nature—even though the process is more often implicit than explicit. Proponents of this position argue that the debate is to some extent a contrived one, fueled by theorists who are upset because they are ignored in field settings and practitioners whose anti-intellectual biases need expression.

In an early discussion of this problem, Jacob Getzels began by setting down three possible views of the nature of educational administration.[17] The first evolved from the ancient attitude that leaders appear naturally, that they are "born, not made." The second centered on the belief that school administration is essentially a matter of human engineering, where the central task is developing more effective prescriptions for schools and school personnel. The third assumed that the conceptual understanding of the administrator is what needs to be stretched. Getzels opts for the third view, using this argument:

> To be sure, theories without practices like maps without routes may be empty, but practices without theories, like routes without maps, are *blind*. The prescription-centered approach to the solution of fundamental educational issues (which I hope is the business of the school administrator) seems to me not only delusive but impossible. So-called practical principles cannot be either meaningfully formulated or effectively applied outside a supporting conceptual framework. Indeed, the inevitability of theorizing or "map-making" in *all* human affairs must be clear to anyone who has inquired into the sources of his own behavior or examined carefully the behavior of others. The question of whether we should use theory in our administrative behavior is in a sense as meaningless as the question of whether we should use motivation in our behavior.[18]

There may be a gap between theory and practice, but there is no rationale for it, and every effort should be made to eliminate it. Getzels makes a basic point when he says that the conceptually sensitive administrator works to achieve a "strategic position not only to understand what is going on, but also to make decisions for himself, rather than to follow the mob, call in the 'expert' or just do nothing at all."[19]

One of the most satisfying discussions of the relationship between theory and practice in educational administration was prepared by Joseph Schwab.[20] Schwab viewed the practicing administrator as all-too-often "living in a narrower well than most of us," restricted not simply in the capacity to use theory, but also curtailed in the ability to understand experience within that well. For Schwab the singular efficacy of theory for practitioners lies in its liberating impact.

> Thus, every administrator needs a variety of bodies of theory about a variety of bodies of phenomena, not only to guide his interpretation of events and of the problems he sees, but to magnify and diversify what he can recognize as a problem, and similarly to magnify and diversify what he is prepared to recognize as a viable solution to a problem.[21]

He saw two underlying causes of the gulf between theory and practice. The first involves the differences *among* theories, forcing upon the practitioner confusing variations in terms. Without a metatheory the practitioner either fails to see such discrepancies, or, seeing them, is unable to resolve them. The second is the abstract nature of theory. "All general knowledge," Schwab writes, "is achieved at the expense of some measure or another of the richness which characterizes particular events."[22] Even some future metatheory will not restore that richness.

Nonetheless, says Schwab, theory and practice are compatible. They complement each other, and he draws an unusual metaphor in describing their union.

> The practitioner, the administrator, must be, then, the outcome of a complex marriage, interaction, and tension between theory and practice.
>
> Theory brings three things to the marriage:
> 1. A depth and breadth of coherent knowledge beyond anything which experience can supply.
> 2. A breaching of the walls of personal and social class prejudice in the practitioner—urbanity, in short.
> 3. Continuing refreshment and enlargement of what is admitted to experience —antidote to complacence, rigidity, and obsolescence.
>
> Practice, meanwhile, brings the two gifts we have already named:
> 1. The wit which brings theory to its matter—quite literally to make sense of ideas.
> 2. The wit which bridges what theory has yet to make coherent.[23]

That "developed wit variously known as deliberation, calculation, prudence, common sense, practical wisdom, and experience"[24] must exist in the *practitioner* if the marriage is to work. The bridge may be envisioned by the scholar, yet it is built by the practitioner. The wedding proposal may be offered by the scholar, yet it must be accepted by the administrator in the field setting.

Halpin seems to concur with the view that the practitioner and not the scholar must offer leadership here.

> "How can administrative theory be applied by the superintendent?" I think that when we pose the question in this form, we invite confusion. This is the wrong question, or at least it is a premature question at this juncture. It would be better to ask, "How can the practitioner use the social scientists' findings to sharpen his analysis of the social situations with which he must deal?"[25]

Halpin's view is that theory sensitizes the administrator rather than prescribing courses of action to him or her. It is a position we wholeheartedly support.

Coladarci and Getzels carry this line of reasoning at least one step further by proposing that

> Theory and practice constitute an integrity—that is, they are *not* different things; most commonly they represent differences in the point at which interest and attention are momentarily directed. . . . Theorizing is always present in human behavior, if only implicitly, and an explicit concern for theory is necessary to and has patent values for successful practice—indeed, without a theoretical dimension, practice can be only accidentally successful.[26]

The integrity noted here is something more than Schwab's marriage. One can see theory and practice as different, they say, but that is a problem of perception rather than one of substance. Particularly interesting is their discussion of the administrator's inductive construction of theory. Working theory is developed from experience and then is applied to new experience. What is determined inductively is tested deductively. Thus, grounded theory is as available to the administrator as to the scholar. Coladarci and Getzels add that in this process the administrator has "a moral obligation to make the bases for his acts explicit and examinable."[27] The term *moral* may be a bit too strong, but we concur with the general point, and it is a suggestion to which we return in the final section of the book when cases are offered to the reader for consideration.

But let us not be distracted from our argument. "Theorizing and practicing do coexist. Each is an aspect of the process of inquiry and, intelligently pursued, *each constantly redefines the other.*"[28] This summary statement from Coladarci and Getzels represents a major premise of our book. The theoretical sections which follow are intended to inform and redefine practice rather than to prescribe it. Perhaps this is a more gentle view than some readers will prefer, yet it is one that we feel to be realistic. In addition, our view implies that the administrator is under no more pressure from the admonition of a social scientist than from the influence of a philosopher or an artist. Ramseyer reminded us that science is not absolute and infallible. "It merely provides us with ways of thinking."[29] It tells us what the world appears to be like, not what it actually is like. And in telling us that, science only elicits our interpretations, for scientists—like everyone else—"cannot disassociate themselves from values in any act they perform, even the selection of their own assumptions."[30]

When all is said and done, it may not be the nature of either theory or practice that strains their interaction, but rather the temperament and inclination of the scholar as opposed to that of the administrator. C.P. Snow knew a good deal about both worlds:

> A great many scientists have a trace of the obsessional. For many kinds of creative science, perhaps most, one could not do without it. To be any good, in his youth at least, a scientist has to think of one thing, deeply and obsessively, for a long time. An administrator has to think of a great many things, widely, in their interconnections, for a short time. There is a sharp difference in the intellectual and moral temperaments.[31]

Perhaps it is difficult for an individual in one role to understand the thinking of an individual in the other role, as different as it appears to be, and to accept the contributions of knowledge which might be readily exchanged otherwise. The Canadian novelist, Robertson Davies (who in his lifetime helped Tyrone Guthrie develop the Stratford Festival Theatre, and then later was Master of Massey College at the University of Toronto), commented on "the ordinary disposition of the intellectual to prefer the complex to the simple, and the distant vision to what is directly under his nose."[32] In contrast, the administrator may prefer the simple to the complex, and what is directly at hand to the distant vision. Regardless of these contrasts, and regardless of the starting points of theory, we are certain that theory has similar uses for the scholar and the administrator. It generates problems, questions, and hypotheses. It points to certain data sources. It assists in the analysis of data. It helps describe what exists. It aids in the making of decisions. And revised, it encourages the raising of further problems, questions, and hypotheses. This is enough.

## *NOTES*

[1]See L. Bolman, "Theory, Practice, and Educational Administration: Bridging Troublesome Dichotomies," *Education and Urban Society*, 9:1 (1976): 67–80.

[2]L.E. Whitehead, "Administration: Theory and Practice; Response to Duhamel," *Interchange*, 13:2 (1982): 62–66.

[3]Robin H. Farquhar, *Preparatory Programs in Educational Administration* (Columbus, Ohio: University Council for Educational Administration, 1975).

[4]Donald J. Willower, "Theory in Educational Administration," *Journal of Educational Administration*, 8:1 (May, 1975): 77–91.

[5]R.E. Clark, "Spanning the Gap Between Theory and Practice," *Innovator*, 19:4 (February, 1982): 16–18.

[6]Whitehead, p. 65.

[7]Andrew W. Halpin, *Theory and Research in Administration* (New York: Macmillan, 1966), pp. 294–295.

[8]Ibid., pp. 295–296.

[9]R. J. Duhamel, "Administration: Theory or Practice?" *Interchange*, 13:2 (1982): 60.

[10]Whitehead, p. 65.

[11]T.B. Greenfield, "Theory about Organizations: A New Perspective and its Implications for Schools." In M. Hughes, ed., *Administering Education: International Challenge* (London: Athlone Press, 1975), pp. 71–79.

[12]Daniel E. Griffiths, "Some Thoughts about Theory in Educational Administration—1975," *UCEA Review*, 17:1 (October, 1975): 12–18.

[13]W. Walker, "Values, Unorthodoxy, and the 'Unscientific' in Educational Administration Research," *Educational Administration*, 6:1 (Winter 1977–78): 62–66.

[14]Willower, "Theory in Educational Administration."

[15]See Charles E. Bidwell, "The School as a Formal Organization," in James G. March, ed., *Handbook of Organizations (Chicago: Rand McNally, 1965);* Daniel E. Griffiths, "Administrative Theory," in R.L. Ebel, ed., *Encylopedia of Educational Research* (Toronto: Macmillan, 1969); and Ronald G. Corwin, "Models of Educational Organizations," in Fred M. Kerlinger and John B. Carroll, eds., *Review of Research in Education 2* (Itasca, Ill. Peacock, 1974).

[16]Willower, p. 83.

[17]Jacob W. Getzels, "Theory and Practice in Educational Administration: An Old Question Revisited," in *Administrative Theory as a Guide to Action* (Chicago: Midwest Administration Center, University of Chicago, 1960), pp. 37–58.

[18]Ibid., p. 42.

[19]Ibid., p. 58.

[20]Joseph Schwab, "The Professorship in Educational Administration: Theory- Art-Practice," in *The Professorship in Educational Administration* (Columbus, Ohio: University Council for Educational Administration, 1964), pp. 47–70.

[21]Ibid., p. 63.

[22]Ibid.

[23]Ibid., p. 64.

[24]Ibid.

[25]Halpin, p. 285.

[26]Arthur P. Coladarci and Jacob W. Getzels, *The Use of Theory in Education Administration* (Stanford, Calif.: School of Education, Stanford University, 1955), p. 4.

[27]Ibid., p. 6.

[28]Ibid. (their italics).

[29]John A. Ramseyer, "Reflections on the Use of Theory as a Means for Improving Research and Practice in Educational Administration," *Theory into Practice*, 9:4 (October, 1970), p. 227.

[30]Ibid.

[31]C.P. Snow, *Science and Government* (Cambridge: Harvard University Press, 1961), p. 72.

[32]Robertson Davies, *One Half of Robertson Davies* (New York: Penguin, 1978), p. 144.

# TWO

## ORGANIZATIONAL THEORY AND EDUCATIONAL ADMINISTRATION

# 4

## The Production of
## School Outcomes

### A PRINCIPAL AT THE COUNTER OF THE HOTEL COFFEE SHOP

I've always thought about my job as if I were an artist going to paint a picture. When you start you don't quite know what you're going to do, you don't quite know how it's all going to come out. I guess I could get all romantic with this metaphor. But you really do begin *de novo*. You confront the canvas, but nothing is clear at that point.

**But how do you get results with this approach? How do you solve problems?**

I've always thought you had to develop loyalties to common things in a school. Personally, I'm not goal oriented. That's an insult to an administrator; it limits you too much. You end up being so autocratic, as if you're going to control the course of events. You can't always do that, you know. I like to be part of a group. The boss, sure, but in a working, living environment. You have some jobs to do as the principal, and you do them or people will be disappointed. But you really want to be in a position to learn from the group and with the group, because that's the way you get things done. I consider myself a good politician—and if I have political goals and skills, I can work in any school. I've been able to do that.

**Well, tell me a story about how you work.**

One that comes immediately to mind has to do with the standardized tests. Some years ago—it must have been in the late 1960s—I announced to the assistant superintendent that our school was not going to test the kids that year. He couldn't understand my logic. I remember his response was to threaten to move me out. I said, "Ralph, this *building* isn't going to test the kids. I'm just the person who is saying it." And the system did away with standardized testing for five years. Wasn't that silly?

**Wait a minute. You're going too fast. Go back to the beginning.**

I didn't want to be a test burner. But the tests were so culturally biased. And our school had one of the largest concentration of black kids in town. I had gone down into the classrooms and administered the tests personally. I knew the kids, and many of them were bright enough. But they didn't do well on the tests. It just wasn't right. I knew what the system wanted. They wanted to be able to compare schools. Who's on top? We were the dummies that made the other schools look good. I always oppose this kind of competition. I always have and I always will.

In a situation like this I want to be an independent agent, but with a group I work for. Let me put it another way. I want a political constituency that's stronger than the people who are trying to run me from the top of the school system. Well, even if not stronger, one that would be respected, that would support anything that is reasonable. And on this matter of the testing, I had the staff and the school community with me, I can assure you of that.

I sent over a memo telling the folks in central administration that we were not going to test. Actually, it was the second one I had sent. I had given them one the year before, and they had ignored it, and I hadn't pushed it the first time around. I soon got signals that they were very angry. The word came through secretaries and custodians. They know what's going on, and they'll tell you if you work with them quietly. So, I knew my bosses were stirred up. I decided to let them come see me. I wasn't going to make any inquiries. You have the meeting in your own office when you can. It's territorial, like the jungle. You're at your best in your own territory. So, Ralph called me on the phone. We can work it out. That was his message. I stood firm. They were trying to figure out if I meant it this time. I reminded them that I had raised this issue before. "Yes, but you didn't propose any alternatives." I told Ralph not to come to me for the solution to a problem that was not of my making. My exact words were, "I can recognize cancer even if I can't treat it." That pretty much ended the conversation.

Two weeks after the tests were due in central administration, Ralph came to the school. He said that tests had been received from all the schools except ours. He acted like we hadn't had the telephone conversation. Were we going to be late? I replied, "You're not going to get them, Ralph." Well, he suggested that the superintendent might have to talk to the board of education. I knew that was a lie—that he had already done that—because board members had called me. I told him that the teachers were with me, but that I didn't want to go public on the whole thing, yet. Ralph was damned unhappy with me. He just didn't know how to respond.

### But the system did respond?

Oh, yes. They decided to stop the testing until they could figure out what to do. They didn't change the policy, they just instituted a moratorium. What we did in our schools was kind of like a sit-down strike. Listen, the issues troubled them, too. As we argued over the next few months, they admitted that. They just didn't like my way of getting what I wanted. Making an exception of one school got to them. I told them to find some tests that weren't culturally biased. Then we'd be glad to test our kids again. Well, they looked, but they couldn't find them, and that justified our position. Five years later the tests had improved, and so the whole system started testing again, including our school. You know, good organizations will permit moratoriums when there are some legitimate objections to a particular policy or procedure.

### And you believe that the school constituency is critical to all this?

Absolutely. When I *do* think about the central office, it's usually how to protect my teachers from them. My teachers went to a district-wide meeting not long ago where the teachers from other schools were complaining about the forms they had to fill out which took them two hours each. My teachers were puzzled since they had not received the forms, and they came back and asked me about them. I explained that when I received requests from the central office which would waste their time, sometimes I threw them away. A few I sent to them to complete. But in other cases, and this had been one of them, I simply fill out the cumulative forms and return them. "I know you all pretty well; I know pretty much what you would have to say. But if you want me to send you all these forms. . . ." They cut me off. No, I should just keep doing what I had been doing. That was fine. Protecting them helped me build the constituency. Then when I asked them all to attend three 3-hour *evening* in-service sessions that were voluntary, they all did it. There are tradeoffs.

 Another thing: It's important not to administer against all excesses. You have to have structure and rules for teachers—when to sign in and out and so on. But you have to encourage them to break the rules sometimes. It gives them the sense of freedom and well-being they need. One teacher in our school was separated temporarily from her husband because he was required to take work on the other side of the country. They were both feeling lousy, she told me. I said, "You've got an unhappy husband. Take six days and go see him. I'll put it down as illness." She responded emotionally: "I can't say I'm sick." I told her it was my decision, and off she went. She would never take advantage of anything. But she was better with her kids when she returned. You build loyalty to the school. An administrator has to be concerned with that. Schools are still families, very important social units where people care about each other. Many people who work there don't have churches and families to offer this kind of support. That's why an administrator has to *think* about what he or she is going to do to help people. It has to be conscious. You have to be able to drop something that *seems* important to do something that *seems* unimportant.

**You sound like you could get along without the central office.**

The system is necessary, but for purposes that are not relevant to education at the local school level. Certainly not for day-to-day issues. If a teacher needs a pencil, I should take the pencil to her room for her. The superintendent isn't involved with teachers and kids. He has to gather the resources; I understand that. But he doesn't ultimately care about anyone except the board. They are in charge of his survival. I'm not complaining, I hope you understand that. It's a mistake for an administrator to try to be a popular figure outside his own constituency. It's our local school community that I care the most about.

In a way systems don't exist. They really don't exist. How many principals get fired? None. How many principals stay up late nights worrying about getting fired? Most. It's kind of a fantasy if you think about it very long.

You have to have a sense of the ridiculous. I was at a boring meeting of all our administrators recently. We were in a big library, and I'll bet there are twenty mobiles hanging from the ceiling. I was sitting under one of them. The superintendent was talking about millage. All superintendents seem to feel obliged to talk about millage. No one was listening. I looked up at this mobile. It had three levels of little airplanes. I blew up toward the ceiling, and the bottom level started rotating. I blew again and the middle level started moving *in the other direction.* I was delighted. I stopped and looked across the table, and there was Ralph staring at me. I knew he was really annoyed. But I couldn't stop, I couldn't act guilty. So I stage-whispered, "Ralph, see if you can get that third level going." He didn't know what to do. When someone tells me I'm behaving like a child, I'm complimented. Thank God, you recognized it. There was a child-like quality to Gandhi. It was wonderful. That's why the elementary principalship is the best administrative job of all for educators. You can do the Gandhi trick all day long.

## *FROM PRACTICE TO THEORY*

Educational administrators are familiar with the language of goal-setting. Establishing objectives, planning lessons, accomplishing instructional purposes, setting priorities, and evaluating achievements—these are terms that give comfort to them and to the professors who train them. Perhaps the emphasis upon goals is in direct contrast to the overwhelming confusion of purpose that actually characterizes the profession of education. We try to establish some objectives, and we certainly spend a lot of time examining students, with tests that may or may not respond to those objectives. But, in reality, we are spinning somewhat like that mobile—one level in one direction, a second in another, a third level waiting for a breath of fresh air.

Despite its emphasis upon *outcomes* (and that emphasis is growing), the technology of education is filled with uncertainty. A technology is a process designed to transform a raw material into a product. Simple. Straightforward. And yet, the technology of education and educational administration seems to be poorly understood. There is a lot of pressure on administrators now to *produce*—to exert a strong influence upon student achievement. But what do we really know, in theoretical terms, about our own professional technology? If we knew more, would our influence over process and product increase?

## THE PRODUCTION OF SCHOOL OUTCOMES

### Introduction

In the last fifteen years, a large number of studies investigating the relationship between school resources and student achievement have been conducted. This research has looked at a number of variables, including the attributes of teachers and student peer groups, class size, instructional time, physical facilities, instructional strategies, and curriculum.[1] The conclusion of this research is that schools make a difference. Teachers and the student peer group are regarded as the primary resources for improving student outcomes. Secondary resources affecting student learning include class size, curricula, instructional strategies, and physical facilities. These primary and secondary resources make up the knowledge, materials, and operations relevant to the transformation process in schools. In response to research findings, educational systems are being asked to design policies and practices that will contribute to the increased learning of students. Many of the same findings suggest a need for reshaping these resources. However, constraints in ongoing systems are obvious, and they make changes difficult to come by.

> Resource configurations in ongoing systems result from a large number of instructional mechanisms, internal labor market rules and customs, and from responses of teachers and students and families to these mechanisms. For example, the allocation of teachers to schools is determined by seniority rules and the decisions of the more senior teachers. Which children attend particular schools is determined by rules concerning attendance boundaries, and by family location decisions.[2]

Despite such apparent obstacles, society is hopeful. Programs continue to be initiated at local, state, and federal levels to improve the outcomes of schooling.

School improvement programs and legislative reforms of the 1980s are directed toward tightening the linkages between school programs and their effects. The chain between educational policy, school structures, administrator behavior, teacher behavior, and student behavior is weak and inconsistent, and the farther these components are removed from the student, the weaker their connection with student achievement. For example, California is offering incentives to districts that implement a teacher mentor program (a form of differentiated staffing designed to assist probationary teachers). But no one knows if this particular program is effective, since it was not pilot-tested; if it can be implemented, given the opposition of teachers' unions and the restrictions of collective bargaining agreements; and if it can achieve its goals, since teacher mentors will be distributed sparsely. Further, no one has considered what changes in the school culture or structure may be necessary preconditions for the successful implementation of this program. Still, California administrators are asked to ensure the success of this change in the structure and work of schools. If program goals are not realized, then poor motivation, faulty communications, missing school ethos, inadequate funding, and ineffective instructional leadership may be cited by observers as the cause(s) of failure. But just how responsible is the administrator for the learning that takes place in the school, or for controlling the performances of teachers? What is within the control of the administrator? What is not?

To consider this issue, we must inspect the work of educational organizations. Just what is it that educational organizations do? Often, texts on educational administration do not discuss this subject. This silence is perhaps due to the career ladder of the occupation. Most administrators were formerly teachers, and it is easy to conclude that administrators probably know what teachers do, how they organize their work, and how students learn. But we believe that it is crucial to step back and examine the work of schools from the perspective of organizational theory.

What is the work of the school? Let us examine several illustrations. To be sure, schools deliver a service—instruction. Few would disagree with the argument that it is the work of the school to teach Johnny and Judy to read, do sums, and write in grammatically correct sentences and paragraphs. At a higher level, the expectation generally is that schooling imparts an array of useful knowledge of many kinds, and through many methodologies. Basic understandings in chemistry or algebra are important, but so are library and laboratory research skills, as well as the ability to think creatively, to read critically, and to argue with well-developed logic.

The service provided by the educational organization does not reside solely, of course, in the delivery of a storehouse of knowledge. Schools are also expected, as a second major component of their work, to be "people-changing" institutions. They are expected to prepare young people for responsible adulthood, to encourage the mores and values of the larger society, (e.g., a respect for law and order) and even at times to correct aberrations in the development of the young (through providing drug abuse education, family life courses, and psychological counseling and the like). At the level of higher education, furthermore, educational organizations are expected to be "society-changing" institutions—to produce new knowledge rather than simply passing it on, to advance ways of knowing about our world, to protect those who serve as a conscience for our society.

As a third major element in the work of the schools, it should be recognized (perhaps cynically, but realistically) that educational organizations also serve a custodial service. Millions of youngsters are warmed, fed, and kept busy each day of the year while their parents work. Compulsory attendance laws remove potentially troublesome young people from the streets and from the marginal labor force. And, the long span of time encompassed in formal schooling offers individuals and their families something to do while society delays (sometimes well into the third decade of life) the difficult decision of how to employ them.

On the topic of employment, it should not be forgotten that education is a sizeable industry— a fourth element in the work of schooling is in no small measure the establishment of jobs. Although its many services such as instruction, custodianship, and the like are valued products, the provision of opportunities for adult employment is also a significant focus of activity. Educational administrators find that a sizeable portion of the work of their offices must be spent in garnering and guarding the resources needed to pay staff members, finding the wherewithal to add staff, and adjusting to organizational rules that protect staff (e.g., a maximum class size provision in the teachers' union contract). In higher education, not the least of motives in the active grantsmanship of academic departments is the acquisition of "soft money" to add jobs to those departments.

Finally, as a fifth illustrative element in the work of schools, consider the services educational organizations supply their surrounding communities. Not the least of these services is entertainment. The winning football team, the band's half-time performance at the big game, the drama club's production of *Our Town*, the annual art fair—all these are community events of important entertainment value, and also activities which require a great deal of work. This particular work of the school helps stabilize a community. It adds to the attractiveness of a town, it gives people much to talk about, it provides a bit of the social glue that holds a community together. It is not just pure obstinacy that lies behind the battles many rural communities wage against those who would consolidate their schools into larger and larger school districts.

We see, then, that schools engage in varied forms of work. In pursuing their work, the persons employed in educational organizations are guided by their notions of desired outcomes on the one hand and cause-effect relationships on the other.[3] Considerations of cause-effect relationships are wrapped in the technologies that schools employ—that is, in the transformation processes that bring raw material to finished product. Schools are complex organizations, and they can be shown to use differing technologies to accomplish differing aspects of their work. In this chapter, we shall focus particularly upon the problems of technology and administrative effort surrounding attempts to improve the instructional programs of schools. This chapter defines the concept of technology, identifies three characteristics of technology (uncertainty, interdependence, and complexity), and discusses how these characteristics apply to educational organizations. Further, it presents two classical typologies of technology, and then analyzes the opportunities for administrators to influence teacher work and behavior with the hope of improving school outcomes (that is, realizing the expectations this society holds for its schools).

## Technology Defined

By technology, we mean the processes designed to transform any raw material (whether material, human, or symbolic) into goods or services. For example, the raw material can be silk, values, alcoholics, or steel, and the products can be garments, governmental decisions, reformed alcoholics, or automobiles. Technology encompasses the knowledge, materials, and operations relevant to the transformation process. Specifically, the technology of an organization includes: (1) the background, knowledge, and skills of personnel, (2) the techniques used for analyzing the characteristics of raw material, (3) the procedure(s), methods(s), program(s), and tools (machines and equipment) used in the transformation process, and (4) the arrangements of the work flow. The concept can be applied to human service organizations as well as industries. In a school, for example, the teaching of mathematical functions at any grade level requires some knowledge of human behavior, motivation, and subject matter. The teacher may have a bachelor's degree in education with a master's degree in mathematics. Applying this knowledge, a teacher assesses the ability and achievement level of students, makes judgments about how the students should be instructed, develops lesson plans, selects appropriate materials, groups students for instruction, and then proceeds to teach.

Some theorists have argued that an organization's formal structure (e.g., roles, rules, and authority) is dependent on its technology[4] and that both organizational effectiveness and human satisfaction are dependent on how well suited the organization's structure is to the accomplishment of its tasks. This proposition is called the technological imperative. It is interesting to recall that over the years proposals for alternatives to the traditional cellular organization of schools (such as the open space concept) stem from a belief that the traditional structure and authority relationship between teacher and students is not well suited to teaching and learning. From the perspective of the technological imperative, the key role for the administrator is in maintaining or changing an organization's structure to enhance the efficiency and effectiveness of the organization's work. Of course, that process can be quite different as seen by a principal in a low-income school and people in the central office when their goals are in conflict.

To understand technology and its application to school organizations, three dimensions of technology are considered in the following pages. They are: (1) uncertainty or unpredictability, (2) interdependence, and (3) complexity or diversity. The dimensions "isolate the most critical variables needed to predict structural features of organizations."[5] We discuss each dimension from a theoretical perspective, relying on typologies developed by Charles Perrow and James D. Thompson, and we apply each to the school context.

## DIMENSIONS OF TECHNOLOGY

### Uncertainty

All organizations face some uncertainty as they perform their work. This uncertainty may stem from a variety of sources, including the technology of the organization. With respect to the public schools, the scarcity of financial and human resources, the unclear goals of schooling, and the difficulty of isolating and measuring the effect of schools on students may create uncertainty. The nature of public school finances in some states (district income based on the collections of tax receipts and the allocation of federal grants to supplement state and local funds) creates serious contingencies for their operation. State-level funding is set on a year-to-year basis, rendering long range planning difficult. Lacking sufficient resources, a district might continue to use out-dated textbooks, reduce the number of teaching positions, or eliminate special programs viewed as tangential to the schools' central mission. The Columbus (Ohio) Public Schools were forced to eliminate art programs and art specialists for the elementary schools in 1970 due to a lack of funds and to close school doors in the winter months of 1977 due to severe energy shortages in the Midwest. Another example of uncertainty stemming from scarce resources is witnessed when legislation mandates new programs or procedures without sufficient educational resources, as in the case of California's current legislation requiring instructional reform primarily at the secondary level. Similarly, limited resources often make it difficult for local schools to comply with federal program regulations.[6] A study of the implementation of Public Law 94-142 (The Education of All Handicapped Children Act) in Massachu-setts concluded that the time needed to coordinate testing, to hold meetings for discussions of individualized educational programs, and to write individualized programs took time away from students who needed instruction.[7]

The unclear goals of schooling create another kind of uncertainty for education-al organizations. Organizations are instruments for achieving specific purposes and goals. Goals specify desired future end results and identify where present energy and efforts must be directed.[8] Thus, goals guide decision making and the selection of alternative courses of action, and they serve also as a basis for evaluating an organization or its members.[9] When schools are described as having unclear goals, it is suggested that the school has multiple goals which may be incongruent or inconsistent. Do we want all students to attain the same achievement level? Is religious instruction to be separated from other instruction? Do we want all students to graduate from high school, or do we want to increase graduation standards? Are we interested in maintaining a system of winners and losers at the student level, as the principal in the coffee shop suspected? The lack of agreement about goals and the priorities for their attainment often means that the mission for our schools changes as new winds blow.

Lack of agreement about goals, as well as problems of measurement and the evaluation of output, makes it difficult to assess whether or not schools have accomplished what they set out to achieve. In recent years, the assessment of student achievement in reading and mathematics on standardized tests has served as an indication of school effectiveness and success (a fact of life that was unacceptable to the principal who spoke at the beginning of this chapter, particularly if a test loaded against his students was being employed by the district). This is troublesome for several reasons. First, there is an overwhelming relationship between achievement and the socioeconomic status (SES) of students. Thus, if one assumes that successful school districts are those which score higher than predicted by SES, entire districts or even states may be labeled unsuccessful. According to this standard, fewer than 20 elementary schools in the entire state of California can be regarded as successful. On the other hand, if one looks at increases in test scores or determines the consistency of scores over time, that list of schools would be quite different.[10]

Relying solely on the standardized test scores in a limited number of subject areas for evaluation suggests that the responsibilities and functions of schools are quite narrow. Erickson points out, "Quite a bit of research evidence suggests that schools which are effective in developing basic skills in mathematics and reading may be lousy schools for developing higher orders of cognitive ability, creative thinking, synthesis, and analysis."[11] Perhaps organizational effectiveness needs to be measured on a variety of dimensions, not just student outcomes or productivity in reading and mathematics. Beyond this, it is difficult to sort out the influence or impact of schools from that of other social institutions in the development of the individual. How much credit or blame should the schools accept? We often equate schooling with education, yet there are other educative influences such as the church, the family, and the media which cannot be discounted.

The key task for the administrator, according to Thompson, is the management of uncertainty stemming from technology. Technological sources of uncertainty for educational organizations include unpredictability and variability in students (raw material), in teaching tasks (operations), and in educational professionals (task performers). To understand the relationship between organizational technology and uncertainty, we draw upon the work of Charles Perrow.[12]

An organization's technology is labeled uncertain based on (a) the uniformity or variability of its inputs (raw material), (b) the number of exceptions encountered in the work process, and (c) the number of major product changes experienced.[13] The characteristics of the raw material an organization transforms will determine whether it performs routine or nonroutine work.[14] Work is said to be routine when it meets two conditions: Well-established techniques are known to produce the desired outcome or result, and these techniques can be applied to essentially similar raw materials over and over. Nonroutineness in work refers to work conditions in which there are few well-established techniques to produce the desired result, and exceptions are made in the work process because the raw materials are not alike or the products must be custom made.[15] An organization faces degrees of uncertainty to the extent that its raw materials are not uniform and stable and the techniques used to transform the inputs are not codified in the written or oral histories of the organization. The work of any organization (or subunit within an organization) will fall on the continuum ranging from routine to nonroutine.

Perrow proposes a model based on two technological dimensions. The first is the extent to which problems are encountered as one is performing the work of the organization. A worker may contend with few or many problems depending on the stability of the raw material. The second dimension is the extent to which the worker knows how to solve the problem presented by the exceptional cases. Faced with an exception, the worker must search for the appropriate response. If the individual is familiar with the problem and knows automatically what to do, or can turn to instructions, a manual, a computer, or other personnel for information, the search is called analyzable. The search is unanalyzable when the individual must rely on experience, judgment, wisdom, or intuition to solve the problem.[16] These two dimensions—exceptions and search procedures—are dichotomized and cross-classified by Perrow to yield four types of technology which are labeled craft, nonroutine, routine, and engineering (see Figure 4.1). From this typology, a technology is labeled craft when few exceptions are encountered, but when exceptions do occur, the search for solutions must take place without written instructions or a manual. The worker must feel a way to the solution. The craftsperson selects the tools, methods, and pace at which he or she works. The work is characterized by variety and personal control over it. A technology is labeled nonroutine when it is high on variability (due to customer needs) and search is also unanalyzable. The worker encounters many exceptions for which solutions have not been developed. An engineering technology

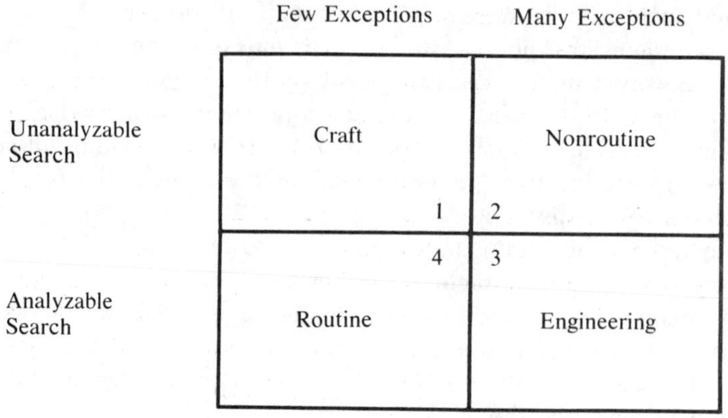

Few Exceptions        Many Exceptions

| Unanalyzable Search | Craft | Nonroutine |
|---|---|---|
| | 1   2 | |
| | 4   3 | |
| Analyzable Search | Routine | Engineering |

**FIGURE 4.1**    Technology variables

is high on variability, but programs guide the selection of the appropriate techniques to create the custom-made products. A routine technology is low on variability, and search is analyzable. In the mass-production assembly line, many workers watch and facilitate machine operation or assemble parts by hand. The individual exercises little control over the work. The rate of work, selection of tools, and product to be assembled are outside the individual's control.

This analysis can be extended to people-changing organizations, including schools. The nature of the raw materials varies along two dimensions—its uniformity and stability, plus its understandability (see Figure 4.2). In this grid the conceptions, rather than the objective realities, of the raw material are crucial. That is, we move from a concern with the objective facts to the organization's (or task performer's) phenomenological response to the raw material.

Perrow makes this point skillfully in his comparison of two juvenile correction institutions which differ dramatically in their concept of the nature of the delinquent and what is necessary to transform (i.e., rehabilitate) the youngster. In one institution, the staff believed all delinquents lack proper respect for adults, have not been trained to be obedient, and are not trustworthy.[17] Thus, all youngsters were treated in a uniform manner, and strict discipline was administered to rehabilitate them. In addition, personnel did not have specialized training, for anyone could follow the routines designed to instill respect and obedience. In the other institution, each adolescent was considered unique psychologically. It was believed that the reasons for delinquency vary from individual to individual. Programs and activities were selected after information was gathered (through testing and psychoanalysis) on each individual. Because judgments had to be made about each case, personnel were professionals—psychologists and social workers. Perrow observes, in summary:

> If you perceive a delinquent as simply lacking in respect for adults because he has never been made to obey adults, your way is clear. The raw material is simple and known, and the techniques are readily available from military or prison history. . . . If you perceive delinquents as complicated, self-activating, unique individuals about whom not a great deal is known, search is unanalyzable and must rely upon vague processes, such as empathy, understanding, or interpreting early childhood experiences.[18]

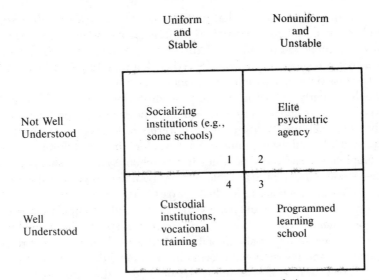

FIGURE 4.2    Raw material variables (people-changing examples)
From *Organizational Analysis: A Sociological View*, by Charles Perrow. Copyright © 1970 by Wadsworth Publishing Company, Inc. Reprinted by permission of Brooks/Cole Publishing Company, Monterey, California 93940.

The conceptions of the raw material dictated the technology used, the personnel hired, and the programs selected.

The carryover into education is readily apparent. One school and its faculty may view its raw material as eager, alive, and instructionally receptive children who must be challenged, plied with learning alternatives, and provided with room and time to explore on their own. The faculty assumes that the children want to learn, and they work to facilitate learning. A second school, alternatively, may view its raw material as resistant, passive, and uninterested in learning. The children must be force-fed that which they need to know, in a carefully structured and closely controlled curriculum that seeks to cover thoroughly each important body of knowledge. Such a curriculum must blanket its subject well, because it cannot be assumed that anything that is missed will be discovered by the child later, on his or her own volition.

Uncertainty in a people-changing organization can be reduced if its clientele or work processes become more predictable. This can be accomplished in two ways. First, the variability of clientele can be managed by regarding it as immaterial to the transformation process (as in the example of the correctional institute which treated all delinquents identically). Second, the work can be made more predictable through the hiring of highly trained or experienced personnel. Training and experience help the worker discern patterns in the variability which permits him or her to respond in predetermined ways.[19] For example, Mintzberg points out that

> becoming a skillful clinical surgeon requires a long period of training, probably five or more years. An important feature of that training is "repetitive practice" to evoke "an automatic reflex." So automatic, in fact, that . . . a series of surgical "cookbooks" list, even for "complex" operations, the essential steps as chains of 30 to 40 symbols on a single sheet, to be reviewed mentally in 60 to 120 seconds at some time during the day preceding the operation.[20]

This is not to suggest, however, that professionals do not exercise discretion. One would probably find that no two surgeons perform an operation in precisely the same way; however, some degree of standardization or routinization is essential. The surgeon cannot proceed as an inexperienced cook attempting to prepare a Chinese meal for the first time. Chaos must be reduced sharply.

Schools similarly reduce uncertainty by clustering clients and hiring teachers with special training and experience. Students pose unique problems for public schools because they are highly variable in terms of intelligence as well as social, economic, and cultural backgrounds. Each student brings different attributes to school, completely apart from variables in the school system. Schools must determine which student differences are relevant and then find ways to deal with them. In addition to differences among individuals, a particular school may receive the same number and kind of students over the years or the student population may change gradually or quickly. How a school organization responds to individuality and changes in the demographic makeup of its student body depends on the relevance of the difference for the instructional process or outcomes, the number of exceptional cases, and the availability of resources to accommodate the exceptions.

In total institutions (so called because they assume total responsibility for the inmate) such as prisons, military academies, and seminaries, de-individualization processes are employed to strip away the distinctive characteristics of individuals and emphasize their common qualities.[21] For example, inmates may wear uniforms or be called by a categorical appelative rather than individual names. This, of course, would not be tolerated in the public schools, where the interests of the state in ensuring that its youth receive an adequate education must be weighed and balanced with the parents' rights to direct the rearing of their children as well as with students' rights as citizens today.

There are acceptable ways of controlling uncertainty stemming from student variability. Public schools, as a result of compulsory attendance laws, are likely to sort students within a particular school to achieve greater homogeneity.[22] Independent schools may restrict admission to certain kinds of students, and schools with religious affiliations may attract an identifiable student population to achieve a similar effect. The effect of sorting is to reduce the variability with which the teacher has to deal, to provide a protective environment for the patrons, and to build and maintain categories. Grouping of students is needed because the teacher works simultaneously with a large number of students (as opposed to other professionals such as social workers, attorneys, or physicians, who work typically with clients on a one-to-one basis). Following an assessment of needs, a student will be categorized. When school personnel are confronted with exceptional cases, a decision must be made as to how to treat the variability.

> The problem of dealing with variability in student abilities and accomplishments during a school year . . . is vested in the classroom teacher, and one important component of his professional skill is the ability to handle day-to-day fluctuations in the response of individual students and collectively by the classroom group.[23]

The professional requires considerable work discretion. An autonomous decision may be made by the teacher at the level of instruction, but at other times it may be guided by educational policy set by the board of education. The decision also may be guided by state or federal laws.

For schools, responding to exceptions is often expensive because it means adding personnel. Education is a labor-intensive industry. For example, within the broad category of handicapped children, there are specialized credentials for teachers of the learning disabled, mentally retarded, and emotionally disturbed. Based on an assessment of a student's ability and the availability of program alternatives, a handicapped pupil may be placed in a class with a teacher who holds a specialized certificate, or may receive additional educational services, or be integrated into the regular program (i.e., mainstreamed). Each option has a different price tag attached to it.

Decisions about the treatment of exceptional cases, however, may not be guided solely by the judgment of educational professionals. Cultural, economic, social, and political forces come into play. For example, while it was once acceptable to sort boys and girls into different classes and programs in some areas (e.g., physical education, home economics, drafting, sciences), Title IX of the Education Amendments of 1972 removes sex barriers to equal opportunity in school admissions, athletics, counseling, and class assignment. Also, although students are typically grouped into grades according to age—a typical fourth grader is nine to ten years old—other schemes like nongraded structures have been promoted.

This notion that pedagogy is, in part, a function of cultural, economic, social, and political forces can also be illustrated by examining how public schools cope with the presence of language-minority students. The *California Education Code*, Article 3, Section 30 stipulates that:

> English shall be the basic language of instruction in all schools. . . . It is the policy of the state to insure the mastery of English by all pupils in the schools.

When language-minority children are of school-age, the public schools in California must find some way to manage this variability. One option might be to require that before a child could enter school, he or she must have already acquired basic English skills. However, laws passed in California in 1976 and 1980 (stemming from the Supreme Court decision in *Lau* v. *Nichols*)[24] limit a school district's discretion and require that all limited English-speaking students who are in a grade with ten or more children of similar language ability must be enrolled in a bilingual program. However, identifying and serving students may be more difficult than it appears.

The problem of determining which children should receive additional resources or assistance and what kind of program they should receive is further exacerbated when the demographic makeup of a school changes. For example, in Parker Elementary School in San Francisco, where Kinney Lau attended school at the time of the Supreme Court decision, 98 percent of the students were of Chinese extraction. Now, ten years later, the school is 45 percent Chinese, 25 percent Hispanic, and the remaining 40 percent are white, black, Filipino, Cambodian, Indian, Burmese, and Arabic.[25] The changing character of many California schools requires continual adjustment in the number and kinds of bilingual teachers and paraprofessionals, not only from year to year, but often within the school year (all of which is complicated by the severe shortages of qualified personnel).

After determining which students have special needs, the question of instructional methods needs to be resolved. Three approaches are used to instruct language-minority students in the public schools. Language-minority children are taught in their native language until they learn English (transitional bilingual); in their native language in academically demanding classes while also attending English classes (English as a second language or structured immersion); or are placed directly into the regular program where English is the only language of instruction (submersion). The controversy over how to deal with language-minority students and the best method of instruction is not resolved, or even adequately guided, by research data. Research findings and testimonies about the effectiveness of bilingual programs are mixed.[26] In fact, the U.S. Commission on Civil Rights is currently reassessing existing policy on bilingual education to clarify its possible role in the increasing isolation of Hispanic students. On the other hand, many minority leaders call for an end to the policy of linguistic intolerance in the United States.

The selection of appropriate methods, thus, is intertwined with broader ideas of personal and cultural identity and validation of cultural pluralism. Educational experts, politicians, parents, and community members may disagree over matters of educational policy depending on their political beliefs. The example of bilingual education illustrates clearly that political considerations influence pedagogy. This case also reveals the interaction effect of technological and environmental uncertainty in that decision makers are faced with conflicting goals of core constituencies and incomplete knowledge about which strategy would lead to high student achievement.

## Interdependence

In addition to the uncertainty or unpredictability of raw materials, the interdependence of work processes is an important consideration, because interdependence affects the amount of coordination needed among personnel to get the work accomplished. Weick notes that interdependence exists between two workers when the task performance of one worker poses contingencies for the performance of the other.[27] This relationship shapes the amount of supervision needed and the number of administrators (i.e., span of control) required to carry out planning and supervision both to achieve organizational goals and to define the character of the work group.

Educational organizations are structured in a manner that assumes considerable interdependence. In theory, we assume that the learnings at lower grades must be completed before one passes to a higher grade—and we often hold children back who fail to meet this criterion. Algebra teachers assume that the fundamentals of multiplication and division have been mastered; sophomore English teachers assume that the basics of punctuation are well in hand; science teachers assume that other teachers have successfully taught the rudiments of correct spelling; even first grade teachers assume that already, in kindergarten, youngsters have been taught to sit still for short periods of time, to listen, and to raise a hand for recognition. Indeed, one of the central characteristics of schooling is the feeling it imparts that people build an education one layer at a time, sequentially, over many years of closely interwoven instruction.

On the other hand, interdependence in education is not as tight as many have believed. To be sure, the pupilflow in educational organizations is equivalent to the workflow in industrial settings, and teachers are the primary workers. The pupilflow refers to the movement of students from one teacher to another teacher within some time frame, such as day, week, month, or academic year. This notion can be applied to elementary and secondary schools as well as post-secondary institutions. For example, at the high school level teachers are linked with other teachers by the sharing of students. A particular student may be studying English, calculus, physics, and French with four different teachers. This pattern is known as departmentalization and reflects a minimal level of task interdependence. Within this pattern the performance of one teacher is generally not influenced by another. Similarly in a university, the instruction of the anthropology professor is not affected particularly by the instruction of the English literature professor. Also, some teachers in a school may be linked together while remaining quite isolated from others.

To understand task interdependence, we draw upon the work of James D. Thompson. There are three basic kinds of interdependence—pooled, sequential, and reciprocal. Interdependence is inclusive. Thompson observes: "All organizations have pooled interdependence; more complicated organizations have sequential as well as pooled; and the most complex have reciprocal, sequential, and pooled, although an organization will have a dominant form."[28] Thus, pooled is the least and reciprocal the most complex form. Each type of technological interdependence is described in the next several sections.

**Pooled Interdependence.**   Some organizations have as their primary function the linking of otherwise independent elements, such as clients and customers. This type of technology is called mediating, and the work is accomplished through pooled interdependence. The work performed is interrelated only in that each process contributes to the overall objective and is based on the sharing of resources.[29]

Insurance companies, post offices, banks, commodity brokers, and real estate agencies offer some examples of organizations using pooled interdependence. The commercial bank links depositors and borrowers. The real estate agency links those who would like to buy property with those who would sell property. Thompson notes that the complexity in the mediating technology comes from the necessity of operating in standardized ways. For example:

> The commercial bank must find and aggregate deposits from diverse depositors; but, however diverse the depositors, the transaction must conform to standard terms and to uniform bookkeeping and accounting procedures. It must also find borrowers; but no matter how varied their needs or desires, loans must be made according to standardized criteria and on terms uniformly applied to the category appropriate to the particular borrowers. Poor risks who receive favored treatment jeopardize bank solvency.[30]

Examples of pooled interdependence also can be found in educational organizations. The media specialist in the junior high school links instructional materials and media with users (teachers and students). The College of Education at the state university may not interact with the College of Business, and neither may have contact with the College of Medicine. But the poor performance of one college may jeopardize the funding level for the whole university and thus the other colleges. In schools, pooled interdependence often takes the form of resource interdependence for teachers who draw upon the same scarce resources required for teaching, such as materials, equipment, physical space, or the services of specialists and paraprofessionals.[31]

**Sequential Interdependence.**    Another type of interdependence is evident when tasks are ordered in serial fashion. This is best typified by the mass-production assembly line in a manufacturing firm (known as long-linked technology). Some tasks, operations, or motions must be successfully completed before others can begin. One task feeds into the next. In sequential interdependence, relationships between workers are asymmetrical. One worker poses contingencies for another, but not vice versa. As a matter of necessity in our schools, students are grouped or batched according to grade level, ability, or classroom. Students proceed in a regularized manner from one lesson or activity to another in temporal sequence —hour after hour, day after day, semester after semester, and year after year until they leave the system, hopefully as well-educated graduates.

Two kinds of sequential interdependence operate in the school organization —throughput and instructional.[32] Throughput interdependence is similar to Thompson's serial form. Consider the situation in a middle school where pupils flow from one class period to another throughout the school day. If the art teacher holds students beyond the class period to clean up, the social studies teacher (or other receiving teacher) will not be able to start her lesson on time. However, the social studies teacher is not dependent on the completion of the *content* in the art class.

In long-linked technologies, workers often stockpile materials to enable them to adjust to breakdowns in the line. While at first glance it may seem difficult to imagine stockpiling students, Jackson suggested that the waiting which students spend a good deal of time doing is akin to stockpiling.[33] Students wait in line, wait for assistance from the teacher, and do extra-credit work until the rest of their classmates catch up with them. Through these means, teachers are able to control the pace of their work, a quality of worklife believed to be psychologically important. It is interesting to note that suggestions to improve time on task are directed at reducing the amount of waiting or noninstructional time in schools through shortening lunch and recess periods and time between classes. However, the Chicago Public Schools, faced with an oversupply of students during the early 1960s, double-promoted higher-achieving students to spread the bulge through the system. In other words, production was speeded up to accommodate an oversupply of raw materal and smooth out operations. Thus, teachers did not have to be retrained, reassigned, or dismissed, nor did new classroom and buildings have to be constructed.

As noted earlier in this section, workflow interdependencies have implications for required coordination mechanisms. In the case of regulating pupilflow, scheduling is the coordination mechanism. After the master class schedule for a school is built, its maintenance is low in cost, impersonal, and generally effective. Assembly schedules are also designed in advance for days when special programs are offered. Teachers can plan in advance for a shortened class period. But teachers are not dependent on one another as workers in a production line are, where their success depends on the successful completion of the immediately preceding activity. Thompson notes that long-linked technology "approaches instrumental perfection when it produces a single kind of product, repetitively and at a constant rate."[34] When only one product is turned out, the selection of materials and tools, construction of workflow arrangements, acquisition of raw materials and selection of human operators is simplified.[35]

This does not appear to be descriptive of schools. We know that promoted first graders often arrive incomplete (by someone's definition) for second grade—yet, the second grade teacher can and must act. The interdependence in school is not so direct as it is in a petroleum refinery. Students conceived as inputs and outputs are not standardized, and even though many things must be taught and learned in a specified serial order (the alphabet is taught before reading can begin), readjustment is necessary if any student acts improperly or fails to meet educator expectations. Further, students may pass through various courses or component parts (English, math, science, history), but when these parts are assembled into a single functioning unit (as represented by the student's transcript) a standardized end product is not guaranteed. Although they are graduates, students read and compute at different levels, and some are college-bound while others will enter the workforce immediately.

Efforts to increase interdependency are evident in competency-based education and in the improvement of scope and sequence for subjects and levels. Nonetheless, only in gross ways are the instructional activities and plans of one teacher dependent on another. Coordination often is achieved by teacher talks with one another about their ideas and intentions. If overlaps or discrepancies occur, mutual adjustment is required. Thus, instructional interdependencies depend on personal relationships. For example, in the teachers' lounge, a second grade teacher of students with a wide range of reading levels may suggest to the first and third grade teachers that they divide students for reading instruction. They think this is a good idea because it will reduce the number of different preparations they make. To do so, the teachers schedule reading for the same block of time and coordinate topics and materials. Such interdependence of instructional efforts may be accomplished informally. In addition, within the formal system, teachers may be assigned to school units or teams which may be headed by a leader. Teaming may assume many varieties—teachers linked together in a department without sharing students, or, in its purest form, "two or more teachers are given responsibility, working together, for all or a significant part of the instruction of the same group of students."[36] The degree of task interdependence can be ascertained by determining the frequency with which teachers exchange students who impose contingencies for each other.

This team organization is in stark contrast with the traditional, cellular organization of schools. Instructional interdependence is not a predominant reality of the American school, as the following example illustrates. A committee of teachers and administrators in a suburban district was using a technique called curriculum mapping to analyze the entire curriculum. In the course of discussions, the committee learned that the same sex education film was being used in the health, home economics, and biology classes for sophomores. The teachers involved had used this film for years but never mentioned it to their colleagues. It is probably even more surprising that the students never complained.

Teaming changes the visibility of the task performances of teachers and alters their social relationships. In contrast with external scheduling, coordination by mutual adjustment is high in cost, time-consuming, emotionally charged, and unpredictable. Coordination must survive frequently brittle relationships. Nonetheless, the implications of team teaching for educational administrators become apparent when one considers the effects of a closely-knit collegial workgroup on the organization. The teacher now shares pedagogical issues with other teachers in that workgroup. This creates an organizational level existing between the classroom teacher and the principal. A study of the effects of team teaching noted consequences in the instructional program, including a shift of power over the design and operation of the educational program from the administrative hierarchy to the teaching faculty; a reduction in the isolation of the individual teacher from the teaching ideas, problems, and activities of colleagues; and an increase in the teachers' feelings of control of work and satisfaction derived from occupation and job.[37] In this kind of organization, the principal's ability to control or direct the activities of others or attend to the social needs of teachers may be reduced. This notion is addressed in more depth in Chapter 8.

**Reciprocal Interdependence.** Reciprocal interdependence is the most complex of the three forms, and it is characteristic of intensive technologies. In this technology, "a variety of techniques is drawn upon in order to achieve a change in some specific object; but the selection, combination, and order of application are determined by feedback from the object itself."[38] In reciprocal interdependence, the outputs of one unit become inputs for others; work is passed back and forth between units; and each unit potentially poses a contingency for the other.

> The intensive technology is most dramatically illustrated by the general hospital. At any moment an emergency admission may require some combination of dietary, X-ray, laboratory, and housekeeping or hotel services, together with the various medical specialities, pharmaceutical services, occupational therapies, social work services, and spiritual or religious services. Which of these, and when, can be determined only from the evidence about the state of the patient.[39]

It is clear from the example that each worker renders a discrete contribution to the complex task. For schools to operate as intensive technologies, the selection, sequence, and mix of techniques used to get the student to learn must be affected largely by feedback from the student. Perhaps the most obvious example of reciprocal interdependence is witnessed in the identification, placement, and education of handicapped children. A regular classroom teacher refers a child with learning problems to a specialist such as a psychologist for testing. Following a battery of tests (which may include a physical examination), a review team composed of the psychologist, counselor, principal, special education teacher, regular class-room teacher, and parents meets to discuss the placement of a student. If certified for special services, the special education teacher in consort with other professionals will develop an individualized educational program (IEP) based upon the assessed strengths and deficiencies of the child. Other specialists—such as a speech therapist or physical therapist—may be called upon as needed.

The notion of interdependence is important for the administrator because tasks are grouped to minimize the costs of communication and coordination. Each type of interdependency places different burdens on communication and decision making.

> With pooled interdependence, action in each position can proceed without regard to action in other positions so long as the overall organization remains viable. With sequential interdependence, however, each position in the set must be readjusted if any

one of them acts improperly or fails to meet expectations. There is always an element of potential contingency with sequential interdependence. With reciprocal interdependence, contingency is not merely potential, for the acts of each position in the set must be adjusted to the actions of one or more others in the set.[40]

Each type of interdependence has an appropriate method of coordination. Pooled interdependence is coordinated through standardization—routines or rules specify how decisions are to be made, or how work is to be processed. In schools with limited audio-visual equipment, procedures must be established to allocate movie projectors, for example. When more teachers want projectors than are available on a particular day, someone must decide who will be satisfied and who will be deprived. Sequential interdependence is coordinated by plans or schedules specifying the time period in which activities are to be carried out. In schools, a class schedule is developed to regularize the flow of pupils from teacher to teacher. Reciprocal interdependence is coordinated by mutual adjustment. Teachers of various sections of Algebra I may agree to teach the same concepts in the same order at the same time to prepare students for Algebra II. Recall, too, the principal's story of the teacher who needed to visit her husband. Here were a variety of goals—loyalty, self-renewal, improved teaching—which were approached and realized through the mutual adjustment of principal and teacher.

Finally, numerous scholars agree that only gross interdependencies in the workflow—or what has been identified as structural looseness or loose coupling —exist in school organizations.[41] Teachers work rather independently from their colleagues even while they work quite closely with students. "Teacher autonomy is reflected in the structure of school systems. The teacher works alone within the classroom, relatively hidden from colleagues and superiors, so that he has broad discretionary judgment within the boundaries of the classroom."[42] The challenge for the administrator is to get all teachers centered on the task of improving the school program and focused on the priorities set for the school. We return to this point at the end of the chapter.

## Complexity

Another dimension of technology which affects the hierarchical authority structure is complexity. The indicators of complexity include the total number of different major tasks performed; the number of occupational specialties in an organization; the length of training required for each specialty;[43] the number of different geographic locations at which work is carried out; and the extent of professional activity of specialists.[44] These indicators represent a composite from the variety of conceptualizations of technical complexity. Complexity has been defined narrowly as the degree of occupational specialization[45] and, more broadly, as the degree of internal segmentation.[46] The social structure of an organization becomes differentiated as the organization pursues a number of distinct goals as well as more than one major organizational activity.[47] To coordinate these activities, divisions or departments and numerous authority levels are created (horizontal differentiation). Thus, as complexity increases so do coordination problems, and there is need for more administrators to solve them.

As expected, complexity varies across industries as well as within one type of organization. Thus, schools may be more or less complex than hospitals, and elementary schools may be more or less complex than secondary schools. In examining this question more closely, we need to consider the variety, specialization, and spatial dispersion of the tasks of schools. The teacher is engaged in a variety of activities in his classroom performance. The activities or subtasks may be grouped in a number of ways. Thomas Green categorizes the activities of teaching into logical, strategic, and institutional acts.[48] Robert Dreeben identifies four aspects of the teaching technology—the instructional process, motivation, classroom control, and social arrangements.[49] Dornbusch and Scott add character development and record-keeping to the list of tasks performed by teachers.[50] If one were to shadow a teacher for a day, noting the various activities in which she engaged, one could develop a list of what a teacher does. After eliminating such activities as eating lunch, drinking coffee, or making a personal telephone call, Green suggests that the remaining activities fall under three general headings (see Table 4.1). The logical acts are related to thinking or reasoning in the conduct of teaching, such as explaining, concluding, inferring, or demonstrating. Strategic acts refer to the plan or strategy in teaching, such as motivating, counseling, disciplining, or questioning. Institutional acts are those activities which are part of the teacher's work organized by the institution of the school. These activities include collecting money, chaperoning the dance, maintaining attendance records, monitoring the lunchroom, patrolling the hall, supervising study hall, and consulting parents.

Green's framework discriminates between activities of teaching and the office of the teacher. Institutional acts are not necessary to the activity of teaching, but they are necessary to the running of a school. The logical and strategic acts must be present for teaching to be going on. If one wants to improve teaching, one would focus on improving either the logical or strategic acts, if not both. The logical acts of teaching are displayed by the teacher during the course of a lesson, whereas strategy may be evidenced over a longer time frame, such as a series of lessons in a semester.[51] A principal may be able to assess the teacher's ability to provide good explanations or demonstrations based on the single observation of a class, but the same teacher's ability to motivate or discipline students would necessitate a series of observations, discussions, and review of accomplishments to make judgments. The

*TABLE 4.1*     Activities of teaching

| The Logical Acts | The Strategic Acts | The Institutional Acts |
| --- | --- | --- |
| Explaining | Motivating | Collecting money |
| Concluding | Counseling | Chaperoning |
| Inferring | Evaluating | Patrolling the hall |
| Giving reasons | Planning | Attending meetings |
| Amassing evidence | Encouraging | Taking attendance |
| Demonstrating | Disciplining | Consulting parents |
| Defining | Questioning | Keeping reports |
| Comparing | | |

From Thomas F. Green, *The Activities of Teaching* (New York: McGraw-Hill, 1971), p. 71.

emphasis on logical or strategic acts may also vary with the level of the curriculum or talents of the teacher.[52] The expertise or authority of administrators to evaluate the performance of teaching is questioned often. Many teachers, especially in secondary schools, suggest that anyone who has not taught their subject matter is not able to evaluate their performance. Some administrators concede this, yet others defend their role, claiming that teaching is a generic process which can be evaluated independently of subject matter. Green suggests that the logical acts will have more to do with subject matter, but the strategic acts tend to be associated with the nature of the student.

> A teacher's reasons regarding the logical acts of teaching will have more to do with the subject to be taught and the ways of knowing within that field. The teacher's strategic reasons will more often be related to the nature of the students to be taught; how well they understood what was done before; whether they are tired, anxious, motivated, prepared to advance, and so forth.[53]

This analysis has implications for the principal's role in improving teaching. Principals may call upon master teachers, department chairs, team leaders, or central office subject-matter specialists to coach less experienced or talented teachers in the logical acts. However, administrators could assist personally in the improvement of strategic teacher acts. It also might be more appropriate to sponsor school-wide inservice activities in the more generic strategic aspects of teaching. A science teacher who is unable to use experiments to demonstrate scientific principles could be coached by another science teacher known for being expert with this method. If the same science teacher wastes a lot of time at the beginning of the class period due to student misbehaviors, either the principal or another teacher knowledgable in behavior management techniques could provide assistance. Topics related to motivation, school climate, discipline, or questioning strategies would cut across subject matter areas and so have wider appeal.

In addition to the number or variety of tasks performed, role specialization is another indicator of complexity. Specialization results when major tasks are divided into discrete subtasks and personnel are assigned to complete those subtasks. A number of different occupational classifications are designated to perform various activities. In schools, the complexity of the scheme for dividing the instructional workflow suggests the degree of staff specialization. There are two major roles in schools— teachers and administrators. The teaching occupation obviously is distinguished according to levels—elementary, secondary, college. It is believed that teachers do different things at the different levels, although they also do many similar things. There is a modest amount of specialization at elementary and secondary levels. Beliefs about occupational specialization can be inferred from the nature of training programs, certification standards, and assignment practices in schools. In some states, teachers at the elementary level receive a generalist education leading to certification for all subjects from kindergarten through eighth grade (although frequently a distinction is made between primary and intermediate grades). Teacher skills are also believed to be interchangeable here—a third grade teacher this year may be assigned to teach first grade or sixth grade next. This is not to suggest that there is absolutely no difference between grade levels. Teachers of first graders are likely to remark on their freedom to initiate their own routines, while third grade teachers tend to talk about the enthusiasm and maturity of their students, and so on. However, most states do not certify a person to teach only first grade, because our current knowledge about learning, motivation, and child development does not suggest this fine a specialization. Some increasing specialization or division of labor is apparent in the areas of special education, mathematics and science at the elementary level. On the other hand, at the high school level one sees subject matter specialization. An art teacher may not be reassigned to teach chemistry unless this teacher is properly credentialed in both areas. For the most part, the operatives in schools at all levels are given the broad classification of teacher. As an occupation, teaching seems to be rather undifferentiated.

Another aspect of technology believed to contribute to its complexity is the number of different locations in which the work is carried out (spatial dispersion). School districts often are complex by this indicator (tempered by enrollment levels and the geographic location of the district). A one-room schoolhouse in an isolated rural area is not complex, but an urban district with forty elementary, twenty-five middle, and ten high schools would be. The distribution of work among a number of centers creates problems of coordination for upper-level managers. The difficulty of standardizing all fourth grade programs in 100 elementary schools in a district covering a large geographic area is obvious. This problem of coordinating the activities of teachers dispersed through a number of schools is ameliorated by the standardization of knowledge of skills of professionals. Institutions of higher education train teachers at a relatively homogeneous level. Administrators expect that teachers will perform appropriately. "The system works because everyone else knows roughly what is going on."[54] A logic of confidence operates so that higher levels need not directly supervise what the lower levels are doing. Collegial controls are used in favor of hierarchical controls.

## OPPORTUNITIES FOR ADMINISTRATOR CONTROL

In our earlier discussion we identified different phases of the work process—inputs, the transformation process, and outputs—and different facets of that process—raw materials, operations, and knowledge. We examined these through the consideration of three dimensions of technology: complexity, uncertainty, and interdependence. Also, we presented the notion of a technological imperative—the assumption that the structure of an organization reflects the demands of its technical system.[55] Such an interpretation is criticized by some scholars. Other forces, especially the environment, are believed also to influence structure, as the recent work by John Meyer and others suggest. Although this chapter focuses on the implications of technology for structure, environmental influences are considered briefly and explored more fully in Chapter 7.

We expect some fit between the type of task to be performed and the work arrangements appropriate for regulating a task. Scott suggests these predicted relationships are:

1. The greater the technical uncertainty, the lower the degree of formalization and the lower the degree of centralization.
2. The higher the degree of technical interdependence, the more resources must be devoted to coordination.
3. The greater the technical complexity the greater structural complexity. The structural response to technical diversity is organizational differentiation.[56]

Structures used to coordinate the workflow include rules and programs, schedules, departmentalization, hierarchy, and delegation. The appropriateness of a structure is determined by the nature of the task. Tasks which are high on clarity, predictability, and efficiency are allocated by directives, while those low on these three dimensions are allocated by delegation. In the first category, directed tasks can be subdivided and assigned to individuals who then follow established rules and programs. Extensive specialization leads to a high division of labor and a proliferation of rules. The lower the technical uncertainty, the greater the degree of formalization and centralization. A large administrative component is then needed to allocate tasks; design performance programs; recruit, train, and supervise the work force; and direct the flow of activities.[57] Delegated tasks, on the other hand, affect structure differently. Because performers exercise discretion, the subdivision of tasks is less feasible. "Since problems cannot be predicted in advance, arrangements for dividing labor in these tasks cannot be predetermined."[58] The performer makes decisions based on feedback from the task, not based on a predetermined schedule or program. It is easier to have a single person (or group working together) carry out the entire sequence of required activities. Workers are permitted discretion because of longer training periods and their greater competency. This means that a smaller administrative component is needed because less planning, supervision, and coordination are required.[59]

Curiously, public education also contains pressures toward large administrative components. The profession has become increasingly specialized—and the job of the formerly self-contained classroom teacher now is well supported by experts in remedial reading, learning disabilities, music, art, speech therapy, testing, computer assisted learning, and physical education. With greater specialization, more administrative time and more administrators are needed to plan and coordinate schedules and to allocate resources. At the same time, the increase in the amount of specialized expertise on hand in the public school markedly enhances the amount of individual discretion that can be exercised by teachers. Few school-site administrators feel that they have sufficient knowledge to supervise closely the work of specialists in behavioral disorders, trainable mentally handicapped, hearing impaired, instrumental music, the mathematically gifted, and the use of computers. At best, the administrator can seek to provide opportunities for each specialist to use personal discretion to best advantage in her or his program.

An organization's structure (e.g., hierarchy, formalization, centralization, coordination methods) corresponds to the demands of its technology and its environment. Administrators use structural devices to constrain the decisions of individual subordinates.[60] Many descriptions of influence relationships emphasize the tight coupling between superordinate behavior and subordinate behavior and the organization's output or product. Administrators lead, subordinates follow; administrators decide, subordinates implement decisions; administrators plan, subordinates carry out the necessary tasks. However, subordinates often resist close supervision and bureaucratic rules.[61] The principal in our opening vignette reminded us that such subordinates can be administrators themselves. In reality, control systems are not so tightly coupled as early organizational theorists professed.[62]

Not all formal structural devices, however, need tight coupling of work activities. We suggested, for instance, that teachers often exercise their expertise independently from administrators. The administrative structure is concerned with organizational maintenance. Professionalization, decentralization, and delegation permit some control and coordination while allowing for the exercise of independence. Through these arrangements, flexibility is built into the system. Therefore, the levels of organization—technical, managerial, and institutional—are not directly controlled by the next level higher, but rather within the levels. The higher level is too distant from the work being performed to exercise direct control.[63] This is precisely the argument advanced by the principal in the hotel coffee shop.

## Institutional Perspective of Schools

Certain features of organizations influence the decision to use different control mechanisms.[64] It is easier to directly observe and supervise subordinates for the administrator who has expertise or knowledge of the transformation process, when the culture of the profession or organization supports those activities.[65] It is frequently reported that most principals do not supervise teachers, and the explanations given are many—the principal's lack of expertise, the myth of professionalism, the spatial isolation of teaching tasks from the administrator, norms of autonomy and the logic of confidence, and collective bargaining agreements which stipulate the manner and frequency of evaluation (see Table 4.2). A variety of controls, however, appears to be available for administrators to improve school programs (see Table 4.3). Input control refers to the use and flow of resources to teachers or principals. Behavior controls structure work activities through standard operating procedures, plans, and directives. Examples in schools would include curricular scope and sequence delineation and the adoption of single textbooks for subjects and levels. Output control involves evaluating the quality or quantity of performance, output, or results; for instance, the holding of teachers accountable for the achievement of students or principals for attaining district objectives. In selection-socialization, workers internalize norms of a colleague group and supervise themselves. A superintendent might encourage potential administrators to attend a favored university or select teachers who graduated from particular institutions. Environmental control gives the administrator leverage not available from the internal organization.

What does the research evidence suggest on the topic of control? Leithwood and Montgomery note that fewer than "50 percent of elementary principals actually attempt to assist the teacher in improving instruction."[66] They reviewed research studies on the principal's role, change and innovations, and school effectiveness to determine if effective principals are different from typical ones.[67] After reviewing this research, they concluded that effective principals are different. These differences are

**TABLE 4.2**    Principals' self-reported obstacles

The Teachers

□ Lack of teacher knowledge/skill in new practices
□ Uneven backgrounds of professional training
□ Disincentives or lack of teacher motivation to change
□ Collective bargaining and teacher union contracts

The Principal's Role

□ Role ambiguity and conflict (lack of clear expectations, conflict about responsibilities, no defensible criteria for assessing principal's performance)

The Principal

□ Lack of knowledge, skill, or motivation
□ Lack of influence within system
□ Inability in assessing student needs
□ Deficient leadership skills
□ Lack of skills for handling routine administrative tasks
□ Unwillingness to take risks

The District

□ Priorities, policies, and procedures are too rigid or ambiguous
□ Procedures for evaluation/dismissal of teachers excessively elaborate and time-consuming
□ Lack of adequate support and resources
□ Excessively hierachical

The Community

□ Too little or too much parent interest
□ Pressure of special interest groups
□ Conservative views about the nature of school programs

Based on the work of K. A. Leithwood and D. J. Montgomery, "The Role of the Elementary Principal in Program Improvement," *Review of Educational Research*, 52 (Fall 1982): 309–39

**TABLE 4.3**    Control mechanisms

| | |
|---|---|
| Supervision | Directly observe teacher (or principal) behavior to provide supportive or corrective feedback |
| Input | Control amount, use, and flow of resources—funds and personnel (e.g., discretionary budget, hiring decisions) |
| Behavior | Structure activities to restrict range of acceptable behaviors/tasks (e.g., mandate curriculum objectives, textbook adoption, job descriptions, reports) |
| Output | Monitor or evaluate performance, output, results based on quantity or quality (e.g., standardized achievement test scores, number of National Merit scholars) |
| Selection-Socialization | Rely on norms and values of professional or colleague group (e.g., recruit personnel from particular institution, rely on training and self-supervision of professional) |
| Environmental | Use information (and assessments) derived from outsiders (e.g., parent complaints) |

Adapted from Kent D. Peterson, "Mechanisms of Administrative control over Managers in Educational Organizations," *Administrative Science Quarterly*, 29:4 (December, 1984): 573-97.

displayed on Tables 4.4 and 4.5. A careful examination of these lists reveals that effective principals use a variety of control mechanisms to improve the school program. For example, they are involved with teacher selection and ensure the availability of teaching materials (input controls), they use frequent and regular staff meetings (behavior control), and they closely monitor student progress (output control).

> Effective principals are able to define priorities focused on the central mission of the school and gain support for these priorities from all stakeholders. Their actions impinge on almost all aspects of the classroom and school that are likely to influence achievement of these priorities. They intervene directly and constantly to ensure that priorities are achieved. Such principals nicely fit the widely held image of the British head teacher."[68]

This description reflects the priority given to the instructional management behavior of principals. Bossert and associates suggest several areas of instructional leadership: goals and production emphasis, power and decision making, organization and coordination, human relations.[69] They note further that effective principals do not seem to favor one leadership style over others. Their research suggested that

> no single style of management seems appropriate for all schools. . . . Reviews of the successful schools literature intimate that principals must find the syle and structures most suited to their own situation.[70]

Summarizing the findings of numerous studies, Bossert and colleagues[71] report that principals in effective or successful schools are strong programmatic leaders (they know the learning problems in the school and allocate resources effectively) and coherence providers (they conceptualize instructional goals, set high standards, make frequent classroom visits, create incentives for learning, and maintain student discipline).[72] Further, "successful schools are places where teachers have substantial instructional autonomy."[73] Bossert and colleagues raise this question: How can a principal be a strong programmatic leader and grant a maximum of autonomy? Drawing on the work of Thompson and March and Simon, they suggest the following:

> Principals could constrain and structure classroom instruction in a number of ways, including developing an organizational culture, imposing formal rules that program instructional decisions, manipulating and standardizing instructional inputs such as materials and students, setting goals and monitoring outputs, and utilizing communication channels.[74]

They offer two strategies the principal can use to influence the instructional program. One option is to work directly with teachers and their classroom problems, which is called clinical supervision. The other is to examine the instructional organization to determine how factors shape the classroom's organization. Because clinical supervision is labor intensive and the demands on the principal's time are excessive, they suggest manipulating school-level policies to provide a more supportive structure.

One area of the instructional program in which principals might exercise their discretionary authority is time. Time, a notion common to many models of learning, is central to the control of schools. "States define minimum instructional periods as the number of minutes; high school diplomas are awarded on the basis of 'time served'; dollars are allocated on the average daily attendance."[75] Administrators can exercise some discretion through determining the length of class periods, whether all subjects require equal class periods, the amount of time between classes, and whether pullout programs will be used. In these ways the decisions properly made

*TABLE 4.4* Effective principal behaviors

GOALS

- □ Places first priority on achievement ("the basics") and happiness of students
- □ Describes self as instructional leader
- □ Establishes norms for risk-taking
- □ Articulates high expectations for teachers/students
- □ Seeks parental/community support for goals

FACTORS (potentially affecting student experiences)

- □ Involved with teacher selection
- □ Ensures good fit between teachers and students
- □ Concerned about instructional strategies and resource material, amount of class time devoted to instruction, instructional orientation
- □ Ensures availability of adequate materials and resources
- □ Influences coordination of teachers regarding goals and methods
- □ Attends to staff competence, procedures for selection and placement of staff
- □ Views governmental agencies, external project funds, or special financial arrangements with own board as money sources
- □ Uses program priorities as a criterion for allocating out-of-classroom materials and resources
- □ Focuses school-community relations on communicating school goals

STRATEGIES (influencing in- and out-of-class experiences of students)

Interpersonal

- □ Institutes mechanism for staff participation to achieve principal's priorities
- □ Seeks staff advice on important issues, encourages early and continuous participation in decision-making through period of program development
- □ Treats teacher as equal partner in decision-making
- □ Uses regular and frequent staff meetings
- □ Attends teacher in-service sessions
- □ Selects team leaders, attends planning meetings, hosts social gatherings
- □ Provides clear focus for teachers' professional goal setting
- □ Encourages teachers to spend time in instruction
- □ Expresses support for new practices related to program improvement
- □ Is available as sounding board for teachers' problems or new ideas

Other

- □ Works closely with teachers on issues identified during classroom observations in which principal has special expertise
- □ Assists staff in gaining access to consulting staff/district resources and visiting with other teachers
- □ Provides new-teacher orientation
- □ Collects information about teachers: their values and expectations for the principal; their instructional performance as basis for hiring; success in instruction and implementation of innovative activities; and relations with other staff
- □ Closely monitors student progress (reviews test results)
- □ Uses vested authority to prevent intrusions into high-priority school activities
- □ Provides information to staff on school goals and program priorities
- □ Establishes close contact with parents (holds meetings and conferences, builds parent-teacher groups, becomes integrated into the school community)

Based on the work of K. A. Leithwood and D. J. Montgomery, "The Role of the Elementary School Principal in Program Improvement," *Review of Educational Research*, 52 (Fall 1982): 309–39.

*TABLE 4.5*    Typical Principal Behaviors

GOALS
- Has primary goal of smooth-running school
- Has administrative orientation
- Acts as major school disciplinarian
- Emphasizes harmonious interpersonal relationships
- Is distant from curriculum or instructional decisions
- Initiates few changes in the school's programs

FACTORS (potentially affecting student experiences)
- Places emphasis on existing professional competence of teachers and "leaves teachers alone to teach"
- Leaves decision of whom to teach to teachers
- Looks to established budgets/procedures/fund-raising as money sources
- Focuses school-community relations on establishing unobtrusive, friendly relations

STRATEGIES (influencing in- and out-of-class experiences of students)

Interpersonal
- Does not encourage teacher participation
- Requests teacher participation in decision-making late in the process
- Does not treat teacher as equal partner in decision-making
- Participates limitedly in teacher in-service
- Uses formal and authoritarian style of interaction
- Withdraws support or tolerates teacher problems to avoid confrontation

Other
- Makes mechanical arrangements for in-service
- Does not orient new teachers
- Does not provide feedback after teacher visitations/observations
- Uses vested authority to speak and act on behalf of the school staff, to apply pressure for productive output from teachers, to exercise discretionary power in responding to parent requests
- Provides information to staff on individual professional matters or messages from the district office
- Reports being drowned in a sea of administrivia with no time left to attend to program improvement

Based on Leithwood and Montgomery, "Role of the Elementary School Principal" 309–39.

by teachers in the daily conduct of their work (e.g., grouping students, sequencing of instruction and activities) can be constrained by decisions and policy made at the managerial and institutional levels of the school organization.[76]

Bossert and colleagues suggest also that principals should crystallize production goals and clarify the means to these goals (e.g., the path-goal theory of leadership presented in Chapter 8). The principal should manage interdependency in workflows by creating rules and committees to coordinate the overall production (classroom instruction). Synthesizing findings from the change and innovation literature, they pinpoint several administrative activities which influence school success:
- Direct discretionary funds to instructional efforts
- Control scheduling of staff meetings
- Select staff for committees
- Publicly reward teachers associated with improved programmatic efforts

- □ Selectively protect teachers from outsiders and regulations
- □ Demonstrate attitude toward the program
- □ Control flow of information inside and outside school
- □ Limit competition between program efforts
- □ Represent school interests to district administrators
- □ Promote instructional projects outside the school.[77]

In sum, principals can make decisions about school-level factors that will affect the instructional program and student learning. These factors include procedures and policies regarding curriculum material selection, student course selection, class size, pullout programs, homework, scheduling, and use of classroom aides. The principal has freedom to work on these matters provided there are no restrictions in state and local policies or collective bargaining agreements.[78] Principal-instructional management behavior affects two basic features in the school—its climate and instructional organization.[79]

Recognizing the classroom as an autonomous unit shielded from external influences, Deal and Celotti present options for administrators to increase their influence over classroom activities and procedures.[80] They suggest that the administrator act as myth-maker, structure-builder, or symbolic leader to respond to this challenge. The administrator as myth-maker or myth-user relies on the myths of the community or staff to influence events and achieve desired ends. This view is reflected in the earlier work by Iannaccone and Lutz which described the cycle of incumbent defeat and subsequent involuntary separation of the superintendent.[81] Utilizing Becker's classification of community power structures along a sacred –secular continuum, Iannaccone and Lutz recommended strategies for introducing educational innovations in different communities. For example, in a sacred community bound by traditional values, a superintendent should demonstrate how an innovative program is similar to existing programs and rely on the testimonies of respected administrators and school board members in other districts describing their successful experiences with a similar innovation. Deal and Celotti suggest that by "judiciously cultivating a few time-honored myths, the administrator might make a difference."[82] The principal in the hotel coffee shop saw protection of teachers from unrealistic central office demands as a school goal, and he used the incident of the forms which he filled out *for* the teachers to help build the supporting myths at the school level.

Another approach to counter the loose coupling of schools is to build structures. By defining goals and objectives and creating policies and rules to achieve them, the administrator tightens linkages and "by carefully delegating responsibility, adroit administrators can actually increase their control over outcomes."[83] Thus, the purpose of delegating is not to manage one's time more efficiently, but rather to create relationships. For example, in a small, semi-rural district, the superintendent reorganized the administrative staff into a team and specified 47 objectives for the year. Administrators were given responsibility for developing activities and due dates to achieve the objectives. The objectives created reasons and opportunities for the superintendent to meet with the administrators and teachers as well as the community. Thus, the management-by-objectives strategy created linkages between the organizational roles.[84] It is possible for the administrator to combine both styles and to act as symbolic and formal leader by utilizing myths and structural elements. However, Deal and Celotti warn that a haphazard administrative style may inadvertently incorporate varying degrees of the two modes; but it is a deft administrator who consciously recognizes and taps innate sources of personal influence in concert with the sources of energy inherent in the school organization.[85]

Although schools possess the trappings of bureaucratic controls (e.g., written rules, hierarchy, division of labor), the actual instruction of students is not well coordinated and controlled by administrators.[86] Rowan notes that formal controls are exercised by administrators in schools in the areas of finance, personnel, scheduling, pupil placement, and grouping,[87] and he concludes that "district administrative staffs have evolved principally to control financial transactions, personnel problems, and auxiliary student services."[88] These observations support the notion that schools are loosely coupled systems.[89] Meyer and Rowan both suggest that schools selectively decouple their formal structures from technical core activities precisely because of the uncertainty they face—conditions of ambiguous goals and unclear technology.[90] A logic of confidence and the myth of professionalism hold the organization together.[91] Such rationalized beliefs (or myths) play a primary causal force in creating and supporting organizational structure. These rationalized beliefs are socially constructed definitions of reality.[92] Thus, education has both technical and institutional ingredients. According to John Meyer and colleagues, the structural composition of schools is determined largely by institutional sources—the political environment —and not the demands of its core technology.[93] For example, since it is difficult to specify precisely what being a high school graduate guarantees, attention is given to evaluating conformity to established norms of practice—titles of courses in the college preparatory program and number of credits earned, for example. These categories can prescribe order and meaning, and rational myths can supply rationales for choices and action in an organization in which it cannot be demonstrated regularly that certain outcomes occur.[94] Likewise, the quality of the educational program might be assessed by the number of teachers with graduate degrees in their discipline, the computer-student ratio, the number of National Merit scholars, the expenditure per pupil, the percentage of graduates who go on to college, or selectivity in student admissions.

Some scholars argue that structure actually may not be responsive to task and technology. "Structure and activity seem to be unrelated, and both are loosely linked with the environment."[95] This is a topic which is discussed in more detail in Chapter 5. "The symbolic view suggests a number of noninstrumental purposes that structures can serve. One purpose is to express prevailing values and myths of the society. In many organizations, goals are multiple and elusive, the technology is underdeveloped, the linkages between means and ends is poorly understood, and effectiveness is almost impossible to determine."[96] From this perspective, schools gain public acceptance by conforming to the legal and social expectations for them.

## CHAPTER SUMMARY

It is possible to consider school-improvement proposals from their underlying beliefs about the nature of students (raw material). National reports call for a standardization in curriculum such as graduation requirements and a replacement of the track system with a core curriculum. As a consequence of these proposals, many state legislatures have mandated an increase in the total number of credits for all students and stipulated the apportionment of these credits into English, math, social studies, science, foreign languages, and computers. One state has mandated a full-day attendance requirement for all high school students. The belief is that all students will benefit from the same core educational program which embraces a liberal arts tradition. It is not clear whether these reforms actually will result in a high quality program for all students; what arrangements will be made to handle exceptional cases; or if the consequence of these policy changes will be an increase in dropouts. We also witness the beginning of a shift in task operations from individualization to whole-group methods of instruction as research begins to confirm the superiority of the latter approach.

Our current educational reform movement assumes that dissimilarities among students are of little consequence; it is believed that specified methods will work for all. Further, the desired outcome is the same for all students—mastery of the core curriculum. The foremost goal for most reformers is to produce an educated person for the technological workforce, thus enabling the United States to regain its dominant position in the international marketplace. The enrichment of individuals and the achievement of equality and opportunity for all, while still important and worthwhile goals, are apparently being subordinated at this juncture in history. Nonetheless, Walberg notes that "Two humanistic questions recur in the history of education: What are the ends of education? And, do the education means, that is, manipulations of the environments, justify the ends? These philosophical questions concern values, morality, and ethics."[97] The recent national reports, and future generations of such reports, eventually must be placed in this context.

The process-product ambiguity of teaching and learning makes educational policy development difficult. As a result, policies and decisions are often based on "wisdom, tradition, guesswork or authority, but not systematically applied scientific principles."[98] We suggested that the technology of schools has both subjective and objective qualities. What teachers do as work is, in part, shaped by beliefs about students and the goals of schooling. These beliefs may be possessed by society, politicians, parents, and administrators, as well as teachers. Thus, schools are built on differing technological models. The work of any school—the nature of the teacher-learning process there, the characteristics of its students, and the organization of the pupilflow—greatly affects the administrator's opportunity for influencing it.

## FROM THEORY TO PRACTICE

The principal said, "I'm not goal oriented," and then he confessed that "if I have political goals and skills, I can work in any school." Was he contradicting himself? No, he was making a distinction among types of goals from his vantage point in the school system. He did not want to be identified with the management by objectives, PERT-charted, highly rational approach to goal setting that probably was the standard in his district. His sense of the idiosyncratic and the spontaneous would not let him sit still for *that*. But the principal could become single-minded in his goal orientation when the outcome suddenly became crucial to him. He made a decision—and a tough one at that—not to give the boys and girls in his school the district standardized tests, and his desire to get the district to accept that decision, in some form, became a clear-cut goal. A goal that had welled up out of the school community, one that responded to a sense of inequity rather than a sense of standardization.

It is interesting to think about the plight of the central-office administrators who undoubtedly spent a good deal of private time cursing the principal. The goal was a pretty clear one from that part of the bureaucracy: Test *all* of the kids, collect the tests, analyze the tests, and compare the results. What the principal was providing was the uncertainty that drives administrators up the wall, and it probably rankled even more because it was the act of an organizational dissident. There are enough problems without administrators piling some more on each other. But the principal's refusal did more than raise a different goal—it tapped into a common latent concern, for the central office administrators apparently had been worrying more than they had been willing to show over the biases built into the tests. And even though the conflict evolved into a long district-wide moratorium, eventually the resources were found in the form of new tests that permitted the new common goal to be realized. Of course, it is more time-consuming and expensive for the system to respond to the exceptions; you have to find the new tests, purchase them, administer them, and then start from scratch in analyzing *them*.

The system was depending upon pooled interdependence, expecting the principal to be the mediator between the central office and the clients (in this case, the students), trusting in standardization as the appropriate method of coordination. And it was on this last point that the principal upset the apple cart, for he was forcing a kind of reciprocal interdependence on the situation, quite ready to pose a contingency for the central office, seeking coordination not through standardization but through mutual adjustment. In all likelihood he was not surprised by the moratorium; he may have been disappointed by the lack of a more creative central office response.

The principal uncoupled the system, even if briefly. He might have challenged the curriculum, protecting his own local domain, and never had a serious response. But the standardized tests—now he was squarely on the central office turf. "When I do think about the central office, it's usually how to protect my teachers from them." He acknowledged that rules even down at the school level are important (for the adults) in regard to certain outcomes. But when the outcome changes, then you break the rule with equanimity, without blinking (even when the teacher with the distraught husband is uncomfortable with claiming to be what she is not). The principal may not be goal-oriented, but it is the change in goal he was seeking and eventually brought about that transformed him from a manager into an insurrectionist. He poses the nonrational alternative to his rational colleagues. How do you get the third level on the mobile moving?

It's an alternative to listening to a boring commentary by the boss, even if it leaves Ralph gasping for air one more time at the principal's open challenge to the system.

## NOTES

[1]Richard J. Murnane, "Interpreting the Evidence on School Effectiveness" (New Haven: Yale University, mimeographed, 1980).

[2]Ibid., p. 14.

[3]James D. Thompson, *Organizations in Action* (New York: McGraw-Hill, 1967), p. 14.

[4]Charles Perrow, "A Framework for Comparative Analysis of Organizations," *American Sociological Review* 32 (April, 1967), p. 94; Joan Woodward, *Management and Technology* (London: Her Majesty's Stationery Office, 1958); and James D. Thompson, *Organizations in Action* (New York: McGraw Hill, 1967).

[5]W. Richard Scott, *Organizations: Rational, Natural, and Open Systems* (Englewood Cliffs, N.J.: Prentice-Hall, 1981), p. 211.

[6]L. S. Sproull, "Responding to Regulations: School Superintendents and the Federal Government," in S. Bachrach, ed., *Organizational Analysis of Schools and School Districts* (New York: Praeger, 1981), p. 7.

[7]R. A. Kegan, *Regulating Business, Regulating Schools: The Problem of Regulatory Unresponsiveness,* (Project No. 81-A14). Paper presented at the IFG Seminar on Law and Governance in Education, Stanford, Calif., July 1981, p. 83.

[8]Amatai Etzioni, *Modern Organizations* (Englewood Cliffs, N.J.: Prentice-Hall, 1964), p. 6.

[9]Scott, p. 262.

[10]Donald A. Erickson, "The Central Question in Government Regulation of Private Schools Is What Is Plainly Essential for Good Citzenship," *ISACS Magazine* (Autumn, 1983), p. 27, citing work of Bossert and Rowan at Far West Laboratory.

[11]Ibid., p. 27.

[12]Charles Perrow, *Complex Organizations: A Sociological Review* (Belmont, Calif.: Wadsworth, 1970).

[13]Scott, p. 211.

[14]Perrow, *Complex Organizations*, p. 75.

[15]Ibid.

[16]Ibid., p. 76.

[17]Ibid., p. 34.

[18]Ibid., pp. 76-77.

[19]Scott, p. 211.

[20]Henry Mintzberg, *The Structuring of Organizations* (Englewood Cliffs, N.J.: Prentice-Hall, 1979), p. 350.

[21]Erving Goffman, *Asylums* (Garden City, N.Y.: Doubleday, 1961).

[22]Richard O. Carlson, "Environmental Constraints and Organizational Consequences: The Public School and its Clients," in Daniel E. Griffiths, ed., *Behavioral Science in Educational Administration Yearbook, Part II*, National Society for the Study of Education (Chicago: University of Chicago Press, 1964), pp. 262-276.

[23]Charles Bidwell, "The School as Formal Organization," in James March,ed., *Handook of Organizations* (Chicago: Rand McNally, 1965), pp. 972-1002.

[24]Lau v. Nichols, 414 U.S. 563 (1974).

[25]Charlie Euchner, "Languages, *Lau* and San Francisco," *Education Week* III (January 25, 1984), 12.

[26]Susan Walton, "Research and the Quest for Effective Bilingual Methods," *Education Week* III (February 8, 1984), 18-19.

[27]Karl E. Weick, "Educational Organizations as Loosely-Coupled Systems," *Administrative Science Quarterly* 21 (March, 1976), 1-16.

[28]Thompson, p. 55.

[29]Scott, p. 213.

[30]Thompson, pp. 16-17.

[31]John S. Packard, *Management Implications of Team Teaching* (Eugene, Oregon: Center for Educational Policy and Management, 1976), p. 155.

[32]Packard, *Management Implications of Team Teaching.*

[33]Philip W. Jackson, *Life in the Classrooms* (New York: Holt, Rinehart & Winston, 1969).

[34]Thompson, p. 16.

[35]Ibid.

[36]Judson T. Shaplin, "Description and Definition of Team Teaching," in H. F. Olds, Jr., ed., *Team Teaching* (New York: Harper & Row, 1964), Chapter 1.

[37]Packard, p. 5.

[38]Thompson, p. 17.

[39]Ibid.

[40]Ibid., p. 55.

[41]See Bidwell, Weick.

[42]Bidwell, pp. 975-76.

[43]William A. Rushing, "Organizational Rules and Surveillance: Propositions of Comparative Organizational Analysis," *Administrative Science Quarterly* 10 (March, 1976), 423-443.

[44]Jerald Hage and Michael Aiken, "Routine Technology, Social Structure, and Organization Goals," *Administrative Science Quarterly* 14 (September, 1969), 366-376.

[45]Hage and Aiken, "Routine Technology, Social Structure, and Organization Goals."

[46]Robert H. Hall, J. Haas, and H. J. Johnson, "An Examination of the Blau-Scott and Etzioni Typologies," *Administrative Science Quarterly* 12 (June, 1967), 118-139.

[47]Peter M. Blau, "A Formal Theory of Differentiation in Organizations," *American Sociological Review* 35 (April, 1970), 201-218.

[48]Thomas L. Green, *The Activities of Teaching* (New York: McGraw-Hill Book Co., 1971).

[49]Robert Dreeben, *The Nature of Teaching* (Glenview, Ill.: Scott, Foresman and Co., 1970).

[50]Sanford M. Dornbusch and W. Richard Scott, *Evaluation and the Exercise of Authority* (San Francisco: Josey-Bass Publishers, 1975), p. 18.

[51]Green, p. 8.

[52]Green, p. 9.

[53]Ibid.

[54]Karl E. Weick, "Educational Organizations as Loosely-Coupled Systems," quoting John Meyer.

[55]Woodward, *Management and Technology.*

[56]Scott, p. 212.

[57]Dornbusch and Scott, p. 84.

[58]Ibid.

[59]Ibid., p. 85.

[60]James G. March and Herbert Simon, *Organizations* (New York: John Wiley, 1958).

[61]See Frederick J. Roethisberger and William J. Dickson, *Management and the Worker* (Cambridge, Mass.: Harvard University Press, 1939); and Alvin W. Gouldner, *Patterns in Industrial Organizations* (Glencoe, Ill.: Free Press, 1954).

[62]See Max Weber, *The Theory of Social and Economic Organizations*, eds., A. H. Henderson and Talcott Parsons (Glencoe, Ill.: Free Press, 1947tr); Henri Fayol *General and Industrial Management* (London: Pitman, 1949); and Frederick W. Taylor, *Principles of Scientific Management* (New York: Harper, 1911).

[63]Talcott Parsons, *Structure and Process in Modern Society* (Glencoe, Ill.: Free Press, 1960), p. 656.

[64]The discussion that follows relies on the work of Kent D. Peterson, "Mechanisms of Administrative Control in Educational Organizations: An Exploratory Study," which summarizes a manuscript developed under a grant from the National Institute of Education (photocopied, no date).

[65]See Dornbusch and Scott, *Evaluation and the Exercise of Authority.*

[66]K. A. Leithwood and D. J. Montgomery, "The Role of the Elementary School Principal in Program Improvement," *Review of Educational Research* 52 (Fall, 1982), 309.

[67]Ibid., pp. 309-339.

[68]Ibid., p. 335.

[69]Steven T. Bossert, David C. Dwyer, Brian Rowan, and Ginny Lee, "The Instructional Management Role of the Principal," *Educational Administration Quarterly* 18 (Summer, 1982), 34.

[70]Ibid., p. 38.

[71]Ibid.

[72]Ibid.

[73]Ibid., p. 35.

[74]Ibid.

[75]Ibid., p. 43.

[76]Abraham F. Daniels and Emil J. Haller, "Exposure to Instruction, Surplus Time, and Student Achievement: A Local Replication of the Harnischleiger and Wiley Research," *Educational Administration Quarterly* 17 (Winter, 1981), 48-49.

[77]Bossert et al., p. 51.

[78]Steven M. Goldschmidt and Leland Stuart, "Teacher Educational Policy Bargaining and its Implications for School Responsiveness," paper presented at the annual meeting of the American Educational Research Association, New Orleans, April 26, 1984.

[79]Bossert et al., p. 40.

[80]Terrence E. Deal and Lynn D. Celotti, "Loose Coupling and the School Administrator: Some Recent Research Findings," (Stanford, Calif.: Stanford University, 1977), p. 3.

[81]Laurence Iannaccone and Frank W. Lutz, *Politics, Power and Policy: The Governing of Local School Districts* (Columbus, Ohio: Charles E. Merrill, 1970).

[82]Deal and Celotti, p. 23.

[83]Ibid.

[84]Nancy J. Pitner, "Descriptive Study of the Everyday Activities of Suburban School Superintendents: The Management of Information" (Columbus, Ohio: The Ohio State University, unpublished doctoral dissertation, 1978).

[85]Deal and Celotti, pp. 23-24.

[86]John W. Meyer, "They Also Serve: Organizations as Ideological Systems," paper presented at Conference on Administrative Leadership, University of Illinois at Champaign-Urbana, 1981.

[87]Brian Rowan, "Instructional Management in Historical Perspective: Evidence on Differentiation in School Districts," *Educational Administrator Quarterly* 18 (Winter, 1982), 44.

[88]Ibid., p. 47.

[89]See Bidwell, 1965 and Weick, 1976.

[90]John W. Meyer and Brian Rowan, "Institutional Organizations: Formal Structure as Myth and Ceremony," *American Journal of Sociology* 83 (September, 1977), 340-363.

[91]Meyer and Rowan, "Institutional Organizations."

[92]Peter L. Berger and Thomas Luckman, *The Social Construction of Reality* (New York: Doubleday, 1967).

[93]John W. Meyer, W. Richard Scott, Terrence E. Deal, "Institutional and Technical Sources of Organizational Structure: Explaining the Structure of Educational Organizations," in Stein, ed., *Organizations and the Human Services: Cross-Disciplinary Reflections* (Philadelphia: Temple University Press, 1981).

[94]Lee G. Bolman and Terrence E. Deal, *Modern Approaches to Understanding and Managing Organizations* (San Francisco: Jossey-Bass Publishers, 1984).

[95]Ibid., p. 169.

[96]Ibid.

[97]Herbert Walberg, "Introduction" in *Educational Environment and Effects: Evaluation, Policy and Productivity* (Berkeley: McCutchan Publishing Co., 1979), p. 1.

[98]Ibid., p. 2.

# 5

## Control and Coordination in Education

## DONALD RIDDLE

*He was Chancellor of the University of Illinois at Chicago Circle, now the University of Illinois at Chicago, as the big-city branch and the university medical center were being combined under a single chancellor. There is a quiet satisfaction with his career that one senses as somewhat unusual within the ranks of top university executives these days. He believes that administrators in higher education should pay their professional dues and remember from whence they came. As a consequence, he is comfortable with the pace of his career from World War II veteran to the office of an urban university administrator in a midwestern city, and he has great respect for the individual professor and for the role of faculty governance in the university. The pipe smoke swirling about him and the twinkle in his eye belie the man's political fortitude. He views his skills as being those of an administrator effective in developing institutions and in mediating situations that need the hand and mind of a peacemaker. He is nearing the end of a substantial career, but that is not of particular concern to him.*

**Tell me about your career and how it developed.**

I guess I started later than most. I graduated from high school in 1938, but I couldn't afford to go to college. We were married in 1942, and I was in the Army six weeks later—at Miami Beach for basic training. Then I spent four years in what was then the Army Air Forces. When the war was over, I started at Princeton University on the GI Bill and went straight through.

**You mean to the Ph.D.?**

Yes. I had full tuition of $500 a year and my wife helped a great deal. I earned my B.A. and then a Ph.D. in political science. After that I went to Hamilton College where I taught for six years, from 1952–1958. I took a leave for a year, without pay, to work with Senator Paul Douglas—that was in 1955–1956—and I actually completed the dissertation the same year. My study had to do with the Truman Committee, which had monitored the war effort, and while I had done most of the research in 1952 and had a pretty good draft by 1955, it was in the summer before I started working with the Senator that I pulled everything together. I holed up in the National Archives for a couple of months and read the complete records of the Committee.

   After that I went to the Eagleton Institute of Politics at Rutgers University where I headed a project supported by the Fund for the Advancement of Education to produce better materials for high school social studies classes. None of them is in print today, but when I left Rutgers I thought the work there might be the most useful thing I'd done in my life. A good deal of it involved editing, and it was a lovely place to work—in a big, old house. I had fine academic colleagues there. My project director was a superb editor, and I'll never forget his telling me that he wouldn't hire anyone he wasn't willing to have lunch with every day. I'm the only one still alive of the five of us who worked so closely together on that project. I stayed there seven years, until 1965.

   By then I had been at Rutgers long enough. I could see that the school project was pretty much finished. What I really wanted to do was to revamp the world history course. How could you teach world history in one year, and usually to sophomores? I thought you would have to give up chronological, political history. Then you could focus on five or six things that people had done across the face of the world. Perhaps the growth of science and technology. You'd bring in the diverse cultures, east and west, naturally. The development of religion was another, and something like artistic expression. The development of government through democracy, and you could add several more. These are the major things that man has been about. But the publisher thought it was too radical for the schools, that it placed too heavy a demand on most teachers.

   Then I received a letter from New York telling me about a new college of police science that was looking for a dean of faculty. Apparently I'd been nominated for the position. I was interested, but I thought, "So what?" But the letter contained a telephone number, and I thought, "What the hell. It's worth a call." I called and I was interviewed. I was offered the job and I took it.

**Why was this so intriguing to you?**

I didn't know much about cops, but I did know that the police have a lot to do with the quality of life in any society. The notion of a college for them sounded like a good idea. You know, liberals think police need to be educated, and the conservatives think give them what they want. There was support from both sides of the political fence. So, I started in the spring of 1965 as the dean of faculty at John Jay College. There was no president at the time, and the local police commissioner was serving as acting president. Well, he couldn't handle both jobs, and from day one I was really running the place. They called it police science then, but the term criminal justice is used now. The field was really taking off. Almost all the people I was involved with were ex-practitioners. For a couple of reasons I soon had some national prominence in the field. John Jay was the only college that was devoted entirely to this subject. And I was the only person around in the field with traditional academic credentials. That's a heady brew. They handed me a platform, one that commanded attention, and I used it.

Our curriculum was heavy in the liberal arts, and the place began to change. It wasn't done by one person, of course. Initially the students were all cops, and it was open to all. We started out in the police academy—and that was a good building, but we quickly outgrew it. Finally, we went into some rented space and then eventually to the present, permanent location. In October of 1965 we had a president named. He was a lawyer who had been a deputy commissioner in the police department, and as the dean of faculty, I was his executive officer. I was the inside man, and he was the outside man. In the fall of 1967 he died very suddenly of a heart attack, and I became the acting president. His wife called me at 4:00 A.M. to tell me of his death. I didn't go back to sleep. I concluded right then that I was much more content doing what I was doing than what he had been doing. But things don't always work out the way you want them to, and my only choice was to be acting president. Then, as the search proceeded, I discovered that there were few individuals being interviewed who were going to let me continue to do what I was doing. Most of the faculty wanted me to be president, but from the scurrying around, you'd have thought half the lawyers in the city of New York were trying to get the job. Frank Keppel was chairman of the board's search committee. It was a board of distinction, very good indeed. Keppel was named because it was thought he might be most resistant to political pressure. And so, eventually, I was named as president.

I served there for ten years, until 1975, and then I concluded ten years was long enough for me and for John Jay. I didn't actively go seeking a job. It's kind of funny that the only person I knew at the University of Illinois at Chicago nominated me for the chancellorship. He was a professor of criminal justice. Actually, I had nominations at two places, but the other university needed talents that I don't have—promotion, money-raising. But here there was political turmoil. They needed someone to pull things together, and I thought that played to my strengths. So when they offered the job I accepted it. The place had aspirations that I shared. The faculty, or at least parts of it, was at war with the administration. The internal power was in the hands of a very small number of people, and that power had to be much more widely distributed. The arts and sciences faculty was contesting with the faculties of the professional schools. And the state of management was dreadful. We were operating at a deficit, and you can't do that with public funds. The administration had to be gotten hold of and shaped up. I had to do whatever a president can do to restore a sense of trust. One of the nicest things that happened was that when my wife came to Chicago three months later, one of the deans pulled her aside. He said, "Don was not my first choice for chancellor, but in three months he has done more good than is believable. He's got people talking who haven't done that in years." I saw that as some progress in the right direction.

Another problem was our attitude toward the University of Illinois at Urbana. As a branch, even though we're a big one, we were expressing some inferiority feelings. And there were some unreasonable expectations. Couldn't we solve our money problems by taking some funds from the parent university? Some thought so. You can't do that, of course. We're much more confident now.

## What are the really important lessons you have learned about educational administration?

I've never seen anything in print in the literature of educational administration that mentions instinct, and yet this is one of the most important characteristics of the effective administrator. You see nothing that points out the importance of knowing what *not* to do. I don't mean by that the decisions you decide not to make or the things you delegate. I mean the vast array of things you decide to leave alone, to let other people do. Sometimes they are small things. Like parking and space allocation—I refuse to have anything to do with these. Sometimes they are much more consequential things. Ah, how much pain I've been spared! The principal of an elementary school has to keep a much tighter hold on the school, because there's not much substructure. I'm talking about the things you let go of completely, whether the outcome in those areas is what you've wanted or not. You just don't worry about them in a big organization like this one. You learn this through an evolutionary process. When I had a vice president and a dean of faculty at John Jay it took me a while to learn to tell people that there are others who can help you. But I finally told them, "Call me on it when I make decisions that should be yours." And they did. I gradually weaned myself away from making decisions on their behalf. Somewhere along the line I not only realized that I couldn't keep my finger on every button, but that it was unreasonable to try.

## How would you describe your administrative style?

Easy-going, low key, relaxed. It's more of a personal style than an administrative style, as I describe it. There's one thing I'm hard-nosed about. No surprises. My subordinates learn that in a hurry or they don't stay around very long. If they try to sweep a problem under the rug and it bursts in my face—or theirs—I'm very unhappy.

## How do you exercise control from the top of a large university?

Let me tell you about the chancellor's reserve fund. This place grew pretty fast, as you know. When I arrived in the winter of 1976 there was still a lot of money available, and it wasn't being handled very tightly. Many units were in the habit of running a deficit, and the chancellor's reserve had money to bail them out when they did. The chancellor's reserve depended largely on unused personnel funds. You just couldn't hire faculty fast enough in those days. For example, let's imagine that in a given year a college had ten new faculty lines and they could only fill eight. Well, that money that was left over didn't just sit there. It came back to the chancellor's reserve, and then I used the money to cover a whole range of deficits or emergencies around the campus. There were pretty large balances in the reserve in those days.

### So everyone was sitting pretty?

Not at all. It didn't take me long to discover that the whole *campus* was running a deficit. I had to stop that. So we tried to get people managing their unit budgets more carefully. The business office set up a monthly monitoring system, and the red flags would go up and then we would have some conversations. Lo and behold, the deans and department chairmen got a lot better at handling their budgets, including their personnel lines. But because they did, the chancellor's reserve began to shrink.

### Was that a problem?

Yes, it was, because there were emergencies that cropped up every year that had to be handled out of the chancellor's reserve. It was a contingency account that had to be available for the whole campus, and the chancellor had to be in a position to decide how to allocate it. If it were spread around in a lot of smaller accounts, you would never have been able to find it and pry it loose when a big expense came along. There wasn't very much argument over the *necessity* of the chancellor's reserve. There were some other disagreements about it, as you'll see.

It all came to a head a few years later. We had an academic resources board that was broadly representative of the university, and one of its major tasks was to help the chancellor build the academic budget each year. The board actually reported to the vice chancellor for academic affairs, who would be like the provost in many other universities, and the board asked each college and department to present and justify its budget each year. Unfortunately, the *board* counted on $275,000 each year to be located in the vice chancellor's budget for contingencies in the *academic* area. I say unfortunate because that $275,000 came from the chancellor's reserve, and I had discovered that there was no way to provide it in this particular year and still have money left for me to deal with unforeseen campus-wide problems. I wasn't going to have a chancellor's reserve at all unless I did something.

### What was your strategy?

Well, there was nothing wrong basically with the way we were organized. I surely wanted to keep people working together cooperatively, and I wanted the money to be available in the right places to get the job done. For instance, I had no quarrel about the need for the $275,000 and the prerogative of the vice chancellor to handle it. But as we were getting better at managing the university, we had to work with more sophistication in maneuvering our resources into place so that faculties and their administrators could make decisions that worked.

So, I started talking to people, and one idea that emerged from these chats was that I ought to require that a portion of salary-lapsed funds in each campus unit be turned over to the chancellor's reserve every year.

**What's a salary-lapsed fund? Is that the same as the money that was left over from unfilled positions in the earlier days?**

No, it's a little different. When you're not hiring as much, it means the money not being used with relation to current personnel lines. As when someone goes on leave or sabbatical, or a new secretary doesn't cost as much as the former one did. Most budgets accrue some savings of this kind every year. The point, though, is that I would *require* the colleges and departments to share some of this money with me. Then I would be able to make my routine contribution of $275,000 to the vice chancellor, and, in effect, to the academic resources board. So I scheduled a meeting with the board to discuss this problem. The word began to get around as to what I was likely to propose. One faculty member called me to share a message he had received from a faculty colleague: "Be sure to come to the academic resources board meeting and watch Riddle get chopped to pieces." It sounded like it was going to be fun. Before the meeting I let the word get around that I was ready to negotiate.

**Were you backing down?**

Oh, no. But I wasn't sure I had *the* answer, after all. At the meeting I laid out the idea, and I set it in the context of three points. First, there was no way I could give the $275,000 to the vice chancellor unless we did something to shore up the chancellor's reserve. Second, I explained what I needed and what I did with the whole reserve fund. Third, I kept the focus on the vice chancellor's fund, not mine. Incidentally, I didn't notice any chopping of Riddle taking place. We were able to agree that both the chancellor and the vice chancellor needed reserves. And it was easy to sense that I was willing to consider alternatives. The dean of liberal arts and sciences, or LAS, was uneasy, though. He looked like the person with the most at stake.

During the next week I met more or less continuously on this issue with key groups and individuals. No one took the thing lightly, let me assure you. Finally the LAS dean came in. He made an interesting counterproposal to "tax" the personnel base of each unit every year to generate the needed monies, and to phase in the tax over a period of a few years. We both realized that this idea would eventually cost LAS more than my proposal, because it was a huge unit, but LAS had severe budget problems at that time and it was important for them to have a transition period. So I went back around the trail with my colleagues to test the idea with them.

**Did you have the votes?**

Well, I thought so, but you can be surprised. What I spelled out in detail in these informal conversations was a 1 percent tax on the personnel base of all units, to be phased in over two years, with the exception of LAS where it would take three years. A number of deans were concerned about the preferential treatment for LAS, but when I pointed out that LAS would make larger contributions proportionally over the long haul that satisfied them. When I went back to the academic resources board with the refined proposal, there were only two negative votes.

### Was there anything else that tipped the scales?

Well, they certainly preferred a tax that they'd know about, that was up front and predictable year by year. This way of doing it left the management in the hands of the units, and it gave them an incentive to manage that salary-lapsed money efficiently. And over the years it has worked out very well. The vice chancellor told me beforehand that I'd lose. He didn't support the various proposals or oppose them, but he was gratified as to how it all worked out.

### How much money do you have to work with in the chancellor's reserve today?

It all boils down to maybe $100,000 *uncommitted* at the beginning of each fiscal year. That's not very much for a university of this size. The reserve gets some money from grants overhead and some hard money, but the big bucks are the salary-lapsed monies. That was a difficult *political* job for me. There was a period of only two weeks between those two meetings of the academic resources board, but once I had the other key committees and the deans convinced, I knew they couldn't turn me down. You keep banging away on the premises, but you also stay flexible and listen. That's the way you try to keep it together.

### How do you feel about the consolidation of campuses that is taking place in your university system in Chicago?

The campus chancellor will do a lot more of the deciding now. The president inevitably will be the outside person as we reduce the number of chancellors. As the two chancellors get more and more equal, and if they get together on an issue ahead of time, they will prevail. The idea of consolidation is sound—I'm still convinced of that. But I'm increasingly uneasy about the implementation. Some things are happening now, in the transition, that may have to be undone. Some people who have had too much power will try to hold on to that power.

### Your job will vanish with the consolidation. What impact will that have on you?

I think they will go outside for a president for the two merged campuses in Chicago. I wouldn't want to be a divisive factor. On the other hand, I don't think it's a particularly attractive job for an outsider. He's going to need some experience. The first new chancellor is going to be highly expendable. The average tenure of the leader in a truly merged institution has been about two years. I don't think Jesus would last much longer. I'm at an age where I am expendable. Maybe you could put this place together in several years with a good chancellor and a lot of push, but if there's resistance from one campus or the other it could take ten. Of course, I can retire. I know where I can go, and I've been wanting to go there for a long time. If I were sitting outside and I came to understand the problems, the new job would not be particularly attractive to me. On the other hand it would be more challenging than going to a place where you'd just preside.

**Where is that place you'd like to go?**

In the Adirondack region of New York. We have a place in Keene Valley. We spent our honeymoon near there in 1942 when there was no gas for the car and we had to take a train. We visited again over the years when a colleague shared his place there with us, and finally, in 1966, we bought some land and built a house there. A gorgeous view. We get up there about twice a year, at Christmas and for a while each summer. Our kids get up there all the time; they use it more than we do now.

**What counsel would you give to a young man or woman who is considering the possibility of a career in higher education administration?**

*Pay your dues.* Do some teaching first. You can learn all the other things. But your level of credibility is much higher if you've done it. That may change—maybe we're moving more rapidly than I see to a period where there will be professional administrators who do nothing else in their careers. We share a lot of authority with our faculty here, and it really helps if you can talk to the faculty and be respected by them as one who has paid his dues as a faculty member. It's a good idea to start out as an assistant to someone who is really good at a job. You can learn a lot that way, and pretty fast. It's stuff you can't teach in class. I'm sorry about that, but it's true. Finally, master the arts of human relations—of managing people. If you are good at this, most other shortcomings will be forgiven. If you fail at this, no other strengths will get you by.

## *FROM PRACTICE TO THEORY*

The top executive in an institution of higher education—a person in control. Nominally. In reality, administrative control must be earned, negotiated, discovered, shared. Certainly, there are weapons readily available to the person in charge: the budget, some key appointments, deciding what and to whom to delegate, access to information, outside contacts. But these weapons comprise a weak armory, admits Don Riddle, if they aren't backed by the much more powerful forces of credibility, availability, and even good *instinct.*

To what extent can an educational organization be controlled? To be sure, a college or university may be more anarchic than a public school district, but do all forms of organization in education share some capacity for control or noncontrol that is of important theoretic interest? Some mechanisms—hierarchy, formalization, centralization—would appear to give managers a direct influence over the productive activities of the educational organization. Other common qualities—decentralization, delegation, professionalization—seem to legitimate and support the exercise of independence. How within the swirl of dependence and independence does the educational administrator bring it all together? Is there a helpful theoretical approach to the task of administrative control?

# CONTROL AND COORDINATION IN EDUCATION

## Introduction

Popular images of schooling across the years portray the education institution as persistently rooted in pedagogical structure and control. We remember eighteenth century schoolmasters as tight-lipped, grim-visaged young men, willow whips firmly in hand, supervising standardized recitations of lessons laced with a healthy dosage of Puritan morality. A picture of turn-of-the-century schooling in the city shows a multistoried edifice of solid stone, teeming with the ill-clad progeny of recent immigrants—heads bent in neat rows over oak desks, seventy or more to a room, pronouncing English in rehearsed unison. Our modern schoolmasters, despite a leavening of midcentury liberalism, still march pupils into their respective elementary buildings in well-disciplined lines (often boys on one side, girls on the other); distribute them egg-crate fashion into look-alike classrooms of graded ability lying along both sides of long, long hallways; and treat the children, arms raised in a competitive supplication of teacher approval, to read-and-recite teaching that would have made their predecessors proud.

Control is a word of comfortable familiarity in education. Parents expect it, teachers depend upon it, pupils need it, administrators work hard to ensure it. Events that get out of hand—accidents, conflicts, acts of rebelliousness, inefficiency, breakdowns in communication, excessive noise, disorder—all are believed to interfere substantially with the educative process. Not the least of the duties of the site-level school administrator (as well as the classroom teacher) is the maintenance of a secure, trouble-free learning environment. Indeed, teachers and administrators are much more likely to be dismissed for failure to maintain control than for failure to educate.

## The Problem of Control

While control is a word of great importance to the profession and describes much of what educators do, it is, interestingly, a term of confused meaning in the governance and administration of education. Widely varying perspectives have long held educational organizations to be rather poorly coordinated and ineffectively controlled. Some observers, for example, have suggested that education is effectively out of control because it tends toward *over-bureaucratization*. David Tyack argues persuasively in *The One Best System* that the delivery of educational services was changed fundamentally by modernizing forces in the late nineteenth and twentieth centuries into a corporate, centralized model of decision-making that cut off the profession from some of its laudable, rural American roots, particularly those related to preserving local communities.[1] It is not by accident, he notes, that our earliest schools resembled churches, with their steeple-like bell towers—for they were at the center of the educational, social, cultural, political, and even religious activities of their immediate communities. Nor is it by accident that school buildings in the rapidly industrializing twentieth century came to look very much like factories. Like the factory, they are "separate from family and community, hierarchical in organization, planned, purposive, consequential."[2]

Such critics point out further that the education profession seems to have succeeded all too well in a reform movement (with foundations established early in this century in an era of managerial efficiency)[3] in generating an elaborate, centralized, and rationalized structure of administrative control. With the growth of state and federal programs and regulations, with the increased interventions of the courts, and quite simply with the development of one urbanized nation, the tendency over time has been toward an over-elaboration of bureaucratic rules and regulations, procedures and paper work, standards and criteria—to the point where educational organizations are ponderously (even pathologically, say some observers)[4] overcome by their own complexity and inertia.

However, a second perspective, quite the opposite, tells us that educational organizations are out of control or only partially controlled because they are decidedly *under-bureaucratized*. Far from being closely monitored and tightly structured, the typical educational organization is decidedly "loose." The administration of education is now characterized by such a fragmented pulling and tugging of disparate interests that administrator control has become politicized and unpredictable to a dangerous extreme. The press of parental demands, equal rights activists, "watchdog" groups, the media, advisory councils, business interests (e.g., textbook publishers), governmental officials (e.g., the federal bureaucracy, the state education department), lawyers, unions, academic "do-gooders," and even a now politicized student clientele surrounds educational officialdom with a great deal more confusion than rationality, and guides leaders more often to conflict than to control. Like the central figure in a children's video game, the educational administrator today can be found in rapid-fire action, dodging death-filled missiles, leaping alligator-packed pits, and in self-defense occasionally downing a destruction-intended intruder a split second before Armageddon. This is a long historical leap from the administrator's childhood memory of honest, laconic cowboys in white hats on faithful horses restoring close-knit communities to rural tranquility by out-maneuvering the town's one recognized bad guy.

From this perspective (that education is under- rather than over-bureaucratized), observers argue that educational organizations internally are in fact much more anarchic than centralized. Teachers' decisions on how and what to teach are not much affected by administrative oversight.[5] It is not unknown for building principals to engage in a bit of "creative insubordination" when directives from above conflict with what is deemed best for their own schools.[6] Innovative ideas are often far from recognizable by the time they reach classroom or site-level implementation.[7] And board of education policy pronouncements are not infrequently torn apart and sharply redefined by warring elements within the educational bureaucracy, as they wind their interpretive way down the organizational hierarchy.[8] Whatever control there is within the administrative framework may be more a function of accident than design.

Thus, the control of educational organizations is claimed to be both stultifyingly rational and confusingly irrational, both fragmented and centralized, both tight and loose. School organizations are criticized as hierarchies and anarchies, open but also closed, unchanging systems as well as impulsive, bureaucratized and profession-alized, goal-centered and directionless, authoritarian and undisciplined.

Confusingly, each of these criticisms has merit. Educational organizations *are* both tightly structured and loosely coupled, both centralized and decentralized. This combination of apparent incompatibilities presents a snarled dilemma in the establishment of administrative control. On one hand, the educational organization can be considered amenable to *rational action,* to the pursuit of an intended, goal-oriented sharing of organizational life, under administrative direction, by its many participants. On the other hand, the educational organization can be perceived as an unsteady and discontinuous *coalition* of disparate actors, so filled with ambiguity and uncertainty that intent and conscious foresight in administration is well nigh impossible. Seen from the first perspective, the best efforts of a conscientious administrator to take firm control of school system behavior may be well advised; seen from the second, the same set of administrative actions may well be considered part of the problem.[9]

In this chapter we discuss implications for the control and coordination of educational organizations that flow from both of these conceptualizations. We are concerned with the degree to which an organization in education *can* be controlled. We suggest that valuable understandings can be gleaned from both the rational and the coalitional models. Some mechanisms of rationality—hierarchy, formalization, centralization—help ensure that administrators can even influence and shape the behavior of other participants charged with carrying on the production activities of the organization. Other devices more common to the coalitional perspective —decentralization, negotiation, professionalization—ensure only *some* coordination and control, while legitimizing and supporting the exercise of independence. The human struggle between determinism and free will has not been brushed aside in the late twentieth century.

In no small measure, this chapter faces the problem that there is no widespread consensus on just what it means to control, or even to coordinate an educational organization. Definitions of these key terms are typically left vague in the manage-ment literature. Furthermore, the word control often carries a pejorative quality, conveying the image of a boss dictating worker behavior, demanding swift obedience under the ever-present threat of dismissal. Even with such negative connotations removed, the fact certainly remains that to exercise control is to exert *influence* over the behaviors of other persons. Indeed, we shall use a quite simple definition borrowed from Herbert Simon in suggesting that: (a) control is found in the manner in which the decisions and behaviors of employees are influenced by their surround-ing organization; while (b) coordination is seen in the degree to which all (or most, or many) members of the organization reach the same decisions or exhibit the same behaviors.[10]

We also follow Herbert Simon in suggesting that an organization's influence is many faceted—both in the degree to which one individual affects the behavior of another and in the means whereby such influence is exercised.[11] Control can be exerted directly or indirectly, consciously or subconsciously, from the top down or from the bottom up. In the examination of the first of our two theoretical perspectives, we propose two major avenues toward the rational control of the educational organization—direct and indirect. Both paths are concerned with the attainment of organizational goals, but from differing points of departure. Within each of these approaches we offer three strategies for administrative control. Direct control under rationality is pursued through an organization's rules, communications, and evaluation procedures; while indirect control under rationality flows from administrative talk, socialization, and manipulation. Afterwards, with less elaboration and fewer options, we suggest in turning to the coalitional model that two administrative strategies prevail in the control of education. These are negotiation and good faith.

## CONTROL FROM THE RATIONAL PERSPECTIVE

One of the more insistent facts of life in educational organizations is the extent of order and coordinated regularity.[12] Despite the relative isolation of classroom teachers from one another; despite the complexity of productive roles in education; and despite the difficult logistics of moving and protecting pupils, matching pupils and curricula, and assembling an array of necessary resources (from books to desks to hot lunches) on time and in place—there is remarkably little confusion. For the most part, education from preschool through the university is quite well organized. Teachers are in place when their pupils complete a skillfully negotiated journey by bus from a street corner close to home. Somehow, after the usual bit of chaos on opening day, there is a schedule of learning activities for everyone, and these schedules intermesh surprisingly well. Lessons end simultaneously, begin again four minutes later in new locations with new instructors, and carry on through staggered lunch periods, teacher breaks, and occasional fire drills—all with considerable efficiency. Even the unexpected (a gym class injury, a bomb threat, a post-game melee, a bad-weather day) is generally handled with professionalized dispatch, with scarcely a moment's break in the education of students.

Little of this happens by accident. It takes anticipation and planning to stay ahead of events, especially those that are unpredictable. Education has a special rhythm—a school year with fixed dates of registration, end-of-semester, holiday break, and graduation. Budget making, personnel selection, facilities preparation, student scheduling, record-keeping, grade-reporting, and materials purchasing must conform to this cycle, must be synchronized with the flow of activity through the academic day and year. In short, the educational organization flirts with chaos, leans toward confusion, but emerges surprisingly well coordinated and seemingly under control.

### Development of the Rational Perspective

**Scientific Management.**    According to a number of historians, it was the effort to bring the increasingly complex function of schooling under control that gave initial impetus to the development of rational structures of educational organization.[13] Joseph Cronin, for example, traced the consolidation and centralization of city school systems from ward-based schools and school boards to central boards and superintendencies. As the twentieth century dawned, a reorganization movement, solidly rooted in a spirit of municipal reform, laid the groundwork for a strong superintendency. Reformers struggled to remove education from the corrupting influence of machine politics sometimes exploiting ethnic immigrant diversity into the hands of appointed, conservative, and elitist school boards who in turn would choose strong-minded, exceedingly able administrators to direct the schools. A philosophy of administration quite conveniently at hand during this reform era was the scientific management approach advocated by industrial engineer Frederick W. Taylor.[14] This approach, with its stress upon efficiency, caught on well with educators wishing to claim that there were indeed special skills and areas of knowledge available to those who administer schools. Taylor claimed that it was possible to analyze scientifically the nature of each person's job and to discover the one best way to maximize work output at least cost per input. Standardized methods of performance with standardized tools and conditions of work would be planned, developed, and enforced by a management that was itself specialized for maximum efficiency (e.g., into repair foremen, quality control supervisors, "gang bosses").

In his *Education and the Cult of Efficiency*, Raymond Callahan traces the impact of Taylorism upon the early years of educational administration. Time and motion studies of teachers, cost-cutting hints in supplies purchasing, examinations of pupil study habits, standardized accounting methods, the measurement of student abilities and achievements, and the comparative costs per hour of curriculum offering—such was the stuff of school administration in the profession's formative years.[15]

**The Weberian Ideal.**   Although his turn-of-the-century work was not formally translated into English until 1946, the German sociologist Max Weber provided a conveniently idealized administrative *structure* that fit very comfortably around Taylorist notions of administrative *behavior*.[16] The oft-maligned word *bureaucracy* was to Weber a special form of social organization designed to maximize administrative rationality. Its key ingredients are:

- The organization of offices (and officials) should be according to a principle of hierarchy, with each lower office controlled and supervised by a higher one.
- Conduct in office should be governed/bound by sets of (usually explicitly written) rules.
- Officials should act only within their own specified spheres of competence as part of a systematic division of labor.
- Officials must be selected on the basis of their technical qualifications (their competence).
- Employment in an office constitutes a career, with promotion (dependent upon the judgment of superiors) according to achievement.
- Officials must function impersonally, without favoritism or arbitrariness— ensuring predictability, conformity, and equality of treatment.
- Each official is to be subject to strict and systematic discipline and control in the conduct of office.[17]

Weber's idealized model suggests that a rational administrative structure includes many interrelated elements of control designed to ensure that employees will perform with maximum efficiency in the pursuit of specific goals. Lines of authority tying superiors to subordinates from the top to the bottom of the hierarchy, standardized performance according to rules and formalized procedures, stable and predictable patterns of recruitment and promotion, impersonality, a career orientation, and role specificity—all of these elements combine to guide the production activities of the organization toward acceptable forms of efficient task accomplishment.

Lest Weber be blamed for the charges of red tape, mismanagement, ineptitude, and sluggishness that describe our contemporary stereotypes of bureaucracy, it should be noted in his defense that he saw the bureaucratic employee as an individual *freed* rather than constrained by rationality. Guided by a framework of rules and impersonality, the lower administrative official should be able to exercise much greater initiative, discretion, and independence of judgment than would be the case under a system of confusing organizational procedures. If there is failure, Weber would argue that it is because there is too little bureaucracy—as he defined it—not too much.

## The Rational Model

Both the scientific management and Weberian ideals have been the subject of heavy criticism and considerable theoretical revision over the years. Such scholars as Robert Merton and Alvin Gouldner showed that the formal characteristics of bureaucracy (e.g., explicitly written rules) may cause unintended consequences ("dysfunctions"), leading the organization away from rather than toward rationality.[18] Philip Selznick and later Michel Crozier showed that the necessary delegation of authority in bureaucracy creates divisions of interest and departmentalized turf —with the latent effect of introducing the pursuit of a variety of goals and values (e.g., along departmental lines) in place of the common goals of the organization.[19] Herbert Simon added the concept *bounded rationality* to the lexicon of organizational life, suggesting that man's search for rationality involves a willingness to settle for that which "satisfices" in the midst of overwhelming complexity and constraint.[20] Don Riddle's instinctive understanding of the bounded rationality of a large university certainly was one of the factors that prompted him to sort out what he would and what he would not try to control.

Nevertheless, despite criticisms and revisions, the rational perspective remains a powerful model of organizational behavior and administrative control. W. Richard Scott has assembled a number of definitions of organizational rationality, pointing out that the definitions all have the common features of:

1. *Goal Specificity.* Organizations purposefully pursue specific goals—and function amidst clear criteria for choosing among alternative activities toward the attainment of these goals.
2. *Formalization.* Organizations are deliberately structured in terms of their goals—with explicit rules and performance roles, under central coordination, designed to elicit the conscious cooperation of organizational participants.

Scott's summarizing definition is that:

> An organization is a collectivity oriented to the pursuit of relatively specific goals and exhibiting a relatively highly formalized social structure.[21]

Under rationality, the structure of the organization (its chain of command, its distribution of resources, its allocation of work, its reward system) is tightly articulated in terms of its goal directedness. Employees donate cooperatively to a clearly defined corporate product; the contributions of organizational members are closely monitored with efforts toward efficiency in goal attainment properly rewarded; and career advancement opportunities (movement up the corporate ladder) are understood clearly to depend upon evidence of exceptional service to the organization's stated purposes.

Applying all this to education, the rational model would suggest *first* that educational organizations are guided by shared goals—goals that originated at the top of the hierarchy, as policy, and have been steadily translated and transformed downward into carefully articulated tasks for progressive layers of subordinates. This is what Don Riddle was after when he asked the business office of the university to step up its monitoring of unit budgets. And in a high school, teachers are giving technological voice (e.g., an algebra lesson) to a set of objectives (math literacy) that permeate the entire institution.

*Second*, the educational organization has a formal system for controlling and coordinating behavior downward through a command hierarchy in terms of its goals. Organizational rules and procedures are the central mechanisms of control, they are incorporated in curriculum guides, administrative directives, communication channels, union agreements, data collection forms, budgeting procedures, and personnel policies. A modern understanding of the organization will also recognize elements of control such as tradition, employee socialization, the quality of executive leadership, and the organizational reward structure as critical parts of the goal attainment mixture.

*Third*, the educational organization has clearly delineated roles and areas of differential responsibility, such that its separate parts contribute in coordinated fashion to overall institutional performance. Each level of responsibility (e.g., principal, department head, teacher) is provided with a downward delegation of authority commensurate with that level's task specifications.[22] The assumption is that a local board of education will establish a matter of school district policy. The policy will be translated into administrative rules by a superintendent and her staff. The rules will be communicated to school principals, passed on to classroom teachers, and implemented by teachers in daily interactions with pupils. Ostensibly the impact of the board's policy can be assessed by examining changes in pupil behavior.

### Rationality and the Control/Coordination of Education

How does an administrator control and coordinate the educational organization from the rational perspective? There are two ways. The administrator may either (a) establish *direct* mechanisms of control over the behaviors of subordinates, or (b) establish *indirect* mechanisms. The rational model commonly is portrayed as a system for the direct (and authoritarian) specification of required behavior, communications channels, task limits, work products, and the like. However, such a portrayal provides a misrepresentation of the other side of rationality, the side that would proceed indirectly toward organizational goals by structuring the premises and conditions of employee behavior.[23] In terms used by Edward S. Herman, the administrative use of direct control may be thought of as *literal* control, where there is explicit power to make key decisions and guide the behavior of one's subordinates. The use of indirect control, alternatively, resides in the added power of administrators to exercise a *constraining influence* upon other persons.[24] The difference is between an administrative order (e.g., "Teachers will be in their classrooms thirty minutes before each day's opening bell") and a process of socialization (e.g., collegial norms of classroom preparedness are shared by old-timers and learned by newcomers).

## Direct Mechanisms of Control

Frederick W. Taylor's efficiency perspective received theoretical elaboration as an approach to organizational management in the later work of Henri Fayol and Luther Gulick.[25] These theorists sought to rationalize the organization from the top down, with the development of explicit principles for organizing, commanding, and controlling the flow of work from the apex to the base of an administrative pyramid. The famous acronym POSDCORB came out of Gulick's work—complete with explicit principles for such activities as task specialization, staffing and staff training, the proper span of control, and the nature of a command hierarchy. POSDCORB is a shorthand list of what it is the able administrator must do in running the organization: Planning, Organizing, Staffing, Directing, Coordinating, Reporting, and Budgeting. With these important responsibilities, the administrative official must necessarily be a person in charge, or as Gulick captured it so eloquently: "The problem of organization thus becomes the problem of building up between the executive at the center and subdivisions of work on the periphery an effective network of communication and control."[26]

Nearly every educational organization is formally organized in a manner that would have made these early theorists proud. The organization typically has a single head (albeit one who is responsive to some form of board) who directs the work of a small number of subordinates, each of whom is in charge of a crucial, but separable component of the organization's mission (e.g., curriculum, personnel, finance, academic affairs, administrative operations). These officers, in turn, direct the work of immediate subordinates with even more specialized responsibilites (e.g., research, outreach and public service, data processing, facilities management). As one proceeds downward through the pyramid, the organization further departmentalizes into an array of units directly servicing the organization's clientele, each of which is similarly topped by a single head (e.g., dean, principal) who watches over the work of a radiating web of middle-level and, finally, street-level subordinates.

Within this framework, the most important mechanisms of control and coordination are the educational organization's rules and orders, its information and communication process, and its procedures for evaluation. Anthony Downs developed these three elements into a basic control cycle for bureaucracy:

1. An official issues a set of orders. The official then:
2. Allows subordinates time to put each order into effect.
3. Selects certain orders to evaluate subordinates' performance.
4. Seeks to discover what has actually been done at lower levels as a result of the orders.
5. Compares the effects of each order with original intentions.
6. Decides whether these results are effective enough to require no more attention, ineffective but unlikely to be improved because of severe obstacles encountered, or partially effective and capable of being improved by further orders.
7. In the last case, the official issues further orders, starting the cycle again.[27]

From Downs' perspective, effective control in an organization begins with the issuing of orders. They are as often as possible in the form of elaborately written rules and regulations which can be consulted again and again by lower level personnel, thereby reducing the number of decisions that topmost officials are asked to make. Whether written as rules or passed on verbally as directives, orders should be distortion-proof messages that can be communicated down an authority chain with minimal leakage. As the orders are implemented, written reports of performance (using objective measures) should feed back upward. Top-level officials cannot review everything, but what they do decide to review should not be easily forecast by subordinates, and it should cover areas of importance for the organization (e.g., that which can stir outside criticism, that which deviates most significantly from preplanned performance targets, that which generated disagreement among subordinates). The monitoring or evaluation portion of the control process is further assisted by the employment of antidistortion devices to insure subordinate compliance. Such devices might occasionally involve some report redundancy (duplicate reporting as a check of accuracy) or some overlapping of responsibility (requiring upper-level coordination).[28]

Educational organizations certainly have not been criticized for lacking direct control of the type outlined by Downs. There are many, often quite elaborate rules emanating from state and federal program guidelines, union agreements, court decisions, matters of organizational history and tradition, board of education policies, and of course top-level administrative initiatives. There are also reports. Reports on students, teachers, facilities usage, expenditures, parental involvement, site-level needs (e.g., textbook requisitions), accidents, state school code compliance (e.g., inoculation records), and federal programs—these are just a few of the voluminous number that are produced. Public school personnel, from the classroom on up, also claim rather vociferously that they are closely monitored, despite professional norms of autonomy. Checks on lesson plans, classroom visits, standardized tests of pupil achievement, sign-in/sign-out procedures, end-of-year evaluations, recordings of disciplinary incidents, records of grades awarded, and checks on the fulfillment of non-teaching assignments (e.g., cafeteria duty, hall guarding)—all are common elements of supervision over a profession raised on respect for pedagogical freedom.

Nevertheless, from this direct-control perspective, it is difficult to claim that educational organizations are under effective control. To explore this point, let us examine more closely the three elements of rules, communication, and evaluation.

**Rules.**   Alvin Gouldner studied the functions fulfilled by bureaucratic rules. An important one is that rules specify the obligations of subordinates and, specifically, draw their *attention* to managerial expectations. When he moved to change the rules regarding the reserve fund, Don Riddle attempted to re-specify the obligation of his fellow managers to his office through a "tax" that eventually would contribute to the common welfare. He expressed a new expectation to them, and he met resistance that was both collective and individual. We will explore such resistance to Gouldner's first function below. A second factor is that rules remove a necessity for the repetition of orders. Standing rules apply to similar circumstances—thereby providing a sameness, a uniformity of action under repetitive conditions. Third, this uniformity facilitates control-from-a-distance within the organization. One can tell at a glance whether rules are or are not being followed. Fourth, bureaucratic rules legitimize the utilization of punishments. As statements of expected behavior they provide an advance warning of sanctions that will follow acts of noncompliance. Fifth, rules provide managerial leeway. Managers can play them as chips (either sticking to rules or bending them) to secure worker cooperation. However, sixth, one can turn the leeway notion around and find that rules may stimulate worker apathy. Subordinates become aware of how little they can do and still remain secure in their jobs.[29]

Gouldner's list provides a useful point of departure in examining the difficulty of controlling educational organizations directly through the rules and the administrative orders process. Let us look at the first of Gouldner's points. While rules and directives do draw the *attention* of employees, that attention is seldom, as rationality would imply it, aimed at the specific, unitary goals of an administrative hierarchy. Rather, rules in education reflect its diversity, its fragmented structure of governance. They come out of the hard bargaining of a union contract. They reflect education's strange legal setting, wherein the state controls (e.g., sets standards, regulates, monitors), but the locality has autonomy (e.g., to tax, create a budget, hire a superintendent). And similarly, they reflect all the many and often conflicting cross-currents of a policymaking process deeply embedded in court decisions, ideological debates (e.g., Darwinism vs. Creationism), demographic realities (e.g., white flight), local community politics, and the exigencies of state-federal funding. Administrators on the firing line commonly complain that their attention is drawn in just too many different directions. The expectations are overwhelming, and are often in conflict. Whom do you really work for? It is not easy to tell.[30] Whose attention are you being drawn toward? Whose rules do you follow?

Some scholars would argue that it is precisely in situations where there are these crosscurrents of policy that administrators most decidedly need rules. If an administrator is confused, she or he seems to love to pay attention to a rule that will relieve the difficulty. In chaotic circumstances, rules take on a much greater significance than would be the case in more serene, manageable situations.[31] The rule becomes a convenience, something to fall back on, something to use as an explanation to those who press for special consideration. Nevertheless, this pragmatically correct observation turns Gouldner's notion of attention-getting on its head. Rules are not drawing the attention of administrators to organizational expectations; they are, rather, providing a convenience to administrators in drawing attention away from areas that are filled with managerial ambiguity and conflict. Administrators may select some rules and ignore others, they may devise their own, or they may interpret those of the organization in strange ways to meet their own administrative needs. Attention is diverted, not focused.

Gouldner's second function of rules (furnishing a uniformity of action) may also cut two ways. There is much in the delivery of educational services that is predictable, ongoing, and repetitive; administrative rules appear to apply rather well in most of these areas. Procedures for the purchase of instructional materials, the registration of pupils, the maintenance of student records, and the processing of pay checks are just a few of the key arenas in which standing rules facilitate an efficiently administered enterprise. In many other task areas, however, standing rules call for a uniformity of action that may not match reality. The need sometimes is for variability, not uniformity. In their research on the implementation of collective bargaining agreements, for example, Mitchell and colleagues observed a modern trend toward the production of tighter and more comprehensive work rules in the course of school district translation of contract agreement into contract administration. These central office rules reflect an understanding of the need for scrupulous consistency and uniformity of contract interpretation throughout the district. Nevertheless, the researchers found that on the bottom of the hierarchy, school principals require flexibility. In order to manage their schools effectively (e.g., keeping close personal relationships with teachers), principals need the option of treating each individual union contract situation on its own idiosyncratic merits. In fact, maintaining the loyalty and cooperation of their school staff necessitates a bending of the rules quite as often as an application of them.[32]

Similarly, the third and fourth functions of a rules framework (control-from-a-distance and warnings of sanctions) raise pivotal questions in education. Control of what? Sanctions for what? Pitner and Ogawa write that male local school district superintendents have been found to devote most of their attention to "structural aspects of school systems such as programs, budgets, facilities, and schedules."[33] That which is at the heart of the educational enterprise, its instructional activity, receives relatively little direct attention. Two major reasons for this appear to be that (a) the technology of instruction is so uncertain it is hard to know what to try to control and how; and (b) there is so little consensus among a school system's constituents regarding preferred outcomes that standards of performance (necessary to the exercise of control) never really surface.[34] Thus, superintendents turn to that which *can* be controlled. They build and repair schools, prepare budgets, engage in public relations, seek extra funding, hire staff, and push new programs or educative wrinkles (e.g., year-round schooling, desk-top computers, teacher in-service, a winning athletic program). Such control from a distance as there is in education is more commonly tied to rules and regulations in the support areas of the educational mission than in its domain of central purpose, instruction.

And, for this reason, we may observe that Gouldner's fifth and sixth functions of rules (allowing managerial leeway and, sometimes, worker apathy) are similarly turned around in education. Administrators undoubtedly use options that are available to them in securing subordinate cooperation. School principals, for example, have been observed to bend rules on special education placements, teachers' leave days, extra-duty assignments, class size limits, and pupil discipline procedures in the course of accommodating teacher self-interest. Similarly, rules in such areas as student enrollment, attendance, standardized testing, and purchasing/accounting occasionally are waived in order to serve the interests of the school as a whole.[35] Few rules, however, and consequently few options apply to the technology of classroom instruction. Principals occasionally create their own rules (e.g., by checking teachers' lesson plans, specifying procedures for the recording of student marks, requiring teachers to assign homework); however, even these rules only peripherally affect what really goes on behind the classroom door. Teachers generally are left alone to teach—in their own way, through their own devices. Consequently, there is little opportunity for teachers to feel secure within a rules framework. In counterpoint to Gouldner's suggestion that rules serve worker apathy by defining how little one can do and remain secure, teachers are faced with the problem of rarely knowing how much or what they *have* to do. Beyond the security offered by tenure (now of diminishing value), the teacher knows the stress of rulelessness far better than the apathy supposedly provoked by organizational rules.

In sum, despite cries that educational organizations have become bogged down in rules and are over-centralized and over-controlled, we would observe that direct control through the rules process is of problematic value in the administration of education. Rules come from many sources beyond the simple authoritative hierarchy of the organization, and they are often in conflict. The need for local flexibility and our still primitive knowledge of a teaching-learning technology augur poorly for a specification of tight rules that would guarantee a close monitoring of classroom effectiveness. Finally, the absence of rules in an underdeveloped technology may serve the organization well by generating more stress than apathy—by keeping employees on their toes within an uncertain environment.

**Communication.** The control of an organization is in large part lodged within the effective *coordination* of its many activities. Coordination is impossible without a system of information and communication. Although size and complexity of organizational structure are linked generally with the severity of the coordination problem, any organization, whatever its size, must seek to understand what its various parts are doing.[36] Because educational organizations, from tiny to enormous, evidence structural looseness, the control of their activities through a process of effective communication looms large as a critically important element of administration.

In the late 1960s and early 1970s, the development of highly sophisticated (usually computerized) management information systems (MIS) captured the enthusiastic attention of administrators in many fields of public service, including education. Program or performance budgeting systems (PPBS), program evaluation review techniques (PERT), and management by objectives (MBO) were a few prominent creations in an era of managerial optimism occasioned by the discovery of a new science of systems analysis in organizational life. Educators, from building principals through college presidents, began experimenting with some—often radical—ideas (e.g., zero-based budgeting, linear responsibility charting) aimed at improving their grasp of what was really going on in the organization below them.

Much interest in the 1970s was given to the notion of cybernetic control in organizations.[37] Basic to the cybernetic model is the collection and use of information as *feedback*. The organization is viewed as a collection of interacting variables (with cause and effect relationships between them) that require rather close monitoring. The idea is to ensure that organizational performance stays in line with institutional goals. Cybernetics employs the metaphor of a thermostat, keying in on such variables as conflict or deviance to see that the organizational atmosphere continues to operate conducively toward its productive purpose. A cybernetic approach could be extremely complex or inordinately simple. In *The Productive School* (1971), J. Alan Thomas offered a simplified feedback model for the individual school, which urged building principals to (a) develop procedures for measuring school outputs at various stages, (b) compare these findings with desired levels of performance for the school, and then (c) use differences between actual and desired levels of performance as standards of comparison when altering school inputs and procedures.[38]

By the early 1980s, however, the bloom was well off the rose of systems analysis and educational cybernetics. Scholars like Martha Feldman and James March offered some revisionist insights into information usage within organizations that indicated much more complexity inherent in the communications element of administrative control than had been recognized.[39] Linkages between the information collected and the problems confronted or goals pursued by organizations may be quite weak. Much information is collected routinely that cannot be used. Information that was once useful is still assembled, but it is now no longer relevant. Other information is gathered and processed by organizations to justify decisions already made, to survey the outside environment for surprises, and to serve the self-interest of individual managers (e.g., the hoarding of information can be an instrument of intra-organizational power). Furthermore, bad information seems to drive out good objectives, in a kind of Gresham's Law of communication as control. Information by its existence carries a symbolic value that legitimates some areas of bureaucatic endeavor while undermining others. This is not unlike the educator's dilemma in permitting that which can be measured (e.g., factual recall) to drive out of the curriculum that which cannot be measured (e.g., creativity).[40]

Despite its newly appreciated complexity, the control and coordination of the educational organization through its communications is nevertheless a central tenet of the administrative effort. As Downs' basic control cycle indicated, seeking to discover what has been done at lower levels perhaps is the sine qua non of rational managerial effectiveness. Don Riddle was not interested in surprises, or failures of communication. In taking such a hard line on this matter, he placed substantial pressure on subordinates to communicate with him. It may be suggested in this regard that the cybernetic idea of feedback is still the key variable. The cybernetic model in its complete and ideal form, though, assumes that each of the many parts of the organization is too easily responsive to changes elsewhere and too easily amenable to control from the top through some form of information system. However, the maintenance of some system or procedure whereby information can be collected and used to improve goal-attainment is still of vital importance to those who would seek to exercise direct, administrative control.

Recent studies a la Mintzberg[41] of educational administrators at work have led to some revised notions concerning the feedback process. Administrators (including educators) rely heavily upon verbal (most often face-to-face) information, spend large portions of the working day away from their own desks amidst the work places of others, encounter frequent interruptions and changes in the focus of their attention, and accomplish much of their decision-making in episodes of brief duration.[42] Van Cleve Morris and his research colleagues described the workaday world of the school principalship, for example, as follows:

> For the most part, the tempo of life in a principal's workday is not conducive to serene reflection and ordered, thoughtful decision making. There is a certain tumble of events, one after another, which requires the ability to move abruptly from one subject to another. The principal's day allows little rank-ordering of priorities, everything seems to blend together in an undifferentiated jumble of activities that are presumably related, however remotely, to the ongoing rhythm and purpose of the larger enterprise. In one instance, a principal was wrestling with a critical problem—the freshman history sequence. And yet, the entire matter was elbowed aside, denied a position of deserved prominence, by a cascade of other concerns—vandalized auditorium seats, a foul-mouthed girl intimidating her teacher, bomb threats by anonymous phone callers, and cockroaches in the locker room.[43]

Within this real world of administrative behavior, the organizational information system takes on a different flavor. Mintzberg writes that getting information *rapidly* can be more important than getting it absolutely *right*. Gossip, hearsay, and speculation are valuable staples in the feedback diet. Furthermore, managers at work prefer their information to be tangible, to address specific events and problems and observed phenomena. Finally, verbal information is the central medium, with the result that informal feedback channels assume more saliency than the formalized system of reports and communications.[44]

In keeping with these realities of managerial behavior, Lee Sproull and David Zubrow have suggested an administrative performance information system (APIS) for educational organizations that addresses communication toward (a) a variety of sources (e.g., students and parents as well as teachers and principals); (b) many "collection modes" (including personal observation and conversation); (c) flexible timing; and (d) varying usages (e.g., symbol management as well as problem solving). The authors argue that a behaviorally grounded information system can reintroduce many elements of rationality-guided administration into organizations. If administrators at work rely heavily on observation and face-to-face communication, they should systematically incorporate these modes into their feedback procedures. Also, nontraditional practices, such as placing random calls to one or two parents (or teachers) a day to ask about how things are going, could broaden an administrator's base of information as well as serve "the symbolic purpose of demonstrating administrative attentiveness."[45]

In sum, the use of communication in the direct control and especially in the coordination of many activities of the education organization has been seen in recent years in a clearer and clearer light. From a flirtation with PPBS-type approaches, we have moved to an improved understanding of the many complexities and subtle nuances that surround the flow of information into and out of the sensibility of administrators. Based upon keener knowledge of what it is that administrators really do and the continuing importance of feedback, broadened conceptions of rationality-guided communicative behavior have emerged. Thus administrators are urged to employ creatively a variety of communication modes and channels that in an earlier era might have been considered well beyond the pale of what the rational administrator should do.

**Evaluation.**    Achieving prominence in Anthony Downs' basic control cycle is a set of actions that together provide an *evaluation* of organizational performance. A sample of administrative orders is selected. The behaviors of those who carried out the orders are examined, and the effects of each order are compared with the consequences originally intended. If the results prove ineffective, attention is given to improvements (e.g., removing obstacles) which will redirect actions toward the intended effects.

Students of organizations (most notably Dornbusch and Scott) identify the evaluation process as one of the most powerful elements of administrative control. They observe that nearly all organizations seek in some manner to monitor the performance of their participants. The evaluation of employee performance according to how well their actions meet organizational expectations is a prime mechanism whereby administrators focus the attention of lower-level employees. Evaluation leads employees to orient their efforts toward success on whatever endeavor is selected to be measured.[46]

The education profession is no stranger to the use of evaluation. Testing and measurement techniques have long been elements in training programs for educators, and such tools of the trade as standardized, nationally normed examinations have received widespread acceptance as indicators of such qualities as college aptitude, teacher preparedness, student interests or attitudes, subject-area knowledge, and high school competency. Furthermore, evaluation is a well-accepted element in the management of education. Principals are expected to observe and pass judgement on classroom teachers; principals themselves are often subjected to school-by-school comparisons (e.g., percentages of pupils performing at grade level, student attendance rates); college instructors are only tenured and promoted following thorough evaluations by academic peers; and the object of all this attention, the student, is awarded a diploma only after undergoing years of evaluative screening, sorting, profiling (e.g., with IQ scores, occupational interest inventories), and grading.

Nevertheless, the use of evaluation as a technique to control educational organizations has not been numbered among the strongest of administrative tools. Some major reasons for this were discussed earlier in Chapter 4. *First,* such assessments have focused on input typically, often to the point of being confused with (or used in lieu of) measures of output. Schools which manage to obtain the brightest students or garner the largest amounts of scarce resources, for example, often are thought by definition to be the best schools. *Second,* educational goals are decidedly ambiguous and diverse, and are often in conflict. *Third,* even when educational goals are clear, we find that means-ends relationships in education are poorly understood. The technology of defining organizational tasks in terms that clearly contribute to goal-attainment remains a decided mystery. *Finally,* education has a long tradition of awarding considerable personal autonomy in the one area (instruction) that is thought to be its purpose in life. Because teachers are left alone to teach, they are not easily touched by administrative evaluations.

A framework that appears to fit the problems associated with the use of evaluation in controlling educational organizations has been offered by William Ouchi.[47] Figure 5.1 suggests that the type of control an organization employs is related to a knowledge of its means-ends relationships—that is, knowledge of the process whereby inputs are *transformed* into outputs. Furthermore, the organization should have reliable and valid measures of the desired outputs available.

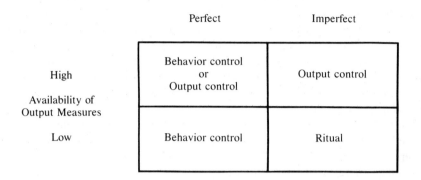

FIGURE 5.1     Control Type and its Antecedent Conditions

Adapted from William G. Ouchi, "The Relationship Between Organizational Structure and Organizational Control," *Administrative Science Quarterly*, 22:1 (March 1977): 98.

The matrix identifies four separate types of control under differing antecedent conditions. With perfect knowledge of the processes for transforming inputs into outputs (transformation processes), an organization can exercise close control over both the behaviors of people engaged in the work of the organization and the outputs which result from their behavior. However, if knowledge of transformation processes is imperfect while good output measures nevertheless are available, the organization's control structure will focus upon output to the neglect of behavior. Conversely, if there is sound knowledge of transformation processes but an inadequacy in the measure of output, the organization can be expected to focus upon behavior control. However, in the final cell, where the transformation process is not known *and* outputs are unmeasurable, it is suggested by Ouchi that "only ritualized control is possible."[48] Here, the organization controls its workers through means that give the appearance of rationality but are in reality simply part of a time-tested ritual of institutional control. As noted by Meyer and Rowan, an example of ritualized control may be identified in the detailed, definitive specifications (training and credentialing) that surround who may be permitted to teach in which types of classes and schools. This ritualized selection process is used *in place* of some means whereby the performances of teachers or schools are evaluated from student achievement data. Similarly, rituals governing student classifications (e.g., grade-levels, units completed, ability levels) are used in place of effectively determining exactly what the students have actually studied and learned.[49]

It may be suggested that educational organizations have struggled mightily between the two right-hand cells of Ouchi's matrix. From its earliest foundations in a scientific management era, educational administration has had an on-again, off-again flirtation with accountability methods of controlling employee behavior. There are many quantifiable measures of output in education (e.g., test scores, students graduated, pupil attendance rates, student job-placements), and at one time or another nearly every conceivable indicator has been employed in some fashion to give the enterprise an evaluative flavor. Nevertheless, despite all of its counting and measuring, educational administration depends little upon evaluation as a means for institutional control. Meyer and Rowan suggest that despite its profusion of tests, education, in reality, avoids a close inspection of its instructional activity. The counting, summing, and percentiling of results serve a goal of public legitimation (making the organization look good) rather than a goal of evaluation-based rationality in the conduct of administration.[50] Natriello and Dornbusch say that if there is a weakness in the control system in education, the fault lies in the failure of the evaluation system to link up sufficiently with the distribution of valued rewards and penalties.[51] Teachers, principals, even college professors may be monitored and their students tested, but seldom do any real sanctions (or rewards) accompany deviations in educator performance. Interestingly, a former dean of a college of education has remarked how surprised he was to discover during his term in office how unduly receptive members of the college faculty could be to miniscule pay increases. Even a meager sweetening of the paycheck conveys meaningful, positive signals from the dean's office that are seldom otherwise received in academia.[52] It might not take much for the reward and evaluation systems to blend meaningfully together in education. With the extensive standardization and equality that is build into teachers' pay schedules, a few informal sweeteners gain considerably in motivational power.

In sum, the evaluation of organizational performance is considered one of the administrator's most powerful tools of direct control. However, despite professional attention to skills of testing and measurement, education has not been successful in using evaluation in the governance of its own productive efforts. Among the oft-cited reasons for this failing are ambiguities and conflicts regarding just what *should* be evaluated, education's poorly understood technology (means-end relationships), a historical focus upon input quality rather than output quality, and the long tradition of educator autonomy in the one area—instruction—that is central to the enterprise. Finally, educational organizations as yet have not linked their evaluation and reward systems sufficiently—and this is a situation which well might be corrected. Efforts to provide such a linkage (e.g., merit pay for teachers) generally have not been successful.

## Indirect Mechanisms of Control

*Direct* control over the behaviors of subordinates may involve establishing and enforcing rules, paying attention to communications, and closely evaluating worker performance. *Indirect* control, no less firmly rooted in rationality, proceeds toward the attainment of organizational goals by structuring the premises and conditions of employee behavior.

The indirect control perspective owes much to the human relations view of administration—a counter-movement of the 1930s and 1940s that developed in reaction to the top-down authoritarianism of Frederick Taylor. Mary Parker Follett, one of the intellectual leaders of the movement, argued that organizations are amalgamations of groups in potential conflict whose separate views and interests must be *integrated* if the organization is to function well.[53] While it is more person-to-person and more relaxed as an approach to administrative control, nonetheless the indirect perspective shares the press of the rational model toward organizational goal attainment. It is the administrator's job to counteract potentially disintegrating forces among employees by indirectly controlling the nature of their work—by influencing and motivating productive effort rather than directly ordering it.

Some of the most provocative thinking of the period came from Chester Barnard in his *The Functions of the Executive.*[54] Barnard suggested that an organization must be viewed as a cooperative system. Cooperation, the willingness of people to contribute to the operation of the organization, to a common purpose, is dependent upon the capacity of the administrator to bring together (reconcile) conflicting forces, interests, desires, needs, and viewpoints. The notion of the organization as a cooperative system (that is only with difficulty held under administrative control) is best illustrated in Barnard's definition of authority. In contrast with the direct-control assumption that authority resides with the person giving an order, Barnard contends that authority is present only when other persons *accept* that order. People must be willing to comply with administrative orders, and their compliance is by no means assured, even if they are formal underlings in the administrative hierarchy.[55]

As an example, consider a local superintendent's relationship with her building principals. A new board of education policy on student discipline has been promulgated. The policy takes the form of a uniform discipline code, spelling out in careful detail the procedures to be followed and the sequence of disciplinary measures (punishments) to be used for each infraction of school rules. As it is enacted, the discipline code receives considerable attention in the local press, and the superintendent of schools makes it clear that the code constitutes a procedural directive that school staff members are to follow to the letter. Nevertheless, nearly a year later, only a few teachers in the district's elementary schools are discovered to be even aware of the existence of such a code. Their principals, while aware, confess that the code is not of much use to them in their situation.[56]

Why have not building principals and their school staffs *accepted* the authority of the superintendent and, for that manner, the board of education? There could be many reasons, of course—serious inconsistencies in the code; the failure of the central office to provide resources required for its implementation; heavy political opposition to the code's implementation (e.g., from the teachers' union); bureaucratic in-fighting (e.g., which headquarters department will administer it); even widespread insider recognition that the code was media oriented to begin with, and never meant to be implemented. Whatever the explanation, the point is that the cooperation of employees is by no means assured via the formal and direct structure of organizational authority. How do you get people to *accept* orders from above?

James D. Thompson wrestled with this question in *Organizations in Action*, suggesting that control under rationality rests in the ability to control the decision premises (the belief systems) of persons serving within an organization. Specifically, he suggests, the purpose of a rationally oriented leader should be to control two major dimensions of behavior: (a) the beliefs people have about cause-effect relations and (b) the preferences of organizational actors regarding possible outcomes.[57] With Thompson's framework as a point of departure, we would suggest the close examination of three elements in the *indirect* control of education— talk, socialization, and manipulation.

**Talk.** Peter C. Gronn writes: "Control is an aspect of administration for which talk is a key resource, particularly for staff relations, and in schools, talk is a potential

instrument of control for both principal and staff."[58] Just how important this resource
is has become clear in study after study of what it is that educational administrators
really do. Some two-thirds of the working day of the school principal or superintendent is normally spent talking and listening, usually in the form of close, face-to-face
interaction with a rather wide array of other persons.[59] Each encounter is typically of
short duration (just a minute or two), a snatch of conversation while the administrator
is literally on the run from one activity to another.[60]

The importance of verbal interaction may be at least in part a function of
physical surroundings. Educational administrators spend a lot of time away from
their own offices. They are as likely to be found in the vicinity of teachers' "offices"
(i.e., their classrooms), for teachers are not easily able to break away from the task of
monitoring children. A great deal of the administrative work of the school is done in
its corridors.[61] With work space distributed along both sides of such thoroughfares,
the school principal can be found in constant motion—popping into and out of
classes, catching teachers (or being caught) for a moment between periods, having a
chat on the threshold of a class while students troop in, keeping tabs on student
behavior in the halls while classes are in session. Morris et al. report that a common
phenomenon in educational administration is the "peripatetic committee meeting"
—where, for example, principal Johnson may receive a question about a scheduling
conflict from teacher Greene, climb a flight of stairs to discuss the matter with head
librarian Masters, and work out a proposed solution in separate talks with three other
teachers at their respective work stations before returning later in the day to inform
Greene of the answer to the question.[62]

Gronn suggests that talk as a form of control fits not only the physical but also
the normative environment of education. Teachers (and especially college professors)
cannot be expected to comply automatically with the directives of administrators.
Deference to administrative action is not a natural part of the way of life in many
educational circles. Furthermore, because of its peculiar professional dynamics,
where teachers tend to be in isolated curricular contact with students while
administrators are isolated in their own way in being removed from such contact,
each participant is likely to have his or her own subjective understanding of school
life.[63] Removing an extremely troublesome pupil from her classroom may be a prime
consideration for Miss Jones, for the child's behavior intrudes heavily upon the
learning time available to the other children in her class. To Mr. Smith, the principal,
the student's bothersome effect upon his classmates is of less concern than whether
the school will be on firm ground legally and politically in its handling of the
troublemaker.

Amid a physical and normative environment that emphasizes verbal interaction, administrative control through talking things over assumes a place of central
importance. The fact that Don Riddle encouraged colleagues who had not been
talking to each other to do so, involved much more than social niceties. A key
consequence of such administrative action is that talking almost necessarily involves
listening (although some persons are much better listeners than others). And
listening usually leads toward some degree of sharing. Thus, while the administrator
wishes to impose his will, to get it done his way, strategies are more likely to
resemble some form of accommodation. Indeed, in their study of the bases of
supervisory power among public school principals, Guditus and Zirkel note that

effective control in schools can be perceived as a win-win, or reciprocal, situation rather than something that is fixed in the hands of one group at the expense of another. They conclude:

> Principals who interact with teachers and solicit their opinions can obtain more responsiveness and better morale. Thus, this research challenges some of the traditional practices that have grown out of the "all or nothing law of power."[64]

Beyond its opportunity for providing a sharing of control, talk also fits a function of educational administration only recently recognized for its importance—symbol management. Pitner and Ogawa, for example, have reported that "superintending is communicating." Superintendents translate community preferences into the organizational structures of their school districts.[65] Maintaining constant contact with key sources of information, paying close attention to ceremonial activities, doing a good deal of politicking and persuading, choreographing smoothly the activities of participants and the timing of events, and occasionally using such ploys as diversion (e.g., creating one issue to draw attention away from another)—such are strategies used by superintendents to gain control over their own organizations. It would appear, the authors conclude, that superintendents "exert limited and, at best, indirect influence on organizational performance." However, their symbolic leadership, expressed in their ability to communicate (specifically, to mediate between community and organization), is in reality the essence of the job.[66]

**Socialization.** The careful selection and socialization of organization members can represent a potent mode of control. Indeed, Amitai Etzioni suggests that if an organization could somehow recruit and train individuals to perform as required quite adequately without supervision, there would then be no need for a structure of control. The work of the organization would be delegated, and people left alone, with confidence, to do their jobs.[67] In effect, the organizational and professional *culture*, passed along from one working generation to another, would build in a powerful structure of control.

To a large extent, this is exactly what education *attempts* to do. Elementary and secondary teachers are trained according to state requirements specifying the course work and clinical experience (classroom observation and student teaching) required to be certified (and therefore presumably prepared) to teach. There is also a powerful, shared understanding within the culture of the profession regarding what it is that youngsters should learn that shapes teacher training courses and experiences. Classes in the methods of teaching, educational psychology, and the foundations of education, are much the same whatever the college or university. In higher education there are few legalisms but more tradition, with the long period of apprenticeship needed to acquire the union card of a doctor's degree serving as a time of pervasive occupational socialization. After the initial training is completed, selection procedures will vary. Standardized tests sometimes screen teacher candidates, letters of recommendation and college transcripts are generally important, and an interview is usually mandatory. In higher education where one studied and whom one studied with is of initial importance, followed by the obligatory seminar where the candidate presents an academic paper (or otherwise makes a presentation) before his or her peers-to-be. A recruit's early years are monitored closely, and tenure is eventually awarded, although in higher education only after the trauma of rigorous peer evaluation.

In keeping with Etzioni's suggestion, education places a loose structure of work supervision around this socialization. Educators are assumed to be properly attired, as a result of their training, in a "broad mantle of professionalism."[68] The central difficulty with this, as Lortie and others have pointed out, is that education is still an incomplete profession. There is no well-defined body of knowledge that only educators (unlike lawyers and doctors) can lay claim to; there is, despite its credentialism and its press toward certification, only a truncated period of preparation and indoctrination; there has yet to be developed a strong culture for the profession marked by specific norms and operational values; and there is an inadequate separation politically between education and the laity.[69]

Thus, education has some of the trappings of professionalism (e.g., weak supervision, much classroom autonomy) but as yet an inadequate system of *control* through professionally directed socialization. Lortie points out that (a) teachers tend to be justifiably skeptical of the practical usefulness of their college training courses; (b) the brief period of practice teaching is not followed up by the protracted internship or apprenticeship found in other occupations; and (c) beginning teachers are asked to continue to develop their skills in virtual isolation from their colleagues.[70] Consequently, institutionalized controls that would be expected to flow from the application of specialized expertise and collegially shared values are not widely in evidence.

Curiously, despite its tendency to be structured as if it were highly professionalized, education has not given much attention to the role of the school administrator as socializing agent.[71] Although their study was not focused specifically upon socialization, the Morris team developed some observations as an interesting by-product of their research on the principalship in one large-city school system.[72] As chance would have it, the researchers began their field work at a time when sizable numbers of classroom teachers were being transferred between schools for the purpose of city-wide teacher desegregation. The research team had an opportunity to observe the ways in which principals in place in the receiving schools helped (or failed to help) newcomers learn the ropes in their new buildings. Although the transferees were all experienced teachers within the school system, the move was often an emotional one. With racial balance as the objective, many teachers found themselves shifted from majority to minority status in their new teaching situations. Indeed, some schools in white areas of the city received at this time (the fall of 1977) their first black teachers.[73]

Not all principals gave the transferees any special attention. They were treated like every other experienced member of the school staff. Others recognized the need for a bit of socialization—especially as they observed separate white and black tables in the faculty lunch area, heard complaints from parents about a new teacher's methods, or became aware of strains between the old and new faculty. The transferred teachers had lost the status they had achieved over time in their previous schools and often encountered resentment as they tried to regain favorable positions (e.g., a teacher of gifted pupils, a free period to develop the reading curriculum) in their new assignments.[74]

Strategies used by principals in these city schools to socialize newcomers included techniques of dependency, identification, and instruction.

1. *Dependency.* Transferred teachers often remarked about the many differences between their old and new schools, even though they were all part of the same, overarching school system. Policies and procedures important to teachers' lives and their relations with principals seldom were spelled out (e.g., in the form of a staff handbook). They had to be learned quickly and thoroughly on the job. In one's old school the norms might have been to send all discipline problems to the principal; submit reports late if need be, for the children come first; report to school each morning just a few minutes before classes begin; take the duty of hall or playground monitoring with a grain of salt; teach while sitting down, if you wished. In the new school, the same set of behaviors might earn one an immediate word of censure, or worse, an early reputation around the school (tough to shake later on) as a bit of a slacker.

The unstated and unwritten norms served principals well. In a situation not unlike the condition of "status degradation" used by the military academies as a first stage of socialization,[75] teachers entered their new schools bereft of the social support they had known and feeling decidedly unwelcome. Perceptive principals used the opportunity to establish a special dependency relationship with their incoming (albeit experienced) teachers—by intervening with parents, by overlooking (conspicuously) some early transgressions of the school norms, by helping the newcomers with special problems that accompanied their transfer situation (e.g., obtaining paychecks that had been sent to the old school), and by occasionally offering a bit of special recognition (e.g., a committee chairmanship) to a newcomer as a step in establishing status.

2. *Identification.* Amitai Etzioni suggests that "organizations which rely heavily on indentitive power are the most successful in terms of socialization achievements."[76] However, minimal differences between schools offer administrators few opportunities for providing newcomers with a firm—and hopefully attractive—school identity. Educators are not accustomed to the public relations or advertising that is often used in the private sector to generate a special image for an organization.

Nevertheless, a number of principals in the Morris study seemed to understand (perhaps intuitively) the value of creating something special in the way of a school identity. Fortuitously, the teacher transfer project coincided with a city-wide effort to desegregate students via open enrollment. Consequently, many principals worked hard to secure special definitions of their schools as back-to-basics units, foreign language academies, classics or humanities centers, gifted centers (emphasizing math and science), and the like. In schools without this heavy thrust toward identity, principals were found to engage in other activities that provided at least a modicum of identitive value. Among these were student festivals where the faculty also would enter in (e.g., a Halloween costume contest for pupils *and* faculty); a series of principal-organized coffees for parents (held in the parents' homes), with a couple of teachers accompanying the principal to each afternoon affair; the inauguration of a committee-based overhauling of the school curriculum, with every teacher serving on one of many committees (meeting weekly); and, special efforts by some principals to introduce transferred teachers to the history and circumstances of their new school with walking tours of the building and auto rides around the neighborhood. Despite their sameness, the city's schools did provide opportunities for the development of a sense of something special—a feeling that a school is more than just a building, that it can have its own separate identity.

3. *Instruction.* Later in Chapter 11, we will discuss at some length the role of the administrator as a teacher of his or her own staff. It would appear that instructing others in the school regarding expected patterns of behavior can be one of a principal's prime tools of teacher socialization.

A brief example from the Morris study shows an interesting, indirect way in which this can occur. Principal James Herron was worried that the teachers transferred into his school might not be thoroughly sensitive to, or adequately prepared to teach, the school's slowest readers. Yet Herron knew that as experienced teachers in the system, the transferees would resent the usual, direct approach of classroom observation followed by an evaluative conference. Instead, Herron asked the teachers to send their poorest readers to him for an hour a day, to receive extra tutorial help. In his hour with the pupils Herron pulled out all the stops. He worked hard, used some curriculum materials that he knew were effective, and sent the pupils back to their regular classrooms in an enthusiastic state. Within a few weeks the teachers began approaching Herron—asking for copies of his worksheets, his advice vis-a-vis particular pupils, and some hints as to his methods.[77]

**Manipulation.**    Our third indirect mechanism of control wears, in some quarters, a rather sinister cloak of nonrespectability. Indeed, analysts employing a Marxist approach to the study of educational organizations proceed from this perspective in arguing that educational bureaucracies are constructed on the basis of maintaining conscious, rational control by the capitalist class over society's workers.[78] In their control over students, so the argument goes, schools replicate the social relations of their future workplaces—by differentially allocating educational opportunity along class lines (e.g., tracking); by training future workers in habits of obedience, punctuality, and good discipline; and by cooling out those whose aspirations are at odds with their origins.[79] In the bureaucracy's control over its staff, it is argued that the employment relationship in education is similarly rooted in upper-class and business mores. Teachers are rewarded for patterning their behavior in conformity with the dominant class interests of the society.

Additionally, manipulation carries a connotation of the unethical. It seems to suggest that administrators are seeking to mold the decisions of their subordinates in directions that go against the subordinates' wills, that the organization's work force is somehow being bent and shaped by alien forces of which it is blithely unaware. To manipulate is to do damage to the trust and good will that form the heart of the employer-employee relationship. Furthermore, to manipulate is to place oneself in danger of being manipulated. As Mowday has suggested, school principals are not at all unknown (especially under conditions of organizational uncertainty) to use covert methods of influence (e.g., withholding important information) upon upper-level administrators.[80] Similarly, the Morris et al. research team has documented the acts of creative insubordination engaged in by building principals in their implementation of orders from above.[81]

In the view of most people, manipulation is a decidedly political act. Educational administrators are most adept at structuring situations and encounters between people in ways that serve effectively to control the outcomes of others' interactions. A dissident on the school faculty can be played off against the building's union representative; a controversial issue among a college faculty can be assigned to a notoriously slow-moving committee; a reorganization of a college can produce new departmental groupings of the faculty, each with a bare majority of the dean's supporters over his detractors; an especially troublesome member of a faculty can be placed in charge of an unimportant but time-consuming office, thus co-opted into management.

Despite its connotations of dirty politics, it may nevertheless be suggested that manipulation offers a viable form of indirect control in education. Its roots lie in an administrative understanding and use of the *reward system* of the organization. People may be guided, in their own rationality, by the allocation and distribution of incentives. Curiously, administrative control over (and manipulation of) the reward system has not received a great deal of research attention in education. At least in part, this may be attributable to the belief that educators are perhaps more heavily influenced by intrinsic rather than extrinsic rewards.[82] Thus the tendency has been to concentrate upon ways in which people become internally (i.e., psychologically) motivated to work, using as a conceptual point of departure the needs hierarchy and job satisfaction theories of Abraham Maslow and Frederick Herzberg.[83] In recent years in other fields, however, there has been a decided movement away from needs-based toward rewards-oriented studies of motivation.[84] Among the newer approaches are studies of behavior modification, social learning theory, and expectancy theory.[85]

Cecil Miskal is one theoretician in educational administration who has become interested in expectancy theory.[86] In brief, this conceptualization (based heavily upon the work of Victor Vroom)[87] suggests that the efforts people put into their work will depend upon (a) their expectations of outcomes or consequences that are likely to occur; (b) the value they place on the expected rewards associated with these outcomes; and (c) the probability that such reward(s) will actually be received if the work is done.[88] Hoy and Miskal note that there have been few efforts to date to test expectancy theory in education—but one study of their own concludes that educators do appear to be more highly motivated if they perceive that the work they do is likely to lead to desirable rewards.[89]

A closer examination of the rewards (and sanctions) available to educational administrators is needed. It is a highly complex topic—one that will not yield easily to an improved understanding. In their study, for example, Miskal and his research colleagues observe that for teachers the motivational force of intrinsic rewards still seems to be high. Thus, they speculate that teachers' expectancy of outcomes may be greatest when rewards are self-administered.[90] Another (somewhat contrary) warning, however, stems from research by O'Reilly and Weitz on the use of managerial sanctions. Sanctions (and rewards) have a social context. Their impact is dependent upon how members of the organization as a group interpret the benefits or losses collectively. Individual rewards are rooted in wider perceptions of value and are therefore to a large degree group-administered.[91]

As illustration, consider the problem of a local school district superintendent who is trying to raise the standardized test performance of pupils in reading within his district. Teachers throughout the district, in *all* subject areas are offered (urged into) special workshops on how to teach reading effectively. The response among teachers is decidedly mixed, varying markedly from school to school, and seems to be unconnected to the college-credit incentive (in that teachers looking toward a step increase in pay are no more likely than others to attend the workshops). Upon investigation, the superintendent concludes that the key variable is the degree to which the teachers as a group within each school share the value that reading improvement is important. Some faculties do, while others do not.

### The Rational Perspective: A Summary

We turn to an essay by Arnold Tannenbaum. In all likelihood, it has been the most frequently cited article on control in organizations over the years. It is only now recognized that Tannenbaum understood well the need to exercise control through indirect methods. He pointed out that control carries a good deal of symbolic importance, it rests on the willingness of individuals to accept it, it is a variable rather than fixed element, and it is distributed widely among workers as well as bosses.[92] Despite the continuing modernity of Tannenbaum's suggestions, students of organizational behavior still have not given sufficient attention to the exercise of indirect administrative control in the pursuit of an organization's stated objectives. In education, with its bureaucracy and semi-professionalism in uneasy juxtaposition, one would expect much interest in indirect approaches to control, yet this has not been the case. To some extent it may have taken a new line of research to produce some of the insights that are beginning to surface and may now be used more consciously by the educational practitioner. Researchers are increasingly entering and observing the world of the educational organization as a culture to be most carefully interpreted and understood—a world no less foreign in many ways than that observed in the earliest investigations of Samoan or Trobriand Islanders. "Thick description" is being used in place of the "thin" research of large-sample questionnaires and focused interviews. Consequently, recent studies of schools in depth reveal that the time devoted to the face-to-face encounter (talk), the instructionally and/or symbolically significant moment (socialization), and the application of properly placed rewards, may be elements of managerial behavior that have great potential significance for organizational control.

## CONTROL FROM THE COALITIONAL PERSPECTIVE

Control from the rational point of view assumes organizational goal-directedness. Administrators are busily engaged in trying to lead (or at least orchestrate) the activities of other persons in pursuit of a common set of objectives. But what if such commonality in goal-directedness cannot be assumed? What if we find, instead, that organizations are collectivities of participants who share common goals not nearly so often as they pursue several (possibly conflicting) ends within a structure that is marked more by diversity than conformity? What if the organization can better be described as a cluster of shifting interests and ongoing struggles over means and ends, than as a shared pursuit of common purposes? The typical elementary school may be less a cohesive whole than a battleground of upper-primary teachers at odds with lower-primary, of subject-centered versus child-centered teachers, old guard against the new, dissident parents disputing satisfied ones, principal supporters countering principal detractors, disciplinarians versus self-expression types, strong unionists fighting non-unionists. How, within this environment, does the school administrator exert control?

We prefer to call our second conceptualization of the organization a *coalitional* perspective. However, other terminology has been used quite frequently. Scott, for example, suggests two models as alternatives to the rational. These are the natural system and the open systems perspectives. Where rationality assumes the pursuit of specific goals and posits a highly formalized social structure, the natural system (taken from Gouldner, 1959) is much more people-oriented—viewing the organization as a "collectivity whose participants are little affected by the formal structure or official goals."[93] It is only under the rubric of the open systems perspective that Scott suggests the organization can be considered "a coalition of shifting interest groups that develop goals by negotiation"[94] (albeit with a strong outside influence from environmental forces).

While Scott suggests that organizations can be viewed as rational, natural, and open systems, Firestone and Herriott counterpose just a single image against the rational model. They propose, using strong language, an image of the organization as "anarchy"—where "goals are ambiguous, hierarchies of authority are not effective mechanisms of integration, technologies are unclear, and participation is fluid."[95] James G. March is the principal theoretician of this perspective—suggesting that as "organized anarchies" educational organizations are lightly controlled, unstable, filled with ambiguity, and are in many ways nonrational (e.g., administrators begin with solutions, with bags of tricks, and go looking for problems to fit their answers, rather than dealing logically with real problems).[96]

Our choice of the word coalition represents our view that despite their frequent looseness, fluidity, and ambiguity, organizations nevertheless are collectivities. Their participants may not be as hierarchically ordered or as single-mindedly goal oriented as the rational view would assume, but they do have at least some commonality. They are *organized* anarchies.

## Development of the Coalitional Perspective

The origins of the coalitional model are more difficult to trace than those of the rational. There is not so easily an identifiable progression of thought and research behind it, and the model has received little attention in the professional (as opposed to the scholarly) literature.[97] Nevertheless some important sources of the coalitional viewpoint may be suggested.

*First*, Chester Barnard opened a valuable line of scholarly inquiry into organizational life with his observation in *The Functions of the Executive* that formal organizations also have lively (sometimes competing) informal structures. Certainly it has its formalized allocation of roles and responsibilities (as typically depicted in an organization chart), but the real work of the organization is found in its friendship linkages and is reflected in matters of who is most closely in touch with whom, where the power lies, and who is "in the know" within the organization. The important point from Barnard's contribution is that individuals are busily engaged within organizations in constructing their own versions of social reality—a reality that often may contrast decisively with the formal charting of roles and responsibilities. Indeed, in recent years those who analyze behavior from a phenomenological view maintain that understanding must *start* with the individual—for the organization itself is merely an artifact of the meanings and intentions that people bring to it. Greenfield observes: "The phenomenological view leads to the concept of organizations as 'invented social reality.'"[98]

*Second*, during the 1950s and 1960s a number of now classic studies in the sociology of organizations used Max Weber's concept of the bureaucracy as an ideal to compare against the real world of organizational structures. Robert Merton, suggested that amidst its manifest functions (those it intends or is well aware of), the organization may also be involved in latent functions (which are unintended and unrecognized.)[99] Some of these may even be dysfunctional for the organization, as when, to use Merton's example, an organization manages to raise the esprit de corps of its own members but this enhanced esprit results in a neglect of the organization's clientele.[100] Of late, such tendency to glance beneath assumed reality has continued, producing some notable contributions to our understanding of educational organizations. Karl Weick, as we noted earlier, depicts the educational organization as a loosely coupled organization. Far from being closely constrained via such standard mechanisms of control as rules, rewards, directives, and administrator supervision, educators at all levels of the organization typically are left alone to do their jobs as they define them. Even at the bottom of the hierarchy, where control presumably should be tight, teachers have broad discretionary power in deciding what to teach, whom to reward, and when to punish.[101]

*Third*, it was during the 1950s and 1960s period of critique of the Weberian ideal that a reference was made to the organization as a *coalition* by Richard Cyert and James March. Although not yet ready at that time to drop the view that the decisions organizations make flow out of agreed-upon goals, Cyert and March farsightedly suggested that these goals are not necessarily established from the top down. Rather, goals emerge from within the organization, through a process of bargaining and side-payment (e.g., money or prestige granted in exchange for acquiescence) among individual participants. The suggestion is that the organization may be better described by using political models of choice than by using the rational model. In the political model, goals to be pursued are the outcomes of a conflict of preferences among organizational subgroups, emerging in the form of a loosely linked coalition of shifting interests. Although these coalitions can be remarkably stable (protecting themselves with controls over valued resources), the process of goal setting is certainly less fixed and less intendedly rational than earlier believed. The bargaining process goes on more or less continuously, as demands made by individuals on the coalition change with experience.[102]

### The Coalitional Model

With its roots in academic revisionism, our coalitional perspective cannot be defined as clearly or as easily as the rational model. Indeed, no real agreement exists as to just what is rational in organizations and what is not.[103] The rational approach places emphasis upon the individual's adaptation to organizational structures, but the coalitional reverses this—emphasizing the importance of participant behavior and, in fact, the organization's adaptation to the individual. The organization is created by its members, not the other way around. Where the rational perspective assumes that the organization can be managed in such fashion as to permit the pursuit of a unitary set of objectives, the coalitional view finds the organization just as likely to be moving in many different directions all at once with only problematic managerial direction.

Summarizing from Scott's comparison of alternative (natural and open systems) models and the rational ideal, we would suggest that the coalitional perspective has the following features:

1. *Goal ambiguity.* Organizations seldom pursue explicitly stated goals. They are more likely to be found (a) serving such generalized ends as "survival," (b) engaged in continuous political struggles over means and ends, and (c) serving many (sometimes contradictory) objectives all at once.
2. *Informality.* While organizations do have formal structures with policies, rules, and regulations, they are much better defined and understood through their behavioral systems—the actual behaviors of participants. Scott writes: "Individual participants are never merely 'hired hands' but bring their heads and hearts: they enter into the organization with individually shaped ideas, expectations, and agendas, and they bring with them differing values, interests, and abilities."
3. *Looseness.* There are many parts to, and many "heads" within, the organization. These parts are engaged in interdependent and collective action but also pull and haul, with separate interests in dynamic tension, against one another. The organization is a politicized environment, with each of its many parts pursuing its own preferences and objectives.[104]

In application to education the coalitional perspective would suggest *first* that educational organizations pursue multiple ends, seldom explicitly stated, often in conflict, and as much formed from-the-ground-up as from-the-top-down. Teachers at the bottom of the hierarchy are street-level bureaucrats who *make* policy in the course of implementing it. As persons charged with the all-important task of delivering educational services to clients, classroom teachers produce discretionary decisions that can guide significantly the direction of the entire organization.[105] Some children (e.g., the brightest, the lightest in color) may receive more teacher attention than others; some portions of the curriculum may be highlighted to the neglect of other portions; some pupil behaviors may be rewarded and others punished (e.g., competition over cooperation, docility over agressiveness); and some parents may be listened to (e.g., the college educated), while others are ignored. Furthermore, throughout the hierarchy, not just at its bottom, offices and bureaus may be in a continuous struggle with one another over valued resources and means/ends. Particularly in the university environment, departments and schools are continuously engaged in the protection of turf, the saving of professorial lines in the budget, an expanded (through course-offerings) appeal to students, and the grabbing of limited research dollars. Negotiations and compromised settlements between departments (e.g., a jointly administered degree program; the creation of a new research center) can lead the university in directions never imagined at the top of its hierarchy.

*Second*, the educational organization, while not without many elements of control and coherence, is a kaleidoscope of behaviors—a multi-hued, not always harmonious blending of values and interests. Two quite opposite objectives can be pursued at the same time. Two or more departments can receive resources to perform exactly the same job. Information collected at great cost by one unit can be collected again three weeks later, at great cost, by another, both of which are supervised by the same upper-echelon official. A committee formed to mediate between two offices can develop a survival interest of its own—seeking formally to become a third unit, with duties and staff weaned away from its parent departments. In conditions such as these the administrative problem of coordination looms large. It is not enough to know what people are supposed to do, what the rules prescribe for them to do. The administrator tries to find out what people are *actually* doing, what is going on behind the scenes of the formal organization.

*Third*, the educational organization is a loosely structured amalgam of roles and areas of responsibility, with an accompanying looseness in its distribution of authority. As Weick cautions, such looseness should not be considered a dysfunction. It often serves the organization well to have units that can provide unique, localized adaptations to the environment (as local schools, for example, learn to fit their immediate neighborhoods) or units which can be sealed off without affecting the rest of the system when there are breakdowns.[106] On the other hand, looseness in its definitions of roles can be filled with problems. Many a university dean has discovered that efforts to secure an enlarged budget for his college, gain university approval of new programs, add office and classroom space, and bring in students, are rewarded with his own dismissal as dean by a faculty who are upset with the dean's *process* of administering (e.g., its lack of collegial consultation) and unimpressed with his *products*.

### Coalitions and the Control/Coordination of Education

What are some key elements of control and coordination in educational organizations from the coalitional perspective? Two are negotiation and good faith. Each of these, it is important to note, proceeds from the assumption that despite their looseness, educational organizations are nonetheless interdependent webs of people. Teachers, students, building administrators, district-level administrators, support staff, even parents share *something* in common—thus work gets done; differences get ironed out; new ideas get introduced; and people enter, live out their productive years, and leave with a sense of having contributed to something, some entity, that transcends the personal in the process of becoming the organizational. Educational organizations may be loosely coupled, but they are certainly not uncoupled.[107] The practice of negotiation and the existence of good faith provide some very important couplings.

**Negotiation.**  As we noted earlier, Firestone and Herriott observe that while the image of the rational bureaucracy permits consideration of strong administrative leadership, the image of the organization as anarchy suggests a much more passive administrative style. At best, it is suggested, the administrator may be able to create conditions where individuals can improve their own effectiveness.[108] Nonetheless, there are those who urge, to the contrary, a very active and forceful role for the coalition-wrapped administrator. In their unusual textbook, David Wiles, Jon Wiles, and Joseph Bondi have proposed some notions of practical politics for school executives.[109] The educational organization should be viewed as an arena where political gaming abounds and where decision making is imbedded in messiness and confusion, much instability, and a web of continuously changing issues and situations. In this setting, the educational administrator performs best as an astute and rather crafty poker player—never holding a sure hand, winning some and losing some, working for the long haul, and gradually accumulating as many chips as possible.[110] To Wiles, Wiles, and Bondi the exercise of educational administration is an exercise in political gamesmanship. The practical administrative politician is adept at forming strategic alliances with "predominant pyramids of power" within the organization, without getting too close to any of them. Additionally, the stuff of administrative control for the practical educator is a capacity for effectively brokering and mediating conflicts between others, for presenting proposals in language that speaks compromisingly to all political interests, and for carefully and judiciously using available power (e.g., not going to the same well too often).[111] We should recall how effective Don Riddle was in negotiating (privately) acceptance for his proposal from university unit administrators, as well as in working out a collectively agreeable exception for one dean. He had more chips available to him than some of the other players in the game anticipated when they first sat down at the table, and he accumulated more as the game unfolded.

The metaphor of the administrator as poker player fits well within a conceptualization of the educational organization as a negotiated order. Introduced and popularized by sociologist Anselm Strauss, the idea of the negotiated order suggests that the social structure of an organization is developed from the ground up by participants explicitly and implicitly negotiating the conditions of their own status and participation.[112] In hospitals, patients negotiate with nurses for services and amenities; nurses and physicians have separate stakes in the hospital environment; and a tenuous balance of power, with many issues to be resolved, characterizes relations between physicians and the hospital administration.[113] Similarly, in education it may be suggested that negotiations between pupils and their teachers, between teachers and parents (for "outsiders" also enter heavily into the political contest), between teachers and other teachers, and between teachers and administrators define the very nature of the social order that is the school.

Becker (1961), Summerfield (1971), Wolcott (1973), Barsky (1975), and Lortie (1975) have all suggested, for example, that a school principal's ability to negotiate successfully with teachers and pupils is critical to his status and authority within the school, and even within the larger school system.[114] Howard Becker noted that a principal is expected by his faculty to back them up (e.g., in pupil discipline situations) and is expected furthermore to respect the faculty's professional independence. Teachers, on the other hand, are supposed to go along with school policies (e.g., submitting reports as expected) and to pitch in cooperatively for the good of the whole school (e.g., doing one's share of committee work). Conflict surrounds a failure to meet these expectations, and both sides have a variety of means for controlling one another's behavior. Principals can refuse to support teachers in crucial situations and can employ the powerful sanctions of allocating the worst rooms, textbooks, pupils, equipment, and duties (e.g., lunchroom supervision) to recalcitrant faculty members. Teachers, in turn, can ignore the principal or resist passively (e.g., with shoddy committee work and poorly prepared reports); they can threaten and request transfer; and they can use close contacts with pupils and parents to create sentiments against the principal. Becker concludes that

> an institution like the school can be seen as a small, self-contained system of social control. Its functionaries (principals and teachers) are able to control one another; each has some power to influence the others' conduct.[115]

Similarly, Barsky noted that the process of negotiation between principal and teacher can involve subtle give-and-take. Principals may work hard, for example, to add to their own stature and authority by doing many little things (e.g., helping with a non-school-related problem, finding a large desk for an oversized boy, running the ditto machine for a harried teacher, taking a young troublemaker out of the classroom for awhile). Lortie observed that the practice of negotiation in schools has some important rules, including the practice of variable zoning, where it is well understood that some matters (e.g., in-class affairs) clearly are in the teachers' zone of influence while others (e.g., records and money) just as clearly are within the principal's zone. Conflict arises only when hegemony is unclear. Finally, Wolcott pointed out that the success of a principal in negotiations within his own school is reflected in his stature vis-a-vis the rest of the school district, where additional rounds of negotiation occur (e.g., to secure resources, get the school repaired, add a teaching position). Conversely, a successful negotiator with the central office enlarges his power back within the school.

The coalitional perspective attracts sufficient evidence to suggest its importance for extending administrative control.[116] As Bacharach and Aiken note, the model does not make the mistake of equating power with authority. Although organizations certainly have formalized structures of authority, there are many, separable processes of *influence* that exist far outside of the authority structure.[117] Because influence is widely distributed, with some amount of it in the hands of nearly everyone, and much more of it in the hands of people who band together, the educational administrator (even though well wrapped in formal authority) has to negotiate widely and continuously in order to get the job done. Negotiation, however, breeds compromise, with results that are often far from what one would rationally intend or even what might be considered sound for the organization. It is a tricky business, and not one that is well understood.

Jeffrey Pfeffer provides assistance to us in his analysis of *Power in Organizations* (1981).[118] Although his descriptions are not drawn from education, the application to our field of endeavor has at least some feasibility. Pfeffer suggests, for example, the following sources of power in organizations:

> ☐ *Power from providing resources.* Organizations are resource dependent; a continuing flow of money, manpower, materials, and information is critical to their operational lives.

The essential understanding is that resources flow into the organization from many sources. In education, students (even if just counted as "bodies") are valued resources which institutions at all levels (from preschool through graduate school) strive mightily to attract and hold. Instructors (from the kindergarten level through the university professorship) bring resources of expertise, commitment, and energy to their institutions. Administrators have know-how and also close contact with the acquisition and distribution of funds. Specialized personnel (e.g., school clerks, data processing people, cafeteria workers, security officers, janitors) often serve at rather vulnerable spots in the organization, where the loss of their services would seriously disrupt the flow of work. Each of these roles, from student to janitor, brings a supply of resources to the educational endeavor—and with these resources, an element of power.

□ *Power from coping with uncertainty.* Organizations are open systems engaged in the ongoing task of coping with uncertain environments.

Power accrues to those who assist the organization well in handling uncertainty; and, although a duly constituted board of education or of trustees is formally charged with the policy-making (i.e., coping) function, we find that dealing with uncertainty occurs all up and down the organizational hierarchy. Teachers and principals, as street-level bureaucrats, bend rules to meet the special needs and interests of a neighborhood clientele. Specialized units (e.g., a university extension service, a community relations office, a winning football team) may serve successfully to buffer the rest of the educational organization from the need for more thoroughgoing public respon- siveness. Chief executive officers (e.g., college presidents, school district superinten- dents) may acquire power internally within their institutions by performing well externally (e.g., on the lunch-and-lecture circuit) with political constituencies.

□ *Power from affecting the decision process.* Choices are made throughout the organization; and despite their formal, hierarchical frameworks, organizations find that the control of decision premises, of decision alternatives, and of usable information rests with many actors, in many farflung locations.

A standing judgment among teachers is, "It's the school secretary who really runs my school." Many a staff member in education has asked why a change (e.g., in student accounting procedures) cannot be made—only to be told that the institution's record-keeping system is just not programmed to handle the new direction in policy. Not infrequently a new directive from the top in an education organization is transformed measurably as it wends its way toward the bottom—by encountering standard operating procedures that remain the same no matter what the policy.

□ *Power from consensus.* Organizations are comprised of aggregations of individuals in subunits.

It is not uncommon for subunit attachments to be greater than organization-wide attachments—as when a professor shows greater loyalty to his own department than to his college or to his university. Where individuals share common perspectives, sets of values, definitions of right and wrong, and act and speak consistently together (that is, they achieve consensus), the individuals in concert are likely to acquire power. Thus some departments of the university, with subunit consensus, advocate their interests with more clarity, consistency, and success than others. Some school buildings in a public school district have more parental support, teacher cohesive- ness, and a better sense of identity, and are considered stronger than others. And, some categories of organizational participants (e.g., tenured professors, unionized teachers) have interests and perspectives that are sufficiently shared to warrant strong attachments (with considerable power) that cut broadly across the entire organization.

☐ *Power from political skill.* Organizations are affected by the capability and willingness of some of their actors to provide political leadership.[119]

Successful politics is promoted somewhat by being a member or head of a politically powerful subunit; it is also assisted somewhat by the structure of formal authority in the organization (e.g., it is easier for a superintendent to acquire power than a classroom teacher); and it is helped particularly by the personal, individual skills that good school politicians are able to bring to bear. Individuals differ in their abilities to compromise, carry on convincing arguments, exercise judgment (e.g., timing a political move just right), and in their political appeal or charisma. In every educational organization there may be many persons with political skills and political followings which are poorly reflected in their formal job-titles—as many a college dean knows well, in having to tiptoe carefully around the sensitivities of one or more superstars on her faculty.[120]

From this vantage point, the hard currency of educational administration is power. The allocation of power within an educational organization is not synonomous with its formalized structure of authority. In fact, the shape and configuration of an organization (its negotiated order) may be in many respects a result of many powers in conflict. As organization theorist Michel Crozier has pointed out, power is one of the most difficult of problems for students of organizations—for it deals with relationships, and is multidimensional, loaded with values, and wrapped in unpredictability. Yet an organization's "system of power arrangments" (i.e., its political rather than its formal structure of control) appears to affect substantially the nature of its work.[121] It is the *use* of power in processes of negotiation that determines the currency's value. Some administrators will negotiate wisely and find the marketplace to be an increasingly splendid array of affordable opportunities for action, while others will negotiate poorly and find the value of their currency steadily eroded.

**Good Faith.** All educational organizations are tightly bureaucratic in many respects. Procedures for student accounting and grade reporting—but not grade assigning—are fully standardized. The scheduling of activities (e.g., when classes begin and end, where each individual is supposed to be, when final grades are due) is carefully coordinated and fully buttressed by ringing bells, hall guards, student ID cards, up stairs and down stairs, three-minute passing periods, even washroom monitoring. The health and safety of individuals is of central concern, and thus bureaucratic procedures abound to ensure that parental permission accompanies off-school excursions; that immunization is complete; that fire safety is complied with; that accident reports are filed; and that foodstuffs are kept fresh. Of signal importance to staff members, the organization's attention to matters of payroll, benefits, promotional opportunity, and employee rights (e.g., a chance to grieve) is efficiently bureaucratized.

Nevertheless, behind the classroom door the district-wide curriculum may never find its way into a daily lesson plan; the committee-adopted textbook may be left on its shelf much of the year; guidelines on grading policy may be ignored; and standardized tests may be used for coaching more than for testing. Despite its many rules and procedures, the educational organization will be found upon close examination to be an ill-tended garden of profusely blooming policy inconsistencies and ever-encroaching political weeds. George receives an A (for his effort and attitude) while Bill, who performed better, receives a B (for his lackadaisical effort and poor attitude). Mrs. Jones complains and her daughter, Judy, is assigned to gifted English; Mrs. Farmer does not complain, and her daughter, Betty, is bored in regular English. Ralph Johnson, principal, works the system for an extra teacher while Don Hargrove, principal, makes do for the year although two teachers short.

What is it that holds many scattered elements of the educational organization together? Weick provides an answer to his rhetorical question in suggesting that members of loosely coupled systems spend much time constructing (or negotiating) a social reality that they can all accept.[122] Similarly, Ranson, Hinings, and Greenwood say that the members of an organization construct their own provinces of meaning (interpretive schemes, shared assumptions and values) that are used to structure members' relationships.[123] Likewise, March argues that a search for order in the face of confusion and complexity is the central phenomenon of organizations—a search that leads individuals toward the development of commonly held interpretive rituals and symbols as a way to give meaning and control to their corporate lives.[124] Finally, Meyer and Rowan claim that educators depend upon a logic of confidence to integrate the organization, a presumption that useful work is being done throughout the institution, without the need for others to monitor it closely or to interfere.[125]

What all of these observations share is a cultural perspective on the nature of organizations. The quality of its culture can significantly affect an organization's success or failure. Consider, for example, the finding of Joanne Martin and her colleagues that organizations differ from negative to positive in the kinds of "stories" employees tell one another. Organizations encounter common problems in relations between individual employees and the administrative hierarchy (e.g., How will the boss react to mistakes? Can the little person rise to the top?), and stories of past behaviors and episodes are passed along for years, as a continuing saga of "what it's like to work here." The message is usually clear: "A first mistake will be graciously forgiven." Or, alternatively, "Mistake makers will not be forgiven." The story-wrapped message becomes an integral part of the ongoing belief system of the organization.[126]

Such stories are part of the organizational culture. It is not entirely clear just what an organizational culture is; and, as Linda Smirchich indicates in her review of the literature, there are at least five different ways in which culture theory (drawn largely from anthropology) has been used by researchers to study organizations.[127] Nevertheless, a definition drawn from Smirchich is useful. She writes:

> Culture is usually defined as social or normative glue that holds an organization together. It expresses the values or social ideas and the beliefs that organization members come to share. These values or patterns of belief are manifested by symbolic devices such as myths, rituals, stories, legends, and specialized language.[128]

The most important point, as Smirchich goes on to note, is that a cultural analysis leads us to question much that is often taken for granted about organizations (e.g., their underlying values) and leads us to examine matters on which the "rational model of organization analysis is largely silent."[129]

Seymour Sarason provides an excellent example of this point in his book, *The Culture of the School and the Problem of Change.*[130] All too often, notes Sarason, we have failed to ask ourselves the simplest but most important questions about programmatic and behavioral regularities in our schools. A visitor from outer space might ask, for example, why our schools are so densely populated for five consecutive days and devoid of humans on two days. Why this 5-2 pattern? Why not a 4-3 or a 3-1-3? Additionally, why do so many small people tend to be in schools during the day while big people only come together at irregular times in the evenings? Why do the small people tend to do little talking while one big person in the front of the classroom talks much? This is especially confusing because as the small people leave their rooms, they speak a great deal, with much variety of facial expression.[131]

A central value of the cultural perspective, observes Smirchich, is that it is directly in tune with the key problem of organizational leadership: "How to create and maintain a sense of organization, and how to achieve common interpretations of situations so that coordinated action is possible."[132] In similar terms, we would contend that educational organizations are held together in large measure by controlling the *good faith* of their participants. College students and the parents of elementary/secondary pupils accept (on faith) the assumption that by spending time in school one is preparing well for a productive future. Educational administrators by and large assume in good faith that behind every closed classroom door there is a conscientious effort to guide learning. Students (and their parents) assume that hard work, conformity, a competitive yet cooperative spirit, and proper habits and attitudes (all part of the Protestant ethic) will be rewarded with good grades and success. Teachers assume that the slices of knowledge which they impart are important and considered by other persons to be important. Administrators and teachers share in the faith that effective learning requires pupil discipline, a blending of rewards and punishments (centered heavily upon grades), a curriculum, and a bit of pedagogical freedom, with action by administrators occasionally to back up the teacher.

Frank Lutz claims that universities are loosely coupled in ways that preserve their institutional status quo. Academic freedom and program autonomy, for example, help preserve the powers of older, tenured professors over the new and untenured and preserve the powers of stronger departments over weaker. He observes, "Untenured professors attempt to be amiable and unchallenging of the status quo in order to survive."[133]

Weick argues that

> under conditions of loose coupling one should see considerable effort devoted to constructing social reality, a great amount of face work and linguistic work, numerous myths and in general one should find a considerable amount of effort being devoted to punctuating this loosely coupled world and connecting it in some way in which it can be made sensible.[134]

These acts, of *keeping the faith* within the culture of the school, may fall in large measure within the lot of the educational administrator. Indeed, some scholars suggest that a perpetuation of reigning "mystifications, myths, and cover-ups" in the school setting is the central focus of the administrative role.[135]

Without going quite that far, it can be argued, with Weick, that the educational administrator does provide much of the good faith that holds an organization together.[136] Keeping the faith successfully may require a heavy reliance on the personal resources of managers (e.g., the face work necessary to gain respect and affection from one's staff) rather than on the technical resources of control (e.g., directives, rules, job descriptions). It may also mean that educational management is more an art of creating and maintaining an organizational belief system than it is a science of shaping contributions toward specified goals.[137] In the last analysis, could Don Riddle have obtained consensus on the revised reserve fund without a general belief that somehow the university would benefit from the change?

Richard Brown has suggested to us that an organizational culture can be conceived as a paradigm. A paradigm is a set of shared understandings "about what sorts of things make up the world, how they act, how they hang together, and how they may be known."[138] Lee Sproull observes that such paradigms or belief systems are likely to be identified in four cultural elements of organizational life. These are: (1) the *general sociocultural beliefs* that people bring with them into the organization and within which the organization operates (e.g., the Protestant ethic); (2) *beliefs about work processes and technologies* (e.g., ability grouping facilitates teaching and learning); (3) *beliefs about organizational identity* (e.g., the mystique of a Harvard or Yale as opposed to the weaker aura of a former teachers' college now become state university); and, (4) *beliefs about environmental characteristics* (e.g., schools must be kept out of politics).[139]

As an illustration of the importance of keeping the faith, we turn to a comparative case study (from the late 1960s) of two recently desegregated junior high schools, labeled Chauncey and Hamilton, by Mary Haywood Metz.[140] Consider, specifically, the issue of the pledge of allegiance to the flag. The school year was 1967–68. The Vietnam war protest was at its height, and both schools began experiencing an increasing reluctance (bordering on refusal) on the part of students to recite the pledge of allegiance each morning at the beginning of the first-period class. A number of teachers added their voices to the protest, suggesting that the pledge was increasingly becoming a rather empty ceremony. The issue spread to each of the schools in the community, leading eventually to a ruling by the school district's board of education and its attorney. The board affirmed that state law required the pledge of allegiance (or equivalent patriotic reading) in every school during the first period of the day. Children could be excused from recitation only with a parental letter of request.

Metz reports that the principals of the two schools handled the issue and the board's reaffirmation of its policy quite differently. The principal of Chauncey firmly cut off faculty debate of the board's policy and responded to faculty questions (e.g., "What do we do about self-styled conscientious objectors?") by telling them the law makes no allowances, and they should follow the teachers' handbook to the letter. Metz observes that:

> Had the principal [of Chauncey] allowed an open discussion of this issue, the division among the faculty would have become evident and the debate probably would have been heated. Thus a carefully nurtured public unity of the faculty would have been threatened.[141]

The principal of Hamilton, in contrast, passed out copies of the board's policy statement to his faculty, and announced that forms would be available in the main office to be filled in by parents who wished their children to be excused. Teachers then flooded the principal with questions (e.g., "Are children who are excused required to stand?"), and a heated debate developed. At one point the principal commented that the board's policy statement seemed to be extremely vague, and there was a great deal of latitude offered teachers (e.g., to define for themselves what constituted an "equivalent patriotic reading"). The faculty became increasingly divided and began taking a number of nondecisive votes on subissues (e.g., splitting thirty-two for and thirty-two against on whether objectors could remain seated). Metz concludes that the behavior of the principal of the Hamilton school served to add to faculty differences and factionalism.[142]

Whether or not one agrees with Metz' conclusions, her case study shows the power of an administrative role in supporting, defending, and guiding sets of belief systems which hold educational institutions together. Showing the flag (sometimes both figuratively and literally) is a critical element of the job.

## The Coalitional Perspective: A Summary

Educational organizations are like the busy streets of a city—full of interests and perspectives in conflict. Central office administrators cannot be assumed to share the viewpoints of school site-level personnel; elementary teachers share some but not all of the interests of secondary teachers; parents are frequently split into factions; and separately identifiable interests are likely to surround the roles of teacher aide, maintenance employee, school nurse, librarian, and secretary. In higher education, departmental power struggles, administrator–professor disputes, disciplinary rivalries (e.g., the humanities versus the physical sciences), and philosophical differences (e.g., basic research versus public service orientations)—all of these conflicts often make the politics of electing a mayor in Chicago look like town-meeting democracy by comparison.

Rational models assume organizational goal-directedness and a structure of rules and procedures sufficient to coordinate staff member activity toward the shared goals. The coalitional model of the organization finds the organization pursuing many goals all at once, or really pursuing few after all, and discovers the organization pulled hither and yon by the competing interests, expectations, and agendas of its own membership (often in coalition with outside forces). The educational organization is loosely coupled, and it is only with great difficulty—and sometimes not at all—brought toward a semblance of coordination and control.

The educational organization as coalition is not uncoupled, however; it is wrapped in sets of relationships, and it has a social reality that makes sense to those who serve within it. Each of these truths suggests that despite its complexity, the organization does provide opportunity for administrative direction. Its many relationships constitute a negotiated order, with central attention given to the political currency of power as a key to administrator impact. Its social reality, its culture (the provinces of meaning which its members share), offers the administrator the vital task of keeping the faith for the organization, and thereby, the opportunity for exercising control.

## CHAPTER SUMMARY

Educational organizations have been criticized for being over-bureaucratized—so full of red tape, forms, performance objectives, guidelines, and administrator checks and counterchecks that the effective delivery of educational services is somehow lost in the paper shuffle. Educational organizations have also been criticized for being under-bureaucratized—so loose and politically fragmented (even anarchic) that children are not as well served as are the interests of those who manage to hold power. In truth, educational organizations are both. They are both rational and irrational, amenable to administrative control and out of control, tightly structured and loosely coupled, ruled by procedure and ruled by politics. Neither a rational (control from the top down) model nor a coalitional (control from the bottom up) model of the educational organization is, by itself, a sufficient framework for an understanding of the administrative role. Both models are useful, and in fact, necessary. Throughout this chapter we have concentrated on identifying ways in which educational administrators might possibly exercise a modicum of control over the work that surrounds them. From a rational perspective, there are opportunities for both direct and indirect control. Direct mechanisms include the rules and regulations framework of the organization, as well as its communication system and its procedures for evaluation. No less important is the indirect route to rationality, with recognition that the talk administrators engage in on the job, plus the socialization and reward and sanctioning opportunities that accompany their jobs are central features of the control function. Finally, we suggest that from a coalitional perspective the exercise of administrative control takes on a different coloration. The educational administrator is just one player among many in a political game, but one with considerable influence. Played one way, the game typically concludes with winners and losers. Played another way, the game can enhance the whole organization. It is with this second possibility in mind that we find ourselves most interested in the educational administrator's symbolically important role of faith keeper for the organization—for it is in no small measure the good faith of its participants that is the amorphous stuff which holds the educational organization together.

Perhaps that was all that Donald Riddle was trying to do. To be sure, the chancellor's reserve fund was important to him. An uncommitted, even though small sum of $100,000 gave the chancellor a valuable lever in trying to move others, in providing someone a bit of a carrot and someone else a few dollars to bail out a flooding institutional boat. People in organizations can sometimes be motivated by meager add-ons—just a nudge here, a bit of seed money there. But more than the amount of the fund, it was the existence of the reserve and the compromising that was necessary to secure it that provides the real message. Despite his position atop the hierarchy, the chancellor does not have a franchise on control; he has to acquire it, to negotiate and bargain for it. Once you have the control associated with the money, its dollar amount is not all that important. Don Riddle's careful victory showed that the chancellor had control, that he was in charge, that he could move the organization.

## FROM THEORY TO PRACTICE

The young administrator moving up in the complex organization encounters executives who act like they want to control everything and everybody, to keep a finger on each movement of the operation—even as the young administrator begins to suspect that these titans cannot really do this. These executives exude a preoccupation with control, as if it were an exotic perfume. Much of this kind of control is a facade, a game; nevertheless, it releases fear in the organization. Not cooperation, but fear. But Donald Riddle is not one of these executives. He is ready to share control with his colleagues. He has a stubborn streak, and one senses that there are some things he would fight for to the bitter end. Yet he understands that no leader can have it all his or her own way. He is not weighed down by responsibility that is not his.

In protecting the meaning and substance of his reserve fund, Don Riddle moved easily within both the rational and coalitional models of control. With regard to the first, he understood that when it comes down to money, and when that resource is increasingly scarce, direct control is essential. But even here the application of direct control opened the door to the indirect technique of talking things over. "The business office set up a monthly monitoring system, and the red flags would pop up and then we would have some conversations." As a matter of fact, the fund itself provided Don the means for exerting power through manipulation. "It was a contingency account that had to be available for the whole campus, and the chancellor had to be in a position to decide how to allocate it." You get this much, you get that much, and in return I actually get more than a balanced budget. The game yields some extra chips for the chancellor as well as tightened lines of cooperation in the university.

The counterpoint between the two models continued. "Before the meeting I let the word get around that I was ready to negotiate." And in the aftermath of the showdown meeting, a reliance on face work to carry the argument. "During the next week I met more or less continuously on this issue with key groups and individuals." He helped the Dean of the College of Arts and Sciences protect that administration's turf appropriately. And then, ultimately, he depended on good faith—the shared conviction that the chancellor's reserve fund was an administrative necessity. That was the rock bottom premise he established at the outset of the negotiation, and it became the anchor for his exercise of control. Donald Riddle—writing detailed high school social studies programs at one point in his career, later learning how to be responsible on top of a large university by deciding not simply to delegate well to others, but to release from his personal concern whole sections of the operation. The rational in counterpoint with the nonrational, always. Taylor versus Follett, Follett versus Simon, Simon versus

Argyris—on and on the dialectic chain seems to be forged. But for the administrator who survives, who produces, who leaves some footprints in the sand, the synthesis is necessary and the struggle for it is constant. Intellect and instinct, the reasoned and impulsive sides of the mind, and both crucial to a leader like Donald Riddle.

## NOTES

[1]David B. Tyack, *The One Best System* (Cambridge, Mass.: Harvard University Press, 1974).

[2]David Tyack and Elisabeth Hansot, "Hard Times, Hard Choices: The Case for Coherence in Public School Leadership," *Phi Delta Kappan*, 63:8 (April 1982): 512.

[3]For two excellent histories of the transition in control of education during the "efficiency movement" in America, see Joseph M. Cronin, *The Control of Urban Schools* (New York: The Free Press, 1973); and Raymond Callahan, *Education and the Cult of Efficiency* (Chicago: University of Chicago Press, 1962).

[4]See, for example, David Rogers, *110 Livingston Street* (New York: Vintage Books, 1969).

[5]T.E. Deal and L.D. Celotti, "How Much Influence Do (and Can) Educational Administrators Have on Classrooms?" *Phi Delta Kappan*, 61:7 (1980): 471-473; also, J. Hannaway and L.S. Sproull, "Who's Running the Show? Coordination and Control in Educational Organizations," *Administrator's Notebook*, 27:9 (1979): 1-4.

[6]Van Cleve Morris, Robert L. Crowson, Cynthia Porter-Gehrie, and Emanuel Hurwitz, Jr., *Principals in Action: The Reality of Managing Schools* (Columbus, Ohio: Charles E. Merrill, 1984).

[7]See Dale Mann, ed., *Making Change Happen?* (New York: Teachers College Press, 1978).

[8]See Rogers, *110 Livingston Street*.

[9]Firestone and Herriott anticipate our organization of the chapter in this manner, in their discussion of two prevailing "images" of schools: (a) rational bureaucracy and (b) anarchy. The use of the term "image" helpfully provides an ideal type that assists in discovering reality. See William A. Firestone and Robert E. Herriott, "Two Images of Schools as Organizations: An Explication and Illustrative Empirical Test," *Educational Administration Quarterly*, 18:2 (Spring, 1982): 39-59.

[10]In a historical review, Richard Edwards has suggested that control processes in organizations have evolved through three phases. Initially, the emphasis was upon hierarchical control, with bosses exercising arbitrary power over workers. A later stage of technical control saw control embedded in the technology of work processes themselves (e.g., the assembly line). The third stage is "bureaucratic control," with control emerging as a complex and complicated aspect of the total organizational structure (e.g., with organizational rules or "laws" in place of a boss's charisma). See Richard C. Edwards, *Contested Terrain: The Transformation of the Workplace in the Twentieth Century* (New York: Basic Books, 1979).

[11]Herbert A. Simon, "Decision-Making and Administrative Organization," *Public Administration Review*, vol. IV (Winter, 1944): 16-30.

[12]See Seymour B. Sarason, *The Culture of the School and the Problem of Change* (Boston: Allyn & Bacon, Inc., 1971).

[13]See Cronin, *The Control of Urban Schools*; Callahan, *Education and the Cult of Efficiency*; Tyack, *The One Best System*; and Diane Ravitch, *The Great School Wars: New York City, 1805-1972* (New York: Basic Books, 1974).

[14]See Frederick W. Taylor, *The Principles of Scientific Management* (New York: Harper, 1911).

[15]Callahan, *Education and the Cult of Efficiency*.

[16]Max Weber, *From Max Weber: Essays in Sociology*, eds. Hans H. Gerth and C. Wright Mills (New York: Oxford University Press, 1946 tr [first published in 1906-1924]). Also, Max Weber, *The Theory of Social and Economic Organizations*, eds. A.H. Henderson and Talcott Parsons (New York: The Free Press, 1947 tr [first published in 1924]).

[17]Max Weber, *The Theory of Social and Economic Organization*, pp. 329-336.

[18]See Robert K. Merton et al., eds., *Reader in Bureaucracy* (Glencoe, Ill.: The Free Press, 1952); and Alvin W. Gouldner, *Patterns of Industrial Bureaucracy* (London: Routledge and Kegan Paul, 1955).

[19]Phillip Selznick, *TVA and the Grass Roots* (Berkeley: University of California Press, 1949); also,

Michel Crozier, *The Bureaucratic Phenomenon* (Chicago: University of Chicago Press, 1964).

[20]Herbert A. Simon, *Administrative Behavior*, 3rd edition (New York: The Free Press, 1976). The first edition was published in 1945.

[21]See W. Richard Scott, *Organizations: Rational, Natural, and Open Systems* (Englewood Cliffs, N.J.: Prentice-Hall, 1981), pp. 20-21.

[22]See Firestone and Herriott, pp. 39-59.

[23]For discussion of these two inversely related forms of control, see John Child, "Organization Structure and Strategies of Control: A Replication of the Aston Study," *Administrative Science Quarterly*, 17 (1972): 163-177.

[24]Edward S. Herman, *Corporate Control, Corporate Power* (London: Cambridge University Press, 1981), pp. 19-20.

[25]See Roald F. Campbell, "A History of Administrative Thought," *Administrator's Notebook*, 26:4 (1977-78): 1-4. See also Bertram M. Gross, "The Scientific Approach to Administration," in Daniel E. Griffiths, ed., *Behavioral Science and Educational Administration*, Sixty–third Yearbook of the National Society for the Study of Education (NSSE), Part 2 (Chicago: University of Chicago Press, 1974), pp. 33-72.

[26]Luther Gulick, "Notes on the Theory of Organization," in *Papers on the Science of Administration*, Luther Gulick and L. Gurwick, eds., (New York: Institute of Public Administration, Columbia University, 1937), p. 7, as quoted in Campbell, "A History of Administrative Thought," p. 2.

[27]Anthony Downs, *Inside Bureaucracy* (Boston: Little, Brown & Company, 1967), p. 144.

[28]Ibid., pp. 144-157.

[29]Alvin W. Gouldner, "About the Functions of Bureaucratic Rules," in W. Richard Scott, ed., *Social Processes and Social Structures* (New York: Holt, Rinehart & Winston, 1970), pp. 320-328.

[30]See Morris et al., *Principals in Action*. pp. 390-391.

[31]Personal conversation with Professor Van Cleve Morris, University of Illinois at Chicago. See also Theodore J. Lowi, *The End of Liberalism* (New York: W.W. Norton & Co., 1969), pp. 287-314.

[32]Douglas E. Mitchell, Charles T. Kerchner, Wayne Erck, and Gabrielle Pryor, "The Impact of Collective Bargaining on School Management and Policy," *American Journal of Education*, 89:2 (February 1981): 162-164.

[33]Nancy J. Pitner and Rodney T. Ogawa, "Organizational Leadership: The Case of the School Superintendent," *Educational Administration Quarterly*, 17:2 (Spring 1981): 45-65.

[34]Ibid., p. 63.

[35]See Morris et al., *Principals in Action*.

[36]Edward E. Lawler III and John Grant Rhode, *Information and Control in Organizations* (Pacific Palisades, Calif.: Goodyear Publishing, 1976), pp. 2-3.

[37]See, for example, Jerald Hage, *Communication and Control: Cybernetics in Health and Welfare Settings* (New York: John Wiley & Sons, 1974); also, Lee S. Sproull and David Zubrow, "Performance Information in School Systems: Perspectives from Organization Theory," *Educational Administration Quarterly*, 17:3 (Summer 1981): 61-79.

[38]J. Alan Thomas, *The Productive School: A Systems Analysis Approach to Educational Administration* (New York: John Wiley & Sons, 1971), pp. 98-103.

[39]See Martha S. Feldman and James G. March, "Information in Organizations as Signal and Symbol," *Administrative Science Quarterly*, 26 (June 1981): 171-186; also Andrew M. Pettigrew, "On Studying Organizational Cultures," *Administrative Science Quarterly*, 24 (December 1979): 570-581.

[40]Feldman and March, "Information in Organizations."

[41]Henry Mintzberg is given much credit for a reorientation of research on administration into the close observation of what managers "really do" on- the-job, day-by-day, minute-by-minute. See Henry Mintzberg, *The Nature of Managerial Work* (New York: Harper & Row, 1973).

[42]For some studies of what it is that school administrators do, see Morris, et al., *Principals in Action*; Kent D. Peterson, "The Principal's Tasks," *Administrator's Notebook*, 26:8 (1977-78): 1-4; William T. Martin and Donald J. Willower, "The Managerial Behavior of High School Principals," *Educational Administration Quarterly*, 17 (1981): 69-90; Nancy J. Pitner, "Descriptive Study of Everyday Activities of Suburban School Superintendents: The Management of Information" (Unpublished Ph.D. Dissertation, The Ohio State University, 1978); John T. Kmetz and Donald J. Willower, "Elementary School Principals' Work Behavior," *Educational Administration Quarterly*, 18:4 (Fall 1982): 62-78; and Jill S. Berman, "The Managerial Behavior of Female High School Principals," (Unpublished Ph.D. Dissertation, Teachers College, Columbia University, 1982).

⁴³Van Cleve Morris, Robert L. Crowson, Emmanuel Hurwitz, Jr. and Cynthia Porter-Gehrie, "The Urban Principal: Middle Manager in the Educational Bureaucracy," *Phi Delta Kappan*, 63:10 (June 1982): 689-692.

⁴⁴Mintzberg, pp. 148-152.

⁴⁵Sproull and Zubrow, pp. 61-79.

⁴⁶Sanford M. Dornbusch and W. Richard Scott, *Evaluation and the Exercise of Authority* (San Francisco: Jossey-Bass Publishers, 1975); also, Scott, *Organizations: Rational, Natural, and Open Systems*, pp. 283-286.

⁴⁷William G. Ouchi, "The Relationship Between Organizational Structure and Organizational Control," *Administrative Science Quarterly*, 22:1 (March 1977): 95-113.

⁴⁸Ibid., p. 98.

⁴⁹John W. Meyer and Brian Rowan, "The Structure of Educational Organizations," in Marshall W. Meyer and Associates, eds., *Environments and Organizations* (San Francisco: Jossey-Bass Publishers, 1978), pp. 78-109.

⁵⁰Ibid.

⁵¹Gary Natriello and Sanford M. Dornbusch, "Pitfalls in the Evaluation of Teachers by Principals," *Administrator's Notebook*, 29:6 (1980-81): 1-4.

⁵²Personal conversation with Van Cleve Morris, former Dean of the College of Education, University of Illinois at Chicago. See also, Van Cleve Morris, *Deaning: Middle Management in Academe* (Urbana: University of Illinois Press, 1981), pp. 46-66.

⁵³See Bertram Gross, "The Scientific Approach to Administration," pp. 46-50.

⁵⁴Chester I. Barnard, *The Functions of the Executive* (Cambridge, Mass.: Harvard University Press, 1938).

⁵⁵Roald Campbell, "A History of Administrative Thought," p. 2.

⁵⁶Patricia Ann Brieschke, "The Tentative Process: A Study of the Implementation of Regulatory Policy in the Urban Elementary School" (Unpublished Ph.D. Dissertation, College of Education, University of Illinois at Chicago, 1983).

⁵⁷James D. Thompson, *Organizations in Action* (New York: McGraw-Hill Book Co., 1967), pp. 132-143.

⁵⁸Peter C. Gronn, "Talk as the Work: The Accomplishment of School Administration," *Administrative Science Quarterly*, 28:1 (March 1983): 1.

⁵⁹Ibid., p. 2.

⁶⁰See Morris et al., *Principals in Action*.

⁶¹Gronn, p. 6.

⁶²Morris et al., *Principals in Action*, pp. 211-212.

⁶³Gronn, pp. 17-18.

⁶⁴Charles W. Guditus and Perry A. Zirkel, "Bases of Supervisory Power Among Public School Principals," *Administrator's Notebook*, 28:4 (1979-80): 4.

⁶⁵Pitner and Ogawa, "Organizational Leadership: The Case of the School Superintendent," pp. 45-65.
Note that a much more pessimistic explanation of the same observed phenomenon, however, has been offered by Jane Hannaway and Lee Sproull. Hannaway and Sproull suggest that top-level educational administrators devote themselves in large part to a fostering of the "legitimacy of the organization with those in the external environment from whom it is dependent on resources." See Jane Hannaway and Lee S. Sproull, "Who's Running the Show? Coordination and Control in Educational Organizations," *Administrator's Notebook*, 27:9 (1978-1979): 4.

⁶⁶Pitner and Ogawa, pp. 62-63.

⁶⁷Amitai Etzioni, "Organizational Control Structure," in James G. March, ed., *Handbook of Organizations* (Chicago: Rand McNally & Co., 1965), p. 655.

⁶⁸See Stewart Ranson, Bob Hinings, and Royston Greenwood, "The Structuring of Organizational Structures," *Administrative Science Quarterly*, 25:1 (March 1980): 6.

⁶⁹Dan C. Lortie, "The Balance of Control and Autonomy in Elementary School Teaching," in Amitai Etzioni, ed., *The Semi-Professions and Their Organization: Teachers, Nurses, Social Workers* (New York: The Free Press, 1969), pp. 1-53; also Myron Lieberman, *Education as a Profession* (Englewood Cliffs, N.J.: Prentice-Hall, 1956); and, Howard S. Becker, "The Nature of a Profession," in Nelson B.

Henry, ed., *Education for the Professions*, Sixty-first Yearbook of the National Society for the Study of Education, Part 2 (Chicago: NSSE, 1962): 27-46.

[70]Lortie, "The Balance of Control and Autonomy."

[71]Despite some valuable research in medicine and police-work, the study of socialization in the work-place has generally been of only recent interest. See John Van Maanen, "Breaking In: Socialization to Work," in Robert Dubin, ed., *Handbook of Work, Organization, and Society* (Chicago: Rand McNally & Co., 1976), pp. 67-130.

[72]See Morris et al., *Principals in Action*; also, Cynthia Porter- Gehrie and Emanuel Hurwitz, Jr., "The Role and Response of Principals in Implementing a Faculty Desegregation Plan," in George W. Noblit and Bill Johnston, eds., *The School Principal and School Desegration* (Springfield, Ill.: Charles C. Thomas, 1982), pp. 113-133. *Note:* Approximately one out of every eleven teachers in the city system was transferred.

[73]Porter-Gehrie and Hurwitz, p. 124.

[74]Ibid., pp. 129-130.

[75]See, for example, Sanford M. Dornbusch, "The Military Academy as an Assimilating Institution," *Social Forces*, 33 (1955): 316-321.

[76]Etzioni, "Organizational Control Structure," p. 658.

[77]See Robert L. Crowson, "The Desegregation of School Administrators: Reactions and Adjustment of Transferred Principals," in George W. Noblit and Bill Johnston, eds., *The School Principal and School Desegregation* (Springfield, Ill.: Charles C. Thomas, 1982), pp. 96-112.

[78]See Richard Edwards, *Contested Terrain: The Transformation of the Workplace in the Twentieth Century* (New York: Basic Books, Inc., 1979); also, Stewart Clegg, "Organization and Control," *Administrative Science Quarterly*, 26:4 (December 1981): 545-562; and, Martin Carnoy, ed., *Schooling in a Corporate Society* (New York: David McKay Co., 1972).

[79]See Samuel Bowles, "Unequal Education and the Reproduction of the Social Division of Labor," in Carnoy, ed., *Schooling in a Corporate Society*, pp. 36-64.

[80]Richard T. Mowday, "The Exercise of Upward Influence in Organizations," *Administrative Science Quarterly*, 23:1 (March 1978): 137-156.

[81]Morris et al., *Principals in Action*, pp. 149-156.

[82]See Dan C. Lortie, *Schoolteacher* (Chicago: University of Chicago Press, 1976).

[83]See Cecil G. Miskal, "Motivation in Educational Organizations," *Educational Administration Quarterly*, 18:3 (Summer 1982): 65-88.

[84]Ibid., p. 80.

[85]See Roger L.M. Dunbar, "Designs for Organizational Control," in Paul C. Nystrom and William H. Starbuck, eds., *Handbook of Organizational Design*, vol. 2 (New York: Oxford University Press, 1981): 85-115; also, Jeffrey Pfeffer, *Organizations and Organization Theory* (Boston: Pitman Publishing, 1982), pp. 80-96.

[86]See Cecil Miskal, Jo Ann DeFrain, and Kay Wilcox, "A Test of Expectancy Work Motivation Theory in Educational Organizations," *Educational Administration Quarterly* 16:1 (Winter 1980): 70-92; also, Wayne K. Hoy and Cecil G. Miskal, *Educational Administration: Theory, Research and Practice*, 2nd edition (New York: Random House, 1982), pp. 155-161.

[87]See Victor H. Vroom, *Work and Motivation* (New York: Wiley, 1964).

[88]Miskal, DeFrain, and Wilcox, "A Test," pp. 71-72; also, Robert G. Owens, *Organizational Behavior in Education*, 2nd ed. (Englewood Cliffs, N.J.: Prentice-Hall, 1981), pp. 127-130.

[89]Hoy and Miskal, *Educational Administration*, pp. 160-161.

[90]Miskal, DeFrain, and Wilcox, "A Test," p. 88.

[91]Charles A. O'Reilly III and Barton A. Weitz, "Managing Marginal Employees: The Use of Warnings and Dismissals," *Administrative Science Quarterly* 25:3 (September 1980): 467-484.

[92]Arnold S. Tannenbaum, "Control in Organizations: Individual Adjustment and Organizational Performance," in L.L. Cummings and W.E. Scott, eds., *Readings in Organizational Behavior and Human Performance* (Homewood, Ill.: Richard D. Irwin, 1969), pp. 667-679.

[93]W. Richard Scott, *Organizations: Rational, Natural, and Open Systems* (Englewood Cliffs, N.J.: Prentice-Hall, 1981), p. 22. See also Alvin W. Gouldner, "Organizational Analysis," in Robert W. Merton, Leonard Broom, and Leonard Cottrell, Jr., *Sociology Today* (New York: Basic Books, 1959), pp. 400-428.

There is some difficulty, however, with the use of the word "natural" as an alternative model. The implication is that the rational perspective is somehow unnatural. Moreover, confusion increases when we find some scholars (e.g., T. Barr Greenfield) applying "natural" as a descriptor to the *rational* model, because, as he claims, the assumptions under rationality are that organizations are shaped by powerful, natural forces "which in large measure act independently of man." See, T. Barr Greenfield, "Theory About Organization: A New Perspective and its Implications for Schools," in Vincent Houghton, Royston McHugh, and Colin Morgan, eds., *Management in Education* (London: Open University Press, 1975), pp. 59-84.

[94]Scott, pp. 22-23.

[95]Firestone and Herriott, "Two Images of Schools," pp. 39-59.

[96]See James G. March and John P. Olsen, eds., *Ambiguity and Choice in Organizations* (Bergen, Norway: Universitetsforlaget, 1976); also Michael D. Cohen, James G. March, and Johan P. Olsen, "A Garbage Can Model of Organizational Choice," *Administrative Science Quarterly*, 17 (1972): 1-25.

[97]A significant exception, from the how-to-do-it genre, is reflected in the current interest in processes of negotiation. See, for example, H. Cohen, *You Can Negotiate Anything* (Secaucus, N.J.: Lyle Stuart, 1980); also, R. Fisher and W. Ury, *Getting to Yes: Negotiating Agreement Without Giving In* (Boston: Houghton-Mifflin, 1981).

[98]T. Barr Greenfield, "Theory About Organizations," p. 67.

[99]Robert K. Merton et al., *Reader in Bureaucracy* (Glencoe, Ill.: Free Press, 1952).

[100]Robert K. Merton, "Bureaucratic Structure and Personality," in Amitai Etzioni, ed., *Complex Organizations: A Sociological Reader* (New York: Holt, Rinehart and Winston, 1961), pp. 48-61.

[101]Karl E. Weick, "Educational Organizations as Loosely Coupled Systems," *Administrative Science Quarterly*, 21:1 (March 1976): 1-19.

[102]See Richard M. Cyert and James G. March, "A Behavioral Theory of Organizational Objectives," in Mason Haire, ed., *Modern Organization Theory* (New York: John Wiley & Sons, Inc., 1959), pp. 76-90; also Richard M. Cyert and James G. March, *A Behavioral Theory of the Firm* (Englewood Cliffs, N.J.: Prentice-Hall, 1963).

[103]For example, in our chapter on the environment (Chapter 7) we note Meyer and Rowan's argument that those aspects of schools that appear to be most rationally controlled are its myths and ceremonies—aspects of the educational organization that are seldom thought of as formalized and institutionally goal-directed. See John W. Meyer and Brian Rowan, "Institutionalized Organizations: Formal Structure as Myth and Ceremony," *American Journal of Sociology*, 83 (1977): 340-363.

[104]Scott, *Organizations*, p. 83.

[105]See Michael Lipsky, *Street-Level Bureaucracy: Dilemmas of the Individual in Public Services* (New York: Russell Sage Foundation, 1980).

[106]Weick, "Educational Organizations as Loosely Coupled Systems," p. 6-9.

[107]See W.W. Charters, Jr., "The Control of Microeducational Policy in Elementary Schools," in Samuel B. Bacharach, ed., *Organizational Behaviors in Schools and School Districts* (New York: Praeger Publishers, 1981), p. 308.

[108]Firestone and Herriott, "Two Images," p. 44.

[109]David K. Wiles, Jon Wiles, and Joseph Bondi, *Practical Politics for School Administrators* (Boston: Allyn & Bacon, 1981).

[110]Ibid., pp. 12-16.

[111]Ibid., pp. 35-57.

[112]Anselm Strauss, *Negotiations: Varieties, Contexts, Processes, and Social Order* (San Francisco: Jossey-Bass, 1979). *Note:* Strauss coined the term "negotiated order"; however, other terminology is used as well. Jeffrey Pfeffer, for example, suggests an image of the organization as a "relational network," involving many forms of patterned transactions (e.g., involving flows of goods, expression of likes and dislikes, information, and influence between actors). See Jeffrey Pfeffer, *Organizations and Organization Theory*, pp. 271-277.

[113]See Anselm Strauss, et al., "The Hospital and Its Negotiated Order," in E. Friedson, ed., *The Hospital in Modern Society* (New York: Holt, Rinehart & Winston, 1966), pp. 243-251.

[114]Howard S. Becker, "The Teacher in the Authority System of the Public School," in Amitai Etzioni, ed., *Complex Organizations* (New York: Holt, Rinehart and Winston, 1966), pp. 243-251. Also, Henry Barsky, "The Political Style of an Urban Principal: A Case Study" (Unpublished Ph.D. Dissertation, University of Pennsylvania, 1975); H. L. Summerfield, *The Neighborhood-Based Politics of Education* (Columbus, Ohio: Charles E. Merrill, 1971); Lortie, *Schoolteacher*; and, Harry F. Wolcott, *The Man in the Principal's Office* (New York: Holt, Rinehart & Winston, 1973).

[115]Becker, pp. 250-251.

[116]There have been a number of studies of budgeting in institutions of higher education, for example, with the common conclusion that the coalitional model is a powerful descriptor of resource allocation within a university. Despite formalized procedures for budgetary equity (e.g., based upon enrollments and credit-hours generated), some departments typically get much more than their "fair share," others less. See, for example, Jeffrey Pfeffer and Gerald R. Salancik, "Organizational Decision Making as a Political Process: The Case of a University Budget," *Administrative Science Quarterly*, 19 (1974): 135-151.

[117]Samuel B. Bacharach and Michael Aiken, "Structural and Process Constraints on Influence in Organizations: A Level-Specific Analysis," *Administrative Science Quarterly*, 21:4 (December 1976): 623-642.

[118]Jeffrey Pfeffer, *Power in Organizations* (Marshfield, Mass.: Pitman Publishing, 1981).

[119]Ibid., pp. 97-135.

[120]See Van Cleve Morris, *Deaning: Middle Management in Academe* (Urbana: University of Illinois Press, 1981), pp. 25-45.

[121]Michel Crozier, *The Bureaucratic Phenomenon* (Chicago: University of Chicago Press, 1964), pp. 145-147.

[122]Weick, "Educational Organizations as Loosely Coupled Systems," p. 13.

[123]Ranson, Hinings, and Greenwood, "The Structuring of Organizational Structures," pp. 4-7.

[124]See James G. March, "Emerging Developments in the Study of Organizations," *The Review of Higher Education*, 6:1 (Fall 1982): 1-18.

[125]John W. Meyer and Brian Rowan, "The Structure of Educational Organizations," in Marshall W. Meyer and Associates, eds., *Environments and Organizations* (San Francisco: Jossey-Bass Publishers, 1978), pp. 78-109.

[126]Joanne Martin, Martha S. Feldman, Mary Jo Hatch, and Sim B. Sitkin, "The Uniqueness Paradox in Organizational Stories," *Administrative Science Quarterly*, 28 (September 1983): 438-453.

[127]Linda Smirchich, "Concepts of Culture and Organizational Analysis," *Administrative Science Quarterly*, 28 (September 1983): 339-358.

[128]Ibid., p. 344. See also Terrence E. Deal and Allan A. Kennedy, *Corporate Cultures* (Reading, Mass.: Addison-Wesley, 1982).

[129]Smirchich, p. 355.

[130]Seymour B. Sarason, *The Culture of the School and the Problem of Change* (Boston: Allyn & Bacon, Inc., 1971).

[131]Ibid., pp. 62-66.

[132]Smirchich, p. 351.

[133]Frank W. Lutz, "Tightening Up Loose Coupling in Organizations of Higher Education," *Administrative Science Quarterly*, 27:4 (December 1982): 653-669.

[134]Weick, "Educational Organizations as Loosely Coupled Systems," p. 13.

[135]See Martin Burlingame, "Protecting Private Realities by Managing Public Symbols: Mystifications, Cover-ups, and Martyrdom," Paper presented at the annual meeting of the American Education Research Association, Boston, April 1980; also, Jane Hannaway and Lee S. Sproull, "Who's Running the Show? Coordination and Control in Educational Organizations," *Administrator's Notebook*, 27:9 (1978-79): 1-4.

[136]Karl E. Weick, "Administering Education in Loosely Coupled Schools," *Phi Delta Kappan*, 63:10 (June 1982): 673-676.

[137]See, for example, "Management Viewed as Art," *New York Times*, Jan. 7, 1983.

[138]Richard Harvey Brown, "Bureaucracy as Praxis: Toward a Political Phenomenology of Formal Organizations," *Administrative Science Quarterly*, 23:3 (September 1978): 365-382; see also, Jeffrey Pfeffer, *Organizations and Organization Theory*, pp. 226-253.

[139]Lee S. Sproull, "Beliefs in Organizations," in Paul C. Nystrom and William E. Starbuch, eds., *Handbook of Organizational Design*, vol. 2: 203-224.

[140]Mary Haywood Metz, *Classrooms and Corridors* (Berkeley: University of California Press, 1978).

[141]Ibid., p. 205.

[142]Ibid., pp. 209-211.

# 6

## The Management of Organizational Commitment

||||||||||||||||||||||||||||||||||||||||||||||||||||||||||||||||||||||||||||||||||||||||||||||||||||||||||||||||

### ANNE DENIER

*She's back in the old neighborhood. The house where she lived while she grew up is a trim and inviting two-flat in light brown brick, only two blocks away from the school. Her face peers down at the visitor to the school from the Class of 1952 picture on the corridor wall next to the office. Friendly, determined. She dresses casually and comfortably, looking most of all like the high school counselor she once was, or a mother in to check on her son's attendance. But the command presence is there. She listens to everything you say. She speaks quickly and fluidly, revealing a mind with nuance, and quicker than most. She finds opportunities to laugh and uses them. Her pride is in the people who inhabit the school, not its clean corridors, imaginatively used spaces, and the unobtrusive attention to rules that make the school work well. Anne Denier continues to teach—a course each semester—and directs the annual student musical. Without the sugar that would turn it sour, she talks about happiness. It's something that everyone should have more of in this school community. The down-to-earth, tough-minded principal is involved in the pursuit of happiness.*

**Tell me about your growing up, your family, your early schooling, things like that.**

I had a Catholic school background, and I was crazy about school. I started here in the elementary school next door and went all the way through high school. I was

**115**

90—maybe 100—percent happy in school, and I give the credit to my parents and to the nuns who were in the school then. You know, in those days nuns weren't allowed to go many places, so they had lots of time available, and they were in the school for *us*. They involved me in intramural activities. They were very interested in kids, and they let us know that they loved us. I never really knew much about frustration and disappointment. And I wanted to learn *everything*. I can remember times I'd be out at a basketball game until shortly before midnight, and then I'd study until 3:00 A.M.

I didn't especially want to be a teacher. I thought I would get married, probably. And then, after a few days in chemistry class, I realized I was entranced with chemistry. So after I graduated, I headed for college to study chemistry. But it wasn't long before I realized, through prayer, that God wanted me to be a nun.

### How does a decision like that happen?

It's hard to explain. Maybe it's something like two people falling in love and deciding to get married. I found the yes in myself. We often prayed in the chapel. And as I was praying I realized that this was right, that this was where I belonged. I made the decision peacefully, and I have never changed my mind.

One of the major tasks of my order was teaching, and so it was not long before I assumed that I would become a teacher. In 1956 I began as a third grade teacher in a school in a conservative neighborhood in St. Louis. After that I taught in another elementary school in St. Louis, but this time in a rough and tumble neighborhood. We had difficult times there financially. I remember one year when we started the year without paper. We just had to assume that it would be provided, by some person or by God, and it was. Then I moved into a junior high school, but I just didn't think I could handle junior high school kids, work with them effectively. However, the principal persuaded me to try one more year. I did, and I guess I learned some things because suddenly things were going well, and I stayed there five more years.

During the period of my junior high school teaching I earned a B.A. in Chemistry. Soon after I was off to Minnesota to teach in a high school—chemistry, supervising the yearbook. I loved it. I was very comfortable. The next year I was teaching a section each of chemistry, physics, and earth science, and counseling as well. Some of the kids had really heavy problems, and I'd keep one of their problems three weeks after it was solved. By now I was studying in the university again, toward an M.A. in Chemistry, and then I was given a full year away from the school to study educational administration.

### Had someone begun to suggest to you that you might want to think about being an administrator?

No, no one had. But I had always succeeded at school things, and this was the logical next step. Actually, the order must have been short of high school principals. I scheduled most of my courses in the evening, and that brought me into contact with a number of educators from the Chicago Public Schools, people who were working and studying for administrative certification, and that was really enjoyable for me. Then I became principal of a high school in the inner city. The climate there was much like it is here—and I have to credit that to our religious community. We are warm and loving people. By the third year, I had been involved in hiring all the members of the faculty, and that was important to me. I stayed there a number of years, and then I gave advance notice that I would be leaving. I think you have to give an organization at least six months notice to make a decent transition in leadership. I had been there long enough, and I needed a "breather" from administration.

## Do you get together with the other members of your order?

As a sister, I always look forward to our annual assembly. I suppose it's like a convention might be for other educational administrators. We get together to talk, to pray together, to do some business, but mainly to renew our friendship and our community. We're so spread out that it is very important to us. But let me tell you about the rest of my travels. I went to a school in Iowa for a year. It was a terrific place, full of pride over everything from debate to football. I worked as a counselor for a year, and then I was offered the principalship. I was flattered. The school seemed ripe for curriculum change, and there was a lot that I might have been able to do there. But that same spring I had a chance to return to the city as a counselor in a high school. I knew that in the long run I wanted to come back to a large city environment, and maybe you don't realize it, but there are few chances to make such a move. I might have had to wait another eight years for a similar opportunity. And so I came back to the city. I served as counselor for two years, and then the principalship opened. I applied and was interviewed by the board and offered a three-year contract.

## Why did the board decide to hire you?

Most of all, they thought I could bring spiritual values and goals to the school. They wanted a religious leader badly. In addition to that, they knew me. They are a wonderful mix of people. I answered all of their questions, from the spiritual ones to those about spaghetti suppers. Frankly, I was concerned about changing roles from counselor to principal. I think it was a good concern. I think I have made the change, but maybe not enough. I don't counsel anymore; I send the kids to the counselors when they need that kind of help. But I don't feel like I'm spending enough time yet doing real research, helping teachers.

## What do you mean by real research?

Well, right now I feel like I'm a curriculum manager, and I really want to be a curriculum leader. I need to dig in even more to understand the teachers and the students and the different curriculum options that exist. I'm talking about the practical research that lies behind a teaching program. The other big issue for me is getting the development program in better shape. We just squeaked through on this year's budget, although we had predicted it was going to be very tight. But next year we can do better, and we will. We just had our first full-time fund drive, and bingo is bringing in $25,000 a year. But we don't have a development director yet, and we're going to have to hire one soon.

### What do you consider the high point of your own career so far?

The ability to build community among the people who work together in an organization. It involves maintaining an atmosphere. That's much more than schedules and plans. I believe in kids as eternal human beings who can be happier and better and lead deeper lives if they've been in the right school. We talk about God out loud here. We pray to him, or her. And we deal with each other as we learn, as we grieve, as we win championships. Prayer is a tremendous part of it all. You can't drench an adolescent in this sort of thing, but they have to know that it's part of what is happening to them. I'll get a note in the morning from a student saying that his mother had a baby the night before and could the school say a prayer for his new brother. I mention that over the PA during the announcements, and we pray together. You just work it in. But the school is a school first. We have some high achievers here. But we have some low achievers here, too, kids who had problems in other schools and come to us in search of help and support. We put a lot of focus on them.

### I was struck by the diversity of the school as I walked through the halls.

About half of our kids are white—Irish, German, Polish, Italian. Then the Spanish-speaking students—quite a few from Cuba, percentage-wise—and those with roots in Mexico, Puerto Rico, Central America and South America. Black kids, Assyrian kids, kids from Thailand and Pakistan. About two-thirds of them live fairly close to the school, and then the other third come from a tremendously wide range of communities throughout the metropolitan area. Some of our students are the ones who get lost elsewhere. We'll get a kid who had 110 days of absence the year before. So we have a very tough attendance policy. If you don't come to school, you're gone. We tell them that when they come, so there are no surprises. We don't have too many big rules. You can't fight. You can't use drugs or alcohol here. That could be it. Just a very modest dress code. On the fighting we've said that the second time you're out of school.

### How do you get results? How do you get people to do things?

Well, all you do is ask them. I just can't imagine that there is something that needs to be done and there is no one to do it. But it goes deeper than that. Rule number one is HIRE WELL. I only hire people who will do the extra things that are necessary with our kids. I know sometimes I will just do it myself—I err in that direction. But I am far more interested in the process than I am in the end result. As a principal you need to hire teachers who will carry things out to the end. I'd rather spend time with a person on a new idea than with someone who needs the third reminder. The people whom you hire have to be self-directing. I want to be able to stand up in front of parents and say, "I don't know how we could have a better faculty than the one we have here." I can say that now. I stand in such awe of parents who trust us to work with their children. I have very positive feedback from them here. I don't really know what negativism from parents is.

## What are the big lessons you've learned as a school administrator?

Be able to make a decision within a timeline, but not on the spot. Don't be too quick to say yes or no. Next, be a good listener. There are a lot of publics, and every one of them is wiser about some aspect of what you do than you are. Be grateful with those who disagree with you. And get away from it sometimes when you're stressed, or it will blow up in your face. Be consistent. Pray. What we're about is not what *we're* about. We're part of a much bigger picture in this world and in eternity.

## Where do you go from here?

I have a sense of what I should be deciding. I want to be here no fewer than three and no more than ten years. I don't know quite what I'll do. I could be a principal somewhere else. I'm not sure I'd want to teach five classes a day again, even though I realize that contact with fresh, young minds on a regular basis is good for me. If I semi-retired, I might want to be a chaplain in a hospital, or just help out in a school—like our secretary on the phones who gives such good support every day. But most of all I'd think about teaching one kid at a time. Boys and girls who have *great* difficulty learning, who have trouble producing in a group.

## Have you ever had a transcendent experience?

There have been good moments, ones when I have been moved to tears. But nothing I would call mystical, and that's how I would define transcendent. I've been touched deeply.

## What advice and counsel would you give to a young person who came to you with the idea of becoming a school administrator?

Probably, "Oh, great. If you could get half the fun and satisfaction that I have. . . ." No, actually, it would be, "What makes you say that?" I'd listen. It would depend upon what I knew about the individual. I'd be encouraging. Test it out. Being a principal takes stamina. It's a hard job. You need to love it, or you will hate it.

---

## JESSE LAMBERT

*When he shakes your hand and looks you dead in the eye and speaks in his earnest, intriguing voice, you are disarmed. There is a quiet charisma to the man that is compelling. He is in his mid-40s, far removed in time and space, but not commitment, from the black inner city where he grew up. Today he is a top executive within the*

*United States Department of Education. He looks as if he might still be formidable on the basketball court, a place where he once earned his living as a professional. His ambition and talent combined with the chinks of opportunity suddenly available to black men in the late 1960s to propel him into a remarkable career as an educational administrator at the local, state, and federal levels. But now he feels somewhat out of the mainstream, increasingly isolated in his three-piece suit and twentieth-floor office, uncomfortably cut off from the people and issues that motivated him in his drive to the top of his profession. He realizes that he has come to another turning point, one that may prove to be even more difficult than the earlier ones.*

### Tell me something about your life as a child and young man.

I grew up in Norfolk, Virginia—went to grade school and high school there. And I eventually went on to college. In fact, I was the first one in my family to do that. I never saw my father, never knew him. I was raised by my mother and grandmother. The idea that a lot of people gave me was that I ought to get out of high school and get a job. But there were some teachers and coaches who saw more potential in me than that, and they began to encourage me and pull it out of me. We didn't have any money, so the only avenue to college that I had was to get a scholarship. I was a very good athlete—football, wrestling, baseball, and basketball. And I was fortunate enough to be offered scholarships in wrestling and basketball. I also had the opportunity to get a pro baseball contract right out of high school, but I had teachers who told me that I'd be worth a whole lot more with a college degree than I would with a baseball contract.

### And they were right.

You had better believe it! And every chance I get, I go back to thank them for that kind of advice. Some of them have passed on now, of course, but a few of them are still at the high school. I had a terrific basketball coach. He was a white man who knew how to work in a black school and a black community. I mean, he would come around in the evening and check up on us to make sure that we were following the training rules. I think that was where my lifelong respect for discipline and organization really began. The other thing was that I was able to steer clear of the gangs, and that wasn't always easy. I was captain of many of the teams, but I was also busy in other activities, like the drama club. And I remember how atrocious my English was. One of my English teachers took a liking to me, and she gave me the job as editor of the school newspaper, mainly to help me to improve my ability with the language. She also would have me do odd jobs around her house on weekends, partly, I realize now, so that she could correct what I said. She reached me, I can tell you that.

I had something like 26 basketball scholarship offers, but my strong desire was to go to the state university. So I went down with my coach for a visit. But the university coach didn't even know who I was. He said, "You've got to play more than one sport." Heck, I was playing four at the time. Or "If you get hurt, I can't help you." I just looked at my coach, and we thanked him politely for the interview and left. That was that. I got a lot of advice to go away from home, and so I eventually chose the University of Tennessee. I had some idea that I wanted to be an aeronautical engineer. I had been part of the Civil Air Patrol, and I had a civilian pilot's license by that time. But those college engineering courses were too much for me—particularly the math courses. The kids from other high schools were so far ahead of me. I decided to switch to biological sciences. The idea of med school floated around in front of me for a while. But the thing that really got under my skin as I moved through college was the desire to pay the debt. I know it sounds like Boy Scout stuff, but I really vowed that someday I would teach or coach or do both. And so I started taking education courses for my minor. By the end of my junior year I really had completed most of my graduation requirements, so I started taking some graduate courses in education and teaching on the side as a substitute in the local public schools. At the end of my senior year I completed my practice teaching. During that process I also had internships—I think that's what they called them—at both the elementary and secondary level. I still think that was a terrific idea for exposing the prospective teacher to the range of opportunities.

### Were you playing basketball all this time?

Oh, yes. Doing very well, too. So well that I was drafted by the NBA. I played first in Los Angeles, and then I was traded to Philadelphia. It seemed like the bottom fell out then because I had a conflict with the coach, and I was sent down to a farm team at Harrisburg. But actually some good things began to happen. I was married by this time, and Harrisburg was not a bad place to settle down for a while. The size of it reminded me more of Norfolk than Philadelphia or Los Angeles had, and so it become more of a hometown. And in Harrisburg we practiced and played our games at night, so I found a job as a teacher.

### Do you mean a full-time job?

Absolutely. I taught all the time I was playing. Not many of my fellow pros could do that. Then, at least, there weren't many who had degrees. I was teaching fourth and fifth graders at the elementary level. There was nothing available at the high school level or in coaching, and it was pretty clear that there was only one high school where blacks were working. I must say that I soon realized I lacked some skills as an elementary teacher. My penmanship, for example, was terrible. It still is. The experience made me realize that I couldn't do it all, and that was a good lesson for me as a future administrator. So I'd get other teachers to help me in areas where I needed it, and then I'd teach things that I was strong in for them, like science. In addition to playing pro basketball and teaching, I started coaching some junior high basketball in the school system, and I also enrolled in some college courses in elementary methods to improve my teaching.

### You must have had an incredible amount of energy.

I don't know how to relax to this day. You can't, not if you're willing to accept a challenge. Another one came along very quickly. I was told that I was going to be transferred to the high school. It was *the* high school in the city, one that had been formerly all white, but now there was about a 12 percent black student population. Actually, I was located in a junior high school, one that was on the same campus with the high school. I was to coach track, basketball, and football and teach physical sciences, health, safety, and physical education. That kept me busy, and by now I had decided that I wasn't going back to the NBA, so I devoted my energies to my educational career.

There had been a heavy turnover of principals in the junior high school. The current principal was a really good man. I respected him. However, as well as he could handle white kids, he simply couldn't deal with minority kids. So he started using me as an assistant to him to help with the black students. Before long he was just doing the scheduling and the paper work, and I was really doing the things a principal really has to do with people. And it was during this period that I went back to the university for a master's degree in educational administration and supervision. I knew I needed a master's degree to get into high school work, and I was beginning to see a future in administration.

Things happened so quickly in those years. My basketball team was undefeated, and then they asked me to move with them up to the ninth grade. So I was a high school teacher at last, as well as the freshman basketball coach and the assistant coach in wrestling and baseball. And we were undefeated again. For the first time I was feeling somewhat overloaded, mostly because I had become an unofficial counselor for the black kids, and that really took a lot of time and energy. The kids would come to me rather than going to their assigned counselors, and more and more of them would come out for the teams if they knew I was coaching. And my basketball teams kept winning big. But you won't believe how I became an administrator.

## Why not?

The powers that be preferred me as an administrator to being the basketball coach at the high school, which should tell you something about where the values were there. I was clearly in line to be the head coach for the varsity, and I had just finished my master's degree. One day the principal came down to the gym and found me on the court and asked me if I would be assistant high school principal. I told him I had never taken the exam. He said, "We can work it out." And they did, and so I was an assistant principal in charge of various things, including black discipline. That was upsetting to me. I wanted to be an administrator for all the students. I had never even heard anyone talk about *black* discipline. That never sat very well with me, but I did my best in the new position, and before the end of the next year I knew I was being considered for a job at the central office. But I knew it would be in something like human relations or government programs, and that wasn't what interested me, at least not in that district.

Before that could jell, I was approached— quietly—by an administrator who had worked in the public school system but who now worked for the state department of education, which was right in Harrisburg. He asked me if I wanted a job with them. I told him that I just didn't think that I could fit in. He said, "Yes you can. Think it over. You can have more influence at the state level than in a local school or school district." It was that last part that hooked me. Whatever else I wanted to accomplish as an administrator, I knew that I wanted to have influence over the course of events. And the money was right. So I accepted, and that was the end of my experience at the local level.

I was the state consultant for equal educational opportunity, an issue I could really sink my teeth into, and eventually I worked up to director of that area, which was at the assistant superintendent level. I was involved in science education and in Title I, too, particularly at the evaluation end. I was the only black male up at that level, and I was very visible. But I was uncomfortable with my job description. I had the old-fashioned idea that you were supposed to be qualified for a job you took. They gave me a budget with no strings attached, but I could see that they weren't very serious about equal educational opportunity. So I took a year to educate myself—really it was a lot of staff development for me and all those around me. I called in experts from everywhere to help us think it through, including some from the United States Office of Education. In the second year I felt I was ready to do my job.

I knew that as the token black I had more leeway than others, and so I started doing what my job description said I was supposed to do—going out to local districts and getting them to comply with the law. I'm sure there were a lot of phone calls back to my bosses, and I'm just as sure those bosses pacified a lot of school superintendents at first. They probably told them to listen to me and then go back to business as usual. But I was developing a style about it. Here's the law. You need to comply with it. I can give you some suggestions. If you don't make some movement, the next people who visit with you will do more than make suggestions. You turned the screws, but slowly. It got tougher.

By that time, just a few years after being in the state department, I was getting offers at the national level. I resisted at first, but then one federal administrator told me that I ought to come to work for him and try to work on my doctorate at the same time. He pushed the right button because that had been in the back of my mind. I knew I had to have the doctorate to do what I could do in education. So, eventually, I accepted the offer to come to the federal level and do the same kind of work, and they assigned me to this region, here in Kansas City, and I've been here now for the last ten years.

## Were you able to do what you wanted to in your new job, to get at the problems that really were of interest to you?

Desegregation was where it was at in those days, in the late 60s and early 70s. I was really attuned to that. My commitment was intense. I knew, or felt that I knew, that everyone was in the same game, from the Commissioner on down. It was not a sham or an idle dream then. You felt that this nation was going to strive to really make some changes in the way people lived and worked together. Here I was—a young man in my early 30s—and I had a chance to be deeply involved in all that. It's the biggest thrill I've ever had, maybe that I'll ever have. You could get out there in the field, work shoulder to shoulder with people who shared the same values and goals, watch the problems get solved. You began to have an appreciation for the work of the educational administrator in this particular field. It was so exciting. I know this sounds corny, but you felt like you were on the cutting edge. A new dawn was coming. And you'd have something to do with it.

### Have these been ten good years?

I can't really say that. It's begun to slip away. Public sentiment has changed. There was a time, and not so long ago, when education seemed to be a priority and everyone was paying attention to civil rights, even if some were fighting against them. Then, they let you go forward if you were working for the federal government. With all deliberate speed. You worked just like that phrase that is related to the Brown decision. But that has changed. I'm still trying to get back to that, and I don't know if I ever will be able to.

### It wasn't all peaches and cream, was it?

Oh, no, not at all. You ran into hostility. The reluctance of people who said they were dedicated to education to do the right thing. I encountered a lot of school administrators who were quite willing to stand in the way of progress. But other people were even more vicious. Once a colleague and I had finished our day's work in a school district, and we started to drive back to the motel where we were staying, twenty-five miles away—really because of fear of physical harm. And we found the brake line on our car had been cut. Another time our car was stoned. It got kind of rough. But all of that only showed the need for what we were trying to do. That opposition to what is morally right convinced me that I was on the case. It made me hang in even harder.

### What was the high point of your career?

That's a difficult one. This might sound vague, but to me it isn't. It has been working behind the scenes in districts where—through joint efforts— we have been able to get more commitment to equal educational opportunities for children. Times when I wasn't even around for the results, but where I knew looking back that I had played my minute part in it all.

### What was the low point?

That's easier. Getting to the top, or near to it, and finding out what it's really like. At least in the federal government you discover that you can't use your skills because you're a part of someone's master plan that begins and ends with a political platform or a speech. I feel totally oppressed by this kind of situation. You end up spinning your wheels along with everyone else, making a show. And worst of all, you've been taken away from any contact with kids, from a chance to improve their lives and their futures. What it comes down to is that you really don't have a lot of work to do. You're manipulated by those who don't have any real interest in education. Business as usual, vicious games, everyone hand-picked by someone above them. You feel like a sausage.

### Did you get that doctorate?

Yes, I did. After four or five years with the federal government, I began to take classes at nearby universities. But I wanted the best instruction in law and finance—I knew that from my field work. No kidding around. I had to find a university that was strong in those areas and that would accept some of my credits from the local universities here. I ended up at the University of Illinois, and I spent one year in residence there plus some summers. Once I even flew back and forth on the plane to take classes when that was necessary. Believe me, it was cheaper than paying the tuition to some of the private universities around here!

## What are some of the important lessons about school administration that you learned along the way?

There are two that are the most important. First, don't be impetuous. If you're going to fight, make darned sure you're right. Second, you have to be a listener. A lot of school administrators shouldn't have their jobs because they only got them because of who they know. That can make you more egotistical, and if you believe that you know it all then you don't have to listen.

## Have you ever come near the breaking point?

Yes, through my involvement in my present job. I'm so far away from what I know how to do to be a really productive educational administrator. Several times I've come close to saying, "To hell with it." I want to stay in education, but it will have to be something different from this. There was a time when I thought I wanted to be the first black United States Commissioner of Education, but I don't want that now. I might be a superintendent of schools, and I've toyed with the idea of being the president of a small college. Whatever, it will be as an educational administrator at some level.

## What counsel would you give to a young man or woman who came to you for advice about pursuing a career in educational administration?

I would tell them that if they were honestly dedicated and if they wanted to pay the price to help people, go for it. In preparing yourself, you should study with the best. And even though you evaluate others, you have to evaluate yourself first, and you must be yourself above all.

## Has your work made a positive difference in the field of education?

I know that a lot of it has. My teaching, my coaching, my work as a school administrator. I'm getting enough years under my belt now to see that I've influenced others who have now become topflight educators, and by that I mean my former students. Behind the scenes I've influenced a lot of administrators, too. They still search me out in the evenings, and we brainstorm: Why should I do this? How can I do that?

## *FROM PRACTICE TO THEORY*

Anne Denier and Jesse Lambert—two individuals from widely different backgrounds, but nevertheless with much in common. Is it their shared capacity for hard work? To be sure, both do work hard; they do not just accept, they *pursue* responsibility—observing that there is a job to be done, and staying with that job determinedly to completion. Is the common element their ability to learn from experience? Both *have* grown in their careers. The past is something to learn from, to analyze, to build upon in a worklife that continues to unfold, to reveal new dimensions, new opportunities. Is the secret of their commonality a shared idealism? "It gets to you after a while," laments Jesse Lambert. Nevertheless, you have the sense that Lambert, and certainly Denier have not lost their vision, their dedication to the creation of a better future.

Hard work, growth in the sense of a deepened awareness of occupational purpose over time, idealism, dedication. Is there a body of theory that captures these elusive qualities? The idea of *commitment* is reemerging as a most important element in organizational theory. It is not a well-understood or well-defined term, but it does seem to include the special combination of ingredients that Anne Denier and Jesse Lambert represent. Commitment involves the willingness of people to give their loyalty and energy to social systems. Anne's loyalty is religious in its intensity, Jesse's is more dependent upon the loyalty that is shown him in return. Are there theories that explain and build upon both of these forms of commitment, that tie the careers of Denier and Lambert together in understandable symmetry?

The securing of commitment from organizational members is crucial to the success of the organization, and it represents a key activity for the educational administrator. Increasingly, we are also becoming concerned with the commitment that organizations, in turn, make to their employees. The condition is reciprocal; it flows back and forth between the individual and the organization. How does the educational administrator secure the commitment of those who work within and serve the schools? How does the organization show its own commitment to its employees?

## THE MANAGEMENT OF ORGANIZATIONAL COMMITMENT

### Introduction

The educational profession is widely known and generally respected for its high level of commitment. A popular image of the schoolteacher is that of a woefully underpaid yet still devoted public servant spending long hours and undergoing much frustration to lead some thirty-five immature minds a step or two along the difficult road toward responsible adulthood. A poster seen often in teachers' lounges shows a picture of a teacher standing on his head, twirling rings with his feet, and performing magic tricks with his hands in an effort to gain the attention of a roomful of totally disinterested youngsters. The poster's caption reads: "No one ever said teaching was going to be easy." Similarly, our image of the college professor is of an individual wearing threadbare tweeds that represent genteel poverty, hunched near-sightedly but enthusiastically over the notes for his next book, and absent-mindedly forgetting to eat, return phone calls, or pay his bills.

Both of these images are overdrawn. Nevertheless, they have a forceful impact upon reality. People are drawn to the profession at least in part by its images of commitment and purpose. Working with kids, helping others by being a teacher, molding young minds, saving youngsters from the handicaps of poverty and environmental neglect, contributing to the betterment of society—these have been the attractions for many who have embarked upon careers as educators. Doing what is thought to be good and just is part of what being an educator is all about.

Because commitment to the profession is so much a part of its ethos, a loss of commitment becomes a heavy loss indeed. When a teacher's rose-colored glasses give way to clearer images of the dark shapes, forbidding presences, and contending forces that surround the profession, his or her commitment suffers. One major difficulty with the concept of commitment is that there is not a great deal of consensus as to just what it is or how one measures it.[1] To assist an improved understanding, three alternative approaches to commitment are considered in this chapter. On one hand, commitment may be viewed as a state of loyalty and shared purpose that is deeply internalized within the psyche of each organizational participant. This sense of commitment comes from within—often with a feeling of sacrifice appended to it, of something that is given up personally in favor of the pursuit of a higher value, a worthwhile collective goal. A typology of commitment offered by Rosabeth Moss Kanter proceeds from this loyalty-from-within perspective. As a second alternative, commitment may be viewed less as an internalized state of being than as the product of a special relationship between individual and organization. Commitment is not the product of sacrifice so much as it is the outcome of an interactive relationship where the incentives provided by an organization must match the needs and interests of the employed person. We discuss in this chapter a conceptualization of commitment by Amitai Etzioni that develops such a relationship-oriented approach. Finally, as a third point of view, commitment may be seen to be lodged not within the individual but within the organization. It is initially the *organization* that must be committed—to the individual—so that in the employee's view the complex of behaviors pursued exhibits a match between the goals and interests of the institution and the goals and interests of the individual. We draw some theoretical understandings from a classification scheme by Lyman Porter and Raymond Miles to illustrate this third perspective. As the chapter unfolds, we discuss first (as background) some of the special constraints surrounding the development of commitment in education and a few of its observed characteristics. The bulk of the chapter is then devoted to our three alternative theoretical perspectives.

## The Context of Commitment in Education

Commitment is something educators are supposed to bring with them, ready-made, to their jobs. It is part of the mystique surrounding the teaching profession. Glowing brightly within the young newcomer to the profession is a strong spark of identification with what is perceived to be a noble profession. Both Anne Denier and Jesse Lambert stepped into the classroom with this brand of commitment. Improperly nourished or inadequately fueled, however, that flame of devotion dies, or worse, turns inward to consume itself. There are many constraints in the nature of the profession and in its relationships which make the maintenance of commitment a problematic endeavor. Let us examine a few of the major barriers.

**What Is Commitment?**　As a first constraint, there is the problem of definition. Because commitment is not a sharply defined term, it is linked with questions of group cohesiveness, integration, socialization, morale, leadership, and loyalty, as well as power or influence.[2] The term can be used to describe a person's commitment to oneself, to another individual, to a group of people, a particular organization, an idea (e.g., democracy), or a societal institution (e.g., public schooling). It has been used to assist in the analysis of such widely varying phenomena as utopian social movements, political systems, armies, religious orders, schools and colleges, governmental bureaucracies, the established professions, labor unions, and manufacturing corporations.[3]

　　A number of definitions have placed an emphasis upon loyalty as the key dimension. Lee, for example, defines commitment as "some degree of belongingness, loyalty, or shared characteristics."[4] Similarly, Kanter, with just a slight variation, views commitment as "the willingness of social actors to give their energy and loyalty to social systems, the attachment of personality systems to social relations which are seen as self-expressive."[5] Commitment from this perspective is viewed as a purely cathectic relationship between organization and individual. The individual demonstrates an ongoing loyalty and attachment whatever the direction and purpose of the organization. Leadership may change (e.g., a new superintendent of schools is appointed) and policies may undergo revision (e.g., because a new board of education majority has surfaced), but the employee remains, despite shifting organizational winds, in steadfast institutional loyalty.

　　Other scholars recognize the importance of loyalty, but suggest that commitment also includes some elements of goal-directedness. People are usually committed *to* something—to some sets of ends or values that draw them together in common cause. Brown writes, for example, that commitment "has a special predictive potential, providing predictions concerning certain aspects of performance, motivation of work, spontaneous contribution, and other related outcomes."[6] In clearer terms, Porter et al. bring the loyalty and goal-directedness dimensions together in defining commitment as "the relative strength of an individual's identification with and involvement in a particular organization." They go on to note that commitment is characterized by at least three elements: "a strong belief in acceptance of the organization's goals and values; a willingness to exert considerable effort on behalf of the organization; and a strong desire to maintain membership in the organization."[7]

　　However, commitment is not a one-way process. Traditionally, commitment has been analyzed from the organization's viewpoint to be that set of problems related to the securing of loyalty and compliance from individuals in the organization. However, individuals come to organizations with needs and skills. They expect to find a work environment in which they can satisfy those needs and utilize those skills. From the employee's perspective, the more favorable this exchange, the greater one's commitment can be to an achievement of the organization's goals. Increasingly —and it is a growing phenomenon of contemporary organizational life world-wide— employees are questioning the organization's commitment to them. To what extent is the organization showing its employees the same loyalty and attachment that it expects from them? Is the organization committed? There is, furthermore, a growing acknowledgment that commitment may find its roots in neither individual nor organization, but only in the quality of relationship between them.

**How Does Commitment Apply to Education?** An article in *Time* magazine reported the widespread abuse of sick leave by teachers in the Boston public school system. About 20 percent of the system's 4,200 teachers reportedly used more than the 15 annual sick days provided under their contract, costing the school system an estimated $10 million a year.[8] Teacher absenteeism is considered to be a nationwide problem, not just a phenomon to be found in city schools. It is claimed that approximately 75 million hours of contact time are lost annually because teachers have failed to report for work.[9] As every educator knows, a substitute teacher typically provides the children with little more than adult supervision.

High rates of absenteeism have been attributed to teacher burnout, the emotional, attitudinal, and physical exhaustion that results from the stress of classroom teaching. Disrespectful students, unresponsive bureaucracies, budget-based layoffs, an inflation-driven decline in the teacher's standard of living, increased parental litigiousness, an erosion of the security offered by tenure, increasingly conflictual labor-management relations, a decline in citizen respect for the teacher, and restrictions arising out of state and federal regulations—all of these factors have been linked with the phenomenon of burnout that some observers claim has reached epidemic proportions.[10]

Whether it be attributed to teacher absenteeism due to work-related stress or evidenced by such other behaviors as lowered job performance, a greater intrusion of personal problems into the work setting (e.g., alcoholism), or simply a lot more griping to be heard, the commitment once thought to define and inspire the educational profession appears to be evolving into one of its most critical problems. If this is so, how can the organization reintroduce the corporate loyalty, the devotion to duty, the self-sacrifice, and the attachment to the welfare of others that presumably have long defined the profession of education?

A second category of constraints arises out of the nature of education as a profession. How does commitment apply to education? There is *first* the central question of professional versus bureaucratic loyalty. To illustrate, consider the not-so-divided allegiance of the college professor. The professoriate is known for its traditional, primary loyalty to the various academic disciplines (e.g., physics, philosophy, sociology) as distinct from its secondary loyalty to the particular institution of employment. Other physicists or sociologists or political scientists (wherever they are located) are considered the professor's closest colleagues rather than the members of other departments located within his or her own university. Even the nature of the organization to which loyalties adhere can better be described in the professor's mind as a community of scholars than as Riveredge U.[11] At best, the loyalties of a professor related to academic profession and institutional affiliation are apt to be shared; they are never directed totally toward the organization. Educators are professionally trained individuals who happen to work in bureaucracies. There are typically tensions between professional norms and values and bureaucratic goals, between professionally nurtured images of behavior (e.g. individual automony) and bureaucratically established definitions of role (e.g. rule-guidedness, responsiveness to supervisory directions).

Elementary and secondary schoolteachers no less than college professors are well equipped with professional loyalties and notions of professional purpose that transcend their employment as teachers in a particular organizational setting. It is not inconceivable for a teacher to be equally committed to her profession and to School District #163, for there is a sense in this instance of goals in common orbit. But where such goals are on a collision course, commitment is unclear and problematic, even stress-producing. How does the committed educator teach inner-city third-graders how to read when budgetary cutbacks have increased her class size from 26 to 35, when increased paperwork intrudes upon student learning time, when instructional materials are months late, when the upkeep of school facilities is sacrificed to cost-cutting necessity? Why should a teacher be loyal to such an unsupportive organization?

It has been suggested, also, that the length and the nature of professional training is a prime cause of tension. This training is a long process of socialization into the attitudes and behaviors of the profession—many of which mores conform poorly to bureaucratic authority.[12] A tendency to resist bureaucratic rules and hierarchical supervision and a tendency to provide only partial loyalty to the bureaucracy find their roots in professionalized training that (in Becker and Carper's words) values

> . . . expertise as a result of prolonged training in a body of abstract knowledge, an internalized code of ethics, a collegial maintenance of standards, autonomy or self-control over one's decisions and work activities, a commitment to a calling, and an identification with the profession and fellow professionals.[13]

College instructors, with their lengthy period of apprenticeship as doctoral candidates, are likely to hold strong professional identifications. Elementary and secondary teachers are somewhat less totally immersed in the professional ethic; nevertheless, the spirit of teacher autonomy is a heavily valued commodity that provides a foundation for much conflict with and resistance toward bureaucratic controls.[14] Schoolteachers no less than college professors are described aptly in W. Richard Scott's comment on the effect of professional training.

> The worker exposed to such a training program often comes to develop a professional self-image in the sense that he values his skills highly and is more concerned with getting and maintaining a reputation among his peers than he is with pleasing his organizational superiors.[15]

The professional ethic tends toward an instrumental view of the organization. The organization is to function primarily to serve the professional—to provide the facilities and support services that will permit the professional a maximum use of his or her special skills. Loyalty to the organization is conditional upon the adequacy of its support.[16]

A *second* point regarding the maintenance of commitment centers around the question of just who or what it is that should be the object of the educator's allegiance. At first blush the answer seems quite simple. The central focus for the educator, like the physician, should be upon the client. Doing what is best for children, devotion to one's students, pupil-centeredness, concern first for the welfare of the kids, attending to students' needs—these are among the most common catch-phrases in the profession. The commitment of the teacher should be directed first and foremost toward the recipient of educative services: the young person of growing mind and personality, the immature individual searching for some help and guidance in the difficult task of growing up.

There is much truth in this popular image, but it is far too simplistic. Teachers at the high school level, and even more in college positions, are renowned for being subject-centered rather than pupil-centered. The commitment to an academic discipline takes precedence over service to the students seated in front of them. Where there is a focus upon the student, opinions differ regarding which students merit what or how much attention. The profession has struggled mightily over the years with questions concerning the relative professional time and energy to be devoted to the gifted, the physically or mentally handicapped, the non-English speaking, the job bound, and the late-bloomer. While a neat image of educator commitment might portray an all-or-nothing focus upon the child, in reality commitment must be parceled out, divided among a number of competing claimants. The students, yes. But the educator also owes allegiance to his or her own family, to academic peers, and to the community, the larger society, and even the organization.

Also there is evidence that commitment is something that changes over time. As individuals enter the profession, as they are socialized and mature, their attitudes toward their jobs and their students are altered. Buchanan has suggested that a person's experiences during three key stages of on-the-job socialization stimulate a progressive development of organizational commitment. These experiences (see Figure 6.1) include, in stage one, personal attitudes toward the organization amidst a first-year job challenge; in stage two (second through fourth years), self-image reinforcement and personal importance; and in stage three (fifth year and beyond), group attitudes toward the organization, a realization of expectations, and the internalization of work commitment norms. The central point is that as member commitment develops over time, the experiences provided by the organization may necessarily need to change in order to build and sustain a worthy level of commitment.[17] The first-year teacher and the mature employee march to quite different drumbeats of job attitude and work-place motivation.

As a *third* problem, consider the question of a relationship between commitment and job performance. Intuitively, it would appear, that the committed teacher

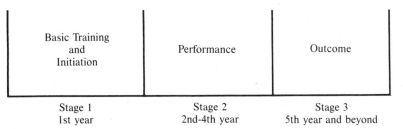

| Basic Training and Initiation | Performance | Outcome |
|---|---|---|
| Stage 1<br>1st year | Stage 2<br>2nd-4th year | Stage 3<br>5th year and beyond |

*FIGURE 6.1*    Stages in the development of organizational commitment

Based on Bruce Buchanan II, "Building Organizational Commitment: The Socialization of Managers in Work Organizations," *Administrative Science Quarterly*, 19 (1974): 533–546.

is the better teacher. Long hours in the evenings and over weekends spent grading papers and preparing lessons; thoroughly organized and substance-filled lessons presented in the classroom with the verve that stems from pleasure taken in one's job; a love of children and a capacity to communicate that love together with demands properly made upon children to learn and to grow—these are the marks of a committed educator and, simultaneously, the indicators of an effective educator. Conversely, the unprepared, the bored, the indifferent are not only uncommitted, but ineffective.

Nevertheless, Mowday and others report that "the least encouraging finding that has emerged from studies of commitment is a rather weak relationship between commitment and job performance."[18] To some extent this finding is based on uncertain measures of performance. It has been difficult to measure effectiveness in education because of the spatial arrangements of the work, the lack of clarity in goals, and the complexity of the teaching task.[19] However, such measures as we do have allow for the distinct possibility that the bored teacher who cannot stand his job and dislikes kids sometimes may be a highly effective educator—long remembered by scores of youngsters as that tough, lazy, cynical, and unfair "old goat" who was roundly hated but inordinately respected as an effective teacher. There are so many other variables in a judgment of quality of teaching performance (e.g., ability to communicate, personal charisma, intelligence, command of subject-matter) that efforts to trace a simple linear connection between commitment and job effectiveness may be unwise.

Mowday and his colleagues suggest that the outcomes of employee commitment are more discernible and more valuable to the organization if visible elsewhere. It is precisely, for example, in those types of organizations where the quality of job performance is less tangible and more difficult to quantify that one needs the most evidence of employee commitment. Evidence of teacher commitment or lack of it can have a sizable impact, for example, upon the *perceptions* that parents hold for their schools. Miss Jones may be a fine educator, but if she is absent a great deal, lackadaisical in grading papers, and unresponsive to parental communications, she is likely to be regarded as a poor teacher. Whatever the reality of Jones' actual instructional performance, it is the *image* of her commitment held by parents that is used to form judgments about the school.[20]

In another illustration, Mowday suggests that the desirable outcome(s) of employee commitment may vary with changing times. When an organization is under threat environmentally or budgetarily, for example, it may wish to call upon the deep-seated commitment of its employees to see it through such troubled times. In a sense, this is what the federal government asked of Jesse Lambert. Alternatively, when the organization is secure with regard to such issues, it may be less concerned about matters of commitment. In fact, it may encourage a bit of a weakening of commitment to the extent that it is able to maintain a moderate turnover rate so as "to ensure an influx of new people or opportunities for career advancement."[21] Recent evidence in education of increased absenteeism and tardiness may reflect inadequate organizational and employee response to the unexpected challenge of the 1970s—the decline of students.

A *final* problem that cramps the maintenance of commitment in education is its inadequate level of reward. Slotted in a standardized salary schedule based on years rather than quality of experience, and on an accumulation rather than application of training, the devoted teacher reaps few rewards (other than the psychic variety) that are unavailable to the academic time-server. Admittedly, the psychic rewards that flow from their students are important to teachers.[22] The joy in watching a young mind grasp a previously elusive idea, the satisfaction that accompanies a lesson well delivered, excited voices remaining locked in debate well after a class period has ended, a complacent student who comes alive amidst a science project on rocketry, a few small words of appreciation delivered to a teacher at year's end—each are rewards of considerable value to educators, particularly to those who are the most committed. For many teachers, it is this type of reward alone that makes the job worthwhile.

It may be suggested, however, that the simple joy found in teaching and in teaching well has diminished a bit in recent years. Teachers complain that youngsters have less respect for authority than they used to, that parents no longer back teachers up as they should, that disciplinary controls are becoming overly relaxed, and that changing societal conditions (e.g., many more latch-key children, one-parent families, and unemployment-pressured households) have made teaching more precarious. Simultaneously, the direct monetary rewards realized by the profession have failed to keep pace with middle-class material and cultural standards. The greatest psychic rewards accrue typically to the most committed of educators, but these may no longer offset sufficiently the frustrations of the job and the economic sacrifices that teachers continue to make.

One promise of escape from the standardized salary schedule is to turn inward, for intrinsic reward, to the joys of the classroom. A second route is to turn toward the organization, paying attention to opportunities for advancement, for an upgrading of one's position in some institutionalized sense. Here too, however, the rewards are few. The ladder of upward mobility in education has few rungs. There are not many supervisory positions (e.g., assistant principal, principal, curriculum director) in relation to the numbers of classroom teachers, and there is little in the way of a standardized career path toward ever-increasing responsibility and attendant reward. To move upward organizationally it is usually necessary, furthermore, to move out of the classroom, to discard the primary loyalty to students, as Jesse Lambert learned with some dismay.[23]

In sum, although a tradition of commitment among educators to their profession and to their clientele is widely recognized, it is also apparent that employee commitment to the educational organization is constrained by forces outside their control. Educator allegiances typically are divided between profession and organization, with each attitude requiring a different perception regarding the central purpose of institutional facilities and supports. It is also not quite as clear as tradition would have us believe just who should receive the primary attention of teachers. The teacher whose loyalty is focused unerringly upon the best interests of her children provides the prevailing image; the reality finds educator loyalties highly divided among many competing claimants. Similarly, it has been assumed that committed educators are better educators, yet a coherent relationship between commitment and job performance has not been firmly established. Not the least of reasons for this may be the fact that the reward structure of education, while valuing and even assuming heavy commitment, has not prescribed a meaningful set of incentives with which to honor it.

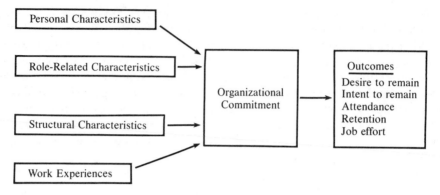

**FIGURE 6.2**    Hypothesized antecedents and outcomes of organizational commitment

Adapted from Richard M. Steers, "Antecedents and Outcomes of Organizational Commitment," *Administrative Science Quarterly,* 22 (1977): 46–56.

## Toward Organizational Commitment in Education

Despite the difficulties associated with it, the development of educator commitment is considered among the most important of tasks for the educational administrator. If teacher absenteeism, burnout, job dissatisfaction, and turnover stem from a break-down in the tradition of a single-minded devotion to work, it behooves the educational administrator to patiently study the vital, but still-imprecise determinants of organizational commitment.

Mowday, Porter, and Steers provide assistance in their report that 25 variables have been found to be related in some way to organizational commitment.[24] Commitment has been shown (as seen in Figure 6.2) to be related to *personal characteristics* (sex, age, education, tenure, achievement motivation, and sense of competence),[25] *role-related or job characteristics* (job scope, challenge, role conflict, and role ambiguity),[26] *work experiences* (organizational dependability, personal importance, met expectations, positive attitudes, and leadership style),[27] and *structural characteristics* (formalization, functional dependence, decentralization, and participation in decision-making).

Mowday, Porter, and Steers have summarized their review of the literature in a table listing each variable and the nature of its correlation with organizational commitment. Although only a few of the studies summarized (from Table 6.1) below have used the employees of educational organizations as subjects, by drawing a few tentative inferences we can identify some interesting implications for education.

**Personal Characteristics.**    Table 6.1 suggests that a person's investment in the organization—as indicated by age, tenure, and position—builds commitment. Hrebiniak and Alutto, for example, found among a sample of classroom teachers that the greater their seniority or experience, the less was their desire to leave.[28] To a considerable extent, of course, any employing organization builds investment. Retirement programs typically penalize the early-leaver, some perquisites accrue with seniority (e.g., the sunniest classroom in the school, the top students, an early lunch period), and close collegial friendships develop over time. Not the least of forces leading toward commitment is the finding that with lengthening tenure

**TABLE 6.1**     Correlates of organizational commitment

| Characteristics | Correlation |
| --- | --- |
| Personal | |
| Age | positive |
| Tenure | positive |
| Educational level | inverse |
| Gender | positive |
| Achievement motivation | positive |
| Sense of competence | positive |
| Higher-order needs | positive |
| Strong personal worth ethic | modest support |
| Work-oriented central life interest | positive |
| Role Related | |
| Job scope | positive |
| Role conflict | inverse |
| Role ambiguity | mixed results |
| Role overload | inverse |
| Structural | |
| Organization size | no significance |
| Union presence | no significance |
| Span of control | no significance |
| Centralization of authority | no significance |
| Formalization | positive |
| Functional dependence | positive |
| Decentralization | positive |
| Worker ownership | positive |
| Participation in decision making | positive |
| Position in hierarchy | no significance |
| Work Experiences | |
| Occupational dependability | positive |
| Personal importance | positive |
| Met expectations | positive |
| Perceived pay equity | positive |
| Group norms regarding hard work | positive |
| Leadership style | |
| Initiating structure | positive |
| Consideration | positive |
| Social involvement | positive |

Based on Richard T. Mowday, Lyman W. Porter, and Richard M. Steers, *Employee-Organization Linkages* (New York: Academic Press, 1982), pp. 30–35.

employees perceive that their opportunities for alternative employment are decreasing.[29] Making the best of what is available may lead many educators to a bit more investment in the job at hand.

A look at a few other personal characteristics reveals that teachers from blue-collar backgrounds exhibit less commitment than teachers from white-collar, managerial, or professional backgrounds. Differences in commitment were also found among male and female teachers. Females exhibit less of an inclination to change employing institutions than their male counterparts; also, married and separated teachers, regardless of sex, see greater costs attached to mobility.[30]

**Role-related Characteristics.** A surprising finding among the list of personal characteristics (with important implications for the teaching role) is the inverse relationship between level of educational attainment and organizational commitment. Hrebiniak and Alutto found that teachers who did not plan to do graduate work exhibited higher levels of organizational commitment than those who did.[31] School districts have long stressed continuing education for their employees, and nearly every salary schedule in the land rewards teachers for furthering their years of formal education. Has this policy been counterproductive vis-a-vis allegiance? Have school districts unwittingly been busily subsidizing their own loss of employee commitment?

Perhaps and perhaps not. An explanation for the apparent contradiction between training and commitment is found, once again, in a special appreciation of the professional role. Sheldon, for example, observed that high levels of commitment to one's profession appeared to be associated with a lack of organizational commitment, at least among Ph.D. scientists employed in a private laboratory. Professional commitment for that group also appeared to increase with work experience; thus, scientists who reported a high commitment to their profession tended not to be committed to the organization regardless of the many investments that it tried to induce.[32] Similarly, school district attention to and investment in further training may add to employee professionalism, but at a cost in organizationalism. One's level of education or amount of professional training may induce a conceptualization of role which in turn may affect the strength of one's commitment to the employing organization.

Numerous scholars have noted the problem of securing the loyalty of professionals who work in bureaucracies and inducing them to work toward the organization's purposes and goals. Basic definitions of role are in conflict; a notion of authority rooted in knowledge and expertise seems to be incompatible with authority rooted in an administrative hierarchy. A resistance to bureaucratic standards and a minimal loyalty to the bureaucracy are the hallmarks of the true professional who, with his or her peers, finds the employing organization more of a hindrance to job effectiveness than a help.[33]

Sometimes an uneasy truce rather than outright resistance is the order of the day—as is often the case in a university environment. Bureaucratic and professional spheres of authority tend to coexist, with faculty submitting to management in many day-to-day administrative matters (e.g., use of the secretarial pool, course scheduling, final grade reporting, use of parking facilities) but, nevertheless, maintaining considerable control otherwise over the conditions under which they work (e.g., deciding individually when to show up at the office, what to teach, what daily activities to engage in, and with whom to interact). The truce is an uneasy one because a maintenance of separate spheres of authority is often managed only with considerable difficulty. Invariably, considerations of budget come to interfere with professorial control of time and energy—with battles developing over teaching load, use of the discretionary dollars raised by research, professorial perquisites (e.g., use of the telephone, computer time, photocopying, travel allotments), and course offerings (e.g., those offerings most attractive to students versus those professors most enjoy teaching).

**Structural and Work Experience Characteristics.**    Table 6.1 suggests that a sense of commitment may develop out of the many ways in which people receive rewards and recognition in organizations. Rewards for the professional (actually, teachers are better described as semi-professionals)[34] is not a simple matter of paying someone a standardized wage based upon position in an organizational hierarchy. Rewards accrue in large measure collegially, and in a complex, decentralized fashion. An opportunity to have a voice in collective decision-making, a sense of efficacy and personal importance communicated by one's peers, a belief that hard work is valued and recognized, a feeling of independence (almost an ownership of one's own job), a feeling of met expectations and involvement in the work of the organization—these are the descriptors of professionalized commitment.

We have suggested earlier that the nature of its reward system is one of the major constraints in fostering commitment in education. Seniority and completed graduate work (the two main criteria by which salary improvements are made) are fixed annually in the teacher contract; teacher rewards are not based on instructional performance; and teachers' salaries are comparatively undifferentiated. Traditionally, as Lortie suggests, teachers have found a major opportunity for reward by turning inward toward the classroom—finding intrinsic (psychic) satisfaction in their day-by-day interactions with students.[35] The classroom, a mini-world all of its own, closed off from the rest of the institution, provides the satisfaction of assignments authoritatively delivered and completed, a close tie to the enthusiasms and energies of the young, a chance to direct and observe the maturation of other persons, and a lot of direct feedback (smiles, hugs, and bright thoughts, as well as tears, restlessness, and overt anger).

The culture of the profession places much emphasis upon these service ideals. Teachers are trained to find their work intrinsically satisfying. Nevertheless, in their review of forces credited with the stimulation of increased unionization among teachers in recent decades, Cresswell and Murphy expose some serious chinks in the armor of the cultural ideal.[36] Teachers just entering the profession tend to be less militant than their more experienced colleagues. With experience, teachers become increasingly dissatisfied (although also more conservative, so that there is an initial rise in militancy, then a long, slow decline). With experience, teachers may become painfully aware of their relative economic deprivation in comparison with other jobholders, many of whom have much less formal education.[37] More to the point, it is argued that teacher militancy has tended to grow in response to managerial centralization. Over time, the development of strong management in education (with increased bureaucratization and routinization) has interfered increasingly with teachers' autonomous decisions vis-a-vis the welfare of pupils under their care.[38] Standardized testing, city-wide textbook and workbook adoption, increasingly complex activity scheduling, mushrooming procedural and legal strictures (e.g., guaranteeing due process, equal opportunity, access, and childrens' rights), and a federally funded specialization of teaching roles (e.g., with specialists in reading, bilingualism, and compensatory education, as well as education for the handicapped and for the gifted)—these are just a few of the centralizing trends in recent decades that have played havoc with education's traditional concept of the autonomous teacher receiving joyful reward from his or her focused commitment to a classroom full of lively children.


## FINDING LOYALTY AND SHARED PURPOSE: THREE APPROACHES TO COMMITMENT IN EDUCATION

The maintenance of commitment has become one of the major problems of education.[39] Traditionally, education has been a high-turnover profession. Many people entered the profession, taught for a few years, and left to raise children, to find better-paying jobs, to return to graduate school. There were typically large numbers of annual vacancies to be filled, and salary schedules usually were "front-loaded" to attract applicants. A dramatic reduction in teacher vacancies began in the 1970s and has continued in the 1980s. As a consequence, persons with low levels of commitment may remain in teaching and may find their opportunities for alternative employment steadily eroding. Teaching has developed during the same period into an increasingly stressful occupation. Although the complexities of interaction between stress, job dissatisfaction, absenteeism, and desired professional commitment are not clear, it is believed by many educational administrators that job commitment and many of the pathologies surrounding the profession are closely interwoven.

How then do we find loyalty and shared purpose in education? How can we reclaim the image of the committed educator? In partial answer, let us examine in some detail three alternative conceptualizations of ways in which commitment develops. These are *first*, the notion, from Kanter, that commitment is lodged within the individual, developing specifically out of the sacrifices and investments that individuals make on behalf of the organization; *second*, the suggestion, from Etzioni, that commitment is formed within an interactive "compliance relationship" between individual and organization; and *third*, the idea, from Porter and Miles, that commitment begins with the behavior of the organization—in the ability of the organization to nurture employee responsiveness.


### Kanter: Commitment as Individual Sacrifice and Investment

Rosabeth Moss Kanter has offered an intriguing typology of commitment based on the sacrifices incurred, and investments made, by members of an organization.[40] She suggests that three key elements of commitment are continuance, cohesion, and control. Continuance is a cognitive form of commitment, wherein a person gives himself or herself to a role with the organization in recognition of both the profits and costs associated with ongoing participation. An individual must make sacrifices and investments to maintain membership. There is a price for membership, and ". . . the more it 'costs' a person to do something, the more 'valuable' he or she will have to consider it, in order to justify the psychic 'expense.'"[41] The process of investment (the other side of the coin of sacrifice) gives an individual a stake in the organization's survival. Investment allows a person future gains from present involvement in the form of time, energy, and economic resources. In other words, when profits and costs are considered, many inhabitants find that the costs of leaving the organization would be greater than the cost of remaining in the organization.

The second type of commitment is cohesion. Cohesion is relationship oriented; it involves the emotional attachment of the individual to the group. Affective ties develop that bind members to the organizational community, with gratification derived from membership involvement. Interaction with other organization members is rewarding in itself, so that leaving the organization means leaving people who are important in the member's life. Kanter suggests that two elements of sacrifice tend to work toward cohesion. These are (a) renunciation, which involves relinquishing outside relationships which are potentially disruptive to group cohesion; and (b) communion, wherein a we-sentiment is formed for the group and individual separateness is relinquished and replaced by identification with the collective whole.[42]

The third type of commitment is control, which is an attachment to the norms, values, and inner convictions of the organization. The individual views his or her identity in terms of meeting the ideal conditions set by the system. Obedience to authority becomes a moral necessity. It was the discovery of the moral hollowness of that authority that was so disturbing to Jesse Lambert. Elements of sacrifice in this category of commitment are mortification and surrender. Mortification involves "the submission of private states to social control."[43] The member molds personality, character, or behavior to fit the organization's ideals. Similarly, through surrender a person gives up decision-making prerogatives to the organization.[44]

Kanter's typology of commitment mechanisms emanated from her research into nineteenth-century utopian communities (for example, the Shakers, and the Amana and Oneida colonies), and her analysis reflects the characteristics of these special communities. Nevertheless, Kanter extends her observations beyond utopian societies and concludes that systems employing commitment mechanisms ". . . whether in the specific forms described or in others which serve the same function, should find their participants dedicated, obedient, loyal, and involved. The conceptual framework is potentially useful in analyzing any organization which seeks to establish strong ties with its members, maintain control over behavior, and in general integrate individuals into social systems."[45] Let us apply Kanter's typology to education more explicitly.

**Continuance.**    By this term Kanter described a cognitive commitment to a role based upon the costs and benefits of organizational membership. The educational profession is well known for its sacrifice of financial well-being in the interest of teaching. Although seldom to be found today, common additional sacrifices extracted from teachers in the past were acts of abstinence and austerity not unlike those found in Kanter's utopian communities. Teachers were frequently expected to abstain from smoking, drinking, profanity, dancing, and even marriage. A residue of these attitudes is that an educator is still expected by the larger society to be above reproach, morally and psychologically. Although some teachers today can be tracked to a Friday afternoon bar, conversations there invariably are laced with guilt-edged witticisms about such matters as embarrassing encounters with parents.[46]

Less fully recognized but no less significant are the sacrifices educators make in esteem and social opportunity. Classroom teaching is not a highly regarded occupation in the American culture, relatively speaking, and teachers become accustomed early in their careers to explaining their work to new acquaintances in subdued, near-apologetic tones. Male elementary teachers talk particularly of the quizzical expressions on the faces of persons to whom they're introduced. Said one: "You can just read what they're thinking. 'He's a second-grade teacher? He looks O.K., but there must be something a bit weird about him. Why isn't he at least an administrator or something?'" Reflected this teacher: "It really gets to you after awhile."[47]

Similarly, like policemen and ministers, teachers tend to have a restricted circle of social acquaintances. A cop's friends, and the friends of his family, tend to be other cops and their families. Likewise, educators stick together in a restricted social orbit that sacrifices many of the benefits and opportunities that come out of wider associations. Seldom do the invitations to join the local country club, to partake of a lengthy, expense-account lunch, to join the board of the local symphony orchestra, or to give a keynote speech at Rotary fall to the classroom teacher. Kanter suggests that the more it costs a person to do something, the more valuable he or she will have to consider it in order to justify the expense. We might conclude from the above examples that being a teacher represents a heavy sacrifice and that, by definition, a person who enters and remains in the profession is giving evidence of a deep commitment, marked by considerable sacrifice.

Kanter also suggests, however, that through its collective sacrifices membership should become more "sacred" to organizational participants. Participation in the organization becomes almost an act of "consecration" to its values and objectives. Despite the many sacrifices and the vaunted dedication of the teacher, one would be hard pressed to argue that teaching has been able to measure up to that standard of motivation. Where consecration does seem to appear, the impetus comes from investment rather than sacrifice. Many teachers make consecrated investments in the special problems of inner-city youth, handicapped children, adolescents in general, athletically inclined children, the maladjusted, or the intellectually gifted.

Reputation was recognized by Kanter as an important area of investment toward commitment, and this element seems especially applicable to education. In higher education, particularly, the professoriate is judged openly and harshly on a standard of academic reputation. To attain the rank of full professor an educator is expected by most institutions of higher learning to have obtained a national reputation in his or her special sub-field. A numerical count of the number of times a professorial candidate's work has been cited by other authors can be a critical consideration for promotion, as can be a weighing of positive against negative book or article reviews by unseen colleagues.

Less easily recognized is the importance of reputation to elementary and secondary teachers. In a profession with few objective standards of comparison, reputation looms large in the motivational environment of the classroom teacher. A poor reputation almost invariably accompanies an inability to maintain firm disciplinary control over one's pupils, a failure to respect the autonomy of one's colleagues (e.g., one should never barge into a fellow teacher's classroom while in progress), or an inability to be professionally self-reliant (e.g., one must always handle trouble-some parents oneself without help from the office). A sound reputation accompanies just the opposite of these attributes. It also can be formed via a grapevine-like communication of pupils to parents, parents to teachers, and teachers to one another. "Miss Jones takes a deep interest in her kids." "Mr. Smith works you hard, but he's fair and interesting." "Mrs. Green really knows her stuff." Insufficiently well recognized among school administrators is the importance of helping a young teacher construct a positive reputation and, with that, the investment that builds commitment.

**Cohesion.**    Kanter defines cohesion as an affective attachment of the individual to the group. She suggests that it involves both renunciation (a relinquishing of outside relationships) and communion (a "we-consciousness" within the group). Educators through the years have been most effective at renunciation, by this effort making some gains in "we-consciousness," but traditionally at a loss in responsiveness to the community. Like other professionals, they have attempted to establish insulating boundaries around their work lives. Parents are always to be kept at their distance (e.g., first names are almost never to be exchanged), conflicts inside the school must not be made public, and education should always stay out of politics.

   This four-walls-of-the-school tradition in education served rather effectively over past years to minimize the influence of the local environment upon the school. With clearly established barriers between insiders and outsiders, a special sense of purpose, of togetherness, of "us-against-them" has permeated the profession. Willard Waller captured the mood well in his examination of teaching. Waller writes:

> The typical large school is overridden with . . . institutionalism. The members of the faculty think of themselves as forming a closed group whose interests are sacrosanct; students must take just what the faculty chooses to give them and ask for nothing more; all members of the faculty unite in condemning any attempt to subject the school to control or regulation from the outside.[48]

But times and things have changed. Over the last decade, particularly, the closed institutionalism that appeared so clearly to Waller has given way to a set of much more vulnerable boundaries between school and community. Teachers often work closely now with teacher aides who live in the surrounding neighborhood; parental involvement and advisement is now common (even mandated in many areas of the school curriculum); school districts increasingly encourage parents to visit their schools (even classes in progress) and to volunteer their services; and parents are no longer reluctant to demand an accounting from their local schools. That which Waller saw as sacrosanct is now considered fair game for parents and other outsiders.

   Teachers have also changed their perspectives. Many more female teachers today than in the 1930s are both the mothers of school-age children and full-time teaching professionals. They understand the concerns on both sides of the old wall. And so do many administrators; Ann Denier has walked an interesting tightrope, stretching out (with great respect) to a shifting, heterogeneous school community, even while protecting the religious ideals and practices of her school (as well as her important personal ties to her church and religious community). Many more teachers of both genders are active politically in their communities—even to the point of representing outside interests as a member of a board of education in one local school district while working inside another district as a classroom teacher.

Thus, it would appear that commitment through a renunciation of the outside world may be a declining characteristic of public education. While greater responsiveness may be the gain, a bit of within-group cohesiveness may be the loss. Teachers are no longer able to renounce, or even to separate themselves far from, the pressures of parental concerns, community politics, even national issues (e.g., questions about desegregation, bilingualism, or competency testing). The insulation from outsiders that in the past alienated parents, slowed responsiveness, and frustrated change has yielded today to somewhat more reaction to the larger community, but at a cost in binding, within-group loyalties among classroom teachers as well as groups of administrators.

There is still a strong sense of "we-consciousness" within teaching, but it may reside more today in processes of communion (Kanter's second source of cohesion) than in acts of renunciation. The structural arrangements supporting communion (fellowship and group consciousness) in education are mixed. On the one hand, an equality and homogeneity among members that Kanter considers essential to communion is supported by education's tradition of a single salary scale and nondifferentiated staffing.[49] On the other hand, there is not a heavy press toward group interdependence in teaching. The isolation of the self-contained classroom, an ideology of teacher autonomy, a tradition of self-sufficiency (i.e., teachers do not readily share ideas or methods), and a typically weak articulation between grade levels and separate areas of the school curriculum do not lead easily toward communalism.

One element of communion (to which Kanter gives substantial weight) that does loom large in education is group ritual. The rhythm of work in the school and patterns of relationship among its members are heavily ritualized. An old joke in education is that a teacher who claims fifteen years of experience in classroom teaching is actually displaying one year of experience fifteen times. The truth in this tongue-in-cheek observation is lodged in the essential sameness and predictable regularity of the academic year. The school calendar is established well in advance of each school year, changes little from one year to the next, and provides a common foundation of grading periods, semester breaks, holidays, and teacher in-service days for all members of the school community. Each portion of the school calendar has its own mini-rituals and shared aphorisms about the best way to do the job. Teachers caution one another to be tough at the beginning of the school year, to grade severely and enforce discipline rigidly, and then to ease up later. As the year progresses, the same bulletin board and window displays, classroom slogans, school assembly programs, sports hoopla, band concerts, reports to be filed, and ceremonies to be endured (the Halloween costume contest, the National Merit Society tea) unfold year after year in a steady progression of events that blend together in comfortable, if eventually mundane, predictability.

Teachers come to depend heavily upon this regularity—establishing a symbolic importance of their own to the opportunities for "communion" that education's predictability offers. One of the high school principals in the Morris et al. study of school administrators, for example, complained of her difficulty in rescheduling teaching assignments. A special clique of experienced teachers on the faculty for years had shared an unassigned second period, spending the hour together in the teachers' lounge. In any rearrangement of class schedules, the principal had to take this group into account. For staff harmony, it appeared necessary to keep this coffee group fully alive.[50] Similarly, teachers use the regularity and predictability of the daily schedule and the yearly calendar to establish special social arrangements before class, during lunch, at recess, and after school. The maintenance of ritual extends as well to questions of who teaches in which classroom, whose pupils troop to the library at which period of the day, who supervises which extracurricular activities, and whose class sits in what location in the school auditorium.

Despite the gains in communion that flow out of its ritualized regularity, commitment through cohesion in education is not strong. Teaching, from kindergarten through graduate school, is a lonely job. Despite some efforts at team teaching, educators are essentially isolated from collegial interaction much of their working day. Privacy and autonomy are respected more than togetherness; the ties produced by good fellowship are not tight; and structural arrangements permit togetherness (e.g., a cup of coffee in the lounge) only at odd moments in the daily routine. Although some educational administrators recognize fully the importance of ceremony, and thus plan astutely for faculty picnics, dinner dances, and golf outings, the tradition of communal sharing is not deeply entrenched in education. We contend that throughout the profession the self has decided preeminence over the group.

**Control.** By this special sense of control, we mean an evaluative commitment of the individual to the organization. An individual becomes attached and obedient to the norms of the social environment, seeing himself or herself as "carrying out the dictates of a higher-order system."[51] Kanter suggests that control involves both mortification (the submission of individual identity to social control) and surrender (an attachment of decision-making prerogatives to a greater power). Both terms as Kanter describes them seem much more appropriate in the religious or monastic environment than education. Mortification "strips away" aspects of an individual's own identity, emphasizing the individual's smallness before the greatness of the organization and making him dependent upon the authority of the organization for direction. In surrender, the individual personally experiences the "great power and meaning residing in the organization," imbuing the social system with rightness and certainty—even a bit of institutionalized awe.[52]

Educators have rarely been known to lose their own identities in their service to the organization, and certainly they have not stood often in awe of the great power and meaning of the surrounding institution. Jesse Lambert is a particularly good example of this point. Nevertheless, there are elements of both mortification and surrender in the educator's world. The student teaching experience, in particular, is notoriously mortifying. Teachers remember for the rest of their professional lives, and recount terrifying tales to one another about the first few days and weeks on their own in a classroom. The experience is too devastating for many, and it is at this point in their training that prospective teachers frequently decide not to enter the profession after all. For others, student teaching is a frightening yet exhilarating challenge—replete with pupils gleefully sharpening their skills of student gamesmanship; supervising teachers looking continuously for new ways to test a novice's creativity and adaptability; and university supervisors seated in grim-visaged appraisal at the back of the classroom. At this point of extreme uncertainty at the beginning of one's career, teachers are most acutely aware of their need for assistance—of their dependence upon significant, professional others. Some receive help, while others do not. The power of mortification as an important step towards the development of commitment lies in the power of its regenerative force, as the individual, in submission, turns to others for help. For those who receive help, some binding ties may be forged. A novice may for the rest of his life pattern his own teaching on the model of a helpful older colleague, may return to that colleague over the years with problems and self-doubts, and may continue to keep in touch with this early mentor throughout a long and varied career. Jesse Lambert spoke with pride about his transition into such a mentoring role.

In general, however, the profession offers little in the way of ongoing, emotional rebuilding. The trial of student teaching is typically followed by an equally mortifying first year on the job. Although educators have experimented fleetingly with buddy systems and sensitivity training, mechanisms for sharing weaknesses, failings, doubts, and innermost concerns about the job do not represent a solid tradition within the profession. The process of socialization into teaching provides more than enough mortification, but perhaps insufficient regeneration into sets of binding ties with and loyalty towards the collectivity.

The situation is quite similar with respect to the mechanism of surrender. Kanter suggests that "institutionalized awe" lies at the heart of surrender. Ideological systems and structural arrangements provide a sense of rightness, of certainty about the demands and commands of the organization. Individuals submit to the organization as they would to "the will of God." Institutionalized awe may be reinforced by increasing the distance and mystery of the decision-making process for ordinary members—through an authority hierarchy well insulated from lower-level membership, through special leadership prerogatives, through an irrational basis for many decisions (e.g., intuition, magic, inspiration), and through a dependence upon charisma as a form of leadership.

Interestingly, institutionalized awe may be more a force in the surrender of the individual to collective authority in higher education than in elementary and secondary education. The arcane process of promotion and tenure within the college or university frequently defies rationality, inspires much fear but also much attachment to the mysterious ways of the collegiality, and roots itself in a centuries-old ideological tradition of a granting of special privilege within a closed system of trial-by-academic-fire and colleague review. Good administrative leadership in higher education, furthermore, probably depends more upon charisma than any other single brand of authority. With its extremes of professional independence, academic freedom, and traditionally weak management, the college or university leans heavily toward the dean, the vice-chancellor, or the president who can inspire respect (even awe) among the faculty; who combines a national reputation as a scholar with the administrative role; and who can articulate objectives eloquently and negotiate their attainment brilliantly within the institution's highly verbal environment.

Thus, while neither mortification nor surrender can be claimed to be strong motivators in education, it appears that elements of both are present. The socialization of beginning teachers provides mortification often without a careful attention to the regeneration that can evolve out of a new attachment to the social norms of the group. And surrender is a not-improbable explanation of the collegial conformity found in higher education among individuals well known historically for their independence and nonconformity.

In summary, we see that Rosabeth Kanter's conceptualization of commitment as an outgrowth of acts of sacrifice and investment provides some important insights into present-day schooling. A valuable historical tradition in the profession has been a notion of commitment that is captured in our classic image of the occupation. Teachers are underpaid and held in low esteem; thus only the most committed of persons are likely to undertake this work. The notion of a special calling to the profession (e.g., "Mary was born to be a teacher") probably always has been overblown. Nevertheless, both sacrifice and investment remain powerful forces in the profession even today. Educators do make large endowments in their jobs (in the children, in the community, in the subject-area of instruction, in their reputations). Teachers have a strong sense of job ownership—speaking often of *their* classrooms, *their* kids, and taking pride in the accomplishments of *their* former students.

This interplay of self-sacrifice and investment is duplicated in Kanter's other approaches to commitment. While the profession seems today to be less closed than in earlier decades, less able to renounce the outside environment, the opportunities for increased communion and control through shared ritual and careful socialization (complete with mortification) are still present and still worth investigating in considerable depth. Although the concept of organizational commitment desperately needs additional, systematic research, there is much evidence in the available literature that many of the special quirks, rules, hazing rites, standard operating procedures, forms of behavior, and long-standing customs of institutions are linked with the need to move employee individuality toward employee commitment. In the 1950s, William F. Whyte described the organization man who had left home, spiritually and physically, to take vows of organizational life.[53] Coser identified greedy institutions that call for undivided commitment from their members by erecting symbolic boundaries between their members and the outside world.[54] Rohlen described the role of company education and training programs in Japan in furthering harmonious relations, company loyalty, high morale, and in integrating the individual "into the ways of the company."[55] Similarly, Deal and Kennedy illustrated how rituals of social exchange govern relationships in corporations. The rituals

> specify how formally or informally individuals are addressed, the long-standing customs that govern conversation, how much emotion or public controversy is permitted, who speaks first in meetings, and who is permitted to end a conversation. . . . Employees learn these rules, in part, through hazing rites that are staged to tear people down before accepting them into a culture.[56]

And Scott and Becker have argued further that the professions generally have compelling ideologies and develop commitment to their values through a lengthy socialization period.[57]

Nevertheless, we are left with the observation that Kanter's model, with its focus upon the sacrifices and investments incurred by the *employee*, leaves something vital out of the equation. Teachers complain that they sacrifice much and invest substantially but secure little evidence that other persons (e.g., students, parents, board members, administrators) are as fully committed *to them*. The tendency of teachers to complain (much as the infantrymen in an army battalion do) and to be occasionally insatiable in their searching for praise and reassurance, may be linked to a perception of one-sided, imbalanced commitment as a hallmark of the profession of education.

## Etzioni: Commitment as a Compliance Relationship

Amitai Etzioni offers, alternatively, a conceptualization of commitment that is rooted in relationships, in (a) the orientations of personnel toward the employing organization (i.e., their "involvement" in the organization) and (b) the kinds of power resources that are utilized by the organization vis-a-vis its personnel. The associations between the power applied and the involvement of lower-level participants represent *compliance relationships*.[58] Again, there is a key distinction between the Etzioni and Kanter typologies that must be noted here. Kanter sees commitment as rather predominantly lodged within the individual, in response to behavioral requirements that emanate from the dominating organization. In contrast, Etzioni views commitment as much more of an exchange relationship. Both individual and organization bring something to trade. The organization seeks to control behavior, but it must contend with employee receptivity (or "orientation"). Employee orientations are not fixed; they run along a continuum of involvement from alienation to commitment with the consequence that the application of power by the organization will have different meanings for different employees. For example, if an employee's orientation is mildly alienated, he or she may display less compliance to organizational directives that employ only symbolic rewards (e.g., a letter of thanks for a job well done) than would an employee who is mildly committed and thus more positively predisposed toward compliance.

**The Importance of Involvement.**    Members of organizations will vary in their involvement in their employing institutions. These orientations can be placed along a scale of negative to positive involvement, as shown in Figure 6.3. For Etzioni, positive involvement is labeled commitment, and negative involvement is termed alienation. Positive commitment of high intensity may be termed *moral involvement*

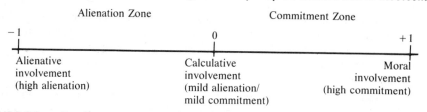

FIGURE 6.3    Involvement

Adapted from Amitai Etzioni, "Compliance Structures," in A. Etzioni and E.W. Lehman, eds., *A Sociological Reader on Complex Organizations*, 3rd ed. (New York: Holt, Rinehart and Winston, 1980): pp. 90–91.

—where an employee has fully internalized institutional norms and an identification with authority or an employee is fully sensitive to the social pressures of colleague groups. Alienation of high intensity is labeled *alienative involvement*—an individual is fully alienated from his or her respective organization. Inmates in prison, prisoners of war, or people in concentration camps are examples of organizational participants who would fall into this category. *Calculative involvement* describes either negative or positive orientations of low intensity. An individual may be either mildly alienated or mildly committed to the organization and is, in this state, particularly sensitive to the inducements offered by upper-level actors.

**The Play of Power.**   While Kanter tends to conceptualize commitment in all-or-nothing terms, Etzioni recognizes that individuals are seldom either fully committed to or fully alienated from their organizations. Most are in that calculative state where some kind of an association between involvement and organizational inducements is possible. Calculative involvement is based upon exchanges between members and the organization, similar to the inducement-contributions theory offered by March and Simon.[59] People will respond calculatively, out of self-interest, to the application of power by persons who are higher in rank within the organization.

Etzioni suggests that the means by which participants are manipulated through the application of power to support organizational purposes include physical, material, and symbolic rewards and deprivations.[60] Specifically, three kinds of power are specified: (a) *coercive power*, which refers to physical means to secure compliance and "rests on the application, or threat of application, of physical sanctions"; (b) *remunerative power*, which refers to material means to secure compliance, using control of "material resources and rewards through the allocation of salaries and wages, commissions, fringe benefits, services, and commodities"; and (c) *normative power*, which refers to the manipulation of esteem, prestige, and ritualistic symbols or the allocation and manipulation of acceptance. Esteem, prestige, and ritualistic symbols are transferred through hierarchical relationships in the organization. The manipulation of acceptance, on the other hand, is more common among participants equal in rank in the organization and is known as social power. Etzioni notes that social power becomes organizational power only when the organization can influence a group's use of power—for example, when a teacher gets class members to use their influence to bring a misbehaving student in line.[61]

Most organizations, notes Etzioni, will employ coercive, renumerative, and normative power; however, most organizations will also tend to emphasize one and rely much less on the other two. When two of these kinds of power are emphasized at the same time, they tend to neutralize each other. The application of force may create so much alienation, for example, that it becomes impossible to use normative power successfully. Thus, traditional prisons rarely achieve successful rehabilitation. Similarly, the use of remunerative power may make it more difficult to appeal fruitfully to idealistic (purely normative) motives. That is not to suggest that an organization should use *only* one of the three major forms of control; the point, rather, is one of relative emphasis. As Etzioni illustrates, the church has more power over the priest than the average parishioner because the priest is controlled by normative and remunerative power while the parishioner is subject to normative power only.[62]

Although Etzioni addresses himself infrequently to education, his analysis of the interplay between power and involvement offers some food for thought to those who study and work in schools. Public elementary and secondary schools employ a healthy dose (some say an overdose) of coercive control. When Jesse Lambert showed the law to segregated local school districts, the coercive power of the federal government was only lightly veiled. Compulsory attendance laws provide the backdrop, while a full panoply of local codes and rules fills in the details of restriction upon students. Teachers, furthermore, typically picture themselves as *teachers* —employed to provide instruction, to guide learning. They consider themselves coerced rather than remunerated when asked to fill out student records, respond to administrative requests for information, serve on committees, take tickets at a school dance, or attend PTA meetings.[63]

Remunerative power figures heavily, too, in the lives of both students and teachers. From their earliest days of school, pupils are trained to expect and to strive for the material rewards of teacher praise, good grades, certificates of accomplishment, special words of recognition, stars on a chart, and diplomas. Furthermore, most come to believe that time spent in learning as a youngster will be rewarded generously with the later-in-life benefits of a good job, steadily increasing income, prestige, and a productive and comfortable future. For teachers, the importance of material rewards has become more salient in recent decades, with the result that such matters as class size, teaching load, pupil discipline policy, teacher evaluation procedures, and leave-of-absence policies are added to salary and fringe-benefit considerations in a steadily growing package of issues which are subject to remunerative negotiation between a teachers union and the organization. Much of what in an earlier era might have been considered a normative part of the job (e.g., teachers will direct the extracurricular offerings of the school) is now the subject of careful negotiation toward material reward.

Nevertheless, normative power remains a forceful control mechanism in the public school environment. Among pupils the peer subculture has a strong hold upon behavior—posing a sometimes impenetrable barrier against the rules, rewards, and normative attractions that are offered by the school (e.g., the teacher as a positive role model, adult recognition and acceptance, parental approval).[64] Similarly, teachers are caught between the normative demands of the profession, the organization, and their immediate colleagues. The profession may tell a teacher to be child-centered, to be warm and nurturing, to help children feel good about themselves in school. However, the employing organization may ask teachers to be subject-centered, to organize the presentation of curricular material carefully, and to guide student achievement toward system-wide goals. Fellow teachers, in contrast, may make it clear that they expect their colleagues to be control-centered, to maintain effective discipline, to be in firm control over their pupils, and to assist other teachers in keeping students well in check.

Thus, all three forms of control over lower-level participants emphasized by Etzioni seem to be present in publicly supported educational organizations. Which is predominant? What are the effects when coercion, remuneration, and the normative are combined? One possible explanation for the elaborate grouping, tracking, placement, and subdividing that occurs in schools is that these allocations of the student clientele permit the organization to match different forms of control with differences in the state of student involvement.[65] The most alienated among the students may receive the closest, most coercive, most watchful attention. The large block of pupils inhabiting the calculative realm of involvement are enticed toward goal accomplishment through widely varying forms of remuneration (grades, the "better" classes, positions of student leadership, special recognition). And, for the highly committed, the institution may respond with honors classes, much individual freedom of movement, special contributory job assignments, and substantial teacher attention.

**Congruence.**    Interestingly, the long tradition and continued strength of private schooling (despite the greater cost to its clients) may lie in some considerable measure in the greater ability of the private school to match form of control with the predominant state of lower-participant involvement. Parents may select a school for their children because of its strict discipline, its attention to traditional education, its religiosity, or its innovativeness. The appeal of this differentiation is apparent in the efforts of educators (particularly those serving urban districts) to provide the same merger of control and involvement in the public sector—with special-purpose schools, alternative schools, and, more recently, magnet schools. There is a congruence between the prevailing mode of institutional control and the predilections of its participants, which could be expanded to include teachers and administrators as well.

Etzioni suggests that power and involvement in interaction constitute a "compliance relationship" (see Figure 6.4). Combining three kinds of involvement with three kinds of power produces nine types of compliance. Some of these types of compliance are *congruent*, in that the kinds of involvement that "tend to be generated by the predominant form of organizational power are the same."[66] Other compliance types are *incongruent*. Remuneration, for example, may be wasted if lower-level participants are highly alienated and therefore not inclined to respond to material incentives; or if coercive power is applied to highly committed participants, the effect may be to alienate them somewhat from the organization.

The messages for schools in Etzioni's typology of compliance relationships are not clear. Hodgkins and Herriott used the typology to study student compliance relationships to age-grade structure and the goals of schools.[67] They noted that as the goal of schooling changes from an instrumental orientation to the transmission of knowledge and skills, the compliance structure changes in emphasis from coercive to normative. They suggest that the shift in emphasis is evident in the importance attached to academic performance versus general behavior in schools. At the elementary level, the problem child is one who misbehaves and acts immaturely, whereas at the secondary level the problem child is likely to be the underachiever.

Different scholars have argued somewhat convincingly on different occasions that student compliance is predominantly normative,[68] utilitarian,[69] and coercive.[70] Compliance can be considered normative because authority in the school is based on the manipulation of esteem, prestige, and other symbols, by virtue of the students' moral involvement. Students accept the legitimacy of the norms governing their conduct within the context of the school and the student work agenda. On the other hand, a utilitarian compliance structure also operates. Students endure school work to secure tangible rewards—to get good grades, be accepted into the right college, or

KINDS OF INVOLVEMENT

|  | | Alienative | Calculative | Moral |
|---|---|---|---|---|
| **KINDS OF POWER** | Coercive | 1<br>Coercive<br>compliance | 2 | 3 |
| | Remunerative | 4 | 5<br>Utilitarian<br>compliance | 6 |
| | Normative | 7 | 8 | 9<br>Normative<br>compliance |

Numbers 1, 5, and 9 are identified as congruent types of power and involvement. They are found more frequently in organizations, and they are believed to be most effective. The other six are called incongruent types and are believed to be less effective.

*FIGURE 6.4*      Compliance relationships

Adapted with permission of the Free Press, a Division of Macmillan, Inc. from *A Comparative Analysis of Complex Organizations* by Amitai Etzioni. Copyright © 1961 by The Free Press.

obtain a high-paying job in their choosen occupation—in return for their involvement in, and submission to, the authority of the organization. Finally, because of compulsory schooling laws, students are coerced into school membership, at least until a certain age. There are important consequences for the organization: public schools get unselected clients. Carlson suggests that the school organization adapts to this situation by segregating clients or showing preferential treatment to some. The student, also, adapts through what he calls situational retirement or side payments —the school is a place where he/she can engage in other activities.[71]

Teachers, similarly, are not easily categorized. There is, as we have discussed earlier, a strong normative component in the profession. Teachers have been known historically for their high levels of commitment and (consistent with Etzioni) for their resistance to coercive forms of administration. Nevertheless, the profession has moved decidedly in recent decades toward collective bargaining and a calculative-remunerative (i.e., utilitarian) relationship between teachers and organization. Normative controls seem to be increasingly out of touch with modern demands for a clear indication (in contractural terms) of staff members' duties and their accompanying monetary rewards. Still more confusing, however, is the evidence of a significant level of high alienation (in the form of job stress, absenteeism, and "burnout") within the profession. Exit and re-entry into teaching traditionally has been quite easy. This is not the case any longer. Increasingly, some teachers feel trapped in their jobs—effectively coerced into staying with employment that they would prefer to leave.

In concluding his remarks on compliance, Etzioni suggests that organizations tend over time to shift their compliance structures from incongruent to congruent types.[72] It would appear that educational organizations have moved decidedly from normative compliance toward the more incentive-loaded state of utilitarian compliance (see Figure 6.4). With the current interest in merit pay and differentiated staffing, this form of the compliance relationship appears to be acquiring even greater importance.[73] Beyond this shift, however, there are some interesting hints that a more coercive compliance relationship may be in the offing for teachers. Contemporary citizen dissatisfaction with school quality has produced many suggestions for more rigorous state controls over teacher training and job entry, tighter evaluation standards and procedures, and a close monitoring of teacher effectiveness in terms of student achievement. Whatever the trend, the key point from Etzioni is that commitment is not generated solely out of the directives and actions of the employing organization, but by those which are in line with the internalized conditions (the state of involvement) of the employee.[74]

Thus, we see that Etzioni's model of commitment has much more of a negotiative perspective than Kanter's. For Kanter it is the employee who acts (through sacrifice and investment) in supplying commitment to the organization. The employee finds loyalty and shared purpose in surrendering to the goals, ideals, and values of the larger whole. The organization uses obedience norms, socialization processes, and in-group acceptance/fellowship as the means to produce (even demand) individual commitment. Etzioni no less than Kanter is interested in the compliance of the individual vis-a-vis the organization, but sees commitment as the product of a compliance *relationship*, rather than one-sided acquiescence. The organization has differing types of power and incentives available to it, but the individual brings a decision concerning his or her own *involvement* that will fit some usages of power and not others. Most individuals act somewhere within a calculative state of employee involvement, where loyalty and shared purpose must be induced (Etzioni) rather than demanded (Kanter).

## Porter and Miles: Commitment as Nurturance

Our third approach completes the swing from individual to organization—turning the notion of sacrifice on its ear to suggest that organizational commitment to the individual must be the starting point. The *nurturance* of employee behaviors (rather than either exchange or sacrifice) is seen here as the key to commitment.

Interestingly, this seemingly most recent of approaches to commitment has its roots in some of the oldest contributions to organizational theory. Employee motivation is one of the most venerable, frequently addressed, and hotly debated topics in the literature on administrative responsibility. At the turn of the century, it was believed that working men and women were sustained in their performance by the quest for reward and the fear of retribution. Workers were seen as responsive to a simple, straightforward carrot-and-stick formula. One of the most successful of all movements in administration was Frederick W. Taylor's scientific management approach, in which employee tasks were defined minutely and programmed for maximum efficiency, and employees then well-rewarded monetarily for high productivity. In short, said Taylor, workers can be trained by administrators to work well and hard—and they will do so if paid adequately for productive effort.[75]

Taylorism spawned a counter-movement in administrative theory that suggested the human element in organizations was being sorely neglected. Workers do not always perform at top effort for a larger paycheck; they have many other needs and interests that should (even must) be attended to if best effort is to result. Among these may be a feeling that the work they do is appreciated or is significant, a sense that they have some control over their own work, a bit of variety in the job, warm relations with co-workers, and feelings of job security.

One of the most powerful and most frequently cited theories of motivation flowing out of this human relations counter-movement was Abraham Maslow's needs hierarchy model. Maslow defined five levels of basic human needs. Lower-level needs may start with the essential physiological motivators of hunger, sleep, thirst, and the like. Progressively higher-level needs to be satisfied are a sense of safety and security; feelings of belongingness, love, and social activity; esteem; and self-actualization or self-fulfillment. The higher-level needs emerge as lower-level needs become satisfied, and organizations must be aware that the higher-order needs of esteem and self-actualization will emerge more strongly as the needs hierarchy is progressively satisfied.[76] In short, contrary to Taylorist assumptions, we become ever more human as workers, requiring *more* rather than less attention to motivational forces, as the needs satisfied by a larger paycheck are met. Well fed by the carrot, we now move toward desiring a share in deciding where to put the carrot patch, when to plant, how often to pick, and to whom to distribute the harvest of carrots.

One of the most popular administrative applications of human relations theory over the years has been Douglas McGregor's conceptualizations of Theory X and Theory Y. Theory X administrators believe implicitly that workers are lazy and disinterested in their jobs; they must be coerced by threats (the stick) or bribed by wages (the carrot) to give a day's work for a day's pay. Theory Y administrators believe that people are psychologically invested in their jobs. They are not lazy; they want to make a contribution to the organization; and, in Maslow's terms, they will respond positively to the satisfaction of higher-level needs.[77]

The human relations counter-movement has itself come under much philosophical and empirical attack. There are now many more-recent theories of work motivation,[78] and McGregor's theories have been criticized as rather naive and oversimplified misinterpretations of organizational reality. Few employees fit either Theory X or Theory Y definitions; more often they are combinations of both. Similarly, few organizations are best administered by either Theory Y or Theory X administrators; administrators need to be masters of both strategies. And, most recently, of course, Theories X and Y have been countered by Theory Z—a proposal that the organization can be treated productively as a clan, with administrative emphasis upon consensus-building and community.[79]

The result is that we still do not know or agree enough about motivating employee commitment in complex organizations. What moves a worker to act or not to act? It is not enough to think philosophically of the generic characteristics of human nature. This line of thinking has not been particularly fruitful in understanding man in the workplace. The modern worker may or may not be a rational creature, but certainly the modern complex organization has been found to be nonrational many times over. What moves a worker to act may be rooted in human nature, but that stimulus moves through a complex interactive system with characteristics of individual personality, the job, the work environment, and the external environment of the workplace.[80] Each worker in a large organization is part of a larger whole, a conglomerate of people, departments, goals, and environments. Each worker is also a member of an immediate work setting—an office, a district, a school—with an immediate superior. One of the tasks of this immediate superior is to find out what moves workers to act both responsibly and effectively, and then to guide them.

If the workplace is a public school in a large, complex educational system, the workers are teachers, and the immediate superior is a local school administrator. What spur and reins are available to get the teachers to begin their work and guide them subsequently? Clark and McKibbon framed the question this way: "Can superintendents, principals, or university deans control the productivity of teachers and faculty? Should they be able to if they cannot? Surely they cannot. But are some administrators more successful at stimulating productivity than others? Unquestionably. What makes the difference?"[81] Here the answers stop. It is not easy to find out what moves workers to act and then to influence them. But it is known that some administrators do it and others do not.

A modern approach to motivation that is more consistent than previous models with the complexity of individual-organization relationships is expectancy theory (discussed earlier in Chapter 5). Expectancy theory, simply put, suggests that motivation is enhanced if people place value in their work and believe that hard work will be rewarded and that top-level performance can be achieved within the organizational context.[82] The burden for the administrator is clear. The commitment reflected in hard work or concerted effort is heavily dependent upon evidence that rewards and the means to achieve valued outcomes are available. If one works hard and finds little reward, or if one finds avenue after avenue toward goal accomplishment blocked (e.g., by red tape, insensitive colleagues, bureaucratic inertia, or "turf" protection), then commitment is likely to be a short-lived affair. The suggestion is that administrative success may flow in large measure from turning the direction of commitment around—portraying a standard of organizational commitment that carries, in turn, a payoff of employee motivation. In short, employee commitment can be an outgrowth of efforts by administrators to *nurture* members' loyalty and shared purpose rather than to demand it (sacrifice) or negotiate it (compliance).

Lyman Porter and Raymond Miles have developed a classification system of variables involved in the management of employee motivation as nurturance. That system includes *individual attitudes, job characteristics, work environment characteristics*, and *external environment characteristics*. Like Etzioni, Porter and Miles point out that employee commitment is affected by what individuals bring to their work situations; and like Kanter, they recognize that what individuals do in their work situations (e.g., acts leading to surrender, mortification, renunciation, communion, etc.) builds commitment. An added ingredient from Porter and Miles, however, is the further suggestion that what happens to the individual in the work situation is a centrally motivating force.[83] Furthermore, it is particularly the array of attitudes and behaviors exhibited by an organization's many managers (e.g., the nurturing required to integrate individual goals into those of the organization) that both guides and displays the organization's commitment to its employees.[84]

**Individual Attitudes.**   First, educational administrators can influence employee commitment by affecting the individual attitudes brought to the work situation.

Educators, from elementary school teachers through university instructors, undergo a long process of professional socialization. Unfortunately, unlike other professions, the formal process of learning-the-ropes tends to stop at the schoolhouse doors.[85]

Quite typically, the beginning teacher or the beginning college instructor is left to fend for himself or herself in the anxiety-laden process of locating a comfortable niche within the organization. Many flounder. Quite often a young, untenured assistant professor uses up three or more of the six years preceding an up-or-out tenure review in simply trying to become acclimated to the professorial role. Some institutions demand collegialism and careful attention to one's committee work; others emphasize fund-raising, placing a heavy value upon externally supported research; still others expect a steady outpouring of published articles in scholarly, refereed journals; while another group may eschew monastic scholarship in favor of the public service role of translating theory into workable practice. Seldom are the expectations communicated openly, in advance, or in clear-cut language. They must be learned subtly, over time. Sometimes the expectations of a college faculty are imbedded within warring factions of the professoriate, and a young instructor can spend his or her entire period of untenured, probationary service responding to clues from an out-of-power faction, thus losing tenure.

In exploring on-the-job socialization, John Van Maanen stresses the enormity of the process that faces the organizational newcomer. Although individuals often may be unaware of the socialization that they are experiencing, in fact, a rather all-encompassing reinterpretation of social reality must be undertaken. For a newcomer, even time can be problematic. When should one take a coffee break, leave work, chat a bit with colleagues, or report for work in the morning? Is there a best time to bother the school principal? Can one take a quick, working lunch or do collegial norms require a more leisurely, business-forgotten interlude with fellow teachers? Beyond the use of time, newcomers must also learn such things as labels, or the categories used by organizational members in referring to clients; work descriptions (the members' own rather than organizational definitions of institutional mission); and accounts, members' own interpretations of why things happen in the organization (e.g., "kids from that neighborhood are all troublesome").[86]

Just as individuals must learn (become socialized into) the expectations of their organizations, those who serve in administrative roles must be aware that their employees approach the organization with expectations and attitudes of their own. Commitment can be nurtured if the administrator succeeds in merging the two. A school principal, for example, can become familiar with teachers' expectations concerning advancement, achievement, and affiliation. Some teachers require more encouragement than others. Some may require assistance and understanding in handling children with learning disabilities or children with cultural backgrounds different from their own (quite clearly an issue for Anne Denier in her United-Nations-like high school). Other teachers, particularly new recruits, may need intensive socialization into the norms and standards of the institution. McPherson and Crowson observe that "the initial identification of, assistance to, and experiential training provided to persons with advancement potential rests typically with a principal who first takes an interest in and 'brings' someone along."[87]

**Job Characteristics.**    Second, educational administrators can affect commitment by influencing job characteristics. This may be a difficult realm for exerting influence, since organizational structures and goals influence the design of jobs. However, job characteristics which are thought to be important are (a) measurability of individual performance, (b) degree of goal clarity, and (c) degree of job challenge.

While performance criteria and evaluation schemes are complex to design, difficult to implement, and notoriously absent or haphazard in large school systems, still an administrator might attempt to generate guidelines for performance at the local level. Teachers can be enlisted in developing tangible performance criteria with which they might be willing to experiment, if not live.

The pursuit of goal clarity, while not without its dilemmas, is another avenue by which the school administrator can influence motivational processes among workers. Although large, complex school systems pursue diffuse and conflicting goals, this need not result in the administrator succumbing to role conflict and role ambiguity in his or her own professional career. The vagueness and intangibility of organizational goals can be overlooked in favor of establishing "goal crispness" at the local level.[88] While the larger school system flounders in goal diffusion, principals and teachers in the local school can rally with strength and determination around objectives which they establish for their own particular situation. Principals must provide support, encouragement, and feedback if the goals are really to be classified at this level.

Job challenge may not be a variable easily manipulatable by school administrators, for they cannot control the intrinsic nature of the task of teaching. However, administrators can guard against teachers slipping into narrow-minded bureaucratic roles. Further, they can try to bridge, or at least not exacerbate, the gap which exists inevitably between routine and idealism. In many ways, despite the enormity of the task, the nurturance of employees toward the acceptance of a special challenge in their work can be among the most commitment-producing of all administrative endeavors. How does one go about doing this? For some persons jobs take on special significance if there is a bit of gamesmanship involved. Morris et al., for example, found school principals gleefully involved in a bureaucratic chess game with the employing organization—taking pride in out-maneuvering the hierarchy and in beating the odds by garnering extra resources for their schools while the board of education was simultaneously cutting budgets back.[89]

Other persons find a challenge in the pursuit of specific, laudable goals. Watching one's physics students receive scholarships to stiffly competitive institutes of technology, producing a winning debate team, helping inner-city youngsters gain admission to top-notch colleges, keeping potential dropouts in school—these have always been among the most inspiring of rewards for teachers. Too often, though, the ideals that permeate the profession are lost in the bureacratic shuffle. They need not be. Malcolm Rutter and his research colleagues found that the simple expedient of displaying examples of the best in student work (e.g., poetry, essays, sculpture, exam papers, drawings) all around the secondary school that they observed, was among the strongest of motivators for students and faculty alike.[90]

Finally, still other persons find a challenge in resolving predicaments and in helping others solve personal or professional problems. Among the most rewarding of administrative efforts can be the knowledge that a classroom teacher has been helped to feel good about improved teaching, or that a serious dispute between factions of the school faculty has been amicably resolved. The resolution of such problems can be communicated as a challenge successfully overcome by superior and subordinate alike.

**Work Environment Characteristics.**   Third, school administrators can affect commitment by manipulating work environment characteristics. The central office of a school district is responsible for the provision of school system rewards, such as salary and health benefits. Local school administrators cannot efficiently control or monitor these organizational actions. Building principals learn to accept deficiencies in these areas. Areas of the work environment over which school administrators have leverage in motivating workers, besides the pursuit of local objectives, include personal significance reinforcement, stability of expectations, and reference group experiences.[91] The overarching organization offers no clear-cut performance indicators. Neither does it recognize teachers' contributions to the organization in any significant way. School administrators shoulder responsibility for reinforcing teachers' sense of personal significance. They must make teachers feel a link between their contributions and the success of the organization. It may be difficult, if not impossible, to make teachers feel like valued members of the organization in situations where system-wide actions seem geared to destroying attitudes of personal significance, such as in times of involuntary transfer. At these times, the school administrator, like the priest whose only recourse when comforting a victim of calamity is to resort to reliance on faith, may be able to offer nothing but a reminder of the missionary roots of the teaching profession. But there are small, unobtrusive ways in which principals can attend to what McPherson and Crowson called the "welfare needs" of teachers:

> Time spent, for example, in "shaking" missing checks out of a downtown payroll office, assisting teachers in obtaining corrections in payment (e.g.,getting paid for the correct number of disability leave days), and "covering" for teachers who need a day off (beyond the number of personal leave days that are usually permitted) are just a few of the welfare actions of the principal.[92]

Stability of expectations, too, is not subject to local school administrators' control, for it involves the frequency with which the central office switches missions or programs. This may come with each new change in office, or even more frequently. Revisions in reading or math programs, the addition of special programs, the establishment of new methods of keeping records, and new procedures come to be seen as the transitory traffic of central-office ideas out in the schools. Teachers are not likely to respond with intense loyalty, and principals must effectively screen directives from the central office and decide which ones teachers can ignore.[93] With this action the principal becomes both a protector and a colleague willing to share consequences.

**External Environment Characteristics.**   The fourth major category which Porter and Miles identified as affecting workers' commitment includes external environment characteristics, that is, demographic, economic, technological, and political characteristics. Weick suspected that "schools are *not* like other organizations, and, consequently, they need to be managed differently."[94] Changes in the outer environment may not follow easily discernible patterns. Not only are school administrators unable to control external environment characteristics, but the organization itself cannot avoid the impact of the outer environment. School site-level administrators, in fact, may be better able to monitor the immediate school community than their central office counterparts are able to monitor the larger society. School administrators must mediate the effect of ambiguous public expectations, particularly for teachers who desire stability and consistency. They must be able to create a shared sense of direction when the outer environment pulls the members of the organization in different directions. In a sense, then, principals become interpreters of both the organization and the outer environment, and from a different vantage point this is also true of superintendents. Administrators need to be concerned with continual resocialization of teachers as they are beset by society's frequent redefinition of educational values. According to Weick, the effective principal must "centralize the organization on selected issues that define the organization, what it stands for, what it can do in its environment, what its boundaries are, what it defends, and who its allies and enemies are."[95] By holding the organization in perspective, keeping the outer environment at bay, and mustering teachers with a shared sense of direction, administrators provide the best possible conditions for sustaining high teacher performance.

## CHAPTER SUMMARY

There is a strong sense that the bonds between the individual and the organization which are termed commitment are vitally important to education. Although the image of the self-sacrificing educator (like that of the family physician who tirelessly made house calls) has been modified over time by teacher militancy, commitment nevertheless remains topmost in a rank-ordering of values in the profession. Educators are supposed to be highly committed. We depend upon their commitment. When there is evidence that they are not, we search for ways to develop it.

The development of commitment is not an easy task at all. Despite its apparent importance, the concept is neither well understood nor consistently and effectively employed in field settings. Within education, a commitment to one's profession or to one's clients may conflict with a commitment to one's employing organization. The commitment of the neophyte may take a far different form from that of the veteran educator. The relationship between commitment and productivity is unclear. Do the most committed teachers tend to be the best teachers? We don't really know. The rewards that sustain commitment over time are not readily apparent. Is the joy of teaching strong enough reward in itself over the long haul? The optimal amount of commitment is not known (too much commitment may be as damaging as too little); and even the direction of commitment is in question. How much commitment *from* the organization fits best with commitment of the individual *to* the organization? To be sure, there are many more questions than answers.

In this chapter we have suggested three different conceptualizations of a commitment relationship between educational organizations and their members. The first, based upon Rosabeth Moss Kanter's conclusions from the study of utopian communities, finds commitment in the behavior requirements (sacrifices) that are imposed upon the members of the organization. Such socializing practices as mortification, renunciation, communion, and surrender bind the individual firmly and comfortingly to the social group. In the second model of commitment, Amitai Etzioni's description of compliance relationships shows the importance of an interplay between the organization's application of control and the individual's receptivity. Some individuals serve within the organization at a higher level of involvement than others. For these persons symbolic rewards (a pat on the back, a letter of thanks) may produce willing and ready compliance with organizational directives. Others, less involved, may require the "harder" rewards and sanctions of money, power, or threat of punishment. The third approach suggests that commitment begins with the behavior of the organization. To the extent that the employing organization is bound to its membership, the commitment of the membership to the organization may be reciprocated. An administrator can nurture employees toward commitment through socialization processes and through efforts to manipulate job characteristics, reward systems, and aspects of the external environment.

Whatever the conceptual approach, educational administrators interested in the management of commitment and in the motivational processes of workers must be concerned with the processes which serve to connect the individual to the formal organization. How does a school administrator encourage this connection and support the commitment *after* it is established? Karl Weick has provided not only an alternative vision of educational organizations, but also a concomitant view of the school administrator's role in establishing and nurturing teachers' commitment. The administrator is still in control, but he or she must perform some different tasks in order to motivate workers. Weick maintains that in loosely coupled systems such as schools, people lack the shared sense of direction for their efforts which exists in more tightly coupled systems. Consequently, "it must be built and reaffirmed in a loosely coupled system. Articulating a theme, reminding people of the theme, and helping people to apply the theme to interpret their work (symbol management)—all are major tasks of administrators in loosely coupled systems."[96]

Administrators whose concerns reach beyond the cause of mere surveillance guide modern workers by applying the spur and reins in challenging new ways. As the workplace develops more and more complexity, old habits of management must fall away. Over the years, as groups of people have developed progressively into complex organizations, explanations for behavior and performance have become kaleidoscopic. School administrators wrestle with conflicting ideas of economic incentives, goal setting, job design, and participation, wondering how they can influence and motivate teachers and other staff when the system of tangible motivation already is fixed by the larger organization. However, while the organization applies the spur and bit at one level, local administrators assume control at another. With astute management of values within the school, coupled with discretionary use of incentives, the administrator can move on to the more energizing tasks of support and encouragement. The school administrator, as nurturing motivator, provides teachers with not only the freedom, but also the challenge to teach.

## FROM THEORY TO PRACTICE

Anne Denier and Jesse Lambert probably will never meet. That is too bad, in a way. They would have a lot to say to each other, a good many notes to compare.

A common feel for the potential power of human heterogeneity, and always scratching to preserve it and build more of it. Dedicated to the kids on the edge for whom a positive school experience may make a real difference, just as it had for each of them when they were young. Hard workers, happiest when the days are long and the challenges seemingly insurmountable. However, even more bound together by that intense brand of commitment that educators seems to have and to need. Yet how differently the wheel of fortune had spun for them in this respect. Anne Denier had fashioned a context of commitment in her life that gave her the strength to administer, while Jesse Lambert had discovered that his one-sided commitment was not nearly enough to make his work meaningful and his professional career worthwhile.

At first glance you could imagine that Kanter was describing Anne Denier's commitment precisely—the loyalty entered into by the volition of the individual, here a young woman turning to a life of the cloth. But it is not as straightforward as the model suggests. Sacrifice? Her commitment to the church was relatively simple, without profound past or present struggle. "I found the yes in myself." On the other hand, she gravitates toward leadership positions in city schools that are on the brink of serious problems, places where her devotion to duty will make a difference. Anne Denier has not renounced the world; her attachments to her family, to a vast array of friends and professional colleagues, even to the neighborhood of her childhood days, keep her engaged, far from a cloistered life. "Some people say that the neighborhood has changed because there are people from different backgrounds living here now. But let me tell you—it's the *same*." The mortification is there, in the sense that Kanter uses the term;  Anne Denier is always trying to move herself and others closer to the values and standards of the Catholic Church. But *surrender*? This woman is hardly the submissive nun of yesteryear. She wants her church to be right rather than triumphant. No, with Anne Denier it is a fascinating blend of the elements of Kanter's model that leads her to the unique and persistent commitment that is at the core of her life and work.

Jesse Lambert became involved in education because of a need for some exchange. " . . . the thing that really got under my skin as I moved through college was the desire to pay the debt. I know it sounds like Boy Scout stuff, but I really vowed that someday I would teach or coach or do both." Organizations were ready to exchange with him at first; because he was competent *and* black, the jobs came to him almost in too rapid a succession, from the assistant principal's office to the Office of Education. Jesse felt the obligation to continue the exchange, to learn more on the job and in the classroom so that he could contribute more. "I had the old-fashioned idea that you were supposed to be qualified for a job you took." Then came the chance to work in the trenches of the civil rights movement. It all came together here for Jesse—the moral involvement and high commitment that Etzioni described as characterizing the most complete exchange between the individual and the organization. "My commitment was intense." And Jesse added, "You could get out there in the field, work shoulder to shoulder with people who shared the same values and goals, watch the problems get solved." Commitment had a payoff. But fifteen years later Jesse is suffering from high alienation, at the other end of the Etzioni continuum. The moral crusade has sputtered in America. Worse than that, the organization to which he was ready to give all that he had now seems to disregard his talents and to trade moral values for political expediencies. "I feel totally oppressed by this kind of situation."

What can you do when you are Jesse in an organization where the purposes changed so radically, where your talents and energy and most of all your commitment now are discounted almost completely? Wait? Struggle with the organization? Quit and find another one to give your commitment to? Jesse had paid his dues, but the isolation he was experiencing now was as devastating as it could get for an administrator. He had been so effective at helping school districts in metropolitan areas adapt to their environments, at getting them to bring the outsiders in from the cold. But now, the string of meaningless work days. "You feel like a sausage." Jesse deserved better.

Ann Denier had made one think about rules. They were supposed to make schools and school systems function more efficiently, but often they only stymied and frustrated people. Yet here in a Catholic school—where the stereotype showed rules clinging to the ceiling like Spanish moss—the rules seemed to be relatively few, quite stringent, and aimed at *helping* students rather than hindering them. She had learned a good deal about decision making, too; take your time in making them, but stick to them when you do. But her big message has to do with faith. Not just personal faith, or the collective faith of a religious community, but the faith that holds schools together. Creating an atmosphere of happiness and building a sense of community which helps people work together cannot be mandated in a series of memos. She had been trying to get people to have faith in the school, in its future, in their abilities to help make it succeed. Anne Denier made it sound pragmatic, not ethereal.

With her you can see the direct line between her religious community ("We get together to talk, to pray together, to do some business, but mainly to renew our friendship and our community") and her school community (where she describes her high point as the "ability to build community among the people who work together in an organization") and the students she is serving ("I believe in kids as eternal human beings who can be happier and better and lead deeper lives if they've been in the right school"). It is hard to imagine Anne Denier, burning out, or even abiding a school where others can burn out. She has been nurtured by her church and her religious community, and now she is able to nurture others, shrewdly and compassionately. Jesse has not found the organization that can nurture him across a career. He is such a long way from where his heart was. "You're manipulated by those who don't have any interest in education." Where are Jesse's boys and girls?

## NOTES

[1]See Bruce Buchanan II, "Building Organizational Commitment: The Socialization of Managers in Work Organizations," *Administrative Science Quarterly* 19 (1974): 533-546; also, Richard T. Mowday, Lyman W. Porter, and Richard M. Steers, *Employee-Organization Linkages* (New York: Academic Press, 1982).

[2]Helen Gouldner, "Dimensions of Organizational Commitment," *Administrative Science Quarterly*, 4 (1960): 468-490.

[3]Howard S. Becker, "Notes on the Concept of Commitment," *American Journal of Sociology* 66 (1960): 32-40.

[4]Sang M. Lee, "An Empirical Analysis of Organizational Identification," *Academy of Management Journal* 14 (1971): 214.

[5]Rosabeth Moss Kanter, "Commitment and Social Organization: A Study of Commitment Mechanisms in Utopian Communities," *American Sociological Review*, 33: 4 (August 1968): 499.

[6]M.E. Brown, "Identification and Some Conditions of Organizational Involvement," *Administrative Science Quarterly* 14 (1969): 347.

[7]Lyman Porter, Richard Steers, Richard Mowday, and P. Boulian, "Organizational Commitment, Job Satisfaction, and Turnover among Psychiatric Technicians," *Journal of Applied Psychology* 59 (1974): 604.

[8]"No Tea Party," *Time*, 12 July 1982, 53.

[9]James Lewis, Jr., "Do You Encourage Teacher Absenteeism?" *American School Board Journal* 168 (November 1981): 29.

[10]Joseph T. Blase, "A Social-Psychological Grounded Theory of Teacher Stress and Burnout," *Educational Administration Quarterly* 18 (Fall 1982): 93-113.

[11]Mowday, Porter and Steers, *Employee-Organization Linkages*. See also Irwin T. Sanders, "The University as a Community," in James A. Perkins, ed., *The University as an Organization* (New York: McGraw-Hill Book Co., 1973), pp. 57-78.

[12]Howard S. Becker and James W. Carper, "The Identification with an Occupation," *American Journal of Sociology* 61 (1956): 289-296.

[13]Ibid., p. 292.

[14]Chester Schriesheim, Mary Ann Glinow, and Steven Kerr, "The Dual Hierarchy: A Review of Evidence and a Theoretical Alternative," in *Proceedings of the Twelfth Annual Conference*, Eastern Academy of Management, 1975. We should note that elementary and secondary teaching is appropriately described by sociologists as a semi-profession. As semiprofessionals, schoolteachers experience a shorter period of training, less autonomy, a lower status, and a more tenuous command of specialized skills than full-fledged professionals. See, Amitai Etzioni, ed., *The Semi-Professions and Their Organization* (New York: The Free Press, 1969).

[15]W. Richard Scott, "Professionals in Bureaucracies: Areas of Conflict," in H. Vollmer and D. Mills, eds., *Professionalization*, p. 274.

[16]Ibid.

[17]Buchanan, "Building Organizational Commitment." See also Kevin Ryan, Katherine Newman, Gerald Mager, Jane Applegate, Thomas Lasley, Randall Flora, and John Johnston, *Biting the Apple: Accounts of First Year Teachers* (New York: Longman, 1980).

[18]Mowday, Porter, and Steers, *Employee-Organization Linkages*, p. 35.

[19]See Sanford Dornbusch and W. Richard Scott, *Evaluation and the Exercise of Authority* (San Francisco: Jossey-Bass, 1975).

[20]Mowday, Porter, and Steers, p. 207.

[21]Ibid., p. 209.

[22]See Dan C. Lortie, *Schoolteacher* (Chicago: University of Chicago Press, 1975).

[23]*Note:* A recent revival of interest in merit pay for teachers has been directed toward differentiating the role so that good teaching *can* be rewarded organizationally. The implications for employee commitment are many, but remain to be seen. Does special reward for the few provide incentive (a goal to attain) for the many? Without a clear agreement as to just what qualities deserve merit, is a reward of extra income likely to be heavily politicized—with a resulting cost in employee commitment rather than gain?

[24]Mowday, Porter, and Steers, *Employee-Organization Linkages*.

[25]See Brown, "Identification and Some Conditions of Organizational Involvement"; Douglas Hall, B. Schneider, and H.T. Nygren, "Personal Factors in Organizational Identification," *Administrative Science Quarterly*, 15 (1970): 176-190; Lawrence Hrebiniak, "Effects of Job Level and Participation on Employee Attitudes and Perceptions of Influence," *Academy of Management Journal* 17 (1974): 649-662; Lee, "An Empirical Analysis of Organizational Identification"; Mary E. Sheldon, "Investments and Involvements as Mechanisms Producing Commitment to the Organization," *Administrative Science Quarterly* 16 (1971): 142-150; Richard M. Steers, "Antecedents and Outcomes of Organizational Commitment," *Administrative Science Quarterly* 22 (1977): 46-56; James G. March and Herbert A. Simon, *Organizations* (New York: Wiley, 1958); Howard L. Angle and James L. Perry, "An Empirical Assessment of Organizational Commitment and Organizational Effectiveness," *Administrative Science Quarterly* 26: 1 (March 1981): 1-14; and Lawrence Hrebiniak and J. Alutto, "Personal and Role-Related

Factors in the Development of Organizational Commitment," *Administrative Science Quarterly* 17 (1972): 555-572.

[26]See Brown, 1969; Buchanan, 1974; Hall, Schneider, and Nygren, 1970; and Steers, 1977.

[27]See Buchanan, 1974; Hrebiniak, 1974; Steers, 1977; Sheldon, 1971; and J. Morris and J.D. Sherman, "Generalizability of an Organizational Commitment Model," *Academy of Management Journal* 24 (1981): 512-526.

[28] Hrebiniak and Alutto, "Personal and Role-Related Factors in the Development of Organizational Commitment."

[29]See March and Simon, *Organizations*; also, Hall, Schneider, and Nygren, "Personal Factors in Organizational Identification."

[30]Hrebiniak and Alutto, p. 562.

[31]Ibid.

[32]Mary E. Sheldon, "Investments and Involvements."

[33]Scott, "Professionals in Bureaucracies."

[34]See Dan C. Lortie, "The Balance of Control and Autonomy in Elementary School Teaching," in Etzioni, ed., *The Semi-Professions and Their Organization*, pp. 1-53.

[35]Ibid., see also, Lortie, *Schoolteacher*.

[36]Anthony M. Cresswell and Michael J. Murphy, *Teachers, Unions, and Collective Bargaining in Public Education* (Berkeley, Calif.: McCutchan Publishing, 1980); pp. 105-144.

[37]On this point, Hirschman in *Exit, Voice, and Loyalty* discusses the importance of the availability of opportunities outside the focal organization as a determinant of member loyalty. The difficulty experienced by the profession can be linked directly with the wide gap in salary and opportunity dividing teaching from private-sector employment. See Albert O. Hirschman, *Exit, Voice, and Loyalty* (Cambridge, Mass.: Harvard University Press, 1970).

[38]Cresswell and Murphy, *Teachers, Unions, and Collective Bargaining.*

[39]Even in the economically uncertain 1980s, however, studies of why job aspirants select teaching as a career find that self-fulfillment and altruistic motives (working with children) remain high. One recent study concludes: "Today's teacher aspirants are influenced by a desire to work with friendly people, and are not especially concerned with 'success.'" See Sandra D. Roberson, Timothy Z. Keith, and Ellis B. Page, "Now Who Aspires to Teach?" *Educational Researcher*, 12: 6 (June–July 1983): 13-21.

[40]Rosabeth Moss Kanter, "Commitment and Social Organization: A Study of Commitment Mechanisms in Utopian Communities," *American Sociological Review*, 33: 4 (August 1968): 499-517.

[41]Ibid., p. 505.

[42]Ibid., p. 509.

[43]Ibid., p. 510.

[44]Ibid., pp. 513-514.

[45]Ibid., p. 516.

[46]See Arthur Blumberg et al., "Learning About Work-Life in the Schools After School: Teachers in Bars on Friday Afternoon," American Education Research Association Symposium, Boston, April 9, 1980.

[47]Private conversation with an elementary-level schoolteacher, Chicago, Illinois, August, 1983.

[48]Willard W. Waller, *On the Family, Education and War*, William J. Goode, Frank F. Furstenberg, Jr., and Larry R. Mitchell eds., (Chicago: University of Chicago Press, 1970); p. 302.

[49]There is much movement at present toward differentiated staffing and merit pay. The unexamined question is whether such action will result in a loss of group consciousness under terms of members' equality.

[50]See Van Cleve Morris, Robert L. Crowson, Cynthia Porter-Gehrie, and Emanuel Hurwitz, Jr., *Principals in Action: The Reality of Managing Schools* (Columbus, Ohio: Charles E. Merrill, 1983).

[51]Kanter, "Commitment," p. 510.

[52]Ibid., pp. 511-514.

[53]William F. Whyte, Jr., *The Organization Man* (Garden City, New Jersey: Anchor, 1956).

[54]Coser distinguishes "greedy institutions" from what Goffman (1961) has called "total institutions." Greedy institutions discourage relationships with outsiders through nonphysical and symbolic mechanisms. Total institutions described are encompassing organizations relying on physical means to separate the inmate from the outside world (e.g., locked doors, barbed wire, forests, or moors). Greedy institutions tend to rely on voluntary-compliance means of activating loyalty and commitment (See, Lewis A. Coser,

*Greedy Institutions: Patterns of Unguarded Commitment* [New York: The Free Press, 1974], and Erving Goffman, *Asylums: Essays on the Social Situations of Mental Patients and Other Inmates* [Garden City, N.Y.: Doubleday-Anchor, 1961]).

[55]Thomas P. Rohlen, "Creating the Uedagin Man," in R. Barnhardt, J. Chilcott, and H. Wolcott, eds., *Anthropology and Educational Administration* (Tuscon, Arizona: Impresora Sahuaro, 1979).

[56]Terrence E. Deal and Allan A. Kennedy, *Corporate Cultures: The Rites and Rituals of Corporate Life* (Reading, Massachusetts: Addison-Wesley, 1982), p. 65.

[57]W. Richard Scott, "Professionals in Bureaucracies: Areas of Conflict," in H. Vollmer and D. Mills, eds., *Professionalization*, pp. 265-275; and Howard S. Becker et al., *Boys in White* (Chicago: University of Chicago Press, 1961).

[58]See Amitai Etzioni, *A Comparative Analysis of Complex Organizations* (New York: The Free Press, 1961); also, Amitai Etzioni, "Compliance Structures," in Amitai Etzioni and Edward W. Lehman, eds., *A Sociological Reader on Complex Organizations*, 3rd ed., (New York: Holt, Rinehart & Winston, 1980), pp. 87-100.

[59]March and Simon, *Organizations*

[60]Etzioni, *A Comparative Analysis of Complex Organizations*, pp. 3-21.

[61]Ibid., p. 61.

[62]Etzioni, "Compliance Structures," p. 89.

[63]Note that there is not an easy answer to the question of what really is or is not "coercive" in human relations. We are indebted, for example, to our colleague Professor Edward Wynne (University of Illinois at Chicago) for the following observation: "In labor law the issue of 'coercion' has often arisen. It is illegal to coerce someone in his or her exercise of the right to join, or not join, a union. And so, what is coercion? Coercion seemed to connote constraining or directing someone's conduct or decisions via force, threats of punishment, etc. But high proportions of our decisions are made under such circumstances. Our parents warn us that if we don't apply ourselves in school, we will not be assured of their support in adulthood, and thus we are coerced into making ourselves eligible for employment by attending schools. Potential union members were told (by employers) that, if they chose a union, they might not reach a contract with the employer, might have to go on strike, and might be out of a job.

"Most discussions of choice relate to the matter of consequences, and pointing out bad consequences inevitably generates fear, and thus may be called coercive. But discussions of choice which ignore the matter of potential bad consequences are vapid.

"Oftentimes, it seems that the issue is not whether people are, in fact, deciding on the basis of warnings or threats, but the degree of tact employed in the process. Does the iron fist have a velvet glove? Not to be taken sarcastically, the velvet glove is a form of consideration which is not without costs for the fist. But if we ask the raw question of whether particular acts are ultimately coercive (unless our definitions are *very* circumscribed), we will discover so many forms of motivation are coercive as to undermine the distinguishing power of that word—which is what happened in labor law."

[64]For an early and still classic discussion of the power of the student subculture, see James S. Coleman, *The Adolescent Society* (New York: The Free Press, 1961).

[65]This point is consistent with Richard Carlson's observation that public schools are "domesticated" organizations, wherein neither the client nor the institution has a choice regarding client participation. The school adapts by placing and segregating pupils; pupils adapt through rebelliousness, finding side-payments, and the like. See Richard O. Carlson, "Environmental Constraints and Organizational Consequences: The Public School and Its Clients," in Daniel E. Griffiths ed., *Behavioral Science and Educational Administration*, Sixty-third Yearbook of the National Society for the Study of Education, Part II (Chicago: University of Chicago Press, 1964): 262-278.

[66]Etzioni, "Compliance Structures," p. 92.

[67]Benjamin J. Hodgkins and Robert E. Herriott, "Age-Grade Structure, Goals, and Compliance in the Schools: An Organizational Analysis," pp. 90-96.

[68]Charles Bidwell, "The School as a Formal Organization" in J. March, ed., *Handbook of Organizations* (New York: Rand McNally, 1965); and Talcott Parsons, "The School as a Social System," *Harvard Educational Review* 29 (Fall 1959): 297-318.

[69]Jesse Burkhead, *Input and Output in Large-City High Schools* (Syracuse, New York: Syracuse University Press, 1967).

[70]See Philip Jackson, *Life in Classrooms* (New York: Holt, Rinehart & Winston, 1958).

[71]Carlson, "Environmental Constraints and Organizational Consequencees," p. 270.

[72]Etzioni, "Compliance Structures," p. 93.

[73]Interestingly, if Etzioni is correct in noting that the form of power should be consistent with type of involvement, it is quite possible that merit pay may be offered quite often to the most morally committed teachers—thereby possibly *reducing* their high levels of commitment rather than adding to them.

[74]Etzioni, "Compliance Structures," p. 94.

[75]For a fascinating account of Frederick W. Taylor's impact upon administrative thought in education, see Raymond E. Callahan, *Education and the Cult of Efficiency* (Chicago: University of Chicago Press, 1962).

[76]See Abraham H. Maslow, *Motivation and Personality*, 2nd ed. (New York: Harper & Row, 1970).

[77]See Douglas McGregor, *The Human Side of Enterprise* (New York: McGraw-Hill, 1960).

[78]For a concise and informative description and critique of competing theories of motivation in educational organizations, see Cecil G. Miskal, "Motivation in Educational Organizations," *Educational Administration Quarterly*, 18: 3 (Summer 1982): 65-88.

[79]See William G. Ouchi, "Markets, Bureaucracies, and Clans," *Administrative Science Quarterly*, 25: 1 (March 1980): 129-141; also, William G. Ouchi, *Theory Z: How American Business Can Meet the Japanese Challenge* (Reading, Mass.: Addison-Wesley, 1981).

[80]Lyman W. Porter and Raymond E. Miles, "Motivation and Management," in J.W. McGuire, ed., *Contemporary Management: Issues and Viewpoints* (Englewood Cliffs, New Jersey: Prentice-Hall, 1974), pp. 545-570.

[81]David L. Clark and Sue McKibbon, "From Orthodoxy to Pluralism: New Views of School Administration," *Phi Delta Kappan* 63 (June, 1982): 669-672.

[82]For a concise description of expectancy theory, see Wayne K. Hoy and Cecil E. Miskal, *Educational Administration: Theory, Research, and Practice*, 2nd ed. (New York: Random House, 1982); pp. 155-161.

[83]Porter and Miles, p. 547.

[84]Ibid., p. 546.

[85]Ibid., pp. 561-567.

[86]See John Van Maanen, "Experiencing Organization: Notes on the Meaning of Careers and Socialization," in John Van Maanen ed., *Organizational Careers: Some New Perspectives* (New York: John Wiley & Sons, 1977), pp. 15-45.

[87]See R. Bruce McPherson and Robert L. Crowson, "Sources of Constraint and Opportunities for Discretion in the Principalship," in Jack Lane and Herbert J. Walberg, eds., *Educational Administration and School Effectiveness* (Lexington, Mass.: Lexington Books, in press).

[88]Bruce Buchanan II, "Red Tape and the Service Ethic: Some Unexpected Differences Between Public and Private Managers," *Administration and Society* 6 (1975): 423-438.

[89]Morris et al., *Principals in Action*.

[90]See M. Rutter, B. Maughan, P. Mortimer, and J. Ouston, *Fifteen Thousand Hours* (Cambridge, Mass.: Harvard University Press, 1979).

[91]See Buchanan, "Building Organizational Commitment"; also, Buchanan "To Walk An Extra Mile: The Whats, Wheres, and Why of Organizational Commitment," *Organizational Dynamics* 4 (1975): 67-80.

[92]McPherson and Crowson, "Sources of Constraint," p. 24.

[93]Morris et al., *Principals in Action*.

[94]Weick, "Administering Education," p. 673.

[95]Ibid., p. 676.

[96]Ibid.

# 7

## The Adaptation
## of the Organization
## to its Environment

### ARMANDO RIVERA

*He is thirty-five and single, an administrator in a community college in Buffalo. His parents came to the United States from Puerto Rico and moved west from New York after a few uneasy years. Armando now realizes that, quietly and without fuss, they gave him an extra edge while he was growing up. He takes pride in his growing capacity as an administrator in higher education, but he knows that he remains an outsider to many of his colleagues. His professional future seems bleak to him, and a job in industry beckons him as much as a promotion in educational administration. He was trained as a social worker, and most of the programs he designs and operates try to help urban adults who are struggling to get more education and better jobs. Armando does not live in the "high rent district" of higher education. He has lost his naivete, and there is more confidence in his voice than there was even a year ago when he was almost fired.*

**Tell me about the jobs you have held in education.**

It wasn't easy finding a job after I finished my master's degree in Cleveland. I came back to Buffalo and held a job briefly as a counselor in a community college. Then I got a chance to be the coordinator of training programs. It was a real challenge to establish a continuing education program for disadvantaged adults. There was nothing there, not even any furniture. I started with the nuts and bolts,

**165**

making something from nothing. And did I make *mistakes*! But that program is still solid, still in place. It began with about $150,000 that I got through a grant. Today they probably work with $500–750,000 per year. Then I was furloughed.

**Furloughed?**

That's what they called it. The system hadn't even begun to look for black and Hispanic administrators much before 1968, and they didn't make any hirings that were of much consequence until 1971 or 1972. Remember, it takes six years to get tenure, so in 1975 when there were cutbacks it was the blacks and Hispanics who lost their jobs. It was brutal. I did a study on it. About three-quarters of the blacks and Hispanics who had been hired in the early 1970s lost their jobs. Including me.

**What happened to you then?**

I only had about two weeks notice, and right after Labor Day I began working in the county jail. Officially I was a counselor trying to persuade the men there to get into an educational program, but we were understaffed and I ended up running the program. Basically it was a GED and literacy program. We tried to accomplish a lot, though—maybe too much. I would talk with an inmate, and then I had to make an informed judgment. It was like a contract. "I'll transfer you to the sixth tier, but don't go unless you're serious." The sixth tier was a privilege, it was desirable. So I'd transfer them. We were trying to establish an educational community in the middle of a jail. It was kind of a monastery, if you know what I mean. I had to interact with these guys. There were no guards with me. I had no supervisor there. I didn't have any trouble, but it was dangerous—I found out later.

**How long were you there?**

Those dates stand out in my mind, I can tell you. March 15 to October 30, 1971. I learned a lot about persuasion. I remember once I was trying to get four guys to come to class. The were playing whist, and they kept saying they'd be right there. What could I do, really? If I'd grabbed them, they would have stuffed me through the wall. Finally I said, very seriously, "If you guys don't come now, I'm going to send you home." One of them looked up at me and said, "What did you say?" Then he got it, and he started laughing. They all cracked up, and then they came to class.

Later I got a call from a director of a community center that was part of the system, and he hired me to be director of student personnel services—admissions, counseling, registration, student activities—all the noncurricular functions. I had a staff of 22, and I stayed there for two and a half years. Then I got another call, and I accepted the job that I'm in now, and I've been here over ten years.

**What do you consider to be the high point of your career so far?**

I haven't had one great accomplishment, although I'd like this job to turn into one. But I don't expect to be a legend in my own time. An administrator doesn't get the appreciation he might want to get from the people he serves. That's the price you pay. One of my staff now has been getting some public recognition, and I want to say "I did that" because I made it possible, really. But you can't, you don't. In one of my jobs I thought I wasn't well-liked by my staff. Then they gave me a going-away party like you wouldn't believe. With them, I used to want to get even for some of the things they said about me in public. I never did, of course, but there were times I wanted to.

**Tell me more about those feelings.**

Well, we were short of resources. And I developed a committee to help me make some tough decisions about how we were going to use what we had. They were honest. They really cared enough to take me on, and I wasn't easy to take on. It was hard on me. Everything was leading to the good solid plan that we drew up, but it was tough. I remember saying, "I reserve the right to get angry in here. Don't take that away from me." It would have been easy to be arbitrary, like the other administrators there. Afterwards, I called each of them in individually and thanked them and put a letter of praise in their files. They couldn't believe it. What I was finding was that maturity is hard to deal with. I'm as mature as any thirty-five year old, but what does that mean? In administration and leadership you really get to the heart of what you are. It's hard growing up. You really have to think about yourself.

**How are you going to recognize that high point when it occurs?**

It will be when I establish real stability in a program, not when I become a dean or a college president. A promotion is just a kick. It will be when this program really gets to be what I want it to be. When I don't have to be the prime program developer all the time.

**Has this all been more difficult for you because you are Puerto Rican?**

It's a heavy responsibility. In a way I've just begun noticing it. I'm the only male Puerto Rican at this high an administrative level in the system. Frankly, I'd rather not have the pressure. People want to use you because you are Puerto Rican, and they will. It's a shame in a city where more and more Puerto Ricans are living, and where the system will enroll more and more of them, and you're the only administrator at even this level. There's a certain amount of competition between blacks and Puerto Ricans, and I can understand that. One group is starting to make it, and the next one wants to, and you have to fight them off. It's always been that way in America. I can't see a clear future for me, though, as a Puerto Rican. I'm getting used to carrying the responsibility, but you get tired. I really believe that everything I've received I had coming to me.

**Tell me about your early days, your family life.**

I went back to the old neighborhood last year, and lot of it has been knocked down, including the hospital where I was born. We lived in a railroad flat, one room after another on a line, and until I was fifteen I slept on a pull-out bed in the living room. I started working in a drugstore when I was fifteen. It was a good job. I worked from 5:00 to 10:00 six nights a week. That helped pay the tuition to the Catholic high school I was attending. I went to Catholic schools all during my childhood. In high school I was one of only two Puerto Ricans in the school. I wasn't a great student, but I wasn't involved in what my friends were into. Some of them were shooting up. I knew there was something better. Something I had to do. I didn't really have a goal, but I wanted to live more comfortably than my parents had. My parents didn't push me that much, although my mother made sure I learned enough English from her to get into a Catholic school when I was in first grade. If I was working and responsible and not on drugs, those were the basics.

When I was eighteen we moved to a larger apartment, and I got a job as a stock transfer teller in a bank. By this time I was in college taking six to eight credits a semester. I quit that job so I could get through college faster. I worked as a waiter and took twelve to fourteen hours a semester. But I ate so much on that job that I gained a lot of weight and finally got fired for being too slow. They were right—I couldn't cut it. All this time I figured I would end up after college with a job in marketing or retailing. That seemed to be a way to make a decent living and have some fun at it.

But at school I realized, while talking with a Puerto Rican girl, how few of us there were on campus. We thought this was wrong. It was the late 1960s, and while I didn't have real social consciousness, it just didn't seem right. Then it became an interesting time in my life. We had a meeting, and we organized a Puerto Rican group, and I was elected president. I'm not really sure why. Well, I did write a guest column in the student newspaper. A black student lent me the column for one week. And what I wrote caused a bit of a stir. That might be it. I was popular, too. I could get along with a variety of people then, and I still can now. That group we formed still exists.

I was working part-time at a community center, and a man I knew there was moving to Cleveland to join the faculty of a graduate school of social work. He persuaded me to come as a student. I had begun to realize that business couldn't be it. It didn't excite me. It didn't have the possibility for letting me make real contributions to society. I was caught up in the jargon, as you can tell. I turned out to be a very good graduate student. I was much more serious, and I think I must have graduated fourth or fifth in my class. In two years I got my master's degree in social work, and I had an internship in the Cleveland Public Schools, in the central office, where I was able to learn the process of program development. I wanted to get a job where I could develop new programs, and that's why that first job was perfect. I didn't think a college would even *have* a job like that. What we're doing in program development in the city community college is critical to the growth and vitality of higher education, but this is not well understood.

### What did you need to know as your career progressed?

Myself. Much of being an administrator you can learn pretty easily. But you really have to know yourself—how you respond under pressure, what your real values are. That you have an ego, like everyone else. I'm still learning a great deal about myself.

## How would you describe your administrative style at this point?

I like to give people responsibility and hold them to it. It's harder to do than you think it's going to be. You make assumptions about other people that are not always true. And if someone makes a false impression about a skill, you have to give the person some training. At the beginning you try to figure out each staff member. What can they do? Sometimes you decide they could do this, but definitely not that. I know who I could send in to a prison to run a program, and it might surprise you who could. You also inherit people who don't fit and can't change. But then there was Georgeanne—a secretary with a B.A., making $8,000 a year. We just started developing a program and I gave her the go-ahead. There was resentment from the staff, of course, and it was just one course with 18 people, but it worked. She lacked confidence, but I said, "Do it." Now she's a great program developer and a strong staff member. I got her a line position—that's unprecedented, too. We usually only add staff on soft money.

But I've been neglecting my staff. We're not going out for a beer at the end of the week like we used to. Something went out of me that I've got to get back. One of my staff tells me that I'm not paying enough attention to them. She's right. She doesn't know that I'm two people, that I have to assuage those above me. I've been talking to you about my *supervisory* style. I'm just realizing my *place*.

## What do you mean by place?

This is politics. I function like a full dean. If you think I'm an assistant dean and young and Puerto Rican and stupid, then I'm going to feed on that. I'll make you think I really *am* that, and then I'll surprise you when it counts, and you'll have more respect for me. I'm realizing now that I'm going to have to be much better at politics with respect to people *outside* the institution who have an impact on it. When someone says something blatantly critical of me or the college, I may think, "You can't say that," but I'm sophisticated in the actual conversation. Is this falseness? It's something I am learning to live with.

There's not a lot I'm going to learn from books. I read the Bible, novels, whatever, but I think I'm going to have a hard time in the doctoral program I've just been accepted into. It's going to be highly structured, and I don't know if I can live with it.

## Do you feel like your hands are tied when you are working with people outside the organization?

I can manage reasonably well when I am there at the beginning, but sometimes things get snarled up before you can get a handle on them. That was what seemed to happen in this instance that I'll tell you about. It all started when I was looking for some space for a Saturday program. I discovered that a community group was using the college facilities for an educational program on Saturdays. When I started poking around a bit more, I was told that it was a cooperative program, but the closer I looked the more one-sided it seemed to be. I had no quarrel with what the program objectives were—teaching English as a second language, typing, preparing students for the GED exam—and I had respect for the community group that was involved. But there were complications. One of our faculty members sat on the board of the community organization, and apparently she had prevailed on the administrator in charge of scheduling rooms to let them use the space. The real difficulty was that there was not supposed to be any charge to students, but it turned out that the community organization *was* charging tuition, and they were paying expenses for the supposedly volunteer instructors and tutors for the program. And they weren't incorporated. All of that spelled trouble for us.

So I went to our president and proposed that we work out an official relationship with the group. We would collect the tuition and pay the instructors and tutors. The program would continue pretty much as it was. There was never any intent on my part to kill it. But we could get FTE credit, which would help us with our budget, and we could possibly recruit from this program into other college programs. In addition, we could have some monitoring of quality, and if we reported the program to the state as one of ours we could get some extra funds for running a remedial program. All I was interested in was trying to figure out how everyone could get something.

### What kind of community are we talking about?

The student body on Saturdays was mainly Hispanic, but there were all kinds of people in the community organization itself—Hispanics from many countries, as well as blacks, whites, and orientals.

### What happened when you went to them with your idea?

It really hit the fan when I proposed a relationship. I asked them to give me an idea of what kind of budget the program needed. From first to last they were unwilling to do this. They thought that would be a loss of autonomy. They felt I would be taking from them the power to appoint personnel, and that I would be dictating pedagogy. I *would* have tried to increase the skills of the tutors in the program through some kind of training program. I'll admit that. Well, they really began a campaign. They wrote letters to the mayor, to our college president, to the local newspapers. They kept repeating that we were simply throwing them out of the space. Some of our students from the college who were involved with the community group came to see me. They didn't know the truth, what I had offered. Once they found out what the facts were, they went back to the community group and started to defuse things. I had given the community organization two alternatives—affiliate with us in an appropriate, legal way or terminate the program and vacate the space at the end of the semester, which was two weeks away.

### What was their reaction to this choice?

They rejected both alternatives and made it clear that they were not going to give up the space. We're talking about 200 students, so this was not just one classroom by any means. There's a lot of political power with a community group plus 200 students in our space, even if they were squatters.

Well, the next Saturday came and at 7:00 A.M. I got a call from our president telling me to get over to the college right away and handle the problem. I knew enough about such situations to realize that any intrusion on my part was really going to cause an incident, and that was the last thing I was interested in. So I stayed out of the way and went to my office, and then I got a coordinator to go to the area where the program was taking place to check things out. The president thought there might be vandalism or theft or fire or something like that. I knew the group wasn't going to do anything harmful; they were interested in rhetoric and speeches, but not destruction. The coordinator said everything was cool, so I called the president's executive assistant and told him that. I said, "I'm leaving the college now. If they know there's a dean here, they'll have a focal point for their protest." Then I asked him to come with me to my apartment where we could both be near the telephone. He wasn't too crazy about that, on a Saturday morning, but he did it. The coordinator would call me if anything went wrong. So, later that morning, the executive assistant called the president and told him everything was all right. The classes finished out the semester without a big incident.

## But you still hadn't solved the problem.

Not at all. It kept going. The next semester they at least agreed to a joint registration. But it didn't go well. They gave the coordinator handling it a really rough time. I should have done it myself. The community people didn't do their usual share, and then they came back to me and complained about the coordinator. I could see what was going on. We knew that we had registered 600 or so students, but the official count from the community organization was 212. We asked for records—and we didn't get them. As the semester wore on we asked for attendance records for the 212—and we didn't get them. The cooperative approach just wasn't working. And through all of this I still couldn't find out what the *real* reasons were for their not simply affiliating with us like I had proposed.

The next semester it fell on me completely. Everyone else backed away. My next strategy was to get together with the Hispanic caucus of college staff and faculty. I told the president I was going to meet them, and he approved that. He really wanted the program to succeed. So we had the meeting, and I laid it all out. The complete history—why we wanted to affiliate, our real interest in continuing a program. The caucus was on my side, and next they went back to the community group, without me. About this time the faculty member who had been on the board of the community organization resigned from the board. As soon as she resigned, I knew I had the situation under control.

## How so?

The vice-president of the community group could not rally the group. The Hispanic caucus was not going to listen to him the way they might have had to listen to the faculty member, the former president, who was Hispanic. The community group could no longer oppose me successfully. And I was right—that's just what happened when the Hispanic caucus went to work. In fact, as far as this educational program is concerned, the caucus actually became the governing board for the community organization. The caucus came back to me and raised some tough questions, and I answered them straight. They were satisfied, and they even worked with the media so that it couldn't be said that we had taken a program away from the community.

Over the last year we have had the affiliated program I wanted from the beginning. There are about 250 students rather than 600, so it's much smaller. It's also more quality based. I think it will grow in time. We're a little more bureaucratic, and that may turn some community people off. But not all of them by any means.

Also, during the last year some members of the community board prepared an expose of our college administration—me, mainly—with respect to working with the community. Once again they sent it to everyone, including our college board of trustees. I may have to go with the president to meet with them in executive session about it. No problem.

### What did you learn from all of this?

The college learned something about *me*. That I could do my job. Some people expected me to fall on my face. I already knew how to work with the community, but I learned how to deal better with the college administration, how to make the connections between the inside and the outside. That's really important. There was something in it for me that I didn't see at the beginning—better visibility, as a result of my being responsible.

If we hadn't made this effort, we could have looked bad. If we had decided simply to cut the program, it would have been a serious political mistake. We acted in part out of self-interest, but we wanted to provide a good service, too. The motivations on both sides are not as important as the results. What we did tells people we are a responsible college.

You have to understand that it's not just one homogeneous community out there. It's an amorphous mass. You can't work with the mass. You have to find the need. Sometimes that means you have to wait, and you have to dig through the nonsense. For example, that community group thinks it needs English as a second language, but what they really need more than that is counseling. If we could do that, then we could begin to find out the other things people in this particular part of the community really need. The counseling could be a direct benefit in itself, but we could learn a lot in the process. But they're not ready for this yet. I'll have to wait.

The adults bring their kids here on Saturday. We look the other way. If the program grows, it will be harder to do that. Maybe we can figure out a way to open up our new day care center for them on Saturdays. If you go by the book, you don't have a program for community people. We take what for us is a risk and what for them is real life.

### How do you get people to do what you want them to do?

Everything is a negotiation. If you're running 90 courses, every one is separate. You have to negotiate space, the teacher, utilities, "free" spots. For example, I needed some space in a library at our college for one course. The librarian was reluctant. I had to figure out what she really wanted. You know what she wanted? First, security. That meant that I had to get free guards around there when my class was in session. Second, she wanted locks on some cabinet doors so expensive tapes wouldn't walk away. Did I get them? Sure. I had to figure out if they were legal. Then I had to figure out how to buy them and have them installed. I got the space for the class. Negotiation is exactly what it is. It's a big part of administration. I don't supervise this librarian, and she doesn't feel I could affect her negatively. That's when you have to negotiate.

### Have you ever had what might be called a transcendent experience in your work?

When I left that job in the prison. One guy was angry when I said I was going, but I reminded him that I had said from the beginning that I was only there as long as it took me to get a job back in a community college. He agreed. As I walked out 60 inmates stood up and gave me a standing ovation. One patted me on my back. Another squeezed my arm as I went by. It was really something. I was going to get full of tears, so I had to get out of there quickly.

### If two young Puerto Ricans—a man and a woman—came to you for advice about moving into careers as educational administrators, what would you tell them?

I wouldn't encourage them. I've had a lot of good opportunities, and I've been lucky. But there's not much of a career path for me from this point on. Can they take a lot of discouragement and a lot of compromising of their ideals? I'd tell them to think again, go into it with your eyes wide open. Even with a doctorate it's going to be tough for me. They are not looking for Puerto Ricans, and they are not going to hire Puerto Ricans. I've been interviewed by a major insurance company. They want me to run a training program for them. It would be more money and fewer headaches. I'll consider it. If I get the doctorate, maybe I could teach eventually. That would be more fun, and I think there'd be more acceptance of me.

### Here's one last question. What's the big lesson about organizations that you've learned so far?

The rational organization chart? That's not the way it is. Everything is shifting on every issue. Sometimes you're the supervisor and sometimes the subordinate. Sometimes the vice-president and sometimes the administrative assistant. It fluctuates with the issue. People change, and organizations are made up of people. Robert Townsend—the man who wrote *Up the Organization*— made it clear that the position should not dictate how you act every time. Answer your own phone! Sometimes an administrator has to act a little pompous for the politician. But the same thing is not good if you're working with a student. Education and the world around it are in a state of flux. It won't be the same in ten years. Being president of a community college won't mean the same thing. The skills you'll need are those of a negotiator, but you were trained as a supervisor.

## FROM PRACTICE TO THEORY

Most managers hold positions *within* the organization. But a portion—sometimes a good deal—of their time is spent in communication, interaction, and negotiation with people *outside* the organization—with the environment. The job of working within an organization but spanning an institutional boundary to serve, represent, or bargain with those without is one of officialdom's most difficult positions. Boundary-spanners live in two worlds: claimed, but easily distrusted, by both; expected by both to serve *their* interests; and sensed by both to be serving the other party's interests.

Armando Rivera is a boundary-spanner of multiple dimensions. He represents a minority group not yet fully accepted in educational administration. He also finds himself placed in liaison, even fire-fighting, relationships between community groups and other administrators. He has been active in grant-in-aid administration, with attendant negotiations between funding agencies and the receiving organization. He socializes fellow administrators or institutionalized inmates (not fully dissimilar categories) into the larger world that lies beyond their own limited backgrounds and experiences. He tries to open up his organization—toward a broader perspective with the world existing beyond its borders.

What do we have in the theoretical literature to offer an Armando Rivera? Educators have only recently moved from a closed-system to a more open-system view of their work—brought kicking and screaming to this awareness, claim some scholars, by the turbulence of the 1960s and the unanticipated decline of the 1970s. Consequently, the theoretical literature on the relationship between organization and environment in education is still developing. Systems theory has received attention, but what can be learned from other perspectives? How does one begin to sort out, as a manager, the many-sidedness, the unpredictability, and the politics of it all? Are there some alternative frameworks, some lenses of differing focus or sharpness, that might help Rivera find at least a bit of understanding—if not direction—as he struggles with an almost overwhelmingly uncertain environment?

## THE ADAPTATION OF THE ORGANIZATION TO ITS ENVIRONMENT

Although both the theory and practice of educational administration long assumed that education could and should be walled off from community pressure, that education must be kept out of politics, the realization today is that schooling is in close interaction with its surrounding environment. It is an open system. Parents, judges, state and federal bureaucrats, newspaper reporters, textbook publishers, members of citizens' groups, people in business, local politicians, police officers, and welfare workers—these are just some of the many individuals who affect the educative process significantly and almost daily.

Indeed, some scholars suggest that the constraints imposed upon educational organizations by outside forces are greater today than ever before— that administrators are not just surrounded by external pressures, they are, what is quite worse, *hamstrung* by the many demands, interests, and ideologies in conflict. David Tyack, for example, has suggested that school governance is now characterized by a new, conflict-laden, "hyperpluralistic" politics of education—a politics of crossfires, fragmented interests, protest movements, demands for redress, factionalism, litigation, and a good deal of plain, old-fashioned contentiousness.[1]

All organizations, we have learned, no matter how hide-bound or protectively garbed in standards of meritocratic professionalism, are in reality open systems. Their internal affairs are sensitive to outside forces. Armando Rivera's Saturday morning was not his own. Political, economic, educational, and cultural vectors in the organization's surrounding environment provide subtle pressures which are accommodated, as well as hard-currency resources which are used internally in the production of sets of outputs. These outputs enter the larger societal dynamic, becoming inputs into the productive processes of other organizational systems.

The recent literature in educational administration has plugged in to the open-systems perspective with much pleasure, and perhaps with a feeling of relief. Administrative theory in education moved from an early emphasis upon the scientific efficiency of a Federick Taylor into the human relations tenets of a Rensis Likert, and forward to the study of organizational behavior and improved decision making a la James March and Herbert Simon.[2] Although careful review of the writings of such seminal thinkers as Max Weber and Chester Barnard discovers their solid appreciation of the importance of environment, the formative development of administrative thought has been criticized justly for bringing a closed-systems perspective to the study of organizations.[3] Internal reward and motivation strategies, the hierarchical authority structure, and the decision/coordination mechanisms of the organization received far more attention for decades than any questions of adaptation to outside pressure. However, when outside pressure developed into a cacophonous roar of disapproval during the turbulent 1960s, theorists found a vital new conceptual framework at hand in the open-systems (particularly the systems-analysis) perspective. As its name implies, the systems model argued that the institution the administrator was trying to manage and the pressures coming from outside should be viewed as part of the same overall framework of decision making. Such an image suggested that the decisions made inside schools might never be entirely free from politics, but it also suggested (conveniently) that the rational organization can be meshed productively with a seemingly irrational environment. The environment can be influenced from within, just as the internal organization is pressured from without.

Despite the developing interest in the open-systems perspective, the relationship between organization and environment in education has yet to be adequately conceptualized. Samuel Bacharach has suggested that one unfortunate legacy of the keep-education-out-of-politics spirit of the past has been the development of two separate bodies of literature, one focused upon school board and community, the other focused upon the school as an organization. It is Bacharach's view that these two research traditions must be merged, to reflect much more adequately "the dilemma school district administrators face in trying to satisfy political and administrative imperatives simultaneously."[4] Seldom, in the real world of school administration, does one encounter either a purely political or a purely administrative decision. Allocating instructional resources efficiently may mean asking Miss Jones rather than Mr. Brown to teach fourth grade. Jones is the better teacher, did well this past year, and likes fourth-graders. Brown, however, has seniority on the faculty, wants to try his hand at fourth grade, and presents the male role model that parents have requested. Which choice is best? The better teacher, or the expedient teacher?

In the same vein, it may be suggested that the failure to merge political and administrative perspectives has resulted in a failure to address adequately two very fundamental questions about the nature of education's interaction with its outside environment: (a) Where does one draw a boundary between the internal and the external in education? and, (b) What is the essence of the relationship between educational organization and environment? Let us examine each of these questions in a bit more detail.

## The Problem of Boundary

At first glance it seems quite simple—either one is a member of an organization or one is part of its environment. The open-systems perspective has made us aware of the permeability of the educational organization and has suggested that there is an identifiable line of separation or differentiation between the institution and others who relate to it but exist outside it.[5]

Bertram Gross has developed a conceptual framework that makes a distinction between an organization's "immediate environment" and its "general environment." The immediate environment would include the organization's clientele, suppliers, advisers, controllers, adversaries, and publics. Clients include both those directly served by the organization (e.g., parents) and those less visibly served (e.g., employers). Suppliers include the providers of needed resources (e.g., homeowner tax dollars) but also "associates" and "supporters" (e.g., helpful local political leaders). Advisors (e.g., PTA leaders) provide relevant information and help delineate future courses of action; while controllers (e.g., governmental agencies) exercise supervisory or regulatory authority. Adversaries may include competitors (e.g., public vs. private institutions) as well as rivals and enemies (e.g., property tax resisters). Finally, every organization is surrounded by a panoply of public opinion.[6]

In its general environment, according to Gross, each institution is affected additionally by broad societal considerations. Among these are (a) the national resource base (current outputs of goods and services, societal wealth, and the scarcity or abundance of such key elements as skilled professional workers); (b) aspects of the larger social organization (such as the current health of families, governmental institutions, political parties, and voluntary associations in the society); (c) matters of power structure (who controls what and whom); and (d) conditions in the value structure of the society (beliefs, loyalties, interests, allegiances, etc.).[7]

Although it is sensibly organized, the Gross framework reveals (at second glance) that a delineation between the immediate environment and the organization is sometimes difficult. Are students, for example, members of the organization or are they (as clients) part of the environment? While students certainly are clients, they are also integral to the definition of institutionalized schooling. In fact, sociological analyses of education by Waller, Bidwell, and Lortie emphasize the degree to which the actual structure of the educational organization is colored by fundamental dichotomies between student and staff roles *within* the organization.[8] The student's role is that of conscript: Students are compelled by society to receive educational services. On the other hand, the teacher is an employee who has achieved his or her position after specialized education.

The demarcation between organization and environment, however, does not suggest a lack of influence between the two. Gerald Salancik and Jeffrey Pfeffer document the impact made by department success in outside fund-raising upon the distribution of "subunit power" *within* a state university. The best *outside* fund-raisers (e.g., faculty members who obtained research grants) also were found to garner a greater proportionate share of the university's available *internal* (e.g., state appropriated) resources.[9] Likewise, claims can be made that a competition for students in recent years of declining enrollment has fostered many structural alterations (e.g., a reluctance to suspend pupils, an increased popularization of school curricula) designed to attract and hold student bodies;[10] that governmentally mandated parental advice (e.g., in special education) has given rise to new forms of administrative protectionism;[11] and that school curricula reflect a heavy competition between publishers for the lucrative textbook market (what kids learn is what publishers have decided will sell).[12]

The observation that lines of demarcation between organization and environment can easily become blurred is even apparent in the realm which Gross calls the "general environment." John Meyer and Brian Rowan claim, for example, that institutionalized rules, norms, and myths of the larger society are fully reflected in the formal structure of the educational organization—in the ways schools classify students, for instance, or avoid a close evaluation of their instructional outcomes. In an argument we will return to later in this chapter, Meyer and Rowan conclude:

> Both "closed-systems" and "open-systems" views of organizations tend to see them as encountering the environment at their *boundaries*. We see the structure of an organization as derived from and legitimated by the environment. In this view, organizations begin to lose their status as internally interdependent systems and come to be seen as dramatic reflections of—dependent subunits within—the wider institutional environment.[13]

In sum, there is a lack of clarity regarding what is environment and what is organization. Where does one establish the boundary? On the one hand the problem of boundary definition is complicated by the existence of many roles that are not easily classified. Is the board of education, for example, housed mainly in the organization or in its environment? How about students, parents who volunteer as teacher aides, the teachers' union president, PTA leaders, the school security guard who is also employed by the city police department, the day-by-day substitute teacher, the private psychologist who has been hired as a consultant? Armando Rivera is a member of the Puerto Rican community he wants to serve. Where does he fit?

On the other hand, and in a deeper sense, the problem of boundary definition is complicated by evidence of a close interactive relationship between the organization's formal structure and its immediate as well as general environment. Some scholars view the educational organization as an entity that encounters the environment at its boundaries and is engaged in many different ways in the task of adapting to external uncertainty. Others view the organization as so deeply imbued with societal norms, the common folklore, social myths, or the power structure that the delineation of a boundary between organization and environment loses all theoretical importance.

## The Problem of Organization-Environment Relationship

The notion of environment is, nevertheless, an extremely useful term in any effort to explain the complex process of interaction between an organization and those forces that do not appear to be integral to it. Just as there is no agreement on the nature of education's boundary, there are differing interpretations as to what it is that forms the *essence* of the organization-environment relationship. We explore four different explanations of this relationship.

One explanation of organization-environment has been offered by Jeffrey Pfeffer and Gerald Salancik and labeled a resource dependence perspective.[14] Pfeffer and Salancik note that the first order of business for any organization is "to manage to survive," and that organizations survive to the extent that they are able to acquire and maintain sufficient resources (including such intangible resources as good will and public trust, as well as the more tangible budget and talented workers). Organizations depend on their outside environments for these resources and must engage in transactions to insure their continued flow. Unfortunately, the environment is seldom stable and not altogether dependable. Survival "comes when the organization effectively adjusts to, and copes with" the many constraints in its external surroundings.[15] Colleges and universities, for example, are heavily dependent upon the availability of students. This important resource is neither in constant supply nor is it constant in quality. As student availability ebbs and flows, the university must adjust to survive. If it finds itself with fewer numbers of students interested in the liberal arts but more students interested in business or engineering courses, it must move organizational resources toward those latter areas of study. Alternatively, the university may cap enrollment in professional schools and increase arts and sciences requirements for all students to insure survival of the liberal arts college and faculty.

A second and closely related explanation of the organization-environment relationship has been offered by James Thompson.[16] Thompson also suggests that organizational survival is the central goal and that meeting environmental uncertainty is at the cutting edge of the survival function. Organizations meet environmental uncertainty, however, from a stance of instrumental rationality. That is, whether dependent upon or interdependent with their environments, organizations are basically goal-directed, and they attempt to control the environment strategically to achieve their goals. Colleges and universities devote a great deal of attention, for example, to the task of maintaining flows of students to their doorsteps. They do not just wait for alterations in student supply and adapt accordingly; rather, they reach out by recruiting students, revising admissions standards, advertising new programs, initiating off-campus or evening classes, and easing registration procedures. Instinctively this is what Armando Rivera was trying to do. From his earliest days as an administrator he was acutely interested in program development that would draw new populations of students into the still traditional institutions that were giving him a paycheck. One does not have the luxury to simply wait; one must initiate an idea and then be patient with its unfolding.

A third view of the environment would suggest that *both* organization and environment are engaged in the pursuit of *many* special purposes or interests (with attendant conflicts and adjustments transpiring between them). The interests may or may not be instrumentally rational and may or may not be linked with matters of organizational livelihood.[17] Exigencies, tensions, and stresses within *both* the internal organization *and* the external environment bring about transactions and negotiations out of which emerge alterations in organizational structure or policy. Deviance and disorganization may emerge just as easily as adaptations assisting organizational maintenance or survival.[18] Sociologist Walter Buckley, for example, writes:

> Any notion that a sociocultural system is self-regulating cannot mean a guarantee that—regardless of men's decisions and actions—stabilizing or adaptive control mechanisms will automatically come into play when 'disturbances' occur in the system. We have to be prepared for the possibility that a social system may generate and maintain deviant and disorganizing forces in just as 'automatic' a way as it generates mechanisms of conformity and organization.[19]

In short, organizations negotiate continuously with their environments but not always in a manner that meets the presumably best interests of their own adaptive stability or survival. A college or university may believe that its own long tradition of a highly specialized program of study, aimed at a special kind of student, is much too valuable a tradition to give up despite evidence that this market no longer exists. Similarly, a private elementary or secondary school sometimes tries to cling to a clientele that has long since moved away from the area of the city served by the institution.

Finally, a fourth explanation of the organization-environment relationship proceeds from an ecological or "natural selection" perspective. Michael Hannan and John Freeman, for example, have argued the need for careful study of the lives and times of *populations* of organizations (e.g., schools, hospitals, universities).[20] Studies of aggregates of organizations yield understandings on the shared fates and common environmental linkages of institutions as part of a "collective adaptive process."[21] From this perspective, such elements as the historical origins of organizations and the place, or niche, each species of organization fills in the overall culture of the society are quite as important as the adjustments organizations make to environmental contingencies at their boundaries. Theoretically, the ecology model often stands other notions of the organization-environmental relationship on their heads. Hannan and Freeman point out, for example, that it is commonly held that individual organizations seek to adapt to changing environments; but, alternatively, it may in fact be the environment that is doing the managing, selecting out "optimal combinations of organizations" for continued contributions to societal survival.[22]

In sum, opinions differ on how organizations adapt to their external environments. Some scholars see organizations engaged in a struggle for survival, amidst a condition of dependency upon the environment for the resources requisite to survival. Other scholars similarly posit a survival goal, but with quite a bit less dependency. Organizations actively (and rationally) reach out to create and control their own environments in their own best interests. Still others suggest that interaction between organization and environment occurs without respect to goal-directedness (even the supposedly critical objective of organizational survival). An exchange process occurs that may lead just as easily to deviance as it does to goal attainment. Finally, a fourth scholarly view argues that such goal directedness as there is in the relationship comes not from the organization—but from the environment. Classes, or populations, of organizations are structured in terms of their niches in the larger society.

## THEORIES OF ORGANIZATION AND ENVIRONMENT

These perspectives on the nature of the relationship between organization and environment are wrapped in differing theoretical interpretations. Those theoretical points of departure bring, in turn, alternative meanings to the administrator. The management of adaptation depends significantly upon how individual administrators view their responsibilities in relation to their world. In the remainder of this chapter we shall examine three major theoretical points of departure and their differing administrative ramifications. The theories are (a) the political systems approach to organization and environment, (b) the public choice approach, and (c) the organizational ecology model. Implications for the administrator's role within each theoretical perspective will also be discussed.

### A Political Systems Interpretation

Systems theory has had a far-reaching impact upon our understanding of organizational life. Although often criticized for being more meta-theoretic than useful in generating specific, testable hypotheses, there is no doubt that the systems approach has been close to a revolutionary advance in the management literature. In its simplest and most easily grasped form, the systems model is represented by one of its major theoreticians, political scientist David Easton), as shown in Figure 7.1.[23] Although Easton was interested in explaining the behavior of political systems, his analysis fits our understanding of organizations quite as easily. The environment provides inputs in the form of both demands upon the organization and support for it. These inputs are converted by the organization (qua political system) into decisions, actions, and statements of policy—which as outputs provide feedback into the larger environment. Constituencies react to these outputs, generating a new list of demands and supports with which the organization must contend.

In education one would expect a local community to provide support for its school system in the form of tax dollars, good will, educable children, voluntarism (e.g., people willing to serve on a board of education), supportive services (e.g.,

The Environment

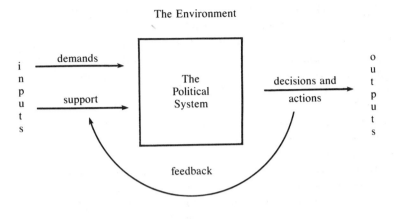

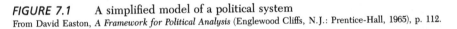

The Environment

**FIGURE 7.1**    A simplified model of a political system

From David Easton, *A Framework for Political Analysis* (Englewood Cliffs, N.J.: Prentice-Hall, 1965), p. 112.

police and fire protection), and obeisance (e.g., a willingness to go along with school rules). The community will also, of course, make many demands upon its schools (often expressed as values, interests, expectations, and preferences) regarding curricula, staffing, the allocation of resources, institutional purposes, and outcomes. These demands are often in conflict (or at least represent issues laden with potential conflict), forcing the organization as a political system into balancing, adapting, or compromising actions which feed back into the creation of new demands and new supports. Local school districts even in relatively homogeneous communities face conflicting pressures from conservatives and liberals, sports enthusiasts and classic-minded academicians, people with school-age children and retired citizens, math/science devotees and humanities advocates, those concerned about pupil control and those pursuing enhanced freedom of expression. In its absorption and digestion of varying preferences, the school district establishes courses of action which convey new messages to the surrounding polity and new orderings of local preferences. Football team boosters, for example, may feel that last year their interests were slighted by a decision not to light the high school athletic field in favor of the purchase of a bank of desk-top computers. This year, when information surfaces that the computers are little used by teachers and students, the demand to illuminate the football field resurfaces and gathers editorial support in the town newspaper.

Despite its relative simplicity, the systems model contains much elegance and widespread appeal, particularly in terms of its unusual flexibility. The model can be used to analyze the nationwide system of public education in America as well as in a study of a single element, or subsystem, of a larger order (e.g., a single classroom). Each of the various parts of an organization can be examined as a system in microcosm as well as a vital element of an integrated whole. Furthermore, the systems approach provides flexibility as a useful conceptual catch basin for the development of fine-grained organizational theory. Approaches as diverse as social-psychological models of the school (a social system, with interlocking personal and institutional dimensions of behavior) and economics-based approaches to educational administration (e.g., schooling as a "production function" with a mathematical relationship between outputs and inputs) are both enveloped in the overarching rubric of the systems analysis perspective.[24]

Beyond its appeal and flexibility, there are two key aspects of the systems approach that are of major importance to this comparative appraisal of theory relating the organization to its environment. These are the concepts of *interaction* and *equilibrium.*

**The Importance of Interaction.**   A rather common misconception in thinking about organizations is the assumption that the demands upon and the support provided an institution run essentially along a one-way street. One often hears this refrain in conversation with school administrators. The administrator complains of the pressures he or she is under and talks plaintively about the many constraints from outside forces (e.g., court actions, voter refusal to raise property taxes, vociferously vocal community leadership, declining numbers of school-age children, new state or federal regulatory mandates). To be sure, the feelings of school administrators that they are being increasingly battered and bruised by forces beyond their control often are accurate. The effects of some significant demographic changes, a serious economic recession, a shaken national confidence in the quality of public schooling, and an increasingly stiff competition for limited tax-dollar resources were some of the inescapable forces pressing upon the educational administrator in the 1970s and early 1980s. For many if not most educators, it was a puzzling milieu, because they had been raised professionally on a diet of steady growth.

A central and vitally important contribution from systems theory, however, is the realization that the open organization is not characterized by a one-way relationship. The notion of feedback between organization and environment is often misunderstood or misinterpreted as little more than an almost automatic stimulus and response. A set of inputs are converted into some outputs which communicate back into an altered pattern of inputs. As one of the earliest, and still classic, studies of the politics of organizations found, however, the feedback relationship between organization and environment is much more than simply reactive. Indeed, Philip Selznick (1949) found the Tennessee Valley Authority (TVA) actively engaged in a practice of "co-optation"—of reaching out to, and even creating its own supportive political milieu. In the process, however, the organization in its turn became deflected from its original goals into a pattern of performance that continued this close symbiosis between organization and environment. The feedback relationship was a convoluted, two-way process in which there was organizational as well as environmental initiative, and in which both sides incurred change.[25]

To make the same point in another fashion, we may note, with Easton, that organizations do not engage their environments successfully through a simple absorption of forces from their surroundings. To persist amidst pressures from outside, the organization as a viable system must "have the capacity to transform its own internal structure and processes."[26] Thus, the very design of the organization and the structuring of its internal managerial dynamics are wrapped in a give-and-take relationship that is open in much more than just a reactive sense. As Easton suggests, the system has the capacity to "take measures."[27]

This observation is addressed and fleshed out in practical terms for educational administration by Mark Hanson in *Educational Administration and Organizational*

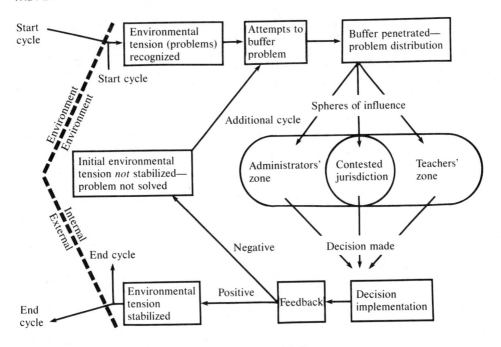

*FIGURE 7.2*    The problem-solving process as cycle of events
From E. Mark Hanson, *Educational Administration and Organizational Behavior* (Boston: Allyn & Bacon, 1981), p. 367.

*Behavior* (1979). Hanson developed a model of the problem-solving process in school administration which is reproduced here as Figure 7.2. Contingencies in the environment (growing tensions) are recognized by administrators as problems to be addressed. Administrators attempt to screen out or buffer the organization from a problem, but once a problem has penetrated the buffer, it is distributed to persons with appropriate spheres of jurisdiction or influence. Decisions are made and implemented. Consequently, the environmental tension may be stabilized, or if not stabilized, the problem-solving cycle may be reactivated. Throughout the process there is the understanding (integral to the model) that both the environmental constraints and/or contingencies and the organizational responses are highly variable and unpredictable. Both internally and externally there are many indeterminancies; some problems will fall into "contested" areas of organizational jurisdiction; and such forces as "lack of information, time, interest, and resources" may make implementation a much more difficult job than finding the initial solution of a problem.[28] Throughout, there is the clear notion that environmental interaction is a two-way boulevard. Both sides (organization and environment) reach out, both sides change, both sides adapt.

**The Idea of Dynamic Equilibrium.**    Hanson's model of a problem-solving process (Figure 7.2) also illustrates a second, key aspect of the systems approach, which is dynamic equilibrium. According to Hanson, as a problem arises and is recognized, there is an initial effort by the organization to protect and insulate itself. When problems are accepted, decision-making activity occurs (sometimes in multiple cycles) until the environmental tension is stabilized.[29] Research on local school boards, for example, has shown that a change in the membership of a local board (e.g., two new members elected to a seven-person board) is typically followed by a concerted and immediate effort on the part of the school district superintendent and existing board members to "socialize" the newcomers. Special orientation sessions are held in the superintendent's office, there are carefully guided tours of school facilities, and there are clear messages (e.g., a bit of chiding, some paternalism) at board meetings to indicate to new members that they are considered freshmen for a while (listeners rather than speakers).[30] The stabilizing of a problematic environment and even the protective activity of buffering represent elements in a process of environmental adjustment or adaptation that James Thompson terms survival; that David Easton calls the capacity to persist in a world of stability and change; and that Walter Buckley labels "remaining viable as an ongoing system."[31] Whatever the terminology, the point is that systems theory posits a special goal-directedness in organizational behavior that is aimed at maintaining the life of the institution. This is not to suggest, as Buckley takes pains to point out, that the search for viability requires a drive toward absolute permanence or stability of outside relationships. And, it certainly does not imply a balancing of organization and environment such that the system, like a child's swing, will always return to a kind of steady state or static equilibrium after being disturbed.[32] Rather, the notion of dynamic equilibrium includes organizational change, adaptiveness, and variation as inherent and necessary ingredients in system persistence. The persistence of a system is not akin to the simple maintenance or retention of existing patterns of relationships and procedures. Although it certainly attempts to buffer itself, and will undoubtedly seek to co-opt parts of its own political environment, the organization must be in motion, must change and adapt, in order to stay in place.[33] Persistence, as used by Easton, has meaning far beyond system maintenance, for it implies change as well as stability and infers a dynamic rather than static response to the stresses produced by an uncertain environment.[34]

How do organizations learn about their environments? In a review of research on this intriguing subject, Bo Hedberg noted that organizations act as experimenters; they blend an adjustment process of adapting to environmental forces with a manipulative process of selecting signals from and actually enacting their own external worlds.[35] Conditions of either information inundation or information scarcity are both troublesome. On the one hand, organizations program themselves to avoid uncertainty. They filter the outside world through rules and standard operating procedures that limit or simplify what might otherwise be an overload of incoming stimuli. On the other hand, organizations actively attack environmental uncertainty; they map their environments and learn from them. James March pointed out that organizations are remarkably adaptive and enduring. Most changes in organizations occur not from unusual incidents or crises, but rather from the operation of "relatively stable, routine processes."[36]

A case drawn from higher education is illustrative. Efraim Gil analyzed the efforts of a struggling, new state university to plan its survival in an era of altered demand and retrenchment.[37] The university was established as a senior-division (junior, senior, and graduate level) institution in the late 1960s. The new institution attracted students by being an innovative and experimental place of higher learning. This mission spawned an open admissions policy; the elimination of traditional letter grades in favor of course-end evaluative comments by faculty; a contemporaneous renaming of traditional departments and disciplines (for example, arts and sciences became cultural studies); and an emphasis upon community service rather than the traditional values of research and publication in hiring and promoting faculty.

As the more conservative 1970s unfolded, the university found that its environment had changed. Student enrollments failed by a wide margin to reach expectations of institutional growth; serious rumors of inferior instructional quality were abroad; state revenues entered a period of stringency with accompanying demands for accountability; and a strongly supportive local political constituency failed to develop for the community service/activist faculty. The institution, in trouble by the late 1970s, replaced much of its top-level administration, and began planning a new organizational purpose.

The planning process was given a good deal of attention—with a heavy investment of administration, faculty, and staff time. By the early 1980s, a new statement of university mission emerged, with accompanying changes in institutional structure and function. And therein lies the point of the case, for the new mission of the university reflected well the combination of change *and* stability that characterizes an adaptive process. The new mission statement represented the institution's effort to survive in a changed environment—but *on its terms*. Change was tempered by a mapping of the external environment as well as a process of learning from it that filtered messages through ongoing institutional structures and standard operating procedures. The open admissions policy of the institution was continued, for example, but an honors program was initiated to track and "challenge" the more "highly qualified scholars," and a "developmental program" was started for poorly prepared entrants. A more traditional practice of awarding letter grades for coursework replaced the earlier innovation, but students were still permitted to elect instructor comments and pass/fail in place of a letter grade if they wished.

Steps were taken toward the provision of a more traditional liberal arts curriculum for undergraduates, but the university continued its policy of trying vigorously to attract to higher education populations of students who were "underrepresented in the attainment of college degrees." The community service emphasis of the institution in its experimental infancy was rechanneled (consistent with the new sense of mission) into a set of enrollment-generation and continuing-education activities. "Outreach" efforts were developed to entice the registration of senior citizens, adult part-time students, and housewives seeking employable skills. Similarly, community service was also redirected into the provision of branch learning sites and a profusion of short courses or workshops "at company sites" for local business and industry. Finally, the university tried to define for itself a new local political constituency that moved toward sets of firmly established institutional (rather than community activist) relationships. Area community colleges were particularly cultivated, as were local business, industry, health care facilities, and schools. By the early 1980s the struggling institution had redirected itself, and it was still trying, step by step, to come to terms with a changing environment.

**The Systems Approach: A Summary.**   The systems approach pictures educational organizations in reciprocal interaction with their social environments. Using the Easton model, we see the environment producing inputs of demands and supports which are converted by the organization into outputs, which in turn feed back into the formation of new inputs. Drawing upon Easton in their statement of a politics of education, Frederick Wirt and Michael Kirst suggest that demands will most often be accompanied by a mobilization of resources so as to influence the disposition of the system, while supports

> take the form of a willingness to accept the decisions of the system or the system itself. A steady flow of supports is necessary if any political system is long to maintain its legitimacy.[38]

Both demands and supports are usually mediated by interest groups which communicate the wants, urgings, and values of the citizenry, as well as the special values of narrowly defined private interests, to the school polity.[39]

There is a continuous (and, of course, reciprocal) interaction between the organization and its environment; and while organizations may strive as Wamsley and Zald suggest for a "bland and benign environment,"[40] the equilibrium of interest between organization and environment typically is in dynamic tension. There is an ebb and flow to the distribution of interests and to the power that accompanies demand and support communication. Armando Rivera watched the apparent power of the community organization he was contending with seem to decline, but had someone won and someone lost? Would this particular state of detente be permanent? He was smart enough to know that new environmental challenges to the objectives and procedures of the college were just around the corner. You worked toward a balance, but the scales seemed never to be quite steady. While organizations display considerable ability to co-opt environmental forces, to deal with contingencies, to smooth out turbulence, and to change while remaining much the same, the process of ensuring organizational persistence is a constant battle that is never really won. The central and most important contribution of the systems approach is the thesis of a constant dialectic of adaptation between organization and environment—a continuing struggle toward equilibrium, as the organization responds to the complex and changing surprises of demand and support in its external milieu.

## The Public Choice Approach

Systems theory is focused upon the behavior of *collectivities*—groups, or subsystems, which form an organizational whole with persistence or survival as a central objective. The organization is considered to have a life of its own, with norms, expectations, and goals that transcend those of the particular individuals serving within it. The organization contains characteristics which represent something more than the behaviors and performances of its individual actors.[41]

An alternative theoretical perspective, that uses the *individual* as its point of departure, is the public choice or political economy approach. This approach uses a rationality of human behavior paradigm from economics to ask how self-interested individuals seek to maximize their own welfare within the context of an organizational reward structure. Although the behavior of people in groups is of no less interest to public-choice than to systems theorists, it is the action of the individual (even when operating collectively with others) that provides the basis for an understanding of the organization.

In an article examining the utility of this conceptual approach for the study of public school administration, William Boyd employs the work of Charles Perrow as a basis.[42] Perrow argued that organizational theorists often fail to distinguish adequately between the *professed* goals of human service organizations and their *operative* goals. While organizations may state a special set of objectives, their actions often clearly indicate an entirely different institutional direction. Specifically, we find that employees, interest groups, and other organizations *use* human-service organizations for their own purposes. People exploit the organization for increased power, greater security, eased upward mobility, an enhancement of employee benefits, a deepening of collegial friendships, and for many other very human reasons. Thus, schools seek to improve the reading performance of elementary school pupils but incur tradeoffs in the process in the need to protect teachers' jobs, make principals look good, spend scarce resources on other pet projects of top administrators, or ratify a curriculum favored by a powerful minority of school system actors.

The public choice approach, argues Boyd, provides a route toward the explanation of Perrow's conclusions. The rational choice paradigm "calls attention to the difference and tension between the goals of individuals (maximizing their own welfare) and the professed goals of organizations."[43] The key to individual behavior resides in the incentive structure of the organization—in the pressures and opportunities surrounding the employee that dramatize such rewards as prestige, job security, advancement, an avoidance of conflict, a sense of efficacy, power, autonomy, a higher salary, collegialism, and personal safety.[44]

Illustrations of Perrow's argument abound in the literature on school administration. David Rogers' analysis of the New York City Public Schools conveys a message of an unhealthy, even moribund bureaucracy so steeped in its own internal pathologies that goal displacement surrounds every effort by the board of education to program a bit of change. Rogers' examples, however, convey *rationality*, not pathology. An order to implement pupil desegregation through a voluntary, open enrollment transfer of pupils was sabotaged by building principals who feared the loss of their best achieving pupils in an organizational milieu that judged principals on test-score evidence of school quality; who feared looking bad if too many parents transferred their children out; and who feared budget loss within an enrollment-driven resource allocation procedure.[45]

Similarly, Van Cleve Morris and his research associates examined acts of "creative insubordination" by school principals within the reward structure of another large-city school system. Rules were bent, regular channels short-circuited, information held back or reworked, directives ignored, and special ploys utilized to meet such reward-related expectations as (a) keeping the school site under control and free of sticky problems that have to be brought to the attention of hierarchical superiors; (b) obtaining and retaining faculty cooperation; (c) protecting the school and the bureaucracy from parental pressures; and (d) smoothing the downward flow of resources to one's school with minimum hierarchical conflict, such as overcoming a short supply of textbooks through informal collegial contacts.[46]

Public choice theory attempts to apply traditional economic analysis and its behavioral assumptions (rational, utilitarian man) to the nonmarket decision-making world of government. It recognizes key differences between the behavior of those who supply and demand services under market conditions and those who act under nonmarket conditions. Under nonmarket conditions, for example, an organization's clientele must rely more often on a voicing of complaint rather than a search for alternative suppliers. Parents of public school children are likely to express dissatisfaction verbally or in writing, organize a bit of political opposition, and cast a No vote or two at election time long before they make, in large enough numbers to be heard, the rather drastic and costly decision to seek education elsewhere. Voice is a less potent weapon than exit—much less so if the people who manage public organizations can secure and protect themselves (particularly their budgets) against client attack.[47]

The *first* component of the public choice approach is its focus on the utility-maximizing (self-interested) behavior of individuals (or collections of them) as they make decisions amidst a system of incentives. It is a theory that recognizes the importance of a managerial reward structure in shaping the decisions of public organizations. *Second,* the theory pinpoints supply and demand characteristics in an organization's environment. Both political elements (e.g., interest groups, the media, the judiciary, legislative bodies) and economic forces (e.g., facilities costs, labor supply, the economic state of the nation, current demand for the organization's output) are examined as part of an *exchange* relationship between organization and environment. As Dennis Mueller puts it: "Probably the most important accomplishment of economics is the demonstration that individuals with purely selfish motives can mutually benefit from exchange."[48] *Third,* the public choice approach examines the special circumstances and consequences of the economic model of behavior in the absence of market controls. Niskanen argues, for example, that without a market's built-in pressures toward efficiency, the central incentive for the public bureaucrat is to maximize the budget of his own organization or unit. Although budget maximization is not always inconsistent with output efficiency, often the effect is that too much is produced at too high a cost.[49]

**Public Choice Theory and Education's Environment.**    Public choice theory is being studied as an informative alternative approach to the conceptualization of influences upon educational administration.[50] We suggest two key points of departure in appreciating the message of this approach. Systems of incentives *external* to the organization guide and constrain the educational organization's exchange with its environment. Furthermore, a reward structure *internal* to the educational organization determines its environmental relations.

**Incentives External to the Organization.**    Economist Charles Tiebout offered one of the earliest contributions to the development of public choice theory in the mid-1950s. Tiebout contended that there is a market for such locally supplied public services as education, which is evidenced by the opportunities people have to vote with their feet in the selection of communities in which to live.[51] People move into communities having educational programs (plus a package of other services) that suit their individual preferences. Consumers exercising residential mobility create pressures toward efficiency and consumer sensitivity in the delivery of local services. That is, a useful competition will be waged among jurisdictions for desirable residents; moreover, demand and supply conditions will lead toward an optimally desired ratio of service delivery to taxation cost. Rationally economic householders choose a preferred community in which to live on the basis of how well the costs of residence are offset by the benefits of such desired services as good schools, nice parks, effective police protection, and clean air. Bish and Nourse observe that

> Families who place a high value on good schools locate where there are good schools. They then continue to vote, lobby, etc. for the maintenance of good schools. Families who place a lower value on good schools (perhaps preferring lower taxes) will locate where schools are not as good but taxes are lower.[52]

To the extent that Tiebout's hypothesis holds true, the incentive in any geographical area will be for people to sort themselves out according to their preferences into small and relatively homogeneous school districts that provide educational programs particularly to their liking. This often results, particularly in metropolitan areas, in a proliferation of communities and school districts that proceed to maintain their uniqueness and isolation through zoning regulations and real estate prices.[53] In Illinois, in the suburban areas of Chicago, one of the unexpected side-effects of high school closings due to enrollment decline (in the early 1980s) was a rash of attempts at de-annexation. Residents in the attendance area of a high school slated for closing petitioned to withdraw their property from District A and join a more compatible District B. De-annexation efforts by householders proceeded apace with efforts by state education department officials to urge just the opposite—i.e.,a consolidation of local school districts for managerial efficiency.

The simplistic elegance of the Tiebout hypothesis breaks down when one considers the fact that many residents would like to choose the right community in which to live from their standpoints, but cannot. Their mobility is restricted, by virtue of their poverty, racial characteristics, or ethnicity; and, although they value good schools, they frequently find themselves in the incongruous position of suffering poor schools *and* high taxes.[54] The incentives toward residential segregation coupled with constraints limiting the mobility of the poor have created huge inequalities between cities and suburbs and between rich and poor school districts. Furthermore, as Paul Peterson points out, the favorably placed school districts are able to maintain and even strengthen their competitive advantages (through policies aimed at developing their local economies), while central-city school systems, with their size and heterogeneity, find themselves having instead to *redistribute* scarce resources to overcome the handicaps of poverty. A redistributive policy transfers money, services, and attention from the better off to the less well off segments of a community. Thus, "more prosperous families living in the central city are subsidizing the education of their poor neighbors."[55] The incentive over time will be for these wealthier persons to move to other locations (the suburbs) where there is a more favorable ratio of taxation to benefits received.[56]

In sum, the collective actions of individuals who are making choices on the basis of incentives (e.g., the benefit/tax ratio) result in environmentally determined constraints upon educational organizations and their administrators. From this perspective, we see that the nature and population characteristics of a surrounding community, the range of policy options open to consideration (e.g., developmental vs. redistributive), the limits upon tax-resource availability for schools, and the dangers of pursuing a course of action that might add to householder mobility (e.g., white flight due to busing) all represent very real considerations for the school administrator that flow directly from the choices that individuals make in weighing their gains and losses associated with living here rather than there.

If constraints associated with the market for educational services represent one key dimension of the environment according to public choice theory, a second key element is the economy of political representation. In *The Logic of Collective Action*, (1965) Mancur Olsen observed that many kinds of public goods or services are distributed broadly in the community as collective benefits. Because these benefits (e.g., clean air, tree-lined streets) are available to all, it is not in the self-interest of rational individuals to participate in or voluntarily contribute toward their provision. They can enjoy a free ride and obtain the benefits without the cost of personal involvement.[57]

The same holds true for public education. Although parents with children in the public schools do have more incentive to participate in decisions on public schooling than those without, the majority of these can continue to enjoy educational services without having to become politically involved. Whether or not you join the PTA, attend board meetings, contribute to a bake sale, chaperone a school dance, or volunteer to help out in the school library, you will continue to enjoy the fruits of other people's volunteerism and activism, and to depend upon the services of just a few members of the community in the relative certainty that the interests of the majority will continue to be served.

On the debit side of the ledger of collective action, however, there is the greater ease with which special interests can be served. Such broad-based, education-oriented organizations as the PTA have difficulty securing participation, but groups more narrowly focused are inclined to become potent lobbies. There is a much greater stake in joining and supporting a group selectively involved in securing benefits for athletes, musicians, or the gifted than in identifying with an umbrella organization that is looking out for the community at large. In their classic study of politics in New York City, Sayre and Kaufman found the schools of that city responding differently to "core" and "satellite" groupings of political interest. Groups with a long history of educational activism and with interests that paralleled the board's own had much more leverage in the enactment of board policy than others.[58]

Thus, educational administrators must contend with the delivery of services in a free-ride atmosphere. It is difficult to secure public-spirited participation or involvement in the general welfare of the organization when issues of significant import, such as a property tax referendum, are before the community. Special interests (e.g., textbook censors, unionized teachers, special education promoters) which have a clear sense of the payoff associated with a commitment of time are much more likely to seek to influence school policy. Even those persons formally designated as representatives of the community at large, such as local board of education members, easily become a special interest group of their own with increasing detachment from the wider polity. Furthermore, Boyd observes that educational organizations must necessarily be concerned with securing the resources needed to maintain themselves, and therefore they become "vulnerable to manipulation by the professionals in school systems and other agencies upon whom they may depend, to a greater or lesser extent, for such resources."[59] Local school administrators turn symbiotically to like-minded professionals in university departments of education, state or federal agencies, lobbies (e.g., a state administrators' association), or private educational consulting firms for advice on matters of school quality, management, personnel policy, and in-service training. Educators all, they tend to share a common language, frame of reference, and sense of the possible. "Stupid" questions—for instance, why increase teachers' pay for years of experience and education when there is no evidence that these factors make an impact on instructional quality?—do not get asked.

**Incentives Internal to the Organization.** In *The Bureaucratic Phenomenon* (1964), Michel Crozier provided a fascinating account of the actions of maintenance workers to achieve effective control over their own work roles. The maintenance people were strategically placed within an industrial organization (albeit a governmental monopoly) that had as its most unpredictable sore spot a tendency toward machine failure. Machine stoppages hurt the entire organization. Maintenance workers, through an adroit manipulation of the repair function (e.g., they could take a long time or just a short time to fix a machine), acquired considerable power and influence within the larger organization.[60] Similarly, a study by Alvin Gouldner, *Patterns of Industrial Bureaucracy* (1954), explained how the risks associated with the hazardous, low-status job of below-ground miner in a gypsum plant gave these employees much more control over their own work lives than their corporation co-workers who served above ground.[61] And, worthy of another mention here, in *TVA and the Grass Roots* (1949), Philip Selznick showed how managers of the Tennessee Valley Authority successfully reached out to co-opt people in outside pressure groups and, thereby, added to their own status and security within the organization.[62]

Each of these selections from the classic literature on organizations illustrates the incentives that individuals have to reduce (or gain control over) central sources of uncertainty in the organizational environment. James Thompson argues that coping with uncertainty is *the* fundamental problem for the complex organization.[63] To the extent that individuals acting rationally in their own self-interest can acquire some degree of control over elements of uncertainty, they may enjoy the rewards of job security, the loyalty and cooperation of co-workers, power, better pay, physical amenities, and enhanced prestige. As we noted earlier, using Perrow's argument, such actions may lead the organization toward, and be indicative of, the pursuit of operative goals in place of professed goals.

In a study of the use of information in organizations, Feldman and March have provided us with an interesting illustration of how all of this works. While the conventional wisdom suggests that information is collected to assist informed decision making, in practice this is not always so. Administrators may collect information less to improve their decision making than to survey the environment for surprises—to guard themselves from sneak attack, sudden changes, or unforeseen shifts in clientele preference. Similarly, individual incentives for gathering information might selfishly include (a) the accumulation or hoarding of intelligence in order to enhance one's own power or status in an organization; (b) the collection of too much information lest one be accused whenever errors are made of having collected too little; and (c) the strategic misrepresentation of information that is sent to others so that the collector will be sure to look good.[64]

In their study of the working days of large-city principals, Van Cleve Morris and his research colleagues observed school administrators busily managing the news in just this fashion. In a special census of bilingual teachers, for example, school district headquarters learned from building principals that there was apparently a serious shortage of this specialized category of personnel in the school district. Actually, principals throughout the city had under-reported their own stock of bilingual personnel, deliberately withholding the names of qualified persons who had been cultivated as substitutes, were known to be in the neighborhood, or who were already on board as regular classroom teachers. The authors concluded: "Each principal figured that every other principal, in his right mind, would have done the same thing; hence the staff report was meaningless, and reported a severe shortage when in fact none actually existed."[65]

An additional interesting observation on managerial incentives vis-a-vis the uncertainties of the environment can be developed. John Freeman has noted that a fundamental problem in education is that its central technology of instruction and learning is poorly understood. No one appears to know what techniques work best, with whom, for what reasons. Second, because their range of expertise is recognizably limited, professional educators are especially vulnerable to outside criticism. It is hard for schools to demonstrate their effectiveness, and there is no lack of interest groups with their own answers to educational quality. The tendency for school administrators under such conditions is to try to manage their public relations in such a manner as to redirect or thwart outside criticism.[66] Indeed, we see an example of this in Rick Ginsberg's analysis of three major twentieth century surveys of the Chicago Public Schools, which shows that in each case the motive was to restore confidence, quell criticisms, and quiet public discontent.[67]

One further central effect of the absence of a normal economic exchange with the environment is the tendency for self-interested employees to engage in behaviors that turn inward toward the maximization of their own welfare. Jacob Michaelsen points out that bureaucrats must satisfy politicians, not customers, for their resources. In lieu of such clear bottom-line indications of efficiency as company profits, public-sector managers (including educators)

> seek instead to survive, to enlarge the scope of their activities, to gain prestige, to avoid conflict, to control the organization and content of their daily round as much as possible.[68]

Michaelsen continues succinctly, "Budgets rather than profits are maximized."[69]

Such a conclusion is not to suggest, with undue pessimism, that altruism and working hard to achieve the organization's professed goals (e.g., improved pupil achievement) are totally lost, for there are also many rewards in doing good and in striving for excellence. It *is* to suggest that the nature of the market in public schooling and the structure of incentives for educators heavily encourage, as Michaelsen puts it, "pervasive goal displacement."[70] Alliances may be fashioned with influential external agencies; bargains may be struck with employee groups; public access to information may be shut off; board of education members may be co-opted; and state legislators may be lobbied by administrator groups—all done in direct conformity with a reward structure in public service that makes such action highly rational. As Boyd puts it: "There is little need or reward for doing otherwise."[71]

**The Public Choice Approach: A Summary.** The public choice approach finds educational organizations guided by the self-interested actions of individuals. A structure of incentives in the external environment is reflected in choices (e.g., where to live, whether to participate) that collectively surround the organization with sets of administrative constraints and uncertainties. A school district serving a wealthy suburb with restrictive zoning ordinances is keyed-in not only to the exclusionary interests of its community clientele, but also to the community's norms and values, its expectations and aspirations. Indeed, in some early research on the local politics of education, David Minar found that even the attributes associated with presumably effective school administration (e.g., conflict-management skills) vary with the social environment of the community.[72]

Similarly, a structure of incentives within the milieu of the organization (for those who work or serve within it) is reflected in the decisions that are made by these individuals to pursue increases in budget, to attend to the expectations of parents, to provide useful information to administrative superiors, to implement a new directive, to be innovative, to take on conflict. The organization's responsiveness to its environment is closely tied to its structure of rewards for the individuals who serve within it. Moreover, we find a good deal of the research to date in the arena of education telling us that existing systems of reward quite often lead toward operative, in place of professed, goals. It is now an old story in higher education to note that the publish-or-perish syndrome of professorial advancement leads *away* from the popularized university mission of public service, and indeed, even of good teaching. Similarly, it is now well recognized that elementary and secondary principals are prone to back teachers up in conflicts with parents even if the parent is right, and that building an atmosphere of pupil control in schools tends to be a first priority over the guiding of student learning.[73]

An important observation from the public choice perspective for those who manage educational institutions is captured in the recent use of the term *boundary spanning* to describe jobs performed at the institutional periphery.[74] Persons in boundary-spanning roles (such as Armando Rivera) are in direct contact with the environment. They interpret the organization to its clientele; they socialize outsiders into the ways and norms of the institution; they collect, massage, and pass on information about what is going on externally; and they are a first line of organizational defense or point of attack. In the language of Michael Lipsky, these roles are often performed at the street level of the organization—at the lowest point in the managerial and professional hierarchy, where the organization is engaged in its most frequent and significant contacts with citizens.[75]

Of key importance is the understanding that street-level bureaucrats are *individuals.* They work at the nethermost levels of the bureaucratic structure in defined roles, but they exercise the discretion necessary to a job filled with the unpredictability and uncertainty of client interaction. That discretion, as Armando Rivera discovered, often is limited. Recall that in his case he exercised independent judgment (based on experience and special knowledge) often, but that the concerns of his boss had to be taken into account continually. Street level administrators find themselves serving some clients more thoroughly than others; they may discover occasionally that it is necessary to develop special simplifications or routines to reduce the strains of public contact (e.g., as police officers learn to stereotype offenders); and they may learn to redefine their own roles (e.g., investigating some crimes more than others) in a manner that suits their own special sense of work efficacy.[76] In short, these individuals, while representing the organization at its environmental boundaries, are coping with their own work-related pressures and understandings of institutional incentives. They contribute to the organization's adaptation to its environment (they span its boundaries, after all), but they also respond to an individualized rationality of their own.


## The Organizational Ecology Model

Some two decades ago, Richard Carlson anticipated the most recent of our three theoretical perspectives, in his observation that elementary and secondary school systems are thoroughly "domesticated" organizations.[77] Schools are unlike types of institutions in which either the organization or its clients has a freedom of choice in selecting the services of one another. Children are forced to attend school, and the school is forced to take them.

Domesticated organizations can be contrasted with "wild" ones—those which must compete for clients (who participate voluntarily), and, as a result, must constantly struggle even harder to survive. With their existence guaranteed by law, the public schools are not quite as caught up as other organizations in a struggle for survival; however, they do (as a consequence of their lack of control over the selection of clients) display some special adaptive mechanisms. Schools may try to control their unselected clientele by ability grouping, by differentiating the curriculum (e.g., college preparatory or vocational), and by over-emphasizing disciplinary norms (e.g., through grades, attendance and tardiness controls, and numerous codes of good conduct). Students, for their part, may adapt to their lack of choice by engaging in open rebellion, by situational retirement, or by attending school for side payments of athletics, music, or peer stimulation.

Brian Rowan suggests that another feature of domesticated organizations is that they are highly "sensitive to normative standards developed externally."[78] Agencies that provide support, endorsement, and/or regulation to an institution also supply definitions of purpose. The domesticated organization is particularly sensitive to innovations that have captured popular and especially legislative attention. These innovations encourage a rapid and usually widespread diffusion of alternative structures with, almost invariably, a rather short life span. Coming and going just within the last few decades have been major and usually nationwide innovations in new math, teacher-proof curricula, the nongraded elementary school, the open classroom, programmed learning, pass/fail grading, performance budgeting, and free schools. At present, back-to-basics, computer literacy, science education, and mastery learning are hot educational items, doomed perhaps to similar fates.

The notion of the domesticated organization fits our third theory of organization and environment. The organizational ecology approach returns to the organization as a whole as its unit of analysis. It argues, as its central theme, that organizations are the creatures of their environments. Unlike theories that tie the outcomes of organizations to a certain, institutionalized goal-directedness or to the internal rationality of individual actors, the ecology model suggests that conditions and constraints *in the outside environment* guide organizational behavior. Marshall Meyer writes:

> The ecological approach assumes that external events determine population characteristics of organizations, but the transaction cost approach favored by economists treats organizations as maximizers and envisions both internal and external sources of organizational arrangements.[79]

The organizational ecologists do not hedge; they unequivocally tie internal structure and process to environmental forces.[80] The approach borrows heavily from notions of natural selection in biology and incorporates concepts of competition, the struggle for existence, adaptive variation and retention, cultural habitat (or niche), and species mortality.[81] Unlike other theoretical approaches, the ecology perspective is as much interested in organizational failure and demise as success.

The approach upsets other theoretical notions of environmental adaptation. While it is commonly held that organizational decision makers reach out to control or adapt to their environments, the ecology perspective denies this contention. It is the environment that selects out, that controls, that engages in optimizing behavior.[82] Meyer and Rowan have applied this point to public schooling. They observe that schools are renowned for exerting incongruously light bureaucratic control over their most important activity—instruction. While some would reply that this is evidence of the "loose coupling"[83] that characterizes educational organizations, Meyer and Rowan suggest to the contrary that such weak control is possible only because schools are really quite "tightly, not loosely, organized."[84]

Tight coupling comes from the controls schools exert over "ritual classifications" surrounding the curriculum, students, and teachers. Students are classified and move through the educational system in standardized ways—by grade-level, by type (e.g., educationally handicapped, college preparatory), by previous education, and often by residence, ability, and ethnicity. Teachers are surrounded by institutionalized classifications according to subject area, credentialing, level of instruction, background, and training. There are also many curriculum-related rituals that define assignments of teachers, students, and resources to available space (e.g., a fourth-grade classroom); that define topics of instruction (e.g., all fourth graders learn math); and that even define a school (e.g., all schools keep detailed records of students).

Meyer and Rowan argue that tight organizational controls in such areas as "the credentialing and hiring of teachers, the assignment of students to classes and teachers, and scheduling" conform to institutionalized rules (and societal myths) about what is proper and valid in education. When all of this seems to be in evidence and properly assembled, then learning is understood to be going on.

> Educators (and their social environments) decouple their ritual structure from instructional activities and outcomes and resort to a 'logic of confidence': Higher levels of the system organize on the *assumption* that what is going on at lower levels makes sense and conforms to rules, but they avoid inspecting it to discover or assume responsibility for inconsistencies and ineffectiveness. In this fashion, educational organizations work more smoothly than is commonly supposed, obtain high levels of external support from divergent community and state sources, and maximize the meaning and prestige of the ritual categories of people they employ and produce.[85]

The organizational ecology model thus tries to persuade us that organizations are created, defined, and moved by their outside environments. Internally, the structures and the processes that describe the work that its people do are merely representative of externally generated forces—the many outside conditions and constraints, including cultural norms and rituals, that surround each societal institution. Could Armando Rivera have killed the program begun by the community squatters? Certainly, we might argue; after all, the key to the door belongs to the college. But, others might contend, a *community* college has to serve that community, however obstreperous or erratic its representatives may be. Maybe Armando had lost the conventional key; perhaps the community upstarts had even more power than they realized (or even wanted). As much interested in explaining organizational failure as success, the ecology model adds that institutions, like living organisms, undergo adaptive efforts, or die. Thus, those who are saying that the public schools are in trouble, that public schooling may go under, are suggesting that education and its environment are somehow losing touch, that a drive toward species mortality is somehow outpacing the adaptiveness of public education.

**Population Ecology and Education.**     There are two key variations in approach to issues of organizational ecology that are of central interest as we examine education and its environment. The first of these commonly has been termed *population ecology,* and the second consists of the understandings that are labeled *resource dependence theory.*[86]

The population ecology model examines species of organizations in the aggregate (e.g., all public schools, all universities, all parochial schools). To be considered part of a common population, part of a species, the organizations must share common properties. How do such organizations adapt collectively to the larger environment? Population ecologists point out that traditional management theory has assumed that organizational change or innovation is consciously directed or planned —usually in connection with some operative goals, preferences, or ambitions that are articulated within the structure of the organization. To the ecologists, change can be both planned and unplanned. In the final analysis, new organizational forms occur as the result of environmental constraints, through a tendency among all organizations to vary with, select from, and retain that which best fits them (vis-a-vis their environments) for survival.[87]

One of the key concepts of population ecology is the idea of *niche,* the notion that a species of organization may inhabit a distinct arena or space in the environment, in which it outcompetes all other organizational forms for resources and ultimately survival.[88] This concept can be useful in explaining why some organizations appear to specialize while others generalize. Certain institutions of higher education, for example, have been well known for their special focus upon certain programs of study, (teacher education, engineering, four-year liberal arts degrees); or certain populations of students (women, city-dwellers, blacks); or certain approaches to learning (Antioch, Tuskegee). Many other institutions develop into reasonably comprehensive, broad-based houses of learning—each of which seeks to build a balanced curriculum under one large organizational roof.

Hannan and Freeman have argued that specialization and generalism are closely related to uncertainties in the organizational environment. Specializing organizations are likely to do well when uncertainty is low but also when uncertainty is exceedingly high. Generalizing organizations will often accumulate excess resource capacity and increase their capacity to deal with a variable environment, but at a cost in efficiency. When the environment is changing quite rapidly, the specializing organization can ride out the turbulence, while generalizing organizations tend to waste time and energy adjusting structures to short-lived conditions (e.g., a program budgeting fad, an ethnic studies phase, a student activism period).[89] Many private secondary schools, for example, define themselves narrowly (e.g., as laboratory schools, Catholic girls' schools, military academies). While such institutions certainly are quite vulnerable to environmental change, they are not as likely as public high schools to expend resources responding to environmental crises (e.g., calls for minimum competency testing, PSSC physics, learning disabilities) that soon pass from the societal and educational scene.

Finally, the population ecology point of view has been used by Laura Salganik and Nancy Karweit to explore characteristics distinguishing private from public education.[90] In response to the Coleman II finding that private schools outperform public institutions,[91] Salganik and Karweit note that fundamental differences in their social environments suggest that these are really two separate populations of organization. Private schools derive their legitimacy as institutions, for example, from being accepted as schools by a willing clientele who decide voluntarily to enroll their children. Furthermore, the private school's legitimacy is continuously being reaffirmed by families; its legitimacy is respected. Public schools have their legitimacy conferred upon them by governmental authority, but this legitimacy is quite separable from considerations of respect. Children may attend the public school without the value consensus and mutual trust that typically accompany such respect. In schools supported by consensus and trust, the authors suggest we will find that ". . . parents are more likely to support specific decisions made by the school, and to trust that the staff will act in the best interests of their children."[92] Salganik and Karweit conclude that quite simply "because private schools are voluntaristic and public schools are run by the government, the educational process is intrinsically different in public and private schools."[93] Although both types certainly deserve the label *school*, they inhabit separate niches and are vitally different forms of organization.

**Resource Dependency and Education.**    Population ecology examines the characteristics of *groups* of organizations and their life cycles (including birth and death processes) in response to conditions and constraints in the external environment. A perspective that places no less emphasis upon the effect of the environment but returns to the analysis of *individual* organizations is labeled resource dependency.[94] The unit of analysis is no longer the species; it is, once again, each unique organization.

Resource dependence theory argues that an organization is most critically attentive to those elements in its environment that provide the resources important to its survival. The demands of groups that control critical resources will receive the most attention.[95] Not at all unlike political systems theory in this regard, the resource dependence model suggests that at the input level demands and support from the environment are converted by the organization into outputs that seek a life-prolonging equilibrium for the organization(see Figure 7.1). And, again, in recognition of political reality, both theories realize that those who have the most power (e.g., through their control over dollars, public opinion, regulatory mandates, votes) will have much more pull upon the organization than those who are powerless.

Resource dependency and systems theory also share another important observation—an element not recognized by the population ecologists. This is the notion that the relationship between organization and environment is an interactive one. Those who run organizations, according to both theories, do not just sit back and take it. They reach out as administrators to try to alter their own environments—to manage, as Pfeffer puts it, "their external dependencies, both to ensure the survival of the organization and to acquire, if possible, more autonomy and freedom from external constraint."[96] Both theories recognize that in their dependency upon their environments, organizations are rewarded if they can somehow acquire a bit of their own power and discretion over that dependency. Quite often, important roles are developed by the organization for just that purpose. College and university presidents typically devote less time to the internal management of their organizations and give more time to fund raising lunches with alumni groups and (in the case of public institutions) sessions with legislators. School district superintendents typically put a great deal of time into managing the agendas of their local boards of education. What gets before the board and what does not, what gets read and what does not, what comes up first and what last—these are important issues in the lives of school administrators.

Where the systems theory and resource dependency points of view part company is with the latter's contention that the managerial framework of an organization (particularly its internal distribution of power) is a reflection of environmental contingencies. In short, the resource dependence model links the internal politics of an organization (and thus its structure and function) to environmental effects; internally, the organization reflects its external constraints. Administrative actions are influenced by the distribution of power within the organization and this distribution, in turn, is an outgrowth of resource dependencies in the outside environment. Armando Rivera wanted the budding community program under the college aegis because (in part) it could generate additional state funds. Not much, perhaps, but every dollar counts when they are doled out by a state bureaucracy. Systems theory and resource dependency agree that survival is a prime goal for the organization and that organizations tend to reach out and manage their own survival; the resource dependence model, however, incorporates from ecology the added notion that it is the environment that essentially creates the conditions for intraorganizational behavior. To understand the behavior of an organization internally, one must first understand its resource dependence linkages with its environment.[97]

Jeffrey Pfeffer and Gerald Salancik provide an illustration from their study of resource allocations within a large state university.[98] They asked under what conditions some university departments were likely to receive larger proportionate budget allotments than others. While on the surface, resources were distributed to the departments on the basis of differences in instructional work load (departments with more students were to receive more dollars), in practice another measure of departmental power came heavily into play. Academic departments receiving larger proportionate allocations (more than their workload promised) of legislatively appropriated (or general) funds were those that had been most successful over time in bringing *outside* grants and contracts into the university. The best money-raisers from outside sources were rewarded with more money from inside sources.

An important observation from resource dependence theory, then, is that our old, closed-system notion that organizations can be studied and understood through the examination of internal behavior needs to be reversed. D.J. Hickson, et al., for example, operate from this perspective in offering "A Strategic Contingencies Theory of Intraorganizational Power."[99] They suggest that the many subunits of an organization acquire power within the organization to the degree that each helps the organization cope with its most critical and pervasive environmental uncertainties. Although not yet systematically applied to public elementary and secondary education, such a perspective implies the importance of studying closely the activities of school administrators at times and points of special uncertainty. In one portion of their book on large-city principals, for example, Van Cleve Morris and his colleagues documented the "survival tactics and the scramble for power" among principals under conditions of unusual turmoil (e.g., major budgetary cutbacks amidst a financial crisis, a system-wide reordering of the elementary curriculum).[100] Some principals learned to use the period of turmoil (a "shifting bureaucratic chessboard") to their own advantage—to add staff, for example, even while designing cutback orders, or to implement the new curricular procedures in a way that would send a flood of positive messages of results up the hierarchy. The authors concluded that

> our inquiries into principaling behavior reveal a new form of entrepreneurialism: the ability, in states of corporate uncertainty, to turn confusion to one's own advantage. Indeed, some principals find bureaucratic chaos the most exciting and productive period in which to practice the art of principaling; it is precisely in those periods, when everybody else is in a state of semi-shock, that artful maneuvering through the hierarchical maze can yield the greatest gains.[101]

While seemingly losing power, the more knowledgeable chess players among the city's principals emerged not only unscathed but even strengthened politically within the aging bureaucracy.

**The Organizational Ecology Model: A Summary.** The organizational ecology approach emphasizes the extraordinarily heavy influence of the external environment. "Organizations are constructed by their environments" and "selected by them," writes John Meyer.[102] It is the environment which is the central actor—the key determinant of organizational form to which organizations must continuously adapt.

From this viewpoint, organizations can be studied in the aggregate, as populations with common characteristics; and they can also be studied productively individually, with attention to their internal adjustments to resource dependencies. The population approach, with its concept of niche, is a useful tool in seeking generalizations about the common characteristics of schools, their effects, and their relationships with the larger societal culture.[103] It is also a helpful way to develop instructive comparisons between subspecies of the same organism (e.g., public vs. private education, city vs. suburban schools). One of the more interesting concepts borrowed from the Darwinian origins of ecology is the belief that within its niche a population will successfully outcompete all other populations. Quite surprisingly, however, despite a recent interest in voucher plans in financing education, the research literature has not given much attention to competition in education. Nevertheless, the *vocabulary* of the educational administrator is filled with allusions to this phenomenon, as references are made to magnet schools, attendance boundaries, turf (particularly in higher education), student recruiting, and attracting better faculty.

Resource dependence theory emphasizes the importance of the external environment in the formation of internal (and essentially political) decision-making processes. One critical observation in linking resource dependency with ecology arises from its notion that organizational adaptation occurs in much more of a biological manner than in a rational, ordered, goal-directed fashion. James March speaks to this in "Footnotes to Organizational Change."[104] Organizational change, notes March, is an ecology of many responses in various parts of an organization to many elements in the environment. Organizations can be quite imaginative in their adaptations but rarely change in ways that are fully intended. In fact, most change occurs

> because most of the time people in an organization do about what they are supposed to do; that is, they are intelligently attentive to their environments and their jobs.[105]

Change can occur quite simply through the following of rules that accompanies the evolution of new procedures (new rules) out of competition and survival. Contagion can be a source of change (actions spreading from one organization to another). Learning, particularly from the responses of clients and customers, can also be important, as are the actions that result from conflicts between diverse interests controlling different resources. Sometimes, summarizes March, we even find that reigning organizational superstitions, myths, or elements of "manifest foolishness" direct the course of change in organizations—and it is not uncommon for solutions (those things that appear to work) to direct the organization selectively toward those problems that fit the available answers.

## Education and Environment: A Comparative Summary

Samuel Bacharach has noted that the central dilemma confronting school administrators is the problem of how to be responsive to the political imperatives (external demands) surrounding education in a democracy, while not compromising the internal control (and certainty or rationality) that is required to be administratively effective.[106] In this chapter we have presented a brief description of three theories of organization and environment which provide three different perspectives from which to view Bacharach's central dilemma. From the point of view of each theory the external environment is closely tied to the internal management of the organization, but, in each case, in quite a different way. While all three of our theories acknowledge the modern attitude that educational organizations are open systems and cannot be understood thoroughly without an acknowledgement of environment, each theory brings a vitally different set of understandings to light.

In closing this chapter, we shall compare the three theories and then summarize their respective managerial implications. We shall examine particularly the differences between the theoretical approaches in three important arenas of organizational behavior in education: (a) the nature and direction of the relationships between organization and environment; (b) the production of organizational outcomes; and (c) the sources of organizational change. A summary of our comparative analysis is provided in Figure 7.3.

Systems theory places a heavy emphasis upon interrelatedness. Both organization and environment are engaged in a continuous give and take, a mutuality of input and output, of feedback and adjustment. The organization, as a political system, is surrounded by a complex array of demands and supports (from interest groups, the courts, state and federal governments, the media, the student and parent clientele, private businesses, other educators). But the educational organization as a political system is an actor in its own right. It joins the fray. It reaches out in response to environmental stress; this response creates new conditions, which call in turn for some new responses—all as part of a continuous feedback loop, an ongoing dynamic between organization and environment.

From the perspective of systems theory, organizations do not just adapt blindly and automatically to the stresses in their environments. They operate with some degree of intelligence, and the adaptation that occurs is mediated and guided by goals. These goals are rooted in the values that are dominant in the organization. With feedback, organizations are able to study the effects of past behaviors and can transform old goals into new ones. The transformation of goals, and hence the changes that occur in organizations serve a drive toward equilibrium. Equilibrium is not defined in static terms. It is a concept that allows much room for (and even necessitates) change through a dynamic restructuring of the organization under environmental stress. The concept employed by Easton to describe the end result of change is "system persistence"—a term that suggests much more than survival as a goal, for it communicates survival *on the organization's terms*. Members of the organization process their environments selectively, offering a chance for continuity along with adaptive variability.

While systems theory shows a reciprocal adjustment between organization and environment, the public choice approach places much more emphasis upon individual, managerial initiatives—albeit guided by incentives and constrained by external conditions. Individuals may seek to gain prestige or to avoid conflict. They may enlarge the scope of their activities and enhance their own power through increases in budget. They may acquire greater control or freedom from control inside their

| Theory of Organization and Environment | Nature and Direction of Relationship with the Environment | Organizational Outcomes Are a Result of | Organizational Change Is Closely Tied to |
|---|---|---|---|
| **Systems Theory** | Both organization and environment directed | Goal-directed behavior | Equilibrium needs |
| **Public Choice Theory** | Management directed under constraint | Incentive-guided behavior | Reward structures |
| **Organizational Ecology** | Environmentally directed | Adaptive behavior | Resource dependency conditions |

*FIGURE 7.3*     A comparison of the three theories of organization/environment

own bureaucracies by forming special alliances outside. They may enjoy better pay, greater physical comfort, and enhanced job security if they can lead the organization toward their own sets of operative rather than organizationally professed goals. While certainly constrained by outside forces (by and large pressure groups who of course respond to their own sets of rewards), the central figure in the organization-environment relationship is the managerial official, who is stepping to the tune of an incentive structure located deep *inside* the organization. Although there are restrictions as a consequence of the nature of the surrounding market (e.g., the problem of the free rider, or the effect of a poorly understood technology of instruction), initiatives in meeting the environment emanate from within the organization more than from without.

In contrast with systems theory, the public choice approach warns us that organizational change in adapting to the external environment may be related to tendencies toward imbalance and/or nonpersistence rather than in the almost automatic adjustment process suggested by the systems framework. Reward structures are embedded within an organization's history, personnel policies, mythologies and sagas, and standard operating procedures. The culture of an institution is defined in large part by its incentives, and these incentives are hard to change. Not uncommonly they lag far behind a changing environment. Survival seems to come about *on the terms of the organization and the environment.*

The ecology model concludes that the central thrust in the organization-environment relationship is that of environment. For one thing, the external milieu erects heavily fortified barriers around managerial autonomy simply in the nature of the culture of the larger society. Educational organizations may play out their role only within a limited life space (or niche)—with their raison d'etre, their patterns of behavior, their structures of activity and authority necessarily adapted to conditions in the social environment.

Ralph Turner illustrates this point nicely in his now classic article on the ways in which American and English systems of education are patterned after their differing norms of upward mobility.[107] In the United States, he notes that the predominant mode of mobility is through an open *contest.* Elite status is a prize to be earned through one's own efforts, with accepted rules of fair play and an agreement that each contestant should be permitted to compete on an equal footing. In England, the rule is *sponsored* mobility—which rejects the notion of the contest in favor of a controlled selection process. Individuals are sorted out, often fairly early in life, on some criterion of merit and are given specialized training for elite status. Formal education under these alternative norms of mobility will be shaped quite differently. American high schools, for example, avoid sharp separations between superior and inferior students and keep channels of movement between courses of study as open as possible. Schooling is presented as an opportunity, with the student urged to be enterprising and to display initiative. The English system separates out the promising from the unpromising, giving the former special training for the higher standing they will claim in late adult life. Not just the structure but the educational content of schooling differs under the two norms. Induction into elite culture under sponsored mobility, writes Turner, "makes for emphasis on school esprit de corps, which can be employed to cultivate norms of intraclass loyalty and elite tastes and manners." In contrast, under contest mobility, schooling tends to be measured for its practical, vocational benefits; it is not valued as a good in itself as much it is in providing "skills necessary to compete for the real prizes of life."[108]

Below the societal level, at the level of the individual organization, adaptations will be most heavily influenced by whatever characterizes the control of resources that are critical to institutional survival. As Figure 7.3 indicates, organizational outcomes within the ecology perspective may often be an outgrowth of the adaptive behavior of units rather than institutionalized goal-directedness or incentive-guidedness. One strength of the ecology approach is that it, like public choice theory, allows the consideration of varieties of adaptive behavior within the same organizational context. It also allows for many varieties of and directions in organizational change. In writing from this perspective and in pointing out, for example, that educational organizations tend to be "loosely coupled" systems, Karl Weick has suggested that loose coupling provides a number of positive adaptive mechanisms. First, it allows some portions of an organization to change while others remain stable. In fact, such an arrangement often quite efficiently permits localized adaptation and a chance to experiment with "mutations and novel solutions" to environmental stress without forcing the entire system to be drawn in. Second, loose coupling provides a "sensitive sensing mechanism" that keeps organizations in tune with their environment, to know them better than would be the case under tight control. Third, loose coupling permits an organization to isolate or break off any of its portions that collapse—to localize its trouble spots without excessive danger to the rest of the organism.[109] In short, the ecology approach permits organizations all of the natural selection avenues toward adaptation and change that are found in the broader world of human beings. But it is *the terms of the environment* that must be honored first and foremost.

## Managing the Environment

Let us return now to Bacharach's central dilemma: How can an organization be responsive to external imperatives while at the same time retaining the internal control that is necessary to administrative effectiveness? From the systems perspective, Bacharach's central dilemma might be answered:

> You must try somehow to be responsive to the outside and try to retain control inside *at the same time*—and this requires a very delicate administrative balancing act.

This is not at all easy. A lack of clarity and understanding regarding the best way to administer the educational organization as an open system has fostered a number of contemporary efforts to define a revised, more environmentally aware managerial role for the educator. Wiles, Wiles, and Bondi, in *Practical Politics for School Administrators*, for example, (as we noted previously) suggest the administrator take the role of an adept poker player. As such, the school administrator recognizes the fluidity and indeterminacy of the managerial environment. The administrator is just one player among many in the larger environment. He or she rarely holds a sure hand, analyzes each situation and the stakes involved before jumping too heavily into the game, and accumulates chips gradually, winning some and losing some, while playing for the long haul.[110]

The political arena includes not only the politics of an external environment but simultaneously the internal politics of the organization. The arena may be stable or unstable; it may involve players acting as the representatives of ongoing interest groups; it may involve individual players in hard-fought struggles for new coalitions. It may involve few, predictable interactions across organizational boundaries or many, unpredictable ones. It may be wrapped in a clarity of organizational rules, sanctions, and elements of authority or in a confusion of purpose and control. Administrative strategies in stable arenas may need to be different from those in unstable ones, but in both situations a leader's role is to assist a search for continuity, to provide security amidst uncertainty.[111]

In contrast, the answer to Bacharach's dilemma from the public choice perspective might be:

> **Environmental responsiveness flows from achieving internal control as a first priority. Start inside the organization, not outside.**

Although aware of constraining conditions in the external environment (e.g., the free rider phenomenon), the educational administrator recognizes the need to start with some inside questions about the rewards organizational participants receive and the consequences for organizational effectiveness that ensue. Granted, some of these rewards may come from the environment—as people who play boundary-spanning roles interact positively with clients, receive recognition from persons in the wider community, or are treated with deference by the representatives of pressure groups. Developing a thorough understanding of these and other elements in the reward structure, however, may be a precondition to administrative effectiveness, that ought to precede any concern with environmental responsiveness. Mark Hanson's portrayal of the problem-solving process in schools (note again Figure 7.2) demonstrates that the bureaucratic distribution of spheres of influence *within* the organization (e.g., the recognized domain of the teacher vs. the domain of the administrator) determines substantially how an externally generated tension will be recognized and addressed.[112]

Finally, from the organizational ecology perspective, one might quite easily argue:

> **It's well-nigh impossible to be environmentally responsive *and* simultaneously in internal control. Start with the environment.**

Educational organizations are the institutionalized creatures of the society. Public schools are vulnerable organizations in a political sense, and so familiar to all of us that our intervention as a citizenry into their affairs comes naturally. As strategy, the educational administrator might be best advised to follow Dale Mann's suggestion to open the organization to a much greater sharing of control. Shared control, preferable to buffering the organization from or accumulating chips against the external environment, adds to the probability that commonly accepted goals of public schooling will be achieved. It is a carefully monitored process of community involvement toward common ends, not a giving away of the educational store. In the contemporary political environment, the shrewd administrator provides a regular opportunity for meaningful community participation and the inclusion of all points of view in matters that affect children and the school (including questions of curriculum, budget, personnel, and student behavior) through such structures as school advisory councils, school-based management, and ad hoc committees. Far from diminishing an educator's power, shared control adds to it—for strong schools require strong community support.[113] Long used to protectionism, educators would be more effective if they based their own controls upon the commonly accepted goals and understandings that come from actively reaching out to the surrounding community. Granted, resource dependencies can be managed and the administrator need not place himself completely in the hands of others; however, internal control and effectiveness can come *from* responsiveness to the environment rather than of necessity being threatened by it.

In conclusion, we remind the reader once again that an open systems view of education has replaced the long-standing belief that the educational organization can be studied and improved apart from its environment. This new perspective has also replaced the old idea that education can and should be kept out of politics. As the most recent of our areas of concentration in the study of organizations, the question of how educational institutions adapt to their environments is one of the least well understood topics in the field. In this chapter we have presented three theories of organization and environment in education—with the message that from each theoretical perspective there are instructive managerial implications. If an educational administrator's central dilemma is in fact how to be responsive to the environment while at the same time staying in control as a manager, the message clearly ought to be that each theoretical interpretation of our complex organizational world has its own strengths and weaknesses, and the creative administrator will use all three.

## FROM THEORY TO PRACTICE

It is easy for administrators to *underestimate* the rationality of the environment and to *overestimate* the rationality of the organization. Armando Rivera has less trouble with this dilemma than many of his colleagues. He understood the rational thrust of the community group as it literally moved into the college, even if he could not accept all of the group's premises and objectives and procedures. Simultaneously, he was prepared to invent means of handling unpredictable actors and coalitions within the college as their interests collided with his own or with those of the community group.

The community? "You can't work with the mass. You have to find the need. Sometimes that means you have to wait, and you have to dig through the nonsense." The organization? "The rational organization chart? That's not the way it is. Everything is shifting on every issue." So when Armando says that "education and the world around it are in a state of flux," he is giving us a description of *his* theoretical framework. It's an unsettling one—rationality and nonrationality in a maelstrom of events in both the environment and the organization, with no anchor that can be thrown down surely anywhere. Perhaps Armando stands closer to the public choice perspective than to systems theory or the organizational ecology model, but in his corner of the managerial world instability seems to be an especially intense shaping factor. Armando has to *become* the anchor, and as a result he spends some time under organizational waters.

The dominant technique for Armando as he tries to establish order out of apparent chaos is not supervision, but rather negotiation. Whether it is with his boss or the caucus or the community group or the librarian or even his respected mentor, Armando takes the stance of an educational politician. He wrestles with self-interest. He tries to find points of mutual interest. He digs for compromises, he stretches for creative solutions in the context of stalemate and anxiety. The issue reconstructs the organization for him as roles and role expectations fluctuate. Actors change places, and personal needs and tendencies to respond vary. But perhaps most of all Armando struggles to stay in position to negotiate. Often this means underplaying advantages, nurturing an unobtrusive posture, avoiding a confrontation, permitting a momentary adversary to underestimate his competencies. If you are not sitting at the table, you cannot play in the game, and Armando is not one to throw in his cards prematurely. He negotiates with specific people within the organization and in the enviroment on specific issues, but he is also shuffling another set of variables which he never reveals completely—his sense of an appropriate balance between the interests of the organization and its particular educational community.

Educational administrators talk about their "professional growth and development" but few use the words "growing up" the way Armando does. For him it is personal rather than professional growth that is critical to his improving performance as an educational administrator. This point of view permits him to stay in touch with the personal side of the organization, which is the important side, after all is said and done. Any administrator has difficulty helping others learn and grow unless he or she is going through the same process, consciously. At least in part because he wants a slice of responsibility and leadership from his superiors, Armando is willing to try to provide one for his subordinates. He finds that this is not always an easy task, and he worries about doing more of it. His personal survival seems linked to his abilities to survive error; to massage his colleagues without resentment; but, most of all, to keep learning and sharing with others.

Where is Armando's allegiance? He devotes it somewhat more to the community than to the organization. That seems natural enough. As a Puerto Rican administrator, he is an intrusion himself into the framework of the college, a burr under more than one saddle. Furthermore, he was trained as a social worker rather than as an educational administrator, and the predilection for service in the community rather than in a school seems to have survived. His interests in higher education from the beginning have been to develop programs for poor, disenfranchised urban adults. The role he has carved out as a consequence—that of a street level bureaucrat or boundary spanner—is never a comfortable one, but his willingness to be a community advocate *increases* his value to the organization, even as that organization resists him periodically because it senses his allegiance is more external than internal.

It is all a far cry from the traditional textbook world of managerial objectives and rational steps toward the attainment of goals. It is the politics of education, clearly and simply—intriguing, confusing, even rather dangerous (for there can be serious political mistakes). Although we do not yet fully understand the nature of the relationship between education and its environment, it is certain that a profession recognizing (at long last) that education cannot be kept out of community politics shall never again be the same.

## NOTES

[1]David Tyack and Elisabeth Hansot, "Conflict and Consensus in American Public Education," *Daedalus*, 110:3 (Summer 1981): 1-25. See also Arthur E. Wise, *Legislated Learning: The Bureaucratization of the American Classroom* (Berkeley: University of California Press, 1979); and, Michael Kirst, "Organizations in Shock and Overload: California's Public Schools, 1970-1980," *Educational Evaluation and Policy Analysis*, 1:4 (July-August 1979): 27-30.

[2]Roald F. Campbell has provided a brief but insightful and comprehensive review of the progressive development of administrative theory in education, in Roald F. Campbell, "A History of Administrative Thought," *Administrator's Notebook*, 26:4 (1977-78): 1-4. See also, Jacob W. Getzels, James M. Lipham, and Roald F. Campbell, *Educational Administration as a Social Process: Theory, Research, Practice* (New York: Harper & Row, 1968),pp. 23-51.

[3]Campbell, "A History of Administrative Thought," p. 3.

[4]Samuel B. Bacharach, "Organizational and Political Dimensions for Research on School District Governance and Administration," in Samuel B. Bacharach ed., *Organizational Behavior in Schools and School Districts* (New York: Praeger Publishers, 1981), pp. 3-43.

[5]David K. Wiles, Jon Wiles, and Joseph Bondi, *Practical Politics for School Administrators* (Boston: Allyn & Bacon, 1981), pp. 113-135.

[6]Bertram M. Gross, *Organizations and Their Managing* (New York: The Free Press, 1968), pp. 113-135.

[7]Ibid., pp. 136-166.

[8]See, Willard Waller, *The Sociology of Teaching* (New York: Wiley, 1932); also, Charles E. Bidwell, "The School as a Formal Organization," in James G. March ed., *Handbook of Organizations* (Chicago: Rand McNally, 1965), pp. 972-1022; and, Dan C. Lortie, *Schoolteacher: A Sociological Study* (Chicago: University of Chicago Press, 1975).

[9]Gerald R. Salancik and Jeffrey Pfeffer, "The Bases and Use of Power in Organizational Decision Making: The Case of a University," *Administrative Science Quarterly* 19 (1974): 453-473.

[10]See Van Cleve Morris, Robert L. Crowson, Cynthia Porter-Gehrie, and Emanuel Hurwitz, Jr. *Principals in Action: The Reality of Managing Schools* (Columbus, Ohio: Charles E. Merrill, 1984).

[11]See, for example, Richard Weatherley, *Reforming Special Education: Policy Implementation from State Level to Street Level* (Cambridge, Mass.: MIT Press, 1979).

[12]Personal discussion with Van Cleve Morris, Professor of Education, University of Illinois at Chicago.

[13]John W. Meyer and Brian Rowan, "The Structure of Educational Organizations," in Marshall W. Meyer and Associates, eds., *Environments and Organizations* (San Francisco: Jossey-Bass Publishers, 1978), p. 109.

[14]Jeffrey Pfeffer and Gerald R. Salancik, *The External Control of Organizations* (New York: Harper & Row, 1978).

[15]Ibid., pp. 2-20.

[16]James D. Thompson, *Organizations in Action* (New York: McGraw-Hill Book Co. 1967).

[17]*Note*: Walter Buckley has written critically of Talcott Parsons' tendency to overemphasize system maintenance and the attainment of organizational equilibrium. Parsonian theory has had a major effect

upon scholars' notions that "survival" is *the* central concern of the organization. Buckley suggests that George Homans, on the other hand, correctly permits deviance, ambiguity, and nonconformity to persist within organizations even when they appear to be dysfunctionally related to organizational survival. Survival, or even continuity, may not be conditions sought by every system. See, Walter Buckley, *Sociology and Modern Systems Theory* (Englewood Cliffs, N.J.: Prentice-Hall, 1967), pp. 23-36.

[18]Ibid. pp. 159-161.

[19]Ibid., p. 163.

[20]Michael T. Hannan and John H. Freeman, "The Population Ecology of Organizations," in Meyer and Associates, *Environments and Organizations*, pp. 131-171.

[21]Ibid., p. 139.

[22]Ibid., pp. 144-145.

[23]David Easton, *A Framework for Political Analysis* (Englewood Cliffs, N.J.: Prentice-Hall, 1965), p. 112.

[24]See, for example, Jacob W. Getzels and Egan G. Guba, "Social Behavior and the Administrative Process," *School Review* 65 (Winter, 1957): 423-441; also, J. Alan Thomas, *The Productive School* (New York: John Wiley & Sons, 1971).

[25]Phillip Selznick, *TVA and the Grass Roots* (Berkeley: University of California Press, 1949).

[26]Easton, A Framework, p. 25.

[27]Ibid., p. 109.

[28]E. Mark Hanson, *Educational Administration and Organizational Behavior* (Boston: Allyn & Bacon, 1981), pp. 366-380.

[29]Ibid., pp. 369-372.

[30]Norman D. Kerr, "The School Board as an Agency of Legitimation," *Sociology of Education* 38 (Fall 1964): 34-59. See also, Laurence Iannaccone and Frank W. Lutz, *Politics, Power, and Policy: The Governing of Local School Districts* (Columbus, Ohio: Charles E. Merrill, 1970).

[31]See, Thompson, *Organizations in Action*, p. 4; also, Easton, *A Framework*, p. 77; and Buckley, *Sociology*, p. 5.

[32]Buckley, p. 56.

[33]For an interesting compilation of papers and exemplary cases on change processes in educational organizations, see J. Victor Baldrige and Terrence E. Deal eds., *Managing Change in Educational Organizations* (Berkeley, Calif.: McCutchan Publishing, 1975); also, Dale Mann, ed., *Making Change Happen?* (New York: Teachers College Press, 1978).

[34]Easton, pp. 88-89.

[35]Bo Hedberg, "How Organizations Learn and Unlearn," in Paul C. Nystrom and William H. Starbuck, eds., *Handbook of Organizational Design*, vol. 1 (London: Oxford University Press, 1981): 3-27.

[36]James G. March, "Footnotes to Organizational Change," *Administrative Science Quarterly*, 26:4 (December 1981): 564.

[37]Efraim Gugel Gil, "Institutional Planning at Public Universities: An Analysis of the Governors State University Planning Process" (Unpublished Ph.D. Dissertation, University of Illinois at Chicago, 1981).

[38]Frederick M. Wirt and Michael W. Kirst, *Political and Social Foundations of Education* (Berkeley, Calif.: McCutchan Publishing, 1975), p. 15.

[39]Ibid., pp. 50-59.

[40]Gary L. Wamsley and Mayer N. Zald, *The Political Economy of Public Organizations* (Lexington, Mass.: Lexington Books, 1973), pp. 30-32.

[41]For a discussion of both sides of the argument regarding "Are organizations anything more than the actions of individuals?" see Richard H. Hall, *Organizations: Structure and Process* (Englewood Cliffs, N.J.: Prentice-Hall, 1972), pp. 10-14.

[42]See, William Lowe Boyd, "The Political Economy of Public Schools" *Educational Administration Quarterly*, 18:3 (Summer 1982): 111-130. Boyd's reference to the work of Perrow is drawn from Charles Perrow, "Demystifying Organizations," in R. C. Sarri and Y. Hasenfeld, eds., *The Management of Human Services* (New York: Columbia University Press, 1978). pp. 105-120.

[43]Boyd, p. 114.

[44]The individual self-interest of the marketplace approach should not by pessimistically interpreted as a denial of altruism in public service. To the contrary, many individuals reap very heavy "psychic

rewards" in serving others. For a discussion of this point, see Richard B. McKensie and Gordon Tullock, *The New World of Economics* (Homewood, Ill.: Richard D. Irwin, 1981), pp. 11-12.

[45]David Rogers, *110 Livingston Street* (New York: Vintage Books, 1969), pp. 309-310.

[46]Morris, et al., *Principals in Action*, pp. 141-181.

[47]See Albert Hirschman, *Exit Voice and Loyalty* (Cambridge, Mass.: Harvard University Press, 1970).

[48]Dennis C. Mueller, *Public Choice* (Cambridge: Cambridge University Press, 1979), p. 11.

[49]William A. Niskanen, Jr., *Bureaucracy and Representative Government* (Chicago: Aldine-Atherton, 1971).

[50]Boyd, "Political Economy," p. 112.

[51]Charles Tiebout, "A Pure Theory of Local Expenditures," *Journal of Political Economy*, 64 (October 1956): 416-424.

[52]Robert L. Bish and Hugh O. Nourse, *Urban Economics and Policy Analysis* (New York: McGraw-Hill Book Co., 1975), p. 128.

[53]For a well-developed discussion of this argument, see Boyd, pp. 117-122.

[54]See Robert L. Lineberry, *Equality and Urban Policy: The Distribution of Municipal Public Services* (Beverly Hills, Calif.: Sage Publications, 1977).

[55]Paul E. Peterson, *City Limits* (Chicago: University of Chicago Press, 1981), p. 99.

[56]Ibid., pp. 93-106.

[57]Mancur Olsen, Jr., *The Logic of Collective Action* (Cambridge, Mass.: Harvard University Press, 1965).

[58]William Sayre and Herbert Kaufman, *Governing New York City* (New York: Russell Sage, 1960).

[59]Boyd, "Political Economy," p. 121.

[60]Michel Crozier, *The Bureaucratic Phenomenon* (Chicago: University of Chicago Press, 1964), pp. 58-111.

[61]Alvin Gouldner, *Patterns of Industrial Bureaucracy* (Glencoe, Ill.: The Free Press, 1954).

[62]Selznick, *TVA and the Grass Roots*.

[63]Thompson, *Organizations in Action*, p. 159. See also, Michel Crozier and Erhard Friedberg, *Actors and Systems: The Politics of Collective Action* (Chicago: University of Chicago Press, 1980).

[64]Martha S. Feldman and James E. March, "Information in Organizations as Signal and Symbol," *Administrative Science Quarterly*, 26:2 (June 1981): 171-186.

[65]Morris, et al., *Principals in Action*, p. 173.

[66]See John Freeman, "Going to the Well: School District Administrative Intensity and Environmental Constraint," *Administrative Science Quarterly*, 24:1 (March 1979): 120-121.

[67]Rick Ginsberg, "The City School Survey: Why Has The Practice Continued?" *Administrator's Notebook*, 29:8 (1980-81): 1-4.

[68]Jacob B. Michaelsen, "Revision, Bureaucracy, and School Reform: A Critique of Katz," *School Review*, 85:2 (February 1977): 239.

[69]Ibid. See also, Boyd, "Political Economy," p. 115.

[70]See Jacob B. Michaelsen, "A Theory of Decision Making in the Public Schools: A Public Choice Approach," in Samuel B. Bacharach, ed., *Organizational Behavior in Schools and School Districts* (New York: Praeger Publishers, 1981), p. 221.

[71]Boyd, p. 117.

[72]David W. Minar, "The Community Basis of Conflict in School System Politics," *American Sociological Review*, 31 (1966): 822-835.

[73]See Donald J. Willower, "Schools and Pupil Control," in Donald A. Erickson, ed., *Educational Organization and Administration* (Berkeley, Calif.: McCutchan Publishing, 1977), pp. 296-310.

[74]See Thompson, *Organizations in Action;* also, Mary T. Moore, The Boundary- Spanning Role of the Urban School Principal" (Unpublished Ph.D. dissertation, University of California at Los Angeles, 1975).

[75]Michael Lipsky, *Street-Level Bureaucracy: Dilemmas of the Individual in Public Services* (New York: Russell Sage Foundation, 1980).

[76]See Richard A. Weatherley, *Reforming Special Education: Policy Implementation from State Level to Street Level* (Cambridge, Mass.: The MIT Press, 1979); also, Robert L. Crowson and Cynthia

Porter-Gehrie, "The Discretionary Behavior of Principals in Large-City Schools," *Educational Administration Quarterly*, 16:1 (1980): 45-69.

[77]Richard O. Carlson, "Environmental Constraints and Organizational Consequences: The Public School and Its Clients," in Daniel Griffiths, ed., *Behavioral Science and Educational Administration*, Sixty-third Yearbook of the National Society for the Study of Education, Part II (Chicago; University of Chicago Press, 1964): 262-278.

[78]Brian Rowan, "Organizational Structure and the Institutional Environment: The Case of Public Schools," *Administrative Science Quarterly*, 27:2 (June 1982): 261. See also John W. Meyer and W. Richard Scott, *Organizational Environments: Ritual and Rationality* (Beverly Hills: Sage Publications, 1983).

[79]Marshall W. Meyer, "Introduction: Recent Developments in Organizational Research and Theory," in Marshall W. Meyer and Associates, eds., *Environments and Organizations* (San Francisco, Calif.: Jossey-Bass Publishers, 1978), p. 14.

[80]The ecology perspective of course offers a strong sense of environmental determinism. Most theorists prefer to argue that organization and environment relationships are much more symbiotic. John Kenneth Galbraith claims, for example, that it is only through the internal exercise of power that an organization acquires the ability to impose its will externally. See John Kenneth Galbraith, *The Anatomy of Power* (Boston: Houghton Mifflin, 1983), pp. 57-64.

[81]See Amos H. Hawley, *Human Ecology: A Theory of Community Structure* (New York: Ronald Press, 1950); also, Karl E. Weick, *The Social Psychology of Organizing*, 2nd ed. (Reading, Mass.: Addison-Wesley, 1979).

[82]See Michael T. Hannan and John H. Freeman, "The Population Ecology of Organizations, in Meyer and Associates, eds., *Environments and Organizations*, p. 144.

[83]The term comes from Karl E. Weick, "Educational Organizations as Loosely Coupled Systems," *Administrative Science Quarterly*, 21:1 (March 1976): 1-19.

[84]John W. Meyer and Brian Rowan, "The Structure of Educational Organizations," in Meyer and Associates, eds., *Environments and Organizations*, pp. 78-109. On the other hand, Karl Weick argues that structural looseness facilitates trial and error behavior and adaptability. Furthermore, ecological changes favor adaptive actions that are loosely structured. See Weick, *The Social Psychology of Organizing*, pp. 177-188.

[85]Meyer and Rowan, "The Structure," p. 80.

[86]See Jeffrey Pfeffer, *Organizations and Organization Theory* (Boston: Pitman Publishing Inc., 1982), pp. 178-207.

[87]Howard E. Aldrich, *Organizations and Environments* (Englewood Cliffs, N.J.: Prentice-Hall, 1979), pp. 26-55.

[88]See Pfeffer, pp. 181-182; also, Hannan and Freeman, "Population Ecology," pp. 151-164.

[89]Hannan and Freeman, pp. 152-170.

[90]Laura Hersch Salganick and Nancy Karweit, "Volunteerism and Governance in Education," *Sociology of Education*, 55 (April/July, 1982): 152-161.

[91]James Coleman, T. Hoffer, and S. Kilgore, "Summary of Major Findings for Private and Public Schools," Report to the National Center for Education Statistics (Chicago: National Opinion Research Center, 1981).

[92]Salganick and Karweit, "Volunteerism," p. 153.

[93]Ibid., p. 158.

[94]*Note*: We follow Michel Crozier in suggesting that resource dependency fits legitimately within the organizational ecology model of organization and environment. See Crozier and Friedberg, *Actors and Systems*, pp. 67-96.

[95]See Jeffrey Pfeffer and Gerald R. Salancik, *The External Control of Organizations: A Resource Dependence Perspective* (New York: Harper & Row, 1978); also, Pfeffer, *Organizations*, pp. 192-207.

[96]Pfeffer, *Organizations*, p. 193.

[97]Ibid., pp. 202-204.

[98]Jeffrey Pfeffer and Gerald R. Salancik, "Organizational Decision Making as a Political Process: The Case of a University Budget," *Administrative Science Quarterly*, 19 (1974): 135-151; also, Gerald R. Salancik and Jeffrey Pfeffer, "The Bases and Use of Power in Organizational Decision Making: The Case of a University," *Administrative Science Quarterly*, 19 (1974): 453-473.

[99]D.J. Hickson, C.R. Hinings, C.A. Lee, R.E. Schneck, and J.M. Pennings, "A Strategic

Contingencies' Theory of Intraorganizational Power," *Administrative Science Quarterly*, 16 (1971): 216-229.

[100]Morris, et al., *Principals in Action*, pp. 162-170.

[101]Ibid., p. 289.

[102]John W. Meyer, "Strategies for Further Research: Varieties of Environmental Variation," in Meyer and Associates *Environments and Organizations*, p. 353.

[103]One theoretical point of departure with much to say about the role of schooling (writ large) in our society comes out of a Marxist orientation. In brief, the Marxists claim that public schooling gives lip service to the American Dream while functioning in fact to preserve an established economic and social structure. Children are channeled and socialized into patterns of behavior and social roles that fit and maintain ongoing corporate inequalities throughout the culture. See Martin Carnoy, ed., *Schooling in a Corporate Society*, 2nd ed. (New York: David McKay, 1975); also, Samuel Bowles and Henry Gintis, *Schooling in Capitalist America: Educational Reform and the Contradictions of Economic Life* (New York: Basic Books, 1976).

[104]March, "Footnotes to Organizational Change," pp. 563-577.

[105]Ibid., p. 564.

[106]Bacharach, ed., *Organizational Behavior in Schools*, p. vii.

[107]Ralph H. Turner, "Modes of Social Ascent through Education: Sponsored and Contest Mobility," in A.H. Halsey, Jean Floud, and C. Arnold Anderson, eds., *Education, Economy, and Society* (New York: The Free Press, 1961): 121-139.

[108]Ibid., p. 132.

[109]Weick, "Educational Organizations as Loosely Coupled Systems," pp. 1-19.

[110]See Wiles, Wiles, and Bondi, *Practical Politics*, pp. 12–14.

[111]Ibid., pp. 42-48.

[112]Hanson, *Educational Administration and Organizational Behavior*.

[113]Dale Mann, *The Politics of Administrative Representation* (Lexington, Mass.: Lexington Books, 1976), pp. 129-159.

# 8

# The Evolution of Leadership
# in the Organization

## JOHN MROZEK

*He grew up in a poor section of Troy, New York, and he gets back at least once every year to see his mother, who is still living in the old family home. He was a scholarship student at Williams College, a Phi Beta Kappa and an English major, and then he spent a dozen years on Long Island as a teacher, coach, counselor, dramatics instructor, and principal. During that period he completed his M.A. and Ph.D. degrees at Teachers College, Columbia University. One of his mentors there helped him get a job with the state department of education in Virginia, a position in which he knows he really cut his administrative teeth. Now he is teaching in a large state university in its school of education. You look at him and have the feeling it was inevitable. He is handsome, casually but carefully dressed, in good shape, grey at the temples—every casting director's first choice for the role of college professor. He speaks softly but urgently. You learn quickly that the twinkle in his eye is a bit deceptive, because he is interviewing you before you can develop your own line of questions. But you feel comfortable with him because he seems genuinely interested in you. The man has integrity written all over him.*

I can see you have a list of questions there. But frankly, I'd rather not get involved in a conventional interview. After NASA contacted me to set up this meeting with you, I gave some thought to what I'd like to share with you, and it really boiled down to an experience I had in Virginia as well as some of my thoughts about what I'm doing now. Would you mind if we simply concentrated on that?

**Not at all.  Go right ahead.**

When you get out of graduate school you are really politically naive. Or at least I was. We were going to save the world, of course. But the problem in graduate school is that you learn to look at *all* the factors, *all* the variables. That attitude turned out to be quite a problem when I tackled the problem of setting up a state assessment program in Virginia. We knew that there would be evidence from such a program for changing the pattern of state school financing. It would have to become more equitable. But we thought that to *really* get at the equity question we needed to collect SES data—for groups, not individuals. Yes, it had to be good research even if it was in the middle of a highly politicized environment. And so we plunged in with really no sense at all of how people out there in the schools and communities of the state would perceive the questions we were asking, to get at that measure of group SES. The minute people started filling in the forms in Norfolk, we knew we were in trouble. I remember one question where we asked if there was a television in the home, and it turned out that welfare families thought we were checking up on them. Straightforward political naivete. The community organizations came at us from one direction, and the right-wingers came at us from another. I recall one conservative arguing that the assessment program was promoting divisiveness, that there were poor and there always would be. We just shook our heads.

**What would you have done differently, given the chance?**

We should have avoided SES and attitude measures. We should have bitten the bullet. Okay, here are the achievement data, and it is going to be difficult to make any comparisons across the state. The other possibility was simply not to test kids, not to worry about achievement at the state level. Table it. But that was difficult to do, too—politically, I mean. Accountability was in the air then. Lots of policies and procedures were being questioned. The state board was uneasy, for example, with the accreditation power that the universities had built up. And they wanted to know if the local school districts were doing their jobs in educating the children.

I had one of those once-in-a-lifetime opportunities. After a few years at a lower level position, I became Director of Policy Planning and Evaluation. No one really had a clear idea of what the office ought to be doing. There were two people there when I took over, one filling out forms and the other grousing because he thought he should have been given my job. We found other spots for both of them. But we had some money. There was $250,000 in unused Title III funds that were there for the spending, and at the encouragement of the state superintendent we used that to begin to put together the assessment program. The state superintendent moved the state board away from the accreditation issue, and we were on our way. Being the researchers that we were, we set up a nice three year plan with all of the logical steps and instrumentation. The board's response was that it was a lovely plan, but we had to start testing kids within the next six months.

We didn't think we needed a legislative mandate to implement the assessment program. Any bill would stir up a hornet's nest, so the state superintendent decided to go the appropriations route. We tacked a brief paragraph on the appropriations bill that was in the legislature, and no one except the members of the appropriation committee and a few other legislators knew what had happened.

**The way things worked out maybe it would have been better to stir up the hornet's nest.**

I really can't argue with that line of reasoning, because after the uproar in Norfolk it all came right back into the legislature anyway. One of the key black legislators from Norfolk, a savvy guy with a lot of respect all around the state, took the hook for us in the Senate. We owed him a lot when it was all over. Then we went through a switch in state superintendents, but the new man was a stronger advocate for the assessment program than my first boss. He really latched onto it like it was his.

But there were even more political lessons to be learned. We tried to use the SES and achievement data to pump more money into Norfolk and Richmond, figuring that's where the need was for more state support. Well, each district would have to do pre- and post-testing, and each student would have to make a certain gain each year for the per capita allocation to be made. Of course, the districts counted the money before they got it—budgeted for it, actually—and, wouldn't you know, the first year Norfolk was going to lose $2,000,000. So we postponed the program penalty for a year; we just gave them the money. The next year their kids didn't achieve well, either, and so we gave them another year to toe the mark. But by the next year we were talking three-year averages. The system we had just wouldn't work for fixing accountability and allocating monies the way we had envisioned. Norfolk might lose other things, but it couldn't lose money. That was not going to happen.

**How have you come to define leadership, then?**

For me, I guess. . . . it has a lot to do with cooperation, or persuading people to come along in a certain direction. I think Harry Truman said it was getting people to do what they didn't want to do in the first place and liking it. I always feel like I'm trying to work a finesse in a poker game or around a bridge table. In fact, when I feel that way I usually recognize that action like that is leadership, and not the routine stuff. That's not very scientific, is it?

**Maybe not, but I have a sense of what you mean by leadership. Can you give me another example from your own experience?**

Sure. One that I'll never forget—because there was a mysterious quality to it as well as incredible pressure. We were trying to get a deseg plan for Richmond. It's really tough when everything is in one place—the local school district, the city political structure, the state department, and the legislature. You don't even have to use the telephone, as you'll see as this story unwinds. You put all of that in the mid-South where there are some strong racial feelings still at work, and you have a challenge.

**What was your job then?**

It was before I moved up to associate superintendent. I was one layer below that, spending my time mostly on liaison with—why should I beat around the bush, I was lobbyist for the state department of education. It was fun. I never learned more in my life. When I was roped into this one the state board and the local school superintendent were already at loggerheads. The board had him in a corner. He had to come up with a pupil desegregation plan by April or the board had said it would take away state funds from the school district. That would cost the district a lot of money. It had never been done in Virginia, and I think a judge probably would have thrown it out. But nobody was counting on that. The lines were drawn, and no one was budging. Like an old-fashioned game of chicken that kids play in cars. Dangerous.

      The state superintendent called me in and asked my opinion. I told him that I thought they were on the wrong course. The state board had a chance of being exposed as impotent; they were going to look silly. I remember telling him, "They should have stayed with a game of inches." My boss told me he couldn't get the state board to buy it. They had a taste of blood now. Then I found out the real reason he had called me in. "Everything's being done in the press," he told me. "We've got to figure a compromise somehow. You know Bonus, don't you? How about having some private talks with them?" Well, that would be a challenge, me an intermediary with Sam Bonus, the local school superintendent. That's what I thought. What I said was, "Tell me what the minimum plan is that you and the state board can tolerate. Then tell me what you'd like. I need to know what the range looks like."

**Did you get enough room to move?**

Oh, sure. Or at least I *thought* I did. So I called Sam and told him I wanted to talk. He said that was fine as long as it was at his home. When I arrived there that evening we had a drink, and then I got on the case. "I have a job. You and I are going to work out a plan." He said that he was willing to try, but that we couldn't be seen meeting together. That was no problem for me. I told him I had a trench coat, and he laughed. But I'll tell you, it really was like a spy story. We met in all kinds of places over the next two weeks—in restaurants, at a bar in a country club, at both our houses, even in a couple of school basements, and once almost leaning on the boiler.

**How do you get some give and take started in a touchy situation like this one?**

I'd say, "What can you do on this issue?" And he'd come back and say "I can do this." He had to talk to his people, of course. On several issues he gave far more than we needed. On others, I'd say, "That's not enough." If the gap was wide, I'd deal with my boss's minimum. If the gap wasn't wide, I'd ask for more. Not very complicated, and reasonably fair, I'd say. So point by point we hammered it out, and my respect for Sam grew. He really wanted to do the right thing, and his word was his bond. So we got all the elements lined up—the plan was there. "Sam, you have my word that the state superintendent will argue like a tiger for this plan, and we'll put the arm on every board member." He asked me if I could guarantee that. I said I couldn't guarantee the board yet, but I'd call him back about four days before he would bring the plan to the board and let him know what the vote would be.

### Did you get the support of the board?

Hang on. I'll get to that. A couple of days later I had a phone call from Sam. "There's a snag." So we were meeting again, this time in a meeting room down at City Hall. I walk in, and, without a word, three men walk out the other door. After letting me see them. The mayor, the city's most powerful representative in the legislature, and the staffer from the governor's office. I knew Sam had been working hard. The snag, as Sam had called it, had to do with the first sentence of the draft plan. It was kind of a dramatic sentence, I'll admit, but I didn't see all that much trouble with it.

### What in the world did it say?

I can give it to you word for word. "Under the proposed voluntary desegregation plan both white and black children who have attended schools in racial isolation will soon attend desegregated, integrated schools." I asked Sam what was wrong with the sentence. He told me that some people believed that it sounded like forced busing. I knew which people. I said that maybe we ought to use some different language, and so we started trying to iron out that marvelous sentence. I'd leave the room and pace through the corridors of the building, and then I'd come back to the meeting room and we'd parley, and then I'd walk again. Finally we came up with it: "Under the proposed voluntary desegregation plan many more white and black children will spend the majority of their instructional time in desegregated settings." He had been on the phone, and he said this would do it.

### Were you backing off from the state board's position?

Not at all. They weren't pressing for forced busing, and Sam's plan wasn't calling for that. We just had to convince people that there wasn't something hidden between the lines. The superintendent and I called our board members and told them we had a deal. The board president was ecstatic because he knew the board was a long way out on a thin limb. You see, Sam Bonus was a good superintendent and he just wanted an agreement that wouldn't put him out on the street. His independent power base was in the political framework, and they had to buy it. When I called him a few days prior to his coming to the board meeting, I could tell him that we had all the votes, with just one question mark. He was pleased, of course.

When he came into the room about 2:00 in the afternoon, the flashbulbs were popping. Both our television channels were grinding. He put a big stack of the plans up in front of him, and then he turned to the board. "The first sentence of this report is the most important one." Then he read it, and all you *could* hear were media noises. No one else was even breathing hard. Then he followed that with, "My signature is on this report. This is what I'm committed to." The board was all smiles. We had 13 board members, and the vote was 12–1 to accept the plan.

## Your leadership here seems to have been critical.

Maybe you won't believe me, maybe you'll think it's false modesty, but I never remember this whole process and think about what I did. Look at it this way. Sam Bonus had the toughest job, the most to lose all the way along. He could have stonewalled me when I called the first time, but he knew that wasn't what the city needed. So wasn't he the leader here? Or how about my boss and his board, putting the pressure on in the first place—with a good chance to be wiping a lot of egg off their faces? And what role did the pols play, telling us what a lot of people couldn't and could accept? I finagled the compromise, yeah, I did that. But don't tell me I was the leader. It's a lot more complicated than that.

## Why did you exchange that rather vigorous environment for campus life?

I wanted to get into a university where I could think about the things I had been encountering on a daily basis. What's the old saw—those who do not study history are doomed to repeat it? Well, there were some things that I had studied, but I hadn't *understood* them. And I wanted to.

## And it's worked out well for you?

Not really. I've been here three—no, it's into four years now—and I'm still struggling with it. It seems like there's a leadership vacuum in the university, and I've always had a penchant to get involved. That tendency to manage things. I was elected to the graduate studies committee, and then I was elected chairman. It starts chewing up all that time when I was going to think, and read, and write. Then I was asked to chair the administration program, and now I'm chairing the division.

## Why did you say yes to all these requests?

Part of you wants to do scholarly work, but then you look around at the people who are doing the leading, and you say to yourself, "I can do it better than those guys." There's that kind of tug between the two. Once you've been in administrative harness, it's hard to get out of it.

## But how are you dealing with that tug?

I think we can make this division better and it excites me to be able to orchestrate some of that. Now we're going to be looking for a new dean, and if the search is primarily an inside search then I know that my name is going to be brought up for that position.

### Is that what you want?

Not really. What I really want deep down is to try to see if I can become a professor. I love to teach, and I'm good at that at this level. But I've really had to force myself to do some writing. Once I get into it the writing excites me, but it doesn't come as easily as I thought, and the time doesn't always seem to be there. I was caught up with the myth of the college professor: You come to the university, put your feet up, read books, and go home in the aftenoon to cut the grass. That's a lot of nonsense. I'm as busy as I've ever been. I tell my old running buddies this, and they won't believe me. "You've got it made now." That's what they say. But the work of the college professor—you can't get away from it. It's consuming. You can't leave it on the desk at work the way you could when you were a school administrator.

### Well, you have fifteen to twenty years left. How are you going to approach them?

Actually, I suppose not much differently from the way I approached the last fifteen to twenty. I didn't plot them out. I reacted to opportunities, if you want to know the truth. There were a lot of gut-level decisions that made up my career; it wasn't a calculated plan. On one hand, I could stay right here until I retire. On the other hand, I could see someone saying to me within a year, "Hey, do you want to do *this*?" And I might decide to do it. I've conquered a lot of worlds, but I'm getting near fifty now. And I've come to realize that if good things happen in an organization they do so really because of incrementalism—the work of a lot of people over time. It's not the one person who comes in and leads the troops to new heights. You have to build up to a critical mass of people and effort. I'm not one to lead a lot of charges up the hill.

### This conflict you feel in yourself between the administrator and the professor—it reminds me of the old strain between practice and theory.

Theory has meaning for the practitioner, I'm convinced of that. Graduate school, particularly at the doctoral level, can teach you that. At least the best graduate schools in educational administration do. You may finish with some naivete about the political world, but you are better prepared to stand back and look at problems and organizations. Any kind of a construct helps you think about how things fit together. Cookbook graduate school teaching just can't do that. If anything, I could kick myself for not making better use of the broader theoretical resources of Columbia University. I just didn't take advantage of the *whole* university the way I should have.

    Now here, when I'm teaching, I start every course by stripping away some of the mystique of theory and trying to diminish the fear of theory that many graduate students in education seem to have. Theory can help you find systematic explanations of phenomena, and for those of us in educational administration, that usually means behavior, and usually behavior in organizations. Different sets of glasses, different appreciations, different handles on reality. Maybe I wouldn't have this view if I'd come through a doctoral program other than the one I did. I feel a little frustrated because I don't know if our graduates see theory as useful or if they can apply it to different situations in their work. That's an issue I'd like to look at in a serious way

It's interesting, that as the decline comes to higher education, universities want the schools and colleges of education to be more research oriented. But that's hard to do with the people whom we have on the faculty, and I'm not sure it's the right thing after all. We're a *professional* school, and that makes us different from other faculty units in the arts and social sciences and physical sciences. My colleagues across campus don't seem to understand that in addition to research and the production of knowledge we have to prepare practitioners, and we have to provide services to those practitioners after they are at work in the field. Some people would like to shut us down completely. But others want us to continue only if we can be like them, and that doesn't mean maintaining a professional orientation. I don't think they can close us out. That just doesn't seem to be in the cards politically. We can at least save the undergraduate program. I hope I'm right.

Our dean has been trying to cut some money out of our budget that supports our relationship with superintendents in this area. I told him that would be a big mistake. Not only should we be helping them, but they provide real political support for us when the university wolves come after us. Here we are struggling, and we are thinking about cutting off our allies. It doesn't make sense.

## FROM PRACTICE TO THEORY

We so often think of *a* leader, *an* individual. Someone who stands above the crowd, charismatic and forceful—a person to look up to, who can rally followers to a cause. John Mrozek's leadership suggests that the concept is far more complex. There is a decidedly mysterious quality to it, warns John. It is as bound up with cooperation and persuasion as it is with pure force of personality or charismatic directiveness. When something worthwhile happens, you know that a modest amount of leadership has taken place. But you find, upon examination, that many people—not just one or two—are involved. Each person adds something, makes a contribution. In the end, leadership has occurred. But who's the leader? One person? Two? Or many?

Then, there is the other side of the coin. It seems, says Mrozek, that there is often a leadership vacuum in organizations. Neither the collectivity nor an individual provides direction. In the end, someone (or ones) decides to get involved. Is that what leadership is? Involvement? The word involvement has many political connotations. The art of compromise, a capacity to bridge competing interests, skill in negotiation, an ability to communicate one-on-one and to instill confidence. Are these political attributes the subtle qualities of good leadership?

Leadership seems to be of vital importance to organizations, but it is a baffling construct. We realize that there are good leaders; and we often agree, usually in retrospect, as to who those good leaders are. We have paid fairly substantial theoretical attention to the question of leadership, and there are, consequently, a number of interesting theoretical approaches to the subject. Each offers insights and perspectives but few concrete answers for practicing administrators. What does it mean to be a leader? Under what conditions or situations does leadership emerge? What is the relationship between leader and follower? Does good followership lead organizations, rather than the other way around? How do you lead a seasoned professional like Sam Bonus?

## THE EVOLUTION OF LEADERSHIP IN THE ORGANIZATION

> I believed . . . that a leader could operate successfully as a kind of advisor to his organization. I thought I would avoid being a "boss.". . . . I thought that maybe I could operate so that everyone would like me—that "good human relations" would eliminate all discord and disagreement. I couldn't have been more wrong. It took a couple of years, but I finally began to realize that a leader cannot avoid the exercise of authority any more than he can avoid the responsibility for what happens to his organization.

This statement by Douglas McGregor as he left the presidency at Antioch College points to the misconceptions and ambiguity commonly surrounding leadership. What does it mean to "provide leadership" or to "exercise leadership in an organization"? When we know that things are not going well for an organization (or a nation state, for that matter), we often attribute its distress to a lack of leadership. But what do we mean when we render this judgment? What *is* good leadership?

Douglas McGregor is well known as a proponent of a people-centered approach to management, yet in his own experience it was necessary for him to become a boss. Are the best leaders those who take command in an organization, who authoritatively establish goals and somehow—through the force of personality, the power of position, the ability to wheel-and-deal—force others along paths that *they* have selected? Or, are the best leaders those who move people from behind—who build consensus toward group goals, who smooth differences of opinion, who engender warmth and trust, who offer a sympathetic ear—coaxing others along paths the group has selected? There is no clear answer. The management literature is filled with comparisons of authoritarian vs. democratic leaders, of task-centered vs. people-centered administrators, and of commander types vs. team players. The results are inconclusive; there are no consistent winners.

What does persist is the belief that leaders have powerful effects on organizational functioning, as well as malfunctioning. Educators have given substantial attention over the years to questions of leader effectiveness. For example, much of the current school improvement research suggests that the leadership of the building principal is critical in promoting student achievement.[1] A widely disseminated proposal for the improvement of city schools calls for a style of school administration that emphasizes (a) strong leadership; (b) the development of teacher expectations that their pupils *can* succeed; (c) instruction centered heavily on basic skills acquisition; (d) a safe school climate; and (e) an ongoing evaluation system.[2] In reality, studies of the on-the-job activities of administrators and studies of communications between educational leaders and their subordinates, find that administrators actually exert only limited influence in the area of classroom instruction. The one dimension of the organization that seems to be central to its basic, societal purpose apparently is among the least closely attended to by practicing educators.[3]

Is this to imply that school administrators occupy positions of supposed effectiveness but that *real* leadership in instruction in education comes from some other source (e.g., classroom teachers, parents, pupils' peers)? Or, can we suggest that administrators do exercise leadership, but in areas other than instruction (e.g., budget, personnel, facilities) that eventually result indirectly in instructional improvement?[4] Again, there are no crisp responses. Leadership is an inchoate process, long the subject of speculation. We assume in the notion of leadership that something happens as the result of the work of a leader, but we are not sure why that something occurs. As James McGregor Burns observes, leadership is "one of the most observed and least understood phenomena on earth."[5]

In this chapter we examine leadership in the context of formal organizations, or what can be termed *managerial leadership:* the influence exercised by hierarchical superiors. Within educational organizations, we refer, for example, to presidents and deans of universities, and superintendents and principals of schools. We recognize that managers do more than just lead. Some scholars believe that leadership is actually just a subset of day-by-day management,[6] and that we have tended to focus primarily on the leaders' moments of glory rather than on their daily (seemingly mundane) activities and routines.[7] Likewise, not all the leadership that is exercised in a group can be attributed to one individual or the hierarchical superior.[8] Leadership emerges in the informal organization as well. We will limit our discussion, nonetheless, to the influence exercised by hierarchical superiors at the managerial and institutional levels of organizations. The purpose of this chapter is to review prior theory and research about leadership and to present new ideas and concepts regarding leader effectiveness. This survey is necessarily broad, but we also include recommendations for improving leadership in schools.

As in our other chapters, we suggest alternative perspectives derived from organizational and administrative theory—asking how each of three separate notions of leadership in educational organizations provides a few differing insights into this most perplexing of administrative arts. We begin our discussion by considering the nature of leadership. The remainder of the chapter is devoted to an extended discussion of three related theoretical perspectives.

## LEADERSHIP DEFINED

Why do some persons fail as leaders while others succeed? Are leaders born or made? Why does an effective leader in one setting so often seem to do poorly in another?

Are leaders generally people of imposing stature and verbal fluency, or can leadership be offered just as effectively by the small, the meek, and the relatively inarticulate? These and many other questions have bedeviled the scholarly community for many decades.

Leadership is a term often used interchangeably with administration, management, power, and authority. Leadership has been defined in terms of individual traits, behavior, and influence over other people; interaction patterns; role relationships; occupation of an administrative position; and perception of others regarding legitimacy of influence.[9] Some representative definitions of leadership illustrate this confusion. Hemphill and Coons note that leadership is "the behavior of an individual when he is directing the activities of a group toward a shared goal."[10] Katz and Kahn "consider the essence of organizational leadership to be the influential increment over and above mechanical compliance with the routine directiveness of the organization."[11] In this latter sense, individuals perform well not because it is required, or because they fear the consequences of non-compliance, but because they want to.[12] Such definitions imply that leadership does not exist alone. Dubin asserts that "leadership must surely mean followership," that leadership cannot exist in the absence of people who respond to the leader.[13] In fact, a frequent admonition to young managers reflects this notion: Find out where the group is headed and jump quickly in front of the line. Despite the variety of definitions, two assumptions appear in most. These are that (a) leadership is a group phenomenon involving the interaction between two or more persons, and (b) it involves a process whereby intentional influence is exerted by the leader over the followers.[14]

As one of the oldest of topics in the study of administration, leadership theory has proceeded through a succession of alternative conceptualizations. With attention justified by the firm belief that leadership has a powerful effect on an organization's viability,[15] the images of good leaders have ranged over time from superman to orchestra conductor, quarterback, prince, hero, coach, and partner.[16] Understandably, a favorite and certainly reasonable approach to the study of leadership over the years has been the observation of the special traits and behaviors of those persons who fill leadership roles. This, the first of our three theoretical perspectives, would argue that leadership can be discovered most readily in the qualities and actions of persons who do the leading. People will tend to follow those who exhibit certain traits (e.g., charisma, abundant energy, a cool head, great personal warmth) or those who exhibit a certain style of behavior (e.g., facilitative, dictatorial, consultative, initiatory, collegial). Trait and behavior theories recognize that leaders are usually quite special people. They stand out. They may differ in their appeal (some are aloof and aristocratically distant, while others are back-slapping, gregarious types), but their leadership qualities are readily apparent. Other people follow them; they command respect (and often affection); they get things done.

The second of our three theoretical perspectives retorts that it is not uniquely the special behavior of the leader that is the key to leadership, but, alternatively, the nature of the leadership situation (where there is an interaction of leader behavior and situational context). People who exercise leadership must do so in a context of differing colleague or staff relationships, organizational constraints, political circumstances, and time and place conditions. Within these differing situations, the capacity to exercise leadership may vary. An effective leader in one context may be a poor leader in another—as when a former army general performs inadequately as a college president, or a successful basketball coach at one school finds that he is unable to motivate the players at another. While leadership style (trait and behavior) is certainly important, it is the situation (the context in which leaders perform) that determines success.

Finally, our third theoretical perspective responds that leadership resides in the eye of the beholder. People are not considered leaders until leadership is somehow attributed to them by their followers. To be sure, one attribute of a good leader may be his or her ability to convince others that leadership is being exercised, to create some proof or an illusion of leadership. However, the significant idea in this third point of view is that leadership can be discovered most readily in the attitudes and behaviors not of those persons who do the leading, but of those who do the following. Successful outcomes are typically attributed to a leader, and it is those who supply these attributions who best explain what leadership is.

## LEADERSHIP TRAITS AND STYLES

Early efforts to understand leadership led researchers to identify personal character-istics and traits that consistently were present or were shared by effective leaders in formal and informal organizations. As the study of leadership matured, the search was focused further upon the behaviors and managerial styles of persons in leadership positions. Both of these approaches assume that leadership can be discovered and explained quite simply through a study of the qualities and actions of leaders.

### Trait Theory

Are there identifiable traits that distinguish leaders from nonleaders? Traits often and early suggested as important to leadership include physical characteristics (such as height, appearance, energy level), personality (such as self-esteem, dominance, emotional stability), and ability (such as general intelligence, verbal fluency). The U.S. Army field manual, *Military Leadership*,[17] and the popular bestseller, *The Managerial Woman*,[18] are representative of the perspective that leaders—whether army officers or women executives—who succeed in their occupations have identifia-ble traits in common.[19] Whatever the context, the person with special traits will display leadership quality. And these traits will live on, serving their possessor in context after context. The leader in school is more likely to be the leader in adulthood; the leader in one crisis (e.g., military conflict) is more likely to display leadership in another (e.g., corporate competition).

However, after a review of seven decades of such research, Stogdill concluded that only a limited number of traits appear to correlate with effective leadership.[20] These are intelligence, initiative, self-confidence, energy and activity, and task-relevant knowledge. For example, several of the studies showed that leaders who are more intelligent (as measured by intelligence tests) than their subordinates are more effective. A wide discrepancy between the IQs of the supervisor and subordinates, however, lessens the influence of the managerial leader.[21] Good leaders seemingly should be bright but not too bright. A review of studies conducted from 1900-1957 focusing on personality traits of leaders concluded that leaders tend to be more extroverted, dominant, masculine, conservative and better adjusted, and to have greater interpersonal sensitivity than nonleaders.[22] In addition, "most successful leaders appear to have good health, be above average in height or well below it, and come from the upper socio-economic levels in society."[23]

In another review of the trait literature, House and Baetz[24] drew three general conclusions. First, leadership exists only with respect to others; thus interpersonal skills are likely to be essential for successful influence attempts. Second, "leadership requires a predisposition to be influential,"[25] which means that such traits as dominance and ascendance are likely to be positively correlated with leadership. Finally, task objectives and organizational goals are usually a part of the exercise of leadership, and thus a "need for achievement," "desire to excel," and "task-relevant ability" are hypothesized to be related to leadership.[26]

Recent studies in a large international company have added another trait to these lists—the helicopter factor. This is the "ability to rise above the particulars of a situation and perceive it in its relation to the overall environment."[27] The helicopter factor can be likened to the difference between how the mouse and the eagle view the same country field. The effective leader is able to see the gestalt, while less effective leaders focus on the details.

It is interesting that although the major focus on traits of leaders which was prominent in the 1950s was somewhat discredited, scholars are returning to this ground. House and Baetz contend that trait research needs to be continued because "the magnitude of the correlations between leader traits and criteria of leadership are as high and often higher than correlations between leader behavior and leadership criteria."[28] A recent study by Warren Bennis emphasizes traits that leaders exhibit. Based on interviews with ninety successful executives, Bennis identified five characteristics or traits these leaders shared:

1. *Vision.* They had a strong vision of where the organization needed to go. They also had a strong outcome orientation.
2. *Communication and alignment.* They were able to communicate their vision to their followers in special ways, perhaps through the use of metaphors.
3. *Persistence.* They were able to "stay the course." They viewed failure as an opportunity to learn.
4. *Organizational learnings.* They found ways and means to change.
5. *Empowering others.* They created a social system and environment that encouraged workers to do their best. They gave their workers the sense that they were at the heart of things, that they were an integral part of the organization and its progress.[29]

Yukl also suggests that the investigation of leader traits has been more productive in recent years: "Greater progress can be attributed to the inclusion of more relevant traits, use of better measures of traits, examination of trait patterns rather than looking only at individual correlations, and the use of longitudinal research."[30]

Interestingly, a current approach to the selection of educational administrators for their jobs depends heavily upon trait-related characteristics. In the late 1970s and early 1980s, the concept of an assessment center began to receive serious, nationwide attention as a vehicle for measuring and advancing managerial potential in education. With support from the National Association of Secondary School Principals (NASSP), the Assessment Center Project conducted job analyses of administrators and concluded that twelve key skills are required for performing well in school management. Among these are judgment, decisiveness, sensitivity, stress tolerance, organizational ability, personal motivation, and oral and written communication.[31]

Edwin Bridges notes that the study of administrator traits and personal attributes (demography, experience, and personality) dominates the research in educational administration.[32] Thus, we discover that American school superintendents are predominately white and male (1.2 percent are female and 2.1 percent are minority), with a median age of 48.7, and married. Approximately two-thirds of superintendents attribute their selection for their current positions to their personal characteristics (e.g., relationship-oriented, businesslike, hard working, a risk-taker, a good listener).[33] Nevertheless, there are curiously few school district superintendents with memorable traits who live on in the memory and folklore of the profession. A few do come to mind, of course: Willard Wirt in Gary and William T. Harris in St. Louis, early in the century. Later, we have Ben Willis in Chicago, Harold Spears in San Francisco, Mark Shedd in Philadelphia, Carl Hansen in Washington, D.C., and Carleton Washburne in Winnetka, Illinois. But in the main, school superintendents tend to be grey and shadowy figures, behind-the-scenes types, public servants—good administrators, competent individuals, but not by reputation societal leaders.

Additionally and surprisingly, with the renewed interest in trait theory, there has been little investigation to date into sex differences in school administration. However, an intriguing study by Joan Meskin reviewed the available literature on male-female differences in the school principalship. Meskin found that (a) women principals tend to use democratic administrative styles (as opposed to authoritarian or laissez-faire styles) more frequently than men; (b) women principals perform better in evaluating the performance of new teachers and in providing instructional leadership; and (c) women perform as elementary school principals (as judged by teacher ratings) in an overall fashion superior to men.[34] Why do women appear to be more successful? Meskin suggests that one psychological characteristic of women that is often sensed as a weakness, but that in reality could be a greater strength, is "their supposedly greater field-dependence."[35] Meskin describes this trait as follows:

> Field-dependence is the quality of orienting one's self to the context of a problem rather than to the problem's object. It has been measured in several technical ways; the best known of these is the rod-and-frame task in which the subject, sitting in a darkened room, must "adjust a luminous rod to the true upright when both it and a surrounding luminous frame are tilted." If he adjusts the rod to the "true upright," he is classified as more field-independent; if he adjusts it perpendicular to the tilted frame he is more field-dependent. The quality is a perceptual one, but it is related to many other attributes, for example, cognition, personality, and social behavior. It is generally considered better to be field- independent; it is an attribute children seem to acquire as they mature, and the principal researcher of field-independence and field-dependence,

H. A. Witkin, considers field-independence as representing a higher level of psychological development. In several dozen studies women and girls have performed in a more field-dependent fashion than men and boys.

It is quite possible, however, that field-dependence, supposedly a negative characteristic, may be one of the qualities that accounts for the special approaches that women administrators take to problems which, in turn, brings them greater success in their jobs.[36]

Specifically, concludes Meskin, women's habits of being more consultative and relationship-oriented than men, and of exchanging information more often, may be related to their field-dependence and may "be an important key to the success of female educational administrators."[37]

Despite the renewed interest, criticism of trait theory persists. Are personality traits antecedents of leadership, or do they develop as individuals assume leadership roles? As with the Presidency of the United States, is it often the nature of the job that brings out traits of outstanding leadership, or do persons with the right traits exhibit leadership whatever the job? In addition to failing to identify a well-defined list of traits which are necessary and sufficient conditions for successful leadership, trait theory appears to run counter to democratic norms prevalent in our culture. It implies that good leaders are more likely to be born than made—that leadership tends to be an ingrained quality (some persons have it, others do not); that it is largely unteachable; that it is in short supply; and that it belongs only to those with leadership talent. Because scholars, in large part, have failed to identify a set of personality traits that correlate with effective leadership, they have turned to the leadership *styles* of managers. The assumption behind the style and behavior theories is that subordinates will perform more effectively for managers who use a particular style of leadership.

## Leader Style and Behavior Theory

Can persons with differing traits (e.g., both the extroverted and the introverted) find an identifiable style of leadership to share? Put another way, if the traits of individuals are not its clearcut determinants, can leadership nevertheless be discovered in individual behaviors? Certainly, people of quite different personalities can be found to act in many of the same ways— and these similarities of action may be the key to leader effectiveness, rather than capacities and predilections which may be lodged somewhere deep within the individual psyche.

As would be expected, style and behavior theorists have studied and described the activity patterns of people filling managerial roles. Managerial behavior has been investigated by asking managers to maintain a record or diary of their activities;[38] by observing managers as they work for a sustained period of time;[39] by observing managers for brief intervals of time on random occasions;[40] by collecting critical incidents of managerial behavior from subordinates, supervisors and peers;[41] and by asking managers, their supervisors, or subordinates to respond to questionnaires that describe specific managerial behavior.[42] We will restrict our discussion to the theories and studies of managerial style that have attempted to identify leader behavior or style involved in the attainment of group and organizational goals. Specifically, we consider (a) the Ohio State University Leadership Studies, (b) Likert's contributions, and (c) the Managerial Grid. In addition, because there is little agreement across studies as to the categories of leadership behavior, we review an attempt by Yukl and his colleagues to integrate the studies and fill this void.

**The Ohio State Leadership Studies.**   Among the best-known studies of leader behavior has been the series of inquiries that started at Ohio State University in the 1940s.[43] They include several instruments designed to measure leader consideration (concern for subordinates' well-being, comfort, and status) and initiating structure (structuring and defining the leader's and subordinates' roles).[44] These instruments include the Leader Opinion Questionnaire (LOQ), Supervisory Behavior Description Questionnaire (SBDQ), and the Leader Behavior Description Questionnaire (LBDQ). While consideration and initiating structure are only two of the twelve scales that measure leadership behavior on the LBDQ, most of the research has focused narrowly on these dimensions.

The appeal of the concepts of initiating structure and consideration as prepared by John Hemphill lies in their suggestion that successful leadership includes two distinct categories of behavior. Leaders should, on the one hand, pay attention to people—to consider the satisfaction, the needs, the wishes, and the contributions of their followers. They should be relationship oriented. On the other hand, leaders should also provide direction—taking initiative in defining organizational goals, outlining the roles of other persons, and communicating expectations. They should be production oriented.

Many studies of school administrators have relied on the Leader Behavior Description Questionnaire. For example, a Midwest Administration Center study used the constructs initiating structure and consideration to analyze and classify incidents collected in structured as well as unstructured observations.[45] In their study of suburban superintendents, Roald Campbell and colleagues used the LBDQ dimensions as a screen in observing the behavior of the superintendents, and as a scheme for a post-hoc analysis of the incidents recorded during observations. They found that three-fourths of the superintendents' interactions were unclassifiable into the consideration- initiating structure framework, with a range of 50 to 90 percent of behavioral incidents from which neither of these dimensions could be inferred. Another "startling finding was the paucity (less than 4 percent) of incidents from which the dimension of initiating structure would be inferred."[46] In other words, only a limited number of superintendent behaviors were aimed at directing subordinates, planning, coordinating, problem solving, criticizing poor performance, or pressuring subordinates to perform effectively. Perhaps the nature of the work performed in schools—exhibiting as it does a weak technological base and unclear goals—or the characteristics of educational professionals makes structuring behaviors less necessary.

In looking at the impact of the leadership behaviors of school principals on teacher performance, different studies report that principals take either a facilitative role or a directive role. Seldom do they manage to combine both. (John Mrozek seemed to be a learner in this respect. In the state assessment program, there was

sufficient structure, but too little consideration. During the desegregation bargaining, he came much closer to striking that elusive balance.) Teacher morale appears to
be related to the consideration dimension of administrative behavior, as measured by
the LBDQ.[47] In particular, personal interaction and encouragement by principals has
an impact on teachers. The perception teachers hold that the principal works closely
with them on instruction correlates positively with teacher job satisfaction and
positive attitudes.[48] The administrative functions most relevant to job satisfaction
include the provision of encouragement and support, the removal or reduction of
irritants, and the granting of reasonable requests.[49] While this research indicates that
administrators do have an impact on teacher morale and satisfaction, other factors
such as staff cohesiveness and personal challenge may have a greater effect on
morale.[50] Several studies report that supportive leadership had no relationship to
performance ratings, productivity, or the motivation of subordinates.[51]

In addition to the consideration dimension, structure also seems to be related
to teacher satisfaction. Although a favorite self-characterization of the profession is its
freedom to teach, in reality, teachers generally desire definite rules and react
favorably to administrative structure.[52] With the immaturity of their clients and the
constant threat of unforeseen events, teachers appreciate administrative actions that
make the workday predictable, that remove busywork, and that ensure order. Yet it
must also be noted that excessive supervision and tight reinforcement of rules
produce teacher resentment and dissatisfaction. This concurs with Lortie's observation that teachers want principals to use their authority to facilitate teacher work. In
the teachers' words, however, this means that they want principals to support them.[53]
Coordination appears to be important in school settings.[54] Effective principals were
found in several inquiries to coordinate, discuss, and advise on instruction, while
ineffective principals did none of these things. Teachers judged that the ineffective
administrators made poor decisions. It is noteworthy that the earlier studies
concluded that the principal should be supportive and facilitative while leaving
responsibility with the teacher, but more recently the effective schools studies
suggest that the principal ought to take responsibility and be much more directive
with regard to the school's instructional program.[55]

What are the more important reservations about the LBDQ instrument? First,
despite the word *behavior* in the name of the instrument, the LBDQ contains items
far removed from specific behaviors; it is more concerned with skills, traits, and
personality attributes of the leader (such as uncertainty tolerance, predictive
accuracy, persuasiveness, and demand reconciliation).[56] Second, the items, for the
most part, measure discretionary leader behavior as opposed to behavior which the
leader can neither help nor control. This point is important in light of the
work-activity studies of school administrators, which portray administrators as
adapting and reacting to the requests of others, not initiating and manipulating
opportunities. Third, items usually ask about the frequency of leader behaviors, less
often about their magnitude, and never about the timing or appropriateness of
structure or consideration to a particular task or work context.[57] Fourth, a serious
deficiency of the research using the LBDQ stems from problems of inferring or
determining the direction of causality. In other words, do considerate principals
cause teachers to be more motivated and productive *or* do principals behave in a
more considerate fashion when teachers perform well? The research findings do not

clarify the direction of this relationship. Schriesheim and Kerr conclude, after a thorough review of the instrument, that the LBDQ "cannot be considered sufficiently valid to warrant [its] continued usage in leadership research."[58] Yet, as Bridges notes in his review of research in educational administration, we continue to rely heavily on the LBDQ in our field.[59] That this is so may be in part because a better instrument has yet to be developed.

**The University of Michigan Studies.**    During the same period of time when the Ohio State research was in full swing (the 1950s and early 1960s), a series of studies on leadership behavior was conducted at the University of Michigan Institute for Social Research, leading to conclusions that parallel closely those of the Ohio State group. Rensis Likert and his colleagues focused upon the productivity of work groups and the supervisory behaviors of managers in groups of varying performance. They asked, for example, whether high-producing managers behave with subordinates in ways distinctively different from low-producing managers.[60] The resulting Michigan model of leadership was made up of four factors rather than the two (initiating structure and consideration) which received central attention at Ohio State. The commonalities between the two sets of research are readily apparent.

1. *Support.* Behavior which increases subordinates' feelings of being worthwhile and important people.
2. *Goal Emphasis.* Behavior which stimulates an enthusiasm among subordinates for getting the work done.
3. *Work Facilitation.* Behavior which actually helps subordinates get the work done by removing obstacles and roadblocks.
4. *Interaction Facilitation.* Behavior which builds the subordinate group into a work team.[61]

The University of Michigan approach appears to emphasize consideration rather than initiating structure. In *New Patterns of Management* (1961), Likert concluded that the most effective leaders are employee-centered rather than job-centered: "Superiors with the best records of performance focus their primary attention on the human aspects of their subordinates' problems and on endeavoring to build effective work groups with high performance goals."[62] With foresight that can be appreciated only now, Likert warned that increasing competition from industrializing countries throughout the world requires new attention to the development of a better system of managing the human resources of an organization.[63] Power and responsibility should be shared with employees for enhanced group productivity. The effective leader "must always adapt his behavior to take into account the expectations, values, and interpersonal skills of those with whom he is interacting."[64]

In fleshing out the Michigan model, one of Likert's more interesting contributions is his concept of the linking pin function.[65] The suggestion of the linking pin is that a supervisor can be effective with his subordinates only to the degree that the supervisor in turn has sufficient influence over his or her own superior's decisions. The capacity to exert influence upward is essential if one is to exercise leadership successfully downward. Up and down the organization, when an individual member fails in his leadership role, "the group or groups under him will not be linked into the organization effectively and will fail in the performance of their tasks."[66]

The notion of the linking pin may be particularly important to our consideration of leadership in education. As a consequence of our appreciation and understanding of the loosely coupled nature of educational organizations, there is a tendency to consider leadership in terms that are defined too narrowly. The effective-schools literature prescribes a role for the school principal, for example, that assumes successful leadership is turned inward upon one's own school—motivating teachers and pupils, creating a positive climate for learning, paying attention to the school's curriculum. That same literature does not suggest that successful school-site leadership might be turned outward (or upward) as much as inward.

**The Managerial Grid.**  A third and widely disseminated approach to leadership style has been that offered by Robert Blake and Jane Mouton. Again, there is a parallel with the Ohio State research, for the managerial grid offers two central dimensions of leader behavior: a concern for production (or institutional performance) and a concern for people. The Blake and Mouton theory is thoroughly developed in their 1964 book *The Managerial Grid.*[67] However, in 1981 the authors focused their attention more specifically upon problems of leadership in colleges and universities, with a specific adaptation of the notion of the Managerial Grid to higher education settings.[68] We use this more recent model to guide our discussion.

The production or performance oriented administrator is concerned with the achievement of institutional outcomes and goals. Alternatively, the administrator who is concerned with people is attentive to interpersonal relations, to the self-worth, esteem, and needs of others. Each of these two dimensions can be placed along one axis of a grid of academic administration, yielding combinations of leadership style as shown in Figure 8.1. Although the grid indicates the possibility of eighty-one leadership behaviors, Blake and Mouton confine their discussion to five major grid styles.

*Style 1,1—Caretaker Administration.* As the label implies, the caretaker administrator has little concern for task accomplishment and exercises little of the power or authority of his or her position. The caretaker is putting in time and going through the motions of administrative routine. The approach to the job is custodial, with general indifference to institutional purposes. "The goal of this administrator," observe Blake and Mouton, "is to maintain organizational membership and continuity for his or her own personal advantage."[69]

*Style 9,1—Authority-Obedience Administration.* This style combines a high concern for institutional performance with low concern for people. The 9,1 administrator is highly directive and unsparingly judgmental of others. He or she strives mightily to be in complete control, works hard, attends to the smallest details of the institutional endeavor, does not admit defeat, takes full credit for any successes, and expects subordinates to be readily obedient to his or her administrative authority. Blake and Mouton conclude: "The 9,1-oriented administrator is likely to initiate action, then take the ball and run with it."[70]

*Style 1,9—Comfortable and Pleasant Administration.* This administrator places people above institutional performance. Gaining the warmth and approval of others is a high priority, as is seeing to the comfort and job satisfaction of subordinates. The 1,9 administrator "believes that when people are happy, results will take care of themselves, and there will be little or no need for supervision."[71] In the academic

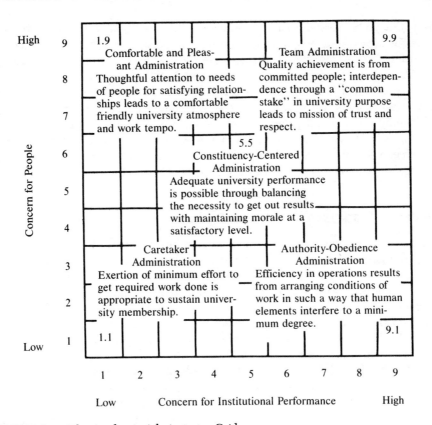

**FIGURE 8.1**    The Academic Adminstrator Grid
From Blake, Mouton, and Williams, *The Academic Administrative Grid,* p. 12.

environment, an administrator with this style will be attentive to, even solicitous of faculty opinions and interests and will engage in "unending efforts to create a harmonious social atmosphere."[72]

*Style 5,5—Constituency-Centered Administration.* This style displays both a moderate concern for institutional purpose and a moderate concern for people. The central effort is to be equally responsive to the demands for institutional performance (emanating usually from hierarchical superiors) and to the demands for human consideration (that arise generally from relations with colleagues and subordinates). The 5,5 administrator does not direct others to get jobs done so much as he or she tries to motivate people into wanting to perform well.[73]

*Style 9,9—Team Administration.* This is the style that Blake and Mouton prefer. The 9,9 administrator combines a high concern for institutional purpose with a high concern for people, all in a collegial approach to academic administration. The involvement of subordinates in the work of the institution is emphasized, with consideration given to a meshing of both individual and institutional goals. Careful attention is devoted to full consultation with persons who can contribute to a decision, and, although teamwork is emphasized, conflicts are not avoided or ignored. In fact, confrontation is not uncommon, for it "permits tensions and emotions to be fully resolved through understanding and insight."[74]

Although it is based upon the same (possibly overworked) dichotomy between goal-centeredness and people-centeredness, the Blake and Mouton approach is of special interest because it is both more descriptive (in a down-to-earth sense) and more blatantly prescriptive than the other models. Few individuals with experience in educational organizations can fail to recognize and probably attach names to the prototypical styles of "caretaker" or "authority-obedience." Furthermore, the authors unabashedly provide and promote a preferred-choice administrative style that, to their minds, is "the soundest approach to university management."[75] Whether or not one agrees with such a claim, the approach is at least refreshing in its attempt to move from theory and research toward the reality of practice.

## Summary: Leadership Traits and Styles

In this section, we have reviewed ideas and studies of school administrators that fit within the genre of leadership trait and style theory. There is some evidence to suggest that certain traits of leaders are worthwhile topics for further investigation and that leadership style does correlate with a number of other, important measures of organizational behavior. However, there appear to be several problems with leadership trait and style theories. First, most such theories specify the result of desired leader behavior, not the behaviors that lead to desired outcomes. The manager is told what the finished product should look like, but not what to do to obtain the results. This is analogous to a cookbook full of photographs of gourmet meals but without the recipes. Second, the consistent assumption underlying the style and behavior theories is that a single leadership style (such as team management or Theory Y) is superior to other styles in all kinds of organizations (such as schools, hospitals or business corporations) and under all kinds of conditions cutting across cultures, environmental factors, or task characteristics). Such a premise is suspect. Third, each major study of leadership behavior has led to a different behavior taxonomy with only modest agreement across studies, making it difficult to compare the findings. While the consideration and initiating structure categories are the most widely used in educational organizations for understanding managerial leadership in a variety of contexts, they have been criticized for presenting too general and simplistic a picture of leadership. As Yukl points out, "They fail to capture the great diversity of behavior required by most kinds of managers and administrators."[76] This diversity is highlighted in the work activity studies. Finally, Stogdill makes an insightful observation about theory development in the area of leadership.

> An almost insurmountable problem is the question of the extent to which, in new theorizing, we pour old wine in new bottles. Julius Caesar's descriptions of his own leadership style are clear, succinct endorsements of the need for what Blake and Mouton (1964) would see as a "9-9" style, a style that Fleishman (1953a) would describe in terms of high initiation and consideration, and that in the year 2000 some young theorist will have given new names. When does a field advance? Are we beyond Caesar's understanding of how to lead infantry shock troops?[77]

In an attempt to reconcile the diverse findings of the these studies and to identify meaningful and measurable categories of leadership, Yukl has isolated twenty-three categories of managerial behavior.[78] These behavior categories are identified in Table 8.1.

To be sure, Yukl's list includes the usual attention to consideration (e.g., decision participation, interaction facilitation) and to structure (e.g., goal setting, performance emphasis). But his new taxonomy of managerial behaviors also gives refreshing attention to such activities as training-coaching, praise-recognition, and the structuring of rewards. In anticipation of some implications for practice to be addressed later in this book, Yukl suggests that managerial leadership may involve a stress upon *teaching subordinates and rewarding them.* Curiously, much of the emphasis upon consideration in the earlier literature assumed that acts of sharing decision-making or building teamwork carried their own payoffs. People who felt themselves to be involved in the work of the organization were rewarded automatically. To the contrary, the achievement of common purpose and teamwork, if unaccompanied by other rewards (e.g., promotion, better pay), may lead to a disenchantment with current leadership rather than to its advocacy and support. Also to the contrary, teachers who receive constant consideration (e.g., much committee work, lots of discussion) may actually feel punished. They would often prefer administrators to go ahead and make many decisions, leaving them free to teach.

The categories in Table 8.1 do not appear to be situation specific or overly broad and abstract, but sufficient research has yet to be conducted using the instrument both in educational and noneducational settings. A recent study of elementary school principals using the Yukl categories suggests that some appear meaningless in this particular situation.[79] Because of the failure of style and behavior theories generally to take the context of a leadership situation into account, scholars began to speculate about the interaction of environment and leadership behavior. Do all leadership traits and behaviors work as effectively in every situation? Are there some behaviors that are appropriate in one organizational context but not another?

## SITUATIONAL THEORY

Situational or contingency theories of leadership posit that no one leadership style will prove effective in all contexts; instead, a person who displays qualities of leadership in one organizational environment may be judged a poor leader in another. Traits that seem to be effective in military organizations, for example, may be decidedly inappropriate to an institution of higher education. Conversely, a person who has the consultative, deliberative, let's-talk-things-over style of a university administrator may be a poor choice to head an agency (e.g., a city police department) that operates on a principle of tight hierarchical authority and by-the-book decision making. In short, contingency theories suggest that it is not leader behavior alone that is the key to understanding leadership so much as it is the *context* in which this behavior occurs.

### Fiedler's Contingency Theory

Fred Fiedler developed his contingency theory of leadership because of his disappointment with the results of research conducted on the differences in effectiveness between trained leaders and untrained leaders.[80] In one of these studies

*TABLE 8.1*    Definition of managerial behaviors in new taxonomy

---

PERFORMANCE EMPHASIS:   the extent to which a leader emphasizes the importance of subordinate performance and encourges subordinates to make a maximum effort.

ROLE CLARIFICATION:   the extent to which a leader informs subordinates about their duties and responsibilities, clarifies rules and policies, and lets subordinates know what is expected of them.

TRAINING-COACHING:   the extent to which a leader provides any necessary training and coaching to subordinates, or arranges for others to provide it.

GOAL SETTING:   the extent to which a leader, either alone or jointly with a subordinate, sets specific, challenging, but realistic performance goals for each important aspect of the subordinate's job.

PLANNING:   the extent to which a leader plans in advance how to efficiently organize and schedule the work, coordinate work unit activities, accomplish task objectives, and avoid or cope wth potential problems.

INNOVATING:   the extent to which a leader looks for new opportunities for the work unit to exploit, proposes new activities to undertake, and offers innovative ideas for strengthening the work unit.

PROBLEM SOLVING:   the extent to which a leader takes prompt an decisive action to deal with serious work-related problems and disturbances.

WORK FACILITATION:   the extent to which a leader provides subordinates with any supplies, equipment, support services, and other resources necessary to do their work effectively.

MONITORING OPERATIONS:   the extent to which a leader keeps informed about the activities within his/her work unit and checks on the performance of subordinates.

EXTERNAL MONITORING:   the extent to which a leader keeps informed about outside events that have important implications for his/her work unit.

INFORMATION DISSEMINATION:   the extent to which a leader keeps subordinates informed about decisions, events, and developments that affect their work.

DISCIPLINE:   the extent to which a leader takes appropriate disciplinary action to deal with a subordinate who violates a rule, disobeys an order, or has consistently poor performance.

---

he and his associates "compared a group of Belgian navy recruits and a well-trained and experienced group of petty officers . . . [and] found no overall differences in their leadership performance." Fiedler consequently developed a model of leadership that views group performance or effectiveness as dependent upon the interaction of leadership style and the favorableness of the situation. He identified two significant leadership styles: task-oriented leadership and socio-emotionally oriented leadership. Task-oriented leaders are concerned with accomplishing the task above all else. Socio-emotionally oriented leaders are more concerned with maintaining good relations with their subordinates. Again, these notions are similar to the concepts of initiating structure and consideration.

Fiedler measured leadership orientation with the Least Preferred Co-Worker (LPC) scale (see Figure 8.2). Using bipolar and adjective pairs following the semantic differential technique,[81] a leader was asked to think of and describe the esteem he or she held for a least preferred co-worker. This co-worker would be a person with whom the leader would work least well in getting a job done. A leader who describes

*TABLE 8.1 (continued)*

REPRESENTATION: the extent to which a leader promotes and defends the interests of his/her work unit and take appropriate action to obtain necessary resources and support for the work unit from superiors, peers, and outsiders.

CONSIDERATION: the extent to which a leader is friendly, supportive, and considerate in his/her behavior toward subordinates.

CAREER COUNSELING AND FACILITATION: the extent to which a leader offers helpful advice to subordinates on how to advance their careers, encourages them to develop their skills, and otherwise aids their professional development.

INSPIRATION: the extent to which a leader stimulates enthusiasm among subordinates for the work of the group, and says things to build their confidence in the group's ability to successfully attain its objectives.

PRAISE-RECOGNITION: the extent to which a leader provides appropriate praise and recognition to subordinates with effective performance, and shows appreciation for special efforts and contributions made by subordinates.

STRUCTURING REWARD CONTINGENCIES: the extent to which a leader rewards effective subordinate performance wth tangible benefits, such as a pay increase, promotion, better assignments, better work schedule, extra time off, etc.

DECISION PARTICIPATION: the extent to which a leader consults with subordinates before making work-related decisions, and otherwise allows subordinates to influence his/her decisions.

AUTONOMY-DELEGATION: the extent to which a leader delegates responsibility and authority to subordinates and allows them discretion in determining how to do their work.

INTERACTION FACILITATION: the extent to which a leader emphasizes teamwork and tries to promote cooperation, cohesiveneess, and identification with the group.

CONFLICT MANAGEMENT: the extent to which a leader discourages unnecessary fighting and bickering among subordinates, and helps them settle conflicts and disagreements in a constructive manner.

CONSTRUCTIVE CRITICISM: the extent to which a leader criticizes subordinate mistakes and poor performance in a constructive, calm, and helpful manner.

Based on Gary A. Yukl, *Leadership in Organizations*, © 1981, pp. 120–125. Reprinted by permission, of Prentice-Hall, Inc., Englewood Cliffs, N.J.

the least preferred co-worker in particularly rejecting terms would be considered a strongly task-oriented person—concerned above all with completing a job and, consequently, reacting negatively to someone with whom it is difficult to work. "This is the typical pattern," notes Fiedler, "of a person who, when forced to make a choice, opts first for getting on with the tasks and worries about . . . interpersonal relations later."[82] Relationship-oriented individuals tended to describe the least-preferred co-worker in more favorable terms than task-oriented leaders. Fiedler also contends that a person who favorably describes a least preferred co-worker is able to see him/her as a person who might have some acceptable traits, thus indicating an interest in interpersonal relations.

A central element in Fiedler's theory is the notion that critical elements in the job situation govern leadership opportunity. Fiedler identified three critical dimensions of a job that determine a favorable or unfavorable situation—leader-member relations, task structure, and leader position power. Leader-member relations are favorable when the leader's subordinates are trusting and somewhat obedient. Task

Instructions:
    People differ in the ways they think about those with whom they work. On the scale below are pairs of words which are opposite in meaning. You are asked to describe someone with whom you have worked by placing an "X" in one of the eight spaces on the line between the two words. Each space represents how well the adjective fits the person you are describing, as in the following example:

Very neat:_____:_____:_____:_____:_____:_____:_____:_____:Not neat

               8      7      6       5       4      3      2      1
             Very  Quite  Some-  Slight-  Slight-  Some-  Quite  Very
             neat   neat   what    ly       ly     what  untidy untidy
                          neat    neat   untidy  untidy

Now, think of the person with whom you can work least well. He may be someone you work with now, or he may be someone you knew in the past. He does not have to be the person you like least well, but should be the person with whom you had the most difficulty in getting a job done. Describe this person as he appears to you.

| | | |
|---|---|---|
| Pleasant | :____:____:____:____|____:____:____:____: | Unpleasant |
| Friendly | :____:____:____:____|____:____:____:____: | Unfriendly |
| Rejecting | :____:____:____:____|____:____:____:____: | Accepting |
| Helpful | :____:____:____:____|____:____:____:____: | Frustrating |
| Unenthusiastic | :____:____:____:____|____:____:____:____: | Enthusiastic |
| Tense | :____:____:____:____|____:____:____:____: | Relaxed |
| Distant | :____:____:____:____|____:____:____:____: | Close |
| Cold | :____:____:____:____|____:____:____:____: | Warm |
| Cooperative | :____:____:____:____|____:____:____:____: | Uncooperative |
| Supportive | :____:____:____:____|____:____:____:____: | Hostile |
| Boring | :____:____:____:____|____:____:____:____: | Interesting |
| Quarrelsome | :____:____:____:____|____:____:____:____: | Harmonious |
| Self-assured | :____:____:____:____|____:____:____:____: | Hesitant |
| Efficient | :____:____:____:____|____:____:____:____: | Inefficient |
| Gloomy | :____:____:____:____|____:____:____:____: | Cheerful |
| Open | :____:____:____:____|____:____:____:____: | Guarded |

FIGURE 8.2    Example of an LPC Scale
Adapted from F. E. Fiedler, A Theory of Leadership Effectiveness (New York: McGraw-Hill, 1967).

structure is favorable when leaders (and presumably followers) know exactly what to do and how to do it. It was precisely such clarity that John Mrozek was able to establish prior to and during his negotiation with Sam Bonus. Finally, leader position power is high when the leader can distribute rewards and punishments freely. The higher the three situational factors, the more favorable the situation is for the leader. Fiedler argues, then, that leadership effectiveness or group performance depends on the interaction between leadership style and situation favorableness. For example, a low-LPC leader will be more effective when the situation is either highly favorable or highly unfavorable. A high-LPC leader is more effective in moderately favorable or unfavorable situations. Fiedler contends that when a mismatch between leadership orientation and the situation exists, it is easier to change the situation—through changes in responsibilities and power—than it is to change the leader's personality orientation.[83]

There is some debate as to whether Fiedler's hypotheses have received empirical support. According to Steers, research related to the construct has demonstrated generally that relationship-oriented leaders are more effective when the situation is moderately favorable or unfavorable, while task-oriented leaders are more effective under highly favorable or highly unfavorable conditions.[84] Thus, relationship-oriented leaders do operate best in conditions when the situation is moderately favorable, and task-oriented leaders can take charge in distinctly favorable or unfavorable situations.[85] An assertive principal of a public school might be expected to gain the respect and support of the faculty at a time of serious organizational stress—when pupil discipline is out of hand or parental criticism introduces raucous disharmony. The same principal might be opposed by the faculty when fine-tuning rather than change seems to be the managerial order of the day. Despite the intuitive good sense of its managerial message, however, Schriesheim and Kerr raise serious questions concerning the LPC scale's construct validity, content validity, and predictive validity.[86] Further, quoting Ashour, they assert that "the model is a theoretical empirical generalization—it does not explain why its hypothesized relationship occurs, and it is, therefore, not a theory in almost anyone's sense of the word."[87]

## Normative Theory

A situational model that specifies the conditions under which leaders should employ either autocratic, consultative, or participative decison-making styles has been developed by Victor Vroom and Philip Yetton.[88] Their approach differs from other contextual models in that situational characteristics are considered to be attributes of the particular *problem* at hand rather than more general characteristics of role expectation and situation status. Furthermore, the Vroom and Yetton model is restricted to a narrow range of leadership behavior, that is, decision making. The model is a normative model that views effective leadership as a function of knowing when, to what extent, and in what manner subordinates should participate in decisions that affect them either directly or indirectly.

The central criterion for judging leadership effectiveness in the Vroom and Yetton approach is decision effectiveness. The model indicates that there are three characteristics of decision effectiveness:

1. *Decision quality*—referring to the extent to which decisions under consideration would "make a difference" to the organization (e.g., facilitate group performance).
2. *Decision acceptance*—referring to how important it is for organizational participants to accept decisions in order for them to be implemented successfully.
3. *Time required to reach a decision*—referring to how important it is for decisions to be made slowly and methodically versus quickly.[89]

A key role of the administrator in the Vroom and Yetton model is the task of correctly diagnosing a particular problem that is being faced in order to choose an appropriate leadership style. To diagnose accurately, the manager analyzes eight problem attributes, as shown in Table 8.2. With problem attributes in mind, the manager next proceeds through a decision tree to clarify the problem type and arrive at a feasible and acceptable set of decision methods—the appropriate leadership style. The decision tree is shown here as Figure 8.3. Depending on the leader's answers to each of the problem attribute questions (A through H), he or she will branch off toward a choice of one among five alternative decision-making procedures—ranging

*TABLE 8.2* Problem attributes

A. If decisions were made, would it make a difference to the organization which course of action were adopted?
B. Do I have sufficient information to make a high quality decision?
C. Do subordinates have sufficient additional information to result in a high quality decision?
D. Do I know exactly what information is needed, who possesses it, and how to collect it?
E. Is acceptance of decision by subordinates critical to effective implementation?
F. If I were to make the decision myself, is it certain that it would be accepted by my subordinates?
G. Can subordinates be trusted to base solutions on organizational considerations?
H. Is conflict among subordinates likely in preferred solutions?

from having the leader make a unilateral decision, to consulting another person, to allowing the work group to make the decision after a discussion in which both subordinates and the manager participate. Vroom and Yetton identify some fourteen different problem types (see Figure 8.3) which may call for differing decision methods.

To use the Vroom and Yetton model, a leader must make judgments about the characteristics of problems faced. Judgments are guided by definitions of the attributes, but they are still judgments on the leader's part, with unknown correspondence to the actual properties of the situation. A leader may think he or she has the necessary information to solve the problem only to discover later that there were critical facts which were unobtainable. Or the leader may believe that subordinates will be certain to accept the decision, only to discover later that they actively oppose it. In some cases, the manager's view of the situation may lead to the use of a decision process that is unworkable in practice.

Vroom and Yetton found support for their model in a study of actual decision situations. In the situations where leader behavior agreed with the feasible set of acceptable decision-making styles (reached by working through the decision tree), two-thirds were judged to have been successfully decided. Conversely, in cases in which leader behavior was not in line with the feasible set of acceptable styles, only one-fifth were judged to have been successfully resolved.[90]

A serious limitation of the model is its narrow focus upon decision making as the central context in which leadership is displayed. Mintzberg-type studies of the workaday activities of administrators (what it is they actually do) suggest that managers may be involved just as often in the roles of ceremonial figurehead, spokesperson, information disseminator, and contact (or liaison) person as in the role of decision maker.[91] The non–decision-making characterizing a school principal's speeches and appearances at assemblies, parent meetings, and teacher get-togethers may be quite as important to the aura of leadership surrounding a school as the many decisive actions that are taken in the face of discipline problems, budget crises, personality clashes, and political conflicts.

Nevertheless, the Vroom and Yetton model is useful to educational administrators in suggesting that the kinds of problems they face are important attributes of the leadership situation, and, furthermore, that some kinds of problems may be more

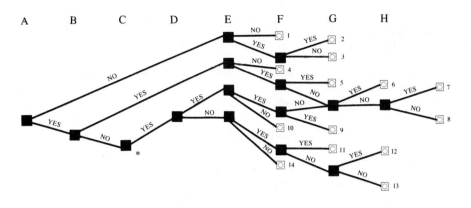

A  B  C  D  E  F  G  H

*If "no," more information is needed or redefine problem before proceeding.

FIGURE 8.3     Decision tree

Reprinted from *Leadership and Decision Making,* by Victor H. Vroom and Philip W. Yetton, by permission of the University of Pittsburgh Press. Copyright © 1973 by University of Pittsburgh Press.

amenable to one style of management than another. Dan Lortie, for example, has drawn our attention to the variable zoning that exists in school system management. Some areas of decision making are generally recognized throughout the school system hierarchy as falling within the zone of influence of the principal (e.g., compliance with record keeping, the enforcement of pupil discipline policy, keeping track of the expenditure of school funds). An autocratic style of decision making in those areas that are considered the principal's special zone may be quite acceptable to teachers; in fact, teachers may even resent being asked to participate in decision making that they think the principal should handle alone. There are, on the other hand, zones of influence (e.g., classroom affairs) that teachers believe are uniquely theirs; there are also zones where hegemony is unclear (e.g., curriculum policy). A more consultative and participatory style of leadership may be necessary whenever administrative problems move out of the clearly administrative domain into the grey areas of the instructional and the professional. As Lortie concludes, the suggestion may then be the preferred administrative ploy, rather than the order.[92]

## Path-Goal Model of Leadership

While other models examine forces associated with personality, situation, and task (e.g., decision-making) a third situational approach to leadership focuses upon end product (i.e., goal attainment). This is the Path-Goal Model of leadership developed by Robert House and colleagues.[93] This model focuses on how managers influence subordinates' perceptions of their work, personal goals, and various paths to goal attainment. Leaders can facilitate task performance by showing subordinates how their performance can be instrumental in achieving desired rewards. The Path-Goal Model builds heavily on the expectancy theory of work motivation.[94] It rests on two propositions: (a) the leader's function is supplemental, and (b) the situation affects the motivational impact of specific leader behaviors.[95] This theory attempts to identify situations in which either directive, supportive, achievement-oriented, or participative leadership would be most effective in promoting subordinate motivations and effort. The effective leader in this model

1. Recognizes and arouses subordinates' needs for outcomes over which leaders have some control.
2. Increases personal payoffs to subordinates for effective performance or goal attainment.
3. Clarifies the path to those payoffs, either through coaching or additional direction.
4. Helps subordinates clarify expectancies.
5. Reduces obstacles or frustrations that inhibit goal attainment.
6. Increases opportunities for personal satisfaction as a result of effective performance.[96]

The Path-Goal Model holds that effective leadership is a function of the interaction between leader behaviors and such situational or contingency variables as subordinate characteristics and/or environmental factors (e.g., task characteristics, the formal authority system, and characteristics of the primary work group).[97]

Little research on the Path-Goal Model has been conducted either in educational or noneducational settings. The studies that are available, however, lend some credence to the model.[98] These studies suggest "that the model is probably more complex than first thought and that additional variables, like conflict and structure, should be incorporated into future versions of the model."[99] It is interesting that "situational approaches to leadership share the assumption that while the style of leadership likely to be effective will vary according to the situation, some leadership style will always be effective regardless of the situation."[100]

Also of interest is Kerr's point that the situational leadership approach that is least dependent upon the assumption that hierarchical leadership is always important is Path-Goal theory. House and Mitchell observe that in certain work situations both goals and paths to goals may be clear. They warn that leader attempts at clarifying in these situations "will be both redundant and seen by employees as imposing unnecessary, close control" which may have negative consequences.[101] Kerr is surprised that House and Mitchell do not themselves conclude that under these conditions leadership may not be necessary. Kerr elaborates that "subordinate attributes such as competence, knowledge, and experience may reduce requirements for leader-provided structuring almost to zero, and that task-related characteristics such as inflexible regulations and invariant work methodologies may have the same effect."[102] These observations lead to the question: Is hierarchical leadership always necessary? Some scholars suggest that sometimes leadership does not matter.[103] Kerr and Jermier propose that there are situations in which hierarchical leadership has no substantial impact on subordinate satisfaction, motivation, or performance.[104]

## Substitutes for Leadership Theory

Steven Kerr and his associates have developed a situational model known as Substitutes for Leadership. They argue that under certain conditions the impact of hierarchical leadership behavior is moderated, depending upon the characteristics of individuals, the characteristics of the work to be performed, or the characteristics of the organizational structure. These variables influence which leadership style will permit the hierarchical superior to motivate, direct, and control subordinates, while other variables moderate the superior's ability to influence subordinates. Kerr and Jermier identify two types of moderators: (a) "substitutes for leadership," i.e., conditions which serve in place of leadership; and (b) "neutralizers," or conditions which counteract leadership or render it pointless.[105] In some cases, the presence of substitutes or neutralizers, not leadership behaviors, may explain the presence or absence of desired end-results, such as commitment, motivation, or performance.

　　　Kerr extracts the substitutes and neutralizers from micro and macro organizational theory. A preliminary set of substitutes and neutralizers for supportive and instrumental behavior based on Kerr's work is displayed in Table 8.3. As indicated in the table, a cohesive work group may well provide a substitute for managerial leadership. This might occur under conditions where organizational goals are well internalized, and where togetherness is consistent with productive effort. Attempts to exert leadership in a hierarchical sense may even detract from task accomplishment; the group is best left alone.

*TABLE 8.3*　　Specific substitutes and neutralizers

| Substitute or Neutralizer | Supportive Leadership | Instrumental Leadership |
|---|---|---|
| Subordinate Characteristics | | |
| Experience, ability, training | | Substitute |
| "Professional" orientation | Substitute | Substitute |
| Indifference toward rewards offered by organization | Neutralizer | Neutralizer |
| Task Characteristics | | |
| Structured, routine, unambiguous task | | Substitute |
| Feedback provided by task | | Substitute |
| Intrinsically satisfying task | Substitute | |
| Organization Characteristics | | |
| Cohesive work group | Substitute | Substitute |
| Low position power (leader lacks control over organizational rewards) | Neutralizer | Neutralizer |
| Formalization (explicit plans, goals, areas of responsibility) | | Substitute |
| Inflexibility (rigid, unyielding rules and procedures) | | Neutralizer |
| Leader located apart from subordinates with only limited communication possible | Neutralizer | Neutralizer |

Based on Gary A. Yukl, *Leadership in Organizations,* © 1981, pp. 120–125. Reprinted by permission of Prentice-Hall, Inc., Englewood Cliffs, N.J.

To illustrate further the principles behind this model, we might consider the literature about professionals in bureaucratic organizations. Professionals tend to resist bureaucratic authority and cultivate horizontal rather than vertical relationships.[106] Professionals generally will not accept directives regarding how to perform their work. They look to the professional peer group for advice and informal evaluation, tending not to refer to the hierarchical leader for recognition.[107] Professionals also tend to take an instrumental view of the organization—their commitment to the organization is conditional upon the adequacy of the organization's facilities and programs.[108] In other words, professional orientation can reduce the importance of an exercise of leadership by a hierarchical superior. Professional orientation substitutes for both supportive and instrumental leadership.

Next, the model can be illustrated by looking at the reward structure of schools, a fairly complex matter. We know from learning theory that reinforcement is a crucial element in behavior change. Rewards are considered to be an important factor in controlling the performance of rats, monkeys, pigeons, and people. The experimenter or leader must, however, be in position to control the allocation of rewards and punishments in order to reinforce desired behaviors and extinguish undesirable ones. Rewards in schools may conceivably be salary, prestige, and esteem. Lortie and others assert that teachers purport to find their work intrinsically satisfying at its best. Further, Lortie notes that the "classroom is the major arena for the receipt of psychic rewards. . . . Much of a teacher's work motivation will rotate around the conduct of daily tasks—the actual instruction of students."[109] Satisfaction derives from attaining desired results with students.

From the Kerr theory we can identify two characteristics of teaching—feedback provided by the instructional task and intrinsic satisfaction—that could potentially act as substitutes for leadership. Task-provided feedback will substitute for instrumental leadership. In this example, the principal may not need to tell the teacher how he or she is doing because the teacher knows this from the evidence or lack of evidence of student progress. Also, intrinsically satisfying tasks substitute for supportive leadership. If teachers find their work enjoyable, the principal does not need to provide supportive leadership to make the job situation tolerable. Of course, the attractiveness of the working environment varies from school to school, suggesting that in some cases and in some school settings supportive leader behaviors may be necessary.

Although we have noted that intrinsic or psychic rewards are important to teachers, extrinsic rewards also are attached to teaching. However, extrinsic rewards are distributed in a way that makes it difficult to influence their flow. For example, the two main criteria by which salary improvements are made (years of service and graduate-level coursework) are determined by the teacher collective bargaining contract. Teachers' rewards typically are not based on performance, and teacher salaries are comparatively undifferentiated. Where teacher collective bargaining has taken firm hold, the principal has relatively little decision-making prerogative in the allocation of salary improvements. The principal probably can allocate instructional materials, and (to the extent not preempted by a collective bargaining contract) can assign a desired group of students or preferred extra duty as small tokens of appreciation.[110] In other words, the principal has a low power position in the organization, and this condition is believed to neutralize the impact of both supportive and instrumental leadership.

The Substitutes for Leadership Model helps us understand the influence relationships between school administrators and teachers. Pitner is currently testing this theory with a sample of elementary schools on the West Coast.[111] She is attempting to clarify those situations in which hierarchical leadership is important to teachers in the achievement of their goals. Specifically, questions worth pursuing are: What conditions mediate or enhance strong connections between the managerial and technical levels in schools? How do these conditions vary from school to school, and how does principal behavior vary in these contexts? Her findings may suggest an alternative to the intellectual leap that has been needed to accept the assertion that effective schools are necessarily led by strong principals who follow a detailed prescription for school improvement.

## Summary: Situational Theory

Four varieties of situational leadership models all agreed that effective leadership depends upon the situation, and they reject any semblance of one best way to lead. Despite this similarity, there are differences among the theories. Fiedler is fairly pessimistic about changing leader behavior and advocates, instead, changing the situation. One wonders how easy this would be in districts experiencing severe decline or in a flat organization with limited specialization of administrative functions at the building level. Vroom and Yetton offer a range of five leadership styles based on the problem at hand. This approach assumes managers are able to change their styles willingly from day to day (or perhaps even within a single day), given the fragmented nature of their work. It also assumes that administrators can conceptualize and articulate the managerial problem in most instances. This model may suggest some problems for organizations like schools, with their changing goals, unclear technology, and fluid participation. House and associates differ from both Vroom and Fiedler in their suggestion that the leader is supplemental. Kerr and associates are even more radical in arguing that the leader may be redundant, not even necessary if personal or impersonal equivalents are available to provide support for subordinates. The assumption that leadership is causally linked to organizational performance has not been consistently verified in research studies, regardless of the theoretical framework.[112] This raises serious questions about the adequacy of dominant notions about leadership—that is, that leadership must somehow always reside in and be related to the behavior of a person whom we shall call leader, and that there is a clear linkage between leader behavior and expected performance.

# LEADERSHIP AS GOOD FOLLOWERSHIP

Our first theoretical perspective posited that leadership can be discovered in the traits and behaviors of persons who successfully do the leading in educational organizations. The second perspective reasoned that the key to understanding leadership can be discovered in the nature of the situation or context in which leadership is attempted. Indeed, as that theory has developed, it is claimed that in some situations the flesh and blood leader may be unnecessary—the situation itself structures effective effort.

The third of our three theoretical perspectives turns to the role of follower as the key to understanding leadership. Good leadership resides in the perceptions of those persons who are being led. Consider, for example, the tale of the ill-fated hot-air balloon pilot who crashed in the land of Oz and became its Wizard.[113] The citizens of Oz believed that the pilot had special powers beyond those of normal individuals and was somehow sent to them. Because the citizens refused to accept his explanation of the event, the pilot adapted to their perceptions by assuming the role of Wizard and creating the necessary illusions to support their beliefs. For example, the citizens wanted to live in an emerald city, so he issued everyone green glasses. The perceptions of followers (supported by shared illusions and mythologies) rather than the special traits of the leader provided the defining characteristic of leadership in that perhaps not so fanciful context.

In what we would now consider a modern approach to the topic, Chester Barnard insisted in 1938 in *The Functions of the Executive* that leadership finds its concrete expression in

> . . . creating faith: faith in common understanding, faith in the probability of success, faith in the ultimate satisfaction of personal motives, faith in the integrity of objective authority, faith in the superiority of common purpose as a personal aim of those who partake in it.[114]

Without faith, the conversation between John Mrozek and Sam Bonus could not have taken place. And indeed, in a later collection of his papers (*Organization and Management*, 1952) Chester Barnard anticipated our three theoretical perspectives and called for their necessary integration. Barnard suggested that leadership depends upon three things: (a) the individual, (b) the followers, and (c) the conditions.[115] Although he did not elaborate upon followership, Barnard did offer, in down-to-earth language, a clear indication of the importance of this role. Quite often, as managers observe operations closely, concluded Barnard, it

> . . . disconcerts them to note that many things a leader tells others to do were suggested to him by the very people he leads. Unless he is very dynamic—too dynamic, full of his own ideas—or pompous or Napoleonic, this sometimes gives the impression that he is a rather stupid fellow, an arbitrary functionary, a mere channel of communication, and filcher of ideas. In a measure that is correct. He has to be stupid enough to listen a great deal, he certainly must arbitrate to maintain order, and he has to be at times a mere center of communication. If he used only his own ideas, he would be somewhat like a one-man orchestra rather than a good conductor, who is a very high type of leader.[116]

Two emerging approaches to leadership that devote central attention to the characteristics of followers, and suggest leadership approaches not unlike those employed by Barnard's orchestra conductor are attribution theory and symbol management theory.

### Attribution Theory

An attribution is a judgment about the reasons for another person's behavior.[117] The teaching profession is characterized by such judgments. Teachers trying to reach reluctant learners may attribute inadequate pupil performance variously to low mental ability, laziness, a broken home, a poor choice of friends, poor health, diet deficiencies, lack of interest, a short attention span, or inadequate prior learning. More introspective teachers may explain (sometimes agonizingly) their pupils' learning problems in terms of their own failures to make learning fun, structure the curriculum effectively, meet pupils' needs, or communicate properly. Perhaps the most infamous example of teacher attribution emanates from the Rosenthal and Jacobson study of teachers' expectations concerning the mental abilities of their students as these expectations impact upon student achievement. They discovered that expectations can be self-fulfilling; when teachers expect pupils to perform well, they do, and when pupils are expected to fail, they oftentimes do fail.[118]

Obviously, as the Rosenthal and Jacobson research illustrates, attributions of behavioral causality can be heavily biased. There may be systematic prejudices in organizational settings that pervade each institution's many role relationships.[119] Rist, and others, for example, have called our attention to the social class biases in schools that determine which pupils tend to receive substantial teacher attention (e.g., in ghetto schools, those displaying observable middle-class characteristics) and which do not (the deep ghetto children).[120] In the context of superior-subordinate relations in schools, it is not uncommon for both teachers and parents to expect high school principals to be male, of large physical stature, of commanding presence, and sternly aloof. Profiles of urban school superintendents reveal that they have tended to be of rural or small-town rather than big-city upbringing, and they come to their jobs armed with the conservative values, work ethic, sense of morality, and political cautiousness that are considered characteristic of small-town America.[121]

Although no careful research has been done on how similar biases might affect the leadership offered by principals to teachers in school settings, one can speculate a bit from knowledge of the culture of the school. Teachers expect principals to support them in disciplinary encounters with pupils and parents; they also expect to be left alone to teach, with minimal managerial intrusion upon classroom activity; finally, they expect principals to intercede on their behalf vis-a-vis the organizational hierarchy. Principals who fail to conform to these expectations—who side with parents against teachers, who spend large blocs of time overseeing the quality of classroom instruction, and who enforce organizational demands upon teachers (in other words, who try to provide leadership as their superintendents and boards of education might view it)—may find themselves left without the allegiance of their followers and labeled (by them) as inadequate leaders.

Thus, the definition of leadership and its proper exercise depends heavily upon the perceptions of followers (which may differ mightily from the perceptions of superiors and outsiders). These perceptions can be seriously biased, often along lines that are built into organizational frameworks. *Followers grant an individual the obeisance due a leader when it is possible for them to explain (attribute reasons for) the behavior of that leader in terms that are consistent with their own preconceptions.* From this same line of thinking, Jeffrey Pfeffer draws upon attribution theory in providing the following definition of leadership:

> Leadership is associated with a set of myths reinforcing a social construction of meaning which legitimates leadership role occupants, provides belief in potential mobility for those not in leadership roles, and attributes social causality to leadership roles, thereby providing a belief in the effectiveness of individual control.[122]

The words myth, meaning, belief, and attribution abound in Pfeffer's definition —painting a picture of a rather murky and intangible construct that is a far cry from the earliest efforts to isolate clearly the special traits of good leaders. Perhaps in few settings is the identification of successful leadership as fog-bound as in higher education. Deans of colleges, for example, have a long history of rapid turnover, despite the fact that the need for successful leadership to secure the good will of its following is part of the structure of higher education. In few other institutional settings are subordinates (i.e., the faculty) involved so carefully in the appointment of their own administrative superiors. Why, then, is there so much coming and going in the job?[123]

Let us suggest a possible answer in three parts, an answer that proceeds in tandem with Pfeffer's definition. *First*, we might note that the mythology surrounding the college professorship places a premium on the preservation of professorial autonomy. Faculty members guard jealously their freedom to teach favorite courses, determine their own use of time, do research on topics of their own choosing, write what they wish, make decisions at their own (usually slow) pace, and consult (often endlessly) with one another on matters of college governance. Their leaders are expected to work hard to preserve these freedoms; nevertheless, the dean must also face quite different expectations and demands from administrators at upper levels of the university hierarchy. From the organizational stratosphere, course offerings should have sufficient student enrollment to justify the expense, research should be encouraged which is supported by outside funding, each faculty member should teach a full annual load of courses, budgets should be pared to the bone (e.g., with restrictions on faculty travel), all decisions should be made quickly and rationally, and programs or courses which lose student demand should be cut back and then dropped. In effect, the dean is trapped—between two separate constructions of meaning, a condition that is pictured precisely on the amusing jacket of Van Cleve Morris' book, *Deaning*. A dean in academic garb is shown walking a tightrope between Corinthian columns—with toothy alligators (the faculty) wielding knives and forks below, while lightning bolts (the upper organizational administrators) flash above. It may be particularly instructive to observe that deans who do survive such peril for long periods of time and who do retain the high regard of faculty members are those who continue their professorial lives despite their administrative responsibilities. They continue to write, publish, do research, even teach, and in the process they retain a sympathy with and reinforce the meaning of the professoriate.

*Second*, leadership in the position of college dean must confront and adapt to the myth that professors are not self-aggrandizing climbers up a corporate ladder. Deans are supposed to accept their jobs reluctantly, and show little ego involvement in the trappings and perquisites of the office. However, no matter how low-key their approach to the job, and no matter how reluctant they appear to be to accept the position, persons who do become deans are immediately suspect. In Pfeffer's terms, the social construction of meaning in higher education *does not* legitimate the leadership role of the dean. Quite the opposite; the role incumbent is considered *illegitimate* until proven otherwise. Those who become leaders in the job tend, we would suggest, to be those persons who manage to build legitimacy over time; that is, they display an increasing ability to let go of their own egos, to communicate a truly dispassionate acceptance of the perquisites of the position, and to espouse a truly

**FIGURE 8.4**
From Van Cleve Morris, *Deaning: Middle Management in Academe* (Urbana: University of Illinois Press, 1981).

ambitionless demeanor vis-a-vis the job. Curiously, this ability to let go, to underplay the deanship, while it may add to the leadership potential of the person, detracts from the appeal and authority of the office. The role incumbent is caught once again—between an office that requires a forceful and energetic acquisition of power and a route toward power that is filled with faculty suspicions of motive.

*Third*, college deans wrestle with a tendency of faculty members to attribute a sort of one-sided causality to their leadership efforts; this attribution often points the blame at failure but seldom recognizes success. Deans are like basketball coaches or baseball managers. A bad year is attributed readily to the quality of the dean's leadership, but a good year is credited just as promptly to the presence of outstanding faculty and their superb teamwork. From the dean's perspective, there is, conversely, a tendency to take credit for success but to blame the environment for failure. That milieu may consist of such forces as a clique of unreasoning and unreasonable faculty members, an upper-level administrator who is trying to do him in, or the intrusion of outside elements (e.g., action by a state accrediting agency, cutbacks in state appropriations). Causality is not easily viewed alike by leader and followers, although we do sometimes recognize great coaches and even, occasionally, great deans.

In sum, college deans can be haunted by conflicting expectations of behavior on the part of their followers and their superiors; by follower suspicions of deanly motive or purpose; and by the placement of blame for results. Indeed, Fox and Staw point out that administrators (in many organizational settings) may often become enmeshed in the defense of failing programs—for to admit otherwise is to increase one's vulnerability in the job and open the door to a placement of blame. Staw conducted a controlled experiment in which people were asked to rate leaders in stories as effective or ineffective. In one story, the leader stayed the course despite contrary information and data, but in the other the leader adapted to changes in the environment and made incremental changes in goals and paths to the goals. The leader who *did not* modify his goals or plans in response to new intelligence was consistently rated as most effective.[124]

Attributions of causality to individual actors and efforts to understand differences in the social construction of meaning between administrators and their followers would appear to be important, emerging notions in the study of leadership. However, in their discussion of attribution theory, Hoy and Miskel refer to a review of the literature by James M. and Ramona S. Frasher, pointing out that the reviewers "did not find a single research application of the theory to educational administration."[125]

## Leadership as Symbol Management

Karl Weick has observed that "an organization is a body of thought by thinking thinkers."[126] From this perspective, concludes Jeffrey Pfeffer, we find that the job of a manager becomes the administration of the myths, images, and symbols which together form a cognitive map shared by those who serve the organization.[127] Weick suggests that standardized rules, operating procedures, chains of command, and channels of communication are far less important to an understanding of managerial direction and control than is the *thought* that surrounds people engaged in common endeavors. When John Mrozek and Sam Bonus grappled over the wording of the key sentence in the desegregation agreement, they revealed different ways of thinking about what desegregation would look like in the city. Language was not being negotiated nearly so much as metaphors and symbols. In fact, the key role for a manager may be that of evangelist far more than that of decision-maker, accountant, evaluator, or negotiatior.[128] What people think and believe, how people view the many symbols of organizational life that surround them, and what moods or messages are conveyed by the many stories that people tell—such may be far more the stuff of effective leadership than forces of personality, style, situational context, or managerial authority. Weick writes:

> The chief responsibility of an administrator [is] to reaffirm and solidify those ties that exist . . . through a combination of . . . symbol management, selective centralization, consistent articulation of a common vision, interpretation of diverse actions in terms of common themes, and by the provision of common language in terms of which people can explain their own actions in a meaningful way and communicate with one another in similar terms.[129]

In an article on leadership and excellence in schooling, Thomas Sergiovanni places heavy emphasis upon symbolic leadership at the school site: "The symbolic leader assumes the role of 'chief' and by emphasizing selective attention (the modeling of important goals and behaviors) signals to others what is of importance and value."[130] Although it certainly lacks the conceptual reality of problem solver or decision maker, the role of symbolic leader is nonetheless real. Sergiovanni suggests that the hours principals spend touring the school, spending time with students, dropping into and out of classrooms, and downplaying paper-shuffling in favor of conveying a presence around the school demonstrate a leader's intuitive sense that "providing meaning and rallying people to a common cause" is the essence of good leadership.[131]

With a bit of reflection, we find that educational organizations are filled with such symbolic emphasis. David Tyack and Elisabeth Hansot suggest (as we briefly noted before) that it is not at all by accident that the one-room school of America's nostalgic past resembled a church, with its steeple-like bell tower. The large urban high schools of a half-century ago looked much like factories, while today's sprawling one-story school in suburbia could as easily be a shopping center. The one-room school, notes Tyack, was an expression of its community, a blending of school, family, church, and neighborhood. The factory-school, to the contrary, was separate from family and community. It was planned, complex, and bureaucratic—single-mindedly aimed at turning its rough-edged raw material into a uniform, societally acceptable product. The modern shopping-center school is

> soft-edged, divided into segments, united mostly by a common parking lot and heating system; it offers nearly endless choices. It is blurred in purpose, adapting to individual tastes but not articulating common values. It is the quintessential educational expression of a postindustrial consumerist society.[132]

From the flag pole on its lawn to its ordered rows of elementary pupils waiting to enter the building, and from its washrooms with all mirrors removed to its centrally located office with chest-high front desk separating staff from clientele, the school is a potpourri of messages regarding acceptable behavior, attitudes toward children, and definitions of organizational purpose. Bulletin boards with pithy slogans, science festivals and spelling bees, report cards with separate grades for achievement and behavior, open houses and parent conferences, good-citizenship and good-attendance awards, homework policies and achievement tests—all convey a sense of what is of value to the organization, a not-so-hidden set of messages regarding a prevailing vision behind the work of the school.

Beyond a bit of evangelism and the hard work involved in modeling valued behavior, it is not at all clear, however, just *how* a manager can provide symbolic leadership. How does one affect the thoughts of those who serve in schools? How can one build a creative and effective managerial career on a foundation of the images, conceptual frameworks, and symbolic values of one's followers? Although an easily understood technology (let alone a clear theory) of leadership through symbol management has yet to be developed, there are some interesting hints that this form of leadership calls for unusual managerial skills. Karl Weick urges administrators to talk a lot—to spend large portions of their time one-on-one with their subordinates, reminding people of shared visions and *teaching* people to interpret their work in common terms.[133] He writes:

> The administrator who manages symbols does not just sit in his or her office mouthing clever slogans. Eloquence must be disseminated. And since channels are unpredictable, administrators must get out of the office and spend lots of time one on one—both to

remind people of central visions and to assist them in applying their visions to their own activities. The administrator teaches people to interpret what they are doing in a common language.[134]

Similarly, John Meyer draws our attention to the importance of ritual in conveying organizational symbols. Although ceremonial functions in schools are time-consuming and often stress-producing chores, their symbolic payoff, while seemingly diverting the educational organization from its real work, may be well worth the price.[135] Michael Cohen and James March urge managers to learn and interpret organizational history. Attend to what gets recorded at staff meetings and what does not, what endures in the telling and re-telling of organizational events and what does not, whose views and initiatives are remembered for years in the organizational events and whose are not.[136] Also, Burton Clark and more recently Joanne Martin et al. identify the functions of managers in creating and maintaining organizational sagas—the many stories, passed along for years, sometimes positive and sometimes negative in implication, that provide employees with insights into their own relationships with management. Martin et al. suggest that stories typically deal with tensions between employees and management in the areas of equality, security, and control. Positive stories may lead toward conclusions that top people in the institution are approachable, competent, caring, and admirable. Negative stories may convey just the opposite.[137]

The symbolic approach to leadership is a relatively new topic, meriting close further consideration. One of the most important yet most difficult of tasks for the symbolically oriented administrator may be the care and feeding of education's sense of its own professionalism. Geoff Esland notes that for some professions (most notably medicine and law) the capacity to acquire and demonstrate the symbols and trappings of professionalism does not present an overwhelming problem. But for other professions (such as teaching, social work, nursing) an acquisition of the symbols of professionalism is central to a continuing and constant quest for status and public legitimacy.[138] Educators at all levels increasingly covet the doctorate and are careful to use formal forms of address ("Good morning, Dr. Smith") with those who hold this coveted degree. Despite their frequent amusement at their own strange terminology, educators are fond of pedagogical jargon and use it with apparent relish with outsiders. Although gleefully critical of one another in private, educators are careful not to criticize fellow educators in front of parents or students, honoring a professional golden rule that sometimes angers parents who feel that when they complain, nobody listens.

The site-level administrator can do little about some of the key trappings of professionalism (e.g., control over entry into the profession). Nevertheless, there may be a number of manipulable symbols that do carry messages of professionalized respect—delivering messages to teachers face-to-face, sometimes rendering them physical assistance, checking with people before changing school routines, or even just lending a ready ear to the humorous incidents, war stories, and tales of woe regarding their pupils that teachers tell to let off accumulated steam in a lonely job. These are examples of administrative acts of potentially important symbolic value in an occupational milieu searching hungrily for added professionalism.

However, it also must be recognized that the symbolic approach to leadership has a dark side. Like the Wizard in Oz, managers may manipulate or even establish symbols that create illusions of progress without significant substance. As John Meyer notes: "Managers may create committees, rules, offices, consultants, and organizational units as a way of getting rid of a problem without any intention that something will actually be done."[139] Educational organizations are well known for their appointment of new advisory committees and their purchases of services from outside consultants when faced with politically sensitive issues. Robert L. Crain has noted that the 1960s-era politics of large-city school desegregation usually involved, first, board of education rejections and, later, only symbolic acquiescence to civil rights groups. Meaningful desegregation occurred often after demands and demonstrations escalated beyond the point where symbolism was adequate; however, in many cities, a symbolic gesture in time was sufficient to cool the issue.[140] Policy changes that are publicized but never implemented, offices that are created (e.g., an ombudsman, an affirmative action officer) but are understaffed or shunted aside organizationally, advisory committees that are established but do not advise—all these can project an image of leadership without real substance. Indeed, Martin Burlingame suggests pessimistically that mystification and cover-up represent two key roles of local school district superintendents. Amidst the ambiguities of unclear goals and weak technologies, superintendents lead if they shape deliberate self-fulfilling prophecies about the work of the schools (mystification). Similarly, efforts at cover-up make the school appear to be rational, well-programmed, and purposeful —despite its reality of irrationality and inconsistency.[141] It is important for superintendents to capitalize on all available images of public success, warns Burlingame, for when doubt enters and begins to spread, education's house of cards falls apart quite swiftly.[142]

## Summary: Leadership and Followership

We examined two similar perspectives on leadership qua followership. Both point toward the need for an improved realization that images, mythologies, perceptions, and visions held in common in organizations can shape the acceptance of leadership effort. Attribution theory adds that leadership is accepted most readily by followers if the actions of those who would lead conform to the expectations of those who would be led. Followers follow when it is possible for them to attribute reasons for the behavior of their leaders in terms consistent with their own views and behaviors. The relationship between leader success and follower expectation is probably most problematic for the many middle management roles which predominate in education. School principals, college deans, even school district superintendents (governed by their boards) must balance controls from above with (often widely) differing expectations down below. To be a good leader, one must find a way to be followed; but to be followed may put a manager in jeopardy with those up above who would have the manager follow them.

In the face of such dilemmas, our second perspective on good followership contends that at least one important attribute of leadership is the ability to arrange the cognitive map of *all* those who serve the organization. The *thought* that surrounds people in common endeavor may well be the effective leader's most potent lever, particularly useful in the form of the many myths, sagas, symbols, and shared visions that surround people who work together. As with the force in *Star Wars*, or the illusions masking the "if-you-believe-it-you-can-do-it" message in the *Wizard of Oz*, the power of symbolism in a leadership effort cuts two ways. A symbolic gesture can be a step toward real leadership and productive outcome, or it can be form without substance, a grand illusion of meaningful effort.

## CHAPTER SUMMARY

Despite the attention it receives and despite its "here's-what-you-should-do" flavor, the subject of leadership in education remains poorly understood and only marginally useful in the day-by-day management of schools. The topic is certainly not bereft of alternative theoretical perspectives. Indeed, there is an almost over-rich abundance of competing definitions, points of departure, researchable questions, and managerial implications. Futhermore, the complexity and confusion surrounding leadership is not at all lessened by its close alliance with similarly mysterious managerial constructs such as power, motivation, job satisfaction, organizational climate, and effectiveness and efficiency.

We would concur with Chester Barnard when he maintains that an understanding of leadership depends upon an understanding of all three of its critical elements: (a) the individual, (b) the conditions of leadership, or situation, and (c) the followers.[143] Our chapter has examined each of these in turn. In our exploration, first, of the characteristics of the leader, it is suggested that this, the oldest of theoretical perspectives on leadership (trait theory), warrants continued attention. Although out of favor for some years and considered too narrowly defined, trait theory bears renewed interest, particularly in the exploration of such modern-day concerns as the possibility of sex-related differences and suggestions that such qualities as vision and persistence are the talents of successful executives.

Similarly in and out of favor for years theoretically, the study of leader style and behavior has been a heavily-criticized yet persistently fruitful perspective. Some managerial styles do appear to work better (e.g., resolve conflict, engender cooperation) than others—and, most encouragingly, it is style more than any of the other perspectives that seems most amenable to managerial application. The prescriptiveness of style and behavior theory recognizes that this perspective offers something that can be taught to prospective leaders.

Four approaches to leadership that stress situational forces were examined. The key point, of course, is that some persons may perform well in some situational contexts but not in others. The central difficulty is that we know little about the nature of situations in organizations. What forces, elements, or conditions in the workplace most readily affect (either facilitate or endanger) a leadership effort? It is this perspective, coming to attain a better understanding of the situation, that is leading to some of the most interesting contemporary work on leadership. Indeed, Kerr suggests that as one begins to understand situational forces better, one discovers that the situation itself plays an important role in neutralizing and even upon occasions substituting for personal leadership. Leadership may not always depend upon either the personality *or* the direct intervention of a leader.

Finally, the chapter concluded with the development of emerging ideas regarding the impact of the follower upon leadership. Both attribution theory and theory regarding the impact of symbolics upon productive effort suggest that the act of creating faith (as Chester Barnard noted four decades ago) is in the final analysis the sine qua non of leader success. A leader is a person to be believed in, to be judged worthy of our attention, to be given obeisance—*if* we have faith in a shared symbolic meaning, a common understanding, and mutuality of purpose. To be sure, such traits of character as determination, steadfastness, and vision may be important attributes of a good leader. A managerial style that unites a goal orientation and a people orientation into a blend of getting-there and caring at the same time can be influential. In the end, however, a leader by definition must be followed, and it is the follower who defines the effectiveness of the leader. To follow well is to have faith.

## FROM THEORY TO PRACTICE

John Mrozek would be six feet under if leadership were a speeding train. He can't seem to get out of its way, even now, when "there's a leadership vacuum in the university, and I've always had a penchant to get involved. The tendency to manage things. It's very hard to say no." A man willing to put his hand on the rudder. How different the two leadership situations were that he discussed, and, in fact, both were atypical with regard to the role of followers. For most administrators working in educational organizations, the followers are right there, often too close for comfort. But in the effort at statewide student assessment the followers were remote, and in the desegregation negotiation John's bosses—the state superintendent and the board—actually became the followers. That happens sometimes, and the pressure and sense of responsibility in those situations can be intense.

In the state assessment case, a major goal of collecting the SES data (at least from John's perspective) was the eventual more equitable distribution of state funds for education, and yet the poor people who would have been helped out attributed quite different motives to John and his colleagues, far away in Richmond. They were viewed as spies, not helpers. A leader has to be in tune with his or her followers, as they are and where they are. You begin with the people's goals and motives and work backwards to the leader's desk. Nor can you be sure that the structure you initiate will be accepted. For John it was a simple formula: student test score gains equal supplementary state aid payments. But the big-city district simply budgeted the extra dollars, ignoring the first part of the formula. From *that* perspective, the money was needed, so why quibble over details? The money was there, in the state budget, ready to be spent, and in the last analysis it was the big city that prevailed. In a game of this magnitude, the followers can dictate the process. It is a little distressing for the educational administrator to read this page from the book on political life for the first time. John and his staff were simply too far away from their hoped-for followers. You had better have an instinct for what long-distance followers want and will accept (like Ralph Lauren *knowing* which shirt will sell millions and which one will bomb out in a month).

Leadership can be played out in one-on-one situations, too. John Mrozek eyeball to eyeball with Sam Bonus in a schoolhouse boiler room. Not a bad scene for a movie at all. Here the qualities and actions of the leader are more important because they are so exposed to the other major actors. Intelligence, initiative, self-confidence, energy, task-related knowledge—John seemed to have all of these attributes. And both the helicopter and linking pin factors came into play here. John was able to get the bird's-eye view, to develop his nose-to-nose strategies out of a clear sense of the total picture. In addition, he was closely linked with his superiors, and from the beginning he was going to have a strong influence over their decision in this circumstance. The bacon that he brought home was going to be cooked and eaten, and it was, by all but one board member. He was careful to put parameters on the clout and confidence given to him by his immediate boss. "Tell me what the minimum plan is that you and the state board can tolerate. Then tell me what you'd like. I need to know what the range looks like." It wasn't easy after he received the answers, but it was possible. Just as Vroom and Yetton posited, the decision quality and means of acceptance as well as the time factor were important for John in pounding out a decision. "I finagled the compromise, yeah, I did that." All effective leaders seem a little nervous, even after a success. What they know is that the next time the combination of leader and followers and situation may not be quite so conducive to winning. Some days you get the bear. Some days the bear gets you.

## NOTES

[1]Wilbur B. Brookover and L.W. Lezotte, *Changes in School Characteristics Coincident with Changes in Student Achievement* (East Lansing: Michigan State University Press, 1979); Elizabeth G. Cohen, et al., "Principal Role and Teacher Morale Under Varying Organizational Conditions," Mimeographed (Stanford, California: Stanford Center for Research and Development in Teaching, 1977); K. Cotton and W.G. Savard, "The Principal as Instructional Leader" (Alaska: State of Alaska, 1980); Ronald Edmonds, "Effective Schools for the Urban Poor," *Educational Leadership*, 37 (October 1979), 15-24; and Neal Gross and Robert Herriott, *Staff Leadership in Public Schools* (New York: John Wiley & Sons, 1965).

[2]See Ronald Edmonds, "Effective Schools for the Urban Poor," *Educational Leadership*, 37 (October, 1979), 15-24.

[3]See, Ronald Corwin, *Militant Professionalism* (New York: Appleton-Century-Crofts, 1970); Robert Dreeben, *The Nature of Teaching* (Glencoe, Ill.: Scott, Foresman and Co., 1970); Dan Lortie, *Schoolteacher* (Chicago: University of Chicago Press, 1975); Van Cleve Morris et al., *Principals in Action* (Columbus, Ohio: Charles E. Merrill, 1984); and T.E. Deal and L.D. Celotti, "How Much Influence Do (and Can) Educational Administrators Have on Classrooms?" *Phi Delta Kappan*, 1980, 61:7, 471-473.

[4]Such a model of indirect (mediatory) leadership is suggested in Charles D. Ellett and Herbert J. Walberg, "Principals' Competency, Environments, and Outcomes," in H.J. Walberg, ed., *Educational Environments and Effects* (Berkeley, Calif.: McCutchan Publishing, 1979).

[5]James McGregor Burns, *Leadership* (New York: Harper & Row, 1978), p. 2.

[6]See Henry Mintzberg, *The Nature of Managerial Work* (New York: Harper and Row, 1973); Chester A. Schriesheim and Steven Kerr "Theories and Measures of Leadership: A Critical Appraisal of

Current and Future Directions," in *Leadership: The Cutting Edge*, eds. James G. Hunt and Lars L. Larson (Carbondale, Ill.: Southern Illinois University Press, 1977).

[7]Morgan McCall, Jr., "Leaders and Leadership: Of Substance and Shadow," in *Perspectives in Behavior in Organizations*, eds. J. Hackman, E.E. Lawler, and L. Porter (New York: McGraw-Hill, 1977).

[8]B.M. Bass, *Stogdill's Handbook of Leadership: A Survey of Theory and Research* (New York: Free Press, 1981) p. 15.

[9]Gary A. Yukl, *Leadership in Organizations* (Englewood Cliffs, N.J.: Prentice-Hall, 1981), p. 2.

[10]John K. Hemphill and A.E. Coons, "Development of the Leader Behavior Description Questionnaire," in *Leader Behaviors: Its Description and Measurement*, eds. R.M. Stogdill and A.E. Coons (Columbus: Bureau of Business Research, Ohio State University, 1957), p. 7.

[11]Daniel Katz and Robert L. Kahn, *The Social Psychology of Organizations* (New York: John Wiley & Sons, 1978), p. 302.

[12]Richard M. Steers, *Introduction to Organizational Behavior* (Santa Monica, Calif.: Goodyear Publishing, 1981), p. 253.

[13]Robert E. Dubin, "Metaphors of Leadership: An Overview," in *Cross Currents in Leadership*, eds. J.G. Hunt and Lars Larson (Carbondale, Ill.: Southern Illinois University Press, 1979), p. 225.

[14]Yukl, *Leadership in Organizations*, p. 3.

[15]Jeffrey Pfeffer, "The Ambiguity of Leadership," *Academy of Management Review*, Vol. 2 (1977), 104–112.

[16]Eugene E. Jennings. *An Anatomy of Leadership: Princes, Heroes, and Supermen* (New York: Harper & Row, 1960).

[17]Headquarters, Department of the Army, *Military Leadership*, FM 22-100 (Washington, D.C.: Government Printing Office, 1973).

[18]Margaret Hennig and Anne Jordim, *The Managerial Woman* (New York: Doubleday, 1976).

[19]The trait theory of leadership is akin to "the Great Man theory," which suggests that some individuals emerge as leaders because of innate characteristics, and the Zeitgeist theory, which suggests a leader is a product of his/her times.

[20]Ralph Stogdill, "Personal Factors Associated with Leadership: A Survey of the Literature," *Journal of Psychology*, 25 (1948), 35-71.

[21]Robert J. House and M.L. Baetz, "Leadership: Some Empirical Generalizations and New Research Directions," in *Research in Organizational Behavior*, ed. B.M. Staw (Greenwich, Connecticut: JAI Press, 1979).

[22]R.D. Mann, "A Review of the Relationship Between Personality and Performance in Small Groups," *Psychological Bulletin*, 56 (1959), 241-70.

[23]Charles B. Handy, *Understanding Organizations* (London: Penguin Books, 1976), p. 90.

[24]House and Baetz, "Leadership," p. 352.

[25]Ibid.

[26]Ibid.

[27]Handy, *Understanding Organizations*, p. 89.

[28]House and Baetz, p. 352.

[29]Warren Bennis, "Leadership Transforms Vision into Action," *Industry Week* (May 31, 1982), p. 55.

[30]Yukl, *Leadership in Organizations*, p. 90.

[31]See Paul W. Hersey, "The NASSP Assessment Center Project—Validation, New Developments," a brochure published in 1982 by the National Association of Secondary School Principals, Reston, Virginia.

[32]Edwin M. Bridges, "Research on the School Administrator: The State of the Art, 1967-1980," *Educational Administration Quarterly*, 18 (Summer 1982), 12-33.

[33]Luvern L. Cunningham and Joseph T. Hentges, *The American School Superintendency* (Arlington, Virginia: American Association of School Administrators, 1982), p. 23.

[34]Joan D. Meskin, "Women as Principals: Their Performance as Educational Administrators," in Donald A. Erickson and Theodore L. Reller, eds., *The Principal in Metropolitan Schools* (Berkeley, Calif.: McCutchan Publishing Corp., 1979), pp. 323-347. A Mintzberg-type study of the behaviors of female high school principals also confirmed that females tend to be more consultative, more "democratic" in style than their male counterparts. See Jill S. Berman, "The Managerial Behavior of Female High School Principals" (Unpublished Ed.D. Dissertation, Teachers College, Columbia University, 1982.)

[35]Meskin, p. 341.

[36]Ibid. Quoted by permission of the publisher. Copyright © 1979 by McCutchan Publishing Corporation, Berkeley, California.

[37]Ibid.

[38]Sune Carlson, *Executive Behavior* (Stockholm: Strombergs, 1951).

[39]Mintzberg, *The Nature of Managerial Work.*

[40]J. Kelly, "The Study of Executive Behavior by Activity Sampling," *Human Relations,* 17 (1964), 277-287.

[41]J.C. Flanagan, "Defining the Requirements of an Executive's Job," *Personnel,* 28 (1951), 28-35.

[42]Andrew W. Halpin and B.J. Winer, "A Factorial Study of the Leader Behavior Descriptions," in *Leadership Behavior: Its Description and Measurement,* eds. R.M. Stogdill and A.E. Coons (Columbus: Bureau of Business Research, Ohio State University, 1957); and Hemphill and Coons, "Development of the Leader Behavior Description Questionnaire."

[43]See, for example, John K. Hemphill and Alvin E. Coons, *Leader Behavior Description* (Columbus, Ohio: Personnel Research Board, Ohio State University, 1950).

[44]Hemphill and Coons, "Development of the Leader Behavior Description Questionnaire."

[45]Roald Campbell and Luvern L. Cunningham, "Observations of Administrator Behavior" (Chicago: Midwest Administration Center, University of Chicago, 1959).

[46]Ibid., p. 48.

[47]M.C. Kalis, "Teaching Experience: Its Effect on School Climate, Teacher Morale," *NASSP Bulletin* (April 1980), 89-102.

[48]Elizabeth G. Cohen, R. Miller, A. Bredo, and K. Duckworth, "Principal Role and Teacher Morale Under Varying Organizational Conditions," Mimeographed (Stanford, California: Stanford Center for Research and Development in Teaching, 1977).

[49]E.A. Holdway, "Facet and Overall Satisfaction of Teachers," *Educational Administration Quarterly,* 14 (Winter 1978), 30-47.

[50]J. Brady, "A Pilot Study of Teacher Morale in Three Secondary Schools in the North of England," *The Journal of Education and Administration,* 14 (May 1976), 94-105.

[51]Allen C. Filley, Robert J. House, and Steven Kerr, *Managerial Process and Organizational Behavior,* (Glenview, Ill.: Scott, Foresman and Co., 1976).

[52]Wayne K. Hoy, W. Newland, and R. Blazousky, "Subordinate Loyalty to Superior, Esprit, and Aspects of Bureaucratic Structure," *Educational Administration Quarterly,* 13 (Winter 1977), 71-85.

[53]Dan Lortie, *Schoolteacher: A Sociological Study* (Chicago: University of Chicago Press, 1975).

[54]Elizabeth Cohen and R.H. Miller, "Coordination and Control of Instruction in Schools," *Pacific Sociological Review,* 23 (October 1980), 446-473.

[55]Ronald Edmonds, "Effective Schools for the Urban Poor," *Educational Leadership,* 37 (October 1979), 15-24; and J.B. Wellisch et al., "School Management and Organization in Successful Schools," *Sociology of Education,* 51 (1978), 211-226.

[56]A.K. Karman, "Consideration, Initiating Structure, and Organizational Criteria—A Review," *Personnel Psychology,* 19 (Winter 1966), 349-361.

[57]Ibid.

[58]Chester A. Schriesheim, Robert J. House, and Steven Kerr, "Leader Initiating Structure: A Reconciliation of Discrepant Research Results and Some Empirical Tests," *Organizational Behavior and Human Performance,* 15 (1976), 297.

[59]Bridges, "Research on the School Administrator."

[60]Rensis Likert, *New Patterns of Management* (New York: McGraw-Hill Book Co., Inc., 1961).

[61]Ibid.

[62]Ibid., p. 7.

[63]Ibid., p. 1.

[64]Ibid., p. 95.

[65]Ibid., pp. 113-115.

[66]Ibid., p. 114.

[67]Robert R. Blake and Jane S. Mouton, *The Managerial Grid* (Houston, Tx.: Gulf Publishing, 1964).

[68]Robert R. Blake, Jane Srygley Mouton, and Martha Shipe Williams, *The Academic Administrator Grid* (San Francisco: Jossey-Bass Publishers, 1981).

[69]Ibid., p. 47.

[70]Ibid., p. 116.

[71]Ibid., p. 14.

[72]Ibid., p. 155.

[73]Ibid., p. 200.

[74]Ibid., p. 276.

[75]Ibid., p. 331.

[76]Yukl, *Leadership in Organizations*, p. 120.

[77]Bass, *Stogdill's Handbook of Leadership*, pp. 6-7.

[78]Yukl, pp. 121-127.

[79]Nancy J. Pitner, "Principal Influence on Teacher Behavior: Substitutes for Leadership" (Eugene, Oregon: Center for Educational Policy and Management, 1982).

[80]Fred E. Fiedler, *A Theory of Leader Effectiveness* (New York: McGraw-Hill, 1967).

[81]Charles Osgood, George Suci, and Percy Tannenbaum, *The Measurement of Meaning* (Urbana: University of Illinois Press, 1957).

[82]Fred E. Fiedler, "The Leadership Game: Matching the Man to the Situation," in Fred E. Fiedler, Victor H. Vroom, and Chris Argyris, *Leadership: Fiedler, Vroom, and Argyris* (New York: AMACOM, 1977).

[83]Fred Fiedler "Engineer the Job to Fit the Manager," *Harvard Business Review*, 43 (September, 1965), 115-122.

[84]Steers, *Introduction to Organizational Behavior*.

[85]Ibid.

[86]Chester A. Schriesheim and Steven Kerr, "Theories and Measures of Leadership: A Critical Appraisal of Current and Future Directions," in J.G. Hunt and L.L. Larsen, eds., *Leadership: The Cutting Edge* (Carbondale, Southern Illinois Press, 1977), pp. 22-27.

[87]Ibid., p. 55.

[88]Victor Vroom and Philip Yetton, *Leadership and Decision Making* (Pittsburgh: University of Pittsburgh Press, 1973).

[89]Ibid.

[90]Victor Vroom, "Leadership Revisited," Technical Report No. 7 (New Haven, Conn.: Yale University, 1974), p. 9.

[91]See, for example, Van Cleve Morris, Robert L. Crowson, Emanuel Hurwitz, Jr., and Cynthia Porter-Gehrie, "The Urban Principal: Discretionary Decision-Making in a Large Educational Organization" (Chicago: College of Education, University of Illinois at Chicago, 1981), 185-201.

[92]Dan C. Lortie, "The Balance of Control and Autonomy in Elementary School Teaching," in Donald A. Erickson, ed., *Educational Organization and Administration* (Berkeley, Calif.: McCutchan Publishing, 1977), pp. 335-371.

[93]Robert J. House, "A Path-Goal Theory of Leader Effectiveness," *Administrative Science Quarterly*, 16 (1971), 321-338; and Robert J. House and T.R. Mitchell, "Path-Goal Theory of Leadership," *Journal of Contemporary Business* (1974), 81-97.

[94]Expectancy theory is based on two premises: (a) people subjectively assign values to expected outcomes, and (b) motivated behavior is explained by ends people hope to accomplish and the extent to which they believe their own actions contribute to producing preferred outcomes.

[95]Schriesheim and Kerr, "Theories and Measures of Leadership," p. 14.

[96]Steers, *Introduction to Organizational Behavior*.

[97]Ibid., pp. 271-272.

[98]Ibid.

[99]Ibid.

[100]Steve S. Kerr, "Substitutes for Leadership: Some Implications for Organizational Design," *Organization and Administrative Sciences*, 8 (1977), 135-146.

[101]House and Mitchell, "Path-Goal Theory of Leadership."

[102]Kerr, "Substitutes for Leadership," p. 3.

[103]Kerr, 1977; Pfeffer, 1977; and McCall, 1977.

[104]Steven Kerr and John Jermier, "Substitutes for Leadership: Their Meaning and Measurement," *Organizational Behavior and Human Performance*, 22 (1978), 375-403.

[105]Ibid.

[106]W. Richard Scott, "Professionals in Bureaucracies: Areas of Conflict," in *Professionalization*, eds. H. Vollmer and D. Mills (Englewood Cliffs, N.J.: Prentice-Hall 1966), 265-275.

[107]Mary E. Goss, "Influence and Authority among Physicians in an Outpatient Clinic," in *A Sociological Reader on Complex Organizations*, ed. Amitai Etzioni (New York: Holt, Rinehart & Winston, 1969).

[108]Scott, "Professionals in Bureaucracies."

[109]Lortie, *Schoolteacher*, pp. 104-106.

[110]Steven Goldschmidt, "Collective Bargaining: It's Worse Than You Think," Paper presented at the annual conference of the American Association of School Administrators, Atlantic City, February, 1983.

[111]Pitner, "Principal Influence."

[112]Kerr and Jermier, "Substitutes for Leadership."

[113]Rodney Ogawa, personal conversation with N.J. Pitner, 1979.

[114]Chester I. Barnard, *The Functions of the Executive* (Cambridge, Mass.: Harvard University Press, 1938), p. 259.

[115]Chester I. Barnard, "The Nature of Leadership," *Organization and Management* (Cambridge Mass.: Harvard University Press, 1952), p. 84.

[116]Ibid., p. 86.

[117]See Wayne K. Hoy and Cecil G. Miskal, *Educational Administration: Theory, Research, and Practice*, 2nd ed. (New York: Random House 1982), p. 165.

[118]R. Rosenthal and L. Jacobson, *Pygmalion in the Classroom* (New York: Holt, Rinehart & Winston, 1968).

[119]See James M. Frasher and Ramona S. Frasher, "The Verification of Administrative Attribution Theory," paper presented at the annual meeting of the American Educational Research Association, Boston, 1980; see also Fritz Heider, *The Psychology of Interpersonal Relations* (New York: John Wiley & Sons, 1958).

[120]Ray C. Rist, "Student Social Class and Teacher Expectancies: The Self-fulfilling Prophecy in Ghetto Education," *Harvard Educational Review*, 40 (1970), 411-451.

[121]See Larry Cuban, *Urban School Chiefs under Fire* (Chicago: The University of Chicago Press, 1976).

[122]Pfeffer, "The Ambiguity of Leadership," p. 111.

[123]For an interesting account of the trials and tribulations of "deaning," see Van Cleve Morris, *Deaning: Middle Management in Academia* (Urbana: University of Illinois Press, 1981).

[124]Frederick V. Fox and Barry M. Staw, "The Trapped Administrator: Effects of Job Insecurity and Policy Resistance upon Commitment to a Course of Action," *Administrative Science Quarterly*, 24 (October 1979), 449-470.

[125]Hoy and Miskel, *Educational Administration*, p. 165.

[126]Karl E. Weick, "Cognitive Processes in Organizations," in Barry M. Staw ed., *Research in Organizational Behavior*, vol. 1 (Greenwich, Conn.: JAI Press, 1979), 42.

[127]Jeffrey Pfeffer, *Organizations and Organization Theory* (Boston: Pitman Publishing, 1982), p. 215.

[128]Weick, "Cognitive Processes," p. 42.

[129]Karl E. Weick, "Administering Education in Loosely Coupled Schools," *Phi Delta Kappan*, 63:10 (June 1982), p. 676.

[130]Thomas J. Sergiovanni, "Leadership and Excellence in Schooling," *Educational Leadership*, 41:5 (February, 1984), 6.

[131]Ibid., pp. 7-9.

[132]David Tyack and Elisabeth Hansot, "Hard Times, Hard Choices: The Case for Coherence in Public School Leadership," *Phi Delta Kappan*, 63:8 (April, 1982), 512-513.

[133]Weick, "Administering Education," pp. 673-676.

[134]Ibid., p. 676.

[135]John Meyer, "They Also Serve: Organizations as Ideological Systems," paper presented at Conference on Administrative Leadership, University of Illinois at Champaign-Urbana, 1981, p. 11.

[136]Michael D. Cohen and James G. March, *Leadership and Ambiguity* (New York: McGraw-Hill Book Co., 1974).

[137]See Burton R. Clark, "The Organizational Saga in Higher Education," *Administrative Science Quarterly*, 17:2 (1971), 178-184; also, Joanne Martin, Martha S. Feldman, Mary Jo Hatch, and Sim B. Sitkin, "The Uniqueness Paradox in Organizational Stories," *Administrative Science Quarterly*, 28:3 (September, 1983), 438-453.

[138]Geoff Esland, "Professions and Professionalism," in Geoff Esland and Graeme Salaman, eds., *The Politics of Work and Occupations* (Toronto: University of Toronto Press, 1980), pp. 213-250.

[139]Meyer, "Organizations as Ideological Systems," p. 11.

[140]Robert L. Crain, *The Politics of School Desegregation* (Garden City, New York: Anchor Books, 1969).

[141]Martin Burlingame, "Superintendent Power Retention," in Samuel B. Barcharach, ed., *Organizational Behavior in Schools and School Districts* (New York: Praeger Publishers, 1981), pp. 429-464.

[142]Ibid., p. 461.

[143]Barnard, "The Nature of Leadership," p. 84.

# THREE

## THE IMPROVEMENT OF
## PRACTICE

# 9

## The Administrator
## as Problem Finder

### THE PROFESSOR

I had finished working up the interviews into a monograph for NASA, and they had been pleased with the results. The cover would feature a photograph of an oil painting that hung on my living room wall. My NASA contact thought it was perfect when I suggested it, and it was. I was a superintendent at the time, and the truth of the matter is, I had my wallet out even before I asked how much it was going to cost. I remembered walking away from the street art fair toward my car with the painting under my arm, and a parent who was active in the schools stopped me and wanted to see it. "Is that your portrait?" The painting is dominated by the figure of a coatless man outfitted in white shirt, tie, and creased pants. He is juggling eight balls while balanced precariously on two wheels, one attached to each shoe. The look on his face is glazed and stoic. There he is—the educational administrator nonpareil.

We didn't have to fuss much after that to find the metaphor for the monograph. The first sentence was still in my head.

> When the school administrator returns to the friendly confines of her own kitchen at dusk, and her husband asks how things have gone, the harried executive says with some accuracy, "It was like a three-ring circus today."

We incorporated the images of the juggler, the tightrope walker, and the human balancing act to reflect the feelings of the school administrator. The circus big top—or, more often now, the indoor arena. Let's face it, the school administrator *is* a performer much of the time, playing to a wide range of interested spectators. Exposed, under the spotlights, a certain number of balls or plates or dumbbells always up in the air. The burdens feel heavy, much like those of the person on the bottom of the four-high human tower. There's the possibility of a loss of balance and a crash to the floor in which art is destroyed and incompetency exposed. And for those true high-wire specialists, the superintendent of schools and the university president, often there is no safety net.

The young child chewing on cotton candy in a tenth row seat relishes the anxiety and excitement of the circus as much as the exotic food. Despite the *appearance* of danger—the near fall, or the missed clasp of the aerialists' hands, or the fury of a caged leopard—the child soon learns that everything is going to turn out all right. The elephants will parade in the grand finale, the lights will fade, everyone will go home for a warm supper. The stage spectacle retreats into nostalgic dreams.

But you only had to talk to a few circus performers to find out that their perceptions are a good deal different. For them the ethos of the circus is built around the flirtation with death. This is what the men and women of the circus and their families worry about every day, in grim anticipation. Death lurks in the wings, claiming few, but collecting debts with suddenness and savagery. Most of America shuddered when the Flying Wallendas fell, but circus people were not surprised.

I was interested in the persistence of organizations, in their survival. But how about the survival of administrators? There was a brutal aspect of their work that we hadn't faced up to yet in the profession. Threat, attack, even death. Somewhere in the pile on my table was an article that a student had shared with me—a worried student—about a berserk man in Florida who had killed eight innocent people before police officers shot him. He had been on his way to a local school in which only the principal and assistant principal were present. Then there was the radio report last week about the suburban superintendent and board of education who had to be protected by security officers from an angry crowd of mothers and fathers during a livid debate over a school closing. Could it have been that important? Most big city superintendents moved through each day accompanied by an armed guard, but that hadn't saved Marcus Foster, the Oakland superintendent, when he was gunned down by the SLA a few years ago. Setting dynamite charges for a living might constitute a better risk.

The tenure of most superintendents is relatively short. If you get five to seven years in one place you think you're doing well, and who can manage thirty years of hassle? Principals come and go, too. I thought about the number of my old running buddies in the field who were retiring at 55. That would have been unheard of twenty or thirty years ago. No, it is difficult to be an administrator, either in one position over time or in a number of places throughout a career.

Now a new manuscript stared up at me from the desk. We had decided to write a book, and we wanted this section of the book to offer some practical help to administrators who were trying to hang in wherever they were. Despite their seeming disparity, three strategies had been chosen because they can help the administrator more directly. We could tie our theoretical positions into actual experiences of some of the administrators I had interviewed in Chicago—John and Martin, as well as an interesting guy I had met over a Reuben sandwich in the hotel restaurant. I had a little trouble tracking him down, but he agreed to let me use his story. In the final chapter, we wanted to look at some broader issues of leadership. The administrator as ringmaster? The NASA metaphor was still on my mind. But in these three chapters it would be the administrator as an artist performing in the single ring. Personal, face-to-face methods for exercising more control over the course of events in the immediate work environment. Not a survival kit, but attitudes and techniques that could make the administrator's daily work more bearable, more interesting, and more effective.

But we had to be careful. Thinking about the administrator as an artist risks misunderstanding. Those of us who are university professors tend to concentrate on thinking and its product of understanding, but at the expense of feeling and *its* product of meaning. For too many practitioners the reverse is true. In addition, practitioners often associate an artistic approach with rationalizing a slapdash, ad hoc way of doing things. But shouldn't professors and field administrators, scientists and artists— all of us—be trying to integrate and synthesize thinking *and* feeling in order to produce understanding *and* meaning? Well, that was easier to say than to do, but the idea ought to guide me while I put this section together.

I thumbed through the drafts of the three chapters on the desk—"The Administrator As Problem Finder," "The Administrator As Negotiator," and "The Administrator As Teacher." These strategies had not followed any neat path from theory to practice. Some practitioners could probably write this chapter as well as we could because they would be talking about their bread and butter. In a professional field such as educational administration—in contrast to one of the academic disciplines—much of what the professor examines and the researcher analyzes is already entrenched in practice. On the other hand, these particular strategies didn't seem as widespread in practice as they needed to be, and reference to more recent research and theory might open up some windows again. Professors do have some advantages, after all. We can be involved in a close study of practice which simply is not possible for the practitioner. New alternatives which flow from a given line of thinking can be explored and extended. We're in a position to disseminate ideas across a field, assuming anyone wants to read what we write or to listen to us. Most of all, though, I think that what we are trying to convey is that the self-conscious use of knowledge is a source of power. That's the real link between theory and practice that makes sense from both the professor's comfy chair and the administrator's hot seat. But how analytical, how thoughtful can you be in the middle of the tempest? It's hard to do, even for the brightest.


## JOHN NIELSON

*He is fifty, big-framed and somewhat overweight. The voice is soft, yet clear. He has worked in a small city district in a sunbelt state. A year ago he was told that his contract would not be renewed. He became a professional casualty when the board of education decided to fire the superintendent and to relieve several second-echelon administrators as well. During the past year he has had few responsibilities within the district, and has spent a good deal of time searching for a new job. A strong thread of concern for the improvement and development of curriculum winds through his entire career, from his earliest days as a teacher to his current responsibilities as a top-level school executive. Over the past ten years he has gained the trust and respect of many teachers and administrators in the district. In his quiet way he remains confident of the future and certain of his own values and working style.*

### What has been the low point of your career?

I imagine it has to be this whole last year. My being a lame duck. You have the office and title but no real responsibility or authority. You end up feeling pretty uneasy. There's some satisfaction in trying. In trying to maintain your dignity and integrity, in trying to do well what's left for you to do. I've been spending my time as constructively as possible. Job hunting is a big part of it—that's been very serious. That whole process has been exhilarating at some times, grinding at others. I've had to learn to convince myself that the rejections are not personal.

### Have you felt any bitterness over what has happened to you?

No, there's been very little bitterness. . . . If there has been any, I've been covering it up, even with myself. Some regret. Certainly some regret. I see something good getting screwed up, and I think, "What a waste." For everyone involved. It's a challenge to keep people around me on task and not feeling that I'm letting them go. Some have become really angry at me, just because they were upset at what was happening. I guess I had to be the scapegoat. They were feeling guilty about pulling away from me. I've had to tell them, "That's OK. I know you have to do that. You've going to be here next year, and I'm not."

### How has this experience changed you?

I think I'll be different after this. I hope so. Moving out of the security of this district and this job will be good for me. I find it interesting that I have looked at mostly the same kind of job that I have held here. It's reaffirmed a lot I believe in, and it's confirmed my respect for a lot that I've done. I'm sure a lot more philosophical about the vicissitudes of this profession. It's made me examine my future directions. I know now that being a superintendent is not really what I want to do. On the other hand, I'm not altogether clear as to what I'll do in the next 10-15 years. I'm pretty introspective, and I wonder if there is an element in me of wanting to recapture what was good here once. The more I look, though, the more I know there isn't going to be a reenactment of this job. Not this one. Yes, there's some ambivalence now. If I can't find the same set of circumstances, then I want the leeway to do the things I like to do and that I think I do well, with trust and respect for what I'm doing from the people I work for. I also want to learn some new things. One job, to head a special school in the medical field, has some appeal for that reason. If I go back to a district, it should be one with a *focus* on curriculum and instruction.

**Have you ever come close to the breaking point?**

Not for a long period of time. There have been some real emotional swings this year—dealing with rejection, times of questioning. I haven't had time to do the good things this year—I haven't been acting like an administrator. It's harder to maintain that confidence in yourself when you aren't doing the work, when you don't have the proof. But I handle pressure times pretty well. You think back and say, "I managed to get through it before." So you gather the pieces, and somehow you finish on time. I always did.

**What are the things that you like to do and that you do well?**

I like to identify problems and work with other people to find the solutions to those problems. I like to involve people who will be affected by a decision in shaping that decision. Let me give you an example. I was interviewing in one district, and they had me go through a simulated problem. I had something to read when I came in. The problem was with a parent, and the high school drama teacher played the angry parent. I knew how much authority I had. I could uphold or overrule the decision of the principal. Videotaped, the whole thing. I really liked it. I listened to the parent, and then I identified a problem that we needed to work on together—what it was that was troubling both of us there, and what we could do about it. Or here's another example. When I was working on our elementary school study it involved taking a group of 25 people and working with them to identify what was good and effective in the present programs, and what we weren't doing so well, and what we could do to make the programs better. I didn't have many preconceptions. It really *was* mutual discovery.

**Tell me about your earlier life and career.**

I grew up in El Paso, Texas: I was a top student in elementary school. When I was eleven we moved to Cincinnati, and I went through high school there. I worked part-time in the stockroom at J.C. Penney's. I remember that once my senior English teacher, who also taught the senior problems course, asked us how much money we thought we'd be making as adults. I told her I thought I'd be earning $25,000 a year as manager of a J.C. Penney store. She was appalled at my career choice. But I really had no plans to go to college. My parents had only completed eighth grade, and there really wasn't any push for me to go to college. But my teacher made me take the entrance exams for Princeton. Then, that next summer, sometime in August I think, I wandered up to Miami University, and I applied and was accepted. Afterward I went home to see if my folks would help support me there. My Dad wanted to know why I wanted to go college at all. But my mother worked on him.

In my junior year I decided to go into the five-year teacher preparation program, in social sciences. I did my student teaching in the fifth year, and then I went to work in a small high school teaching history and English. I found out that I liked English better, so I decided to get a master's degree in English. After that I had a Fulbright in Germany for two years, and when I came back they made me chairman of the English department. Soon I became chairman of a district-wide committee to look at the senior high English curriculum. It was the first taste of what I would later like to do so much. We revamped the English curriculum totally for the district's three high schools. I had to do a lot of negotiating and educating with other teachers then.

## What do you mean by negotiating?

Well, we were all out for a drink once. Most of the people were working on this committee. I happened to be with a teacher who was resisting what I saw as progress. So I started talking. Everything the committee was doing seemed to be stuck. I was asking, "Isn't there some way to try out some of these new ideas?" Not long after that we worked out an agreement to pilot the new program. Somehow this conversation was important. I didn't know exactly what I was doing, but afterwards the log jam was broken. My role was that of facilitator, broker. Rephrasing things to keep the interaction going, identifying conflicts, narrowing down toward a solution, trying to find agreements, always synthesizing. It gave me a real interest in process, in what I think of when I say curriculum development.

While I was chairing that committee, I started looking around for a doctoral program. A professor at the University of Tennessee was doing some of the same things we were considering in our English options program, but at a more theoretical level. We had just hit upon the same thing independently. We had him in for workshops, I remember. So I decided I wanted to do my doctoral work with him. I finished putting all the loose ends of the district's high school English program together, and then I left.

I took courses for three years, and then I got involved in the Upward Bound project on campus as an academic coordinator and tutor, and after I finished my comps I became assistant director of the program. It was my first real administrative job. A couple of years of that while I finished my thesis, and then it was time to get on. I looked around for a language arts coordinator job in a school district. I wasn't preparing for college teaching, although most of the other grad students I hung around with were. We used to argue about it all the time. I always thought that a public school was the place to have the most influence on teachers, not the college classroom.

So I came here eleven years ago as language arts coordinator, and then six years ago I became assistant superintendent. That first job really felt good. There was a supportive atmosphere, and teachers were receptive, and I gave them a lot of involvement. I also became involved in planning programs related to administrators' professional growth. I became director of our gifted program, too. I always have been oriented somewhat more to the academically talented student.

## How did you find out what you were supposed to do as an administrator?

That's the toughest one you've asked me so far. . . . (Long pause) . . . When I was assistant director of the Upward Bound program, I just moved into an existing role. The director had been an assistant director. I shaped it in some ways, I suppose. When I came here I had a pretty free rein. It was a new position, but there were parallel positions, and I could see them. I certainly brought some of my own style to the language arts coordinator job. In fact, I ended up shaping some of these *other* jobs. I can't remember much conscious, deliberate training anywhere. Just a healthy atmosphere, trial and error, here are some limits.

### What did you discover that you needed to know as your career progressed?

I can think of all the mistakes that I made that were a violation of some principle of good administration. I would think, "Ooops—you can't do that." I was organizing a district-wide English study committee here, and for some reason I forgot to include the department heads. Slowly but surely the meetings became a forum for bitching about the leadership at one of the high schools. I was sitting there, listening and learning, but the feedback was getting to that particular department head, too. I got the word. That's no way to operate. There were some principles I learned there about who you include and what you allow to happen in a meeting. Important things for me. I pulled back and did some fence-mending, set up a different framework. I also responded to good behavior around me. I was aware of my boss's thoroughness, his careful touching of bases, his getting accurate reports out and planning ahead.

When I became assistant superintendent, suddenly I was dealing with a much larger public, and there was a new set of considerations. The supervisory responsibilities were different for me, and while it wasn't difficult, there was a shift in my dealing with people who formerly were peers. Now I was the boss, and it reshaped some of our interactions. Even so, I tried to change from being a colleague spokesman to being a boss advocate. By that I mean I wanted to be sure the superintendent really knew what they did, what their concerns were.

### What did you begin to think you could accomplish?

I've always wanted to get whole groups committed to things, to give kids choices, to bring life to programs. And I really wanted to be assistant superintendent. It felt right. I didn't come here with that in mind, but I liked the place and I knew how to do some things. It was a challenge, it wasn't going to be just maintenance. I've always wanted to be in a position in an organization to communicate what's going on and what's important. It's this advocacy thing. I wanted to talk about the value of the jobs that people were doing around me in the office. We were going through cutbacks, layoffs—there were difficult times. But I wanted not just to protect people, but to protect the integrity of the program. To get the decision makers to take a *creative* look at the alternatives. Even this year, when I have had no clout at all, I got an appointment with the superintendent and told him that it was a mistake to take the special education and bilingual programs out of the curriculum office. I told him that their coordinators needed to interact with other curriculum coordinators, that they are subject to a lot of criticism and misunderstanding, and they need an advocate.

### You were developing a good deal of confidence in yourself, it seems.

You can get caught on the blind side, of course. One of those times that I remember most clearly took place during a public board meeting. That afternoon a white student had been attacked—stabbed—by a black student in the locker room at one of our local high schools. It was a serious injury, but the young man was in the hospital and recovering nicely. Regardless of that, the board meeting room was packed that night. After the Pledge of Allegiance, the buzz in the room grew higher. The board always began its meetings with a public participation session, and the first person up to the microphone was the injured boy's father. He screamed at the board,

> **My wife's with my son in the hospital right now, and he almost died this afternoon. What are you going to do about this? You *must* protect our children.**

Then the meeting almost went up for grabs. There was a lot of shouting in the audience, a lot of racial tension among parents and citizens that were there. The board president could barely maintain order. There was some limited discussion, and then the board president said,

> **If we can't expel violent kids like the boy who hurt your son, then we'll have to have some place to put them, to control them while they're in our schools.**

Well, we had several alternative schools in town at the secondary level, and one board member said that we needed an alternative school for the bad boys and girls. It was just about in those words. So a motion was developed and passed easily which authorized the creation of a new alternative high school for disruptive youth. The superintendent was asked—well, *told* would be the better word for it—to present a plan at the next board meeting in two weeks. The superintendent said,

> **We will be happy to comply. Dr. Nielson will take the leadership on this project beginning tomorrow morning.**

**How did you feel about that?**

I was stunned. Everyone knew that I was one of the most liberal members of the school admininistration. My views were often out of sympathy with the board majority. I had a reputation in this respect in the community that went way back a number of years. "Why me?" I thought. This wasn't my cup of tea at all.

**What did you do?**

I knew what the board had in mind. It was kind of a minimum security prison. Maybe there wouldn't be any barbed wire, but it would be close to that. Get these kids out of the way and keep them there. By the next morning, after a night without all that much sleep, I had at least sorted out what seemed to me to be my alternatives. I could fight the whole idea, or at least refuse to be involved with it. Or I could build the prison. Or I could come up with some kind of plan for a school with an educationally justifiable program for these kids. I kept worrying over these alternatives for the next few days, and I think it was over the weekend that I finally turned to my wife over coffee and said,

> **Kids who are suspended from the high schools really do need a program that they can't get now. Maybe I can work one up. Maybe I am the right person for this lousy job.**

**Did you get much help before the next board meeting in working up your plan?**

Actually, I did. I had heard of another program for suspended students in a community across the state, and I drove over there to see it in action, and I got a lot of good ideas from its director. I also sat down with representatives from the local courts and juvenile justice systems in town, and they were encouraging, in a solid way. And a lot of administrators and teachers from the system—old colleagues—called me or came by my office to offer suggestions. The plan emerged. I proposed that the entry of a student into the school could be only by self-referral or court assignment. A low teacher-pupil ratio would have to be maintained so that some decent counseling could take place, about one to four, I thought. The dual objectives of the alternative school would be to move kids back into the regular high schools or out into the community in decent jobs. The school curriculum would focus on basic skills, career education, individual and group counseling, and every effort would be made to help each disruptive boy or girl earn a high school diploma or G.E.D. diploma. I'll be honest—as the night of the next board meeting came nearer, I was more and more pleased with the plan. I really thought it could work.

**Did the board of education buy it?**

Not before I lived through another tornado. I presented the plan, and then the board president opened it up for discussion. It seemed to satisfy most of the liberal and all of the conservative board members, and it certainly took the superintendent off the hook with the general public, but in the section for community comments I was chewed up. One after another, black leaders and civil right advocates came to the microphone to attack the plan. What they were saying was that it was going to be a prison for black kids, and they weren't going to put up with that. I was just crushed. I remember slumping down in my chair and wishing it would all just go away. Someone made a motion to table the plan, and the motion passed, so I knew my plan wasn't dead yet.

Two days later, I met with the black leaders. "What do you want changed?" It turned out that their complaints had to do with process rather than product. As one of them put it, "We thought all the kids in this new school would be black, and you never involved us. You really should have." I apologized profusely and shared with them suspension data supporting my argument that while the school might have a disproportionately large black population, it would not be "all black" by any means. At the next meeting the plan was approved by the board by a 7-2 vote, without community dissent. I should have demanded more time from the beginning, I suppose. But my real mistake was one of ego—thinking I had the ability to transform a bad idea into a good idea magically all by myself. It's not a mistake I would normally make, but in this case I didn't want to share the birth with anyone.

**Has the school been successful?**

That was eight years ago. The alternative school really has become part of the school system. It has served maybe 80 students of whom approximately 60 percent were white. I'm pleased to say that it turned out to be more than a paper plan. Yes, the school has worked well. The kids really are getting diplomas and jobs. It's funny. What seemed to be a disastrous assignment actually turned out to be for me an opportunity to be creative, to put together a program that I'd look upon now as one of the real high points of my career. You never know.

## FROM PRACTICE TO THEORY

An incident, a disruption, a turbulent board meeting. The tendency is to reach for a quick policy decision—to douse the fire, reacting quickly under public pressure, letting someone in administration work out the details later. The solution has been provided. Now, what is the problem?

John Nielson is a problem *finder*. While administrative theory has traditionally addressed the art of problem solving, John Nielson's experience informs us that a solution may often precede a knowledgeable identification of the real problem. The administrator is handed down a solution. How, now, can he redefine an underlying dilemma, an issue, or a conflict into a creative and morally acceptable administrative problem?

Perhaps our whole educational system comes into question a bit here. We are all trained well in finding the answers to problems that others (our teachers) have presented. But are we prepared adequately to find the problems themselves—to probe beneath the surface of a dilemma or a conflict in order to isolate the essential question, then attack it? Problem finding, it would appear, is the first, most critical step in problem solving.

## THE ADMINISTRATOR AS PROBLEM FINDER

School administrators always seem to have experienced a certain strain between their roles as assertive bureaucrats and reflective leaders. The superintendency and the principalship emerged in the nineteenth century as school systems and schools grew larger and more complex, particularly in expanding cities and metropolitan areas. Administrators were expected to be effective organizers and decision makers. But at the same time, citizens increasingly expected their administrators to exercise vision, to identify and shape important problems as well as to solve them. During the twentieth century, the role of manager began to dominate the role of leader. Administrators were more likely to be praised for balancing the books than for improving teacher morale or expanding the educational opportunities of children and youth. Roald Campbell and his colleagues noted that "Administrators, particularly at the top of the hierarchy, must do much thinking before acting."[1] Nonetheless, the reflective activities of the educational administrator often go unnoticed and unpraised.

## Problem Solving and Problem Finding

Visitors to schools at all levels quickly sense the traditional commitment of school people to problem solving. The transmission of problem-solving skills is the goal when a third grade teacher helps children solve simple story problems or when a professor shows business administration students how to analyze and improve a faltering company. Furthermore, problem-solving skills seem to be highly essential to teachers and school administrators in their work. While a teacher puzzles over how to motivate an indolent student, an administrator may ponder how to pacify an irate parent.

The fewer problems a school has, the better the public may judge it. A school without a drug problem or race problem is considered preferable to a school with such problems. Moreover, administrators are linked irrevocably with the assessments of their schools. The public perceives a good principal or an effective superintendent as one who makes the schools run smoothly. One might conclude then, that effective administrators are effective problem solvers. Yet the matter is not quite so simple. In reality, in schools without apparent problems administrators confront difficult problems but frame them in ways which lead to productive solutions before there is a crisis or public notoriety.[2]

The problem-solving perspective is rooted in two assumptions about school administrators and the problems they face. One is that administrators are submerged in a sea of problems which require quick solution to prevent institutional drowning. Indeed, studies of building principals by Harry Wolcott,[3] Kent Peterson,[4] and Van Cleve Morris and his colleagues[5] describe the principal as a harried, peripatetic administrator whose work day is fragmented; whose contacts with colleagues and clients are brief and cursory; and whose dominant mode is that of rapid problem-solver. Another assumption is that most of the problems that school administrators attempt to solve are not of their own making; that is, colleagues and clients control the definition of problems. Both premises make it relatively easy for us to believe in a problem-solving process which begins with a given problem and then moves through distinct stages: the identification of alternatives; the testing of alternatives (typically through a review of personal and institutional experience and through the seeking of advice); the selection of the "best" alternative; action on the part of the administrator and others; and, finally, a period of reaction and evaluation.

This picture of the school administrator as problem solver would be provided by a photographer as easily as an ethnographer.[6] A snapshot portrays the observable behavior of administrators, and, to be sure, a good deal has been learned about educational administrators as problem solvers over the past quarter century by social scientists who have talked to them and watched them at work. Still, we have few pictures of the earliest stages of the problem-solving cycle. The assumptions we have cited need questioning, for there are occasions when school administrators do not act swiftly to solve problems; when the situation does not present clearly defined problems; and when considerable reflection precedes conventional problem solving. While such situations may not be numerous or typical, they do occur, and it is necessary to understand them in order to obtain a more complete assessment of the work of school administrators—their thought as well as their action.

The thought which precedes problem solving has been called problem finding.[7] This area of inquiry is relatively unexplored, for it is difficult to register problem finding behavior either through the camera lens or on the notebook of the researcher. Problem finding is the act of transforming an uncomfortable or irritating situation into a question which can be answered, or into a hypothesis which can be tested. Problem finding is the first and most crucial element of problem solving.

Case examples clarify the reality of problem finding in the work of educational administrators. This chapter began with one such example as it described the effort of John Nielson to define the exact nature of a new school. A second is set in the principal's office in much less volatile surroundings.

> For the fourth year in a row the math achievement test scores of the fourth, fifth, and sixth grade students were two stanines below the reading scores. Both math computation and application were low. The principal of Truman Elementary was concerned about this difference, but a few phone calls to other principals in the district informed him that they faced the same dilemma. He really didn't know what to do. Math was important to him and he had used local fund raising and federal funds to develop a pool of money to support the purchase of two computers in December. Here it was the middle of May, and here were the same lousy math scores. Even a new text adoption two years ago had not improved the scores at all. He looked at the clock and was surprised to see it was nearly 5:00 P.M. He had been thinking about these test scores for over an hour, but he still did not know what to do.

The administrator faced a perplexity, but before he could act he had to identify a specific problem—hopefully the central problem. Framing the problem as "What textbook can I find to improve the math scores?" would have led to a different solution than "How can I get teachers to spend more time teaching math?" The principal also could have posed the problem as "How can we make students enjoy math?" or "Which part of the test contributes to lower scores?" or "Which teaching techniques make one teacher a better math teacher than another?" Successful administrators find the particular problem which can be solved productively for a maximum number of individuals and groups within a school or school community.

Problem finding is an important aspect of all disciplined thinking. Jacob Getzels has maintained that "Pure science, fine art, technological invention, and systematic philosophy are devoted as much to discovering or creating problems as to solving problems."[8] "The formulation of a problem," said Albert Einstein "is often more crucial than its solution, which may be merely a matter of mathematical or experimental skills."[9] Max Wertheimer provided a similar perspective:

> Often in great discoveries the most important thing is that a certain question is found. Envisaging, putting the productive question, is often a more important, often a greater achievement than solution of a set question.[10]

But is problem finding only the province of scientists? Actually, it is a routine human activity which occurs with such regularity as to go almost unnoticed. People engage in problem-finding behavior numerous times daily, in a seemingly reflexive manner—in the seclusion of the mind, in the context of a family setting, and in the more complex social and organizational milieus which we all inhabit. Problem finding is a creative human activity which allows the artist to fill the canvas, the scientist to order his experiment, and the administrator to lead and manage the organization.

## The Problem and the Dilemma

The dynamic relationship between the dilemma (as Getzels would term the uncertainty) and the problem defines problem finding. A dilemma thus is a perplexing, puzzling situation which attracts attention—not the two-horned contradiction of traditional definition. Ominous clouds on the horizon interest the family driving toward the picnic grounds as much as they interest the pilot about to fly in the direction of the potential storm. The issue cannot be avoided: Should the family drive back to the safety of home? Should the pilot wheel the plane back into the hangar? Like most dilemmas, the storm is not the problem. People cannot solve a dilemma, but must wrest from it a problem which is manageable, understandable, and potentially amenable to solution. If the family knows that there is a large shelter on the picnic grounds, their problem may take a particular form. If the pilot senses that the weather hides a tornado, then his problem may assume a particular shape. In these cases, like hundreds and thousands of others, tension between an unclear dilemma and the possibility of a well-defined problem sets the stage for problem finding.

A problem is a question which requires an answer or solution. In many instances problems for educational administrators are overt, and they can be placed figuratively on the office counter. In other situations they are hidden in the minds of others, and administrators must discover what the others are thinking, or the wrong issue may be addressed. A further complication is that a problem may masquerade as a dilemma, and the administrator must convert the dilemma back into a problem —not necessarily the same one—before action can be taken.

Administrators can solve problems; they cannot solve dilemmas. In the case of the alternative school, the problem of dealing with the young man who injured another accelerated quickly into a dilemma of policy for the beleaguered board of education, one which presented different problems for the board members and for John Nielson. For the board members, the problem, or question, became "Can we create a separate unit within the school district in which to isolate violent students?" For John, interested in more than simply custodial care, the problem emerged differently: "Can we develop an educationally sound program for violent students who have been placed in an alternative school setting?" Different vantage points lead to distinctly different problems. Also, some individuals seem more able than others to generate a wider range of problem choices. While the board members appeared to be interested in only one problem, John considered both of the problems stated above as well as a third: "Can I participate in this assignment and maintain my professional and ethical standards?"

Social scientists have begun to explore advancements in the physical sciences, both pure and applied, which have depended on imaginative problem finding. For example, Joseph Ben-David cited the discoveries of Koch which led to the development of a new field—bacteriology.[11] The death of cattle in Koch's community was of overriding practical importance to him. Whereas most scientists had asked

"What can be *done* about illness?", Koch asked, "What can be *known* about this illness?" His intense investigations into anthrax enabled him to discover that bacteria were the cause of the disease. Robert Merton mentioned that Nobel laureates

> invariably lay great emphasis on the importance of problem finding, not only problem solving. They uniformly express the strong conviction that what matters most in their work is developing a sense of taste, of judgment, in seizing upon problems that are of fundamental importance.[12]

Furthermore, they expressed a fervor for finding new, often risky areas of inquiry. James Burke reported that in 1894, C.T.R. Wilson designed a cloud chamber to study the formation of clouds.[13] By passing newly discovered x-rays through the chamber, he formed streaks of condensation. He took photographs of these, and although he noticed that some of the main streaks had secondary ones moving away, he considered them unimportant. In 1912 when he showed these pictures to Ernest Rutherford, his colleague became very excited. The secondary streaks told him that subatomic particles of alpha radiation were being scattered. Rutherford called these photographs "the most original apparatus in the whole history of physics,"[14] for they enabled scientists to study how atoms behaved under bombardment. He had transformed the problem of unexplained streaks in a photograph from a meteorological curiosity into a key discovery of atomic physics. Rutherford's problem finding shaped the guiding theory of subatomic research which eventually led to the development of various uses of atomic energy. Getzels cites another example, from cancer research. For years the focus of curing leukemia had been on killing the cancerous cells. Unfortunately, most of the drugs which killed the hostile cells were also toxic to healthy cells. Leo Sachs framed the problem differently. He asked, "Would it be possible to find a way to make the leukemic cells mature and simply die?" This perspective opened a new area of productive research.[15]

## Roots of Problem Finding

The intellectual roots of problem finding are found in the writings of the American pragmatic philosophers, such as Charles Peirce, George Herbert Mead, and most especially John Dewey. Peirce's term for problem finding was abduction, and the concept formed the basis of his essays on how doubt becomes belief and meaning is ascertained.[16] To Peirce, a belief is an indication of habit in human nature which determines response in a given situation. In contrast, doubt is a state of uneasiness or dissatisfaction. The most important characteristic of doubt is that it incites action. Doubt prompts the struggle which leads to belief. This struggle constitutes Peirce's concept of inquiry. Abduction occurs when the individual pursuing inquiry forms hypotheses from experience and imagination and chooses one of several alternatives. It may take the form of a question or an explanatory statement. Unlike deductive and inductive facets of the scientific method, abduction has no fixed rules of procedure, although it must encompass experience and a scientific imagination.

> Abduction alone gives us an understanding of things. . . . it is still the hypothesis itself that makes the real contribution to the progress of science.[17]

Peirce recognized that knowledge, belief, and thought originate with the formulation of a central question.[18]

Although George Herbert Mead did not place as much emphasis on the process of inquiry as did Peirce or Dewey, problem finding is central to his theory of learning. He conceived of learning as the development of a social act. Reflective thinking begins when acting on impulse is resisted. During this period of thought, the individual considers alternative ways of responding, by considering the environment and the attitude of others. By adopting the generalized attitude of others, and looking through their eyes, the problem finder forms hypotheses or frames questions about how others will regard his actions. During the period of resisting the response of the impulsive "I" and moving toward the final reflective "me," the individual engages in problem finding. Organizing, testing, and selecting responses or reactions and adjusting to the situation leads to the final action of solution or answer to the hypothesis or question. Mead's *reflective thought* is similar to Peirce's *abduction* and Dewey's *inquiry*. All three behaviors are processes which involve the formulation of hypotheses or questions arising from a dilemma encountered in direct experience. To the pragmatists, these processes constitute intelligent thought, which guides one to learning and further discovery.

Dewey's analysis of reflective thinking crisply describes the phenomenon of problem finding. He specified five phases which comprise the problem cycle, encompassing both problem finding and problem solving:

> (1) *suggestions*, in which the mind leaps forward to a possible solution; (2) an intellectualization of the difficulty or perplexity that has been *felt* (directly experienced) into a problem to be solved, a question for which the answer must be sought; (3) the use of one suggestion after another as a leading idea, or *hypothesis*, to initiate and guide observation and other operations in collection of factual material; (4) the mental elaboration of the idea or supposition (reasoning, in the sense in which reasoning is part, not the whole, of inference); and (5) testing the hypothesis by overt or imaginative action.[19]

Dewey acknowledged that the sequence as outlined is not applied rigidly in every instance of reflective thinking. Nonetheless, Dewey's first two stages mirror the process of problem finding. The second stage in particular reveals movement from the dilemma to the problem. After facing a perplexity, an individual must gather the stubborn facts of the situation which will clarify a problem. Assisted by observation and inference, the individual's thought moves back and forth between review of the collected data and speculation about feasible answers to an unclear problem, between recollections of the past and predictions of the future. Suspended judgment must prevail if reflective thinking is to occur.

Dewey dismissed ready-made problems as assigned tasks, but he was intrigued by situations in which a difficulty or dilemma disguises the problem. A true problem is found only through reflective thinking, through a separation (tentative, though it may be) of the problem from its dilemma.

We know what the problem *exactly* is simultaneously with finding a way out and getting it resolved. Problem and solution stand out *completely* at the same time. Up to that point, our grasp of the problem has been more or less vague and tentative. This precarious nature of problem finding is one of its attributes.[20]

Dewey continued his discussion of problem finding in *Logic: The Theory of Inquiry* (1938), in which he defined inquiry as "the directed or controlled transformation of an indeterminate situation into a determinately unified one."[21] Problem finding appeared in the early stages of his model. The indeterminate situation becomes problematic only when it is addressed by an individual:

> Organic interaction becomes inquiry when existential consequences are anticipated; when environing conditions are examined with reference to their potentialities; and when responsive activities are selected and ordered with reference to actualization of some of the potentialities, rather than others, in a final existential situation. Resolution of the indeterminate situation is active and operational.[22]

The problematic situation becomes a determinate situation through inquiry, and the potency of the particular problem, existentially selected, is substantial. Dewey went on to say:

> The way in which the problem is conceived decides what specific suggestions are entertained and which are dismissed; what data are selected and which rejected; it is the criterion for relevancy and irrelevancy of hypotheses and conceptual structures.[23]

This observation may appear obvious to scientists, but it has been discussed rarely in other human affairs, including the management and leadership of schools.


## Problem Finding in Educational Administration

Perspectives on problem finding related more closely to educational administration are found in the inquiry of Jacob Getzels. By the early 1960s he had turned his attention to the interaction of creative thinking and problem solving.[24] Theoretical roots for the study of problem finding reside in this interaction. Getzels' association with Mihalyi Csikszentmihalyi culminated in an important longitudinal study of the thinking and creative activity of young artists at the School of the Art Institute of Chicago.[25] While observing the artists in experimental settings, the researchers defined two distinct kinds of problem situations: *presented*, in which the problem is well-defined and accepted by the individual and where thought can be turned to problem solving; and *discovered*, in which the problem is not defined and where initial thought must turn to problem finding. Art students who eventually became commercial artists felt most comfortable with presented, or ready-made problems, while those who would eventually become fine artists felt most challenged by the empty canvas and its possibilities for discovered problems.

Somewhat like a fine artist being asked to design a Wheaties box, John Nielson was unable to accept the problem that was presented to him by the board of education. He returned to the dilemma and discovered a more professionally appropriate problem. In addition to these modes of *rejection* and *acceptance* in the process of problem finding, at least two other methods may be available to the school administrator. One such method is *initiation*, which involves occasions when the administrator actually stirs up the dilemma or frames problems which challenge the thinking of others. Another method might be termed *prediction*, used when an administrator looks to the future and raises problems which do not require immediate solutions but which have a shaping effect on the institution.

In stressing the dynamic relationship between the dilemma and the problem, Getzels moved somewhat beyond Dewey's understanding. For instance, Getzels distinguished a manifest dilemma from a latent dilemma. Student violence was a manifest dilemma for the board of education members and John Nielson. Yet there are situations in which the problem is clear but the dilemma is not, and finding out what is behind the problem is tantamount to finding an adequate solution. Furthermore, there are problems which have both a manifest and a latent dilemma. Note, as an example, the instance when a superintendent of schools proposes a school pairing plan (problem) within the context of a desegregation crisis (manifest dilemma) only to watch the citizens and the local newspapers exaggerate that plan into forced busing (latent dilemma). Also, Getzels was much readier than Dewey to recognize the manifest (or given) problem, for many problems simply must be accepted at face value by school administrators and solved.

There appear to be several standard modes of addressing dilemmas and problems. But how does an administrator decide whether to engage a dilemma or problem, or how to come to grips with one and solve it? However stoic the administrator appears to be, his or her mind is spinning with questions: Who will win and lose in this situation? How much time do I have? If I don't settle this one, what will follow? How does this fit into the scheme of things in the district? How much clout do I have? Will this one rock the boat as much as the last one? Didn't the board have a policy on this? Why do the ones that look so simple end up so complicated? Does my reputation in this area get in the way of my objectivity? Do I have enough experience to deal effectively with this problem? At first glance, these questions appear to reflect the subjectivity of the problem finder. In this light, Lee Shulman, Michael Loupe, and Richard Piper pointed out that most often the inquirer focuses his ideas and feelings on matters in which he has an emotional investment, much like a doctor with patients, a teacher with students, or a lawyer with clients.[26] Abraham Maslow carried the point a step further by commenting on the deception which a given manager can create when inner problems are projected into the world as outer problems where they are more workable and less subject to anxiety and repression than by direct introspection.[27] In either event, we are forced to be aware of the personal complications which can be conjured up, however unintentionally, by someone else who shapes an organizational problem.

At least three sets of variables guide the school administrator in sorting through an emerging dilemma or problem. The first category includes *personal variables:* individual and professional values; expertise, including training and experience; satisfaction potential; job security; and location within the bureaucracy. The second category includes *organizational variables:* organizational history, norms, policies and goals; the location and influence of the person presenting a dilemma or problem in the community or organization; and the potential impact on continuity and stability. The final category contains *circumstantial variables* which pose both logistical headaches and creative possibilities for the administrator: the amount of time available; the complexity of the dilemma or problem; the potential of physical danger; the newness of the dilemma or problem; and the possibility of stimulating additional dilemmas or problems.

Let us return one more time to John Nielson struggling with the issue of the alternative school for disruptive youth. How might he have proceeded through this sorting process? First, while the proposal of a school solely for students with behavioral problems was clearly contradictory to his own values, he believed that he could satisfy both ideological camps, the board of education and the community (personal variables). Second, he had been ordered to do the job by the superintendent, and tacitly, by the board; he was part of the system, and it was difficult to reject their authority (organizational variable). Third, the time was excruciatingly short, but he thought he could draw together a plan in two weeks (circumstantial variable).

## Towards a Theory of Problem Finding

J.T. Dillon, has argued that no *theory* of problem finding appears ever to have been constructed.[28] Dillon proceeded to identify three kinds of problem situations—those where problems can be identified; those where they are imbedded in context; and those where they simply do not yet exist. He then developed a conceptual schema based on existential concerns (the status of the problem) and psychological concerns (the relationship of the observer to the problem). For Dillon, if a problem exists, then it is evident, and the observer need only recognize it. If a problem is emergent, then it is implicit, and the observer must discover it. If a problem is potential, then it is inchoate, and the observer must invent it. Dillon's ideas provide an interesting refinement of Getzels' presented and discovered problems, but they, too, fall somewhat short of a comprehensive theory of problem finding.

Coming somewhat closer to that mark is a series of insights into problem finding now being developed by David Kolb. Kolb states that problem management is the core task of the organizational executive and that "the vitality and success of organizations are determined, in this view, by 'doing the right thing' (problem finding) and by 'doing things right' (problem solving)."[29] Kolb draws upon theories of experiential learning in developing a reasonably comprehensive model of problem processing, or problem management (see Figure 9.1). He criticizes conventional problem-solving models as being too narrow, too rational and linear, too proactive, and too cognitive. His model, in contrast, includes problem finding as well as problem solving; a dialectic process; both rational and intuitive elements; reflection as well as action; and social as well as cognitive emphases.

The model is formed around four analytic stages—situation, problem, solution, and implementation—which replicate the four stages of experiential learning. The problem is chosen and defined, and the solution is chosen and implemented through a series of sequential dialectical exchanges. Kolb begins with a given problem which is then scrutinized in the *situation analysis* stage in terms of value (or urgency) and priority (or importance). He believes that "the successful leader in situation analysis identifies the values and goals of those in the situation and then holds up those that are most important as priorities for action."[30] If a particular problem is chosen for attention, then it must be defined through the counterpoint between available information and a cluster of hunches or hypotheses about the nature of the problem, or *problem analysis*. "Problem definition is basically a process of building a model portraying how the problem works—factors that cause the problem, factors that influence its manifestation, and factors mediating the application of solutions."[31] Seemingly disparate skills in causal analysis and imagery are critical to this problem

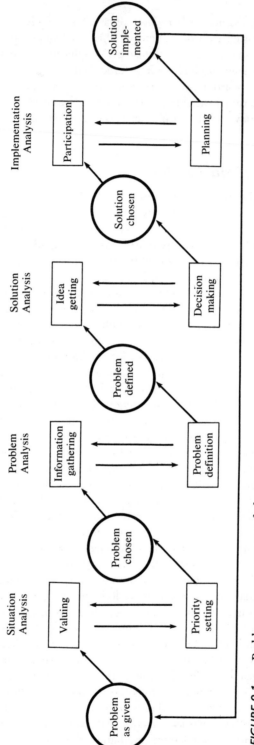

*FIGURE 9.1*    Problem management as a dialectic process

From David A. Kolb, "Problem Management: Learning from Experience," in Suresh Srivastva, *The Executive Mind* (San Francisco: Jossey-Bass, 1983), p. 122.

analysis phase of the process. Kolb adds, "In a sense the problem manager in problem analysis is in the role of a detective—gathering clues and information about how the 'crime' was committed, organizing those clues into a scenario of 'who done it' and using that scenario to gather more information to prove or disprove the original hunch."[32] The problem is now defined, or in the terms we have been using, it has been found. What Kolb has described thus far is what Getzels has called the transformation of a dilemma into a workable problem.

Next the defined problem must be moved toward resolution. In the stage of *solution analysis* possible solutions are related to feasibility factors. Intention is balanced with extension, and it is here that brainstorming can be employed usefully. The solution that passes the test is then considered in the final stage of *implementation analysis*. The administrator attempts to accomplish tasks with the participation and commitment of others. What does the plan look like? Who is going to do what? These are the down-to-earth but somewhat different questions that must be asked and answered. The plan itself develops out of rational considerations, while participation emerges from nonrational aspects of planning in this final dialectic set. The model then concludes with the implemented selection posed as a potential given problem for another cycle of problem management.

Kolb also points out that the dialectic sets involve disparate thinking styles. Valuing, information gathering, idea getting, and participation are "green mode" in the sense that they involve attitudes of appreciation, divergence, feeling, and a sense of release; while priority setting, problem definition, decision making, and planning are "red mode" in that they represent attitudes of criticism, convergence, thinking, and a sense of tautness.[33] The administrator needs to be aware of the counterpoint between these two ways of thinking, and needs to be able to employ them personally and to orchestrate their use by others as problem management unfolds. In summary, then, the administrator as problem finder clarifies goals and sets directions, then creates problem models and obtains information to confirm or reject them. As problem solver the administrator generates new ideas and tests their applicability, then incorporates others in the process as a plan is built and action is taken.

Kolb's emphasis on analysis is akin to Dewey's discussion of reflective thinking, and the psychology of experiential learning is a further link between the two men. The balanced quality of the model is attractive, with as much emphasis on problem finding as on problem solving, and with concern for the dialectic process between the two modes of thinking. The administrator is cast in the servant-leader role, assisting the organization as it solves central value problems but not creating change that cannot be implemented. Kolb's problem management model warrants both empirical research and practical application at this time.

## Problem-Finding Behaviors in Schools

While there has been little study of the problem-finding behavior of school administrators, several inquiries with other foci have provided insights. For example, John Hemphill, Daniel Griffiths, and Norman Fredericksen found that elementary principals with more professional knowledge and higher scores than others on basic ability tests refrained from making quick decisions.[34] Such principals spend increased amounts of time in problem analysis and clarification. Michael Cohen, James March, and John Olsen argued for an unorthodox approach to problem finding, moving from potential solution back to question. They observed that

> In spite of the dictum that you cannot find the answer until you have formulated the question well, you often do not know what the question is in organization problem solving until you know the answer. [35]

From their vantage point, administrators would be guided by a test of practical efficacy: Which problem definition has a potential solution, which will be accepted, and which will work? [36]

Three additional pieces of research focus on the prioritizing and processing activity which is part of problem finding. Wolcott studied the work of a single elementary school principal and compared this principal to a fireman responding to one emergency after another. [37] The principal emerged as an administrator involved with more problems than could be handled easily. In trying to maintain the stability of the school, the principal attended to problems somewhat indiscriminately as they arose. [38] In his field study, Hanson observed seven key stages in a problem-solving cycle (the first three of which involved problem finding): problem recognition, problem screening, problem distribution, decision making, decision implementation, feedback, and problem resolution or renewal. [39] Problems penetrated administrative screens only at certain times: during crises; when central office directives provided support; when they were maneuvered through human "soft spots"; and when a screen was removed voluntarily by administrators. While neither Wolcott nor Hanson addressed the relationship of the dilemma and the problem, Hanson's construct is particularly helpful in sketching some of the ways in which administrators react to dilemmas and some of the problems which enter their purview. Hanson's key stages acknowledge the considerable activity which occurs before problems are solved, and they delineate the modal resistance of administrators to handling new problems. In their identification of the dimensions of problems ordinarily found in school districts, Peter Hall and Dee Spencer-Hall included the situational context; core issue (which may be what we have termed the dilemma); the source(s); the nature of emergence; the magnitude, duration, and intensity; the form of negotiation, if any; and the manner of resolution. [40] They also documented the intense interest of administrators at the top of the educational bureaucracy in controlling and containing problems throughout the school district, a key dimension of problem finding for some school executives.

School administrators who become more conscious of problem finding discover that they can exercise increased influence over issues of stability and change in school and school-system environments. Dewey stated the matter bluntly when he wrote: "A problem well put is half solved." [41] Getzels, too, recognized that problem finding involves selection, and consequently command of the attention and energy of organizational participants:

> The world is, of course, teeming with dilemmas. But the dilemmas do not present themselves as problems capable of resolution or even sensible contemplation. They must be posed and formulated in fruitful and often radical ways if they are to be moved toward solution. The way the problem is posed is the way the dilemma will be resolved. [42]

Framed one way, a problem keeps a school on its present course. Framed another way, a problem moves a school in quite a different direction, perhaps toward radical change. In many instances, both problems may be rooted in an identical dilemma.

In the conventional struggle between school administrators and board of education members over policy-making and managerial prerogatives, board members soon realize that their chief leverage with superintendents resides in the hiring process and in the formation of short- and long-term agendas for planning and action. Effective superintendents counter this leverage with imaginative questions or problems which capture the attention of a wide range of organizational participants and, simultaneously, underscore the leadership functions of the administrative staff.

The sense of being overwhelmed by dilemmas and problems, rather than the inherent difficulties of their positions paralyzes young administrators and continues to press the veterans. While this situation is not unique to school administrators, the context of the school and school system provides a particularly wide range of sources for dilemmas and problems. School administrators discover that problem-finding skills offer the first and most reliable defense against potential chaos. They must become proficient at sensing, defining, screening, and prioritizing dilemmas and problems. School principals often have over a hundred human encounters in a day and make dozens of quick decisions. While they cannot be reflective in each situation, they postpone action on some issues so that additional thought can be applied to a puzzling or complex dilemma or problem. In this manner, school administrators act as partial gatekeepers with respect to the dilemmas and problems which will become concerns of the school or school districts.

Administrators who frame new problems often are responsible for their movement through the problem cycle. Interesting problems may excite attention, but they also promote cynicism when they do not move through the entire cycle. Only administrators are in an organizational position to provide both stimulus and nurture during the problem process. In some instances, the demise of important new problems is brought about by a failure of responsibility, while in others a major failing is the collapse of cooperation. Effective leaders spend a good deal of time and energy developing cooperative modes in every unit and at every level of their organizations. The ability to coalesce support around critical, found problems is an essential task of leadership. A problem which does not provide a rallying point for collective interest and attention will not move through the cycle toward solution in most cases.

Unquestionably, problem finding is a creative human activity. We can be comfortable with the concept of a creative student or a creative teacher but the phrase *creative administrator* appears to many observers to be something of a non sequitur or oxymoron. Rationality is valued in school administrators at the expense of creativity; yet, as R.W. Gerard remarked, "Imagination supplies the premises and asks the questions from which reason grinds out the conclusions as a calculating machine supplies answers."[43] Curiosity and will are both necessary when engaging a dilemma, for the common reaction is to avoid the problematic circumstance, to sidestep still one more distressing, unclear situation. Administrators who are not yet expert problem finders may retreat from a dilemma in the hope that it will disappear or that someone else will engage it. Sometimes administrators accept the definition of a problem which someone else extracts from a dilemma, defining for a moment —regardless of roles—who is the leader and who is the follower. Yet, at still other times, administrators embrace a dilemma with interest, if not always delight, and attempt to define a problem. It is at this point, as problem finding begins, that imagination is a most important ally. The creativity of the problem finder is then essential in determining not only the shape of a particular problem, but also the range of problem possibilities. School administrators who avoid setting up an impassable dichotomy between the nonrational and the rational are at these times likely to find interesting, productive problems that can be guided to solutions.

## FROM THEORY TO PRACTICE

John Nielson says, "I like to identify problems and work with people to find solutions to those problems." In the case of the alternative school he was more effective in finding the problem than he was in including in the process everyone who had a stake in the outcome. His failure to involve black leaders from the community as he planned the new high school almost undermined the effort. Fortunately, John was able to admit his oversight and recoup his losses. Rarely can administrators touch too many bases. What he did manage to do was to find a problem he could work with both creatively and professionally. At the beginning, he had no real *problem* at all. The *dilemma* (in Getzels' terms) was there—violence in the schools. A solution was present, courtesy of the board of education—a separate school for secondary school pupils who upset the operation of the regular high schools. John had to keep both the dilemma and the solution in mind as he tried to find a problem that would permit him to reshape somewhat the presented solution. That's the way it is in school organizations—solutions in search of problems just as often as problems in search of solutions. And in both cases it is often the administrator, sometimes holding only scotch tape and baling wire, who has the responsibility for making the connections. John Nielson was guided in this particular attempt not by mere obedience to the superintendent of schools and the board of education, but rather by his allegiance to the disruptive students and their continuing rights to an education. Problem finding is a creative process that often is rooted in just such moral considerations.

## NOTES

[1]Roald F. Campbell et al., *The Organization and Control of American Schools*, 4th ed. (Columbus, Ohio: Charles Merrill, 1980), p. 239.

[2]The following section of this chapter, as well as several subsequent sections, have profited from the research and conversation of Glenn McGee, Principal of the Fairview Elementary School in Darien, Illinois. His collaboration is acknowledged with thanks.

[3]Harry F. Wolcott, *The Man in the Principal's Office.* (New York: Holt, Rinehart & Winston, 1973).

[4]Kent D. Peterson, "The Principal's Tasks," *Administrator's Notebook* 26 (1978), 1–4.

[5]Van Cleve Morris, et al., *The Urban Principal: Discretionary Decision Making in a Large Educational Organization* (Chicago: University of Illinois at Chicago Press, 1981).

[6]This section, as well as the Dewey and Getzels discussions of problem finding and the case example of the alternative school first appeared in similar form in R. Bruce McPherson, "The School Administrator and Problem Finding," *Administrator's Notebook* 24: 9 (1980-81), 1-4, and are used here with permission.

[7]Within the field of educational administration the term has received particular use by a veteran of theory development, Jacob W. Getzels. See, for example, Jacob W. Getzels and Mihaly Czikszentmihalyi, *The Creative Vision: A Longitudinal Study of Problem Finding in Art* (New York; John Wiley & Sons, 1976); Jacob W. Getzels, "Problem Finding and Research in Educational Administration," in Glenn L. Immegart and William Lowe Boyd, eds., *Problem Finding in Educational Administration* (Lexington, Mass.: D.C. Heath, 1979); and Jacob W. Getzels, *Problem Finding and Creative Thinking* (College Station, Tx.: Texas A & M University, Press 1979). In addition, J.T. Dillon notes its use even earlier in N.H. Mackworth, "Originality," *American Psychologist* 20 (1965): 51-66.

[8]Getzels, "Problem Finding and Research," p. 6.

[9]Albert Einstein and L. Infeld, *The Evolution of Physics* (New York: Simon & Schuster, 1938), p. 92.

[10]Max Wertheimer, *Productive Thinking* (New York: Harper & Row, 1945).

[11]Joseph Ben-David, "Roles and Innovations in Medicine," *American Journal of Sociology* 65 (1959-60): 557-68.

[12]Robert K. Merton, *The Sociology of Science* (Chicago: University of Chicago Press, 1973), p. 453.

[13]James Burke, *Connections* (Boston: Little, Brown & Co. 1978).

[14]Ibid., p. 42.

[15]Getzels, "Problem Finding and Research," pp. 4-5.

[16]Milton R. Konvitz and Gail Kennedy, eds., *The American Pragmatists* (New York: Meridian Books, 1960).

[17]Charles Hartshorne and Paul Weiss, eds., *Collected Papers of Charles Sanders Peirce* (Cambridge, Mass.: Belknap Press of Harvard University Press, 1960), p. 690.

[18]A related but more recent view has been advanced in Donald A. Schon, "Generative Metaphor: A Perspective on Problem Setting in Social Policy," in Andrew Ortony, ed., *Metaphor and Thought* (Cambridge, England: Cambridge University Press, 1979), pp. 254-283. Schon posits that problem setting (or finding) is dependent in a dominant way on metaphors in the minds of problem setters (or finders). He suggests, for instance, that the power of metaphor dictates to most of us that fragmentation is bad and coordination is good. Thus, the values associated with metaphors become powerful determinants of problem finding and problem solving.

[19]John Dewey, *How We Think: A Restatement of the Relation of Reflective Thinking to the Educative Process* (Boston: D.C. Heath, 1933), p. 107.

[20]Ibid., p. 108.

[21]John Dewey, *Logic: The Theory of Inquiry* (New York: H. Holt and Co., 1938).

[22]Ibid. p. 138.

[23]Ibid.

[24]Jacob W. Getzels, "Creative Thinking, Problem Solving, and Instruction," in Ernest R. Hilgard, ed., *Theories of Learning and Instruction*, Sixty-third Yearbook of the National Society for the Study of Education, Part I (Chicago: University of Chicago Press, 1964), pp. 240-67.

[25]Getzels and Czikszentmihalyi, *The Creative Vision.*

[26]Lee S. Shulman, Michael J. Loupe, and Richard M. Piper, *Studies of the Inquiry Process* (East Lansing, Mich.: Educational Publication Services, College of Education, Michigan State University, 1968).

[27]Abraham H. Maslow, *Eupsychian Management* (Homewood, Ill.: Irwin, 1965).

[28]James T. Dillon, "Problem Finding and Solving," *Journal of Creative Behavior* 16 (1982): 97-111.

[29]David A. Kolb, "Problem Management: Learning from Experience," in Suresh Srivastva, ed., *The Executive Mind* (San Francisco: Jossey-Bass, 1983), pp. 109-143.

[30]Ibid., p. 126.

[31]Ibid., p. 127.

[32]Ibid., p. 129.

[33]Ibid., p. 135-136.

[34]John K. Hemphill, Daniel F. Griffiths, and Norman Fredericksen, *Administrative Performance and Personality* (New York: Bureau of Publications, Teachers College, Columbia University, 1962).

[35]Michael D. Cohen, James G. March, and John P. Olsen, "A Garbage Can Model of Organizational Choice," *Administrative Science Quarterly* 17 (1972): 3.

[36]One section of the Midrash, freely translated, reads: "Blessed be he who creates the cure prior to the appearance of the affliction."

[37]Wolcott, *The Man.*

[38]Karl E. Weick, "Managerial Thought in the Context of Action," in Suresh Srivastva, ed., *The Executive Mind* (San Francisco: Jossey-Bass, 1983), pp. 235-236, reminds us, however, that "fighting fires, which managers do all the time, is not necessarily thick-headed or slow-witted. Firefighting has seemed like mindless activity because we have used scientific activity as the ideal case for comparison, because we have thought of thinking as a separate activity that stops when people put out fires, because we have presumed that the only time people think is when they make distinct decisions or solve clear-cut problems, because we have not examined activities closely to see how thought might inhere as if they occurred in sequences rather than simultaneously."

[39]E. Mark Hanson, *Educational Administration and Organizational Behavior* (Boston: Allyn & Bacon, (1979), pp.366-372.

[40]Peter M. Hall and Dee A. Spencer-Hall, *Conditions and Processes of Problem Identification, Definition, and Resolution in Two School Systems: Toward a Grounded Theory* (Columbia, Mo.: Center for Research in Social Behavior, University of Missouri, 1980).

[41]Dewey, *Logic,* p.108.

[42]Getzels, "Problem Finding and Research," p. 5.

[43]R.W. Gerard, "The Biological Basis of Imagination," *Scientific Monthly* 62 (June 1946): 479-99.

# 10

## The Administrator as Negotiator

There's a lot less power in the position with the fancy title than most people believe. If you don't think so, you haven't had positional power. If you have it, and I do now, you know there's less than you expected on the way up. Of course, there are exceptions. John Silber of Boston University, for example. Do you know him?

**Well, I don't know him, but you hear about someone that controversial. Wasn't he at the University of Texas earlier?**

Yes. I have a friend who used to work for him. His intellect and personal dynamism gets people to do things. John Silber doesn't say, "Please." He says, "Do it!" Now *I* say, "Please." I only say, "Do it!" when I'm mad, or if I know you pretty well.

**What's the difference between you and John Silber?**

I've never thought I had enough brains and energy to bowl people over. I'm an assistant superintendent in Ohio. I have to have some other tools in my chest. John Silber loses some, maybe more than he'd have to if he were a little more

**287**

flexible in his style. Sometimes a lighter touch and some patience gets the job done most effectively. For instance, let me tell you a story about the negotiation that came before a negotiation. Very delicate.

**I'm listening.**

The union contract for a big group of our noncertificated personnel had a year and a half to run. We were getting plenty of information from December on from the federal and state levels to let us know that we were in financial trouble, and the contract called for a 6 percent increase in salary on July 1 for every union member. As we sized things up it seemed like we had two options. First, we could keep mum until nearly the end of June, give them the 6 percent, and then lay off 20 percent of the membership. Or, second, we could begin a gradual process of educating the union leaders and get them to think about an alternative. That seemed the better idea.

So, at a social gathering I got the union leader in a quiet corner and told him that it looked bad. I gave him the worst case scenario. We could be megabucks in the hole by June 30 . . . but there's that 6 percent increase. I told him we could talk about it. I got a skeptical look—and not a word of response.

I had the superintendent's agreement to use the strategy I'm going to unfold for you. We started sitting down with the union people—about eight of their leaders—every two weeks or so. "Just to keep you informed," I'd say. And I'd lay it out—the assumptions, the potential impact. And I kept telling them I assumed we would pay the 6 percent and that there would be a reduction in force of a bunch of their members. I also pointed out each time that we'd have to notify the people who were going to lose their jobs sometime in the spring. "Sure," they'd say, "but those are your figures." "Check them out," I'd say. "Anything more I can give you?" But they weren't buying. Yet.

In the early spring a letter went out from the superintendent to every employee saying that we were meeting with all the unions to discuss the financial crisis and all the possible alternatives to meeting it. As the spring unfolded it became even more apparent to us that the federal and state monies weren't going to be there. The union started sending messages to board members telling them we were lying, and a field man from the state union started showing up at some of our regular sessions.

"Do *you* have any alternatives?" I kept asking. Finally, the union decided to send out a questionnaire to everyone. I gave them a whole list of alternatives to use, like employment for ten months of the year with no layoffs, on some kind of staggered basis. But nothing came of this.

**You must have started sweating by this time.**

No, not really. On April 1 we sent out the layoff notices, using the contract provisions. We said they would be rescinded if the money became available to us. As far as the union was concerned, we wanted to give them a chance to find a better solution with us. But they were under a lot of pressure—not only from us, but from the state union—and they were increasingly difficult to deal with. Whenever we met with the union now, we sent a confidential memorandum to all key management people. It was leaked, of course. We knew this was the best way to get the word out. We thought they were willing to talk, but we couldn't afford to get into a public fight, and in the memos we would repeat what had been said, we would lay out the situation, and we even included the names of people in the legislature and in Washington they could call to verify our figures. Believe me, we weren't twisting the truth on those figures. It was bleak, as time has proven.

## Where was the board all this time?

We had a couple of executive sessions with them, one in late March and one in early April. We reviewed the financial situation, and we told them that it was our strategy to get the contract reopened, because rather than laying off people we wanted to hold staffing as close to current as possible. They knew that we had just completed a 20 percent reduction, and we were close to the margin in this area. Also, we wanted to establish some kind of precedent for opening up a contract to renegotiation.

So the board bought it. We also explained that the layoff plan, which we hoped would never come to fruition, would be based on seniority by department, not system–wide. This would give us more leeway in determining where we could best afford to lose people. We pointed out, too, that we were avoiding any disproportionate effect on women and minorities. One board member said, "Just lay them off." I told him that if we could *select* those who would be laid off, we might improve the function of the system. You have to be concerned about worth and competence as much as you can within a contract. Another board member said he was pessimistic but that it was worth a try. "What a lesson for other school districts it would be if we could pull it off. A bargaining unit gives up bucks to keep people on the job and the operation going!" And just to complete the picture, still another board member, who was a union member once, said he thought the whole approach was a mistake.

It was the beginning of June by now. The appropriation level in the legislature was clear. There was no way we'd get enough money for that 6 percent increase. Everyone knew it, but the union still said we were lying. At our next meeting (and remember these sessions were still informal because the contract still had another year to go—it was only that automatic, collectively bargained salary increase that we were talking about), for the first time we suggested reopening the contract and talking about an exchange for that 6 percent. They didn't answer; they just got up and walked out.

## You were running out of time.

Precisely. So we sent the union a letter. One paragraph long. We'd reopen on one subject only, and you know what that was. The offer was good for 24 hours only. At 8:00 P.M. that evening, with time running out, the union president showed up at my house. He was nervous, clearly under tremendous pressure, and he started talking about leadership. I listened for a bit, and then I stopped him. "There's a right way and a wrong way," I told him. "The right way is hard. You know you ought to reopen. If this contract isn't reopened, a lot of people are going to be on the street. And I'm going to remind you about the choice you made for a long time.'' He called the next morning, and they reopened.

**Let me interrupt you there. What kind of negotiation is it when you get your way completely?**

Maybe I didn't make it clear. *Both* sides won. This is what *they* wanted, too. They just couldn't say it out loud. It's difficult for a union to give up anything they have won across the table, particularly money. I just think we had to take the lead in a situation where we could afford to do what was right—to keep people working during a period of high unemployment. Our second priority was to give them as much of a raise as was possible. We promised that any money in the personnel line items beyond what was necessary to keep paying the people on the payroll at their current levels would be used for salary increases.

**So you were home free.**

Not quite, actually. The union had to hold a ratification election. When did they decide to hold it? June 30, of course. Now the shoe was on the other foot, kicking. Layoffs would take place the next day, and the board had to ratify, but its last meeting of the month was long past. As it worked out, people were still voting while others were getting laid off. The union president gave me the results orally, but I told him I wanted it in writing, on union stationery, signed by him. That's the way I got it. It was a squeaker—five or six votes margin in favor, as I recall. In the late afternoon I called the board president; he was pleased, but he wanted the board polled to make the ratification certain. We finished that around supper time, and then we started with the telephone calls and telegrams to those who'd been laid off to tell them to come to work the next day.

**Did any of those who received the April notices go out and get new jobs?**

Only four or five. It was an unreal situation for most people. They just believed the union, and the union told them it wasn't going to happen. Later, when the dust had settled, we got enough money to give everyone a 3 percent raise, and when we announced it, feeling pretty good about the whole thing, the union went through the roof. We had lied to them, etc., etc. Now they've sued us, and we're in court with them. They have to play this all the way out, of course. We got another reaction altogether, from my fellow administrators, of course. I was at a meeting with some of my colleagues from around the state, and they were all moaning over multiyear contracts where they had to pay the increase and then fire a lot of personnel. I told them we had figured out a wage rollback and didn't lay off anyone. "How the hell did you manage that?" one of them bellowed at me across the table. I told them, but they couldn't believe it. What it came down to is that they weren't willing to work for it. They will put in the time in collective bargaining, over the table, but they won't do the negotiating when it counts, when the contract seems solid.

**So you really think both sides come out winners?**

Look at the result. No one lost a job unnecessarily and everyone got a raise that was as much as we had the bucks to pay. Because one party works harder to get it, or is in a position politically to take the lead—does that diminish the final outcome? See, that's what you don't understand about this informal kind of negotiation. Both sides ought to be trying to figure out a way, any way, to get to a solution where everyone gets as much as possible. It's a hell of a lot more positive than collective negotiations. Can you imagine the egg that would have been all over the faces of management if we didn't pull this one out of the hat? Other unions, maybe if they were a little more hardened, would have taken the 6 percent and watched their friends eat beans. And if they didn't have a continuing contract, this would have been quite a different story. It all came down to instinct, believing it just might be possible. And when they sent out that questionnaire, we knew we had them thinking.

## *FROM PRACTICE TO THEORY*

We assume that the nice thing about being a boss is that you can tell other people what to do; you can develop plans, take initiatives, supervise the work being done, and make changes. Not entirely true. Even the smallest change, even the most innocuous work order, even the most straightforward plan may require careful administrative attention to the subtle art of negotiation. The authority of the administrator is earned, through negotiation, more often than it comes naturally as an attachment to the office.

Perhaps it is our frontier heritage or all the John Wayne movies we used to watch. We want our leaders to wear white hats—to be forceful, demanding, and tough, as well as honest and up front. On the other hand, a behind-the-scenes leader, a person who wheels and deals, who bargains and compromises toward accomplishments, who checks bases with others before acting, draws our suspicion. Black hats lie on the table in the smoke-filled rooms of our culture—whether in Dodge City or Baltimore—and we tend to find the indirect approach somehow distasteful and dishonest.

This cowboy metaphor is shifting, in part because of our respect for results. Richard Daley won the respect of thousands of Americans, including many in rural communities, for leading "the city that works," and he was a consummate back-room negotiator. George McGovern seemed to wear a white hat, but he never was able to hang it in the White House, partly because not enough Americans believed he could produce the results he promised. Change your style if necessary, but get the job done. It is a lesson that educational administrators in the 1980s are learning from the politicians.

The administrator in the restaurant makes an important point. Negotiation is seen by many of his colleagues as something to conclude, a distasteful annual experience, best forgotten afterwards. They find it difficult to honor informal, on-going negotiation as an integral part of—even a necessity of—administrative life. This posture may be dysfunctional. Negotiating for the administrator is like dieting for the chronically overweight. You work on it every day to your credit; you ignore it to your peril.

Beyond the formal and now socially acceptable bargaining found in the collective negotiations process, administrative training has given relatively little attention to ongoing, day-to-day negotiation in schools. What do we really know about this brand of negotiation? To what extent can the educational organization be characterized as a negotiated order?

## THE ADMINISTRATOR AS NEGOTIATOR

### Formal Negotiations in Education

For most school administrators—principals, central office administrators, and superintendents—negotiations mean *collective negotiations*. In the United States, this form of developing a contract between labor and management has been familiar in the private sector of industry for a half century, but it is a relatively new phenomenon in the public sector of education. The practice achieved a strong foothold in large city school districts in the 1950s and 1960s and spread rapidly to suburban, exurban, and small city districts, particularly in highly industrialized sections of the country. Bargaining with a teachers union was a rare experience for the school administrator several generations ago; today it is a routine expectation.

Some administrators, particularly superintendents, have enough experience with collective negotiations to take them in stride, but many still experience them as exasperating and fearful. A number of different perspectives lie before the administrator for the choosing. Collective negotiations are a charade; or a game of chance;[1] or a means of splitting up the benefits available; or a method of searching and settling problems in some kind of order, through exchange and agreement.[2] The procedures of bargaining are bound up in governmental regulations that dictate the process for discussion. The process itself is repetitive—it arrives as regularly as the spring lilacs—and highly stylized, controlled at the bargaining table by the "spokesmen" for the two parties, replete with caucuses, predictable threats, and a slow walk toward the final shootout. Furthermore, it is highly specialized; often the superintendent will not "go to the table" with the management bargaining team, but will assign leadership to a member of the board of education or a professional negotiator or a lawyer who has experience in bargaining. The relationship between the union and management (representing the board of education) is adversarial, and often it is compounded by administrator resentment of teachers who have called themselves professionals, yet appear to be acting like steel mill workers. Furthermore, teacher anger—and occasionally their picket line—is not targeted on the board of education, but rather on the superintendent, the bargaining team, and sometimes other administrators in the system. It is small wonder that in a national study of chief executive officers, superintendents identified collective negotiations as one of the major factors inhibiting their effectiveness.[3]

## Informal Negotiations in Educational Administration

The harshness of collective negotiations has obscured a more routine type of negotiation which occurs in schools and school systems every day throughout the year. This kind of negotiation is extralegal, informal, spontaneous and direct, and it can lead not only to compromise, but to real cooperation. Further, it can produce win-win outcomes rather than win-lose or lose-lose results. Both practitioners and scholars increasingly recognize this informal type of negotiation as essential to problem solving and decision making in educational organizations. The question, "Are you negotiating?" begins to assume new meaning. A typical superintendent might respond:

> Yes. I conducted five negotiations this morning, and I have to think the district is operating a little better as a result. I stopped by one of our junior high schools and chatted with the principal who heads the Principals Association; I told him that I didn't want to bargain with the group but that I would be glad to enter into a memorandum of agreement. The editor of the *Herald* called right after I arrived at the office, and he persuaded me that it would make sense to give the education reporter and him a private advance briefing on the changes in the school closing plan that the board will be discussing next meeting. Then I promised one of our very active parents that we would not close *her* elementary school before exhaustive public hearings and that that would mean no action by this September; but I also got her to promise that when the board finally makes a decision, favorable or unfavorable, we are going to have her support and that of her group. The board president and I had lunch together, and I told her that there was nothing to the rumor that I was planning to leave; she offered to talk with me in a week or so about a contract extension, and I said I'd be happy to do that. Probably most important of all, I helped untangle some conflict among the secretaries. A lot of resentment had been building silently over who was and who was not getting the opportunities for overtime work. I saw some smiles of gratitude at the end of that session. Negotiating—is that what you mean?

Negotiating for cooperation is a strategy suited to a fluid, vulnerable organization. An early proponent of this process was a figure prominent in the history of organizational study and administration, Mary Parker Follett. In the 1920s she distinguished among three ways of dealing with organizational conflict—domination, compromise, and integration. She preferred the latter because when desires are *integrated,* neither side has had to sacrifice anything.[4] She had a particularly keen sense of the inadequacies of compromises—their lack of creativity and their failure to set conflicts to rest. Thus, she called for integrative strategies that would eliminate differences; permit desires to be reassessed; uncover the fundamental (rather than the theatrical) features of conflict; break up large demands into their many features; and anticipate (rather than exacerbate) conflict. Integration involved subtlety rather than force; Follett saw it as a matter of "playing the game differently. That is, you integrate the different interests without making all the moves."[5] She had a blunt, sensible, and optimistic way of viewing organizational travail: "We should never allow ourselves to be bullied by an 'either–or.' There is often the possibility of something better than either of the given alternatives."[6]

In the intervening half century, experts in negotiation have moved from admonition to prescription. More specific strategies, guidelines, and techniques for negotiation are now available to educational administrators, fresh from testing in many quite different organizational settings. For instance, Dean Pruitt suggests five methods for refocusing issues in the search for integrative agreements: (a) *expanding the pie*, or developing more negotiable issues; (b) *nonspecific cooperation* (you get what you're after, but I get a completely unrelated benefit); (c) *logrolling*, or giving a concession on a low priority issue to obtain a high priority concession; (d) *cost cutting* (you get what you want, but I get lower costs); and (e) *bridging*, or restatement of an issue which unearths the hidden interests of the two parties.[7]

Negotiation has been championed recently by four influential writers who have approached the topic from quite different perspectives. Anselm Strauss has been associated with the development of negotiated order theory, growing out of his research in hospital settings. His *Negotiations* presents a paradigm for use by researchers in extending inquiry in this area of sociology.[8] Herb Cohen's *You Can Negotiate Anything* was on the *New York Times* bestseller list for several months.[9] Cohen, a professional negotiator, told readers they could shape their lives and improve their lifestyles through negotiation. Roger Fisher and William Ury of the Harvard Negotiation Project were concerned particularly with conflict resolution at a society level, ranging even to the international context, as in the Camp David agreements involving Egypt and Israel.[10] In *Getting to Yes*, they provided principles for negotiation which permit self-interest to be pursued without the usual hostility that surrounds disagreement.[11] Regardless of their vantage points, this social scientist, this practitioner, and these lawyers share a fascinating and important point of agreement. Strauss wrote, "Negotiations pertain to the ordering and articulation of an enormous variety of activities."[12] Cohen argued, "Your real world is a giant negotiating table, and like it or not, you're a participant."[13] Fisher and Ury made almost the identical point. "Like it or not, you're a negotiator. Negotiation is a fact of life. . . . Everyone negotiates something every day."[14] The common theme of these books emerges: Negotiation is a fundamental human activity, much less a fundamental administrative activity.

### Negotiated Order Theory

What is the source of this growing interest in negotiation? One starting point lies in the work of Strauss. In the early 1960s, during his research in hospital wards, Strauss was drawn increasingly to the manner in which agreements were struck by professionals and nonprofessionals on a daily, ongoing basis in order to keep their work coherent and to meet their objectives. He recognized that in the hospital the conflict between social order and the press for change emanated from both internal and external sources.[15] He saw that hospital life was characterized by conflict not only between professionals and nonprofessionals, but among professionals with quite different sets of values and priorities. To get anything done—to bring about any action—meant resolving those conflicts. Social order, thus, "must be reconstituted continually. . . 'worked at' . . ."[16] Rules, regulations, and commands were not really important in this regard, but rather negotiation counted—human give and take, personal diplomacy, and repeated and cumulative bargaining.

For the most part rules for professionals in the hospital were "far from extensive, or clearly stated or clearly binding."[17] In addition, such rules did not seem to be communicated thoroughly in the organization; as a consequence, few people knew all the rules, and even important rules often fell into disuse. A crisis might revive a forgotten rule or call for the invention of a new rule, and the cycle of negotiation was begun once more. From the underside of the hospital organization nurses used rules to counter the direction and demands of physicians, and patients worked around rules for privileges which would make their hospital stay somewhat more bearable. Strauss and his colleagues discovered that

> at the very top of the administrative structure, a tolerant stance is taken both toward extensiveness of rules and laxity of rules. . . . There is a profound belief that care of patients calls for a minimum of hard and fast rules and a maximum of innovation and improvisation.[18]

A good deal of the negotiation in hospitals seemed to occur around the care of individual patients. For while the prevailing ethos suggested that each ill person should be treated as an individual case and hence as someone for whom the rules may not be exactly appropriate, there were disagreements among professionals and nonprofessionals regarding what needed to be done for the patient. Negotiation seemed to take place and seemed to work in an organization where rules could be "stretched, negotiated, argued, as well as ignored or applied at convenient moments."[19] When the rules became "hard and fast"—as often is the case in a contract between a school district and a teachers union—informal negotiation was much more difficult to initiate and sustain. In summary, then, this provocative research suggested that successful client care in service organizations may be related more to professional and nonprofessional creativity in negotiating than to known, time-tested, fixed procedures governing the interaction of staff and clients.

Strauss and his associates concluded that negotiation breeds further negotiation, that if an observer can isolate and recognize negotiation it will appear persistent, sequential, intricate, and pervasive. "In sum, there is a patterned variability of negotiation in the hospital pertaining to who contracts with whom, about what, as well as when these agreements are made."[20] These agreements represent change—not a return to an old equilibrium, but an advance to a new social order, which is itself quickly replaced with yet another new social order. The new order resembles the past, incorporates new elements of the present, and points toward an uncertain future. This kind of negotiation is not a long-distance affair; it involves personal contact, often in one-to-one situations, in planned and unplanned meetings, across the office desk, and over a cup of coffee in the cafeteria. It is the antithesis of the formal, impersonal, inflexible communication associated with pure bureaucracy.

Let us return briefly to our discussion of *collective* negotiations. In their first experience at the table, most school administrators assume that at certain dramatic moments key contract decisions will be pounded out by the chief negotiators, surrounded by their respective teams. This is not the way such decisions are made. Key contract decisions are made away from the table in hallway conversations between the chief negotiators or, in difficult circumstances, through a professional mediator. The bargaining table is where decisions are *ratified*, not where they are made. Informal contacts count, which is why the personal relationship between the chief negotiators is a major factor in the shape, substance, and ease of a settlement. Candor, trust, respect, and a sense of equity become significant even among adversaries who must rage at each other in public (often for the benefit of the two teams, but rarely for the benefit of each other). It is in these ways that informal negotiations become imbedded in formal negotiations in education.

Robert Day and JoAnne Day reviewed the status of negotiated order theory, concentrating particularly on the work of Strauss.[21] They observed that

> the negotiated order perspective calls into question the more static structural-functional and rational-bureaucratic explanations of complex organizations. In their place it presents an interactional model involving a processual and emergent analysis of the manner in which the division of labor and work are accomplished in large organizations. In this framework the informal aspects of organizations are emphasized as much as the formal (Weberian) and, furthermore, there are implied dialectical relationships in which the informal ultimately shapes the formal and vice versa.[22]

The Days found negotiated order theory attractive for its processual, emergent, dialectical qualities. However, they expressed concern on certain other points. Theoretically, its relationship to other perspectives, such as exchange theory, is not clear; its micro focus links it with a major weakness of symbolic interaction theory; and the role of power, both formal and informal, is treated too lightly, in their judgment. Methodologically, the theoretical development of negotiated order theory is closely associated with case studies in a single field (medical sociology), with participants' own assessments of key situations and actions, and with an overreliance on internal phenomena and a neglect of external organizational variables. In calling for a negotiated order theory which moves beyond the micro and middle ranges of efficacy, Day and Day foreshadowed the later work of Strauss.

Before exploring that effort, reference must be made to another point from the Days' critique. They noted that research into negotiated order theory is nestled in the larger inquiry into organizations and theory of the professions. Much of the work in this area was undertaken by sociologists, chief among them Everett Hughes. Weberian theory could not explain to the satisfaction of these investigators what they were observing in organizations. Emerging theory of the professions

> involved an entirely different set of assumptions which emphasized authority based upon knowledge and expertise, flexibility, independent judgment, and adherence to a code of ethics established by the profession which extended beyond any organization.[23]

However, researchers were not satisfied with this explanatory framework either. In fact, tension between bureaucratic and professional constructs—between rule-laden organization and judgment-based organization—nurtured the emergence of negotiated order theory and other paradigms of negotiation.

How does negotiated order theory apply to education? Is a hospital like a school? Is a hospital at least enough like a school for us to assume (in the absence of adequate research in the educational setting) that negotiated order theory is relevant to school administrators? Major characteristics of the hospital setting are worth examining here. First, the Days observed that the work is done in a single locale by individuals from a number of professional and nonprofessional specialties who represent a considerable diversity in training, socialization, and perspective. Second, these individuals share a common goal—to help the patient get well and go home. Third, clear and respected rules are challenged by factors such as temporality, situational context, and contingency strategies. Since power is not strictly a function of hierarchical relationships, it may be exercised by people at the bottom of the pyramid, such as nurses and patients. In school settings, however, the range of professionals and nonprofessionals is not nearly so wide. The backgrounds of teachers, principals, and other administrators are quite similar. Counselors often have moved up from the ranks as teachers. New arrivals such as social workers (required by legislation such as P.L. 94-142) may be based as often in special cooperative districts as in regular school settings. As in hospital settings, individuals working in schools share a common goal: to help each student move as far as possible through levels of schooling. However, in both hospitals and schools, professed goals may be quite different from actual goals. Many patients feel that they are not encouraged to leave the hospital, and many students feel that they are not encouraged to complete high school or move on to college or the university. Finally, the bureaucracy as a prevailing model of organizations is disputed as much in school settings as in hospitals.[24] The underdog in educational organizations—that is, the teacher—increasingly is taking a hand in reshaping both formal and informal rules, and in exercising more power in the work environment.[25]

Enough similarities between hospitals and schools warrant a working hypothesis. The conflict of ethos, value, and prescription in schools and other educational organizations may be much like that in hospitals. Negotiation may be an aspect of the work of many educational administrators—principals, superintendents, or college deans. On the other hand, negotiation between doctors and nurses in a hospital setting represents bargaining between professionals and semi-professionals, while negotiation between principals and teachers represents interaction between bureaucrats and semi-professionals. That is, there is no pure professional in the educational arena. In hospital settings doctors (pure professionals) *work* in wards, in research laboratories, and at the highest levels of policy development. This fact may not alter the reality of negotiation, but it may affect in important ways the form and substance of that negotiation, particularly in schools where teachers view themselves, accurately or inaccurately, as the protectors of the professional flame.[26]

When he wrote *Negotiations,* Strauss realized that an interesting sideshow of organizational research was moving quickly into the main tent. He observed that, "Currently the topic of negotiation verges on becoming fashionable. It is 'in the air.'"[27] He made four major points in his treatise. First, issues related to negotiations must be related to other forms of action, as well as to a variety of social orders. Second, if negotiations are more universal than ad hoc, conceptualizations in this new field of inquiry must acknowledge far-reaching implications. Third, Strauss offered his work as a theoretical paradigm which could be useful to researchers in developing a theory of negotiations. Fourth, social orders—a central issue for sociologists—are, to some extent, negotiated orders. These main arguments challenge the rational models used in the examination and understanding of human behavior, particularly in organizations.

For Strauss, every point within a day when a new negotiation establishes a new informal contract represents a new social order. In organizational life viewed with this kind of flexibility, "there are no final agreements and no ultimate limits."[28] This has been a particularly difficult lesson for school administrators to learn. In their training, many come to believe that they will be backed into uncomfortable corners by individual decisions as their careers progress. And yet, as Philip Jackson discovered, the rhythm of administrative life in schools is somewhat different.[29] Based on his experience as principal and director of an independent school, he reported:

> Most of my actions did not really involve decisions at all. They were dictated by circumstances. I behaved as I did because I had little or no choice in the matter. Indeed, I now have come to believe that the role of the administrator as a final decision maker is too prominent in our stereotype and is overplayed in the research literature and in theoretical writings. Certainly, it does not fit the experience of the school administrator as I know it. He does make decisions, I would agree, but not too many momentous ones.[30]

Thus, an important implication of negotiated order theory or negotiation theory is that practitioners need to pay more attention to the cumulative effect of small decisions and agreements than to those large decisions which may not be so common and encumbering after all.

It is interesting to see how closely Mark Hanson's findings based upon field research in schools and school districts parallel those of Strauss in hospitals. Hanson developed an Interacting Spheres Model to describe what he and his colleagues found at Silverwood High School to be descriptive of the interaction of teachers and administrators.[31] Three turfs (or zones) emerged clearly: a teacher zone where control over in-class instructional matters was protected fiercely; an administrator zone where control over allocation, security, boundary, and evaluative decisions was defined; and a contested zone where collaborative decisions were required and where informal negotiation was the mode of problem resolution. In an almost interminable sequence, first at Silverwood and later at Elmwood High School:

> Students negotiated with teachers for less homework; teachers negotiated with janitors for repairing the light fixtures now instead of later in the day; teachers negotiated with administrators for increased vigilance in the halls; administrators negotiated with parents for increased participation in school affairs or more patience and understanding with the school reading program. The end product of the on-going negotiation process is to bring order and stability to the potentially disruptive contested zone.[32]

Hanson (like Strauss) discovered that the negotiated order is changing constantly, and that it promotes a dialectic rather than assuring a final decision. Indeed,

> at Elmwood High the uncertainties of decisional control were only temporarily abated through informal, interpersonal negotiations. The unpredictable nature of the decisional domain compelled teachers and administrators to constantly shift their energies to other problems and conflicts. Hence, as problems arose, a network of informal negotiations developed until an acceptable agreement on what to do emerged. The next time a similar problem arose, a different solution would often be negotiated.[33]

The administrator in the corner booth developed just such a "network of informal negotiations" in his interaction with the union. And yet, that cast of characters would shift as varying problems surfaced over time.

Let us now look specifically at the Strauss paradigm. The *negotiation* itself involves specific actors, context and dialog, plans, mutual effort, "and embedded negotiation *subprocesses* . . . making tradeoffs, obtaining kickbacks, paying off debts, and negotiating agreements."[34] The negotiations are set within a *structural context* which exhibits certain *structural properties* that are of importance to the negotiation. For instance, the structural context of negotiations at a school district level would include such properties as the federal and state responsibility for education in the public sector, the conflict between lay and professional interests, and the impact of court decisions at various state and federal levels on service delivery in school districts. The *negotiation context* involves the situation within which the parties interact. According to Strauss, this smaller context has certain *negotiation properties:*

> The *number* of negotiators, their relative *experience* in negotiating, and whom they *represent.*
>
> Whether the negotiations are *one-shot, repeated, sequential, serial, multiple,* or *linked.*
>
> The relative *balance of power* exhibited by the respective parties in the negotiation itself.
>
> The nature of their respective *stakes* in the negotiation.
>
> The *visibility* of the transactions to others; that is, their overt or covert characters.
>
> The *number* and *complexity* of the *issues* negotiated.
>
> The *clarity* of *legitimacy* boundaries of the *issues* negotiated.
>
> The *options* for avoiding or discontinuing negotiations; that is, the alternative modes of action perceived as available.[35]

Strauss placed particular importance on the matter of options, arguing that their availability may not only preclude negotiation on occasion, but may also shape the course and nature of the negotiation.

Yet is a paradigm useful only for scientific inquiry? Or is it possible that practitioners develop their own negotiation paradigms to guide decision making, to gather practical data in order to monitor and evaluate their own performances, and to assist in their vital roles as predictors of future action? Let us look, for example, at a recent descriptive passage related to the superintendency in a widely used textbook for students of educational administration:

> The social and educational changes of the last few decades require a new set of management skills for the superintendent. He or she must be a social analyst, an organizational diagnostician, a planner, and a mediator, all rolled into one. The first two of these roles are conceptual and analytical; the last two are also conceptual, but the action components are generally more apparent. As a planner the superintendent must be a logical analyst, as a mediator the superintendent must be a skilled power broker.[36]

It is immediately apparent that these are not the roles which scholars would have commended to practitioners or which practitioners would have subscribed to 30 or 40 years ago. Possibilities for negotiation are inherent for the mediator, and for the skilled power broker who attains such status largely through the ability to resolve organizational disputes and conflicts. But in answer to our question about the usefulness of the paradigm, it should be said that superintendents are quite aware of these roles and of differences among colleagues in enacting them. Their paradigms are not used as explicitly and consistently, perhaps, as the paradigms of behavioral scientists. Nonetheless, elements of the Strauss paradigm are found in the working strategies of many administrators who see themselves, in part, as negotiators, mediators, or even statesmen or stateswomen.

## How to Negotiate Anything

Few superintendents may have turned the pages of Strauss's *Negotiations*, but a certain number probably are familiar with Herb Cohen's *You Can Negotiate Anything*. Cohen's expertise stems from considerable practical experience as a consultant to corporations and government agencies; as a participant in negotiations involving corporate mergers and hostage releases; and even as a lecturer at major universities. Superintendents with scars from collective negotiations would understand and resonate with one of Cohen's definitions of negotiation: "It is the use of information and power to affect behavior within a 'web of tension.' "[37] There is always anxiety in a negotiation, and this fact alone is enough to put off school administrators who simply do not feel effective and creative in such a context, those who find stress dysfunctional rather than stimulating. Accepting the "web of tension" has become an important part of the superintendent's job because anger and resentment make working with momentary adversaries difficult.

Cohen argued that there are three crucial elements of the negotiation process—power, time, and information.[38] He saw power as a number of levers which can affect a particular negotiation, including the power of competition, legitimacy, risk taking, commitment, expertise, knowledge of needs, investment, rewarding and punishing, identification, morality, precedent, persistence, persuasive capacity, and attitude. His most pervasive concern in this area appeared to be with needs, or what Strauss termed "stakes." He made a distinction between *stated needs* (as people negotiate) and *real needs* (which often are not stated). Then he argued:

> If you want to persuade me to believe something, do something, or buy something, you must rely on three factors:
> 1. I have to understand what you're saying. It's imperative that you put your reasons into analogies that relate to my experiences, my particular imprinting. In order to do this, you must enter my world. (That's why it's so hard for you to negotiate with someone who's stupid or who you think is a lunatic.)
> 2. Your evidence must be so overwhelming that I can't dispute it.
> 3. My believing you must meet my existing needs and desires.
> Of these three factors, the third (meeting my needs and desires) is, by far, the most important.[39]

Cohen was interested in needs because he saw them as the vehicle for avoiding Soviet-style, win-lose negotiations and attaining collaborative, win-win negotiations. In the former style, tactics are often emotional, concession is seen as a weakness, and the continuation of a relationship is inconsequential. But in the latter style, conflict is a natural problem to be solved, the complementarity of needs is investigated, and the parties presumably will work together after the negotiation. It was primarily this latter situation that the administrator in the corner booth had forced. He never questioned the intelligence of the union leader, and he never saw the problem as bizarre. And most probably because he knew that the administrators and union members were going to continue as organization participants, he was eager to satisfy the needs of both parties. It is that continuing relationship that is central to the budding collaborative negotiation.

With respect to the second crucial element—time—Cohen observed that the end of a negotiation is always flexible, even if one or the other party has a deadline.

This posture is related closely to Strauss's processual model. Cohen, like Strauss, believed that negotiation is not an event but a process, one for which information must be gathered long before the actual confrontation. Knowing the real limits of the other person is important because a negative response is often a reaction and not a position. Cohen also stressed the importance of listening—comparing what is said with what is omitted.

The formula for effective negotiation was relatively simple for Cohen: "Successful collaborative negotiation lies in finding out what the other side really wants and showing them a way to get it, while you get what you want."[40] This is achieved by building trust, which is critical in a continuing relationship, and which is a product of effective communication. Using ideas advanced by the other party can transform the relationship from competition to collaboration. Every effort must be made to avoid creating visceral opponents—those whose blood is hot, whose self-image is damaged, and whose capacity to reason is diminished.

School administrators often have been told that they must accept their political responsibilities. They also have been taught in the one political science course they may have completed in graduate school that politics is the art of compromise. Cohen disagreed strongly with such a definition, countering that

> many negotiators think that compromise is synonymous with collaboration. It is not. By its very definition, compromise results in an agreement in which each side gives up something it really wanted. It is an outcome where no one fully meets his or her needs. . . . The strategy of compromise rests on the faulty premise that your needs and mine are always in opposition.[41]

Cohen's dominant message to negotiators in complex organizations (not unlike that of Follett) is to enter each negotiation with the idea that the needs of both parties may be in concert. Where you sense opposition and want conflict, often you can create it. Where you sense harmony and want cooperation, often you can develop it.

### Principled Negotiation

A third position related to negotiation was developed by Fisher and Ury of the Harvard Negotiation Project.[42] In *Getting to Yes* they presented the concept of principled negotiation which is neither hard (where the negotiator is interested in winning at all costs) nor soft (where the negotiator is willing to make almost any concession to avoid personal conflict).[43] They wrote that the method of principled negotiation is

> to decide issues on their merits rather than through a haggling process focused on what each side says it will and won't do. It suggests that you look for mutual gains wherever possible, and that where your interests conflict, you should insist that the result be based on some fair standards independent of the will of either side. The method of principled negotiation is hard on the merits, soft on the people.[44]

Principled negotiation incorporates many of the ideas advanced by Strauss, the social scientist, and Cohen, the practitioner, and welds them into a coherent approach to negotiation in any arena, from the front seat of a car, to the principal's office, to a United Nations meeting room.

Fisher and Ury suggested that there are three criteria for judging any negotiation. None of the criteria is satisfied by positional bargaining, while all of them are satisfied by arguing on the merits of the negotiation. Is the agreement wise? Is the procedure efficient? Is the relationship between the parties as strong as it was at the onset of negotiation, or perhaps even stronger? The administrator in the corner booth seemed to meet the first two criteria reasonably well, but not the third. Locked-in positions, prolonged debate, and contesting wills and egos are attributes of positional bargaining which preclude wise, efficient, trust-building decisions, according to Fisher and Ury.[45]

Like Strauss, Fisher and Ury communicated a clear sense of the changing, shifting nature of negotiation, particularly involving the two levels of negotiation —substance and process. They believed that any issue can provide the substance of a negotiation. The process is most important, and they characterized it as

> a game about a game—a "meta-game." Each move you make within a negotiation is not only a move that deals with rent, salary, or other substantive questions; it also helps structure the rules of the game you are playing. . . . Whether consciously or not, you are negotiating procedural rules with every move you make even if those moves appear exclusively concerned with substance.[46]

Negotiation, then, is more like three-dimensional chess than simple checkers. Exercise of control over negotiation by school administrators requires their recognition that both substance and process are actually negotiated simultaneously.

Fisher and Ury claimed that four basic elements comprise principled negotiation. "These four points define a straightforward method of negotiation that can be used under almost any circumstance."[47] First, they began with people: "Separate the people from the problem." The problem is how people on the other side of the table think, not who they are as human beings. The negotiation should be viewed from their perspective, and their intentions kept separate from your fears. They are not to be blamed automatically for the problems brought to the negotiation. Proposals should be made that are consistent with the other party's *values*. The legitimacy of emotions in the negotiation should be acknowledged, and this premise should be on the table. A participant should be allowed to blow his top without concomitant reaction. Active listening will result in understanding what the other party means as well as what is said. Speaking about yourself will help the other side separate you from the problems.

Second, Fisher and Ury urged the negotiator to "focus on interests, not positions." The most powerful of each side's multiple interests are basic human needs, cloaked by the sophistication of contemporary life. Often compromise does not address underlying interests or needs, and Fisher and Ury retell one of Follett's stories to make the point:

> Consider the story of two men quarreling in a library. One wants the window open and the other wants it closed. They bicker back and forth about how much to leave it open: a crack, halfway, three-quarters of the way. No solution satisfies them both.
> Enter the librarian. She asks one why he wants the window open: "To get some fresh air." She asks the other why he wants it closed: "To avoid the draft." After thinking a minute, she opens wide a window in the next room, bringing in fresh air without a draft.[48]

The workable compromise dealt with the interests of the two men, not their positions, and the window which focused their intransigence was ignored by the negotiator as mediator, for it could lead only to compromise at best.

Fisher and Ury's third admonition was: "Invent options for mutual gain." They challenged the creative side of the administrator as negotiator and called for divergent thinking. The number of options tends to decrease when one side or the other believes that its position is the right one. What can be done to keep the options open? Invention may postpone judgment, perhaps through unilateral and mutual brainstorming. Increasing the options in front of the parties may avoid the tendency to narrow the gap and search for the one best solution too soon. Movement between theory and practice is crucial, for an intriguing option on the table "opens the door to asking about the theory that makes the option good and then using that theory to invent more options."[49] Differences in ideology, timing, prediction, and risk aversion sometimes must be accepted for their creative possibilities. When tradeoffs regarding such issues are sought, the other side can be asked for preferences rather than agreements. Decisions should be made easy for the other side, both to avoid patronizing them and giving the impression that the other side created its own problems and will have to solve them alone. Negotiators do this by "walking in the other guy's shoes" and identifying how they might respond to your needs and requests.

What can the parties to a negotiation do when this straightforward method of negotiation is unsuccessful or when conflicts persist and threaten any resolution of differences? Applying power is using a two-edged sword that can cut both parties, either the one exercising her will or the one yielding to pressure. In answer, as a fourth point, Fisher and Ury suggested that "the solution is to negotiate on some basis *independent* of the will of either side—that is, on the basis of objective criteria."[50] Focusing on fair standards or fair procedures creates the possibility of agreement. One approach to irresolution is to restructure the issue as a mutual search for objective criteria. The parties must be willing to reason, and they must be aware that the end of the line is near. If objective criteria can be found and employed by both parties, negotiation can be completed.

## Chapter Summary

The administrator as negotiator has far more at his or her disposal than the contentious attitudes and tools of collective bargaining.[51] James March has reminded us that

> organizations are not simple hierarchies. They are political systems with unresolved, or partially resolved, conflicts of interest. Awareness of conflicts of interest in organizations has led to an elaboration of theories of coalitions, bargaining power, the quasi-resolution of conflict, and implementation.[52]

A working paradigm for organizational negotiation complements, describes, and extends the accumulated experience of the typical practitioner. Continuing renegotiation of order is important to educational administrators whose primary goal of control in schools is maintaining the order which permits teachers to instruct and students to learn. This function assumes that thought must come before action, strategy must come before decision, and creativity must come before a wise decision. On one hand the negotiator looks for objective standards and efficient solutions, yet on the other hand he or she penetrates to the needs of others and transforms adversaries into colleagues. This complex stance draws upon the full human talents of the educational administrator.

## *FROM THEORY TO PRACTICE*

In all likelihood the administrator in the corner booth had not read these books about negotiations. But it is probable that he would devour them if given the chance. Just how well did his efforts in this pre-negotiation case measure up to the criteria of the experts? The fact that the union is extending its argument into the courts suggests that stability has not been found in this particular organization. Is the organization functioning more effectively and efficiently after the negotiation? Yes and no. Of course, the administrator in the corner booth did not have much help from his counterpart in the union in developing a stronger negotiated order. Strauss would have applauded the administrator's refusal to assume that rules, codified in this case in the contract between labor and management, were set in concrete. The administrator was ready to bend and break some rules as a means to a common end.

Cohen's "web of tension" certainly held in this negotiation, from start to finish. The administrator seemed especially adept in his use of information, not simply by figuring out—quite creatively—how to circulate it, but by trying to gain acceptance of a common body of information. He may have been more successful in this regard than he realized. On one hand, you could listen to his version of the events and believe that he had most of the power. But on the other hand, there was a story that we did not hear, and the timing of the union ratification vote—and its closeness—remind us that not all of the chips were on one side of the table. "Successful collaborative negotiation lies in finding out what the other side really wants and showing them a way to get it, while you get what you want." In these Cohen terms, the negotiation in the school district was only partially successful. The administrator knew that the union wanted the jobs *and* the money, however unrealistic that posture may have been. Did they want the jobs more than the money? Perhaps. They might not have gone to court over fewer jobs and more money for those still employed, though. The administrator probably came as close as possible to engineering a win-win agreement. What he did do with great skill was to probe behind the union position—no movement whatsoever—to find the more complex *needs*—protected jobs and higher wages *and* a public posture of noncooperation. The administrator expressed the view of the organization in opting for protected jobs as a priority.

Was this a principled negotiation, in the Fisher and Ury sense of that term? Certainly the administrator kept his focus on the problem rather than the people across from him, and then tried to uncover and match interests. There is not much evidence that the widest possible range of options for mutual gain was devised. The administrator simply was not able to draw the union leader into the kind of creative brainstorming that would have yielded such alternatives. Nor were the participants in this negotiation able to come up with mutually accepted objective criteria for measuring the success of the negotiation. The union ended up in court, still seeking these criteria as well as an objective judgment.

But we should not be too hard on the administrator in the corner booth. In many important regards it was a successful negotiation. The organization found a balance between employment level and compensation; employees held onto their jobs; and the union found private and public paths out of a mire of differences. After all, the administrator was developing a moral position, and that has something to do with principled negotiation. He believed that the number of people working was more important than the level of compensation for all. He was not dealing with statistics. The jobs which were saved were filled by real people who had made important contributions to the organization and who now deserved the allegiance of the organization, including both management and labor. He was unable to develop universal support for this position, but one has to believe that the employees who retained their jobs understood—and were grateful. It was something for the administrator to think about in the back of the courtroom.

# *NOTES*

[1]David K. Wiles, Jon Wiles, and Joseph Bondi, *Practical Politics for School Administrators* (Boston: Allyn & Bacon, 1981).

[2]John G. Cross, "Negotiation as a Learning Process," in I. William Zartman, ed., *The Negotiation Process* (Beverly Hills: Sage, 1978), pp. 29-54.

[3]Luvern L. Cunningham and Joseph T. Hentges, *The American School Superintendency, 1982* (Arlington, Virginia: American Association of School Administrators, 1982), p. 38.

[4]Henry C. Metcalf and Lionel Urwick, eds., *Dynamic Administration: The Collected Papers of Mary Parker Follett* (New York: Harper Brothers, 1940), p. 38.

[5]Ibid., p. 43.

[6]Ibid., p. 49.

[7]Dean G. Pruitt, "Achieving Integrative Agreements," in Max H. Baverman and Roy Lewicki, eds., *Negotiating in Organizations* (Beverly Hills: Sage, 1983), pp. 44-46.

[8]Anselm Strauss, *Negotiations: Varieties, Contexts, Processes, and Social Order* (San Francisco: Jossey-Bass, 1978).

[9]Herb Cohen, *You Can Negotiate Anything* (Secaucus, New Jersey: Lyle Stuart, 1980).

[10]Roger Fisher and William Ury, *Report of the Harvard Negotiation Project—September 1979 —March 1981* (Cambridge: Harvard University Law School, Harvard Negotiation Project, 1981).

[11]Roger Fisher and William Ury, *Getting to Yes: Negotiating Agreement Without Giving In* (Boston: Houghton-Mifflin, 1981); and Roger Fisher and William Ury, "Getting to Yes," *Management Review* 71 (1982): 16-21.

[12]Strauss, *Negotiations*, p. ix.

[13]Cohen, *You Can Negotiate*, p. 15.

[14]Fisher and Ury, *Report*, p. xi.

[15]Anselm Strauss et al., "The Hospital and its Negotiated Order," in Eliot Friedson, ed., *The Hospital in Modern Society* (New York: The Free Press, 1963), pp. 243-251.

[16]Strauss et al., "The Hospital," p. 148.

[17]Ibid., p. 151.

[18]Ibid., p. 152.

[19]Ibid., p. 153.

[20]Ibid., p. 162.

[21]Robert Day and JoAnne V. Day, "A Review of the Current State of Negotiated Order Theory: An Appreciation and a Critique," *The Sociological Quarterly* 18 (1977): 126-42.

[22]Ibid., p. 126.

[23]Ibid., p. 128.

[24]Karl E. Weick, "Educational Organizations as Loosely Coupled Systems," *Administrative Science Quarterly* 21 (1976): 1-19; and John W. Meyer and Brian Rowan, "Institutionalized Organizations: Formal Structure as Myth and Ceremony," *American Journal of Sociology* 83 (1977): 340-63; and Van Cleve Morris et al., *The Urban Principal: Discretionary Decision-making in a Large Educational Organization* (Chicago: University of Illinois at Chicago, 1981), pp. 213-226.

[25]Michael Lipsky, *Street-Level Bureaucracy: Dilemmas of the Individual in Public Services* (New York: Basic Books, 1980).

[26]E. Mark Hanson, *Educational Administration and Organizational Behavior* (Boston: Allyn & Bacon, 1979), pp. 113-137.

[27]Strauss, *Negotiations*, p. 2.

[28]Ibid., p. 260.

[29]Philip Jackson, "Lonely at the Top: Observations on the Genesis of Administrative Isolation," *School Review* 85 (May 1977): 425-432.

[30]Ibid., p. 428.

[31]E. Mark Hanson, "The Professional/Bureaucratic Interface: A Case Study," *Urban Education* 11 (1976): 315.

[32]E. Mark Hanson, *Educational Administration and Organizational Behavior*, p. 125.

[33]Ibid., p. 375.

[34]Strauss, *Negotiations*, p. 98.

[35]Ibid., p. 99.

[36]Roald F. Campbell, et al., *The Organization and Control of American Schools*, 4th ed. (Columbus, Ohio: Charles E. Merrill, 1980), p. 239.

[37]Cohen, *You Can Negotiate*, p. 16.

[38]Interesting commentary on the power variable has been provided by David Kipnis and Stuart M. Schmidt, "An Influence Perspective on Bargaining in Organizations," in Baverman and Lewicki, p. 312, who indicate that managers will use *assertiveness* when thay have a predominance of power, their objectives are organizational (rather than personal), and their expectations about their ability to influence the target are low. Managers will use *reason* when the target and the manager approach equality in power, organizational objectives are sought, and they have high expectations about their abilities to exercise influence. Finally, *ingratiation* is most likely to be used when managers have less power than the target of influence, personal objectives are sought, and expectations of successful influence are low."

[39]Cohen, *You Can Negotiate*, p. 85.

[40]Ibid., p. 161.

[41]Ibid., p. 197.

[42]Fisher and Ury, *Report*.

[43]Fisher and Ury, *Getting to Yes*.

[44]Ibid., p. xii.

[45]Ibid., pp. 4-5.

[46]Fisher and Ury, *Getting to Yes*, p. 10.

[47]Ibid., p. 11.

[48]Ibid., p. 41.

[49]Ibid., p. 69.

[50]Ibid., p. 85.

[51]Looking into a crystal ball, Daniel E. Griffiths, "Another Look at the Research on the Behavior of Administrators," in Glenn L. Immegart and William L. Boyd, eds., *Problem Finding in Educational Administration* (Lexington, Massachusetts: Lexington Books, 1979), p. 58, predicts that "because of the change in authority relationships, the key administrative process is very likely to be bargaining, and not necessarily collective bargaining."

[52]James G. March, "Emerging Developments in the Study of Organizations," *The Review of Higher Education* 6:1 (Fall, 1982): 2.

# The Administrator
# as Teacher

## MARTIN MASON

*He is in his early forties, married to a woman with a flourishing professional career of her own. You are struck by his considerable energy; his interest in people; his irrepressible good humor; and his commitment to a life as an educator. He kiddingly refers to himself as a "golden boy," and yet it reflects his knowledge of himself and his good fortune to have developed a career that has been intriguing and satisfying. Underneath the ever-present wit, however, you sense the soul of a competitor and the zeal of a teacher. He would just as soon teach as administer, and he looks forward to later years in his career when he can do that more frequently than he does now. He has just received a three-year extension of his contract as headmaster of an excellent independent school on the west coast.*

We found a slightly seedy pocket lounge that most of the hotel guests (to their credit) were not going to discover. Its saving grace for me at the moment was that it was quiet. I described my project, and Martin responded, "I've never liked the word *administrator*. I was a teacher so long administrators have a bad name for me." And he laughed in a conspiratorial way.

**Who was the best administrator you ever worked for, or with?**

I can't answer that question. At least I can't answer it the way you asked it. I worked for four very good administrators who were all so different. They came at various times in my career, of course, and I learned from each of them at the time. The first was the most authoritarian. I might not be able to accept his style so easily now. He'd see me in the hallway and tell me I was going to get a $200 raise, and I'd say, "Great!" I worked for him for seven years, eighteen hours a day, and I liked it. I built a language laboratory for the first administrator, and when I came to talk to him about it he'd say, "Don't ask me a lot of questions. Just go *do* it." That attitude has really affected the way I operate now. Number two was in a larger school, and he was quite removed from the daily life of the teachers, although he did become a mentor for me. Number three was a principal who worried about me—often for good reason. He gave me my first administrative job. He had been my predecessor. He had a terrific vested interest in what I was doing. The situation was chaotic, and there were a lot of things that I was doing poorly now that I was in charge. It took a really tough year for me to take hold. I almost got fired. I almost went back to Philadelphia to teach. But you have to gut it out in those situations. And number four gave me a lot of responsibility and left me alone to get the work done.

## How did you find out what you were supposed to do as an administrator?

By achieving success. I needed approval—of course I did, as much as anyone else in the school. I had to deal with not getting praise as much as I was used to. As an administrator you give more than you get. But the key thing is that you find that people respond to you in the role, and then you get comfortable in the role. I remember once when I was a young Turk teacher and an old-timer, a seasoned English teacher, came to me for advice because I had the title of summer school dean. It was the first time that had happened to me, and I noticed it. Then, too, there's the beginning of the realization that you can't take it all personally. You have to take some of it personally, of course. If your stomach isn't churning some of the time, you're losing a bit of the quality that can make you effective.

## Tell me some things about your becoming a professional.

I worked in college to keep myself there, and I took a double major in literature and fine arts. I remember going to summer school in my junior year. I'd have classes from 8:00-12:00, and then I'd work from 12:30-5:00, and then I'd study from 6:00-12:00. I thought it was great. I was a leader in the campus dramatics group during the year. That was fun. Finally I was going to graduate in mid-year, at the end of the first semester. I was taking six courses to make that happen, and two of them were in graduate school at night. And I was working in the development office. The director of the office asked me what I was going to do. I told him, "I'm too tired to think about it. Maybe I'll teach." He said, "You are going to write letters to schools, and you are going to do that now." So I did. I wrote about thirty letters. He was a good friend. Actually, I had only thought a little about teaching. Most of the responses to my letters were negative. The middle of the school year is a hard time to find a teaching job. But then I got a phone call from a headmaster who asked me to come to the school to visit. We had a nice talk. He was charming, and in five minutes I was sold. The pay didn't matter. I was an apprentice teacher for the rest of that year; they had never had one before. I visited a lot of classes and helped out where I was needed. Then the head of the English department had a mild heart attack, and two days later I took over all his classes. And it was *senior* English.

The next year the head said that he needed an American literature teacher. Would I do it? "Sure." All that arrogance! The trouble was that I didn't really know much about the subject. So I got some tutoring that summer from a colleague, and then the following summer I started back in graduate school for a master's degree. And when I could I traveled to Europe in the summer, sometimes with students, sometimes for study of European literature. I learned about independence in those summers. And I took two groups to France in different summers for the Experiment in International Living. All of that contributed to my becoming competent.

Your feeling for the first place you teach is unlike any other. Even so, I told the head of my first school, "George, I'm getting stale." He was so nice about it. I went upstairs that night and wrote some letters and mailed them the next morning. I received a letter offering an interview, I went for an interview, and they offered me a job. One interview, one job. I was a teacher and a drama coach and even a soccer coach. I was a *terrible* soccer coach. They also had me run the bookstore. It was my first administrative job, and I loved it. It was finite. There was this room full of books, and I had to unpack them and stack them up and sell them. I just ran my own store, for the kids and the teachers. I'd work from 8:00 in the morning until 10:00 at night for *weeks* before school started. I was also advisor to the yearbook. I still am, incidentally. But a terrible soccer coach—awful, a *travesty!* They had to cover it; I understand that now. I directed two or three plays a year. And oh, I ran the chapel program. Usually it involved a lot of dreary clergymen from the area, but we took some chances, like jazz groups, and once we invited a Greek Orthodox priest. The man was magnetic. He had tapes and slides and the kids were in his hands the whole time—I recall how they crowded around him at the dinner hour. I got the sense of trying some new things—sometimes they work. It was a busy life. But once again I really did think I was going stale. I could be there the rest of my life doing the same things. They wanted me to stay and become dean, but they made the offer after I had decided to leave.

Suddenly, I was in a larger, more prestigious school, working *in* a dorm rather than heading one, working *in* a department, directing plays, and still coaching soccer—poorly! I started working as assistant head of the summer school. Hiring, advising, programming—I got a real taste for administrative life. I found that I had learned a lot about running something from directing plays. You get a lot of talented people and organize them, and then you don't have to do anything. Some of the same skills pertain. I was coordinator again for the overseas programs of the school. And then a black kid asked me to be advisor to the Afro-American club. It was the most eye-opening thing I ever did. I had had very little contact with black kids, and I had no sense of the anger that was there. I remember that I once learned a lesson from the way the head handled an angry black kid in a meeting I'd set up. All the brass were there, and this meeting seemed to be absolutely necessary as a safety valve. The kid lashed out at the head—he was absolutely vituperative. The head responded quietly, "I'd never talk to you that way." The meeting turned around; it took a positive course. It was one of those incidents where you really learned something.

That head became my mentor, and after my fifth year there he came to me and said that maybe I should begin thinking about becoming an administrator. So we talked to some headhunters, and I ended up being interviewed at a double-martini lunch at some club on Wall Street. I was pretty intimidated. "Have you had any business experience?" "No." They needed someone with more experience. Later I was asked if I would be interested in going to work in Pittsburgh. I said, "Where?" They needed an upper school head in what was in effect a new school. Everything clicked, and so I went. The school didn't even have a name. It was trial by fire.

After that first rough year that I told you about, the people that I hired started doing very good work, and I began to feel more confident. I married Joan that summer. It was a horrible first year for her. She was teaching at an inner-city school for the performing arts—a job that made mine look easy. There were kids who didn't even have instruments, and there were no lockers for storage. Her purse was stolen on the first day. It was really awful for her. But those kids were playing Bach and Haydn by the time we left. In my school there were financial crises, and I learned about cutting budgets, about working *with* people to do that. I learned how to work with people to get a decision made rather than just making it myself.

## How did you get to your school in California?

Well, I looked at a *lot* of schools. There was a boarding school that interested me, but Joan said it was wrong, and she was right. I came close on a couple after that. And then I had a call from the head of the search committee at my present school. Suddenly, I was jetting into the San Francisco airport for meetings. I knew a bit about the school because I had been at conferences with a former headmaster. And the person who was trying to hire me was the president of a major corporation, and he was good at his business. I became quite interested.

I did my homework before the interview. If you're a good teacher, you don't go to class unprepared. So I visited there, and I liked it. And I went back for a second visit with Joan. It all fell into place. This board is very good, and they did *their* homework. They knew my flaws—what training I would need. They hired a consultant to grill my references. I mean they spent about 45 minutes on the phone with each of my references. They knew what they were getting. They visited *me*, too. It was just the right move—good for Joan, too. People are just as nice to us now as they were when we arrived. I've completed my third year, and I've been rehired. And that *really* is a difference. I'm no longer the new headmaster. Folks are not *quite* as quick to tell me how nice the speech was, and a *little* quicker to tell me how I've gone wrong!

## Have you ever come close to the breaking point?

No. The breaking point would mean quitting. The most pressure is at hiring time, in personnel matters. That's the toughest thing. Sometimes you have nasty conferences with very good people. Not long ago I created a personnel committee, but I think it may have been a mistake. It put a group between me and the faculty. Now I'm being *interpreted*. We're too small for that. The *faculty* is uncomfortable with that. We need a new process. If I know the *process,* I can sleep at night. I don't have to know how it will end up, but I have to know the process.

### What do you consider to be the high point of your career?

As a teacher it was probably my last year at Billington. Oh, did you mean as an administrator? Well, your standards for yourself change. I've really liked everything except that first year as an administrator. As an administrator, it's *right now.* I'm living without knowing what I'm doing every minute, or how it will all turn out. And I still love teaching, and I'm teaching *what* I like to teach—European literature. A regular class, every school day. I don't see it as an advancement to go from teacher to administrator. This attitude is kind of rare, I guess, especially in public schools. But all our administrators here are basically first-class teachers. They bridle if they're not teaching; it's a good tension.

### Do you see yourself as a teacher of adults as well as young people?

This is the question I ask: "How can I change people's jobs?" Now some administrators will change a teacher's assignment arbitrarily from third grade to fourth grade to try to prevent staleness. That's a lot more direct than I would be, I guess. But let me give you some examples from our school. Everyone has one extra job beyond the regular teaching or administrative assignments. One teacher had been organizing an annual community project where students, teachers, parents—all of us—did something for the neighborhood around us. She came to me this spring and said that for next year she wanted to tackle the whole issue of service inside and outside the school. I was ecstatic. Do you see how she was changing her job? Service is critical to us, and here is someone who wants to help define it and improve it. Clearly, it fit her skills and interests to make this attempt, and that's an important criterion, too.

Then there's the case of the teacher who had taught only at this school, who had lived only in this particular corner of the world. She came to me to say that she needed to get away. She's a great teacher, and I knew that we stood a chance of losing her. I wouldn't fight that, if it was right for her, but I wondered how I might change her job to make it more interesting and challenging. So I suggested that she apply for a special fellowship program for independent school teachers which would take her east for a year, put her into an entirely different environment. Well, she won the fellowship. Then the question was, what would she do when she returned? I believed that she couldn't come back from a year like that and just do the same thing she was doing before she left. So we sorted it out together. She's going to be director of studies for the upper school. And the administrator who *was* fulfilling that function is going to give us leadership in the area of computers. He had been toying with the idea of leaving for another administrative job, but a couple of interviews convinced him that wasn't what he really wanted. But he still needed a change. He didn't know much about computers, but he was fascinated by them, and once he floated the idea, I really encouraged him. He's going to be a fabulous example for the faculty, and he'll be in a position to teach his colleagues, as he learns. Our lower school director is also going to handle all the admissions for the school, for the first time. And our middle school director is going to give direction to the overall curriculum for the entire school, and that plays right to her strength. You mix it up. You keep things possible.

## What other kinds of teaching situations with adults do you get into?

I talk to all the staff on opening day of school in the fall. It's the only time I give such a speech, and I guess it's the one time they have to sit and listen to me. I spend a lot of time preparing that speech, and usually I talk about teaching. Not techniques, but its importance, what we're striving for.

The administrators spend a lot of time teaching each other. We meet once a week, and it's a meeting that rarely gets canceled. We enjoy being together, in a setting where we can really speak our minds. It gets so candid that sometimes after a meeting I think the whole thing's coming apart. But it's not really, of course. What we keep focusing on in these meetings is process. How to deal with a situation, how to deal with a person or a problem. Not one of us is afraid to say, "I fouled it up this time." That's a *really* important rule of the game if we're going to give and get advice. I told our business manager recently that I had misread the salary schedule and overpaid a consultant, that I had blown it and it was too late to make any changes. He said, "I appreciate your telling me that, saying it that way." The problem is that I have a sneaking suspicion that he doesn't foul things up as much as I do!

With the board members it seems to be a matter of teaching and learning. Some teach *me*. Others call me for advice. Frankly, I enjoy both roles that I'm thrust into with them. I remember making a decision my first year that I thought was perfect, and it really bombed. The chairman of the board told me a month after it was all over, "When you made the decision I knew it was wrong, but I also knew it was your decision to make." Now that's a teacher at work. Parents who aren't on the board often come to me for guidance. I guess I'm still startled at how often they accept my advice. I really am.

## Why do you see yourself as a teacher when so many administrators seem to move further and further away from teaching roles?

Part of it may be because I taught for a long time. It's really in my blood. I had a dream recently. I had just finished teaching my fifth class of the day to students, and I said to myself, "That was *wonderful.*" See what I mean?

If I couldn't continue to teach in all these various ways, I wouldn't want this job. And the new opportunities to teach keep cropping up. We're into a big development program now, and I've been out on the road talking to alumni. You have to tell them what's happening at the school now, accurately, and you have to make friends on an honest basis, just like in a classroom.

Another thing in answer to your question is that many administrators look ahead with some kind of ultimate job in mind. I never have felt that way. I'm very happy with *this* job. That doesn't mean I want to stay here forever. Maybe I'd move to another kind of job someday. But I keep my eye on *this* job.

If I had to go through what many public school administrators do, I wouldn't stand for it. I'd be teaching. I couldn't take it. I talk to enough of them to know. Lots of teachers come here to work for the same reason. If our goals here were different, maybe I'd move on. But people are so *enthusiastic*.

The best administrators have really known how to teach. I taught full time for 14 years. My wife says I'll never go back to full-time teaching, but she might be wrong this time. Lots of heads leave and go to work for foundations. Can you believe *that?* I want to deal directly with kids, always.

This is the situation I'm in right now. But I don't think much about it. It's the way Joan and I both operate. We don't sit around wishing that something else were true. I guess you do begin to wonder about arriving at the age when you don't have as many options. I can get another job If I'm fired here . . . (he laughs and knocks on wood) . . . I'm in my forties now, but I've never mapped out my career.

### How would you describe your administrative style? Has it changed over time?

It would probably be better for you to ask others about that. Colleagueship is very important to it. I *know* where the final decision is made, but I want to know the fallout when that happens. When we meet as an administrative group, everything goes on the table. Even salaries. I use a lot of humor. We take ourselves *so* seriously in this business. At a meeting once one of the principals said that we ought to have a needs assessment. I said, "A *what?*" It's very important not to let each other get away with that. We work for a real sense of compromise in the group. The principals really work hard to make that happen. I don't get involved in discussion of schedule conflicts, for example, and the principals do all the original screening and recommending in hiring situations. As administrators we tend to do too much for other people. That's not all bad, but people resent it sometimes.

### Have you ever had what might be called a transcendent experience?

For me, it's hiring the person you want. They are the ones who will make all the difference. Every September you have to feel that as a school you're better, and it's because of those you hired. You are lowest when the person you really wants goes somewhere else. If I get depressed—and that's rare—it's this sort of thing. Rejection—I guess that's what it's called. Then you have to think to yourself, "This school is not the center of the universe." *That's* very liberating.

## *FROM PRACTICE TO THEORY*

Martin Mason was a superb classroom teacher. His heart is still there—with the kids, teaching English, experiencing the singular joy that comes from teaching well. Most administrators in education had success in the classroom, which brought them to someone's attention, led to additional responsibility, developed their self-confidence, demonstrated their competence. Not uncommonly, one hears administrators talk nostalgically about returning to classroom teaching—giving up the managerial rat race, rediscovering what they enjoy most. Some do just that. Few careers permit a graceful retreat from command, but education seems to understand these motives and actions well.

The tragedy is that administrative training has failed to recognize fully that administration *and* teaching are parts of the same role. Martin Mason has learned, over time, to apply some of his instructional skills to his work with adults, and it has helped him become a better administrator. Still, when asked about the high point of his career, Mason asks: Do you mean as a teacher or as an administrator? The distinction is still there: two different roles, two sets of skills, two reward systems which are often competitive.

Can we reconceptualize educational administration? What happens to our view of, and our assumptions and expectations regarding, the role of educational administrator if we think of executive behavior as teaching behavior? For educators, this reconceptualization would seem to be easy. We were teachers first and administrators second. The skills are still there. Can they be applied from the front office?

# THE ADMINISTRATOR AS TEACHER

The leader in an organization, at whatever level, must fill a teaching role. Few admonitions have been advanced so persistently in the literature of organizational life. Thoughtful observers of executive behavior—theorists and scholars, as well as men and women with considerable practical experience—all understand that leaders cannot merely *expect* certain behavior from others. Expectation must be accompanied by instruction regarding what needs to be done. The executive maintains broader knowledge of the goals of the organization than most of its other members, in substantial measure because of greater access to the sources of those goals. The leader coordinates the work of the organization by helping participants move toward such goals while satisfying their personal needs and predilections. Indeed, by teaching workers the processes and procedures of desirable organizational behavior, the leader can influence institutional and personal performance substantially. This view has deep and extensive roots.

> . . . almost every act of the workman should be preceded by one or more preparatory acts of the management which enable him to do his work better and quicker than he otherwise could. And each man should daily be taught by and receive the most friendly

help from those who are over him, instead of being, at the one extreme, driven or coerced by his bosses, and at the other left to his own unaided devices.[1]

> Frederick Taylor
> *The Principles of Scientific Management*
> (1911)

An executive is a teacher. Most people don't think of him that way, but that's what he is. He can't do very much unless he can teach people. He does it not by any formally organized classes or seminars, but that's what he has all the time. He has conferences that are seminars in which he or other people who are involved do instructing. That's absolutely essential. You can't just pick out people and stick them in a job and say go ahead and do it. You've got to state the goals, you've got to indicate the limitations.[2]

> Chester Barnard
> *Conversations with Chester I. Barnard*
> (1938)

. . . we shall all agree that it is one of the leader's chief duties to draw out from each his fullest possibilities. The foreman should feel responsible for the education and training of those under him, the heads of departments should feel the same, and so all along up the line to the chief executive. . . . I say that it is the part of the leader to educate and train. He must know how to do this.[3]

> Mary Parker Follett
> *Dynamic Administration*
> (1944)

. . . training prepares the organization member to reach satisfactory decisions himself, without the need for the constant exercise of authority or advice. In this sense, training procedures are alternatives to the exercise of authority or advice as means of control over the subordinate's decisions.[4]

> Herbert Simon
> *Administrative Behavior*
> (1947)

Those who act most effectively as administrators do so in part *by* teaching. This does not mean that the teacher-administrators consciously see themselves as such. . . . Intuitively, however, most administrators know that they cannot get organizational action by orders alone. They give more instruction than instructions. They activate people by assisting them in the learning process.[5]

> Bertram Gross
> *Organizations and their Managing*
> (1964)

The only way I know to get somebody trained is on the job.[6]

> Robert Townsend
> *Up the Organization*
> (1970)

For in the long run the executive who makes the greatest contribution to his corporation is the one who is able to release and develop the potential of the human resources that are his organization's principle asset. Thus, according to modern management theory, every manager must be an educator too. So it is not enough for managers to be educators. They must be adult educators.[7]

> Malcolm Knowles
> *The Adult Learner: A Neglected Species*
> (1973)

In the knowledge organization, the supervisor has to become an assistant, a resource, a teacher.[8]

> Peter Drucker
> *Managing in Turbulent Times*
> (1980)

Nor is it likely that this is the last of such testimony. The concept of the administrator as teacher is particularly important in this era of regarding employees as assets in the school's portfolio and recognizing the need to dearly husband all resources.

We draw the reader's attention to two interpretations of the administrator as teacher (or teaching in administration). First, the administrator can continue to be involved directly in the instruction of *students*. Second, administrators tend to become responsible (either directly or indirectly) for the training and development of their *subordinates*, be they teachers or administrators. It is in this category that supervision and career counseling come into play. And, to be certain, the administrator instructs when she builds the cooperative effort of stakeholders in the organization, a theme that is sounded frequently in this book. In this respect the administrator becomes teacher in an almost generic sense.

## The Teaching Principal

A century ago the typical principal was a teacher both of children and adults. The principal had continuing classroom responsibilities, often as the master teacher in the building, and, in addition, the principal taught his ill-trained and inexperienced faculty colleagues about both the process and substance of their teaching. The principal was something like a professor of education in residence. As schools grew larger and more complicated, principals acquired either clerical assistants or teaching assistants to make it possible for them to get both jobs done effectively.[9] It was well into the twentieth century before the idea of a nonteaching principal—one who was no longer a classroom teacher—was well established.

Men and women who had been superb classroom teachers became full-time principals. The gap between the classroom and the principal's office had been established, and in the years that followed it was to turn into a ravine. The siren's song of money, prestige, and power lured some educators away from the core activity of the school. Other enticements appeared in the form of increasing professionalization of the administrative role; growing specialization of the teaching faculty; the accumulating demands of the superintendent and the board of education; as well as multiplying pressures from the local community and state and federal agencies. Even visiting classrooms was to become a rarity for these men and women who once had found their major satisfactions there.

Graduate training which precedes or accompanies socialization to the administrative role is another alienating factor. In his study of the development of graduate study in education at the University of Chicago in the early part of the twentieth century, Woodie White argued that deliberate and specific strategies were used to provide administrators with identities quite different from those of teachers.[10] In developing the early programs of graduate study in education at Chicago, John Dewey envisioned education as the meeting place for all of the appropriate disciplines. White reported that Dewey

> had recognized the necessity of courses in school administration, but he always saw them as part of a larger program of study designed for all educators. It was Dewey's attitude that with the exception of general superintendents, administrators were no more than teachers with general responsibilities.[11]

Thus, the classroom and the development of classroom activities for teachers and students should provide the core for graduate studies for aspiring educators, thought Dewey.

Dewey's successor, Charles Hubbard Judd, moved in the opposite direction. He conceived of schools of education as vehicles for professorial and administrative careers. Graduate students were expected to meet certain prerequisites of race and gender: they should be white and male. For Judd, *teaching* was reserved for women trained in normal schools or second-rate colleges and universities. *Leadership* was reserved for men enrolled in the premier universities where the new sciences of education as defined by Judd—particularly psychology—were beginning to flourish. Special curricula were set up at Chicago by the late 1920s which, according to White, gave administrators "a sense of purpose and power distinct from the impotent classroom teacher."[12] White suggested that the same pattern emerged at Harvard, Columbia, and Stanford as the entire field of educational administration was transformed.

The wedges driven between the administrator and the teacher at the site of graduate training appear to have been powerful ones: white versus black, male versus female, Judd's science versus Dewey's art, power versus impotence, and control versus obedience. Is White's assessment of the Chicago program accurate? If so, were its effects indeed widespread? And, if so, are these effects still potent today? The answers to these questions are uncertain, but the problems that White raises are worthy of our continued concern and study.

Other conditions have widened the breach between administrators and teachers. In the period following the Second World War, teachers developed collective powers. Administrators were excluded from organizations of educators such as the National Education Association, and contract bargaining pitted organized teachers against informally organized administrators. In district after district, contracts spelled out differential responsibilities for teachers and administrators, particularly at the school level. Gertrude McPherson captured the curious ambivalence of the evolving relationship between the teacher and the principal:

> What the teacher is saying to the principal, then, is: "Leave me alone. Don't interfere in my classroom. Don't tell me how to teach. Protect me from all who challenge me. Support my decisions. *And* show you care about and appreciate me."[13]

Over the years schools grew larger, particularly at the secondary level, and principals were compelled to spend more time on bureaucratic duties than in interaction with teachers. In their discussion of the school as an open system, Roald Campbell and his colleagues described how the attention of school administrators at every level turned increasingly to the school community.[14] Raymond Callahan documented the growing cult of efficiency in schools,[15] and Chicago United exemplified the influence of a business community coalition on an urban school board and superintendent.[16] The growth of federal and state involvement in education at the local level demanded the attention and time of administrators in program development, implementation, evaluation, and expenditure accountability. What Arthur Wise characterized as the "hyperrationalization" of schools and classrooms had begun.[17] The accountability movement drew administrators away from teachers and into closer contact with boards of education, citizen groups, and state and federal bureaucrats. If teachers had encouraged administrators to return to their desks, others were closing the office doors.

Esther Shkop currently is studying the developmental ethic in service organizations which encourages administrators to take leadership in the education of their subordinates.[18] She has identified four elements of this managerial possibility: the provision of reinforcement and feedback; the creation of learning opportunities; the instilling of confidence; and the expressing of concern for subordinate career success. In particular, Shkop is investigating the relationship of organizational reward structures to administrative teaching. Are there high costs or risks awaiting the administrator or teacher? In many educational settings, and particularly at the precollegiate level, administrators are not rewarded for being excellent teachers. For example, in many elementary and secondary schools principal supervision of teachers (which is an admirable vehicle for teaching) has become more closely linked with evaluation than with human resource development. The principal who tends to praise and retain effective teachers may not be viewed as favorably from on high as the principal who wants to punish and discharge ineffective teachers. It is another message within a school district which constrains the teaching role of the administrator.

Thus, it is difficult for a school administrator to be a teacher. He or she is separated from the classroom and from front-line teachers. Graduate education tells administrators that they are different from and better than teachers. Social forces over which they have little control lead administrators to cloistered offices, away from the hubbub of classrooms. There is a well-traveled highway from classroom teacher to bureaucrat, but only an unfamiliar path from classroom teacher to educator.

## Administrators Who Teach Students

On the other hand, some administrators continue to teach children and youth in their schools in the face of all these deterrents. Many of them, like Martin Mason, are principals or headmasters in nonpublic schools, although some may be found in public settings. One of the authors called a superintendent recently to find that he was away from the office teaching an elementary science class. As it turned out, every administrator in that district has a classroom teaching assignment. Such administrators may not be working with students in a regularly scheduled class, but usually they will be doing so in a regularly scheduled way—in a tutorial, a community inquiry, a semester-long project, or a remedial section. At least at the level of the principal, and whenever possible at the other levels of the school system, we believe that administrators should participate in the core work of the organization.

Such a commitment to teaching students tells teachers that the principal likes and values the basic work of the school; that some of the early passion that nurtured a career is still there; that the principal feels what it is like to be teaching in that particular school; and that the principal is in a position to give pedagogical advice and counsel on the basis of more than memory. If the principal who continues to teach students is good at it, that word gets around, too. It is a risky but powerful way of measuring up.

The principal who continues to teach students can insist on being viewed as, and possibly respected as, a teacher by the faculty of the school. In such circumstances two attractive possibilities open up. First, if the leadership involves, as Seymour Sarason has suggested it does,[19] challenging others with ideas and being vulnerable in return to their ideas, then the overlapping of roles in schools is desirable and perhaps even necessary. Teachers who have worked with a teaching principal in their midst may have been somewhat surprised, but just as often they have been pleased. They feel more like members of a college faculty which values a dean who prefers the professoriate to a long career as a university administrator, a dean who continues to teach and to be engaged in scholarly activity. In such situations, the administrator tends to take a more collegial and consultative attitude toward his or her *administrative* responsibilities, and a real quid pro quo exchange between teaching and administrative decisions can occur. Second, the principal has a better opportunity as at least a part-time teacher in the school to become what Gertrude McPherson has termed a senior colleague rather than a boss or housekeeper.[20] A senior colleague can enter into a supervisory relationship that is associative rather than merely evaluative or perfunctory. The current national effort to retrain principals and other school administrators as clinical supervisors stems from the unhappy interaction between principals and teachers in many schools, and yet it is doubtful that bosses and housekeepers can become effective clinical supervisors. Respect for the principal as teacher must be the premise upon which clinical supervision is built. Without such regard from teachers, principals will own a new set of procedures and forms but little real participation in shaping and reshaping the essential activity of classroom teaching.

## Problems That Hamper the Administrator-Teacher

The problems that administrators encounter in preserving their roles as teachers are not entirely of their own making. The mere transition from the classroom to the principal's office convinces many men and women that much of what they have learned as teachers must be discarded if they are to perform effectively in their new administrative roles. To be certain, the teacher who has become a beginning principal has acquired much important knowledge—familiarity with the workings of a school, understanding of the priority and ethos of the classroom, a grasp of the nature of reasonable and unreasonable parental concerns, knowledge of the ways in which children learn and fail to learn, and mastery of methods for the control of students. But as Sarason observed, teachers have had considerable experience in leading children and youth, but conspicuous inexperience in leading adults, which is the essential characteristic of administrative life.[21] Kent Peterson[22] and Van Cleve Morris[23] have noted that teachers usually work alone, while administrators interact constantly with the various members of the school community. In addition, teachers grasp only fragments of what administrators do with their time and energy. Consequently, their views of principals, superintendents, deans, and college and university presidents often are distorted. For instance, teachers commonly ascribe more power to administrators than they actually exercise.[24] The classroom is focused and limited, while the world of administration involves more complex responsibility, which is rooted in issues of organizational stability, the necessity of broadly based cooperation, and the inherent danger of initiating and supporting efforts toward change. Administrators protect teachers from numerous internal and external challenges, but who protects administrators from similar threats?

## The Supervisor or Counseling Resource

We have suggested that one way for principals (and other administrators) to build a bridge between teaching and administering is to continue teaching students. There is a second possibility, one that can enhance supervisory and evaluative process over a wide range of staff development activities. What seems to be essential is what Kanter calls "transforming the managerial role from tyrant to teacher." She suggests that

> managers will need to be taught how to be effective counselors. This is particularly important in cultures (a) where a deference barrier exists between superiors and subordinates or, (b) where norms of politeness interfere with a manager's ability to offer criticisms, or (c) where men in authority positions do not know how to talk honestly to women, or (d) where the ideas of evaluation of competence, goal-setting, and planning are not prominent.[25]

Several of these characteristics would appear to describe many school organizations. Through supervision and counseling the administrator helps teachers (or other managers) decide how to improve their skills and develop their talents. It is important to distinguish between routine supervision and the development of human resources. The distinction is one between maintenance and growth, and it is measurably dependent on the capacity of the administrator to analyze the abilities and potentialities of organization members. Schools need to develop encouragement and positive feedback for adult learning, both through systematic performance appraisal systems and more informal talk among professionals. And while we do not propose to discuss the complex issue of personnel supervision in detail here, we do want to talk about some tenets which form a basis for the supervisory or counseling relationship.

Adult education is not new. Over a half century ago Edward Lindeman advanced its basic precepts.[26] Situations which call for adjustment are the starting points for adult learners, rather than the subjects which organize school learning for young students. Experience is the most important resource of the adult learner, not the codified guidelines of the expert. The teacher of adults uses methods which involve those adults both in the quest for practical solutions to problems and in the search for wisdom.

Malcolm Knowles has discussed the four differing assumptions which distinguish pedagogy, the art and science of teaching children, from andragogy.[27] The first has to do with *the concept of the learner*. Where pedagogy prevails, the learner is largely dependent on the teacher; where andragogy is practiced, it is recognized that the learner has matured from dependency to substantially more self-direction. The second assumption deals with *the role of experience for the learner*. Pedagogy emphasizes that the experience of the learner—most often a child—is of far less importance than that of the teacher and of other adults who enter into the learning situation (e.g., the textbook author, the television program director). Given such an assumption, transmittal teaching strategies prevail. In contrast, andragogy stresses that

> as people grow and develop they accumulate an increasing reservoir of experience that becomes an increasingly rich resource for learning—for themselves and for others. Furthermore, people attach more meaning to learnings they gain from experience than those they acquire passively.[28]

Thus, experiential teaching strategies are preferred in an andragogical setting. The third premise focuses on *the readiness of the learner to learn*. The pedagogical teacher believes that students are ready and able to learn what the teacher (and the education profession, and the society) decides they ought to learn. The standardized curriculum becomes the chief vehicle of pedagogical learning. In contrast, the andragogical teacher believes that students are ready and able to learn what they need to, to solve developmental problems related to their social roles. Martin Mason seems to have an unusual sensitivity to his teaching and administrative colleagues on this score. Education is built around actual problems facing the learners; and the curriculum is subjective and personalized. The fourth assumption speaks to the issue of *the orientation of the learner to learning*. Under the rubric of pedagogy "learners see education as a process of acquiring subject-matter content, most of which they understand will be useful only at a later time in life."[29] Under the rubric of andragogy, this sense of postponed application of knowledge is abandoned in favor of a principle of immediate application of knowledge. A new skill is valuable if it is self-actualizing in the here and now. In this manner, then, Knowles draws crisp distinctions between pedagogy and andragogy and suggests that the learning needs and methods of children and adults are quite different. It is small wonder that over the past fifteen years the theory of andragogy has been one of the most powerful influences in the field of adult education.

On the other hand, a competing view of adult learning was developed by Cyril Houle.[30] Houle argued that

> if pedagogy and andragogy are distinguishable, it is not because they are essentially different from one another but because they represent the working out of the same fundamental processes at different stages of life.[31]

Houle created a system of educational design that was derived from the study of the education of adults but which he believed had relevance to education at any stage of life. Houle's system included situation-related categories and then a series of procedural steps: identification of a possible educational activity; a decision to proceed; refinement of objectives; development of a learning format; the relating of that format to the life patterns of learners; implementation; and appraisal. For Houle these steps are as central to the development of an educational program for children as they are for adults.

Interestingly enough, Knowles has modified his position from the early 1970s, and it is now much closer to Houle's stand.

> Originally I defined andragogy as the art and science of helping adults learn, in contrast to pedagogy as the art and science of teaching children. Then an increasing number of teachers in elementary and secondary schools (and a few in colleges) began reporting to me that they were experimenting with applying the concepts of andragogy to the education of youth and finding that in certain situations they were producing superior learning. So I am at the point now of seeing that andragogy is simply another model of assumptions, thereby providing two alternative models for testing out the assumptions as to their "fit" with particular situations. Furthermore, the models are probably most useful when seen not as dichotomous but rather as two ends of a spectrum, with a realistic assumption in a given situation falling in between the two ends.[32]

What emerges from this dialectic, then, is a picture something like this. Typically, and perhaps often erroneously, we teach children in the United States using a pedagogical model. This same model has been used often when adults are the learners, and often with no better than mixed results. Increasingly, adult educators have recognized the value of the andragogical model in preparing learning programs for adults. Furthermore, there are situations where this model will benefit a young child, just as there are instances when the pedagogical model will be successful with an octogenarian. The situation, the particular learner, the precise learning objective—it is these variables that dictate the relative use of pedagogical and andragogical principles, or their mixture. The third grade teacher in a self-contained classroom, the college professor in a seminar setting, the superintendent standing before the board of education for a budget briefing—each should have pedagogical and andragogical strategies available. Such flexibility also finds support in Houle's much earlier research which revealed the range of perspectives just within the category of adult learners: those who are goal-oriented, who find meaning in the end of learning; and those who are learning-oriented, who find meaning in the nature of learning itelf.[33]

Administrators gravitate to the pedagogical end of the pedagogy–andragogy continuum because that is what they have known, and that is what affords them comfort. Teaching from this perspective involves the transmission of knowledge and skills that are proven over time, from a teacher to a learner. Independence, self-direction, the valuing of experience, active learning, the focus on real problems drawn from the lives of learners, immediate application of new knowledge and skills—these are as foreign to some school principals and associate superintendents as were the open classrooms of the 1960s and 1970s where, indeed, many andragogical principles were employed with children and youth in American schools. The demise of most of these classrooms is profound testimony to the strength of the pedagogical model in precollegiate education in the United States.

We believe that the pressure on teachers for immediate performance requires their administrators to treat them as adult learners with predominantly andragogical learning needs. Teachers teach five days a week for nine to ten months a year. They cannot wait to improve their practice. As a consequence, administrator-designed lectures, presentations by external experts, and discussions focused on problems which are not real problems doom in-service programs to failure. Teachers can learn more that will be helpful to them over a cup of coffee and a sandwich with two other teachers, or in a one-to-one encounter with the principal on the playground. In fact, the countless verbal interactions that principals have with teachers can be viewed as opportunities to instruct, coach, counsel, and give feedback. The administrator can create conditions within which organizational colleagues will flourish, often by removing obstacles. Does the teacher lack knowledge or expertise or resources? Andragogical strategies are in order, but so is a flexibility in leadership style that will coincide with the maturity of the individual being helped.

In addition to teaching teachers, a principal teaches future administrators, teachers who eventually will move into the ranks of management. This function of identifying and tutoring one's successors has been recognized in business circles for many years. Harry Levinson observes that the executive teaches in two ways:

> First, he can do what he ordinarily does, enabling others to learn from observing him. This is a hit or miss system which fails to take into account elementary psychological principles about how people learn best. Second, he can do what he ordinarily does, but at the same time build into his daily activities formal teaching circumstances and conditions which facilitate learning. It is the latter that is asked of him.[34]

Most principals are prepared to treat these particular colleagues, these proteges, as adults. Mentorship, then, often is characterized by a masterly blending of pedagogical and andragogical techniques. Unfortunately, that same mentor may resort to almost exclusively pedagogical methods when working with less favored subordinates.

Adult education is an unconsidered topic for most administrators, a graduate school specialization rather than a necessary part of every administrator's training and role. Moreover, average administrators do not encounter many excellent role models in college or while teaching. Even more distressingly, the pedagogical principal has infused a tradition which maintains that teachers are dependent upon administrators; that their experience and desire to learn is limited; and that their seeming inability to convert general pronouncements into specific procedures is nothing more than intransigence.

Supervision is treated with ambivalence by teachers and administrators. Principals—especially secondary schools principals—complain that they have neither the time nor the subject-matter expertise to supervise staff effectively. It is true that some supervision may have to be delegated to other administrators, but is it also possible that supervision may have to occur without the presence of traditional supervisors at this level? Perhaps management functions will be redistributed in much more radical ways in the future. We continue to believe in the importance of the administrator in this culture; he or she is the glue in the mosaic, if not the artist who assembles it. Yet administrators continue to speak of their powerlessness. That they are busy is not at question, but the importance of what they are doing is beginning to be questioned in some corners of the educational enterprise. The debate on how much supervision is required to create and maintain truly effective schools is not over. Certainly it is not necessary to become a convert to clinical supervision in order for an administrator to influence teachers. Day to day, informal, face to face verbal encounters often become more powerful teaching and learning situations than infrequent, formal, restrained, and largely written supervisory encounters which are subject to a district format and recorded on a standardized report form.

## The Concept of an Educator

The administrator who wants to be an educator, particularly a teacher of adults, can find assistance from the conceptual framework of adult educators. Lessons can be applied on the job, but the most critical steps, which involve change in attitude and perspective, can be described here. To become an effective organizational teacher of adults, the administrator as teacher must cultivate an instinct for learning related to professional matters. Continued learning is imperative, regardless of the administrator's experience, age, gender, degree status, or leadership position in the organization. Superintendents of schools and presidents of universities need to hire men and women for administrative roles who exhibit this attitude, who stimulate those who are in positions to cultivate it, and who replace those who continue to ignore its development.

Administrators who are learners can create learning communities in their schools. One does not get the sense that adults are second-class learners in the school that Martin Mason leads. While such communities are rare in elementary and secondary settings, they are more common in university departments and colleges and even in entire universities. Indeed, precollegiate education needs to capture this particular spirit and value of the university—the sense that schools are important as learning institutions for the adults as well as the youth and children who inhabit them. The creation of a learning community takes years and decades, not weeks and months. The task of administrators is to nurture the concept. Robert Schaefer suggested that "The first obstacle to be overcome, therefore, if the school is to become a center of inquiry, is the fear of revealing how little we know."[35] A second obstacle is to reduce the workload of teachers, cutting away tasks which may not correlate to student learning, and to identify tasks which necessitate varying types of teacher-student interaction. Schaeffer also argued that colleague authority is increased while executive authority is reduced in a school that inquires. In the process, skepticism toward administrative tinkering is encouraged on the part of everyone.

Administrators also must distinguish between direct and indirect teaching methods. Speeches, newsletters, and memoranda all have value in releasing potential, yet they are strikingly less effective than informal, eyeball-to-eyeball methods in individual encounters or small groups. Objectives must be matched with teaching techniques as time for teaching is found in the fragmented day of the school administrator. Teachers may need more time for paperwork, but administrators require respite from the paperwork for the task of teaching. The principal who has become this kind of leader sees a different world from the average principal. Sarason observed:

> He judges himself not by the absence of problems but how problems surface and get resolved; he judges himself not only with what teachers do but in the ways they think; he judges himself not only by what teachers do in their classroom but in how they relate and utilize each other; he actively seeks the participation of parents and others in the community rather than viewing them as outsiders or irritants; he distinguishes between pride about the level of children's knowledge and pride about the quality of their thinking; and in relationships between those of differing roles (e.g., parent-principal) he knows the difference between honest give-and-take and the intellectual and personal charade that goes with the spirit of noblesse oblige.[36]

Beyond these perspectives, in the thick underbrush of practice, what does an administrator need in order to be a good adult educator? Allen Tough[37] and Lois Hart[38] both have identified some basic strategies which might be used in a private conference, at a group meeting with faculty, at a parent caucus, or in a session with the boss. Administrators can teach adults that the answers to most problems are rooted in past experience, and that they can facilitate exploration of such experience, not as anecdotal flavoring, but as a source of answers. Presume that the adult really wants to solve the problem. A Socratic, inductive style of dialog is effective in helping to shape and define the problem so that it is amenable to solution in an organizational context. Some problems cannot be handled and others must be reconstructed. Assume that adults work through issues best when the adult teacher and adult learner are colleagues in a cooperative effort. Administrators can depend on adult students' participation in the entire learning cycle, from planning all the way through evaluation. Answers to problems must be in a suitable form for immediate use, a situation which obtains more often than many administrators assume. This sense of immediacy will help the administrator as teacher and the adult as student to avoid extraneous posturing and conversation.

John Whithall and Fred Wood stressed the importance of accurate and immediate feedback. They also cautioned adult educators to be aware of the anxiety which signals like radar to the adult learner when a learning activity is subject to external judgment or to an attack on professional competency.[39] Most adult educators recognize that motivation is centered in the adult learner and not in the teacher.

Roland Barth constructed a taxonomy of response for the administrator as teacher.[40] At the bottom of the taxonomy are the too-familiar behaviors of not listening, vetoing an idea, and listening but not hearing. Then come the still-remembered behaviors of listening and hearing, and then listening, hearing, responding to, and valuing an idea. Finally, at the top of the taxonomy, the rarer combination of reactions include listening, hearing, responding to, and valuing an idea, *and* agreeing to share the risks and consequences. The commitment inherent in this final posture is similar to that of the parent, the brother or sister, or the friend. It is the commitment of the true teacher, an obligation which the administrator as teacher can fulfill.

As we shall elaborate in the next chapter, Chester Barnard (and Mary Parker Follett, whose ideas so influenced his) is credited with understanding that cooperation is the key to organizational control. Purposing plays an important function in securing organizational cooperation, as intention is shaped into reality and then sustained. Sergiovanni and Corbally furnish an interesting example:

> Language is the means by which administrators intervene in the metaphoric and ritualistic aspects of school life. . . . Administrators who seek to increase power by centralizing decision making in the face of opposition can win the battle against aspirants to power equalization by framing centralization as a means to increase accountability and to bring about a more coherent statement of organizational purposes and quality. Those who oppose centralization, once the concept is framed in this manner, oppose as well accountability, coherence of purpose, and quality.[41]

The ritual of the annual school calendar provides regular, predictable opportunities for such instruction of organization members. These occasions are supplemented by the powerful if unpredictable interactions of administrators and their colleagues. There will be conflict, as in the instance above, but there will also be the possibility of building a common vision. How can the goals of the organization be met even while individuals are encouraged to grow and seek their own satisfactions at work? This is a question that has intrigued Jacob Getzels, and in Chapter 12 we will turn to his reflections on the matter.

## FROM THEORY TO PRACTICE

When you have paid your dues, the way Martin Mason has, teaching gets into your bones. You can't move away from it if you want to. Martin is a teaching administrator. "All our administrators here are basically first-class teachers. They bridle if they're not teaching; it's a good tension." Perhaps it is easier to develop this approach in the private sector. Bright young men do not seem to be rushed into administrative posts in independent schools, as so often is the case in public school circles. They show more respect for seasoning, possibly. Martin has a lot of support from others in clinging to his teaching role. In effect, he is a senior colleague for his teachers.

Most administrators can name their mentors, the people who gave them the encouragement and push at the right time, but Martin seemed to have more than most. Mentoring was another way these administrators rather unconsciously returned to teaching—tutoring their successors on a one-to-one basis.

Don't control people, control the process. Martin has that premise well in hand. A school or a school system had goals, to be certain, but the particular outcomes were another matter, and maybe good administrators are willing to let these evolve rather than predetermining them. Let the process find one solution from among many.

Martin had not revealed his undergraduate grade point average, but there were indications that he had been a fine student. Outstanding student, dedicated teacher, teaching administrator—they all seemed so closely and necessarily related. At every step of the way, apparently, he had the capacity to improvise, to plunge ahead without being precipitous, to keep the best interests of the school and its students in mind. Behind that exuberance was a lot of perspiration. "If you're a good teacher, you don't go to class unprepared." He learned what it meant to be self-directed—drawing on his accumulating experience; responding to situational needs; using what he learned to solve the problems of today rather than tomorrow. Andragogy came as naturally to Martin as pedagogy had at an earlier time.

For Martin Mason a central task of the educational administrator as teacher is assisting colleagues in the transformation of their jobs—accepting new responsibilities, facing emerging challenges, avoiding the staleness and boredom that can so often characterize repetitive work in schools. "How can I change people's jobs?" Martin is not tinkering with the work of others; he is opening the way for learning and professional growth. While he may give an occasional speech, and it may indeed be inspirational, it is individualized staff development that is his concern. He takes satisfaction from helping others become teachers of adults within a school of teachers of children. He sees opportunities to teach children and adults in abundance in his environment, and it is this vision that shapes his work as an educational administrator—finding the process, solving the problem, providing the advice, sharing the information, critiquing the plan, building upon error. "You mix it up. You keep things possible." What is it that adults need to know and wish to learn? Martin Mason has discovered the secret that can be shared. Adults in school communities *sense* what they need to learn; they often *know* precisely what they need to learn; and they will *communicate* this to educational administrators who are prepared to listen and to teach.

## THE PROFESSOR

I finished correcting the three draft chapters. They were almost ready for another turn by the typist in the word processing room. Every administrator out there has a fascinating tale to tell—thousands of stories, and just as many lessons for those of us interested in educational administration. We had decided to ask a few of them to share experience and insight with us, and they had spoken to us frankly, and sometimes emotionally. We had wanted to do more than pay respect to the complexity of their professional work and to them as thoughtful professionals. We were hoping to maintain throughout the book that we were preparing the counterpoint between research and theory, on one hand, and the practice of educational administration, on the other hand.

I poked around through the papers in one of the many piles, looking for another clipping. There it was at last. On the evening of July 10, 1982, under a circus roof in Tucson, Arizona, an event took place which stunned circus buffs around the world. The Flying Vazquezes performed a quadruple somersault *in performance.* The first triple somersault had been achieved by an aerialist in 1897, and it is still a difficult trick, but the steel control necessary to complete the "quad" had been a quest for only the most gifted teams of high-flying acrobats. How did Juan and Miguel Vazquez from Mexico finally make this breakthrough? They had entered a moment of precision in which perfect balance and timing were achieved through the exercise of control over their minds and bodies, in combination with

> an almost mystical factor that they refer to as "the feel of the rigging." The rigging is the 33-ft.-tall metal frame from which they work; sometimes it feels solid and sometimes it does not.[42]

They said they know they can repeat their feat, but they are not optimistic about doing it often in front of a circus crowd. Like the top of Mt. Everest, the quad is possible, but still elusive and dangerous.

These three chapters—hadn't they been about an analogous search for control by school administrators? The process by which the administrator can master the "feel of the rigging" and begin to exert some precise control over the internal and external organizations typically is slow and erratic and painful. The training of administrators begins in the graduate classroom, and it is reinforced by the defining perceptions of classroom teachers. The nature of administrative work emerges on the job in a particular role and a particular setting. To survive, the administrator must reconcile differences between learned conceptions of the job and its intruding reality. Only at this point is the administrator ready to ask the question: "What should I be doing to keep this place from flying apart?" Or, put another way: "How can I exercise some control personally over the events that seem to make us all so vulnerable?"

I pulled out my wallet, stuffed with much more paper and plastic than money, and riffled through it. Yes, it was still there—the typed quotation from Willard Waller that I used in a speech whenever I could figure out how to work it in:

> Real leadership is unconscious and informal; it is deeply personal in that it flows out of the man rather than the office. It is domination which the dominant one himself cannot prevent, which he quite possibly did not plan, domination that arises from a mind more complex than the mind of the followers and a hand readier and bolder than theirs. This is a kind of disciplined cooperation into which both leader and follower can enter fully; it is that which is lacking in the school.[43]

This was the way it *felt* to be a leader. But the administrator had to learn Disraeli's lesson. Something like, "I stand behind the people. Am I not their leader?" Or Lao Tse: "And of a good leader we will say, when our work is done, we did this ourselves." Charging up the hill sometimes, and figuring out a way to avoid the hill altogether at other times. Douglas MacArthur had been effective at this.

I recalled a conversation with Steve Mrozek at O'Hare International Airport before we flew back to the East Coast. "Steve, do you *really* think most school administrators have much use for theory? Did you, when you were out there in the field?"

"I think that if you're educated in a university that respects theory and exposes you to it—and that was the case for both of us—then there is an indelible mark. When the local walls are pressing in on you, you tend to look for relationships, connections between the elements of a real-life situation. The administrator doesn't use hypotheses the way a social scientist might, but you're a little less prone to accept the simplistic solution, and sometimes you can predict with more accuracy than the social scientist what might happen if you did $X$ as opposed to $Y$. Also, I think a theoretical posture helps you collect and organize information more effectively, and, goodness knows, this is important to the administrator. You have a hunch when you have too many data, or too few. And I know that there were times when I could go back and think through what we had done more effectively than those around me who tended to downplay the theoretical approach. Now, I know that sounds pretty general, but—"

"Come on, let's be honest. We don't even have much theory that is *unique* to educational administration. We borrow theories blithely from other fields and assume that there is some relevance for educational organizations, but it may not be there. There's not much of a knowledge base for our work, as a result. And most of all we teach administrative theory and organizational theory in the abstract as if—"

"But that's the real problem. We really learn the trade on the job—from mentors and from clumsy experience. I think that's why many superintendents are so cautious. You're feeling your way through a career without the benefit of theory or the wisdom that can be accumulated and codified with its help. Who wants to be the bold leader in circumstances like that? What can either you or I teach from a book in a campus classroom that is going to stick when we're working with professionals, and not budding professors? The clinical experiences at my university are superficial, and I'd guess that yours aren't much better. The administrators who end up doing the teaching in the field are often atheoretical or anti-theoretical. I think they have us in the wrong places. We ought to be stationed out in school districts, teaching there where we could actually show the value of theory to the practitioner. But we're locked up in the ivory tower, writing more and more books and articles that won't do the job as far as professional training is concerned."

"Amen. You know, I feel most comfortable teaching the couple of times each year when I personally take a group of students to a local board meeting. It's like a seminar back there in the fourth row, my students huddled around me firing questions when the board goes into executive session. I feel somehow like a doctor with a group of interns trailing behind me, examining this particular aspect of the organization. It's a powerful shared experience between a teacher and students, and I can bring theory to bear then."

I was convinced that Steve was on the right track in arguing that the locale was critical. The internships at our place were pretty perfunctory. Some state legislatures were passing laws requiring us to give education students more field exposure at various stages in their training, but most of that had to do with teachers. Why did we always have to be pushed?

Educational administrators don't start out pining to become educational administrators. They want to be teachers, educators. It's the impulse to serve that stirs them when they're young—to share, to encourage, to nurture. You could look through several hundred high school yearbooks and never find under the pictures of the seniors anyone saying that he or she wanted to become a principal or a superintendent or a college president. A teacher, maybe. But an administrator? That's not the goal. When you're in high school or college, and you say you want to be a doctor or a lawyer or a minister, somehow it's clearer. Educators aren't reluctant when the opportunities for leadership finally come, though. Most of us are ready and eager. But that original instinct never goes away. You're still trying to help people, as confusing as your attempts may look to others—trying to help younger people get an education and get ahead.

I thought about the men and women I had interviewed in Chicago. It was striking how much more intrigued most of them had seemed to be by means rather than ends. It was as if that was where a great deal of action was, where they wanted to exert control. Few of them had exorbitant egos. They were willing to share leadership, even though they kept trying to control the leadership that came from a hundred sources to make the puzzle whole, or at least closer to whole.

I wasn't sure that their educational organizations had changed all that much across the twentieth century, but their environments had. There didn't seem to be quite the same reciprocity between school and society that had once been the case. The environment seemed to be gaining the upper hand. Declining enrollment in the early 1970s hadn't been just an event, it had been a watershed for administrators in local school districts. But how had educational administrators changed? Were there some new tricks of the trade worth sharing? Problem finding, that early part of the problem cycle, seemed to be one. And I recalled Armando saying, "It's all negotiation." That was another one. Also, reclaiming the teaching role that a lot of administrators had let slip away. All of these seemed to involve the nuance and moxie that were needed now by educational administrators more than ever.

I was tired. It had been a long trip but, I suspected, no longer than the ones that Ike and Martin and John and Anne Denier and Don and Armando and Jesse and Steve had taken already, and were still to take.

## NOTES

[1]Frederick W. Taylor, *The Principles of Scientific Management* (New York: Harper & Row, 1911), p. 26.

[2]William B. Wolf, *Conversations with Chester I. Barnard* (Ithaca, N. Y.: Cornell University, State School of Industrial and Labor Relations, 1973), p. 7.

[3]Mary Parker Follett, *Dynamic Administration, The Collected Papers of Mary Parker Follett*, in Henry C. Metcalf and L. Urwick, eds., (New York: Harper & Row, 1964), p. 267.

[4]Herbert A. Simon, *Administrative Behavior* (New York: Macmillan, 1957), p. 15.

[5]Bertram M. Gross, *Organizations and Their Managing* (New York: The Free Press, 1964), p. 630-631.

[6]Robert Townsend, *Up the Organization* (New York: Alfred A. Knopf, 1970), p. 188.

[7]Malcolm Knowles, *The Adult Learner: A Neglected Species* (Houston: Gulf Publishing, 1973), p. 31.

[8]Peter F. Drucker, *Managing in Turbulent Times* (New York: Harper & Row, 1980), p. 226.

[9]Glenn William McGee, "The Development of a New Procedure for the Selection of Principals in

an Elementary School District" (Unpublished master's thesis, University of Chicago, 1978), pp. 1–25.

[10]Woodie T. White, "The Decline of the Classroom and the Chicago Study of Education," *American Journal of Education* 90 (1982): 144–74.

[11]Ibid., p. 157.

[12]Ibid., p. 157–58.

[13]McPherson, "What Principals Should Know," p. 241.

[14]Campbell et al., *Organization and Control.*

[15]Raymond E. Callahan, *Education and the Cult of Efficiency* (Chicago: University of Chicago Press, 1964).

[16]*Chicago School System: Recommended Actions* (Chicago: Chicago United, Chicago United Special Task Force on Education, 1981).

[17]Arthur E. Wise, *Legislated Learning: The Bureaucratization of the American Classroom* (Berkeley: University of California Press, 1979).

[18]Esther M. Shkop, "Organizational Reward Structures and Human Resource Development," research in progress, College of Education, University of Illinois at Chicago.

[19]Seymour Sarason, *The Culture of the School and the Problem of Change,* 2nd ed. (Boston: Allyn & Bacon, 1982), p. 177.

[20]Gertrude McPherson, "What Principals Should Know About Teachers," in Donald A. Erickson and Theodore L. Reller, eds., *The Principal in Metropolitan Schools* (Berkeley: McCutchan Publishing, 1979), pp. 248–250.

[21]Sarason, p. 141.

[22]Kent D. Peterson, "The Principal's Tasks," *Administrative Notebook* 26 (1978): 1-4.

[23]Van Cleve Morris et al., *The Urban Principal: Discretionary Decision-Making in a Large Educational Organization* (Chicago: University of Illinois at Chicago, 1981), p. 31.

[24]McPherson, "What Principals Should Know," p. 235.

[25]Rosabeth Moss Kanter, *Men and Women of the Corporation* (New York: Basic Books, 1977), p. 274–75.

[26]Edward C. Lindeman, *The Meaning of Adult Education* (New York: The New Republic Press, 1926).

[27]Malcolm Knowles, "Andragogy: The New Science of Education," in R. Gross, ed., *Invitation to Lifelong Learning* (Chicago: Follett, 1982), pp. 149–150.

[28]Ibid., p. 149.

[29]Ibid., p. 150.

[30]Cyril O. Houle, *The Design of Education* (San Francisco: Jossey-Bass, 1972).

[31]Ibid., p. 272.

[32]Knowles, "Andragogy," p. 148.

[33]Cyril O. Houle, *The Inquiring Mind* (Madison: University of Wisconsin Press, 1961), pp. 15–16.

[34]Harry Levinson, *The Exceptional Executive* (Cambridge: Harvard University Press, 1968), p. 116.

[35]Robert Joseph Schaefer, *The School as a Center of Inquiry* (New York: Harper & Row, 1967), p. 60.

[36]Seymour Sarason, *The Culture of the School and the Problem of Change,* (Boston: Allyn & Bacon, 1971), p. 208.

[37]Allen M. Tough, *The Adult's Learning Projects* (Toronto: Ontario Institute for Studies in Education, 1979).

[38]Lois B. Hart, "The Supervisor as Teacher," *Supervisory Management* (January, 1981): 38–41.

[39]John Whithall and Fred Wood, "Taking the Threat Out of Classroom and Feedback," *Journal of Teacher Education* 30 (January-February 1979): 55–58.

[40]Roland S. Barth, "The Principal as Staff Developer," *Boston University Journal of Education* 163 (1981): 144–162.

[41]Thomas J. Sergiovanni and John E. Corbally, *Leadership and Organizational Culture* (Urbana, Ill.: University of Illinois Press, 1984), p. 212

[42]Gerald Clark, "They Caught the Quad!" *Time* (July 26, 1982): 63.

[43]Willard W. Waller, *The Sociology of Teaching* (New York: Russell and Russell, 1932), p. 446.

# FOUR

## CONCLUSION

# 12

## *Practice and Theory: Some Enduring Fundamentals*

||||||||||||||||||||||||||||||||||||||||||||||||||||||||||||||||||||||||||||||||||||||||||||||||

Administrators operate from some theoretical base in every instance. Yet in most situations action is reflexive rather than reflective. An administrator spends more time thinking about crossfire, losses, and counterattacks than about how Vroom and Yetton's decision theory can be applied to the latest crisis. The thought that scrambles through an administrator's mind when the heat is on is cursory, cryptic, couched in strategic and logistical terms. The philosophic and theoretical frameworks are back there at work somewhere, but they are obscured and unrecognized. Even if the administrator read and understood Vroom and Yetton at an earlier time, and even if their ideas may be having a quite potent effect, the administrator usually is unaware of their presence.

It would not be unusual for a high-school principal to say something like this to the superintendent of the district:

> The first thing I tried to do was to get to the heart of the problem. That wasn't easy with all of the static I was getting. After things settled down a bit, I encouraged the teachers and parents to dream up some alternatives. I don't know why I did that, because they gave me about a dozen too many. I wasn't going to tell them what I would do, but one of the options looked like it might work. So I went back to my office and touched some bases by telephone. I think it'll be a possibility. What I want to do is to run it by you, and if you like it I'll make an announcement tomorrow morning.

A powerful theoretical framework is present here. It is doubtful that the principal knew that. The superintendent would have had trouble identifying it. What the superintendent was really interested in was how the principal thought the problem

**334**

could be licked. Occasionally, if administrators are doing some long range planning they might be a bit more systematic about applying a theory (or more likely a model) to help them work out a sensible process, but that is rare. Typically the conceptual perspective of the administrator is hard to identify; its sources are uncertain; and it is a resident of the subconscious rather than the conscious mind.

Does that mean that universities should abandon their courses on organizational and administrative theory? Some students would like that, but one of the best ways to burrow into the subconscious of future administrators is through direct instruction of theories, models, and concepts that have the potentiality for improving their practice of the trade. The professor is not handing out formulas, but rather different ways of looking at the organizational world. It is not the only (perhaps not even the best) way to develop those points of view, of course. Practitioners are constantly developing grounded theory[1] out of their experiences. You observe yourself and your colleagues, your successes and your failures, and you slowly develop theoretical postures that become powerful shapers of future behavior. Some of them would look like Rube Goldberg nightmares if they were transcribed to paper, and many would be idiosyncratic. On the other hand, many of them would work; they would mold and predict behavior and action effectively. Administrators also talk to their colleagues and reflect on common experience. They trade techniques and barter skills, working hard at refining the concepts that guide them.

Joseph Schwab made it quite clear as to who he thought ought to be teaching courses in educational administration and weaving theory and practice together.

> If the professor of educational administration is concerned with the improvement of educational administration and the training of administrators; if defensible administration arises from a subtle, complex interaction of theory and practice on one another; if the experience of practice can be undergone and the interaction instituted only in the act of practice; then the essential professor of educational administration is one who has practiced; he is a professing educational administrator.
>
> Clearly, he is not any educational administrator who has practiced but one who has the theoretical resources as well and has brought his theory and his practice into interaction with one another.[2]

Some professors of this stripe learned a good deal about organizational theory that affected the way they worked as administrators from mentors who would not have lasted a week as a principal in an inner-city school, or even a suburban school for that matter. If you see educational administration as a professional field and not a discipline (and that was Schwab's point of view), then it makes sense to have former practitioners with "theoretical resources" for the most part doing the educating of future administrators. But there are some things to be learned from men and women who never had the twinge of a desire to run a school or school system.

One of these people was Jack Getzels. He was always fascinated by educational administration, but he never claimed to know *how* administrators plied their trade. He has been committed resolutely to the professoriate throughout a distinguished career. He could have become a dean (had he wanted to be one), but his interests lay elsewhere. He was a theorist, first and last. He never argued that a theory *had* to be designed with practice in mind. Yet he was interested across the years in the interaction of theory and practice, and he was just as interested in a practitioner who found his ideas helpful as in a researcher whose study had been shaped by the same ideas. Getzels managed to stick his model into the collective subconscious of a field of study and practice.


## JACOB W. GETZELS

He was born in Poland, and he came to the United States when he was nine years old. After taking degrees at Brooklyn College and Columbia University (and serving with the OSS during the war), he completed his doctorate at Harvard University in 1951, where he studied with Talcott Parsons in the Committee on Social Relations. During the same year he became an instructor in the Department of Education at the University of Chicago, where his entire career was to unfurl. He was a full professor by 1957 (something of a feat even at Chicago, where unusual talent could be recognized and rewarded), and eventually he became the R. Wendell Harrison Distinguished Service Professor. While a lot of other professors preached about civil rights during the late 1960s, Getzels joined the marchers in Selma, Alabama. He is a member of the National Academy of Education now. His research and theory development have fallen into the general academic areas of cognitive and social psychology with particular emphasis on the acquisition of values, on social behavior in social systems, and on creativity, including its relationship to intelligence and its application in the work of such disparate fields as the fine arts and educational administration.

His office on the fourth floor of Judd Hall on the Chicago campus was a quintessential professor's office. He wrote in a canyon carved from huge piles of books, manuscripts, articles and miscellaneous other paper parcels. The light was soft through the Chicago haze, somehow just right for the long conversations where he skewered his graduate students, with cause and with regret. A student came back to the office for the second time with temerity, prepared for his constant graciousness and the twinkle in eye and voice, but never quite prepared for the intellectual surprises and the uncompromising questions that made every encounter with him unique and chastening. He didn't see it as his job to make life easy for graduate students.

But how had he affected educational administrators as *practitioners*? What fundamental ideas did he give us or encourage us to develop? The original Getzels-Guba model was widely familiar, but it had been revised by Getzels over the years. What was the importance of the new shapes it had taken?


### The Evolution of the Getzels Model

The serious study of educational administration in the United States and the development of its dominant theoretical perspective—the Getzels model—had common beginnings. The theory movement sent down strong roots in the Department of Education at the University of Chicago in the mid-1950s. It was there and then that Getzels framed his now-famous model of social behavior in a social system (with the assistance of Egon Guba, who was the first of his doctoral students) and applied it to the field of educational administration. The model represented a useful entrée for both university professors and field administrators to the perspectives of the unfamiliar social sciences, and it helped define the organizations they inhabited, be they universities or school systems.

The study and practice of educational administration have changed significantly as the years have passed. The shift in the viewpoint of scholars and practitioners from closed to open systems has been pervasive. Of course, a veteran school superintendent might point out that his school system was not now open just because a professor or two had said so. There may always be some historical lag between what educational administrators know and do and when scholars find out what they know and do. However, it can be said with some confidence now that the open systems perspective holds sway in our field.

One way of sensing the change that has taken place is to recall part of what happened in the field of social psychology, a discipline that has contributed much to theory and research in educational administration. Two of its leading figures, Daniel Katz and Robert Kahn, criticized closed systems theory in 1966:

> Traditional organizational theorists have tended to view the human organization as a closed system. This tendency has led to a disregard of differing organization environments and the nature of organizational dependency on environment. It has led also to an over-concentration on principles of internal organizational functioning, with consequent failure to develop and understand the processes of feedback which are essential to survival.[3]

Twelve years later they could report a dramatic transformation:

> Our first edition championed the cause of the open system approach to the study of organizations. Today that point of view has gained wide acceptance in organizational research and theorizing. Research is no longer contained within the boundaries of a single organization but crosses those borders to deal with environmental forces, relationships with other systems, and the effects of organizations on individual members as human beings and members of the larger society. That social psychological principles can be applied to all forms of collective organized effort is now acknowledged in many disciplines.[4]

Or we might look at a major textbook in educational administration from this period—Roald Campbell and colleagues' *The Organization and Control of American Schools*. The theoretical backdrop of the first edition of 1965 is similar to that of the fifth edition of 1985 in several important respects. The school and society are seen to be in a reciprocal relationship; administrators are thought increasingly to be dependent upon the understandings of the social sciences; and institutional roles are used as an essential organizing thread for the book. But the 1985 edition provides much more explicit support for open systems theory:

> We view the organization and control of schools from the perspective of open systems. This view emphasizes the interdependence between an organization and its environment. . . . The open systems perspective contrasts with the literature which argues that schools traditionally have been bureaucratic systems which are nonresponsive to their environment.[5]

A second important development in the study of educational administration has been the accelerating loss of faith in the possibility of grand theory. A recent spate of articles and books has been devoted to an examination of the past, present, and future of the field (Roald Campbell,[6] Luvern Cunningham, Walter Hack, and Ray Nystrand,[7] Donald Erickson,[8] Daniel Griffiths,[9] Glenn Immegart and William Boyd,[10] Norman Boyan[11]). Boyan provides a crisp summary of the current situation:

> First, internal specialization has increasingly characterized inquiry. Second, the requirements do not exist for emergence of a new, single, synthesizing paradigm to guide research across the entire territory or even within any of the major specializations. Third, improvement in the states of the several arts has moved unevenly and modestly.[12]

As the overarching view of scholars and practitioners in the field has moved from closed to open theories, the prospects of collectively accepted guiding paradigms seem to have slipped further and further from our grasp.

Such was not always the case, particularly during the heady early days of the theory movement, as can be seen from at least the later judgment on that period of Andrew Halpin. Halpin edited one of the important volumes of the new literature of educational administration—*Administrative Theory in Education*. It was a compilation of papers presented at a 1957 conference sponsored jointly by the University Council for Educational Administration and the Midwest Administration Center at Chicago. Halpin's comments in the original introduction were quite tentative. "We should have no illusions about where we stand. We still just make feeble efforts toward the development of theory."[13] He termed the monograph, somewhat casually, "a progress report by a few of us who have tried to grapple with the task of devising administrative theory. The fact that these formulations are not all polished to a high gloss does not stop us from sharing our ideas with you."[14] However, in an addendum to that introduction which was written nine years later for a new edition of the monograph, Halpin described the same seminar more expansively. "In 1957 the use of the theory-oriented research in educational administration was essentially a novel and hence an alien idea for most professors in the field; the papers have had a dramatic effect in opening up new and highly rewarding research vistas."[15] Taken together, these commentaries by Halpin are a reasonably accurate set of parentheses around a remarkable decade in the development of the educational administration as a field of study. The theory movement had progressed in that time from a tentative birth to a much more confident childhood.

With the advantage of hindsight we can see that two chapters from *Administrative Theory in Education* were of special importance. One was "Some Ingredients of a General Theory of Formal Organization," in which Talcott Parsons discussed his classification of educational organization into technical, managerial, and institutional (or community) levels.[16] The second was "Administration as a Social Process" by Getzels.[17] Both pieces continue to be read and studied in graduate courses in educational administration.

Getzels' most serious concern regarding educational administration had been revealed even earlier in the decade in some of the first words he wrote about the subject. "There is a conspicuous lack of systematic research in the field of educational administration."[18] Apparently, he saw one of his tasks as proposing theoretical ideas that would encourage research and permit an attack on problems in schools that cried out for solution.

> Systematic research requires the mediation of theory—theory that will give meaning
> and order to observations already made and that will specify areas where observations
> still need to be made. It is here that we would place the root of the difficulty in
> administration: there is a dearth of theory-making, and such theories as do exist have
> thus far proved unequal to the task of stimulating research.[19]

Both in this initial article devoted to educational administration and his later
pioneering monograph with Arthur Coladarci,[20] he emphasized three critical theoretical dimensions: authority, affectivity, and role. They would be reduced to two
dimensions—normative and personal—in the Getzels-Guba model.

Getzels noted that "we sought a model that was at once heuristic, operational,
and that had the elegance and power of parsimony."[21] What he and Guba managed to
capture in a simple (but not simplistic) model was the inescapable fact that
administration in organizations involves both nomothetic and idiographic elements
(see Figure 12.1). From the beginning he said that it is the latter set that is most
significant. He observed that "administration always operates in an interpersonal
—or, if you will, *social*—relationship that makes the nature of this relationship the
crucial factor in the administrative process."[22] While the two dimensions of the model
were conceptually independent, they were interactive phenomenally. These ideas
were not entirely new to Getzels (David Bickimer[23] has traced the intellectual lineage
from Parsons to Barnard to Getzels), but their presentation in the form of a model was
particularly compelling.

The original model had limitations, of course. Its emphasis on observed
behavior (termed social behavior in later versions) reflected a particular empirical
bias. Increasingly it has seemed somewhat limiting to believe that all administrative
behavior can be observed and recorded, and it is of some interest in this respect to
note Getzels' recent interest in problem finding, particularly as applied to the work of
educational administrators.[24] The thought of such men and women is a process that
must be examined by imaginative and indirect methods. Another liability of the
original model was its tendency to focus the attention of scholars and practitioners on
the internal organization: "We have tried to show that administration deals essentially with social behavior in a hierarchical setting."[25] In many regards this was a closed
systems model. However, it coincided with a rush of inquiry in a field that largely
had been prescriptive and hortatory, and it was natural enough that initial theory-
building and investigation would start at home, inside the school and the school
organization.

Nomothetic Dimension

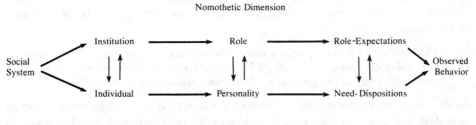

Idiographic Dimension

**FIGURE 12.1**     Original Getzels model

From J. W. Getzels and E. G. Gube. "Social Behavior and the Administrative Process," *School Review* 65 (1957): 429.

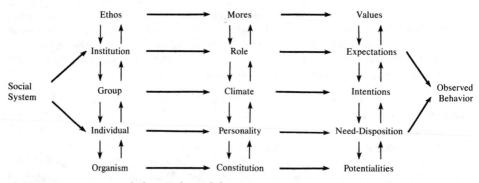

**FIGURE 12.2**     Expanded Getzels model

From J. W. Getzels and H. A. Thelen, "The Classroom as a Unique Social System," in N. B. Henry ed., *The Dynamics of Instructional Groups* (Chicago: University of Chicago Press, 1960), p. 72. Fifty-ninth Yearbook of the National Society for the Study of Education, Part 2.

The Getzels model was expanded almost immediately beyond its sociological and psychological dimensions into a more distinctively open form (see Figure 12.2). Getzels and Herbert Thelen[26] added a biological dimension (accounting for constitutional as well as personalistic elements), an anthropological dimension (focusing on cultural terms and issues), and even a group dimension (surely the contribution of Thelen) which would mediate between the normative and personal dimensions of the model. The evolving model was somewhat complicated, and yet it profited from the additional possibilities which the authors envisioned:

> In so far as there is going to be a "science" of education, it will be related to concepts, findings, and propositions from the whole range of disciplines called social science. It will be an integrative structure of ideas about the ways in which cultural, institutional, group, individual, and organismic factors interact and, in the process of interaction, change and bring about change.[27]

In effect, the revised model had defined the environment of the school as social system more concretely; had related the issues of rationality, belongingness, and identification in the organizational setting; and had predicted the attention of additional disciplines to the study of education and educational administration which would characterize the 1970s. Unfortunately, the "integrative structure of ideas" which Getzels and Thelen envisioned is still remote.

Within a few years Getzels[28] as well as Getzels, James Lipham, and Campbell[29] began to make significant alterations in this more comprehensive model. The group dimension was discarded, but the cultural dimension was seen to be of increased importance:

> The point we want to make here is that mediating between biological dimension and the personality dimension is the cultural dimension; *just as role expectations are related to a context of value, so are personality dispositions related to a context of value.*[30]

In addition, Getzels distinguished between a general model (see Figure 12.3) and an operational model, (see Figure 12.4), the latter of which he hoped would be useful in the study and practice of educational administration. The general model represented an open system with organismic, personalistic, institutional, and cultural elements arrayed in systematic interaction and set in an environmental context. His operation-

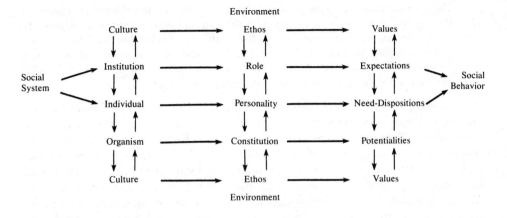

**FIGURE 12.3**  Revised Getzels model: cultural dimension

From J. W. Getzels, J. M. Lipham, and R. F. Campbell, *Educational Administration as a Social Process* (New York: Harper & Row, 1968), p. 105. Copyright © 1968 by Jacob W. Getzels, James M. Lipham, and Roald F. Campbell. Reprinted by permission of Harper & Row Publishers, Inc.

al model expressed his desire not only for parsimony and elegance, but his growing sense of the importance of the cultural dimension in understanding the operation of schools and school systems. He observed that:

> Although the *general* model includes the five dimensions, which must be borne in mind when considering any element of social behavior, the basic *operational* model in the present analysis of administrative processes in the educational context is composed of these three salient factors: the interaction of *role* and *personality* in the context of *value*.[31]

For instance, Getzels (as a social psychologist and not a political scientist) was specifying that the culture of the school and the culture of the child are sometimes compatible (e.g., for the middle-class child) and sometimes incompatible (e.g., for the poor child). The model was relevant particularly for educators who were coming to grips with this politically and socially critical dilemma of the 1960s.

Getzels recognized some of the limitations of the model, and in the late 1970s a further revision was offered to scholars and practitioners (see next page).

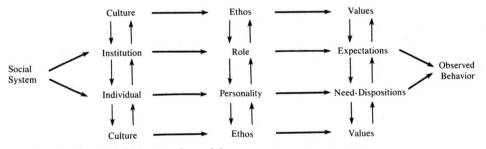

**FIGURE 12.4**  Working Getzels model

From J. W. Getzels, J. M. Lipham, and R. F. Campbell, *Educational Administration as a Social Process* (New York: Harper & Row, 1968), p. 106. Copyright © 1968 by Jacob W. Getzels, James M. Lipham, and Roald F. Campbell. Reprinted by permission of Harper & Row Publishers, Inc.

These formulations may now be seen as too monolithic and in the need of refinement; they were based on the assumption of the self-contained autonomous community, which, if it has not disappeared altogether, is the exception rather than the rule. It is closer to reality to think of the school and the child as embedded not in a single community but in a variety of communities—whose impact fluctuates throughout the life span and even in the course of meeting day-to-day needs.[32]

Here, in its most recent configuration, the Getzels model makes much more concrete the cultural setting of the school as a social system, and, in doing so, extends its potential usefulness as an open system model (see Figure 12.5). The model now characterizes the interaction of institutional, individual, and community elements where six community categories are identified: (a) local community, (b) administrative community, (c) social community, (d) instrumental (or functional) community, (e) ethnic community, and (f) ideological community. These communities of education are not new, but they are newly identified and related to each other by Getzels. The educational administrator who speaks of a homogeneous black community, or the scholar concerned with an individual's ideological community to the exclusion of other community identifications, is cautioned by this last, but perhaps not final version of the model.

The influence of these communities on educational organizations has increased steadily in the past quarter-century. The sophisticated college president or superintendent, dean or principal will know and be able to work with the communities of education, expressed as they are in various combinations in the individuals who work in educational organizations; in the clients of the organizations; and in the cultural contexts of the organizations themselves. The puzzling dilemmas which are the sources of problems for institutions and their administrators often are rooted in the communities of education. Problem solutions must be framed in forms that anticipate consequences for both the internal and external organizations.

What had started out as a closed system model in the mid-1950s had become an open systems model by the late 1970s. In many respects, Getzels' ideas had predated and then paralleled the same shift in the field of education. And while some of the man's more vocal critics would prefer to see the model dead and buried, it keeps being resuscitated. Wayne Hoy and Cecil Miskel[33] organize their current view of the school as a social system around the model, using it as a core for a derivative new

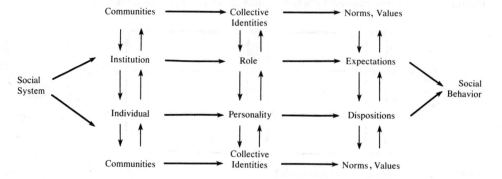

**FIGURE 12.5**    Latest Getzels model: communities dimension
From J. W. Getzels, "The Communities of Education," *Teachers College Record* 79:4 (May, 1978): 673.

model which also contains conceptual elements of bureaucracy, formal and informal systems, and open systems.

## Critique of the Getzels Model

There are a number of reasons why the Getzels model so dominated the field of educational administration, particularly in the 1950s and 1960s. For one thing, it was presented to the profession at the time when there were few serious competitors. Getzels' timing, which was in all probability not premeditated, was impeccable. It was clear and captivating where other theories and models tended to be complex and puzzling. It was discussed in various articles by Getzels in language that was relatively straightforward and understandable. It was explanatory, yet it also stimulated other investigations[34] and provided the conceptual framework for dozens of books and articles in this emerging field of study. Finally, it should be remembered that the model drew from the discipline of social psychology, which was to have a dominant influence on educational administration, particularly in the period from 1955-1970, largely because of its emphasis on role theory and the issue of change.

The Getzels model has not been without its critics. One argument has been advanced by Campbell:

> One can easily ask too much of a single model. Useful as are the concepts in the Getzels-Guba model, they do little to explain the external relationships of an organization. This is not stated to fault Getzels and Guba. Getzels and his colleagues gave some attention to this matter in what they called the cultural dimension. But the development of that dimension was left largely to others. Here political concepts were needed to supplement those in social psychology.[35]

While this assessment would not receive much support from Katz and Kahn, who would hardly exclude the external environment from the purview of social psychologists, it is a serious argument.[36] What Campbell seems to be saying is that the model may have been open in design, but it was never operationalized effectively by Getzels as an open systems model. Other scholars have complained that because it was located in a logical positivist tradition, the model tended to reify the concept of institution, although this was certainly not Getzels' intention. Others have reacted to it as if it were a grand theory or a paradigm, and have been frustrated by its consequent limitations in that regard. Still others have complained that none of the versions of the model has the sense of intensity that often characterizes theory with a cutting edge, no such intensity as *could* be felt in the earliest Getzels commentary on educational administration.[37] One can also wonder—following Paula Silver's[38] line of argument—if the research stimulated by the Getzels model led to the production of widely accepted knowledge that permits practitioners to solve important problems in schools and school systems. Of course, this same objection can be raised with respect to most educational administration models developed since the advent of the theory movement.

But why did the original model remain more closely associated with Getzels than any of its successors? For one thing, there was not all that much theoretical competition for the model in the 1950s, whereas there certainly is today, as scholars from a variety of disciplines—including more recently sociology, anthropology, political science, and economics—bring their theories and methodologies to the study of educational organizations and educational administrators. Social scientists may exhibit the same tendency that we see in shopping teenagers to search for the novel rather than the venerable; thus, by the late 1960s, the evolving Getzels model was viewed by some scholars as old hat. When the field of educational administration finally was ready for an open systems model, it was Easton's political science framework that caught the attention of scholars rather than the expanding Getzels model. Nor can we dismiss readily another possibility, that the real competition for the revised models was the original. The straightforward, gripping power of the first Getzels model could not be displaced by later versions despite their advantage of comprehensiveness of view.

What caught the practitioner's eye were the two dimensions of the Getzels model. Getzels said that while he might be able to tease them apart on a sheet of paper, in actuality they were in dynamic interaction, dependent upon each other for meaning. At first glance, Getzels seems to be interested in the direct control that an administrator can exert. The picture of the administrator that he portrays is one who is comfortably active in the midst of conflict. He saw the job of the administrator, at least much of the time, to be that of resolving differences between the two dimensions of organizational life and of trying to bind them together as much as possible. For Getzels, in the organization that works, collective goals are realized and individual needs are satisfied. If that is so, then administrators (or what he called transactional leaders) are driving toward a kind of internal equilibrium as they carry out their work.

Today, of course, there are organizational theorists who would claim that this representation of an organization is limited and misleading, that there may be many more dimensions than those Getzels named and discussed, or that organizations should not be defined in terms of dimensionality. Others would respond that the *stimulation* of healthy conflict is as much the task of an administrator as the reduction of unproductive conflict, a distinction which Getzels does not discuss. These arguments have merit. Yet for the administrator who goes to work five days a week in a building that is heated and lighted by an organization with a letterhead and a payroll and inhabited by other individuals who also come there regularly—for this man or woman the twin dimensions are experienced just as sharply as Getzels laid them out. The problems that end up in the superintendent's lap often are characterized by a struggle between the collective organization and the individual organization member. The student accused of harming another, the teacher cited for professional inadequacy, and both threatened with expulsion from the organization. The parent frustrated by the board's decision to curtail bus service, the board member angered over the high school principal's policy regarding use of the football field, and both eager to see action reversed. *At the point at which administrative work is defined and undertaken, the Getzels model seemed to have a finger on the pulse of administrative behavior.* And thus, as limited as the theory developed by Getzels may have been in its premises or objectives, or as important and useful as the theoretical explorations beyond it may have been, his model provided the starting points for a field of study. It is as simple as that. Getzels knew, without having been an administrator, what every experienced administrator learns—that the struggle for control in an organization between the collective will and the individual aspiration is perennial and rarely decisive.

Two of the most difficult questions which every practitioner must answer inevitably are linked to the problem of control in the organization. To whom do I owe my allegiance? How wide is my responsibility in the organization? With regard to the first, Getzels suggested three leadership alternatives—one emphasizing the interests of the organization, one emphasizing the interests of the individual, and one emphasizing the interests of both. He was uncomfortable with the administrator as a company man or as a maverick, and he opted for the posture of mixed allegiance. What Getzels is asking the administrator to do is to make a tough moral decision. He knew that the rewards for the established company man or for the established (or occasionally undiscovered) maverick are more predictable and durable than they are for the administrator in the middle who runs the risk of attack from every side and, even more probably, isolation. It takes courage to pursue a course as a transactional leader, with the loneliness, disappointment, and delayed recognition that accrue. But, suggests Getzels, it is the correct direction.

Speaking to the second of these questions, Getzels urged administrators to accept the fact that they are fated to accept the broadest responsibility for the operation and the survival of the organization. The administrator can not permit the organization to wander (or even perish) as the result of unbridled conflict. The school organization often represents the interests of a governing board which is particularly sensitive to the financial interests of clients in the organizational context. Yet the organization also represents a custodian who is concerned about the quality of medical insurance which is protecting his family. The trustee and the custodian need never meet, and for the most part they do not care about each other's possibly disparate goals. But the *administrator* must know both, and he or she must negotiate between the two, advancing and mediating the needs of the trustee and the custodian.

This attribute of the effective administrator was captured by C.P. Snow in his discussion of the development of government scientific policy in Great Britain just before the Second World War.

> On the surface these politics seem very simple. Just get hold of the man at the top, and the order will go down the line. So long as you have collected the boss, you have got nothing else to worry about. That is what people believe—particularly people who are both cynical and unworldly, which is one of my least favorite combinations—who are not used to hierarchies. Nothing could be more naive. . . . To get anything done in any highly articulated organization, you have got to carry people at all sorts of levels. It is their decisions, their acquiescence or enthusiasm (above all, the absences of their passive resistance), which are going to decide whether a strategy goes through in time. Everyone competent to judge agrees that this was how Tizard guided and shoved the radar strategy. He had the political and administrative bosses behind him from the start. He had also the Air Staff and the Chiefs of Command. But he spent much effort on persuading and exhorting the junior officers who would have to control the radar chains when they were ready.[39]

The Getzels model portrays the educational administrator in this same light, as a constantly active organizational negotiator, responsible for the entire turf and not just an isolated corner of it.

Getzels' persistence is to be admired. He was not satisfied with his core ideas as static concepts. Here was a pioneer in the social sciences, working within an established intellectual tradition, who continued to build a model over three decades. Without a doubt he is the scholar who links our past in educational administration—at least our past as a field of study—and our present.

## CHESTER I. BARNARD

*Conversations with Chester I. Barnard* by William Wolf is a slim volume.[40] Wolf, a management professor at Cornell University, had been fascinated by Barnard's *The Functions of the Executive*[41] and had wanted to learn more about the man behind the book. So he arranged for several interviews in Barnard's New York City apartment in early April of 1961, which was, as it turned out, just two months before Barnard's death. Wolf's efforts are fascinating because a few misconceptions about Barnard and his book are cleared up. For instance, readers have always been puzzled by his abstract prose. Surely this was not the natural style of a businessman. Was it the adopted language of a man of affairs who realized he was writing at a theoretical level and wanted to sound like the unversity professor that he admired but was never to become? A good many critics, like Kenneth Andrews, were ready to ascribe this rationale to Barnard's puzzling sentences and paragraphs.

> The ponderousness of Barnard's style is the mark, perhaps, of the amateur scholar. It is more surely an indication of how much he wanted it to be a definitive theory, adequate not only for his own extraordinary mind and experience but for the rest of us as well.[42]

Yet Wolf's interviews uncovered Barnard's apparent rationale:

> A great deal of the knowledge that I have of how things go is confidential knowledge. I just can't reveal it without hurting somebody or creating a disturbance of one kind or another, and my possession of the knowledge is due to a special privilege. It's like servants in the house, they're not supposed to talk about what goes on in the house because they are only there as privileged persons for limited purposes. That's why it's so difficult; or I'll put it another way, that's why my book had to be in highly abstract terms.[43]

It seemed plausible. This was Barnard's way, perhaps, of providing anonymity not only for the hundreds of people he had worked with over the years, but for himself as well. He always claimed to have learned more from conversations with business colleagues than from scholarly treatises.

The *New York Times* obituary that Wolf included at the close of the interviews displayed just how broad the organizational experience of Chester Barnard had been.[44] He was the first president of New Jersey Bell Telephone, named when he was 41 years old. Later in his career he was president of the Rockefeller Foundation, chairman of the National Science Foundation, and a director of the United States Chamber of Commerce. One of his most challenging jobs was as president and then chairman of the board of directors of the United Service Organization (USO) which probably reached its zenith, at least in the public consciousness, during the Second World War. In the late 1940s Barnard worked with the United Nations Atomic Energy Committee, and at the end of his life he was a member of the Board of Health in New York City, where he was instrumental in gaining the adoption of a new public health code. His earlier public service in New Jersey had been substantial and diverse. He had organized and helped implement a model emergency relief program during the Great Depression, and he had been a vigorous founder of the Bach Society of New Jersey and the Newark Art Theatre.

It was a proud record of professional accomplishment and public service, and seemed to be what the obituary editor thought readers should remember. There were only two brief and separate sentences about the part of his reputation that is of most interest to educational administrators. "Mr. Barnard was the author of *Functions of the Executive*, published in 1938 by the Harvard University Press." "He was considered an authority on the practical science of executive management."

An alternative obituary might look like this: Chester I. Barnard was a businessman and a public figure who gave substantial leadership to his community, state, and nation. He wrote two books. The first, *The Functions of the Executive*, was destined to become one of the classics in the field of organizational management. The second, *Organization and Management*, contains several interesting chapters on leadership and an interesting section on the organization of *The Functions*, but it is a patched-together volume which does not add a great deal to the ideas he developed in his masterpiece. The style of *The Functions* annoys many readers; nonetheless, few books have been used so persistently and widely for training managers and executives—in education, in business, in the military, and in government. While not an academician himself, Barnard was associated with such men and women through-out his career, particularly Lawrence Henderson, Talcott Parsons, and Alfred North Whitehead during the time he spent in residence at Harvard while he was writing *The Functions*. He had substantial impact on prominent organizational scholars after the publication of *The Functions*, among whom were Kenneth Boulding and Herbert Simon, for whom he wrote the foreword to *Administrative Behavior*. *The Functions* is now in its twenty-ninth printing, nearly a half century after its first publication, and the demand for the book seems to be increasing.

The book grew out of the eight lectures Barnard delivered at the Lowell Institute in 1937. Barnard did not have the sense of attracting much attention then.

> By the time I gave my lectures they were not popular at all. Nobody ever attended Lowell lectures. I don't believe there were more than fifty people ever in my audience and half of them were my friends and relatives.[45]

Dumas Malone, the renowned Jefferson biographer, was director of the Harvard University Press at that time, and he was an important influence in seeing that *The Functions* was published. It was a highly theoretical work developed by a practitioner —a man who had devoted his life to helping organizations survive and prosper, who had then reflected on what he (and others) had done, and seen, and questioned, and learned. In a way *The Functions* was akin to that literary phenomenon—the one, great autobiographical novel of a person's lifetime.

## A View of the Organization

The reader must find a writer's starting points to have a chance at understanding the writer's arguments. Sometimes the premises hide between the lines, never clearly articulated; at other times they are at the end of an article or essay or book, couched as conclusions. This latter case held true in part for Barnard. The closing pages of *The Functions*, contain his declaration of faith.

> I believe in the power of the cooperation of men of free will to make men free to cooperate; that only as they choose to work together can they achieve the fullness of personal development; that only as each accepts a responsibility for choice can they enter into that communion of men from which arise the higher purposes of individual and of cooperative behavior alike. I believe that the expansion of cooperation and the development of the individual are mutually dependent realities, and that a due proportion of balance between them is a necessary condition of human welfare.[46]

The cooperation for institutional purposes, the development of the individual, and the satisfaction of individual purposes—here were the origins of the twin dimension of the Getzels model.[47]

But where Getzels started with a rational perspective of the organization, Barnard tended to begin with nonrational issues and elements that he recognized as crucial for the administrator. Sometimes this point of view was irreverent and funny.

> I don't know of anything that has done more harm than the rule promulgated by the classical economists that the economic function was the maximization of profits. My God, anybody that has had any experience and absorbed the ways things are done knows that maximization of profits is merely one single over-in-the-corner sort of thing. It applies to horse trading and a few things like that, a pure trading proposition where there isn't any sense except to get the most that you can. I don't think it applies to anything else.[48]

For Barnard it is the provision of services and not the acquisition of profits that powers major industries and businesses, to say nothing of smaller ones. That was simply one of the radical ways he looked at the organization. He must have had some juicy arguments with business colleagues on that point.

For another thing, he was something of a pessimist despite that declaration of faith. Barnard was quite aware of the failure of cooperation. It was the 1930s, and the Great Depression was wiping out businesses and driving their leaders to early graves. Socialism and communism were providing political threats to American capitalism which were almost as dangerous as those in the economic sphere. The rising unions were accelerating what Barnard saw as the potentially destructive, centrifugal forces of human motive. In short, despite his success as a businessman, Barnard could see just how easy it was for organization to fly apart, to perish. This concept of the fragility of organizations, even those that were large and complex, lay at the root of his desire to figure out how to control them so that they could survive.

Wolf's little book adds to our understandings of Barnard's starting points. One such insight was related to that notion of his regarding organizational vulnerability. He seemed to have a keen sense that pieces of an organization tend to operate autonomously.

> Now, the idea of autonomous groups is anathema to businessmen, theoretical military men, and, I'm sure, the intellectuals as a group. They continue to talk about the formalities of organization, as if that were fundamentally the subject with which you're dealing. My approach would be to recognize that that's not the case. The case is that you're dealing with groups that largely are, and almost inevitably have to be, autonomous. You cannot direct from the top the multifarious activities of the groups down below. There has to be a reaction and a response to local conditions that can't be conveyed by anybody at a distance. . . . That's not easily acceptable; that was new stuff when I announced it, and it's still new. It's still new even to people who intellectually accept it. They can't operate on that basis. You put a man in charge of an organization, and your worst difficulty is that he thinks he has to tell everybody what to do, and that's almost fatal if its carried far enough.[49]

As natural as he made their existence sound here, Barnard must have been worried about the potentially disruptive nature of these autonomous groups. Maybe you cannot direct those groups, but can you exercise control over them, even if obliquely and indirectly? If not, did that mean that such groups controlled the organization? What Barnard was getting at is that if an executive recognizes the amount of autonomy that exists in an organization, like it or not, then the functions of direction and control are going to be approached in a particular way.

For Barnard the organization was alive and elusive, and hard for the administrator to harness. He had pointed that out in an early chapter in *The Functions*:

> It perhaps has impressed many executives how indefinitely organizations are located in space. The sense of being "nowhere" is commonly felt. With the great extension of the means of electrical communication this vagueness has increased. To be sure, since the material of organization is acts of persons, and since they relate in some degree to physical objects or are fixed in some physical environment, they have some degree of physical location. This is especially true of organizations in factories, or connected with railroad or communication systems. But even in these cases location is indirect, by attachment to a system of physical things; and in the case of political and religious organizations even mere location is only feebly conceivable. The notion of spatial dimensions of these systems is hardly applicable.[50]

Do you give in to an organization that defies the senses? Or do you work even harder trying to figure out how to control it? It is the latter course that Barnard pursued as a businessman and as a theorist. Not control for the sake of control, but control for the sake of survival.

## The Functions of the Executive

One sentence in *The Functions* that seems to hold the key to the book is this one: "Cooperation, not leadership, is the creative process; but leadership is the indispensable fulminator of its forces."[51] Cooperation is the end of the administrator, and if that is achieved then organizational goals and individual motives will have a chance of being realized. Therefore, the most successful leaders are those in a given organization who can create (a perfect word choice by Barnard) cooperation and who can inspire the faith and hope in others that cooperation will be forthcoming even when it is missing. Barnard certainly was no misanthrope; he was persistent in his belief that people want to cooperate, that many obstacles in organizations prevent them from cooperating, and that an essential function of the executive is to tear down those barriers.

Barnard talks to the reader in two places about the organization of his book. In the introduction to *The Functions* he comments:

> Formally this work is divided into four parts, but in a sense it consists of two short treatises. One is an exposition of a theory of cooperation and organization and constitutes the first half of the book. The second is a study of the functions and of the methods of operation of executives in formal organizations. These two subjects, which may be conveniently distinguished for some purposes, are in concrete action and experience inseparable.[52]

Reflecting in a later book upon the experience of writing *The Functions*, Barnard identified the principal structural concepts as the individual, the cooperative system, the formal organization, the complex formal organization, and the informal organization. He also pointed out that the principal dynamic concepts were free will, cooperation, communication, authority, the decisive process, dynamic equilibrium, and executive responsibility.[53] Then he added a sentence that revealed, once again, where his overarching concern lay: "Roughly, Part I and II are the 'anatomy' or structure of cooperation; Parts III and IV are its physiology or economy."[54] When two or more people cooperate, and where those acts are woven together in some conscious form, you have an organization. This was the building block concept for all that Barnard was to say about organizations and the work of executives in them. Of course, even when he was enumerating this neat organization of *The Functions* he could not resist adding that

> I look upon the structural concepts as stable in the sense that a whirlpool is stable. They are statements of stable relationships between incessantly successive series of acts giving a sense, a feeling, of something fixed.[55]

A whirlpool. And that may be the way it feels to administrators much of the time.

Barnard takes care to relate his theory of formal organization to what he feels are the three central executive functions.

> An organization comes into being when (1) there are persons able to communicate with each other; (2) who are willing to contribute action; and (3) to accomplish a common purpose. The elements of an organization are, therefore, (1) communication; (2) willingness to serve; and (3) common purpose.[56]

> The essential executive functions . . . are, first, to provide the system of communication; second, to promote the securing of essential efforts; and, third, to formulate and define purpose.[57]

It is in these three arenas that administrators should be spending their time if they want to have some influence over what is going on in the organization. The rest of it is peripheral. Barnard always argued that executives do not manage people; rather, they should be about the tasks of maintaining the organization, and here are these three tasks, writ large.

The book proved to be full of surprises—ideas that were either expressed well theoretically for the first time, or that seemed conceptually upside down. In the first category was his eloquent discussion of the informal organization. Others before him had been intrigued by this factor of organizational life—Mary Parker Follett and the Westinghouse researchers, for example, influenced his thinking—but he was the first to understand the integral nature of this latent and potent reality. "Formal organizations arise out of and are necessary to informal organization; but when formal organizations come into operation they create and require informal organizations."[58] And he comprehended just what the informal organization did for the individuals down in the depths of the organization who were so often hidden from the view of topside leaders, noting that "informal organizations are necessary to the operation of formal organizations as a means of communication, of cohesion, and of protecting the integrity of the individual."[59]

In the second category came his definition of authority. It is not really in the domain of the administrator, Barnard argued, but in the province of the subordinate.

> Authority is the character of a communication (order) in a formal organization by virtue of which it is accepted by a contributor to or a 'member' of the organization as governing the action he contributes.[60]

> A person can and will accept a communication as authoritative only when four conditions simultaneously obtain: (a) he can and does understand the communication; (b) *at the time of his decision* he believes that it is not inconsistent with the purpose of the organization; (c) *at the time of his decision* he believes it to be compatible with his personal interest as a whole; and (d) he is able mentally and physically to comply with it.[61]

He was challenging the most central tenet of control that administrators were presumed to enjoy, and in doing so he was redefining the leader-follower relationship in a most profound way. It shifted the initiative back to the administrator, dramatically, and it meshed perfectly with Barnard's sense of the mission of the administrator as a developer of cooperation. And even now, as a field of study, we are starting to come back to this idea in our consideration of motivation and commitment.

Another "upside down" idea can be found in his thoughts about executive reticence, the nuance of the decision not to decide:

> *The fine art of executive decision consists in not deciding questions that are not now pertinent, in not deciding prematurely, in not making decisions that cannot be made effective, and in not making decisions that others should make.*[62]

This idea about decision making collided with prior and later images of the administrator as a decision-making machine, active and assertive in controlling the organization through the decision process.

Many of his readers felt that Barnard had mixed up his terms when he developed his ideas about effectiveness and efficiency.

> What we mean by "effectiveness of cooperation" is the accomplishment of the recognized objectives of cooperative action. The degree of accomplishment indicates the degree of effectiveness.[63]

> Although effectiveness of cooperative effort relates to an accomplishment of an objective of the system and is determined with a view to the system's requirements, efficiency relates to the satisfaction of individual motives. The efficiency of a cooperative system is the resultant of the efficiencies of the individuals furnishing the constituent efforts, that

is, as viewed by them. If the individual finds himself satisfied by what he does, he continues his cooperative effort; otherwise he does not.[64]

Surely he meant that human beings were effective and the organization was efficient. This seeming paradox continues to jar readers, but Barnard was true to his theses in using the word this way, as Christopher Hodgkinson observes.

> Efficiency is a term which has caused some confusion in the classical literature due to its divergent use by Barnard. Barnard related efficiency to the satisfaction of individual motives. This is consistent with his view of organizations as incentive collectivities. Organizations were for him "efficient" insofar as they succeeded in eliciting sufficient individual cooperation. The efficiency of a cooperative system would be its capacity to maintain itself by the individual satisfactions it affords.[65]

Having persuaded someone to join the organization and to participate actively in it, the administrator continued to be faced with the question of incentives that not only maintained but strengthened cooperation. Barnard recognized objective incentives as cold as cash, and subjective incentives as elusive as a feeling about the fairness of the boss—and saw both as necessary to the incentive system of the organization.

The closing chapters of the book remain for many readers some of the most exciting pages ever written about organizational life. Here Barnard becomes virtually poetic in describing leadership and the moral responsibility of the leader. He saw leadership as an intricate set of human actions—a complex that few could tease apart. "I have never observed any leader who was able to state adequately or intelligently why he was able to be a leader, nor any statement of followers that acceptably expressed why they followed."[66] But that did not stop him—a man who clearly had been a leader in a large and complex organization—from making the effort at such a statement. In doing so he abandoned the dry tone of the beginning of the book for a quite different language. You can see this transformation across a few sentences on leadership as he argues that

> the essential aspect of the process is the sensing of the organization as a whole and the total situation relevant to it. It transcends the capacity of merely intellectual methods, and the techniques of discriminating the factors of the situation. The terms pertinent to it are "feeling," "judgement," "sense," "proportion," "balance," and "appropriateness." It is a matter of art rather than science, and is aesthetic rather than logical.[67]

There is science involved in administrative work, but leadership is not of that order. Nor is it simply a matter of technical competence greater than that of others:

> It is the aspect of individual superiority in determination, persistence, endurance, courage; that which determines the *quality* of action; which often is most inferred from what is *not* done, from abstention; which commands respect, reverence. It is the aspect of leadership we commonly imply in the word "responsibility," the quality which gives dependability and determination to human conduct, and foresight and ideality to purpose.[68]

The link between leadership and cooperation, as least as far as Barnard is concerned, becomes responsibility, which he defines as *"the property of an individual by which whatever morality exists in him becomes effective in conduct."*[69] He is talking about a good bit more than being careful not to lose the keys to the boiler room. The leader who is trying to create and maintain and build a cooperative system is not merely trying to get through the difficult days. He or she is interested even more in the *quality* of the human life of the organization. And to get at this quality Barnard says that moral responsibility is what a leader must exercise. It is a little difficult to pinpoint in empirical research, but isn't that what we are probing for when we dissect our past presidents? Truman, a success for helping us understand the morality of the issues he had to face; Johnson, a failure for hiding the moral dilemma of Viet Nam from us; Kennedy, a success because he could touch the moral nerve of the nation; and Nixon, a failure because he brought no uplifting moral view to the office and because his particular morality was anathema to the people. All of these men reaching out into the individual and collective psyches of the American people. "So among those who cooperate the things that are seen are moved by the things unseen."[70] Underneath the rational, the nonrational.

## Leadership for the School and Leadership of the School

David Bickimer was interested in finding out just what Barnard had said. In addition to his content analysis of *The Functions*, Bickimer spent a good deal of time reading Pareto and Parsons, coming to understand their influences on Barnard's thought. Bickimer was after the central motif of the book, and he decided finally that it was leadership, rather than cooperation or responsibility. If Bickimer is correct then we can afford to smile at a later commentary by Barnard:

> Leadership has been the subject of an extraordinary amount of dogmatically stated nonsense. Some, it is true, has been enunciated by observers who have had no experience themselves in coordinating and directing the activities of others; but much of it has come from men of ample experience, often of established reputations as leaders. As to the latter, we may assume that they know how to do well what they do not know how to describe or explain.[71]

In applying Barnard's views on leadership to education, Bickimer teased out two forms of leadership. The first—leadership *for* the school—is related to the organization that is experienced internally on a daily basis, while the second —leadership *of* the school—is expressed in the organizational environment. Bickimer presents an interesting argument for the similarity in shape of internal and external leadership.

*Leadership for the School*

1. The value hierarchy *for* the school, that is to say the nature of the school's code or faith inasmuch as it is considered within the school.
2. The "take" or attitude of respect and responsibility which exists throughout the school toward the value hierarchy.
3. The commonality or sharedness of this value hierarchy (including the "take" throughout the school).

*Leadership of the School*

4. The value hierarchy of the school inasmuch as it is considered to relate to the wider community and its values.

5.  The attitudinal thrust or "take" of the school toward the value hierarchy in relation to the similar "take" of the community.
6.  The commonality or sharedness of the value hierarchy (including the "take") between the school and the wider community.[72]

In other words, leadership in an organization is characterized (at least in part) by its morality (or values), which is ascribed to by its participants with a certain persistence (or responsibility) and with a certain sharedness (or commonality). Had Barnard read any of George Counts' books? Probably not, and yet both seemed interested in having the school lead the community and not vice versa. Perhaps, as Meyer and Rowan have argued, the school is dominated by the environment rather than being even an equal partner.[73] But the practicing administrator begins where people congregate every day, be that a university quadrangle or a network of schools and other facilities in a community. Bickimer and Barnard are saying that the leader starts internally by helping people pay attention to and clarify their values (which are in a real sense the organization's values), by seeing how respect can be coalesced around these values, and by trying to maximize the sharing of those values. Once that has happened, or even while that is happening, the testing of external waters can begin. But the starting point (internally and externally) is values. They are the central concern of the leader—as well as the ideas associated with them. It is not long term plans or public relations programs or innovations or capital building programs, but values—the moral character of the organization or the system. No legacy of Barnard's thought is more significant than this one.

On the other hand, this is a pretty self-centered view of leadership. Why should the school or school organization expect to be taken seriously, particularly out there in the environment where there are some fiercely competitive moralities on the prowl? Bickimer responds to this by describing two hypotheses that he discovers in *The Functions*. The first of these is that not all values will do. Barnard put it this way, near the end of *The Functions*:

> Organizations endure, however, in proportion to the breadth of the morality by which they are governed. This is only to say that foresight, long purposes, high ideals are the basis for the persistence of cooperation.[74]

Persistence of cooperation is only a polite euphemism for survival. So, Barnard contended, if an organization is going to exist and then lead its community, the *quality* of its values is a critical variable. Educational institutions with little foresight, restricted purposes, and modest ideals will be dominated by the environment, even devoured. Bickimer continues:

> A second hypothesis about leadership is evident in *The Functions*. It involves *creativity*. The evidence of this creativity is the development of resolutions to moral conflicts in the school and the creation of new moral codes for men to live by. And so, in Getzels' terms, the values of an individual in the school often come into conflict with the value stance of the school in general. Moreover, the value stance of the school comes into conflict with the wider community's values. Leadership consists in the resolving of these conflicts and the creation of new value hierarchies.[75]

Is there an assumption here, on the part of either Bickimer or Barnard, that organizations work best when conflict is reduced, when people hold the same values, when organizational goal and individual motive coincide? We may conclude so. Organizations that contend with, challenge—and even lead— their communities must depend on adherence to and faith in common purpose more than in a fragmented collection of philosophies and goals. On the other side of the coin, administrators know that strict conformance is always difficult to achieve and usually undesirable to seek. It is this grappling with moral conflict that excites leaders. A leader *wants* to think about and work with issues that inflame subjective passion, that may take the organization to the brink of collapse, that frighten others. The leader is up to his or her ears in the moral life of the organization. As Bickimer concludes:

> In addition, leadership is further categorized as creative and compulsive inasmuch as at its core, and at the heart of the executive experience, rests the non-logical resolution of moral dilemmas and the "drive" to enforce the solutions on the wills of men.[76]

Compulsive. Nonlogical. Leadership involves intellectual activity, and yet it is powered by instinct. It is a readiness to contend with the unseen and to challenge others in a moral dialectic, always moving toward consensus. Struggling away from conflict and toward consensus.

> Cooperation and organization as they are expressed and experienced are concrete syntheses of opposed facts, and of opposed thought and emotions of human beings. It is precisely the function of the executive to facilitate the synthesis in concrete action of contradictory forces, to reconcile conflicting forces, interests, conditions, positions and ideals.[77]

Barnard said it, but Getzels might have written the same words. A resolution exists if only it can be found.

## THE CONTROL OF LEADERSHIP

Two months before his death, Chester Barnard was giving a good deal of thought to an important idea, and William Wolf discovered what it was. Barnard knew—and perhaps he had known for some time—what the serious flaw was in *The Functions,* and he wished he could do something about it.

> In my opinion, the great weakness of my book is that it doesn't deal adequately with the question of responsibility and its delegation. The emphasis is too much on authority, which is the subordinate subject. Now, all the teaching in business circles, and most of it in military and academic circles, is wrong by my standpoint. The emphasis is put on authority which, to me now, is a secondary, derivative step.[78]

The idea reverberates like a drumbeat during Wolf's interviews with Barnard:

> If I were active and had the mood to do it, what I would do next would be to deal with the subject of responsibility: what we mean by it and who's involved in it, the importance of delegation, why the delegation has to precede any question of authority.[79]

> I'm perfectly confident that, with occasional lapses, if I make a date with you, whom I have never met, you'll keep it and you'll feel confident that I'll keep it; and there's absolutely nothing binding that makes us do it. And yet the world runs on that—you just

couldn't run a college, you couldn't run a business, you couldn't run a church, couldn't do anything except on the basis of the moral commitments that are involved in what we call responsibility. You can't operate a large organization unless you can delegate responsibility, not authority but responsibility. Authority comes second.[80]

But, actually, the military men are as much concerned with the intangibles of the actual distribution of responsibility as they are with any question of authority. Any good military man will tell his officers your job is to get this done by persuasion. You can't make it persuasion, you can't label it that; but that's what it must be. Anytime you have to court-martial too many people, there's something wrong with your management. You'd say *that* in any organization. Anytime when the boss can't hold his people, there's no rule of authority that will help him.[81]

He had watched the reaction to his book over several decades, and it was his definition of authority that had captivated his readers—not his views on responsibility, and especially not those on moral responsibility that provided the crescendo for *The Functions*.[82] Those final pages must have sounded like a sermon or a coach's pep talk to more than one reader. Worse yet, Barnard realized that he had not written sufficiently on what clearly was preoccupying him now—the *delegation* of responsibility.

Administrators always have grumbled, "I don't want the authority without the responsibility." We have thought they meant the *right* to do something as well as the total *control* over the situation and the decision, with whatever rewards or punishments might accrue. "Let *me* do it, boss. Leave me alone and back me up. Put the matter entirely within my jurisdiction." Is this what Barnard meant by the delegation of responsibility?

At one level Barnard was arguing that leadership is not simply a function of the top executives in an organization. He stated as much at the beginning of *The Functions*:

The functions of the executive with which the last part of this treatise is concerned are those of control, management, supervision, administration in formal organizations. These functions are exercised not merely by high officials but by all those who are in a position of control of whatever degree.[83]

Well, that would include even the custodian in an elementary school. *Particularly* the custodian, many principals would add. It was an idea that Barnard came back to at the end of the treatise. "The formulation and definition of purpose is then a widely distributed function, only the more general part of which is executive."[84] Setting purposes and directions and goals is not simply the province of the bosses; it is a task that the people of an organization share, whether the bosses like that or not. And the other two key executive functions—eliciting the cooperation of others and establishing communication networks—are shared activities, Barnard would argue. Shared leadership. It is such an admirable view of the organization, but it would not satisfy Barnard. The delegation of responsibility involves more than merely relinquishing control over a decision, more than sharing the basic executive functions. It has something to do with the sharing of *moral* responsibility, or responsibility for the quality of the values of the organization.

Like everyone else, educational administrators start out trying to become independent from their parents, gaining control over their own lives. And if they can do that, and ward off all of those other adults—like teachers—who try to put hooks into them, and especially if they can do that quite successfully, they are likely to assume leadership roles. An administrator in an organization—confident, assertive, in charge. Far too many start out by trying to tell others what to do in a direct, unequivocal manner. The sins of the parents are revisited. Abraham Maslow believed that

> the person who seeks for power is the one who is just exactly likely to be the one who shouldn't have it, because he neurotically and compulsively needs power. Such people are apt to use power very badly; that is, use it for overcoming, overpowering, hurting people, or to say it in other words, they use it for their own selfish gratifications, conscious and unconscious, neurotic as well as healthy. The task, the job, the objective requirements of the situation tend to be forgotten or lost in the shuffle when such a person is the leader.[85]

In their own glut of independence, such young leaders forget about the needs of others for independence and for a share of the control of an organization. Cooperation is maimed and destroyed more often than it is created. Perhaps fortunately, many of these leaders end up in the organizational wastebasket. Where they do not, cooperation becomes perfunctory and minimal.

Those that continue to grow up begin to release control, sharing it sometimes and grasping for it at others, often in a fitful and unpredictable pattern that is confusing to the organization. The struggle is not without its perils, as Hodgkinson has observed.

> Yet, to fuse individual morality with social decision is difficult; it demands much, as Barnard constantly stressed, in the way of moral complexity. In comprehending this complexity, it is necessary to cope with two difficult concepts: self-interest and responsibility.[86]

Sometimes administrators at this point in their careers share too much, relinquishing duties as well as powers in a laissez-faire pattern. No one seems to be in charge, and the missing hand on the tiller is noticed. The mortality rate is high at this stage, too.

For those who persist, control begins to be a matter of nuance and routine. Work is delegated to others. Decision making begins to be shared. Decisions not to decide are made—and even, as Donald Riddle pointed out, decisions are made not to be involved at all in some parts of the life of an organization. Was *this* what Barnard meant by the delegation of responsibility?

Barnard, most probably, would not be satisfied yet. In the simplest terms, Barnard wanted to have his cake and eat it, too. He wanted to share leadership, to be certain, but he wanted to *control* leadership even more, to help the organization not only survive but prosper. Through his experience and his reflection he had discovered the way for a leader to make this happen. *By delegating the moral responsibility that lies at the pinnacle of leadership and gaining the authority that is reciprocated, the leader is able to generate the cooperation and commitment needed by the organization and is able to continue as the formal leader as well.* Winners all around—the leader, the followers, the collectivity. The leader at this stage is not controlling people, at least not directly, and it is much more than delegation and supervision and evaluation that is brought about. If you mature this much, then you can enjoy a new kind of power—indirect, subtle without being manipulative, pervasive, beneficial. The authority that is given by followers to a leader that permits the *persistence* of that particular leader has deep moral roots. What Barnard regretted was that he had not been able to give us this final piece of the puzzle in *The Functions*.

There are many ways to look at the job of the administrator in an educational institution. Increasingly, it is considered unstable if not unsavory employment, although not perhaps as distressing as that of the politician. A contemporary journalist describes the political drive in words that might befit those seeking any administrative role:

> Excepting madness, there seems little reason why anybody should want to be a mayor. Indeed, in the medieval Swedish town of Hurdenburg, the job was looked upon as a curse. Elections were conducted as follows: The leading townsmen sat around a table, bending forward so their beards rested on the tabletop, and then a louse was placed at the table's center. The man into whose beard the louse then crawled was declared mayor of Hurdenburg for the following year.[87]

There is a different point of view, and a Dutch writer of mystery stories has captured it as well as any. A high-ranking police official, the commissaris, is talking to the sweetheart of one of his best detectives.

> "You're his boss," Nellie said.
> The commissaris smiled. "These are modern times, Nellie. Nobody is a boss anymore. We all work together."
> "But he's got to do as you tell him."
> "Well. . . ." the commissaris said. "In a way, perhaps."
> "All the way. Now, suppose Hank won't do as you say. All the time, I mean."
> "That would rather interfere with our cooperation," the commissaris said. "But I don't think I would damn the good adjutant."[88]

It does not matter if it is the Amsterdam police department or the Atlanta Public Schools. Administrators who make organizations tick are after cooperation through the subtle exercise of a new form of control. There are still bosses, but their touch is so much lighter.

Yes, the maturing of the educational administrator is a slow and painful process. First, the administrator is told about the nature of work. "What am I *supposed* to do?" Then the administrator learns what the work really is in a particular setting. "What is it that I *have* to do in order to survive?" As the administrator settles into organizational life, learning the ropes, that question is transformed into "What *should* I be doing to help myself and the organization?" Often it takes years of experience for the question finally to evolve into a more responsible shape. "What is it that the *organization should be* doing?"

Perhaps theory is most useful in providing direction to the practicing administrator, rather than directions. Getzels helps with the answer to the third question above. He tells the administrator to focus squarely on the tension between the organization and the individual; further, he suggests that one means of developing cooperation in the organization is for the administrator to work specifically in reducing role and personality conflicts. Here is an important and enduring lever of control. But for Barnard it is the search for the answer to the fourth question that is even more significant. He is after a commitment that no mere mediator can gain from organizational colleagues. Leadership is his central motif, and he wants to control it for the benefit of the organization. The delegation of responsibility is the link not only between leadership and cooperation, but also between leadership and authority. As responsibility is accepted by subordinates, commitment to the organization and cooperation within it expand, and control and authority return to the administrator. For the administrator this is the essence of organizational control.

# NOTES

[1]Barney G. Glaser and Anselm L. Strauss, *The Discovery of Grounded Theory* (Chicago: Aldine, 1967).

[2]Joseph G. Schwab, "The Professorship in Educational Administration, Theory-Art-Practice," in *The Professorship in Educational Administration* (Columbus, Ohio: University Council for Educational Administration, 1964), p. 67.

[3]Daniel Katz and Robert L. Kahn, *The Social Psychology of Organizations* (New York: John Wiley & Sons, 1966), p. 29. First edition.

[4]Daniel Katz and Robert L. Kahn, *The Social Psychology of Organizations* (New York: John Wiley & Sons, 1978), p. iii. Second edition.

[5]Roald F. Campbell, Luvern L. Cunningham, Raphael O. Nystrand, and Michael D. Usdan, *The Organization and Control of American Schools*, 5th ed. (Columbus, Ohio: Charles E. Merrill, 1980), pp. 5–6.

[6]Roald F. Campbell, "A History of Administrative Thought," *Administrator's Notebook* 26 (1977-78): 1-4.

[7]Luvern L. Cunningham, Walter G. Hack, and Raphael O. Nystrand, eds., *Educational Administration: The Developing Decades*, (Berkeley: McCutchan, 1977).

[8]Donald A. Erickson, "Research on Educational Administration: The State- of-the-Art," *Educational Researcher* 8 (1977): 9-14.

[9]Daniel E. Griffiths, "Intellectual Turmoil in Educational Administration," *Educational Administration Quarterly* 15 (1979): 43-65.

[10]Glenn L. Immegart and William L. Boyd, eds., *Problem-Finding in Educational Administration.*

[11]Norman J. Boyan, "Follow the Leader: Commentary on Research in Educational Administration," *Educational Researcher*, 10 (1981): 6-13.

[12]Ibid., p. 12.

[13]Andrew W. Halpin, ed., *Administrative Theory in Education* (Chicago: Midwest Administration Center, University of Chicago, 1958), p. iii.

[14]Ibid., p. iii.

[15]Andrew W. Halpin, ed., *Administrative Theory in Education* (New York: Macmillan, 1969), p. xv.

[16]Talcott Parsons, "Some Ingredients of a General Theory of Formal Organization," in Andrew W. Halpin, ed., *Administrative Theory in Education*, pp. 40-72.

[17]Jacob W. Getzels, "Administration as a Social Process," in Halpin, *Administrative Theory in Education*, pp. 150-165. See also the earlier and closely related article by Jacob W. Getzels and Egon G. Guba, "Social Behavior and the Administrative Process," *School Review*, 65 (1957): 423-441.

[18]Jacob W. Getzels, "A Psycho-sociological Framework for the Study of Educational Administration," *Harvard Educational Review*, 22 (1952): 235-246.

[19]Ibid.

[20]Arthur P. Coladarci and Jacob W. Getzels, *The Use of Theory in Educational Administration* (Stanford, Calif.: School of Education, Stanford University, 1955).

[21]Getzels, "Administration as a Social Process," p. 151.

[22]Ibid., pp. 151-152.

[23]David A. Bickimer, *Chester I. Barnard and Educational Administration.* (Unpublished doctoral dissertation, Department of Education, University of Chicago, 1968).

[24]Jacob W. Getzels, "Problem Finding and Research in Educational Administration," in Glenn L. Immegart and William L. Boyd, eds., *Problem- Finding in Educational Administration* (Lexington, Mass.: D.C. Heath, 1979), pp. 5-22

[25]Getzels, "Administration as a Social Process," p. 165.

[26]Jacob W. Getzels and Herbert A. Thelen, "The Classroom as a Unique Social System," in N.B. Henry, ed., *The Dynamics of Instructional Groups* (Chicago: University of Chicago Press, 1960), pp. 53-82. Fifty-ninth Yearbook of the National Society for the Study of Education.

[27]Ibid., p. 81.

[28]Jacob W. Getzels, "Conflict and Role Behavior in the Educational Settings," in W.W. Charters, Jr., and Nathan L. Gage, eds., *Readings in the Social Psychology of Education* (Boston: Allyn & Bacon, 1963), pp. 309-318.

[29]Jacob W. Getzels, James M. Lipham, and Roald F. Campbell, *Educational Administration as a Social Process* (New York: Harper & Row, 1968).

[30]Ibid., pp. 104-105.

[31]Ibid., p. 106.

[32]Jacob W. Getzels, "The Communities of Education," *Teachers College Record* 79 (1978): 659-682.

[33]Wayne K. Hoy and Cecil G. Miskel, *Educational Administration: Theory, Research, and Practice,* 2nd ed. (New York: Random House, 1982), p. 65.

[34]See Getzels, Lipham, and Campbell, *Educational Administration as a Social Process.*

[35]Roald F. Campbell, "The Professorship in Educational Administration—A Personal View," *Educational Administration Quarterly* 17 (1981): 14.

[36]See also William L. Boyd and Robert L. Crowson, "The Changing Conception and Practice of Public School Administration," in David C. Berliner, ed., *Review of Research in Education,* Vol. Nine (Washington, D.C.: American Educational Research Association, 1981), p. 317.

[37]Getzels, "A Psycho-sociological Framework for the Study of Educational Administration."

[38]Paula Silver, "The Development of a Knowledge Base for the Practice of Educational Administration," *Administrator's Notebook* 29 (1980-81): 1-4.

[39]C.P. Snow, *Science and Government* (Cambridge, Mass.: Harvard Universiy Press, 1961), pp. 60-61.

[40]William B. Wolf, *Conversations with Chester I. Barnard* (Ithaca, New York: New York State School of Industrial and Labor Relations, Cornell University, 1973).

[41]Chester I. Barnard, *The Functions of the Executive* (Cambridge, Mass.: Harvard University Press, 1938).

[42]Kenneth R. Andrews, "Introduction" to Chester I. Barnard, *The Functions of the Executive* (Cambridge, Mass.: Harvard University Press, 1968), p. xiii.

[43]Wolf, p. 43.

[44]Ibid., pp. 56-58.

[45]Ibid., p. 14.

[46]Barnard, *The Functions,* p. 296.

[47]Getzels and Guba, "Social Behavior and the Administrative Process," pp. 433-435. Getzels uses the terms *effectiveness* and *efficiency* precisely as Barnard defined them earlier.

[48]Wolf, p. 28.

[49]Ibid., pp. 29-30.

[50]Barnard, *The Functions,* p. 80.

[51]Ibid., p. 259.

[52]Ibid., p. xii.

[53]Chester I. Barnard, *Organization and Management* (Cambridge, Mass.: Harvard University Press, 1952).

[54]Ibid., p. 133.

[55]Ibid., p. 132.

[56]Barnard, *The Functions,* p. 82.

[57]Ibid., p. 217.

[58]Ibid., p. 120

[59]Ibid., p. 123.

[60]Ibid., p. 163.

[61]Ibid., p. 165.

[62]Ibid., p. 194 (Barnard's italics).

[63]Ibid., p. 55.

[64]Ibid., pp. 56-57.

[65]Christopher Hodgkinson, *Towards a Philosophy of Administration* (New York: St. Martin's Press, 1978), pp. 183-184. Hodgkinson uses *The Functions* as a pivotal piece of organizational literature in his unique attempt to develop the framework of a philosophy of administration.

[66]Barnard, *Organization*, p. 39.

[67]Barnard, *The Functions*, p. 239.

[68]Ibid., p. 260.

[69]Ibid., p. 267.

[70]Ibid., p. 284.

[71]Barnard, *Organization*, p. 80.

[72]Bickimer, *Chester I. Barnard and Educational Administration*, pp. 209-210.

[73]John W. Meyer and Brian Rowan, "The Structure of Educational Organizations," in J. W. Meyer, ed., *Enviroments and Organizations* (San Francisco: Jossey-Bass, 1978), pp. 78-109.

[74]Barnard, *The Functions*, p. 282.

[75]Bickimer, p. 214.

[76]Ibid., p. 188.

[77]Barnard, *The Functions*, p. 21.

[78]Wolf, p. 15.

[79]Ibid., p. 23.

[80]Ibid., p. 35.

[81]Ibid., p. 50

[82]Hodgkinson, p. 13. Hodgkinson is one of the few contemporary scholars who has been interested in Barnard's views on moral responsibility. He places Barnard (we think appropriately) in the Platonic tradition, and that coincides with Barnard's contention that he was writing what essentially was an essay. Hodgkinson observes: "Barnard, writing out of his own experience, is distinctively different from Herbert Simon in that he is greatly concerned with the *moral* component in executive behavior. This moral aspect is linked to his concepts of responsibility and leadership and would seem to imply that the closer the administrator approximated ideal performance of executive functions, the more he would take on the necessary paragon proportions. Barnard's executive elite is a moral elite, a secular priesthood, one within which Dostoevsky's Grand Inquisitor would feel quite at home. This preoccupation with morality renders him somewhat unique in this field of thought."

[83]Barnard, *The Functions*, p. 6.

[84]Ibid., p. 233.

[85]Abraham H. Maslow, *Eupsychian Management* (Homewood, Ill.: Irwin, 1965), p. 125.

[86]Hodgkinson, p. 175.

[87]Jeff Lyon, "Life After City Hall: What's a Mayor To Do?", *Chicago Tribune*, April 28, 1983, Section 3, 1.

[88]Janwillem van de Wetering, *Streetbird* (New York: G.P. Putnam's Sons, 1983), pp. 125-126.

# FIVE

## THE PRACTICE OF THEORY

The final section of the book contains eight instructional cases, each of which is intended to present further opportunities for the reader to explore relationships between theory and practice in educational administration. By the *practice of theory* we refer to the conscious use of theories, models, and concepts in some manner by practitioners in their day to day work. In pointing to the explicit rather than the implicit use of theory by practitioners, we are raising once again a problem that has been a difficult one for the field. In writing this book we have assumed that theory is useful to principals and superintendents and headmasters and deans in certain forms and in certain circumstances. But must administrators be aware of theory as they act? Must they be able to manipulate theory for pragmatic advantage?

The question is not one merely for the practicing administrator. It appears, for instance, as a substantial issue for administrators in training at the advanced graduate level. Once a doctoral student in educational administration has defined a problem for dissertation research, the question that the dissertation advisor tends to pose next is "What is the conceptual framework for your study?" It is not an easy question for most students to understand, much less to answer, especially not for the student whose background has included classroom teaching and some modest, entry-level administrative assignments. Lacking solid experience as a researcher, the student puzzles over the relationship of a conceptual framework to the problem, as well as the influence of theory on the choice of hypotheses or guiding questions; on the selection of a methodology; and particularly on the analysis of collected data. The student must open up the theoretical base for the study to the scrutiny not only of the dissertation committee of professors, but eventually to readers of the dissertation. This experience can be a jarring one.

William Whyte describes the same problem as it is faced by leaders in organizations.

> When we set out to build an organization, we have in mind a theoretical model of that organization. When we set out to change an organization, we have in mind a theoretical model of what the reorganized structure should resemble. A man of action may deny that he is guided by any theoretical model. That is only to say that his assumptions about organizations remain implicit and are thus not available for conscious analysis and evaluation. . . . Man can act more effectively if he recognizes the organization models he carries around in his head and tests them against the realities of experience.
>
> I believe that many organizational problems arise because the leaders of those organizations are attempting to apply to the human problems they face an inappropriate theoretical model of organization. I also believe that most men carry in their heads an extremely limited repertoire of models. They could act with more understanding and effectiveness if they made their own models explicit and if they could become more flexible and inventive in developing and applying models to the problems they face.[1]

In Whyte's estimation, the practitioner's need to employ theories and models consciously is no less than that of the scholar; the practitioner can be truly efficient and flexible only if theoretically aware.

Cyril Sargent and Eugene Belisle present a somewhat contrasting point of view.

> The important thing is the extent to which the behavior of an administrator in a situation (including the examination of a case) reveals interpretations which are illuminated by

concepts which are included in his mental resources. It may or may not be pertinent —and it frequently is not, in mature administrative behavior—to verbalize the concepts, and particularly to verbalize them in academic language.[2]

While they would agree with Whyte in respect to the crucial linkage between concepts and practice in the life of the administrator, Sargent and Belisle are less committed to the conscious use of theory. Perhaps the professor discussing a case with a student should be able to identify the theories and models lurking in the student's mind, but the student need not do so, and the same might be said for the administrator at work.

We take our stand with Whyte rather than with Sargent and Belisle. We believe that while the practitioner's verbalization of underpinning theory may not need to be as consistent as that of the scholar, it does need to be more conscious and more explicit than is regularly the case today with educational administrators. As a consequence, we suggest that as professors and graduate students and field administrators read and analyze these cases, they quite consciously identify and discuss specific theoretical constructs which open up their understandings of these slices of practice. Among these constructs we hope will be many which are discussed earlier in this book, and indeed the selection of cases here is not unrelated to those chapters. However, we anticipate that analysis of these cases will permit the reader to review and test an even wider range of conceptual knowledge from many sources.

We have heeded Whyte's contention in developing the direction sets following each case. The reader is asked to begin analysis by identifying and specifying the implicit conceptual frameworks with which he or she normally would approach the problem or problems of the case. Subsequently the reader will be asked to delineate alternative—and perhaps less frequently employed—conceptual frameworks. Beyond that point, many readers also may wish to select the framework which seems to hold most promise in application to the basic issues of that specific case.

Making the initial linkage between theory and the data of a given case, which may be the most difficult task of all, should provide focus for the reader in using these cases. We are interested as well, however, in the determination of a course of action (and a sound critique of it) where a wise path is only partially apparent or not apparent at all. Cyril O'Donnell draws our attention to this second major emphasis of case analysis:

> The basic purpose of a case is to provide students with factual information so that they may analyze the situation in terms of the manager's functions and reach conclusions concerning the quality of management and the decisions which should be made if appropriate goals are to be reached.[3]

This counsel is important particularly in its suggestion that any solution of the dilemmas or problems inherent in a case probably will resemble a sequence of decisions rather than a command decision. For the educational administrator decision making is serial and muted more often than it is singular and earth shaking. It must be said, too, that theories and models are not to be discarded once the counterpoint between concept and problem has been established. Jay Lorsch and Paul Lawrence suggest that

> like the problem solver in other fields, the manager concerned with organizational issues

needs analytic tools which will provide him with ways of thinking about the problems he faces and the solutions available.[4]

Even at the point of problem solving or decision making, the administrator finds a prevailing theory or model still useful in the testing of alternative directions and responses.

Those who use case studies must be alert to the cognitive pitfalls which are rooted in the perspectives of the practitioner and the scholar, and thus to some degree in their own experiences. Practitioners have a predilection for action rather than contemplation; as a consequence, they move perhaps too quickly to the solution stage of the problem process. Often they decry theory as impractical, failing to see that theory is not a descriptor of administrative action, but rather a precursor to it. In addition, practitioners often prefer to trust common sense and intuition rather than conceptual frameworks in sizing up difficult situations. We suspect that in some measure this is so simply because most administrators have not been exposed in their professional education to middle-range theories and models which can be applied to leadership tasks in educational organizations. But even more significantly, few have received assistance in job settings, either before service or during service, in exploring theory and practice relationships. Administrative conversation in work settings is only rarely concerned with such matters.

Moreover, theories often contradict each other, as the following two do, and this is confusing to the practitioner.

> If we select a mechanical-rational model, for example, we may place great emphasis on clarifying responsibility and authority and on developing clearly defined reporting relationships from top to bottom of the organizational hierarchy. On the other hand, if we are attracted to models with a natural system or biological base, we may be more concerned with developing an organization where trust and openness are the norms, and where there is the fullest possible involvement of all members in decision-making.[5]

Which is the correct model, and how is a choice to be made, if the position of the central office seems to support the first whereas feelings in the local school community seem to require the second? We urge the reader not only to live with such conceptual complexity, but to *construct it* as these cases are considered. An appropriate conceptual framework for one case and one problem may differ considerably from that needed for the problems of the next case and any one case may demand an amalgam of theoretical perspectives as a prerequisite to understanding and proposed action.

The confusion of theory with policy is another difficulty for certain practitioners. The effective schools movement provides such an instance. Because the movement has an intriguing (if uneven) research base, administrators tend to view its tenets as a theoretical model. They might be described more precisely, however, as a prescriptive set of policy recommendations, attractive especially to educators and citizens interested in the reform of practice in urban elementary schools serving poor children.

Scholars who press their theories upon practitioners bring biases of their own which can be distorting. Some are wedded to a particular theory or model (often their own), and they may be reluctant to consider alternative theoretical explanations applicable to a situation or a case. Others apply theories developed in related

disciplines and professional fields somewhat indiscriminately to educational administration. Sometimes the match is useful (for example, Barnard's theory of authority,
drawn from his business experience), but sometimes the relationship is spurious (for
example, the Lippitt and White model of leadership, drawn from research on
adolescent behavior in clubs). We believe—although an opposite point of view is
available—that theories and models are not related to practice by definition. The
capacity to illuminate practice is neither a criterion for theory construction nor an
unfailing test of a theory's efficacy. In addition, scholars often fail to distinguish
between grounded and ungrounded theory. Grounded theory, such as the Hanson
problem-solving model, often has a better sense of fit for the educational administrator because it is generated out of the interaction of theoreticians and practitioners in
field settings. But even some ungrounded theory—such as the Parsonism levels of
organization—may be immediately useful to the administrator.

For both the student who is remote from practice (for whom the case is the best
possible representation of life in the field) and the harried practitioner who is
submerged in that reality, the analysis of a case encourages logical thought and
stimulates careful judgment. We do not assume that educational administrators
always have time for such reflections, but we do believe that the inclination to reflect
needs to be encouraged rather more than the inclination to act. The actual solution of
a case problem is perhaps less important than an improved understanding of the
sources of the problem, or the implications of the handling of a problem for policy in
the particular social system, or the assessment of whether the problem might have
been avoided, and, if so, how it might have been avoided. Indeed, practice in the
management process is in itself an important application of theory to practice. A final
attribute of case analysis is its indeterminate quality. The discussion of a case among
professional colleagues is a creative experience with unknown ends, dependent upon
the clash of experiences, theoretical perspectives, and insights contributed by the
participants.

Case analysis is not a panacea for the ills of the preparation and continuing
education of educational administrators. As Cyril O'Donnell has noted, no case can
give a student a sense of the real weight of responsibility and pressure for decision
that practicing administrators must bear.[6] Nor can the reader here who has not
served an administrative turn fully comprehend the irreversible nature of most
decisions, set as they are within the web of an organization and its overlapping
collections of decisions made by many actors over time. In addition, the information
presented in any case is limited, and thus a cryptic situation is pictured. To be sure,
administrators often must consider a problem in the light of insufficient data, and to
this extent a case may mirror reality. Yet this is a somewhat facile argument when it
can be applied to virtually every case. Finally, remember that the enveloping idea
which sets the context for the case study is that the central task of the administrator is
to see that problems are solved and to make certain that key decisions are made.

Each of the following cases is drawn from the actual experience of an
educational administrator. In all but one the names and circumstances of the
administrators, as well as details of their experiences, have been changed to preserve
anonymity. As a group the cases picture a variety of key administrative roles at the
elementary, secondary, and post-secondary levels of American education. The
dilemmas and problems that these administrators have faced, as well as the courses of

action they have selected, present a range of issues and themes from differing institutional and community settings for the consideration of the reader. Certain of the cases contain extended passages of dialog as well as field documents, and they vary considerably in length.

The tendency of many case studies for educational administrators is to bring the reader to the brink of decision, to prompt the question, "What should I do now?" Our objective here is somewhat different. Because we wish to promote a reflective, searching behavior in the reader—because problem orientation is more important to us than problem solution—many of these cases do not focus on the controversy and crisis which seem to demand immediate action. Rather they emphasize the conflict for which planning and longer-range decisions are required. Many of the cases lend themselves to a post hoc review of the decisions made by the administrator central to the case.

As much as sound case analysis demands active participants and thoughtful processes, it is called forth even more by the quality of the case itself.

> Cases do not, of course, correspond to the original reality, no matter how faithfully they reflect it. But to the practicing or potential educational administrator, a good case seems to serve as a magnet. All movement away from the case represents attempts to perceive it from new perspectives; the case itself remains the center of attention. Perhaps there is no better definition of a good case in educational administration.[7]

We hope that at least for some of our readers some of these cases will meet this high Sargent and Belisle standard.

## NOTES

[1]William F. Whyte, "Models for Building and Changing Organizations," *Human Organization*, 26 (Spring-Summer, 1967): 22.

[2]Cyril G. Sargent and Eugene L. Belisle, *Educational Administration: Cases and Concepts* (Boston: Houghton Mifflin, 1955), p. 10. This textbook was an early and still singular contribution to the subject of case analysis in educational administration. While inevitably some of the cases are dated, the authors' discussion of the relationship of knowledge, experience, and training is exemplary. Other sources that may be useful to those pursuing the case study method include Kenneth R. Andrews, ed., *The Case Method of Teaching Human Relations and Administration* (Cambridge: Harvard University Press, 1953); Bernard Lubin, Leonard D. Goodstein, and Alice W. Lubin, eds., *Cases in Organizational Development* (La Jolla, Calif.: University Associates, 1979); Richard A. Gorton, *School Administration and Supervision: Important Issues, Concepts, and Case Studies*, 2nd ed. (Dubuque, Iowa: William C. Brown, 1980). This is one of the few recent books devoted exclusively to cases in educational administration. Most of the cases reflect the work situations of elementary and secondary administrators, and some are too brief to stimulate graduate-level dialog. Nonetheless, a good many of the cases are effective as supplements to classroom discussion. Stephen P. Robbins, *The Administrative Process: Integrating Theory and Practice* (Englewood Cliffs, N. J.: Prentice- Hall, 1976); and Leonard D. Goodstein, Bernard Lubin, and Alice W. Lubin, *Cases in Conflict Management* (La Jolla, Calif.: University Associates, 1979).

[3]Cyril O'Donnell, *Cases in General Management* (Homewood, Illinois: Irwin, 1965), p. 3.

[4]Jay W. Lorsch and Paul R. Lawrence, *Organization Planning: Cases and Concepts* (Homewood, Ill.: Irwin, 1972), p. 2.

[5]Ibid., p. 5.

[6]O'Donnell, *Cases*, p. 4.

[7]Sargent and Belisle, *Educational Administration*, p. 6.

# THE CASE OF
# THE MISSING SECOND

Afterward, when the furor over desegregation had cooled down, the new superintendent realized he should have done his homework more thoroughly. He had lived in that part of the state for some time, and he thought he knew his new school district pretty well. During his entry period, he made particular efforts to learn about the black community. One out of every five citizens in the small city was black, and many black families had roots there going back five and six generations. Tension between working class white and black adults and youth in the city was minimal, a situation probably not unrelated to the fact that the city had been a stop on the underground railroad before the Civil War. Many of the black parents and citizens he encountered already were professionals and businessmen with good incomes, but his drives through the city let him know that other black families were struggling economically and socially. What he did not discover until well into his second month on the job was that one elementary school in the community was all-black, and another was moving quickly in the same direction.

As the all-black school was described to him, he realized that it held a special affection in the hearts of many community members. While the standardized test scores of its students revealed consistently low performance, it was thought of as a school that really cared about its children.

**It's as if people were willing to trade achievement for humaneness,**

the superintendent told himself. To be certain, teachers and administrators could point to a number of successful students who had attended the all-black school, including some pillars of the local black community. However, to the superintendent these seemed like understandable exceptions to a pattern of failure that the test data revealed as persistent over the years. On the other hand, he was lulled a bit by the fact that there had been no discontent in the local high school, as there had been in those of neighboring districts. If there was anger in any part of the black community, the superintendent could not sense it.

The seeds of conflict were sown with a certain amount of innocence during late August, only two weeks before the opening of schools. A predominantly white elementary school had become overcrowded. An existing open enrollment policy had

**369**

failed to lure students to other schools, and the pressure to relieve overcrowding was heavy. It was obvious that some kindergarten children would have to be bused to another school. During a conference in his office with a colleague, the superintendent looked at a school district map and observed that the obvious receiving school was the all-black school.

> It's right next door, and it has plenty of space, if the figures I looked at this morning are correct.

The assistant superintendent looked at him in dismay.

> You must be kidding. There is absolutely no way the community will accept that solution. I'm not going to let you stick your head in the noose. We'll find another receiving school.

Thus, on the first day of school, a bus loaded with kindergarten children left the predominantly white school community; drove across town on a street that passed in front of the all-black school; and deposited the boys and girls outside an all-white elementary school a half mile away. If the problem was overcrowding, nothing more than that, then a solution had been dispensed. However, if a larger issue was lurking in the background (as the assistant superintendent seemed to infer), then the school district had continued to ignore it.

One morning two weeks later the superintendent received a telephone call from the president of the board of education.

> There'll be a meeting at the high school tonight—a special meeting of the board. There seems to be some upset over the busing program. I expect a good-sized crowd, so come prepared.

The superintendent knew that 25–50 observers usually attended public meetings of the board, so he was startled by the sea of 400 faces, most of them black and none of them smiling. Although the group was dominated by parents, it was several black school district employees who took the lead in objecting strenuously to the bypassing of the all-black school. One of them summarized the assembled feelings:

> What's wrong with us? What's wrong with our school? We have plenty of space for these white kindergarten children. You hired a new superintendent, and we thought there would be some changes. But now you've done it again.

The assistant superintendent apparently had been thinking about the feelings and reactions of white citizens of the city rather than black citizens.

The board was comprised of five white and two black members. It was in no position in the emotionally overheated environment to reject this new problem. A motion was accepted with no dissenting votes to study the boundaries of elementary schools in the city and to consider reassignment of elementary attendance areas. The meeting ended with no one particularly satisfied, least of all the superintendent. An issue involving the school attendance of a small number of children had been expanded into an issue involving the school attendance of all the elementary children in the city. Moreover, the superintendent could not tell if the board was serious or if it hoped the problem would melt in the warm hands of the inevitable committee.

The board president and the superintendent met two days later to discuss next steps. The board president indicated that he wanted a study committee composed of board members, administrators, and parents to be organized at once. The superintendent looked him straight in the eye.

> Let's not play games. The real problem is desegregation, not just a busload of kids or redrawing lines on a map. We're not going to get away with a new set of elementary school boundaries. And if the issue *is* desegregation, then it includes a lot more than realignment. The impact on racial balance in the junior high schools and the high school is at stake. And the future use of buildings, now that our environment is declining. And, most of all, the achievement of poor kids in contrast with the achievement of middle-class and rich kids. What's it going to be?

The board president was noncommittal. The superintendent proceeded with the formation of the study committee, realizing that its efforts might well be ineffective in dousing the fire. It seemed to the superintendent that he was moving further and further away from concrete solutions.

Soon afterward, the superintendent had another conversation with the assistant superintendent who had given him the original advice on busing the kindergarten children. The assistant superintendent observed,

> If you think that was a tough crowd, you can't imagine what it would have been like if it had been mostly white and you were trying to defend sending their kids to an all-black school. The last superintendent never talked about desegregation, publicly or privately. He always told me that it would take the Supreme Court to bring desegregation here. I still advise you forget it. You think you have supporters, but they won't be there later when you need them. I don't want to be involved. I've lived in this city too long, and I want to continue to live here. But I will say this—if you don't deal with the issue of desegregation now, forget it. You're only going to get one chance.

The superintendent silently appreciated the candor of this counsel.

The study committee met first in October to receive its charge from the board. The president said that the board would accept more than one recommendation, and it reserved the right to accept or reject any part or all of the committee report. No one commented on what the superintendent noted as the glaring absence of teachers from the committee. After receiving the report the board would then ask the superintendent and his staff to consider program implications. The superintendent responded somewhat crisply,

> Regardless of the specifics of the committee recommendations, everyone should expect that there will be some major educational changes.

During the months of late autumn and early winter, the buses continued to roll past the all-black school, and the superintendent had some time to think. What was he willing to risk personally on this very difficult matter? After all, it was early in his career, and if he did not exercise some caution perhaps this would be his last superintendency. On the other hand, his deep commitment to combating racial isolation made it difficult for him to take his predecessor's course. He was not a stranger to such battles in school systems; he had shared in the development of a desegregation program in another city in the state when he was an assistant superintendent. What about the school district and the community? The pride of black parents and educators in a school they saw as their own complicated the problem, and it was going to be necessary to find a solution that recognized this fact of life. The pressures were coming from internal as well as external sources, and they were formidable. The chances of finding an answer to a tough, enduring problem of segregation were never very good, but this was a manageable city. Just imagine what the impact of a bold, successful decision might be. How could an answer to the problem help kids get a better education? That was always the objective, of course, but one that became lost so easily and so often in the adult wars. While the issues seemed to be complex and tangled, perhaps there was a simple key to a solution. Well, anyway, the problem had been around a long time, and no one was pressing for a solution by Monday morning. It was in this manner that the superintendent sorted through the variables and decided to place a high priority label on the issue. He was going to try to solve the problem, on his terms if possible.

By early January, time had become the superintendent's adversary rather than his ally. The study committee was floundering in discussion, seemingly months away from a report. If there were changes to be made, the superintendent wanted them to occur the following September. The implementation process might be an extended one, and he could not pull a rabbit out of a hat in late summer. Thus, at a regular board meeting the superintendent chided the board.

> **Are we going to address these issues ourselves, or do you want the courts or perhaps the state to decide for us? I would prefer to have local decisions made by local people. Isn't it about time for the study committee to report and for us to get on with business?**

Acknowledging his concern, the board adopted a resolution establishing the realignment of elementary attendance areas and the solution of all concomitant issues as a goal of the school system. Privately, the board president prodded the committee into action. By early March, its report was ready for presentation to the board and exposure to the community.

The report made four major proposals: retain neighborhood elementary schools; bus students only when absolutely necessary; pair some elementary schools with limited busing programs; and expand school boundaries wherever possible, particularly when schools were closed as enrollment declined. The superintendent was neither surprised nor disappointed, and apparently the board president felt the same way about the conservative suggestions, for he told the superintendent over lunch the next day,

> **I've thanked the committee. Now it's your baby. Give us a report in June.**

The superintendent almost grinned. It was time to name the game and get his chips on the table. Nothing ventured, nothing gained.

The superintendent decided that his first chore was to make up for the board's error and to get the teachers involved. He met with the president of the teacher's union and asked for the help of her organization. She refused him, without explanation. The superintendent then talked with some teachers he knew would be sympathetic to the plan. Three days later another union officer called him to say that the union would be delighted to participate and would be ready to meet with him at any time. Encouraged, the superintendent enlisted the principals as well as typically unrepresented school district employees—the bus drivers and hourly employees such as the secretaries and the clerks. The coalition within the organization was virtually complete and potentially strong.

At the first meeting of the new planning group, the superintendent confessed that the recommendations of the earlier study were not going to be very helpful, in his judgment.

> I think we have to raise this question and answer it: What is the major *educational* issue in our city? Then maybe we can make some sense out of this situation. I want to work on educational problems, not political problems.

The instant response of the group indicated that he had support. The series of meetings that unfolded began to tease out pieces of the answer. At that time the district ranked at only the 40th percentile among all districts in the state with respect to student achievement, even though the schools served a considerable reservoir of families with professional breadwinners and families associated with a large local university. The superintendent shared data with his colleagues revealing severe within-district achievement discrepancies between children from affluent and working-class neighborhoods. The lowest test scores were found in the all-black school. The superintendent commented,

> What seems clear is that the farther along poor kids go in our schools, the worse they do comparatively. How can we make up for the relatively thin pre-school and early elementary backgrounds of poor kids and still maintain a strong educational program for all kids?

Someone replied,

> Isn't that the the answer to your earlier question? Isn't that our major *educational* problem?

All the heads were nodding.

At a session in early May they confronted the issue of busing. The superintendent said that the problem with the March report was that it concentrated too much on the logistics of moving students. A bus driver spoke up:

> What are we talking about? Kids love to ride buses. I know. I drive a bus every school day, and some evenings to boot. Parents are interested in safety, and we can't ignore that. But we ought to be talking most about what happens when the kids get to school. What are they going to *learn* there?

The superintendent knew no one could have said what needed to be said better.

In May the superintendent planted some political seeds. He talked about new educational perspectives at the regular board meeting. Privately, he met with the local newspaper editor and briefed him on the developing plan and its political implications. What was emerging at the heart of the desegregation plan was electric, and, if the board accepted it, he wanted it reported accurately. He began to share information with the board members as well one by one.

Too quickly the June night arrived. The city knew that a momentous occasion was upon it, and 800 of its citizens came to the high school for the board meeting. It was apparent that the auditorium could not hold the crowd, and the meeting was moved to the cafeteria. The superintendent was constrained but fatalistic. It was his gamble, his roll of the dice, and he was ready to accept the consequences. This would be the first voluntary desegregation plan in the state in fifteen years. Could the board and the city buy it? As he drove to the meeting the superintendent recalled the words of his assistant:

> **Bus all the kindergarten kids in the city? You're absolutely crazy!**

He had responded,

> **We'll make it safer than ever. We'll pick up the kids at their front doors if need be.**

His private straw vote indicated that he had six yes votes for the plan, but he wanted seven. He really wanted a unanimous vote.

An almost melodramatic hush fell over the audience as the superintendent unveiled the plan. The superintendent attacked racial isolation in the schools in the city.

> **Do you realize that 85 percent of the black students in our city do not attend school with white children until they reach seventh grade? Do we want this kind of separation to continue?**

He thanked those who had helped in the development of the plan, and then he outlined a basic premise:

> **Each elementary school should reflect the 80:20 white to black racial balance in our city. We recommend that elementary boundaries be redrawn and bus routes established to make this a reality.**

Then he dropped the bombshell. The all-black school would be disbanded as a neighborhood school. It would be converted to a child development center for the entire district, and all pre-school and kindergarten children in the city would attend its resources-rich programs, with all except those who lived but a few blocks away arriving by bus each school morning.

The reaction to the plan from the floor was vigorous, and while the dramatic proposals had their supporters, soon the opposition from both black and white parents and citizens began to dominate the dialogue. The superintendent watched the confidence of some board members who supported him begin to crumble. He asked for the floor once again in order to re-emphasize the educational advantages of bringing the children together—rich and poor, black and white—from the beginning of their school experiences, and to underline the safety precautions that would be taken in the transportation of young children. This effort was apparently to no avail, for a board member with a furrowed brow moved that the board go into an executive session, and his colleagues agreed eagerly.

The superintendent concentrated on keeping his poise in the caucus room. He hoped that the silence of some board members meant that they were standing firm, but he could not be certain of that. A white board member said that once they entered open session she would offer a motion to table the plan, and a black board member indicated that he would second the motion. The superintendent commented,

> I would really prefer a negative vote to a decision to table the plan. This is it. We need to move forward or forget it for now.

As the superintendent returned to the cafeteria with the board, he realized that he had little idea of what was going to happen, but he did not feel optimistic.

The buzzing room quickly came to a dead silence. A hand was raised, and the motion to table the plan was made. What happened next is that nothing happened. The black board member sat impassively, ignoring the stares of the board president and his colleagues. No one else was prepared to second the motion, and it failed without ever coming to a vote. The electricity in the room began to crackle.

The mother of a former student at the all-black school came to the microphone. Everyone knew her and respected her. Her son had been a good student and an outstanding athlete—a college all-American in basketball who moved into a professional career. She said,

> What you all seem to forget is that my husband is a doctor, and I have a master's degree. Why wouldn't you expect our son to do well? We love that elementary school, but maybe it would have been better for my boy not to go there.

The remark struck home with many in the audience, black and white, and the board seemed to gain some of its composure.

A motion to approve the plan was made and seconded. After a brief but agonizing discussion, the votes were counted. The motion was approved 6–1, the lone dissenting vote coming from the black board member who refused to second the motion to table. Later he would tell the superintendent,

> I listened to what you said, and I decided what you said was right. The plan still places too large a burden on black people, and I wanted my vote against the plan recorded.

A week later one incumbent board member lost his seat in the annual election in what was interpreted by some as a reaction to his support of the superintendent's plan.

A year later a poll of citizens showed that while only 60 percent supported the desegregation plan, 85 percent did not want to return to the old way of doing business in the school system.

Four years later achievement scores were rising steadily in the district's elementary schools, and its improving position statewide was applauded by the local press.

Five years later a bond issue was passed by a 3-2 margin to provide monies to revitalize a school in the old central area of the city where businesses were recovering dramatically from a three-decade economic slump.

## THEORETICAL QUESTIONS

1. What forces or issues within the organization and its environment appear to influence the flow of events within the case and to shape the central problem or problems?
2. What is the central problem, or which are the central problems?
3. What theoretical perspective does the superintendent seem to bring to this situation?

4. What theoretical perspective do you tend to bring initially to this situation?
5. Are there additional conceptual frameworks that might be useful in developing an understanding of this case?
6. What are the implications of these conceptual frameworks for developing solution strategies?
7. Which single or combined perspective do you feel is most appropriate for developing an action strategy?

## CASE SPECIFIC QUESTIONS

8. What line of reasoning seemed to prompt the coalition-building efforts of the superintendent?
9. How was the typically strong professional and citizen resistance to busing for desegregation overcome by the superintendent?
10. How did the superintendent approach and deal with the matter of administrative risk?
11. What insights into the relationship between a superintendent and a board of education does this case provide?

## ACTION QUESTIONS

12. Were the appropriate persons or roles involved in the processes of analysis and decision making?
13. How critical was time as a planning and decision factor?
14. Which key strategic data were discovered by the superintendent?
15. Were solution alternatives available? How might they have been tested by the superintendent?
16. Faced with this situation, what would you have done? Is your guiding theoretical perspective helpful as you consider this question?

# 2

## THE CASE OF THE LAST JUDGMENT

▌▌▌▌▌▌▌▌▌▌▌▌▌▌▌▌▌▌▌▌▌▌▌▌▌▌▌▌▌▌▌▌▌▌▌▌▌▌▌▌▌▌▌▌▌▌▌▌▌▌▌▌▌▌▌▌▌▌▌▌▌▌▌▌▌▌▌▌▌▌▌▌▌

The high school principal parked his car in its familiar spot and entered the building through the boiler-room exit, which he knew would be open. A large clock on the wall near the cafeteria informed him that it was 7:15 A.M. He was right on schedule, about 45 minutes before the beginning of the first period. One of the secretaries would have been in the office for a quarter of an hour, and the coffee would be ready. Moving at a quick pace, he rounded a bend in the hallway and barged into two custodians carrying a heavy oak table toward the front entrance of the school.

> Where are you going with this monstrosity, Fred?
>
> It's for the men who are going to pass out the Bibles.
>
> What are you talking about?
>
> Well, they got here about ten minutes ago and brought their boxes in, and they said it had been O.K.'d, so we were just trying to be helpful. Is there anything wrong?

Bewildered, the principal followed them up the long corridor. Sure enough, a small group of early-arriving students and teachers had begun to cluster around the two men in business suits. They were standing next to at least a dozen boxes which apparently contained the Bibles. The principal introduced himself to the two men and inquired about the purpose of their visit to the school that morning.

> Didn't you get our letter? I brought it over to your office yesterday afternoon, just to make sure there wouldn't be any slip-ups.
>
> No, I'm sorry that I didn't. I was with our swimming team at a meet in Beloit yesterday, and we didn't get back until the early evening. So I didn't come back to my office. The letter is probably on my desk now. Did you discuss this plan to pass out the Bibles with anyone?
>
> Yes, with your Board of Education president—Dave Arlington—at the Rotary Club meeting last Wednesday. He said that he was sure it would be all right.

The principal was stunned. Personally, he was opposed to the idea, and he knew a lot of students and teachers and parents would be on his neck by midmorning if the Bibles were distributed. He remembered vaguely reading about a court decision which prohibited the distribution of religious materials in public schools, but did that decision apply in this state and in this community? Had the board president really given his approval, or were the two men eagerly misinterpreting a friendly conversation? Where did the superintendent fit into all of this? He and Dave Arlington weren't getting along all that well right now—he knew that for certain. The principal did not have much time, but he needed to use a little of it.

> I wonder if you two gentlemen would mind coming with me to my office. I really do need to check with our superintendent before you proceed.

He asked a custodian to stay with the boxes of books, and the three men moved toward the office. The principal knew he was in a tight corner. On the one hand, he wanted to avoid creating an issue within the school, particularly one that had been concocted somewhere else. He could not be certain of the legality of the Bible distribution without advice from the school district lawyer, who never seemed to be available for quick counsel when it was needed. However, he was not eager to countermand a decision of the board president. Would calling the superintendent suggest that he could not handle his own problems? These things really ought to break loose *after* one cup of coffee.

He asked the two men to wait for him in the outer office. Sure enough, there was the letter, propped up against the telephone where his secretary had left it the previous afternoon to catch his attention. He read it quickly as he was dialing the superintendent's number.

> We represent the Christian Community Action Program. As you may know, we distribute free Bibles to the young people in the tri-county area. In the past we have been welcomed into almost every school in this area, although we have never had the pleasure of working in your school. We believe that the many problems facing the youth of today and, particularly, the ones that we know you are facing in your school can be helped greatly if our young people have an opportunity to read the Holy Scriptures.
>
> We are not forcing our program on anyone. Each student can choose to receive a Bible or not, and there is absolutely no charge to the students and their parents.
>
> We will have a large supply of Bibles in the school tomorrow morning. Could you please provide us with several tables near the main entrance? That is all that we will need. I think we can finish up tomorrow and then perhaps we can come back again near the close of the school year.
>
> We have talked with Dave Arlington, and he says this would be O.K., although he said he hadn't had a chance to talk to anyone else about it yet.

The superintendent's secretary said that he was at the state capitol for a legislative hearing and that he would not return to the office until late afternoon. The associate superintendent was available, however. The principal hurriedly reviewed the letter and the facts of the matter with his central offices colleague. As he looked out the window while they were talking, he could see the first buses from the country rolling up the driveway to the traffic circle.

I don't know quite what to tell you to do, Myron. One thing that's for sure though—if I were sitting in your chair I wouldn't cross Dave Arlington.

Shrugging mentally, the principal closed off the conversation and placed the telephone back in its cradle. He would have to decide now, but perhaps keep the options open a little longer, without insulting anyone. He waved the two men back into the inner office.

I haven't been able to make contact with the superintendent because he's out of town today. I wonder if you would be willing to help me out a little bit by waiting until Friday to distribute the Bibles. I'll store your boxes safely right here in the school so that you won't be inconvenienced. That will give me time to touch bases and make certain that everyone agrees with their distribution, which I am sure is what you would want, too.

The two men agreed with remarkably good cheer, and the three of them walked back to the table in the corridor where the principal gave the custodian instructions regarding the security of the Bibles and thanked the two men for their cooperation. He promised to call one of them by Thursday noon with the decision. Three days seemed like an eternity at this point. He would have plenty of time to get this one worked out by then. It was a matter of figuring out who would have the final say. The principal walked back to the office, once again in search of a cup of coffee.

## THEORETICAL QUESTIONS

1. What forces or issues within the organization and its environment appear to influence the flow of events within the case and to shape the central problem or problems?
2. What is the central problem, or which are the central problems?
3. What theoretical perspective does the principal seem to bring to this situation?
4. What theoretical perspective do you tend to bring initially to this situation?
5. Are there additional conceptual frameworks that might be useful in developing an understanding of this case?
6. What are the implications of these conceptual frameworks for developing policy situations or solution strategies?
7. Which single or combined perspective do you feel is most appropriate for developing an action strategy?

## CASE SPECIFIC QUESTIONS

8. What are some of the pros and cons of the stalling tactic employed by the principal?
9. Whose rights must be considered by the principal? Whose rights warrant most respect and protection by the principal?
10. What arguments could be made for a unilateral decision by the principal on Thursday?

## ACTION QUESTIONS

11. Were the appropriate persons or roles involved in the processes of analysis and decision making?

12. How critical was time as a planning and decision factor?
13. What additional information does the principal need?
14. What solution alternatives seem to be available?
15. How can these alternatives be tested? What are their implications? Is your guiding theoretical perspective helpful at this stage?
16. What would you do? What would you advise the principal to do? How would you critique his actions thus far?

# 3

## THE CASE OF
## THE FIVE CAREERS

The superintendent was hesitant to open the manila folder that lay in front of him on his desk. It contained the third draft of a speech that he had struggled to write over the past two weeks. The teachers association was honoring him at a special luncheon during the planning period before the opening of school, and he had been asked to talk about his philosophy as a superintendent. He doubted that he could do that. Even after all those years of leadership, he was not at all certain that he had a coherent view of school administration, or that he could write it down if he had one, or that he could be understood if he did make the attempt. And yet there were some things about leadership that he wanted to say as he reflected on his experience, things that welled up from deep within him. Now, however, he felt uneasy. Superintendents were supposed to be somewhat stoic, and this seemed to be more like a personal letter than a formal speech. He sat quietly for a few minutes, listening with a sense of comfort to the muffled, routine office noises behind the closed door to his office, and then he opened the folder and began to read.

I was forty when I came here to be superintendent of schools. That was sixteen years ago. This district was then and still is one of the outstanding districts in the state. For me it was an exciting opportunity. I was certain that I knew enough about superintending and had enough energy and confidence to be suited to the challenge here. But few administrators had any idea of what was going to happen in the 1970s and 1980s, and I was no better as a prognosticator than anyone else.

At the beginning it was still a boom time. The capacity for growth seemed unlimited. We were just fighting to keep ahead of the demand for schools and classrooms and education. I remember that between 1968 and 1971 we completed the construction of a new junior high school, and we built one additional elementary school and added sections to six others. We were busing kids around the district just trying to find adequate room for everyone. Today half of the schools we were operating in 1971 are closed, most of the buildings no longer the property of the school district. The size of the student population and that of the professional and nonprofessional staff was cut in two as well. Many lives have been changed, and careers have been altered and recast. I can never read these figures or refer to them without shaking my head. It seems a wonder that we have survived this period of unexpected and really precipitous decline. What hurt as much as anything else is that it did not occur because we were doing a bad job or because the competition did a better job than we did. In fact, looking back it is difficult to find any individual or group to blame for the troubles we have battled together to survive.

When I first became an assistant superintendent I was working in a highly politicized school system—one that was not managed as well as it might have been. I learned how to finesse problems, to beat them off. I did not find that very satisfying, to be honest. I thought I had plenty of experience to be a superintendent, but when I reached my first superintendency I realized rather quickly that I did not. What I did receive was a marvelous opportunity to *learn* how to be a superintendent. I had a supportive board that wanted me to try some things. Some changes worked, and we built on those. Others failed, more than I want to admit to you today. Nonetheless, I grew up as an educator and an administrator because I began to test my value system.

Your president wanted me to talk to you today about some of my philosophy related to school administration. I hope that I can do a little of that, but it is difficult to present a philosophy without sounding wooden and pretentious. What I feel more comfortable discussing are my values and maybe even some homegrown theories. Looking back on that first superintendency, I realize that I was trying to build and live a concept of personalized management. By that I mean that I had learned that everything I knew about the school business boiled down to the reality that at its essence it was all people. Kids and teachers and administrators and board members are not interchangeable parts, and you have to work with each of them in different ways.

This belief became the core of my daily work as a superintendent, and I like to think that it still is, through good times and bad times. I came to a sense of how to work with people in a way that helped me personally, as one of the leaders of a school district, and that helped the organization, but that also let those same people become what they could be. I have to admit that working from this premise has been fun. This concept attracted moral principles that were important to me, such as credibility, trust, truth, compassion, sharing, the acceptance of failure, the necessity of humor. Yes, superintendents think about and worry about these values, just as you do every day as you work with your students in your classrooms.

I spent a good deal of time in this district trying to hire administrators and teachers who I felt were good people, and by *good* I mean more than just well-educated or experienced. I wanted to work with men and women who were alert, secure, tolerant of stress, perfectionist enough to never endure defeat. The more of those persons I hired, the more work I could get off my desk. My job then could be more that of pot stirring, stretching, and questioning. Some people liked this and stayed, while others preferred other educational pastures. I tried to encourage people in this district to build upon an ethic of pride. We were mostly really fine educators, and we needed to recognize that and move on from there. What do you want to do? How can we help you do it? These are the questions that I thought we ought to be asking each other.

I did my best to flatten the central office. By that I mean that I wanted to break down the kind of hierarchy you could find on an organization chart. I preferred informal hierarchies for getting things done. In a sense I wanted to make manipulation of the central office acceptable, particularly for principals and teachers in the schools. Use us as you will. If you think that I will foul up something that you are trying to do, stay away from me. By and large you are going to do what you think is best anyway, so why should you have to deal with me as a potential or real threat? I hope that these were the messages we were sending and that you were receiving. I gathered a good deal of evidence over the years to indicate that they were. Someone hearing me speak these words might think that we were shrugging off some of our administrative responsibilities. I would argue in return that we were simply trying to strengthen the most important responsibilities in this district—those of our principals and teachers.

I feel like I have had five careers as a superintendent in this community, not just one. The first career involved the period when we were still *growing,* when we were trying to personalize the management of the district and to set up those informal structures that I mentioned earlier. In effect we were trying to build an organization that would be self-perpetuating. But then, in 1971, we began to see a little flatness in the enrollment patterns, and the Larsen School started to get empty. We dealt with the problem together. Actually, we closed it a year or two before that would have been absolutely necessary. There was very little fanfare, if you recall, and I can remember telling other superintendents who were starting to get worried, "We've already closed one." We rented the building to a special education group and actually made a little extra income for the district in the process.

I did not know it then, but I had begun my second career as we moved from growth to *stabilization.* The pressure of growth in the district was over. What could we do now? Well, for one thing, we suddenly had space for art rooms and learning disabilities classes and crafts centers and a district teacher center. We found ourselves turning our focus even more than we had in the past to the issue of quality of education. What is quality all about in this school community? That was on our minds when we set up building goals and reemphasized our support for classroom teachers. Or, put another way, how do you make a school special? We tried even harder to separate political from functional hierarchies. There was a good deal of introspection on our part, individually and collectively. We were proud of how we corrected errors without feeling guilty. And we really stretched out for help from any source because we had more questions than we had answers. There was a stirring and vitality in that period of years that was exciting. It may have been the calm before the storm, but it was something precious to all of us who were in the district then. We actually started talking about personalized management, most often among the administrative group, but with teachers as well—some of you who are here today.

By the mid-1970's the *decline* was real, and my third career had begun. At the time I thought it was the most difficult period of my professional life, but now I am not so certain of that. We did all of the usual things you have to do regarding school closings, and I believe that we did them well, but we placed our major emphasis on personnel matters. At an organizational level, we tried to find ways to avoid destroying our pride and confidence. At an individual level we became familiar with human anguish. The loss of a job is a ripping, tearing experience. One's family, career, and future life are all affected. On one hand, we tried to be objective in order to be fair. We hired outside management consultants so that our data base would be as politically neutral as possible, particularly as we were forecasting future decline and developing some of the alternatives—not necessarily the answers—that we could consider. We went to the community because we wanted to know what the values and priorities were out there as harsh decline set in. Help us build a value hierarchy, as the board of education and the superintendent begin to make some tough decisions. Help us through this trying time. And I think the parents and citizens of this community responded well to our plea. Then we cut $1 million from the budget in 1976, and 72 jobs were lost. That is where we turned to the helping hand. As much as possible we tried to avoid surprising people. Notification was accompanied by specific aid in looking at job alternatives. We tried to make sure that information went to individuals directly from us rather than through the rumor mill. We printed resumes for people who were leaving. We made personal telephone calls of recommendation. If a teacher comes back after a period of years wanting assistance, we still try to give them just that. They are still part of this school community and school family.

Now we have closed eight schools, and the ninth will be closed this year. Every teacher on the payroll has at least ten years of seniority. In these ways the district in the early 1980s is a very different one from the district of a decade ago. We tried to deal with declining enrollment in a human, creative way—to use personal strengths to keep unity alive regardless of these drastic changes. But I would not be honest unless I admitted that most of us felt like Tinker Bell at one time or another. The light that we felt was important to us was flickering.

I am in the middle of my fourth career, and I can see the fifth career as it comes down the road to meet me. If you want to put a label on the fourth career, try *survival*. And I do not mean this for me personally, as vulnerable as the position of superintendent may seem to be. I am talking about the organization. How do we face and conquer stresses that educators simply have not had to contend with to such an extent before? What does it mean to a professional staff when the young men and women in its ranks are depleted? How do people who have been hanging on by their fingertips from year to year maintain their pride? How does a district get support from a community when only 20–30 percent of the citizens have children in the public schools? The thing that we have fastened onto, in my opinion, is exactly what determined human beings under stress always have found as their solace. We are planning for a bright future even when our fortunes seem to be at low ebb.

Those of us who are committed to public education are not prepared to see it fail in this community and in this country. We can see our enrollments beginning to level out in our district, and there is reason to believe that some modest growth may be a reality later in this decade. If we are going to begin hiring some new teachers, what kind of district will be here to support them when they arrive? We not only have to ask this question now, but we also have to answer it now, before those teachers and their students are in our classrooms and school buildings. Excuse me if this sounds a little evangelical, but I believe that we are moving from a period of survival into a period of *hope and imagination.* To meet that next set of challenges we must dream our dreams now. I hope to live out that fifth career with you in this district and this organization, and I need your help in making the plans that are necessary.

   If one element will hold us together during this period of survival and during the period of new growth to follow, it is our ability to communicate with each other. Communication will enable us to encourage each other, to test ideas for the future with each other. From every corner of the district we need to be able to say, "We're looking at this idea, even if we can't put it into effect yet, and we want you to look at it with us." I also want you to know that I recognize that sometimes, when we are licking our wounds, we want to be left alone for a while. We must be delicate with each other, able to back away momentarily. I think we can do that.

   If I were to give a copy of these remarks to my superintendent colleagues, most of them would disagree with me about many of my ideas, about my philosophy (if it is that) of school administration. Personalized management, as I have come to know it and to be able to describe it, is risky and insecure, even dangerous—that is what I would be told. One superintendent said to me once, "I'm a manager, not a mealy-mouthed educator. Don't ask—get it done. Remind people who they report to, or they'll run you around. They'll kill you." Well, I may have had some difficulty telling you what my philosophy of school administration *is,* but I can assure you that the statement of that superintendent is precisely the opposite of mine. When administrators think that they can control human beings, then they will never exercise very much influence on their organizations. I do not want to control you, but I do want *us* to control *our* future. Together we can really make a difference in our profession. Let's keep at it!

The superintendent made the last of several penciled corrections in the text and turned over the last page. It was only then that he saw the note from his secretary.

   This is the best speech you have written, and I hope you won't change a word. I feel proud just to have typed it.

Well, maybe. He still felt like he was giving away some trade secrets.

## THEORETICAL QUESTIONS

1. What forces or issues within the organization and its environment appear to influence the flow of events within this school district?
2. Which central problem did the district face? To what extent did they seem to be defined by the superintendent?
3. What theoretical perspective does the superintendent seem to bring to his definitions of an organization and the best functioning of educational administrators?
4. What theoretical perspective do you tend to bring initially to this situation?
5. What are the implications of these conceptual frameworks for developing policy positions or solution strategies?

6. Are there additional conceptual frameworks that might be useful in developing an understanding of this case?
7. Which single or combined perspective do you feel is most appropriate for developing an action strategy?

## CASE SPECIFIC QUESTIONS

8. Why does the superintendent use the metaphor of sequential careers in discussing his tenure in the district?
9. Why does the superintendent seem to feel somewhat alienated from his superintendent colleagues in other districts?
10. Why has the superintendent struggled with the preparation of this speech?
11. Which values and relationships does the superintendent believe to be essential when a school organization is under duress?
12. Why has this superintendent survived in a situation where many superintendents have failed?

## ACTION QUESTIONS

13. Which key strategic data can you imagine were important to the superintendent in developing a long-range course of action?
14. What solution alternatives might have been available to the superintendent during his first and second careers?
15. How could such alternatives be tested? How might they have come into conflict with his guiding theoretical perspective?
16. What would you have done to face organizational decline? How would you critique the action of the superintendent here?

||||||||||||||||||||||||||||||||||||||||||||||||||||||||||||||||||||||||||||||||||||||||||||||||

A constitutional convention in the early 1970s reorganized elementary and secondary education at the state level in Illinois. Prior to that time responsibilities for pre-collegiate public education were vested in an elected state superintendent; a patronage-dominated Office of the Superintendent of Public Instruction (OSPI); the School Problems Commission, a body created and dominated by the state legislature (or General Assembly) for the purpose of studying educational problems in Illinois and generating legislative proposals; and, of course, the General Assembly itself. Subsequent to 1975, however, some state-level governance power shifted to a new Illinois State Board of Education (ISBE), appointed by the governor and approved by the Senate, and a superintendent now to be appointed by the ISBE rather than elected by the citizens of Illinois.

The issue of school desegregation appeared quickly on the agenda of the ISBE. It was revealed that only 10 of 21 districts cited for noncompliance with desegregation orders under the tenure of the previous superintendent had filed and implemented acceptable desegregation plans. Furthermore, in the interim, other Illinois public school districts had become racially imbalanced. As a consequence, in mid-May of 1975 the ISBE adopted this resolution by unanimous vote:

> In view of the constitutional imperative, both state and federal, governing this Board's actions, and in light of judicial decisions affirming the primary responsibility of the state in eliminating and preventing racial segregation in public schools, that the Illinois State Board of Education approve and affirm, subject to future review, the *Rules Establishing Requirements and Procedures for the Elimination and Prevention of Racial Segregation in Schools*, adopted in 1971; and further that the Superintendent and staff of the Equal Educational Opportunity Section be directed to proceed with full implementation of these *Rules*, including an examination and assessment of those school districts previously determined to be in a state of non-compliance with these *Rules Establishing Requirements and Procedures for the Elimination and Prevention of Racial Segregation in Schools*.

During its spring work retreat the ISBE pinpointed desegregation as its top policy priority, and its new goals statement in November of the same year reaffirmed this position:

**387**

> The State Board of Education is committed to desegregation of local school districts. Federal and state desegregation regulations shall be implemented to meet the mandated responsibility to eliminate racial segregation in public schools.
>
> The State Board of Education shall do so in an affirmative manner, designed to reduce the likelihood of litigation and community disruption and to provide maximum assistance in the desegregation process.

Enrollment data for the 1975–76 school year had become available, and it was clear that some 40 districts in Illinois contained at least one school which violated the *Rules* which established a ±15 percent ratio in all district schools. The ISBE moved aggressively during the next five years, ordering 20 districts to prepare and implement desegregation plans. The other 20 districts included some, like Chicago and East St. Louis, where full compliance would be difficult if not impossible (because of predominantly minority enrollment), and others which moved into compliance before the arrival of a formal ISBE order.

By the turn of the decade, however, the ISBE was forced to reexamine its policy and procedures. Major resistance cropped up when the ISBE began to press hard upon the Chicago Public Schools. A number of powerful legislators threatened to support a constitutional amendment to eliminate the ISBE and return to the pre-1975 governance status.

An equally significant attack was mounted at the local school district level. Five districts which had been ordered to desegregate filed suits in lower state courts, challenging the validity of the *Rules.* The authority for the *Rules* came to a large extent from *The School Code of Illinois.* The short and rather innocent section on attendance units had been amended in 1963 by the Armstrong Act, to a chorus of both praise and disdain across the state.

> 10—21 § 10—21.3 Attendance units. To establish one or more attendance units within the district. As soon as practicable, and from time to time thereafter, the board shall change or revise existing units or create new units in a manner which will take into consideration the prevention of segregation and the elimination of separation of children in public schools because of color, race or nationality. All records pertaining to the creation, alteration or revision of attendance units shall be open to the public. As amended by act approved June 13, 1963. L.1963, p. 1107.

The lower and appellate courts and, finally, the State Supreme court ruled that while this section of the *School Code* placed appropriate obligations upon local districts vis-a-vis desegregation, it was an inappropriate basis for state compliance procedures. The courts observed further that Section 22-19 of the *School Code* already provided state authorities ample procedures.

The sharp new realities were laid out before the ISBE by its legal counsel following the 1982 ruling:

> In summary, the following points are clear:
>
> (1) Absent legislative action, the State Board of Education has no authority or responsibility to deal with de facto segregation.

(2) The State Board of Education must follow the procedures set forth in Section 22-19 of *The School Code of Illinois* in order to make a determination that de jure segregation exists in a local school district.

(3) Upon finding that discrimination exists and a refusal by a local district to remedy, the State Board could request action by the Attorney General or permission of the Attorney General to act on its own behalf, to compel action by a local school district through the use of legal process. In the event of an arbitrary refusal by the Attorney General to act or grant permission to State Board of Education to act, it is highly likely the State Board of Education would have standing to sue.

(4) There is no rule-making authority delegated to the State Board of Education in the very specific language of Section 22-19.

(5) There is clearly a duty under federal case law for the State Board of Education to take action against local school districts where there is reason to believe de jure segregation is occurring.

The effectiveness of the use of Section 22-19 will be, to a large extent, dependent upon the investigative skills of the State Board of Education staff. However, with adequate manpower and training, Section 22-19 may prove to be at least as effective a remedy over the long haul as the now defunct *Rules.*

The foregoing is applicable to discrimination on the basis of race, color, nationality, religion, or religious affiliation. Discrimination because of sex or handicaps are different issues. Both are prohibited by the Illinois Constitution. In addition, discrimination against handicapped persons is prohibited by federal law. There is, however, no legal procedure spelled out in the law similar to Section 22-19 to provide a means for the State Board of Education to hear complaints or make inquiries into sex or handicap discrimination. If the State Board of Education is to take an active role in enforcing equity in those two areas, legislation should be introduced to include them in Section 22-19.

Considerably hamstrung, the ISBE began to reconsider its positions in mid-1982. A study group was appointed to consider the status of equal educational opportunity; to examine options available to the ISBE; and to make specific suggestions to the ISBE by early 1983. The study group was comprised of educational and community organization representatives with an interest in the social and political issue, as well as several former ISBE board members and a smattering of professional educators. Members of the administrative committee of the ISBE also worked closely with the study group.

At one of its sessions the study group heard from Dr. Charles Green of the Bureau of Equal Educational Opportunity, Department of Education, Commonwealth of Massachusetts, who reported on a new strategy that had evolved in that state related to state involvement in local school district desegregation.

In 1965 Massachusetts passed a "racial balance law" requiring implementation of remedies whenever a school was over 50% "non-white." Early enforcement efforts by the state mostly involved approval of construction programs intended to provide large racially-integrated schools, but by late 1970 only one such school had opened. I was hired at that point to push the effort along, and by 1973 we had implementation orders from state courts for racial balance plans in Boston and Springfield affecting more than 75% of the Black students in the state.

In a vain effort to head off implementation of these plans the state legislature drastically amended the law, taking away our authority to order redistricting and other mandatory measures, and instead providing substantial new funding programs as incentives for desegregation. The plans were implemented on schedule in September 1974 (under state and federal court orders), and our primary efforts over the next several years were to set up and administer the funding programs in support of this implementation, at a rate of $9 million a year for educational programs and magnet schools, about the same amount for transportation reimbursements, slightly less for urban/suburban transfers, and very large cumulative amounts for racial balance construction.

In effect, we got out of the desegregation enforcement business.

About five years ago, however, we began to get our heads above water on grant administration and to ask whether we were meeting our remaining—and very minor—enforcement responsibilities under the state law. As we asked this question, two realities became apparent. First, Hispanic enrollments had been increasing rapidly in a number of districts with which we had never worked on racial balance, and indeed could not under the terms of our state law (which made it possible for Hispanic students to be counted as white as opposed to non-white, and thereby denied protection against de facto racial segregation); and, second, we had been so wedded to a de facto definition of the problem of segregation—basically a lazy matter of reviewing racial proportions—that we had failed to ask whether school systems were committing de jure segregation.Worse, we had failed to ask whether the state education agency itself, and even our office, were supporting de jure segregation.

Once we began to define Hispanic students as well as Black students as our desegregation clients, and to ask about the practices which resulted in racial segregation, a new phase opened in our equity efforts. It quickly became clear, as we taught ourselves to analyze these practices, that each urban school system which we investigated was in fact at least arguably guilty, and that in most instances our own agency was significantly implicated through construction grants and other forms of involvement.

Let me describe a typical process with a school system. It will be clear that this process is labor-intensive and highly sensitive; you will understand why I have been deeply involved in each case myself, and why we can handle only two new situations each year.

Generally we become involved when a city is planning to build, close, or change utilization of a facility with a substantial minority population or near schools with such a population. At that point we advise the superintendent that the actions taken will undoubtedly have some impact upon minority isolation and should be reviewed with care. We provide a planning grant to assist with this review process, including production of data on enrollment trends, transfers, and other relevant issues. A temporary solution is usually worked out, permitting the school system to go ahead with its proposed measures, though often in a different form than first contemplated. It has sometimes been necessary at this stage for the Commissioner to point out the potential liability for the school system—and the state—if the wrong action is taken.

During this first stage we begin our own investigation of the practices of the school systems which might have contributed to minority isolation, and invariably find serious enough issues to warrant briefing our General Counsel. She then usually arranges a meeting with legal counsel for the school system. From that point on in our meeting with local school officials, we ask that local counsel be present; we find their support invaluable in advising their clients to negotiate a remedy without a formal finding of liability and possible litigation.

Our primary objective in such meetings with a superintendent and staff is to outline the areas of potential liability, explain our common interest in finding a solution with a minimum of acrimony, and explore possible remedies. Sometimes the first two points alone must be gone over at a half dozen meetings; I have been tempted to put myself on videotape! Our objective is always to move on to the stage of discussing specifics.

Our approach to the specifics of a desegregation plan is too complex to present here; we have written up our model of principled negotiation on the basis of all the legitimate interests, and would be glad to share that with you. In brief, we seek to gain agreement on all of the constraints and goals before specifics are discussed, to assure broad-based participation in considering options, and to encourage phasing-in over several years, with each stage building upon and going beyond the previous stage.

Needless to say, we keep the Commissioner well briefed throughout this process, but we seek to avoid invoking his direct authority, much less that of the Board, unless an impasse is reached. It is enough for the superintendent to know that I enjoy the Commissioner's general support; direct intervention by the Commissioner would have the effect of "raising the stakes" and thus politicizing the issue, and we try to hold that in reserve. We take it as a distinct mark of success that neither the Commissioner nor the Board has made a finding of desegregation liability or issued a remedial order since 1975—but it is important that superintendents and school committees know that they would if they believed it necessary to protect the rights of minority students.

In this connection, it is extremely helpful if the minority parents in a city with which we are working are represented by legal counsel and prepared to play an active role in negotiation of a remedial plan. We prefer to be in the middle between school officials and parents, helping to find a solution which is mutually acceptable, rather than to have to keep the pressure on ourselves. Such cooperation, we believe, actually reduces the chance of litigation: no desegregation case has come to trial in Massachusetts since 1974.

As we work on a remedy, we encourage the local participants to identify their own goals for the school system, and to incorporate as many of those goals as possible into their plan. Massachusetts cities have reorganized curriculum, changed grade structure, raised reading scores, created linkages with over thirty colleges, and advanced sex equity in secondary schools, as well as creating over fifty magnet schools through the desegregation process.

It is simply good management to take advantage of the changes necessary to desegregate in order to meet other educational objectives.

By the way, no superintendent has lost his job as a result of cooperating with us, and several superintendents were given that position after heading up desegregation planning efforts in their systems. Only Boston refused to develop its own remedy through a negotiation process, and only Boston has experienced extreme community resistance—and superintendent turnover.

All that I have been describing is the second stage, which sometimes results in a comprehensive and stable plan, and other times results in what we regard as an incomplete plan which does not preclude doing what should be done next. In the latter case, a third stage begins with the implementation, and we continue to work with the system until a plan—*their* plan—is in place which meets our criteria of constitutional adequacy and long-range effectiveness. I should note that we do not write these criteria down as guidelines; they remain a matter of ongoing discussion and negotiation.

I have described this process at some length because it has been effective and has resulted in good plans and stable school systems. I have no enemies among the superintendents who—always unwillingly at first—have gone through the process, and the Commissioner and Board have not been forced to use any of their political credit to support our desegregation efforts. To the contrary, our state desegregation accounts are among the very few which received increases last year, and four city superintendents were in Washington with us last week to support a new federal desegregation program.

Let me recapitulate briefly the elements which I have described:
  (a) reliance upon the U.S. Constitution as the legal basis for state desegregation efforts;
  (b) quiet investigation and negotiation around liability and the need for a remedial plan (avoiding charges in the press and so forth);
  (c) broad-based negotiation of a remedial plan, using criteria which all parties are able to accept before getting down to specifics;
  (d) encouragement to include unrelated education and management objectives in the changes associated with implementing the plan;
  (e) avoiding "show-downs," official rebukes from the Commissioner or State Board, or other blows to the credibility of those who will have to carry out the plan;
  (f) maximum involvement of the representatives of minority students, including legal counsel if possible (this includes urging them to avoid rhetorical "victories" which may obscure their real objectives); and
  (g) willingness to accept phased-in implementation (provided that later stages will not require burdening the same students a second time), with later stages building on the confidence produced by successful implementation of earlier stages.

Note that I have discussed "mandatory" versus "voluntary" plans. Suffice it to say that we are very supportive of voluntary approaches which do not themselves create inequities, and believe that a sophisticated mix of voluntary and mandatory measures can be most effective.

**393**

In closing, I urge you to bury de facto as a concern: not only is it legally very uncertain, but it produces inadequate remedies and makes it harder to gain public support. A de jure context identifies specific denial of equal opportunity to minority students, and thus allows and requires a remedy which corrects that denial in very specific ways. A de facto context encourages a quick fix numerical solution which barely scratches the surface of equity issues—and which appears to the public as a numbers game.

Don't seek additional legislative authority, or be prepared to lose on that; all the discussions suggest that you will. Instead, build your legislative strategy around obtaining modest funding authority to assist school systems with planning and voluntary measures, and perhaps support related to construction and transportation (though with declining enrollments the former would have modest impact).

Use the 22-19 process to surface de jure issues, and then you can begin to negotiate solutions and provide funding, hopefully. If enforcement is necessary, use the 22-19 process to build a record before referring a case to the Attorney General. Withholding of funding has proved ineffective.

The ISBE also asked its staff to prepare several documents. The first of these, *Internal Procedures for Implementing Section 22-19 of the School Code of Illinois*, was designed to supplement the external hearing procedures of the code with the appropriate processes within the ISBE structure. *Guidelines for Local School Districts on Implementing Section 10-21.3, The Armstrong Act* provided substantial assistance to local boards of education and superintendents in meeting this particular code mandate. Finally, the superintendent prepared and distributed widely within Illinois a clear, nontechnical brochure for citizens to acquaint them with their rights and available remedies under both code provisions. In a foreword to the second document the ISBE chairman underlined the apparent shift of responsibility from the state to the local level.

During the past seven years the State Board of Education has worked with many local school districts thoughout the State of Illinois to prevent discrimination and eliminate racial segregation in schools. To our great satisfaction, substantial progress has occurred and many children are in improved educational settings because of our efforts. But the task is not completed and the State Board along with the local school districts in the State of Illinois must continue to work toward the day when racial isolation of pupils in our schools has disappeared.

Recently the Illinois Supreme Court clarified the respective roles of the State Board of Education and local school boards concerning the Armstrong Act. In *Aurora East Public School District No. 131, et al.,* v. Cronin, et al., 92 Ill.2d 313, 442 N.E.2d 511 (1982) the Court held that the State Board of Education does not have authority to adopt rules for compliance with the Armstrong Act. Instead, local school districts are charged with the responsibility of enforcing the Act. Consequently, promulgating rules relative thereto is the duty of local school boards pursuant to their rule-making authority under Section 10-20.5 of *The School Code.*

By definition a rule is an established guide or regulation for action. Conditions vary in each school district; therefore, the course of action chosen by each school board to meet the requirements of the Armstrong Act will vary. One thing is clear, however, and that is that it is the duty of each school board to adopt procedures to ensure compliance with the Armstrong Act.

The concern of the State Board of Education has been and continues to be for the schools of Illinois to provide equal educational opportunity for all children regardless of race, national origin, sex, or handicap. Accordingly, staff have been instructed to provide assistance to local school districts to achieve this end.

The report from the equal educational opportunity study group was ready for presentation to the ISBE in the late spring of 1983, but it was deferred until the annual work retreat. When it was sent to the ISBE it was titled *From Technical Assistance to Enforcement: An Equal Educational Opportunity Agenda for the 1980's,* and the introduction and first three recommendations read as follows:

The United States Constitution and the Illinois Constitution mandate certain protections for all citizens. Not the least of these is protection from discrimination on the basis of race, sex, handicap, religion, and national origin. Enforcement action against that discrimination is vested in a variety of state and federal offices. The citizens of Illinois look to the State Board of Education for protection against discrimination when it comes to primary and secondary schools and their operations. Recent court cases around the country make it clear that state boards of education are responsible for protecting these rights. The question that faces us today is how shall we accomplish that task. How shall the State Board of Education protect citizens from discrimination and ensure the equal protection of the law?

This report makes several recommendations as to how this might be done. The study group suggests that changes in organization rather than new legislation ought to be the top priority. The report suggests that the changing political and social climate necessitates a shift in the orientation of the State Board towards combating discrimination. In prior years the Board has assumed what we call a "technical assistance" stance in these matters. This was due, in the main, to the posture of the federal government as the leader in the fight against discrimination. States found themselves assisting local school districts to meet the requirements of the federal law. Now states have a broader responsibility if equal opportunity in education is to become a reality.

The State Board of Education, like any state agency, evolves over time within a social and political context. If we look at that agency today we see an organization shaped by the demands of the last two decades. Its shape, the way it does business, even its notion of itself are consequences of its history and what those around it expect and desire. Like any branch of government, it is both cause and effect of the educational environment it helps to produce.

Currently, the agency finds itself encased with an organizational and intellectual shell which is no longer appropriate to the needs of the 1980's. We are struck by the dissonance between the approach that exists and the agenda which is necessary for further progress. Today we see an agency armed with much of the legislation needed to improve equality of opportunity, but caught within a structure unable to meet these challenges.

Given the context of the last twenty years, the agency has developed an organizational structure which acts as a conduit between federal agencies, which supply resources and sanctions, and local districts, which produce educational services. Current practices rely on a technical assistance orientation. By that we mean the Board sees itself as assisting local districts in complying with federal and state law. The agency is now confronted with a different governmental context in which the federal agencies are no longer pro-active in their stance. Many categorical programs are now combined into block grants which give states more authority and responsibility in the dispersal of funds. The shifts in federal responsibility have left a gap between the law and its enforcement. The State Board finds itself rethinking the technical assistance role in this context. We suggest several approaches to enforcement which fill that gap.

Vigorous state action in this area is a function of how the leadership of the Board construes its authority and responsibility. The Board can become the primary mechanism for increasing equality of opportunity by moving from a technical assistance to enforcement mentality. Local school districts cannot by law discriminate. The Board is in an excellent position to enforce the law. To do this will require commitment and courage, for it involves putting equality of educational opportunity on the top of the agenda. The questions the Board and the Superintendent must ask first are, "Is the district in compliance with federal and state statutes and, if not, how we do produce such compliance or at a minimum avoid complicity in law-breaking behavior?"

The first several recommendations of the study group propose an approach to these questions. The study group seeks to place the E.E.O. agenda at the center of what the State Board is about.

Those with a stake in the status quo will resist the change that this new orientation will produce; that is to be expected. People do not easily give up the privileges they have come to expect. But a democratic society such as ours ignores its own principles at some great peril. Too often the inequality we observe between students results from unfair treatment rather than unequal abilities. The following recommendations are offered to help remedy this situation.

1. The State Superintendent of Education shall report annually to the State Board of Education on the "State of Equal Opportunity in Illinois." That report shall include, but not be limited to, an analysis of race, sex and national origin discrimination in the school districts of Illinois. The report shall describe those districts which currently are not in compliance with state and federal law as they pertain to equal opportunity and civil rights. The report shall focus on three substantive areas: race desegregation, vocational education, and special education. In these areas the report will highlight school districts which are not in compliance with the law.

This report will provide the necessary information to highlight those situations which are, on the face of it, illegal, and alert authorities to those situations which are problematic. The report shall indicate which districts appear to have problems in complying with state and federal law.

After this report is transmitted to the State Board, it shall be disseminated to interested parties throughout the state, including those school districts whose activities appear to be problematic from an equal opportunity perspective. Comments shall be solicited from interested and affected parties.

2. The State Board of Education shall direct the Superintendent to develop procedures to remedy the situations described in the State of Equal

Opportunity Report. Those remedies should follow the Action Plan approach used in Massachusetts. Priority areas for these Action Plans should be racial segregation and vocational education as well as special education. If a district displays substantially disproportionate enrollment patterns that district has the option of developing an Action Plan to remedy the difficulties or they can proceed to a hearing to show that the situation does not violate state or federal law (see recommendation 3).

3. The State Superintendent shall develop mechanisms for implementing procedures set forth in Section 22-19 of the school code of Illinois. The State Superintendent shall develop alternative procedures to remedy discriminatory activity not appropriately covered by Section 22-19 of the code. Those mechanisms shall include, but not be limited to, a pro-active stance towards school districts which are found to be in non-compliance with state and federal law as described in the Annual Report on the "State of Equal Opportunity in Illinois." A procedure shall be developed to investigate the situation thoroughly, allowing for testimony to be gathered from all parties involved. Efforts shall be made to bring the districts involved into compliance without resorting to litigation, but these procedures should expedite litigation if it proves necessary. A district may choose to develop an Action Plan in lieu of this investigation.

After several hours of discussion of the report, the State Board asked the State Superintendent to return to it in October at the latest with a plan which would represent new and defensible strategies for school desegregation in Illinois. The State Superintendent knew that such a timeline would require that a draft be ready in six to eight weeks.

## THEORETICAL QUESTIONS

1. What forces or issues within the organization and its environment appear to influence the flow of events within the case and to shape the central problem or problems?
2. What is the central problem, or which are the central problems?
3. What theoretical perspective does the State Board seem to bring to this situation?
4. What theoretical perspective do you tend to bring initially to this situation?
5. What are the implications of these conceptual frameworks for developing policy positions or solution strategies?
6. Are there additional conceptual frameworks that might be useful in developing an understanding of this case?
7. Is a combination of concepts or theories or models feasible or desirable in this case?
8. Which single or combined perspective do you feel is most appropriate for developing an action strategy?

## CASE SPECIFIC QUESTIONS

9. What are the implications for the policy role of the State Board in the apparently necessary shift of focus from de facto to de jure segregation?
10. How accurate were the framers of the study group report in characterizing the historic posture of the State Board vis-a-vis desegregation?

11. Are there ways for the State Board to reestablish initiative in local school desegregation without inviting renewed attacks from legislators, as well as from local boards and administrators?

## ACTION QUESTIONS

12. Who should be involved in the processes of further analysis?
13. How critical is time as a planning factor?
14. What additional information is needed? Which are the key strategic data?
15. What policy alternatives seem to be available to the State Board?
16. How can these alternatives be tested? What are their implications for action? Is your guiding theoretical perspective helpful at this stage?
17. What would you advise the State Superintendent to do?

November 4, 19___

*Memorandum*

To: Rev. Patrick F. Concannon
Superintendent
Archdiocesan Office of Education

From: Pauline Hugh
Secondary School Liaison Officer
Archdiocesan Office of Education

I am responding to your telephone call of November 13, 19___, in which you requested information about the withdrawal of Leo Gurney from St. Thomas Aquinas High School. I regret that you did not have the two enclosed letters from Mrs. Gurney and Fr. William Showalter, Principal of Aquinas, available to you when the representative of the State Superintendent made contact with you. The two letters are enclosed for you to review at this time.

My first contact with this case came when Mrs. Gurney called me on the afternoon of October 31, 1983. She was distraught, and she wanted to know how to appeal the case. I indicated that I could not make any official statement until after I had talked to Fr. Showalter.

I suggested to him that we might be liable under the Family Rights and Privacy Act, and eventually he did mail a listing of the demerits to Mrs. Gurney. I do not understand her comments about not being informed, since Fr. Showalter assured me that he had talked to her to work out withdrawal as an alternative to expulsion.

I am surprised that you received a telephone call from the state office. In the past, before your arrival, letters like Mrs. Gurney's came to the Office of the Superintendent and then were sent routinely to me. The state never has been interested in pursuing cases of parental support. Perhaps this indicates some change of attitude at the state level. It would be helpful to all of us to know of that.

Please let me know if I can be of any additional assistance.

---

ST THOMAS AQUINAS HIGH SCHOOL
November 1, 19___

Mrs. Marvin D. Gurney
17603 West Pioneer Drive
Mountain View, California

Dear Mrs. Gurney:

In your discussion with me in my office today, you asked me to write a letter reviewing the departure of your son, Leo, from St. Thomas Aquinas High School.

Leo was not expelled. As I explained to you, it is our policy that when a student, male or female, receives either ten major demerits in a semester or eighteen major demerits in a school year, that student is reviewed by the principal with respect to possible expulsion.

After Leo received his tenth major demerit rather early in this semester, I reviewed the situation personally and convened a meeting of our Board of Discipline to assist me in that review. Based on those considerations, I indicated to Leo that it would be best for him to withdraw from St. Thomas Aquinas and enter another high school. He did that, and it is my understanding that he has enrolled at Mount Olive. Both our records and those of Mount Olive will show only that he withdrew from our school, and that is all any transcript in the future from either school will show.

I regret that you understood from one of Leo's teachers that not all of them were in unanimous agreement that he should leave the school. I simply do not know if this is the case, since I have not polled them. But I do want you to know that the Board of Discipline—including the disciplinarian, three teachers, and two students—was unanimous in its recommendation to me that Leo be asked to withdraw.

I prefer not to include a list of Leo's infractions in this letter, but if you will call the disciplinarian he will read them to you over the telephone.

I respect your concern for Leo and for his acquiring an education that will prepare him for college entrance. We shared that concern, and I am truly sorry that he is no longer with us. However, we feel that his withdrawal is in his best interest as well as that of St. Thomas Aquinas.

Sincerely,

Fr. William U. Showalter
Principal

17603 W. Pioneer Dr.
Mountain View, CA
November 4, 19___

State Superintendent of Schools

Sacramento, CA

Dear Sir:

I want you to see a copy of this letter from Father Showalter, who is principal of St. Thomas Aquinas High School in our neighboring community.

On November 1, I asked Fr. Showalter to explain in writing the reason he had not given me parental notification that my son, aged 14, was expelled from school on October 31. Also I asked Fr. to give me a list in that letter of the ten charges against Leo.

In the letter Fr. Showalter says that he permitted my son to withdraw from school and, therefore, it was not necessary to inform me. I guess he is not familiar with the state laws governing compulsory education through age 16. I took the trouble to go to the library and check out a copy of the school code for the state, so I am familiar with the rules.

Also my neighbor is a lawyer and perhaps Fr. Showalter is unaware of the Family Rights and Privacy Act which was passed by the Congress of the United States on November 19, 1974, and which gives me the right to see what is in Leo's file where I am certain that list is.

I believe you should protect my rights under the laws of California and the United States. This is my complaint against the Archdiocese, St. Thomas Aquinas High School, and the people at the school who have hurt Leo's chance to go to college.

Truly yours,

Laurel Gurney

## THEORETICAL QUESTIONS

1. What forces or issues within the organization and its environment appear to influence the flow of events within the case and to shape the central problem or problems?
2. For the superintendent, what is the central problem, or which are the central problems?
3. What theoretical perspective do the principal and liaison officer seem to bring to this situation?
4. What theoretical perspective might be useful to the superintendent in examining this situation?
5. What theoretical perspective do you tend to bring initially to this situation?
6. What are the implications of these conceptual frameworks for developing solution strategies?

7. Which single or combined perspective do you feel is most appropriate for developing an action strategy?

## CASE SPECIFIC QUESTIONS

8. How concerned must the superintendent be over the role of the state vis-a-vis private schools?
9. To what extent must federal laws such as the Family Rights and Privacy Act be respected by private school administrators?
10. How much autonomy on the parts of the principal and the liaison officer should the superintendent support?

## ACTION QUESTIONS

11. Who should be involved in the processes of further analysis and decision making?
12. How critical is time as an action factor?
13. What additional information is needed by the superintendent? Which are the key strategic data?
14. What solution alternatives seem to be available?
15. How can these alternatives be tested? What are their implications? Is your guiding theoretical perspective helpful at this stage?
16. What would you do? What would you advise the administrator in this case to do? How would you critique the actions of the principal and the liaison officer?
17. How could a preferable alternative be tested?

# THE CASE OF
# WRITER'S BLOCK

The Assistant Dean caught herself staring at the wall again. She felt the anxiety gnawing in her stomach, the same nagging concern that had robbed her of appetite at lunch earlier in the day and had stolen too many hours of sleep from her during the past week. Her secretary had been gone for over an hour, and the halls in the School of Education were quiet now. She had decided to stay until she could get a draft of the speech to the faculty on paper. But when she looked at the lined yellow pad in front of her, all she saw were a few words and phrases and some aimless doodles. It was hard to know where to begin these remarks, but the middle and the ending were even more difficult to visualize.

The Dean had resigned unexpectedly in mid-July.

**I wish I hadn't been on vacation then. Maybe I could have talked him out of it.**

The University statutes mandated an evaluation of deans every three years, with the faculty accepting a major portion of the responsibility for the evaluation. The Dean had passed the first such of these assessments with flying colors three years ago, so it was not a process with which he was unfamiliar. But the situation was different now—the complaints were more open, the problems more unyielding. The dean was not prepared for a third season under the spotlight.

**Maybe he was just tired of it all. But he had such a thirst for leadership when he began.**

The Dean was an outsider who came to the University with solid credentials as a respected scholar in comparative education and as an able administrator with prior experience as a department chairman, associate dean, and dean. He had been welcomed by virtually the entire faculty, and his emphasis on research and scholarship had been applauded by his new colleagues, even though they previously had spent the majority of their time working in the areas of teaching, service, and program development. The Dean did not socialize much with faculty members, however.

**Not aloof, exactly, but certainly separate. Always above.**

The Assistant Dean had been entertained in the Dean's home only once in six years, although their working relationship never had been marred by a serious dispute.

**But now I'm in this office, for a year at least. And where do we go from here?**

The call from the Provost had reached her at the cabin in Montana even before she heard from the Dean. The Provost had talked to several senior faculty members who assured him that the Assistant Dean had the confidence of the faculty and could handle the job for a year while a national search was conducted to uncover a new leader for the School.

**I wonder if I'll be considered as a candidate.**

The Assistant Dean cut her vacation short by a few days and hurried back to campus where the final arrangements had been worked out with the Dean and the Provost—the title of Acting Dean, a modest salary increase, the move into the suite of offices in the center of the building. The rituals of reassuring the secretaries and other staff members had been completed, her commitments to teaching and research had been adjusted, and a good many hours had been devoted to meeting University administrators whom she had known only casually before, to poring over the files, and to outlining a rough agenda of events and deadlines for the academic year. But in retrospect that all looked easy in comparison to her speech at the opening faculty meeting, which now was only three days away.

**Do I speak to the real issues? Or should I just make some rather noncontroversial statements, tell a few stories, stroke a few heads, and let it go at that?**

There certainly were some issues to be faced.

**But how much is anybody going to expect me to do in a year? What should I leave for the real Dean to tackle?**

The Dean had settled into a faculty office at the other end of the building. She knew he was embittered. He had offered to assist her when needed, but she was uncertain about whether that would be a good idea, even though she had not told him that.

**What impact will his presence have on the faculty in the coming year? What can I say to the faculty that might ease the situation?**

It would be painful for the Dean if she and the faculty began to address some of the problems of faculty governance that had encouraged his decision to step down. Teaching-load policy never had been specified, and there were certainly some inequities. If all members of the faculty were going to be asked to develop a balanced schedule of scholarly activity and teaching and service and program development, then there would have to be some changes, first of all with regard to teaching assignments. A further complication in this regard had to do with teaching in the summer semester when overload pay was available. Faculty salary increases had been slim in the past three years throughout the University, and the competition for summer assignments was becoming ferocious.

The faculty was troubled, too, by the ad hoc nature of promotion and tenure procedures. The bylaws were vague on the subject, and the Dean had varied the process from year to year. She did not think he had been playing favorites, but that suspicion was abroad in the faculty. Was this the year to begin serious consideration of revision of the School bylaws? That possibility would certainly be raised by several of the powerful members of the faculty who felt that the Dean had never consulted sufficiently with the faculty nor accepted their advice often enough even when it was solicited. They were interested in more than load and promotion and tenure policies.

> Mark, Joyce, Ted—they'll see this as the opportunity to underline the role of the departments, to put the real power at those levels. In many ways I agree with them, and yet this office has to have some flexibility, too. How do we work out truly consensual arrangements?

But the problems bubbling within the School were not the only ones that were important as its future was being shaped. Declining enrollment was a problem for the entire University, but the drop in the School had been particularly staggering. She knew that there had been talk in higher circles of the University of closing the School and reassigning tenured faculty members to other units. She could not think of a more vulnerable part of the institution. Not much had been done in the way of student recruitment or the development of programs to attract new students. The graduate level programs were holding up well, but the undergraduate teacher preparation program was about to perish. In addition, the Provost had told her of his concern and that of the President related to the involvement of School faculty in the local community. She agreed that not much was happening at the present time. The exurban environment of the University simply was not of much interest to the faculty, most of whom gravitated to the nearby city in developing their research and service projects. That was all to the good, and yet she could understand the public relations problems of her new bosses.

She remembered, too, that three faculty members had been lost to colleges and universities in the city that past spring, and only one of the positions had been refilled.

> Do we hang on for a year short-handed, or should I try to move the search processes along? Maybe the new Dean will want some room to bring in a few people. If so, these lines should stay open.

The majority of faculty members felt isolated in the somewhat rural environment, but they certainly had not turned to each other for support. The School was hardly a community of scholars or even teachers. Teach and run seemed to be the order of the day. Students had complained to her before about the unavailability and inaccessibility of faculty members for advice and tutoring. The last colloquium that she could remember had been held two years ago, and it was poorly attended even though one of the giants in the field of education had made the presentation. Many times the hallways seemed as empty during the day as at night.

It was seven o'clock, and it was time to start writing.

## THEORETICAL QUESTIONS

1. What forces or issues within the organization and its environment appear to influence the flow of events within the case and to shape the central problem or problems?

2. What is the central problem, or which are the central problems?
3. What theoretical perspective does the Assistant Dean seem to bring to this situation?
4. What theoretical perspective do you tend to bring initially to this situation?
5. What are the implications of these conceptual frameworks for developing solution strategies?
6. Are there additional conceptual frameworks that might be useful in developing an understanding of this case?
7. Which single or combined perspective do you feel is most appropriate for developing an action strategy?

## CASE SPECIFIC QUESTIONS

8. Do you sense that the Assistant Dean had received adequate help in thinking through the issues facing the School of Education?
9. How much of the obligation for leadership should the Assistant Dean accept? To which particular perils of leadership should she be alert? Are there advantages to being an "insider" at this juncture?
10. What sources of commitment are available to the Assistant Dean?

## ACTION QUESTIONS

11. Which are the key strategic data for the Assistant Dean?
12. What alternatives seem to be available to her in organizing the speech? What are their implications for policy or for action?
13. What would you advise the administrator in this case to do? How would you critique her action thus far?
14. What would you write? You may want to create an outline for the speech or to write a first draft. Is your guiding theoretical perspective helpful at this stage?

# 7

# THE CASE OF
# THE HOMELESS SCHOOL

▌▌▌▌▌▌▌▌▌▌▌▌▌▌▌▌▌▌▌▌▌▌▌▌▌▌▌▌▌▌▌▌▌▌▌▌▌▌▌▌▌▌▌▌▌▌▌▌▌▌▌▌▌▌▌▌▌▌▌▌▌▌▌▌▌▌▌▌▌▌

**Hyde Park Herald**
March 6, 1974

## HAPPY ANIVERSARY, MRS. T—40 YEARS AT HARVARD-ST. GEORGE

You'd never know it by looking at  her, but Anne Tyskling is a fighter.

Always has been, always will be.

She worked for civil rights before there was a name for it.

She pressured for equality years and years ahead of the time that it was  fashionable.

And since 1934 she has bridged the racial, ethnic and religious differences of youngsters here in the name of good education and brotherly love.

First as manager of the St. George School for Girls on 46th and Drexel, then as the director of the merged  Harvard-St. George School on 47th and Ellis, Mrs. Tyskling has always  remained in the forefront of education in this community.

"The kids 40 years ago started out being interested, affectionate, and  concerned. Now it has come complete circle. Up until about two years ago the kids didn't know where they were going, they were unhappy with things in general, they were protesting but they didn't really know what they were protesting for.

"But now kids have settled down and have their own sense of values. And our kids here, I think, are really  concerned about what's going on in the world.

"They know they have to make it in school in order to get anywhere, they have the same concerns as the youngsters before.

They  may  question  more,  but  they  have  the  right  to  question."

Mrs. Tyskling taught first grade for a while in the 30's and then was named business manager of the St. George School. During the Second World War she received special commendation for setting up not only a war time nursery school, but a boarding situation for some of her students.

From 1950 until 1952 Mrs. Tyskling fought one of her famous civil rights battles.

"I took a Hindu child into the St. George School and the people on the board thought she was black. They wanted me to get rid of her. I didn't know there was such strong feeling. We never had a black child apply before.

"But here was this Hindu youngster—and I kept her. Oh, they made all sorts of excuses that they had run out of money, this, that and the other thing, and said we should close the school.

"I refused to go along with that and the people in the community helped me fight. . . ."

**Chicago Tribune**
January 29, 1950

## PARENTS KEEP SCHOOL OPEN TO AID NEEDY

St. George School, 4545 Drexel Blvd., which was scheduled to close at the semester's end last week, will remain open, the board of trustees has announced.

At a meeting of the trustees and members of a parents group in the school an agreement was reached whereby the school would remain open if the parents would help raise the funds necessary to keep its operation out of the red.

### Increased Costs Cited

Previously, it had been announced and parents notified that the school, an endowed, accredited and nonsectarian institution for children from homes broken by death or divorce or where parents must work, would be closed because of lack of funds and the increased cost of operation.

### Parents Pledge All

The parents group presented its case to the trustees and pledged to help obtain more pupils of working parents who can pay tuition, to help raise funds thru a tag day and benefit programs, and to form an organized parent-teacher group to help the school in whatever way is necessary.

St. George, which has facilities for more than 200 children from nursery school thru the 8th grade, now has about 160 pupils. Boys are accepted thru the 4th grade. About 92 of the children are boarders, some placed by the courts, and many of the day pupils stay from early morning to early evening. Tuition rates are based on what parents can pay.

If the school were closed, under the terms of the endowment, there are two alternate beneficiaries for the funds. They are the Home for Destitute Crippled Children and the Chicago Home for the Friendless.

**Hyde Park Herald**
September 5, 1951

## *ST. GEORGE FIGHTS TO STAY OPEN*

The St. George Parents' Committee School opened Tuesday, on schedule in its temporary quarters at the Rodfei Zedek Temple, 1022 East 54th Place. Rabbi Simon and his congregation are cooperating with the committee in providing space for the school until such a time as the Courts see fit to rule on permanent quarters. Mrs. Ann Tyskling, who has been manager of the St. George School for fifteen years, will continue to guide its policies and direct its activities. The school has always had a program designed to meet the needs of children whose parents are both employed during the day.

Because of the school's place in the needs of the community, many local civic leaders have rallied to the cause and have lent their support and encouragement to the parents' group who refuse to give up in the face of defeat.

St. George operated from January 1950 to June 1951 with an injunction obtained by the Committee. The injunction has now been set aside and the Committee, represented by Mr. Abraham Brussell, attorney, will go into court September 10 in an effort to convince the Court that the school is self-supporting and can continue to operate without incurring a deficit, which is the only reason the Board of Directors have given for closing the school. The school covered an 18-month period which ended June 30 without a deficit in school operations.

Mrs. Carl B. Williams, 5017 South Blackstone, President of the Parent-Teacher Association and Mr. Manny Siegel, civic leader and business man, have joined forces with friends, parents of children enrolled in the school, and city-wide civic-minded individuals who feel that the school must not be allowed to close after over 30 years of service to the city.

". . . After two years of court battle we were finally kicked out of the school.

"The second year of the fight I had placed most of the resident children in different homes, different schools, or had to send them home.

"There were 32 however, that we couldn't find any place for. They lived in my own apartment in the school building and every morning we would get up at 7:00 and go over to the old Rodfei Zedek and have classes there. Every time the temple would celebrate a high holiday we'd have to pack up the kids and take them someplace else for meals because we weren't allowed to use the gas stove. . . ."

**Chicago Sun-Times**
September 4, 1952

## EVICT 13 CHILDREN AT PRIVATE SCHOOL

Municipal Court bailiffs Wednesday evicted 13 youngsters and Mrs. Anne Tyskling from the St. George School for Girls, 4545 Drexel. She was the school's business manager.

The eviction ended one phase of a legal battle which has involved the private school for nearly three years. The children, ranging in age from 4 to 11, include boys as well as girls from broken homes or whose parents are working.

### Operated 30 Years

Mrs. Tyskling had sought to keep the school operating in the building. She and the children looked on as movers crated equipment and furnishings. The stuff was carried to the sidewalk and piled there for shipment.

The school was established 30 years ago with a $100,000 trust fund set up by the late George Williams, an attorney and real estate man.

In January, 1950, the board of directors decided to close the school. The directors said there wasn't enough income from the trust fund to run it.

A group of parents carried the case to the Circuit Court. The late Judge Benjamin Epstein enjoined the board from closing the institution.

The Appellate Court then sent the case back to the Circuit Court, where Judge Daniel A. Roberts entered a finding favoring the board. The parents have again put the matter before the Appellate Court, where a hearing is scheduled for October.

### Discharge Manager

The board meanwhile discharged Mrs. Tyskling as business manager —a job she had held for 15 years. She and the children refused to leave.

Last May 28 Judge Raymond Drymalski of Municipal Court upheld an eviction notice obtained by the board. He granted her a 90-day stay, which expired Aug. 26.

Mrs. Tyskling said she will try to get funds for a down payment on another building so that she can resume operation of the school.

**Chicago Tribune**
September 10, 1952

## STUCK WITH 12 KIDS, TAKES IT IN STRIDE

Some women would march down to the Western Union office and send a few telegrams reading, "Come get your child—quick."

But not Mrs. Anne Tyskling, who is caring for 12 children—not her own—at her own expense in a South Side apartment hotel.

Until Wednesday, the 12 were boarding pupils of the St. George School, which Mrs. Tyskling long had managed at 4545 Drexel. That day they were evicted, with six Tysklings, by school directors who say the school cannot pay its way.

"I can't tell their parents to take them back," said Mrs. Tyskling Friday. "They are less able than I to figure out what to do.

"The parents of one little girl are in South America. Except for her, the children have only one parent, who works and has no place to leave the child.

"These youngsters have no family—except my own and each other. I think we will find a place where we can all be together."

On school days, the children leave the limited quarters at the Tudor-Ellis apartment hotel, 43rd St. and Ellis, for classes in rooms rented from Congregation Rodfei Zedek at 5200 Hyde Park.

Seventy other youngsters share classes with them, having lunches and dinners there, too, while their parents work.

St. George School was planned by its philanthropist founder as a school for children of broken homes, and its rates have been low—$80 a month, or less in special cases, for a month's schooling, board and care.

It will be hard to take care of such a crowd in three tiny apartments over the weekend—but invitations for groups of children have been received from generous Chicagoans, and some will be allowed to "go visiting" Saturday and Sunday.

Sunday night will see them all under Mrs. Tyskling's wing once more. Maybe she'll have a happy answer to their question:

"Pretty soon will we have a house again?"

**Chicago Daily News**
October 7, 1952

## NEW QUARTERS READY FOR EVICTED SCHOOL

A new home on the South Side has been found for the pupils of St. George School, who were evicted Sept. 3 from the premises the school had occupied for 32 years.

Sixteen scrubbed rooms at 4810 Ellis already are sheltering the 13 youngsters who were evicted with the family of Mrs. Anne Tyskling, director of the school.

On Thursday, Oct. 16, the 47 pupils will move to the new premises from Congregation Rodfei Zedek, 5200 Hyde Park Blvd.

Its hospitality has been extended the school since a court order prohibited use of the classroom part of the school's former building at 4545 Drexel Blvd. more than a year ago.

Trustees of the school had to resort to court order to get parents and Mrs. Tyskling to cease operating the school on the old property.

The trustees said the operation was financially unsound—but the director and parents didn't agree.

At the new address, Mrs. Tyskling (who has four children of her own, two adopted,) will continue to mother children of broken homes and of working parents who must leave their children alone.

The school charges $50 a month to day pupils who receive three meals, full daytime supervision and schooling, and less to those who arrive early in the morning but are reclaimed by their parents before dinner.

**Chicago Daily News**
June 12, 1955

# ST. GEORGE, NONSECTARIAN PRIVATE
# SCHOOL, SERVES ALL RACES

A variety of complicated reasons cause south siders, both white and Negro, to place their children in private schools. The St. George Parents Committee School, operated by Mrs. Anne Tyskling at 4810 Ellis Ave., is typical of schools in the Hyde Park area meeting a distinct need.

St. George's, a nonprofit, nonsectarian institution, has facilities for about 100 children, 50 to live in, and approximately 50 for all-day care. Those who attend for all-day care are at the school from 7 a.m. to 6:30 p.m. Their ages range from 2 to 14 years, and grades from nursery through 8th grade.

As a nonsectarian institution, the school logically includes Protestant, Catholic, and Jewish children as well as Negroes. There is also a white child born in China, a Negro child born in Germany, and a sprinkling of Chinese, Japanese, and Filipino children.

## Aids Busy Parents

However, the group is predominantly caucasian. The theory behind this composition, according to Mrs. Tyskling, is that the youngster should be prepared to make adjustments to the racial and religious realities of the world they must ultimately enter. Even so, the entrance of Negroes, for example, was both selective and gradual.

By and large, the youngsters come from homes of nearly identical economic and cultural levels. The parents are teachers, professional and business people, the nature of whose work prevents them from giving adequate daily supervision to their children.

St. George's served as a licensed child care center during the war, and after the war cared for children of faculty members and G.I. students at the University of Chicago and other colleges.

## Courses Flexible

The school, with a faculty of seven and two special teachers headed by principal Wanda Kendall, operates under a charter granted by the state. It maintains a high standard of scholarship and is fully accredited.

The courses are flexible, and teachers are given freedom to build interests, guide natural talents, and develop the children's ability to think rationally. But St. George's is not a progressive school in the popular meaning of that term. Actually, it is somewhat old fashioned about children learning to read, learning to give, and learning study habits.

When the late George J. Williams set up a $100,000 trust and established the St. George's in 1919, he could hardly have foreseen the ultimate religious and racial composition of the area. He merely recognized the need for a nonsectarian institution for children whose parents worked and those from broken homes.

## Get Court Order

The original site of St. George's was 4545 Drexel Blvd. But in 1950 a conflict arose between the faculty and trustees as to whether various racial groups should be admitted. The conflict resulted in litigation between the trustees and the children's parents.

The trustees, armed with a court order, finally closed the school and dispossessed Mrs. Tyskling and 28 resident children. She took them to a hotel, until she could establish her own institution, which she did in 1952. Four faculty members joined her in the new venture.

Dipping deeply into her own savings, she bought the 15-room mansion of Judge Leonard Reid and remodeled the building, and with the support of parents established the St. George Parents Committee School.

### Going Concern

Ever since, she has been strongly supported by the parents. For example, they recently cooperated by supplying fluorescent lighting, floor tiling, and graveling the playground, items not included in the school's budget. For these parents are concerned deeply about the future of the institution.

Today St. George's is a going concern. The fireproof structure has excellent ventilation, spacious dormitories, cozy classrooms, and a charming dining room. A well equipped playground is maintained as well.

Mrs. Anne Tyskling, a dedicated woman, is married to Martin Tyskling, who supervises the maintenance of the institution. They have four children: Judith, 21, Karen 19, Martin 11 and Linnea 7. She herself is a product of a boarding school, a fact that inspired her to enter the field.

As a community institution serving a vital need, Mrs. Tyskling's neighbors can be proud of the St. George School and the part it is playing in contributing to integrated citizenship.

---

The reputation of the school grew and soon the 32 students grew to 145. In 1962 when Mrs. Tyskling learned that the Harvard School for Boys was closing she started negotiations to purchase that building. It was decided that the two institutions should merge, combining the elementary and high school levels.

"The merger was extremely difficult because we not only brought girls to this new situation, we also brought blacks. Neither the pupils or the teachers or the administration found this easy to accept. It was something completely strange and new.

"But I've always been concerned about not permitting individual differences, in mind or thought as well as color of skin.

"Each person is an individual. You know, teachers can't just think of integration as one thing—color of skin. They have to combine children who have average intelligence with brighter children and have a good, healthy mixture."

---

**Hyde Park Herald**
October 15, 1973

## THE HISTORY OF THE HARVARD-ST. GEORGE SCHOOL
by Students Jim Ryan and Kyle Fowler

Mrs. Tyskling then bought a building and gave it to St. George and moved the school to 4810 Ellis where there was more trouble for the institution. St. George integrated when it moved in 1951. There was no racial conflict in the school or with parents of the children. It was unfortunate that such a beautiful atmosphere had to be disturbed by harassing neighbors who neither understood nor cared to understand that people are people, all over the world.

Times changed, but unfortunately the Harvard School was left lagging behind. By 1962, the Harvard School for Boys had its own share of problems and wanted to be relieved but not without losing too much. By 1962, the once modern Harvard School building was now inadequate in terms of lighting, plumbing, and in its fire alarm system. The community had changed once again and Harvard was no longer really needed. As an all white college prep school in this community, there were not enough students to keep the school going.

At this time, St. George was expanding again and needed more room. So in 1962, the two schools were only too happy to merge with each other and the St. George School Board of Directors arranged for the purchase of Harvard

School for which the mortgage is still being paid. There were problems involved though. There was opposition on the side of the parents of Harvard students.

Two very large changes were to happen if the two schools merged; one, there would be girls, and secondly, the school would be integrated. There was an agreement finally made in which Harvard insisted on not taking any more new non-white students into the High School than were in the St. George School already. Most opposition was centered in parents meetings which were called because St. George did not live up to its agreement.

As a result, many parents sent their children to other schools such as Morgan Park Academy or Lake Forest or they had to learn to live with things the way they were.

Eventually, this died down by 1965; girls and non-whites were just considered as other classmates. . . .

---

With such an extensive background of dealing with children, Mrs. Tyskling must have words of advice for the teachers in her employ, or for that matter, any teachers.

"First of all, I tell them never to read the children's permanent records until they have formed an opinion. One kid will get along beautifully with a certain teacher. Someone else comes in and the child acts out.

"Each teacher has to evaluate kids, absolutely on her own. Equality of education has to be in light of individual differences."

One of Mrs. Tyskling's big concerns is crime and gun control. She is a member of the Civic Disarmament Committee and the 21st Police District Steering Committee.

She involves her students in both organizations as much as she can. For many years she also worked in a first offender program here to aid youngsters with a one time offense.

The mother of four children, she has at one time or another had 14 foster children live with her and her husband, Martin.

There must be a real love between her and children to always surround herself with as many as she can, both at home and at work.

"Yes I love them," she said. "But I expect something. I have very deep responsibilities, but youngsters do too. They have rights, but they also have to meet their responsibilities."

> And then, with a twinkle, Mrs. T. made what has to be the understatement of the year.
> "Kids? Oh, I get along with them very well."

**Hyde Park Herald**
March 13, 1974

## START FIGHT TO ALLOW GIRLS ON BASEBALL TEAM

Heads of schools belonging to the Independent School League (ISL) were scheduled to meet Monday to decide the fate of young women wishing to play what has traditionally been termed as "boys sports."

The special meeting was called after a sixteen-year-old girl from Harvard-St. George school, 48th and Ellis, tried out for the school's baseball team. The ISL does not allow females on its teams.

According to a memo sent to the heads of schools in the ISL, the student, Beth Walsh, 4804 S. Woodlawn "will probably be on" the Harvard-St. George baseball team this spring.

Beth's father, an attorney, said he is waiting to see what the outcome of the meeting is before a decision is made on whether to file suit against the ISL.

The Harvard-St. George board has already voted "that there be no sex discrimination in sports, specifically baseball" at the school.

If the school heads vote against allowing girls to play, and Harvard-St. George keeps Beth on the team, then the school will have to forfeit all the games it plays against league teams.

In the meantime, coaches of ISL teams have already voted unanimously against allowing females to play in what they term "boys' sports."

Anne Tyskling, director of

Harvard-St. George feels that "if the girls who compete on an equal basis are as good as the boys they have every right to play on the team, and this holds true if a boy wants to play on a girl's team.

"I'm the only woman in an administrative position in the independent schools and I've always felt that if I take my share of the responsibility then I should be in the job. The same thing is true with sports."

Mrs. Tyskling said that girls have never had the privileges that boys have in sports and pointed out that not only were they never allowed to play on league teams, but never had the money that is given to boys.

"We've always had to help the girls raise money for uniforms, but the boys' were written right into the budget," she said.

Richard Walsh, Beth's father, said it is "morally wrong" not to allow girls on league teams if they have the ability.

"If they're not good ball players, whether they are girls or boys, then they shouldn't play," he said.

Interestingly, Beth, who plays shortstop and second base, said that "about 90 percent" of the boys on the Harvard-St. George team are behind her efforts.

"I like to play baseball and I want to play on a 'real team'," she said.

## THEORETICAL QUESTIONS

1. What forces or issues within the organization and its environment appear to influence the flow of events within the case?
2. Which were the central problems over time for the school director?
3. What theoretical perspective does the school director seem to bring to this situation?
4. What theoretical perspective do you tend to bring initially to this situation?
5. What are the implications of these conceptual frameworks for developing policy positions or solution strategies?
6. Are there additional conceptual frameworks that might be useful in developing an understanding of this case? Might any of them yield more success than that achieved by the school director?

## CASE SPECIFIC QUESTIONS

7. How does the school director define the school community? Does that definition shift over time?
8. How effective was the school director in building coalitions?
9. Which were the critical decisions that permitted both the school director and the school to survive?
10. Could the complex sense of obligation of the school director toward the children in her charge provide any guidance to public school educators?
11. How important do the personal attributes of the school director seem to be relative to her professional skills?

## ACTION QUESTIONS

12. What solution alternatives might have been available to the school director?
13. What would you have done to deal with the series of crises faced by the school director? Is your guiding theoretical perspective helpful at this stage?
14. How would you critique the action of the administrator in this case?

# THE CASE OF
# THE DO-IT-YOURSELF PRINCIPAL

||||||||||||||||||||||||||||||||||||||||||||||||||||||||||||||||||||||||||||||||||||||||||||||||||||||||||||||||

The superintendent of schools faced a complicated and persistent issue: How could he build enough schools in the city to eliminate all double sessions? He had constructed 125 new schools in just eight years, but board members and parents, and especially those newspaper reporters, were still on his back.

> **Yes, Mr. Superintendent, we know your school construction program has been a great success, but there are still some schools that are terribly overcrowded, where double sessions force some children to come to school when it's still dark and other children to go home after it's dark. Now, Mr. Superintendent,** *when* . . .

The superintendent was tired of this static. He wanted to be done with the matter.

In checking with his staff, the superintendent reaffirmed that he was coming to the finish line. It was mid-summer, and if two elementary schools currently under construction could be completed by September, or even October, he could turn a nagging controversy into a major public relations windfall. He ordered his assistant superintendent to finish those two schools and open them as soon as possible in the autumn. The superintendent let a smile creep across his mind. *Then* he would have an answer for those critics.

But, as luck would have it, inevitable delays extended the construction schedules for both schools—bad weather, strikes by electricians and plumbers, and the simple need for more time to build the relatively large schools to house more than 1,000 students each. Finally, in late November, the exasperated assistant superintendent reported that the schools should be ready for use in the second semester in January. Principals were selected and assigned to the two schools in mid-December. The two district superintendents were told to do what they had to do to open the schools the next month.

The optimistic view from the superintendent's downtown office could not be shared by the two principals. Principal A stood on her corner and looked at a steel superstructure. Principal B saw a new building on her corner which was closed to the winter snows but many months from readiness for students and teachers. As Principal B remembered later,

> We were behind schedule on the construction. There was a big push—the superintendent was mad for the building. This neighborhood was at peak population—for example, Kerlinger went from 1,000 students to 1,800 in a short period of time. The schools were bursting at the seams.

Almost every school in the area was surrounded by mobile units. During the autumn and early winter months community leaders had been attacking the board of education and the superintendent in an effort to get rid of the mobiles which were believed to be another vehicle for keeping black children in the ghetto and postponing further city-wide integration of the schools. The pressure on administrators at every level of the system was intense, but School A and School B simply were not ready for teachers and students.

Principal A had six teachers and classes for which to provide space. For a short time classrooms were improvised in the auditorium of a nearby elementary school. Despite the best of efforts, this simply proved to be impractical. Within several weeks six mobile units were placed on a muddy corner of the site of School A, where they were to remain until the beginning of the summer. Principal A administered this temporary school for six months while the new building slowly took shape.

Principal B did not have to use mobile units, but her situation was still difficult.

> We were forced into the building sooner than we should have been—under raw conditions. We survived, but I would never want to do it again. There were fistfights in the halls between members of different unions. We opened up in the far wing, and they turned the water on a half hour before the kids marched over.

That was in late January when the first four classes of first and second grade students arrived. Gradually, across the second semester, more students and teachers were assigned to School B as classrooms were finished. By June the school was three-quarters full.

Principal A was coming to her first administrative post, and she found a colleague like herself in the district office:

> I didn't know the district superintendent from Adam. He called and asked me to come and see him. He said, "You know, I didn't want you. I wanted a black man—Chuck Watson." I told him to get Watson, then. He was blunt, and I was, too. It worked out well.

Principal B had one previous administrative experience as principal of two small paired schools; she was not particularly happy there. The fact that both principals had been assigned early was highly unusual in the city school system. More typically principals had only several weeks or perhaps a month to get used to a new assignment, even where opening a new school was involved. To be certain, Principal B was somewhat more occupied with day-to-day operational tasks than Principal A, and yet both had a full semester to influence the shaping of their respective schools. How did the principals use this unexpected gift of time?

Both principals recognized that acquiring a faculty was a first priority. They were aware that when a new school building was opened for the first time in the city, the principal could obtain teachers from three potential sources. The first maximized the principal's opportunity to structure the faculty. The principal could enlist up to one-third of the teachers from anywhere in the system by simple mutual agreement. Of course, one principal's gain was another principal's loss, but the "one-third rule" did acknowledge the difficulties inherent in developing a school from its beginnings. Second, as soon as ground was broken for construction, a transfer list was prepared and maintained in the central office. Teachers who knew that a new school was being built could go to the central office and sign up on the transfer list. A shrewd principal often suggested that teachers sign the list. Finally, when the school was about to open, vacancies in teaching slots simply were filled in a random way by the central office. By using the first two options vigorously, a principal could hope to control or influence the assignments of a majority of teachers for a new school.

Given virtually the same situation, the two principals framed two quite different questions. Principal A asked: "Is there a way that I can get my own teachers —teachers who will work closely with each other, who will work cooperatively with me, who will have common goals for the school?" Principal B asked: "Is there a way that the school system will provide a faculty for my school?" Principal A wanted to select a faculty, while Principal B wanted to receive a faculty. As things turned out, the answer to both questions was affirmative.

The two principals seemed to reach a sense of priority by different means. Principal A had plenty of time but little experience, either in operating a school or creating a new one. As a result, she seemed more than inclined to work carefully with her increasingly supportive district superintendent, who later said:

> She finagled, and I encouraged her. She'd come over to see me every week or call me on the phone. I advised her on what needed to be done to open the school. It was a pleasure to work with someone who listened, who'd take notes, and then act on the advice. I felt that because she had an opportunity to select the staff, if anyone could show after three or four years how to work with inner-city kids, she could. The fact that the building was delayed in construction meant that she could see people. She could identify people who wanted to work with her, and they could tell their colleagues. She had a transfer list of up to 40 names. A lot of people came because they heard of her. The word really spread.

Principal B had almost as much time as Principal A but very little helpful contact with her district superintendent. She had some quite contrasting views about selecting teachers:

> Most of the teachers that I got were from other schools nearby that were closing out classrooms. I never really liked the "one-third rule" because I didn't want anyone to scoop up my teachers if I were in that position. And besides, I didn't feel that I knew enough to make good choices. I got the newest and most inexperienced teachers, but some of them were very good people. It all worked out very well, even if most of them were not certified and many were inexperienced.

Principal A, seeing the entire school system as her domain, began to search for teachers, while principal B waited for teachers to arrive on the doorstep of her new school.

In the wet months of winter and early spring, Principal A was away from the site of the new school most of the time. She visited over 125 classrooms and observed teachers at work there.

> Getting a staff to do the job, that was the first big thing. Then getting texts and supplies, and then organization—it's surprising how much teachers like organization. The people I picked settled matters here. I looked for smartness. I talked with people, and I picked a lot of misfits that were unhappy other places.

Principal A designated one-third of the new faculty, and then began to manipulate the transfer list. For every "good" teacher she added to the list, she subtracted a "bad" teacher. She told teachers whom she had observed and considered mediocre to take their names off the list or to face bleak prospects in working successfully with her. As rough as it was, the tactic worked. She listened carefully to the recommendations of superior teachers who had been recruited, and, as a result, a core group of teachers was developed comprised of clusters of friends and respected professional colleagues. Principal A was uncompromising in her dialogue with prospective faculty members:

> I laid it on the line. First, I told them it would be a terribly hard job. There would be a lot of duty and that the kids are not easy. I said "If you don't want to come to really work and put out, then don't come." I did scare some off. Then I told them what I hoped for—Peace Corps-type teachers.

She went on to tell them she was looking for teachers who understood black children, who had a sense of mission, who knew how to decorate their rooms brightly and beautifully, who had many skills and interests other than those required for standard teaching. Her district superintendent gave a similar report:

> She was impressed by how rooms looked, by how discipline took place in the school, by classroom management, and by what was *going on* in those classrooms. She did two things—she sold herself, and she gave each teacher an indication of the objectives of the new school and what was going to be expected of him or her in carrying them out.

Teachers coming to School A largely were professionals on the move in the city who were searching actively for a school where they could fill the roles of classroom teachers effectively. The teachers coming to School B largely were not viewed as full professionals by their new principal, and often had been human pawns in the shifting personnel milieu of the large city system. Principal B appeared to be much more concerned with adaptation than selection.

> It was important to make the transition as smooth as possible, with the least disturbance for the children. The children in these areas move so frequently. That was my main purpose—for the children primarily, but also for the teachers. They, too, were getting bounced from school to school.

Where most of its teachers made conscious decisions to join School A, a substantial number of School B teachers ended up there through no particular effort on their part.

The work of Principal A did not end with the recruitment of teachers. Early in the summer she sent a memo to the new faculty, asking them to come in and help her, letting them know that she could not pay them any extra salary. Later, a teacher recalled:

> Maybe you know, we went in on our own two weeks before the school opened. In her note to the teachers she just said she would be there. There was no pressure, but if you were interested in coming, she'd be there and would be happy to see you. Most of us were there part of every day—some of us in blue jeans. We knew she had a family, but she'd go out and buy us pop and pizza. You felt as if you had to go or she'd miss you. Here were these people coming to work who did not have to—just because they wanted to. The teachers got along well, and it was a climate that spread.

Thus, through the powerful medium of shared work, the faculty of School A experienced an intensive group activity. It seems doubtful that a more imaginative staff-development program could have been designed to serve the goal of welding individual professionals into a working faculty. How different that was from the situation at School B where there was anxiety and uncertainty to the end, as a teacher recounted:

> I had very little going for me. I was really going to give up. At the other school I was out in a mobile. The principal didn't know us, and she didn't visit the mobiles. We actually went over to the new school, but there was no information from downtown, and all we could do was look. It came down to the last day, and we still didn't know where we were going. Even after we carried the kids over to the new school, we didn't know if we were going to stay.

Here were teachers on the fringe of unemployment—thrust into classrooms at School B with little sense of collegial support and with little knowledge of the principal's expectations—rather than secure professionals in search of a better school in which to teach. The district superintendent remembered helping Principal B push desks and chairs around to get rooms ready for teachers and students who at that moment were walking from their old school to their new school, their arms piled high with books.

Five years later the two schools in the same area of the city seemed at first glance to be very much alike. Both schools were located in segregated black neighborhoods where people lived in similar types of housing and where adults earned similar yearly incomes. Both schools were built at a time when elementary schools were needed desperately to house poor children from the inner city. The budgets for the two schools were almost identical. Both schools were staffed by forty teachers. Yet the distinctly different manner in which the principals of School A and School B organized their faculties had at least one stunning implication for the schools.

In School A, 85 percent of the teachers from the initial faculty remained there after five years, while in School B the comparable figure was 44 percent. The rapid turnover of teachers in School B was not unexpected; it fit a pattern long established in the low-income areas of the city school system. However, the relatively low turnover of teachers in School A was a striking exception to the normal course of events.

## THEORETICAL QUESTIONS

1. What forces or issues within the organization and its environment appear to influence the flow of events within the case?
2. What is the central problem, or which are the central problems for the superintendent? For the two principals?
3. What theoretical perspective does each principal seem to bring to this situation?
4. What theoretical perspective do you tend to bring initially to this situation?
5. What are the implications of these conceptual frameworks for developing solution strategies?
6. Are there additional conceptual frameworks that might be useful in developing an understanding of this case? Might any of them yield more success than that obtained by Principal A?
7. Which single or combined perspective do you feel is most appropriate for developing an action strategy?

## CASE SPECIFIC QUESTIONS

8. What differences in thinking led Principal A and Principal B to develop such different methods of obtaining faculties for their schools?
9. What does this case reveal about the nature of organizational flexibility in the large school district?
10. How many different strategies did Principal A use in drawing the faculty at her school into a cohesive group?

## ACTION QUESTIONS

11. Did each principal seem to involve the appropriate persons and roles in the processes of analysis and decision making?
12. How critical was time as a planning and decision factor?
13. Which key strategic data did the two principals find and use?
14. Are there solution alternatives which were available but not used? Is your guiding theoretical perspective helpful at this stage?
15. What would you have done? How would you critique the action of the two principals in this case?

*Note:* Material for this case was drawn from R. Bruce McPherson, "A Study of Teacher Turnover in Two Inner-City Elementary Schools" (Unpublished Ph.D. dissertation, Department of Education, University of Chicago, 1970).

# INDEX

Gross, Neal, 254
Guba, Egan G., 208, 337, 339, 343, 359, 360
Guditus, Charles W., 88–89, 111
Gulick, Luther, 77, 110
Guthrie, Tyrone, 22

Haas, J., 60
Hack, Walter G., 338, 359
Hage, Jerald, 60, 110
Hall, Douglas, 161, 162
Hall, Peter, 282, 286
Hall, Richard H., 208
Hall, Robert H., 60
Haller, Emil J., 61
Halpin, Andrew W., 18, 23, 256, 338, 359
Handicapped students, 39, 44
Handy, Charles B., 255
Hannan, Michael T., 179, 196, 208, 210
Hannaway, Jane, 109, 111, 114
Hansen, Carl, 225
Hanson, E. Mark, 182–83, 204, 208, 211, 282, 286, 298, 306, 367
Hansot, Elisabeth, 109, 207, 249, 258
Harris, William T., 225
Hart, Lois, 326, 332
Hartshorne, Charles, 285
Harvard Negotiation Project, 294, 301
Hatch, Mary Jo, 114, 259
Hawley, Amos H., 210
Health and safety concerns in schools, 102
Hedberg, Bo, 184, 208
Heider, Fritz, 258
Helicopter factor, 224
Hemphill, John K., 222, 227, 255, 256, 281, 286
Henderson, Lawrence, 347
Hennig, Margaret, 255
Hentges, Joseph T., 255, 305
Herman, Edward S., 77, 110
Herriott, Robert E., 95, 98, 109, 110, 113, 149, 163, 254
Herron, James, 92
Hersey, Paul W., 255
Herzberg, Frederick, 93
Hickson, D. J., 199, 210
Hinings, Bob, 103, 111, 114
Hinings, C. R. 210

Hirschman, Albert O., 162, 209
Hodgkins, Benjamin J., 149, 163
Hodgkinson, Christopher, 352, 357, 361
Hoffer, T., 210
Holdway, E. A., 256
Hospitals
  negotiations in, 294–96
  schools, similarity to, 296–97
Houle, Cyril, 322–23, 332
House, Robert J., 224, 239–40, 243, 255, 256, 257
Hoy, Wayne K., 93, 112, 164, 248, 256, 258, 342–43, 360
Hrebiniak, Lawrence, 134, 136, 161, 162
Hughes, Everett, 296
Human relations view of administration, 86–87
Hurwitz, Emanuel, Jr., 109, 111, 112, 162, 207, 257

Iannaccone, Laurence, 55, 61
Immegart, Glenn, 338, 359
Individualized educational program (IEP), 44
Individual's behavior, theories of. *See* Public choice approach to organization-environment relationship
Infeld, L., 285
Information, administrative use of, 191–92
Information systems in organizations, 82, 83
Input control, 50, 51, 52
Inquiry, definition of, 277
Interacting Spheres Model, 298
Interaction in systems theory, 182–83
Interdependence, 40–41
  pooled, 41
  reciprocal, 44–45
  sequential, 42–44
Involvement, 146–47

Jackson, Philip, W., 42, 60, 163, 297–98, 306
Jacobson, L., 245, 258
Jennings, Eugene E., 255
Jermier, John, 241, 257, 258
Johnson, H. J., 60